Introduction to
LITERATURE
p e a r s o n   c u s t o m   l i b r a r y

Vernice Cain, Ph.D.
Slippery Rock University of Pennslyvania

Pearson Custom Publishing

New York   Boston   San Francisco
London   Toronto   Sydney   Tokyo   Singapore   Madrid
Mexico City   Munich   Paris   Cape Town   Hong Kong   Montreal

Senior Vice President, Editorial and Marketing: Patrick F. Boles
Senior Sponsoring Editor: Natalie Danner
Development Editor: Mary Kate Paris
Editorial Assistant: Jill Johnson
Operations Manager: Eric M. Kenney
Database Product Manager: Jennifer Berry
Rights Manager: Katie Huha
Art Director and Cover Designer: Renée Sartell

Cover Art: Photography by Chris Beaudoin.

Please visit our websites at *www.pearsoncustom.com* and *www.customliterature.com*.

Attention bookstores: For permission to return any unsold stock, contact
us at *pe-uscustomreturns@pearson.com*.

**Pearson
Custom Publishing**
is a division of

www.pearsonhighered.com   ISBN 10: 0-558-28399-3
                           ISBN 13: 978-0-558-28399-5

Introduction to
LITERATURE
pearson custom library

Acknowledgements

A project as broad, far-reaching, challenging, and path-breaking as
The Pearson Custom Library: Introduction to Literature could not be under-
taken or accomplished without the support and participation of many col-
leagues. For their contributions, research, ideas, and suggestions, the editors
particularly wish to thank David L.G. Arnold, University of Wisconsin,
Stevens Point; Lydia M. Barovero, Providence College; Lisa Bickmore, Salt
Lake City Community College; Claire Connolly, University of Wales-Cardiff;
Allison Fernley, Salt Lake City Community College; Lisa Fluet, Boston
College; Clint Gardner, Salt Lake City Community College; Curtis Gruenler,
Hope College; Hilary Justice, Illinois State University; Martin Kevorkian,
University of Texas, Austin; Lynn Kilpatrick, University of Utah; Susanne
Liaw; Mark Lovely, Merrimack College; James J. Lu, California Baptist
University; Sarah McKibben, Cristanne Miller, Pomona College; University of
Notre Dame; Jim Miracky, College of the Holy Cross; Bill Miskinis, College of
the Holy Cross; Bill Morgan, Illinois State University; Mark Morrison,
Pennsylvania State University; John Mulrooney, College of the Holy Cross;
Jamil Mustafa, Lewis University; Lisa Perdigao, Florida Institute of
Technology; Jason Pickavance, Salt Lake City Community College; Robin
Schulze, Pennsylvania State University; Mary Trotter, University of Wisconsin-
Madison; Steve Vineberg, College of the Holy Cross; Helen Whall, College of
the Holy Cross; Mario Pereira, Brown University; and Janice Wiggins.

Your *Introduction to Literature* purchase includes access to online resources designed to complement your readings. This Companion Website is located at the following URL:

http://www.pearsoncustom.com/dbintrolit/introlit/student

When prompted, enter the User Name: **ilstudent** and Password: **illearn**

(*Note:* The User Name and Password are case-sensitive, so be sure to use upper and lower case characters exactly as shown above.)

Once logged in, you will have access to the following resources:

Link Library. A collection of vetted web links organized by key terms and literary figures which offer you background and context for many of the selections you'll be reading.

The Writing Process. Advice that can aid you during the writing process. Included are guidelines and suggestions for each phase of writing, from start to finish.

Plagiarism. Suggestions to help you maintain academic honesty, with illustrative examples.

Grammar Guide. Spells out some of the rules and conventions of standard written English.

MLA Style. A brief guide to help you follow MLA style in citing your sources. The Modern Language Association style is widely used for papers in English composition, literature, and foreign languages.

We invite you to explore!

Contents

Section I: What Is Poetry?

William Blake

[1757–1827]

WILLIAM BLAKE *was born in London to a middle class family, but his bent
toward seeing the world in terms of visions quickly appeared. Blake saw more
than the dirty world of a big city; rather he saw angels and other spiritual beings
as he walked through life. He considered the world he lived in to be corrupted by
its lack of imagination, and he set about creating his own Golden Age of art and
poetry. Showing great artistic talent early in life, by age ten he began drawing in
school and later became an engraver and design artist. He did not earn great
sums as an artist, because his work was strange in an era that loved landscapes
and careful representations of classic events such as Bible stories and historic battles. Blake's art illustrated more that could not be seen than that which could be
seen.*

*He married his wife, Catherine, in 1782. She was devoted to him though the
story goes that she nearly fainted when she first saw him due to his fiery eyes and
passionate presence. From that early era came his first collection of poetry,*
Poetical Sketches *(1783). When his younger brother Robert died, Blake's sense of
connection to the spiritual world was strengthened. He wrote the* Songs of
Experience *(1789) during this time of elation and spiritual growth, and these
poems express his sense of the heavenly and spiritual. This bliss, however, was
short-lived as Blake first followed and then rejected the Swedish theologian,
Emanuel Swendenborg. Blake rejected Swendenborg's ideas about predestination,
and wrote* The Marriage of Heaven and Hell *(1790–1793) as an attack on any
such doctrine.*

*Blake then became connected with the champions of the French Revolution,
including William Godwin, Tom Paine, and the Romantic poets, William
Wordsworth, Samuel Coleridge, Robert Southey, and William Hazlitt. His
protest against those who interfere with the rights of their fellow humans
expressed itself in the most famous of his collections,* Songs of Experience
(1798–1794), and in The French Revolution, America, *and the* Visions of the
Daughters of Albion. *The last poem attacks marriage, which Blake disapproved
of while he continued to be a faithful and devoted husband. The* Book of Thel
*(1783) followed, a tale of a soul that refuses to be born into this wicked world.
His mythology was elaborated and illustrated in* The Book of Urizen, The Song
of Los, The Book of Ahania, *and* The Book of Los.

*From 1800 to 1803, the Blakes lived in a small town called Felpham, sup-
ported by a patron and poet friend named William Hayley, but Blake and Hayley
differed in the nature of the poetry the two wrote, Hayley's being simple and sen-
timental, Blake's being mystical and complex. While at Felpham, Blake finished*

The Four Zoas *and* Milton; *upon returning to London, he wrote the third of his "prophetic" works,* Jerusalem. *After that he spent many years in poverty, even painting dishes for Wedgwood, but was finally rediscovered in 1818 by a younger generation of painters, John Linnell, Samuel Palmer, John Varley, and George Richmond. He began to illustrate Dante and the book of Job, but these remained unfinished at the time of his death in 1827.*

The Tyger

WILLIAM BLAKE

Tyger, Tyger, burning bright
In the forests of the night,
What immortal hand or eye
Could frame thy fearful symmetry?

In what distant deeps or skies   5
Burnt the fire of thine eyes?
On what wings dare he aspire?
What the hand dare seize the fire?

And what shoulder and what art
Could twist the sinews of thy heart?   10
And, when thy heart began to beat,
What dread hand and what dread feet?

What the hammer? What the chain?
In what furnace was thy brain?
What the anvil? What dread grasp   15
Dare its deadly terror clasp?

When the stars threw down their spears,
And watered heaven with their tears,
Did he smile his work to see?
Did he who made the Lamb make thee?   20

Tyger, Tyger, burning bright
In the forests of the night,
What immortal hand or eye
Dare frame thy fearful symmetry?

[1794]

First published in *Songs of Experience* in 1794.

The Lamb

WILLIAM BLAKE

Little Lamb, who made thee?
  Dost thou know who made thee?
Gave thee life, and bid thee feed
By the stream and o'er the mead;
Gave thee clothing of delight,   5
Softest clothing, wooly, bright;
Gave thee such a tender voice,
Making all the vales rejoice?
  Little Lamb, who made thee?
  Dost thou know who made thee?   10

  Little Lamb, I'll tell thee,
  Little Lamb, I'll tell thee:
He is callèd by thy name,
For he calls himself a Lamb.
He is meek, and he is mild;   15
He became a little child.
I a child, and thou a lamb,
We are callèd by his name.
  Little Lamb, God bless thee!
  Little Lamb, God bless thee!   20

[1789]

First published in *Songs of Innocence* in 1789.

Anne Bradstreet
[1612–1672]

ANNE BRADSTREET *was born in England, to the Puritan intellectual, Thomas Dudley, who was by profession a soldier of Queen Elizabeth I. Anne's father like her brother and later, her husband, would eventually become governor of the Massachusetts colony. Anne Dudley married Simon Bradstreet when she was sixteen; two years later in 1630, the family sailed to New England where Bradstreet spent the rest of her life. She, her husband, and her eight children lived in Andover, then the frontier of Massachusetts. Before her move to New England, Bradstreet had the good fortune to grow up in the world of Queen Elizabeth who herself was well educated and encouraged women in her court to be educated, too. Bradstreet learned Greek and Latin, French, theology, and history. Her family included ministers and governors, all of whom encouraged and appreciated her intellectual abilities. Her excellent education provided her with the basis for her great poetic achievements throughout her life. At first her poems were read by her family and friends in manuscript form, but her brother-in-law took one manuscript to be published in England in 1650 under the title of* The Tenth Muse Lately Sprung Up in America. *The poetry in this collection illustrates the proper religious and moral perspective of Bradstreet's family with poems such as "The Four Elements," "Of the Four Humours," "The Four Ages of Man," "The Four Seasons of the Year," "A Man's Constitution," and "A Dialogue between Old England and New." The number four in these titles refers to Bradstreet's representation of a balanced universe ordered by a divine intelligence. Her Puritanism was highly rational and measured in perspective, encouraging readers to appreciate the reasoning behind a world that was just beginning to discover science. This first poetry collection sold well, and in 1678, after Bradstreet's death, a second collection appeared under the title of* Several Poems, *and Included such works as "The Flesh and the Spirit" and "Contemplation." Her more private poems were collected in the "Andover Manuscript Book," but this collection was not printed in the 1600s.*

Though she wrote both public and private poetry, today she is most appreciated for her personal poems. The poems that most move modern readers are not so much those that contemplate the religious life but rather those that talk about the real life concerns of a woman in love, a woman facing childbirth, and a woman dealing with the threats of a new society on a new frontier in an area filled with suffering and disease. Bradstreet's spiritual poetry should by no means be discounted, for it worked through metaphors and imagery that challenge and interest many readers today. She remains among the most versatile and prolific of American poets.

The Author to Her Book

ANNE BRADSTREET

Thou ill-form'd offspring of my feeble brain,
Who after birth did'st by my side remain,
Till snatcht from thence by friends, less wise than true,
Who thee abroad expos'd to public view,
Made thee in rags halting to th' press to trudge, 5
Where errors were not lessened (all may judge).
At thy return my blushing was not small,
My rambling brat (in print) should mother call;
I cast thee by as one unfit for light,
Thy visage was so irksome in my sight; 10
Yet being mine own, at length affection would
Thy blemishes amend, if so I could:
I wash'd thy face, but more defects I saw,
And rubbing off a spot, still made a flaw,
I stretcht thy joints to make thee even feet, 15
Yet still thou run'st more hobbling than is meet;
In better dress to trim thee was my mind,
But nought save homespun cloth i' th' house I find;
In this array, 'mongst vulgars may'st thou roam,
In critic's hands, beware thou dost not come; 20
And take thy way where yet thou art not known,
If for thy father asked, say thou hand'st none:
And for thy mother, she alas is poor,
Which caus'd her thus to send thee out of door.

[1678]

First published in *Several Poems* in 1678.

To My Dear and Loving Husband

ANNE BRADSTREET

If ever two were one, then surely we.
If ever man were loved by wife, then thee;
If ever wife was happy in a man,
Compare with me, ye women, if you can.
I prize thy love more than whole mines of gold   5
Or all the riches that the East doth hold.
My love is such that rivers cannot quench,
Nor ought but love from thee, give recompense.
Thy love is such I can no way repay,
The heavens reward thee manifold, I pray.   10
Then while we live, in love let's so persevere
That when we live no more, we may live ever.

[1678]

First published in *Several Poems* in 1678.

Gwendolyn Brooks
[1917–2000]

GWENDOLYN ELIZABETH BROOKS *was born and grew up in Topeka, Kansas, where her mother, Keziah Corine Wims Brooks, taught school and her father, David Anderson Brooks, provided her with a desk and allowed writing time early in her life. She published her first poem in a local newspaper,* Hyde Parker, *at age eleven and published poems again at age thirteen in* American Childhood. *At sixteen, she was publishing poems regularly in the* Chicago Defender. *At twenty-one she married Henry Lovington Blakeley II, with whom she had two children, Henry III and Nora. They moved to Chicago where she expanded her acquaintances and met famous writers of the Harlem Renaissance, including Langston Hughes who came to give a poetry reading in Chicago, and agreed to read her early poetry. Hughes later became a family friend as well as a mentor. By 1953, when she wrote an autobiographical novel,* Maud Martha, *she was a well-established poet. Her* A Street in Bronzeville *(1945) expressed the development of her powerful voice as she described the traumatized soldiers returning from World War II and the oppressed poor blacks who lived in rundown neighborhoods. In this collection she used the sonnet form to sing the woes of blacks in urban America during the thirties and forties. She described what she saw in Chicago and New York with a power that brought a wider community to feel and comprehend the plight of poor people.*

In The Bean Eaters *(1960) Brooks turned her attention to the civil rights movement, recounting the horrors of that time, for example, the murder of fourteen-year-old Emmet Till, in "A Bronzeville Mother Loiters in Mississippi. Meanwhile a Mississippi Mother Burns Bacon." She was accused by some as having become a political poet, but she wrote with a voice that was needed in the sixties. In* the Mecca *(1968) is a collection of her poems about false spirituality and deception, partially written about the time she worked for a spiritual leader who deceived his followers. During the first twenty-five years of her career, she also wrote many reviews for the* Chicago Daily News, *the* Sun Times, Black World, *the* New York Times, *and the* Tribune. *She taught poetry in colleges in Chicago (Columbia, Elmhurst, Northeastern Illinois) and at Wisconsin-Madison. In 1968, she became Poet Laureate of Illinois. In 1971, she wrote her first autobiography,* Report from Part One. *After this, she began to publish only with black presses and to write even more intensely about the lives of black people in the cities. Two volumes,* To Disembark *(1981) and* Children Coming Home *(1991), collect the poems that speak to black people about their lives. In 1996 she pro-*

duced a second autobiography, Report from Part Two, *which introduces and discusses some of her most well-known poems. Throughout the last years of her life, Brooks was generous with her time, traveling to give readings and to receive the scores of awards she received from admiring readers and listeners. Her work is loved and admired by both academics and non-academics, both in her adopted state and beyond.*

We Real Cool

GWENDOLYN BROOKS

The Pool Players.
Seven at the Golden Shovel.

We real cool. We
Left school. We

Lurk late. We   5
Strike straight. We

Sing sin. We
Thin gin. We

Jazz June. We
Die soon.   10

[1960]

Elizabeth Barrett Browning
[1806–1861]

ELIZABETH BARRETT BROWNING *was born in Durham, England, the daughter of an overly protective father who kept her at home and mostly indoors. The family moved to London where they lived quite unhappy lives. Fortunately for Browning, she had access to her brother's tutor and was allowed to learn and study alongside her sibling. In this way, she acquired the education of a wealthy young man of the early Victorian era. She was well schooled in Greek, Latin, and Hebrew and was well read in literature ranging from the classical texts of Greek and Rome, including Homer and Ovid; to the Romantics, poets including Lord Byron, Keats, Coleridge, and Wordsworth whose lives overlapped her own. At age thirteen, she published her first volume of poetry. She injured her spine at age fifteen, and her beloved brother Edward drowned in 1840. The combination of illness and depression provided ample reason for her father to keep her imprisoned at their house on Wimpole Street in London. When she met poet Robert Browning, she was a well-known essayist, poet, and scholar, having published* Essay on Mind, with Other Poems *in 1826, a translation of* Prometheus Bound *by Aeschylus in 1833 and* The Seraphim and Other Poems *in 1838. During their courtship, Elizabeth wrote sonnets to Browning that became her best-known work,* Sonnets from the Portuguese. *Browning referred to her as his little Portuguese because she was dark complexioned.*

In September 1846, the two poets ran away to Italy where they married and lived together until Elizabeth's death. They had one son, Pim. Their intellectual companionship yielded much writing on both their parts. She published two works on Italian political affairs, Casa Guidi Windows *(1951) and* Poems before Congress *(1860). Her longest poem,* Aurora Leigh *(1857), written in blank verse, covered biographical topics and expressed her beliefs on political, social, and economic issues. Her last book of poems,* Last Poems *(1862), was published after her death. Her physical problems returned as the great romance with Robert began to fade, leading to her death and burial in her beloved Florence. Though Elizabeth was originally more famous than her husband, for many decades after her death her work was considered less important than Robert's. Today she has regained critical interest among women scholars and has been rediscovered for the fine poet and social and political thinker that she was.*

How Do I Love Thee? Let Me Count the Ways

ELIZABETH BARRETT BROWNING

How do I love thee? Let me count the ways.
I love thee to the depth and breadth and height
My soul can reach, when feeling out of sight
For the ends of being and ideal grace.
I love thee to the level of every day's   5
Most quiet need, by sun and candle-light.
I love thee freely, as men strive for right.
I love thee purely, as they turn from praise.
I love thee with the passion put to use
In my old griefs, and with my childhood's faith.   10
I love thee with a love I seemed to lose
With my lost saints. I love thee with the breath,
Smiles, tears, of all my life; and, if God choose,
I shall but love thee better after death.

[1850]

First published in *Sonnets from the Portuguese* in 1850.

Robert Burns
[1759–1796]

The son of a Scottish farmer, ROBERT BURNS grew up in Ayrshire where his family moved from farm to farm in small areas in the lowlands of Scotland. Farm life then as now was hard and demanding. Burns spent his early years behind a plow, toiling alongside the rest of his family to keep the farms going. His early death has been attributed to this hard work and harder struggle. Brief schooling in Kirkoswald introduced him to literature as well as the music and traditions of ancient Scotland. In 1781 he left the farm for work in the textile mills in the town of Irvine where he learned more about city life. He fell in and out of love with Mary Campbell and Elizabeth Paton. His father died in 1784, an event that called Burns back to the farm to work with his brother Gilbert. On the farm, in Mossgiel, he met his love Jean Armore but her father, a mason, discouraged the marriage. In 1786 he published his first volume of poems (Poems) and became a famous poet and a favorite in literary circles. He was invited to Edinburgh where he was wined and dined, and acclaimed as the new poetic rage. The second volume appeared in 1787 and provided him enough money to take trips north to the highlands and south to England. By 1789 he became a tax supervisor and married Jean Armore. In the next few years he collected and edited traditional songs and ballads of ancient Scotland (1792) and wrote not only the lyrics but also the music for these verse poems, once again enhancing his reputation as the leading poet of Scotland. At about the same time he became interested in the French revolution, not a popular event in Scotland, and so he lost some of his following. His health began to decline, and he died at age thirty-seven.

For years Burns was condemned as a drinker and carouser, but in truth he was a hard working farmer and poet, married to the woman he loved and devoted to the music and history of Scotland. He was earthy in his writing when he was at his best, for he brought the life of the common person and the beauty of real work in countryside to the world of published poetry and song. He is the poet of Scottish history and Scottish nationalism, as well as the poet of domesticity and young love. His Auld Lang Syne is still sung when friendship and old friends are praised and saluted. Without Robert Burns the world would be a drearier and more dismal place.

Oh, my love is like a red, red rose

ROBERT BURNS

Oh, my love is like a red, red rose
    That's newly sprung in June;
My love is like the melody
    That's sweetly played in tune.

So fair art thou, my bonny lass,   5
    So deep in love am I;
And I will love thee still, my dear,
    Till a' the seas gang dry.

Till a' the seas gang dry, my dear,
    And the rocks melt wi' the sun;   10
And I will love thee still, my dear,
    While the sands o' life shall run.

And fare thee weel, my only love!
    And fare thee weel awhile!
And I will come again, my love   15
    Though it were ten thousand mile.

[c. 1788]

Composed in 1794 and first published in 1799. Collected in the 1869 *Songs, Chiefly in the Scottish Dialect*.

Lewis Carroll
[1832–1898]

Charles Lutwidge Dodgson, who wrote under the pen name LEWIS CARROLL, was a scholarly and erudite Oxford lecturer whose specialty was mathematics. He was known in this field for his scholarly texts, An Elementary Treatise on Determinants *(1867)* and Symbolic Logic *(1896)*. These are only the best known of his sober and edifying theoretical works. Dodgson, however, was a person who delighted in the company of children, and he was in fact rather shy and retiring in the adult world. He loved children whose imaginations carried them beyond the real world of accounting and proper bedtimes. He was friends with the Liddell family, and often played with the children, particularly Alice, their charming and imaginative small daughter. Dodgson wrote the character of a whimsical friend of Alice who recounts her dream experiences in the world of the imagination. The first of these works appeared in 1865 as Alice in Wonderland. The work was colorfully illustrated by the famous artist John Tenniel so that not only did Carroll provide a wonderful world of words; he also provided, through his illustrator, images that live in the minds of children to this day. The fanciful cast includes Queen of Hearts and the Cheshire Cat, as well as the Mad Hatter (who was likely truly mad—hatters in the Victorian era worked with mind-altering chemicals when dying the hats) and the March Hare. In the book, Alice first meets the White Rabbit and then falls down a deep rabbit hole. The dream quality of the tale is obvious right from the start when Alices sees that the rabbit is wearing a waistcoat and carrying a pocket watch. Soon the ominous nature of this imaginary world becomes clear when the queen's tendency to order beheadings becomes a part of the story. Fortunately, the king quickly and politely regularly countermands his wife's decrees. This world portrays the way that the adult world must look to a child: completely mad and inexplicable. Perhaps the best part of the books are Carroll's satires of instructional poetry that were so popular in the Victorian period for teaching children proper behavior. By the time that Alice and her acquaintances finish with the poetry, it has become both satirical and silly, a fine end for pious instructional verse.

The second volume, Through the Looking-Glass *(1871)* features another dream that begins with a fall through a mirror into a room that only vaguely resembles the world of mundane reality. Alice ends up on a chessboard with a variety of pseudo-military animals and creatures but most especially with the Red Queen who assures her that you have to keep running as fast as you can to stay in place, rather like the academia that was Dodgson's working world. Carroll was clearly the master of parody and satire that still both amuses children and *delights adults. Two other works, though not as widely read and loved,* The Hunting of the Snark *(1876)—yes, snark hunts were Carroll's idea—and* Silvie and Bruno *(1889–1993). Many twentieth-century adults would not be who they are today without nineteenth-century Lewis Carroll.*

Jabberwocky[1]

LEWIS CARROLL

'Twas brillig, and the slithy toves
Did gyre and gimble in the wabe:
All mimsy were the borogoves,
And the mome raths outgrabe.

"Beware the Jabberwock, my son!   5
The jaws that bite, the claws that catch!
Beware the Jubjub bird, and shun
The frumious Bandersnatch!"

He took his vorpal sword in hand;
Long time the manxome foe he sought—   10
So rested he by the Tumtum tree
And stood awhile in thought.

And, as in uffish thought he stood,
The Jabberwock, with eyes of flame,
Came whiffling through the tulgey wood,   15
And burbled as it came!

One, two! One, two! And through and through
The vorpal blade went snicker-snack!
He left it dead, and with its head
He went galumphing back.   20

"And hast thou slain the Jabberwock?
Come to my arms, my beamish boy!
O frabjous day! Callooh, Callay!"
He chortled in his joy.

[1]Carroll provides a glossary to the poem that is just as silly as the poem, maybe even sillier.

First published in *Through the Looking Glass and What Alice Saw There* in 1872.

'Twas brillig, and the slithy toves
Did gyre and gimble in the wabe:
All mimsy were the borogoves,
And the mome raths outgrabe.

[1871]

Helen Chasin

[1940–   ]

HELEN CHASIN, *like many other American poets writing in the 1960s, represents the postwar era through confessional poetry that depicts the changing faces of the country and its individuals. Chasin's grounding in the Northeast, from her early life in Brooklyn and later years in Cambridge, Massachusetts while at Radcliffe College, is depicted in poems that take those familiar landscapes as their subjects. In her first collection of poetry,* Coming Close and Other Poems *(1968), Chasin uses those sites and shows their significance to her life. In "Cambridge as Metaphor," Chasin writes, "Often enough the town's sky hangs about / like a sullen child, giving offense," articulating the physicality of Cambridge, but then turns, by the poem's end, to the construction of poetry itself: "You poets are adept at making do / and more, as if it's easy / to blot up the moist and waxy air / because that serves your purpose." Here, she describes how poets work to represent place and to articulate meaning, and recontextualizes the place of poetry in figurative terms, through metaphor.*

Prior to the publication of her first collection, Chasin had been a Bread Loaf Scholar in Poetry (1965) and was later a fellow at the Bunting Institute at Radcliffe College (1968–1970). As a confessional poet, writing at the same time as and in a similar voice to poets such as Sylvia Plath and Anne Sexton, Chasin occupies a central position in a literary history that is engaged with its historical contexts. In her poems about the 1960s, Chasin is an observer to a decadent culture, to its ideologies about the nation and the role of the individual. While Chasin is not as well known as Plath and Sexton, her career is marked by significant recognition; she was awarded the Yale University Poets Prize for Coming Close and Other Poems.

In the poem "First Sight," from her first collection, Chasin represents the relationship between the individual and a larger world, the presence of utter loss and potential alienation from others. She writes of a "certain / unsurprising comfort, suddenly realized," when "We are informed with one another like memory." In this landscape, individuals can connect and find meaning for themselves, in others. In a similar sense, "Motion Picture" depicts how, through a technological medium, people can connect. She writes, "In this instant we are less than life size, / grainy frame in a home movie." Here, the speaker has become the filmmaker and central character in the film. She states, "Fade / out. The end. I pick at motives / and dreams of broken men / like Band-aids." Although she is able to control and manipulate the medium, the medium is always already artificial. Throughout her poetry, Chasin writes about the changes in the second half of the twentieth century and how they influence the conception of selfhood. Chasin's second collection, Casting Stones *(1975), continues that work and reflects the persistent and consistent vision of a poet who is trying to make sense of her times as well as redefining her voice in response to those moments.*

—Mark Lovely, *Merrimack College*

The Word Plum

HELEN CHASIN

The word *plum* is delicious

pout and push, luxury of
self-love, and savoring murmur
full in the mouth and falling
like fruit   5

taut skin
pierced, bitten, provoked into
juice, and tart flesh

question
and reply, lip and tongue   10
of pleasure.

[1968]

Lucille Clifton
[1936–   ]

LUCILLE CLIFTON *was born in Depew, Michigan to working class parents. Educated at Howard University and later at Fredonia State Teacher's College, she studied drama and worked as an actor as well as a writer. She shares some of the stylistic and thematic characteristics of other poets in the Black Aesthetic school, such as lower case letters, concise lines, sparse punctuation, and patterns of repetition, as well as the valorization of African-American culture and vernacular language. She won the YW-YMHA Poetry Center Discovery Award in 1969—poet Robert Hayden entered her poetry in the competition—which launched her career with the publication of the volume* Good Times. *Her writing career is prolific and much lauded. She has written volumes of fiction, poetry, and memoir, as well as books for children. Her* Generations: A Memoir *(1976) gives an account of her family's history through the period of slavery. Her book* Good Woman: Poems and a Memoir *(1987) collected her poems and was a Pulitzer Prize nominee as well as winner of the Juniper Prize. Clifton served as the Poet Laureate of the state of Maryland from 1979 to 1982. More recent books include* Next: New Poems *(1987) and* The Book of Light *(1993).*

Homage to My Hips

LUCILLE CLIFTON

these hips are big hips
they need space to
move around in.
they don't fit into little
petty places. these hips   5
are free hips.
they don't like to be held back.
these hips have never been enslaved,
they go where they want to go
they do what they want to do.   10
these hips are mighty hips.
these hips are magic hips.
I have know them
to put a spell on a man and
spin him like a top!   15

[1980]

Samuel Taylor Coleridge
[1772–1834]

Born in Ottery St. Mary, Devonshire, SAMUEL TAYLOR COLERIDGE *was the precocious son of the mild-mannered village vicar. The doting father died when Coleridge was nine, and the youth was sent off to school at Christ's Hospital. Both Coleridge's friend, Charles Lamb, and Coleridge himself recount those early years at school as lonely and sorrowful. Coleridge did in fact receive an excellent early education that led him to Jesus College, Cambridge, where he began as a good student but then lost focus, one time even running off with the Light Dragoons (a military outfit) using the pseudonyn, Silas Tomkyn Comberbacke. His friends had to buy him back from the outfit. Eventually he left Cambridge (1794) and joined poet Robert Southey in the strange adventure of setting up a utopian community in Pennsylvania. When this failed, he and Southey married sisters, Edith and Sarah Fricker. The chief claim to fame of these two women is being satirized in Lord Byron's* Don Juan. *Coleridge wandered off to meet the poet William Wordsworth and his sister, just after publishing his first book of poems,* Juvenile Poems *(1796). In 1797 he published two of his best poems,* The Rime of the Ancient Mariner *and* Christabel. *The Rime is one of the best-loved of all poems, but* Christabel *is more obscure, a poem about a hypnotic woman who turns into a serpent. The fragment breaks off leaving the reader entranced but unsatisfied. In 1798 he wrote his famous fragment poem* Kubla Khan *and published the* Lyrical Ballads *with Wordsworth. This work is considered the watershed moment in Romanticism. Before 1798 poets still are a part of an earlier era, but after the Preface lays out a sort of credo, theory, and definition for the Romantic poets, the writers move on within the collective constraints of that definition. The Wordsworth siblings and Coleridge then journeyed to Gottingen where Coleridge quickly learned German, read Kantian philosophy, and translated Friedrich Schiller's drama,* Wallenstein. *Soon he followed the Wordsworths back to England and joined them in the country life in Keswick. There he become addicted to opium and wrote two depressing works,* Dejection, an Ode *(1802) and* Youth and Age *(1828). Having licked his opium habit, he moved on to the lecture circuit and spoke widely about his theories of literature, especially creating a Romantic setting of Shakespeare's plays that still tends to dominate critical opinion. He was far better at talking about his ideas than he was at writing them down. He planned a work on theology and several longer poems, but no more were written, and in fact,* The Rime of the Ancient Mariner *is the only long poem Coleridge completed. He did however write two outstanding prose works, his* Biographia Literaria *(1817), in which he illuminates much about his relationship with Wordworth, and* Table Talk, *conversations written down that are among the best of their kind.*

Kubla Khan[1]
or, a Vision in a Dream. A Fragment

SAMUEL TAYLOR COLERIDGE

THE FOLLOWING FRAGMENT is here published at the request of a poet of great and deserved celebrity [Lord Byron], and, as far as the Author's own opinions are concerned, rather as a psychological curiosity, than on the ground of any supposed poetic merits.

In the summer of the year 1797, the Author, then in ill health, had retired to a lonely farm-house between Porlock and Linton, on the Exmoor confines of Somerset and Devonshire. In consequence of a slight indisposition, an anodyne had been prescribed, from the effects of which he fell asleep in his chair at the moment that he was reading the following sentence, or words of the same substance, in "Purchas's Pilgrimage": "Here the Khan Kubla commanded a palace to be built, and a stately garden thereunto. And thus ten miles of fertile ground were inclosed with a wall." The Author continued for about three hours in a profound sleep, at least of the external senses, during which time he has the most vivid confidence, that he could not have composed less than from two to three hundred lines; if that indeed can be called composition in which all the images rose up before him as things, with a parallel production of the correspondent expressions, without any sensation or consciousness of effort. On awaking he appeared to himself to have a distinct recollection of the whole, and taking his pen, ink, and paper, instantly and eagerly wrote down the lines that are here preserved. At this moment he was unfortunately called out by a person on business from Porlock, and detained by him above an hour, and on his return to his room, found, to his no small surprise and mortification, that though he still retained some vague and dim recollection of the general purport of the vision, yet, with the exception of some eight or ten scattered lines and images, all the rest had passed away like the images on the

---

[1]The poet claims that he took medicine for a stomach upset, then read in a book lines about Kubla Khan's pleasure dome. He says that he woke up in a vision, wrote down what is here, got up to go to his room, and then lost the rest of the story—not exactly "the dog ate my homework" but close. Coleridge was not a finisher.

Composed in either 1797 or 1798 and first published in 1816 with "Christabel" and "The Pains of Sleep."

surface of a stream into which a stone has been cast, but, alas! without the after restoration of the latter!

> Then all the charm
> Is broken—all that phantom-world so fair
>   Vanishes, and a thousand circlets spread,

> And each mis-shape the other. Stay awhile,
> Poor youth! who scarcely dar'st lift up thine eyes—   *5*
> The stream will soon renew its smoothness, soon
> The visions will return! And lo, he stays,
> And soon the fragments dim of lovely forms
> Come trembling back, unite, and now once more
> The pool becomes a mirror.   *10*

Yet from the still surviving recollections in his mind, the Author has frequently purposed to finish for himself what had been originally, as it were, given to him. Αὔριον ἄδιον ἄσω: [tomorrow I shall sing a sweeter song]: but the to-morrow is yet to come.

> In Xanadu did Kubla Khan
> A stately pleasure-dome decree:
> Where Alph, the sacred river, ran
> Through caverns measureless to man
>   Down to a sunless sea.   *5*
> So twice five miles of fertile ground
> With walls and towers were girdled round:
> And here were gardens bright with sinuous rills,
> Where blossomed many an incense-bearing tree;
> And there were forests ancient as the hills,   *10*
> Enfolding sunny spots of greenery.
>   But oh! that deep romantic chasm which slanted
> Down the green hill athwart a cedarn cover!
> A savage place! as holy and enchanted
> As e'er beneath a waning moon was haunted   *15*
> By woman wailing for her demon-lover!
> And from this chasm, with ceaseless turmoil seething,
> As if this earth in fast thick pants were breathing,
> A mighty fountain momently was forced:
> Amid whose swift half-intermitted burst   *20*
> Huge fragments vaulted like rebounding hail,

Or chaffy grain beneath the thresher's flail:
And 'mid these dancing rocks at once and ever
It flung up momently the sacred river.
Five miles meandering with a mazy motion 25
Through wood and dale the sacred river ran,
Then reached the caverns measureless to man,
And sank in tumult to a lifeless ocean:
And 'mid this tumult Kubla heard from far
Ancestral voices prophesying war! 30
    The shadow of the dome of pleasure
    Floated midway on the waves;
    Where was heard the mingled measure
    From the fountain and the caves.
It was a miracle of rare device, 35
A sunny pleasure-dome with caves of ice!

    A damsel with a dulcimer
    In a vision once I saw:
    It was an Abyssinian maid,
    And on her dulcimer she played, 40
    Singing of Mount Abora.
    Could I revive within me
    Her symphony and song,
    To such a deep delight 'twould win me,
That with music loud and long, 45
I would build that dome in air,
That sunny dome! those caves of ice!
And all who heard should see them there,
And all should cry, Beware! Beware!
His flashing eyes, his floating hair! 50
Weave a circle round him thrice,
And close your eyes with holy dread,
For he on honey-dew hath fed,
And drunk the milk of Paradise.

[1797]

e. e. cummings
[1894–1962]

Edward Estlin Cummings, or E. E. CUMMINGS *as he preferred his name to be styled, grew up in Cambridge, Massachusetts where his father taught at Harvard University and later was minister at the Unitarian church. cummings completed a bachelor's and a master's in English at Harvard where he became friends with novelist John Dos Passos. After moving to New York to become a writer, cummings volunteered for service in World War I as an ambulance driver. In France, cummings was wrongly jailed for spying for the Germans simply because he reported stories of the terrible conditions at the front in his letters home. cummings later wrote a fictionalized autobiography,* The Enormous Room, *of events during his stay in the French concentration camp.*

After release from prison in 1917, cummings returned to the United States and began to publish poetry in literary magazines. Unable, however, to find a publisher in the United States for a longer collection because of his frank treatment of sex, cummings left the United States to live in Paris. Realizing that his work would not be published if he pursued sexual themes, cummings sanitized and shortened them and finally saw publication in 1923. He soon published three other volumes of poetry. An avid pacifist, cummings was disturbed by the approach of World War II and produced X1, *a collection of disturbing yet insightful poems about the human condition.*

cummings's poetry is seen as dense and difficult to some, and overly simplistic and even childish to others. cummings's exploration of language and form force the reader to consider the purpose of conventions and their uses. For cummings, understanding the meaning of words and conventions was ultimately important; destroying their thoughtless application the goal. However, for all his experimentation with form and syntax, cummings can be thought of as a romantic and even pastoral poet.

["next to of course god america I]

e. e. cummings

"next to of course god america i
love you land of the pilgrims' and so forth oh
say can you see by the dawn's early my
country 'tis of centuries come and go
and are no more what of it we should worry   5
in every language even deafanddumb
thy sons acclaim your glorious name by gorry
by jingo by gee by gosh by gum
why talk of beauty what could be more beauti-
    ful than these heroic happy dead   10
who rushed like lions to the roaring slaughter
they did not stop to think they died instead
then shall the voice of liberty be mute?"

He spoke.   And drank rapidly a glass of water

[1925]

[Buffalo Bill's]

e. e. cummings

Buffalo Bill's
defunct
    who used to
    ride a watersmooth-silver
                     stallion   5
and break onetwothreefourfive pigeonsjustlikethat
                         Jesus

he was a handsome man
              and what I want to know is
how do you like your blueeyed boy   10
Mister Death

                          [1920]

First appeared in *The Dial*, January 1920. cummings first collected the poem in *Tulips and Chimneys* in 1923.

Emily Dickinson
[1830–1886]

Born to an Amherst, Massachusetts, family in the early Victorian era,
EMILY DICKINSON *has been analyzed and reanalyzed for nearly two hundred
years. She was one of three children of Edward and Emily Norcross Dickinson.
Both her parents encouraged her education, sending her to Amherst Academy
and Mount Holyoke Female Seminary, which she attended until her homesick-
ness sent her home to stay. Her father served a term in Congress, giving Dickinson
the opportunity to visit Washington, D.C. briefly, and an eye problem sent her to
Boston to stay with cousins during treatment. Otherwise, she spent nearly all her
life in Amherst. Her brother, Austin, was a justice of the peace and then succeeded
his father as treasurer of Amherst College, while her sister Lavinia (Vinnie) led a
lively social life in the town. Neither Emily or Vinnie married, both living in the
family home, called the Evergreens, until their deaths.*

*Dickinson has often been described as a reclusive poet whose fame came only
after her death, but she actually lived an exciting life of the mind, corresponding
with many of the poets and intellectuals of her day and discussing world events
and poetry with friends and family in the rich intellectual circle surrounding the
family. Austin married Susan Gilbert and built a stately house, the Homestead,
next door to the Evergreens. Emily and Susan became close friends and writing
collaborators, Susan reading and responding to Dickinson's poems throughout
their lives. Dickinson also exchanged correspondence with Samuel Bowles, editor
of the* Springfield Republican; *Josiah Holland, editor at Scribner's publishing
company; poet and novelist Helen Hunt Jackson; and Thomas Wentworth
Higginson, poet and critic. She lived the life of a private intellectual whose letters
recount a rich life of the mind.*

*Dickinson wrote throughout her life, but dating her poems can be done only
through analysis of her handwriting and though analysis of booklets of her poems
she called fascicles. Also, references to current events sometimes give clues to the
timing of her writing. For example, her most productive time seems to have been
from 1858 to 1865 when the Civil War provided her with both motivation and
topic for many a poem. Some have noted that she wrote about death and sadness,
but these Civil War poems clearly reflect the tragic times through which she lived.
She continued to produce poetry until her death, completing over 1,800 poems. In
1890, after her death, a family friend, Mabel Loomis Todd, and Higginson published* Poems, *followed by a second volume in 1890, and a third in 1896. No other
editors saw her manuscripts until Ralph W. Franklin was given access to them and
produced a version,* Poems *in 1998, which followed her particular punctuation*

and spelling patterns. These patterns give her poetry an extremely postmodern feel and flavor, for Dickinson was experimental in a variety of ways, using complex ideas in simple styles and creating new metaphors that challenge and intrigue readers as much in this century as in the last.

After great pain, a formal feeling comes–

EMILY DICKINSON

After great pain, a formal feeling comes–
The Nerves sit ceremonious, like Tombs–
The stiff Heart questions 'was it He, that bore,'
And 'Yesterday, or Centuries before'?

The Feet, mechanical, go round–   5
A Wooden way
Of Ground, or Air, or Ought–
Regardless grown,
A Quartz contentment, like a stone–

This is the Hour of Lead–   10
Remembered, if outlived,
As Freezing persons, recollect the Snow–
First–Chill–then Stupor–then the letting go–

[c. 1862]

Reprinted from *The Poems of Emily Dickinson,* by permission of the publisher and the Trustees of Amherst College. Copyright © 1998, 1951, 1955, 1979, 1983 by the President and Fellows of Harvard College.

Because I could not stop for Death–

EMILY DICKINSON

Because I could not stop for Death–
He kindly stopped for me–
The Carriage held but just Ourselves–
And Immortality.

We slowly drove–He knew no haste   5
And I had put away
My labor and my leisure too,
For His Civility–

We passed the School, where Children strove
At Recess–in the Ring–   10
We passed the Fields of Gazing Grain–
We passed the Setting Sun–

Or rather–He passed Us–
The Dews drew quivering and Chill–
For only Gossamer, my Gown–   15
My Tippet–only Tulle–[1]

We paused before a House that seemed
A Swelling of the Ground–
The Roof was scarcely visible–
The Cornice–in the Ground–   20

Since then–'tis Centuries–and yet
Feels shorter than the Day
I first surmised the Horses' Heads
Were toward Eternity–

[c. 1862]

[1]A tippet is a cape, and tulle is fine, filmy material.

Reprinted from *The Poems of Emily Dickinson,* by permission of the publisher and the Trustees of Amherst College. Copyright © 1998, 1951, 1955, 1979, 1983 by the President and Fellows of Harvard College.

I dwell in Possibility–

EMILY DICKINSON

I dwell in Possibility–
A fairer House than Prose–
More numerous of Windows–
Superior–for Doors–

Of Chambers as the Cedars–   5
Impregnable of eye–
And for an everlasting Roof
The Gambrels[1] of the Sky–

Of Visitors–the fairest–
For Occupation–This–   10
The spreading wide my narrow Hands
To gather Paradise–

[c. 1862]

---

[1]A steeply pitched roof.

Reprinted from *The Poems of Emily Dickinson,* by permission of the publisher and the Trustees of Amherst College. Copyright © 1998, 1951, 1955, 1979, 1983 by the President and Fellows of Harvard College.

I felt a Funeral, in my Brain

EMILY DICKINSON

I felt a Funeral, in my Brain,
And Mourners to and fro
Kept treading–treading–till it seemed
That Sense was breaking through–

And when they all were seated,   5
A Service, like a Drum–
Kept beating–beating–till I thought
My mind was going numb–

And then I heard them lift a Box
And creak across my Soul   10
With those same Boots of Lead, again,
Then Space–began to toll,

As all the Heavens were a Bell,
And Being, but an Ear,
And I, and Silence, some strange Race   15
Wrecked, solitary, here–

And then a Plank in Reason, broke,
And I dropped down, and down–
And hit a World, at every plunge,
And Finished knowing–then–   20

[C. 1862]

I heard a Fly buzz–when I died–

EMILY DICKINSON

I heard a Fly buzz–when I died–
The Stillness in the Room
Was like the Stillness in the Air–
Between the Heaves of Storm–

The Eyes around–had wrung them dry–   5
And Breaths were gathering firm
For that last Onset–when the King[1]
Be witnessed–in the Room–

I willed my Keepsakes–Signed away
What portion of me be   10
Assignable–and then it was
There imposed a Fly–

With Blue–uncertain–stumbling Buzz–
Between the light–and me–
And then the Windows failed–and then   15
I could not see to see–

[c. 1863]

---

[1]Likely an allusion to Christ the King who appears to the dying.

I Like to See It Lap the Miles

EMILY DICKINSON

I like to see it lap the Miles–
And lick the Valleys up–
And stop to feed itself at Tanks–
And then–prodigious step

Around a Pile of Mountains–   5
And supercilious peer
In Shanties–by the sides of Roads–
And then a Quarry pare

To fit its Ribs
And crawl between   10
Complaining all the while
In horrid–hooting stanza–
Then chase itself down Hill–

And neigh like Boanerges[1]–
Then–punctual as a Star   15
Stop–docile and omnipotent
At its own stable door–

[C. 1862]

---

[1]"Sons of thunder" in Mark 3:17; Jesus gives this name to the apostles James and John.

I'm Nobody! Who are you?

EMILY DICKINSON

I'm Nobody! Who are you?
Are you–Nobody–too?
Then there's a pair of us!
Dont tell! they'd advertise–you know!

How dreary–to be–Somebody!   5
How public–like a Frog–
To tell one's name–the livelong June–
To an admiring Bog!

[c. 1861]

I taste a liquor never brewed

EMILY DICKINSON

I taste a liquor never brewed–
From Tankards scooped in Pearl–
Not all the Vats upon the Rhine
Yield such an Alcohol!

Inebriate of Air–am I–ᅠᅠᅠᅠᅠᅠᅠᅠᅠᅠᅠᅠᅠᅠᅠᅠᅠ5
And Debauchee of Dew–
Reeling–thro endless summer days–
From inns of Molten Blue–

When "Landlords" turn the drunken Bee
Out of the Foxglove's door–ᅠᅠᅠᅠᅠᅠᅠᅠᅠᅠᅠᅠᅠ10
When Buttlerflies–renounce their "drams"–
I shall but drink the more!

Till Seraphs swing their snowy Hats–
And Saints–to windows run–
To see the little Tipplerᅠᅠᅠᅠᅠᅠᅠᅠᅠᅠᅠᅠᅠᅠᅠᅠ15
Leaning against the–Sun–

[c. 1861]

Reprinted from *The Poems of Emily Dickinson*, by permission of the publisher and the Trustees of Amherst College. Copyright © 1998, 1951, 1955, 1979, 1983 by the President and Fellows of Harvard College.

Much Madness is divinest Sense–

EMILY DICKINSON

Much Madness is divinest Sense–
To a discerning Eye–
Much Sense–the starkest Madness–
'Tis the Majority
In this, as all, prevail–
Assent–and you are sane–   5
Demur–you're straightway dangerous–
And handled with a Chain–

[c. 1863]

My life closed twice before its close–

EMILY DICKINSON

My life closed twice before its close–
It yet remains to see
If Immortality unveil
A third event to me

So huge, so hopeless to conceive   5
As these that twice befell.
Parting is all we know of heaven,
And all we need of hell.

[c. 1896]

My Life had stood–a Loaded Gun–

EMILY DICKINSON

My Life had stood–a Loaded Gun–
In Corners–till a Day
The Owner passed–identified–
And carried Me away–

And now We roam in Sovreign Woods–   5
And now We hunt the Doe–
And every time I speak for Him
The Mountains straight reply–

And do I smile, such cordial light
Upon the Valley glow–   10
It is as a Vesuvian face[1]
Had let it's pleasure through–

And when at Night–Our good Day done–
I guard My Master's Head–
'Tis better than the Eider Duck's[2]   15
Deep Pillow–to have shared–

To foe of His–I'm deadly foe–
None stir the second time–
On whom I lay a Yellow Eye–
Or an emphatic Thumb–   20

Though I than He–may longer live
He longer must–than I–
For I have but the power to kill,
Without–the power to die–

[c. 1863]

---

[1]Like Mount Vesuvius, that is, volcanic.

[2]The down of the eider duck (eiderdown).

One need not be a Chamber–to be Haunted–

EMILY DICKINSON

One need not be a Chamber–to be Haunted–
One need not be a House–
The Brain has Corridors–surpassing
Material Place–

Far safer, of a midnight meeting   5
External Ghost
Than it's interior confronting–
That cooler Host–

Far safer, through an Abbey gallop,
The Stones a'chase–   10
Than unarmed, one's a'self encounter–
In lonesome Place–

Ourself behind ourself, concealed–
Should startle most–
Assassin hid in our Apartment   15
Be Horror's least–

The Body–borrows a Revolver–
He bolts the Door–
O'erlooking a superior spectre–
Or More–   20

[c. 1862]

Reprinted from *The Poems of Emily Dickinson,* by permission of the publisher and the Trustees of Amherst College. Copyright © 1998, 1951, 1955, 1979, 1983 by the President and Fellows of Harvard College.

Some keep the Sabbath going to Church–

EMILY DICKINSON

Some keep the Sabbath going to Church–
I keep it, staying at Home–
With a Bobolink for a Chorister–
And an Orchard, for a Dome–

Some keep the Sabbath in Surplice[1]–   5
I, just wear my Wings–
And instead of tolling the Bell, for Church,
Our little Sexton[2]–sings.

God preaches, a noted Clergyman–
And the sermon is never long,   10
So instead of getting to Heaven, at last–
I'm going, all along.

[c. 1861]

---

[1]A long-sleeved gown worn by clergy.

[2]The property manager who also rings the church bells.

Reprinted from *The Poems of Emily Dickinson,* by permission of the publisher and the Trustees of Amherst College. Copyright © 1998, 1951, 1955, 1979, 1983 by the President and Fellows of Harvard College.

Success is counted sweetest

EMILY DICKINSON

Success is counted sweetest
By those who ne'er succeed.
To comprehend a nectar
Requires sorest need.

Not one of all the purple Host   5
Who took the Flag today
Can tell the definition
So clear of Victory

As he defeated–dying–
On whose forbidden ear   10
The distant strains of triumph
Burst agonized and clear!

[c. 1859]

Reprinted from *The Poems of Emily Dickinson,* by permission of the publisher and the Trustees of Amherst College. Copyright © 1998, 1951, 1955, 1979, 1983 by the President and Fellows of Harvard College.

The Brain–is wider than the Sky–

EMILY DICKINSON

The Brain–is wider than the Sky–
For–put them side by side–
The one the other will contain
With ease–and You–beside–

The Brain is deeper than the sea–   5
For–hold them–Blue to Blue–
The one the other will absorb–
As Sponges–Buckets–do–

The Brain is just the weight of God–
For–Heft them–Pound for Pound–   10
And they will differ–if they do–
As Syllable from Sound–

[c. 1863]

The Bustle in a House

EMILY DICKINSON

The Bustle in a House
The Morning after Death
Is solemnest of industries
Enacted upon Earth–

The Sweeping up the Heart   5
And putting Love away
We shall not want to use again
Until Eternity

[C. 1866]

The Soul selects her own Society–

EMILY DICKINSON

The Soul selects her own Society–
Then–shuts the Door–
To her divine Majority–
Present no more–

Unmoved–she notes the Chariots–pausing–   5
At her low Gate–
Unmoved–an Emperor be kneeling
Opon her Mat–

I've known her–from an ample nation–
Choose One–   10
Then–close the Valves of her attention–
Like Stone–

[c. 1862]

There's a certain Slant of light

EMILY DICKINSON

There's a certain Slant of light,
Winter Afternoons–
That oppresses, like the Heft
Of Cathedral Tunes–

Heavenly Hurt, it gives us–   5
We can find no scar,
But internal difference–
Where the Meanings, are–

None may teach it–Any–
'Tis the Seal Despair–   10
An imperial affliction
Sent us of the Air–

When it comes, the Landscape listens–
Shadows–hold their breath–
When it goes, 'tis like the Distance   15
On the look of Death–

[c. 1862]

This World is not conclusion

EMILY DICKINSON

This World is not conclusion.
A Species stands beyond–
Invisible, as Music–
But positive, as Sound–
It beckons, and it baffles–
Philosophy, dont know–   5
And through a Riddle, at the last–
Sagacity, must go–
To guess it, puzzles scholars–
To gain it, Men have borne
Contempt of Generations   10
And Crucifixion, shown–
Faith slips–and laughs, and rallies–
Blushes, if any see–
Plucks at a twig of Evidence–
And asks a Vane, the way–   15
Much Gesture, from the Pulpit–
Strong Hallelujahs roll–
Narcotics cannot still the Tooth
That nibbles at the soul–

[c. 1862]

Wild nights–Wild nights!

EMILY DICKINSON

Wild nights–Wild nights!
Were I with thee
Wild nights should be
Our luxury!

Futile–the winds–   5
To a Heart in port–
Done with the Compass–
Done with the Chart!

Rowing in Eden–
Ah–the Sea!   10
Might I but moor–tonight–
In thee!

[c. 1861]

John Donne
[1573–1631]

The son of a wealthy London merchant and a noblewoman, a relative of Sir Thomas More, JOHN DONNE began life with great advantage. He attended both Cambridge and Oxford and studied law. His father's death when he was nearing twenty left him a wealthy and independent young man. Donne is a fascinating study for he displays many features of the early modern period that coincide with the writing of Shakespeare's plays. He was both a wild young man about town, and a serious religious writer who struggled with the conflicts between his early Catholicism and the Anglicanism that blew in on the winds of change, dominating England throughout the first decade of the 1600s. By the time he was twenty, he had finished the poems in his Divine Poems as well as the first three poems in his Satires. By 1594 he wandered through Europe and by 1596 and 1597, he had served as a soldier in Cadiz and traveled to the Azores. In addition, his travels to Italy and Spain introduced him to the excitement of the literary and artistic Renaissance that swept through the south of Europe. Upon his return to London, he secretly married the daughter of Sir George Moore, lord lieutenant of the Tower of London, an act for which he was thrown in prison by his outraged father-in-law. Sir Francis Wooley rescued him and provided a home for the couple. The poetry he wrote to his wife is among the most treasured of personal writing from husband to wife. He finished his Satires and The Progress of the Soul during this time (1601). He also wrote a defense of suicide, Biathanatos, which was not published until after his death.

Donne then embarked on a mental and spiritual struggle that brought him to take holy orders in the Anglican Church in 1611. He wrote prose against Catholicism, Pseudo-Martyr (1610) and Ignatius His Conclave (1611), as well as his great mystical treatise, The Anatomy of the World. He was a favorite preacher of King James I and was appointed the Dean of St. Paul's Cathedral in 1621, a post he held until his death. His collected poems were printed in 1633, but his prose works, including his Letters and more than 150 Sermons were published in assorted venues from 1633 to 1651.

Donne displayed a range of intellectual and poetic talents as well as a multitude of personal faces. Thus he is remembered and admired as one of the great poets and thinkers of his own era and of the twentieth century as well. Donne has been appreciated for his conceits, his satire, his profound mysticism, and his political insight. Few poets have been so complete and so essentially paradoxical as John Donne.

Death be not proud

JOHN DONNE

Death be not proud, though some have callèd thee
Mighty and dreadful, for thou art not so;
For those whom thou think'st thou dost overthrow
Die not, poor death, nor yet canst thou kill me.
From rest and sleep, which but thy pictures be,   5
Much pleasure, then from thee much more must flow,
And soonest our best men with thee do go,
Rest of their bones, and soul's delivery.
Thou art slave to fate, chance, kings, and desperate men,
And dost with poison, war, and sickness dwell,   10
And poppy, or charms can make us sleep as well,
And better than thy stroke; why swell'st thou then?
One short sleep past, we wake eternally,
And death shall be no more; death, thou shalt die.

[c. 1610]

Published 1635 in *Poems*.

Paul Laurence Dunbar
[1872–1906]

The son of former Kentucky slaves, PAUL LAURENCE DUNBAR *became one of the first African-American writers to achieve national prominence. As a student in Dayton, Ohio High School, Dunbar saw several of his poems published in the* Dayton Herald; *pervasive race discrimination, however, prevented him from obtaining a job in journalism after graduation, despite having been voted class poet and president of his graduating class. Nonetheless, his first collection of poems,* Oak and Ivy, *appeared in 1893 when Dunbar was only twenty-one years old. Working as an elevator operator at the time, Dunbar enlisted the help of friends Wilbur Wright and Orville Wright (the brothers famous for their flying machine) to publish the volume privately. His reputation was enhanced by the recognition of the Western Association of Writers and prominent orator Frederick Douglass, who hired Dunbar to work in the Haitian Pavilion at the World Columbian Exposition in Chicago in 1893. In 1896 Dunbar's second collection,* Majors and Minors, *was published—and reviewed favorably (if condescendingly) by renowned critic William Dean Howells, who later that year convinced the publishing house of Dodd, Mead to publish* Lyrics of Lowly Life, *with an introduction by Howells himself. It was the publication of this collection that established Dunbar's reputation as a man of letters.*

Dunbar's most popular poems were written using African-American vernacular, while his more formal work in standard English received far less critical and popular attention. He expressed his frustration with this situation in "The Poet," who sings "serenely sweet," only to discover that the world praises not this "deep" verse but rather the "jingle in a broken tongue." In other poems, such as "We Wear the Mask," Dunbar unveils the "torn and bleeding hearts" hiding behind "the mask that grins and lies." Similar themes can be found in his short stories, particularly those in the 1898 volume Folks from Dixie, *in which he chronicled the myriad abuses heaped on African Americans both before and after emancipation. Throughout his work in fiction, nonfiction, and poetry, Dunbar reflects on the struggles of his race.*

In 1898, after a reading tour of England, Dunbar married fellow African-American poet Alice Ruth Moore and published another collection, Lyrics from the Hearthside. *By this time, however, his health was failing badly. He had suffered from tuberculosis for some time, and in the ensuing years he fought several bouts of pneumonia and other related illnesses. Dunbar's illness placed a strain on the marriage, and in 1902 he and his wife separated. He continued writing, however, publishing a highly acclaimed volume of poetry,* Lyrics of Love and Laughter, *the following year. This collection, appearing after several poorly* reviewed novels, revived the poet's reputation, but not his health. An increasing dependence on alcohol exacerbated his condition, and Dunbar died in 1906 at the age of thirty-three. His legacy remains strong, however, particularly among African-American writers. Contemporary poet Nikki Giovanni calls Dunbar "a natural resource of our people," and the final line of his 1899 poem "Sympathy" became internationally famous when Maya Angelou selected it as the title for the first volume of her autobiography: "I know why the caged bird sings."

We Wear the Mask

PAUL LAURENCE DUNBAR

We wear the mask that grins and lies,
   It hides our cheeks and shades our eyes,—
This debt we pay to human guile;
With torn and bleeding hearts we smile,
And mouth with myriad subtleties.   5

Why should the world be over-wise,
In counting all our tears and sighs?
Nay, let them only see us, while
   We wear the mask.

We smile, but, O great Christ, our cries   10
To thee from tortured souls arise.
We sing, but oh the clay is vile
Beneath our feet, and long the mile;
But let the world dream otherwise,
   We wear the mask!   15

[1896]

Sympathy

PAUL LAURENCE DUNBAR

I know what the caged bird feels, alas!
   When the sun is bright on the upland slopes;
When the wind stirs soft through the springing grass,
And the river flows like a stream of glass;
   When the first bird sings and the first bud opes,   5
And the faint perfume from its chalice steals—
I know what the caged bird feels!

I know why the caged bird beats his wing
   Till its blood is red on the cruel bars;
For he must fly back to his perch and cling   10
When he fain would be on the bough a-swing;
   And a pain still throbs in the old, old scars
And they pulse again with a keener sting—
   I know why he beats his wing!

I know why the caged bird sings, ah me,   15
   When his wing is bruised and his bosom sore,—
When he beats his bars and he would be free;
It is not a carol of joy or glee,
   But a prayer that he sends from his heart's deep core,
But a plea, that upward to Heaven he flings—   20
I know why the caged bird sings!

[1896]

First published in *Lyrics of Lowly Life* in 1896.

T. S. Eliot
[1888–1965]

T. S. ELIOT *was the seventh child of successful St. Louis merchant, Henry Ware Eliot, and school teacher, Charlotte Sterns Eliot. He showed such great intellectual abilities that he entered Harvard at age eighteen. There he studied English, Latin, Greek, German, and French literature. He also studied history, art, and philosophy, and wrote for the Harvard* Advocate. *After college he traveled in Europe and spent a year at the Sorbonne and wrote his first great poem, "The Love Song of J. Alfred Prufrock" at age twenty-three. He went home to America and studied for a doctorate at Harvard, returned to German to do doctoral research, but moved to London and Oxford at the beginning of World War I. In London he met Ezra Pound who championed Eliot's abilities as a poet and helped him publish "Prufrock" in* Poetry *in June 1915. Eliot also published "Preludes" and "Rhapsody on a Windy Night" in* Blast, *and "Portrait of a Lady" in* Others. *The following year he finished his doctorate but did not return to the United States to become a professor as his parents had expected. Instead he married Vivienne Haigh-Wood and took a job as a clerk in Lloyds Bank. During this era he wrote literary journalism for important newspapers and journals such as the* New Statesman, *the* Monist, *and the* Times Literary Supplement. *He became an assistant editor for the* Egoist *and wrote a short book on* Pound, Ezra Pound: His Metric and Poetry *(1918). His first book of poetry,* Prufrock and Other Observations *had appeared a year earlier. In 1920 he published* Poems *and a volume of essays,* The Sacred Wood.

In 1921, Eliot collapsed from over-work and spent a few months resting in Germany and traveling in France where he wrote The Waste Land *in consultation with Ezra Pound, (Pound mostly crossed out passages of a much longer draft; passages that were to become the starting points for later poems), that appeared in 1922. By 1925 Eliot was a literary celebrity, able to leave the bank and join the publishing house of Faber and Gwyer (later Faber and Faber). In 1927 he became a devout Anglican after years of meditation and study. In 1932, following years of Haigh-Wood's acute depressions, he and his first wife divorced. She died in a mental hospital in 1947. He published* The Hollow Men *and* Ash Wednesday *in 1930 and "Journey of the Magi" in 1931. His selected essays,* The Use of Poetry and The Use of Criticism, *were published in 1933. At that time also Eliot began to write drama, becoming a noted dramatist with* Murder in the Cathedral *in 1935 and* The Family Reunion *in 1939. His last great poems were "The Four Quartets: Burnt Norton" (1936), "East Coker" (1940), "The Dry Salvages" (1941), and "Little Gidding" (1942). He married Esme Valerie Fletcher in 1957 and lived as a celebrated writer until his death in 1965. He received the Nobel Prize for Literature and England's Order of Merit among many other honors.*

The Love Song of J. Alfred Prufrock

T. S. ELIOT

S'io credessi che mia risposta fosse
a persona che mai tornasse al mondo,
questa fiamma staria senza più scosse.
Ma per ciò che giammai di questo fondo
non tornò vivo alcun, s'i'odo il vero,
senza tema d'infamia ti rispondo.[1]

Let us go then, you and I,
When the evening is spread out against the sky
Like a patient etherised upon a table;
Let us go, through certain half-deserted streets,
The muttering retreats   5
Of restless nights in one-night cheap hotels
And sawdust restaurants with oyster-shells:
Streets that follow like a tedious argument
Of insidious intent
To lead you to an overwhelming question . . .   10
Oh, do not ask, 'What is it?'
Let us go and make our visit.

---

[1]"If I thought my answer were to one who would ever return to the world, this flame should stay without another movement; but since none ever returned alive from this depth, if what I hear is true, I answer thee without fear of infamy." Eliot's epigraph comes from Canto 27 of Dante's *Inferno*, in which Dante visits the eighth circle of hell, reserved for evil counselors. The words are uttered by Count Guido de Montefeltrano, also known in Dante's time as The Fox. Montefeltrano is condemned to burn in a prison of fire because of his destructive advice to Pope Boniface. A brilliant political and military tactician, Guido in his youth led troops against the Papacy and was excommunicated. He then repented his sins and retired to a monastery. The corrupt Pope Boniface, however, lured Guido out of retirement by offering him reinstatement in the church in exchange for his cunning services in suppressing the Pope's enemies. Seduced by the Pope's promises of a ticket to heaven, Guido aided the Pope's corrupt designs, only to find upon his death that he had been double-crossed and sent to hell for his efforts. Dante imagines Guido as a man "taken in by his own craftiness."

Published in *Prufrock and Other Observations* in 1917.

In the room the women come and go
Talking of Michelangelo,[2]

The yellow fog that rubs its back upon the window-panes,   15
The yellow smoke that rubs its muzzle on the window-panes,
Licked its tongue into the corners of the evening,
lingered upon the pools that stand in drains,
Let fall upon its back the soot that falls from chimneys,
Slipped by the terrace, made a sudden leap,   20
And seeing that it was a soft October night,
Curled once about the house, and fell asleep.

For indeed there will be time
For the yellow smoke that slides along the street
Rubbing its back upon the window-panes;   25
There will be time, there will be time
To prepare a face to meet the faces that you meet;
There will be time to murder and create,
And time for all the works and days of hands
That lift and drop a question on your plate;   30
Time for you and time for me,
And time yet for a hundred indecisions,
And for a hundred visions and revisions,
Before the taking of a toast and tea.

In the room the women come and go   35
Talking of Michelangelo.

And indeed there will be time
To wonder, 'Do I dare?' and, 'Do I dare?'
Time to turn back and descend the stair,
With a bald spot in the middle of my hair—   40
(They will say: 'How his hair is growing thin!')
My morning coat, my collar mounting firmly to the chin,
My necktie rich and modest, but asserted by a simple pin—
(They will say: 'But how his arms and legs are thin!')
Do I dare   45
Disturb the universe?

---

[2]Michelangelo (1475–1564), the revered Italian sculptor, painter, architect, and poet.

In a minute there is time
For decisions and revisions which a minute will reverse.
For I have known them all already, known them all—
Have known the evenings, mornings, afternoons,   *50*
I have measured out my life with coffee spoons;
I know the voices dying with a dying fall
Beneath the music from a farther room.
    So how should I presume?

And I have known the eyes already, known them all—   *55*
The eyes that fix you in a formulated phrase,
And when I am formulated, sprawling on a pin,
When I am pinned and wriggling on the wall,
Then how should I begin
to spit out all the butt-ends of my days and ways?   *60*
    And how should I presume?

And I have known the arms already, known them all—
Arms that are braceleted and white and bare
(But in the lamplight, downed with light brown hair!)
Is it perfume from a dress   *65*
That makes me so digress?
Arms that lie along a table, or wrap about a shawl.
    And should I then presume?
    And how should I begin?

   . . . . .

Shall I say, I have gone at dusk through narrow streets   *70*
And watched the smoke that rises from the pipes
Of lonely men in shirt-sleeves, leaning out of windows? . . .

I should have been a pair of ragged claws
Scuttling across the floors of silent seas.

   . . . . .

And the afternoon, the evening, sleeps so peacefully!   *75*
Smoothed by long fingers,
Asleep . . . tired . . . or it malingers,
Stretched on the floor, here beside you and me.
Should I, after tea and cakes and ices,
Have the strength to force the moment to its crisis?   *80*

But though I have wept and fasted, wept and prayed,
Though I have seen my head (grown slightly bald) brought in
    upon a platter,[3]
I am no prophet—and here's no great matter;
I have seen the moment of my greatness flicker,
And I have seen the eternal Footman hold my coat, and snicker,   *85*
And in short, I was afraid.

And would it have been worth it, after all,
After the cups, the marmalade, the tea,
Among the porcelain, among some talk of you and me,
Would it have been worth while,   *90*
To have bitten off the matter with a smile,
To have squeezed the universe into a ball
To roll it towards some overwhelming question,
To say: 'I am Lazarus,[4] come from the dead,
Come back to tell you all, I shall tell you all'—   *95*
If one, settling a pillow by her head,
    Should say: 'That is not what I meant at all.
    That is not it, at all.'

And would it have been worth it, after all,
Would it have been worth while,   *100*
After the sunsets and the dooryards and the sprinkled streets,
After the novels, after the teacups, after the skirts that trail along
    the floor—
And this, and so much more?—
It is impossible to say just what I mean!
But as if a magic lantern[5] threw the nerves in patterns on a   *105*
    screen:
Would it have been worth while

---

[3]In the Biblical story of Salome and John the Baptist (see Mark VI:17–28) Salome, the daughter of Queen Herodias hated John the Baptist. Herod, to please Herodias, imprisoned John. Salome danced before Herod and he promised to give anything she wished. Salome asked for the head of John the Baptist on a platter.

[4]Lazarus: Prufrock uses Jesus' parable of Lazarus and Dives told in Luke XVI:19–31. In the parable, Dives, a rich man, ignores the suffering of a poor man, Lazarus, who begs for crumbs from Dives's table. Lazarus dies and he goes to heaven. Dives goes to hell. Dives implores God to allow Lazarus to return from the dead to warn Dives's relatives to repent.

[5]An early form of optical projector.

If one, settling a pillow or throwing off a shawl,
And turning toward the window, should say:
   'That is not it at all,
   That is not what I meant, at all.'   *110*

   . . . . .

No! I am not Prince Hamlet,[6] nor was meant to be;
Am an attendant lord, one that will do
To swell a progress, start a scene or two,
Advise the prince; no doubt, an easy tool,
Deferential, glad to be of use,   *115*
Politic, cautious, and meticulous;
Full of high sentence, but a bit obtuse;
At times, indeed, almost ridiculous—
Almost, at times, the Fool[7]

I grow old . . . I grow old . . .   *120*
I shall wear the bottoms of my trousers rolled.

Shall I part my hair behind? Do I dare to eat a peach?
I shall wear white flannel trousers, and walk upon the beach.
I have heard the mermaids singing, each to each.

I do not think that they will sing to me.   *125*

I have seen them riding seaward on the waves
Combing the white hair of the waves blown back
When the wind blows the water white and black.

We have lingered in the chambers of the sea
By sea-girls wreathed with seaweed red and brown   *130*
Till human voices wake us, and we drown.

                                 [1915]

---

[6]Prince Hamlet: the protagonist of William Shakespeare's tragedy, *Hamlet*.

[7]The Fool, or jester, was a stock character of Elizabethan drama.

Robert Frost
[1874–1963]

The son of a journalist who died when **ROBERT FROST** *was only eleven, the now well-known poet lived with his mother in Lawrence, Massachusetts, where he worked at many jobs while finishing high school, where he was co-valedictorian of his class. While in school, he wrote for the* Lawrence High School Bulletin. *He married his co-valedictorian, Elinor White, and began his college career. Frost attended Dartmouth and Harvard, but dropped out of both shortly before the deaths of his three-year-old son and his mother. In search of financial stability, Frost bought a farm in Derry, New Hampshire, where he and Elinor had four more children while he wrote poetry and taught at the Pinkerton Academy. His first book,* A Boy's Will *appeared in 1913. Frost then sold the farm and moved his family to London where he met Ezra Pound who viewed Frost as a follower and composer of "Imagist" poems—poems of vivid pictoral language and minimal sentiment. However, Frost developed his own theory of the sound of poetry, that is, catching the word as it is heard and spoken. His* North of Boston *(1914) poems characterize his particular view of the purpose and practice of poetry. These poems use dramatic monologues to capture the realities of human life and words.*

Frost returned to the United States in 1915 and bought another farm in New Hampshire, but this time he was not dependent on farm income and minimal teaching. While in Europe, Frost had become friends with powerful editors and publishers, including Ellery Sedgwick editor of the Atlantic Monthly *and Henry Holt of the* New Republic. *He also became friends with the powerful poet and critic Louis Untermeyer. Frost taught at Amherst College and published his third book,* Mountain Interval *(1916). His fourth book,* New Hampshire, *won the Pulitzer Prize, followed by* West-Running Brook *in 1928, and* Collected Poems *in 1930, which won a second Pulitzer. Frost refused to join the political literary movements of the thirties but chose to write another personal and individual book,* A Further Range *(1936), which the critics attacked for lack of social relevance. In spite of its critics, the book also won a Pulitzer. In the late thirties, he suffered the deaths of two children and his wife, and he collapsed for a time. By 1942, however, he completed* A Witness Tree, *winner of yet another Pulitzer. This book was followed by* The Steeple Bush *in 1947 and* In the Clearing *in 1962. Frost spoke to the nation by reading "The Gift Outright" at President Kennedy's inauguration in 1961. He died two years later, a poet whose characters questioned their own comfortable assumptions about the world. With many well-wrought poems that demonstrate effective revisions of years of working and reworking, Frost was above all a craftsman.*

Desert Places

ROBERT FROST

Snow falling and night falling fast, oh, fast
In a field I looked into going past,
And the ground almost covered smooth in snow,
But a few weeds and stubble showing last.

The woods around it have it—it is theirs.   5
All animals are smothered in their lairs.
I am too absent-spirited to count;
The loneliness includes me unawares.

And lonely as it is, that loneliness
Will be more lonely ere it will be less—   10
A blanker whiteness of benighted snow
With no expression, nothing to express.

They cannot scare me with their empty spaces
Between stars—on stars where no human race is.
I have it in me so much nearer home   15
To scare myself with my own desert places.

[1934]

Mending Wall

ROBERT FROST

Something there is that doesn't love a wall,
That sends the frozen-ground-swell under it,
And spills the upper boulders in the sun;
And makes gaps even two can pass abreast.
The work of hunters is another thing: 5
I have come after them and made repair
Where they have left not one stone on a stone,
But they would have the rabbit out of hiding,
To please the yelping dogs. The gaps I mean,
No one has seen them made or heard them made,   10
But at spring mending-time we find them there.
I let my neighbor know beyond the hill;
And on a day we meet to walk the line
And set the wall between us once again.
We keep the wall between us as we go.   15
To each the boulders that have fallen to each.
And some are loaves and some so nearly balls
We have to use a spell to make them balance:
"Stay where you are until our backs are turned!"
We wear our fingers rough with handling them.   20
Oh, just another kind of outdoor game,
One on a side. It comes to little more:
There where it is we do not need the wall:
He is all pine and I am apple orchard.
My apple trees will never get across   25
And eat the cones under his pines, I tell him.
He only says, "Good fences make good neighbors."
Spring is the mischief in me, and I wonder
If I could put a notion in his head:
"*Why* do they make good neighbors? Isn't it   30
Where there are cows? But here there are no cows.

First appeared in Frost's second book of poems, *North of Boston,* in 1914.

Before I built a wall I'd ask to know
What I was walling in or walling out,
And to whom I was like to give offense.
Something there is that doesn't love a wall,   35
That wants it down." I could say "Elves" to him,
But it's not elves exactly, and I'd rather
He said it for himself. I see him there
Bringing a stone grasped firmly by the top
In each hand, like an old-stone savage armed.   40
He moves in darkness as it seems to me,
Not of woods only and the shade of trees.
He will not go behind his father's saying,
And he likes having thought of it so well
He says again, "Good fences make good neighbors."   45

[1914]

Birches

ROBERT FROST

When I see birches bend to left and right
Across the lines of straighter darker trees,
I like to think some boy's been swinging them.
But swinging doesn't bend them down to stay
As ice storms do. Often you must have seen them   5
Loaded with ice a sunny winter morning
After a rain. They click upon themselves
As the breeze rises, and turn many-colored
As the stir cracks and crazes their enamel.
Soon the sun's warmth makes them shed crystal shells   10
Shattering and avalanching on the snow crust—
Such heaps of broken glass to sweep away
You'd think the inner dome of heaven had fallen.
They are dragged to the withered bracken by the load,
And they seem not to break; though once they are bowed   15
So low for long, they never right themselves:
You may see their trunks arching in the woods
Years afterwards, trailing their leaves on the ground
Like girls on hands and knees that throw their hair
Before them over their heads to dry in the sun.   20
But I'was going to say when Truth broke in
With all her matter of fact about the ice storm,
I should prefer to have some boy bend them
As he went out and in to fetch the cows—
Some boy too far from town to learn baseball,   25
Whose only play was what he found himself,
Summer or winter, and could play alone.
One by one he subdued his father's trees
By riding them down over and over again
Until he took the stiffness out of them,   30
And not one but hung limp, not one was left
For him to conquer. He learned all there was

First appeared in the *Atlantic Monthly,* August 1915. First collected in *Mountain Interval*
in 1916.

To learn about not launching out too soon
And so not carrying the tree away
Clear to the ground. He always kept his poise   35
To the top branches, climbing carefully
With the same pains you use to fill a cup
Up to the brim, and even above the brim.
Then he flung outward, feet first, with a swish,
Kicking his way down through the air to the ground.   40
So was I once myself a swinger of birches.
And so I dream of going back to be.
It's when I'm weary of considerations,
And life is too much like a pathless wood
Where your face burns and tickles with the cobwebs   45
Broken across it, and one eye is weeping
From a twig's having lashed across it open.
I'd like to get away from earth awhile
And then come back to it and begin over.
May no fate willfully misunderstand me   50
And half grant what I wish and snatch me away
Not to return. Earth's the right place for love:
I don't know where it's likely to go better.
I'd like to go by climbing a birch tree,
And climb black branches up a snow-white trunk   55
Toward heaven, till the tree could bear no more,
But dipped its top and set me down again.
That would be good both going and coming back.
One could do worse than be a swinger of birches.

[1916]

70

Fire and Ice

ROBERT FROST

Some say the world will end in fire,
Some say in ice.
From what I've tasted of desire
I hold with those who favor fire.
But if it had to perish twice,   5
I think I know enough of hate
To say that for destruction ice
Is also great
And would suffice.

[1920]

First appeared in *Harper's Magazine,* December 1920. First collected in *New Hampshire* in 1923.

The Road Not Taken

ROBERT FROST

Two roads diverged in a yellow wood,
And sorry I could not travel both
And be one traveler, long I stood
And looked down one as far as I could
To where it bent in the undergrowth;   5

Then took the other, as just as fair,
And having perhaps the better claim,
Because it was grassy and wanted wear;
Though as for that the passing there
Had worn them really about the same,   10

And both that morning equally lay
In leaves no step had trodden black.
Oh, I kept the first for another day!
Yet knowing how way leads on to way,
I doubted if I should ever come back.   15

I shall be telling this with a sigh
Somewhere ages and ages hence:
Two roads diverged in a wood, and I—
I took the one less traveled by,
And that has made all the difference.   20

[1915]

First appeared in the *Atlantic Monthly,* August 1915. First collected in *Mountain Interval* in 1916.

Stopping by Woods on a Snowy Evening

ROBERT FROST

Whose woods these are I think I know.
His house is in the village though;
He will not see me stopping here
To watch his woods fill up with snow.

My little horse must think it queer   5
To stop without a farmhouse near
Between the woods and frozen lake
The darkest evening of the year.

He gives his harness bells a shake
To ask if there is some mistake.   10
The only other sound's the sweep
Of easy wind and downy flake.

The woods are lovely, dark and deep,
But I have promises to keep,
And miles to go before I sleep,   15
And miles to go before I sleep.

[1923]

Nothing Gold Can Stay

ROBERT FROST

Nature's first green is gold,
Her hardest hue to hold.
Her early leaf's a flower;
But only so an hour.
Then leaf subsides to leaf.   *5*
So Eden sank to grief,
So dawn goes down to day.
Nothing gold can stay.

[1923]

Reprinted from *The Poetry of Robert Frost*, edited by Edward Connery Lathem. Copyright Lesley Frost Ballantine 1964, 1970, 1975, copyright 1936, 1942, 1951, 1956 by Robert Frost; copyright 1923, 1928, 1947, 1969 by Henry Holt and Company. Reprinted with permission of Henry Holt and Company, LLC.

Thomas Hardy
[1840–1928]

THOMAS HARDY *was born on June 2, 1840, the first child of Thomas and Jemima Hardy. He would be followed by two sisters and a brother. The family lived at Higher Bockhampton, Dorset, England—a hamlet consisting of some ten houses situated in a wooded area on the edge of Puddletown Heath (which Hardy was later to christen Edgon Heath). As a young boy, Hardy memorized large swatches of the* Book of Common Prayer, *and on wet Sundays, he would wrap himself in a tablecloth and lead the family in the Service for Morning Prayer.*

Hardy's mother, not necessarily taken with the religious life, enrolled her son in a nonconformist school, and within a year or two had secured him additional tuition in Latin. He left school at sixteen, with a good grounding in Latin, drawing, ancient history, and various branches of mathematics. The same year he was apprenticed to the local architect in Dorchester, John Hicks. Five years later, in 1861, he set off for London to practice architecture on a larger scale.

In London, he worked at his architectural career while reading English literature and taking advantage of the city's museums, opera-houses, and concert halls. He began to write poems ("Hap" and "The Ruined Maid" date from this period). Desperate to find his way into print, he wrote a first novel, The Poor Man and the Lady, *which was rejected. But the publisher's reader, George Meredith, encouraged Hardy to write another, which resulted in his first published book,* Desperate Remedies *(1871). During this time, he read Darwin's* The Origin of Species *and became an agnostic, adopting a scientific world view touched with a sense of beauty and nostalgia.*

By 1870, he returned to Dorset where he continued to write fiction. His first major hit was Far From the Madding Crowd *(1874). On the strength of this success, he was able to marry Emma Lavinia Gifford, a woman he had met and fallen in love with in 1870. For the next 22 years he wrote and published fiction and became one of England's leading novelists, famous as the sexually frank and socially challenging author of* Return of the Native *(1878),* The Mayor of Casterbridge *(1885),* The Woodlanders *(1887),* Tess of the d'Urbervilles *(1891), and* Jude the Obscure *(1895).*

In 1898, after the stormy success of Jude the Obscure, *Hardy surprised his readers by presenting them with not another novel but instead,* Wessex Poems, *his first collection of verse—a collection that included a good number of those early poems rejected by editors in the 1860s. This book was followed by seven more,* Poems of the Past and the Present *(1901—which included "The Darkling Thrush"),* Time's Laughingstocks *(1909),* Satires of Circumstance *(1914—*

which included "The Convergence of the Twain"), Moments of Vision *(1917),* Late Lyrics and Earlier *(1922),* Human Shows *(1925), and* Winter Words *(posthumous, 1928). He died at age 87 on January 11, 1928, equally famous as novelist and poet.*

—Bill Morgan, *Illinois State University*

The Ruined Maid

THOMAS HARDY

"O 'Melia, my dear, this does everything crown!
Who could have supposed I should meet you in Town?
And whence such fair garments, such prosperi-ty?"—
"O didn't you know I'd been ruined?" said she.

—"You left us in tatters, without shoes or socks,   5
Tired of digging potatoes, and spudding up docks[1];
And now you've gay bracelets and bright feathers three!"—
"Yes: that's how we dress when we're ruined," said she.

—"At home in the barton[2] you said 'thee' and 'thou,'
And 'thik oon,' and 'theäs oon,' and 't'other'; but now   10
Your talking quite fits 'ee for high compa-ny!"—
"Some polish is gained with one's ruin," said she.

—"Your hands were like paws then, your face blue and bleak
But now I'm bewitched by your delicate cheek,
And your little gloves fit as on any la-dy!"—   15
"We never do work when we're ruined," said she.

—"You used to call home-life a hag-ridden dream,
And you'd sigh, and you'd sock[3]; but at present you seem
To know not of megrims[4] or melancho-ly!"—
"True. One's pretty lively when ruined," said she.   20

---

[1] Spading up dockweed.

[2] Farmyard

[3] Groan

[4] Blues

First published in 1866.

—"I wish I had feathers, a fine sweeping gown,
And a delicate face, and could strut about Town!"—
"My dear—a raw country girl, such as you be,
Cannot quite expect that. You ain't ruined," said she.

[1901]

Robert Herrick
[1591-1674]

ROBERT HERRICK *of all poets best displays the transition from the grand atti-*
tudes of the Renaissance—as displayed by William Shakespeare and Herrick's
mentor, the great dramatist Ben Jonson—to the repression of the Puritan inter-
lude and back to the rollicking good humor of the Restoration. Born in London,
he was the son of a goldsmith who died soon after his birth. Herrick's mother took
him off to the village of Hampton to enjoy a childhood in the country. He was
then briefly apprenticed to a jeweler but quickly rejected the work and was sent
on to St. John's College, Cambridge, from which he graduated in 1617. He wrote
poetry with the "tribe of Ben" and enjoyed the life of the city but failed to gain a
court appointment. He then took orders in the Anglican church and served as a
military chaplain to the Duke of Buckingham. Shortly after, in 1629, King
Charles II appointed him Prior in Devonshire where he settled in comfortably
and began to write pastoral songs in addition to his lighthearted courtly lyrics.
These were collected in his first publication, Hesperides, *in 1648. The previous*
year he had refused to sign the Solemn League and Covenant, (a binding agree-
ment between Scotland swearing loyalty to the English Parliament), and was thus
relieved of his role as prior. When the Restoration brought back the crown,
Herrick regained his appointment in Devonshire parish and served there until his
death.

Herrick has been described as thoroughly pagan, a lover of life and good liv-
ing. His poems sing of wine, women, and song, not necessarily in that order. He
commanded all about him to live joyfully and seize the day whenever possible.
His conscience may have bothered him at times, for he was also the author of
Noble Numbers, *poems of praise to the Divine and repentance for transgressions.*
Most of all, though, he was the poet of the joys of the simple life, praising the
English countryside where he grew up and where he spent his happiest years as a
village priest. Herrick was the opposite of the metaphysical poets who dwelt on the
life of the spirit and soul. Herrick dwelt instead on the life of the senses, praising
all of life's richness and all the blessings that come from time spent at the dining
table and wandering through fields of daisies and sunflowers. He also was most
able at praising the beauties of a young woman whether clad or unclad, perhaps
not the ideal image for a priest but certainly the ultimate expression of one who
followed the great tradition of the Renaissance.

To the Virgins, to Make Much of Time

ROBERT HERRICK

Gather ye rose-buds while ye may,
    Old Time is still a-flying;
And this same flower that smiles today,
    Tomorrow will be dying.

The glorious lamp of heaven, the sun,   5
    The higher he's a-getting,
The sooner will his race be run,
    And nearer he's to setting.

That age is best which is the first,
    When youth and blood are warmer;   10
But being spent, the worse, and worst
    Times still succeed the former.

Then be not coy, but use your time,
    And while ye may, go marry;
For having lost but once your prime,   15
    You may for ever tarry.

[1648]

First published in *Hesperides* in 1648.

Delight in Disorder

ROBERT HERRICK

A sweet disorder in the dress
Kindles in clothes a wantonness.
A lawn[1] about the shoulders thrown
Into a fine distraction;
An erring lace, which here and there   5
Enthralls the crimson stomacher,
A cuff neglectful, and thereby
Ribbons to flow confusedly;
A winning wave, deserving note,
In the tempestuous petticoat;   10
A careless shoestring, in whose tie
I see a wild civility;
Do more bewitch me than when art
Is too precise in every part.

[1648]

[1]Linen scarf

First published in *Hesperides* in 1648.

Langston Hughes
[1902–1967]

A major figure of the Harlem Renaissance, LANGSTON HUGHES *was born in Joplin, Missouri. His father left for Mexico in 1903, and after traveling for a time with his mother, Hughes moved to Lawrence, Kansas to live with his grandmother. He graduated from high school in Cleveland—again living with his mother—and then spent fifteen months with his father in Mexico and a year at Columbia University before he shipped on a merchant vessel abroad traveling to Africa. He worked for a year in Paris and Venice before returning to the United States.*

Hughes became interested in literature while still young, and published some of his most important poems before his trip abroad. In fact, by the time he was "discovered," working as a busboy, by poet Vachel Lindsay in 1925, he had already established himself as one of the central poets of the Harlem Renaissance. In 1921 The Crisis, *an important journal of African-American letters edited by W. E. B. Du Bois, was published. "The Negro Speaks of Rivers," and "The Weary Blues" appeared two years later in the* Amsterdam News *(a journal published in New York).*

Hughes worked in many genres, including drama, prose fiction, and journalism. He also edited literary anthologies, and offered support and encouragement for emerging writers such as Alice Walker and Gwendolyn Brooks. His first book of poetry, The Weary Blues, *was published in 1926, and his first novel,* Not Without Laughter, *appeared in 1930. He also collaborated for many years writing children's books with novelist Arna Bontemps. Besides the widely anthologized poems mentioned here, Hughes was also widely known for his sketches in the* Chicago Defender *featuring Harlem sage Jesse B. Semple. With Semple, Hughes created a persona through which he could humorously but pointedly address issues of race relations and the condition of African Americans.*

As a member of the Harlem Renaissance and a noted black man of letters, Hughes created controversy with his rejection of the bourgeois aspirations of upper-middle class African Americans, whose value systems he saw as a slavish imitation of white society. He worked toward a literature that was uniquely African American, rather than one that derived its structures and standards from the literatures of Europe. In poems such as "The Weary Blues" he sought to reproduce the rhythms of the blues and to focus on the realities of African-American life. His was a dominant voice in African-American literature, and he shed light on the concerns of black America far beyond the dissolution of the Harlem Renaissance.

—David L. G. Arnold, *University of Wisconsin, Stevens Point*

Harlem [2]

LANGSTON HUGHES

What happens to a dream deferred?

   Does it dry up
   like a raisin in the sun?
   Or fester like a sore—
   And then run?   5
   Does it stink like rotten meat?
   Or crust and sugar over—
   like a syrupy sweet?

   Maybe it just sags
   like a heavy load.   10

   Or does it explode?

[1951]

Reprinted from *The Collected Poems of Langston Hughes,* by permission of Alfred A. Knopf, a division of Random House, Inc. Copyright © 1994 by The Estate of Langston Hughes.

The Negro Speaks of Rivers

LANGSTON HUGHES

I've known rivers:
I've known rivers ancient as the world and older than the
    flow of human blood in human veins.

My soul has grown deep like the rivers.

I bathed in the Euphrates when dawns were young.   *5*
I built my hut near the Congo and it lulled me to sleep.
I looked upon the Nile and raised the pyramids above it.
I heard the singing of the Mississippi when Abe Lincoln
    went down to New Orleans, and I've seen its muddy
    bosom turn all golden in the sunset.   *10*

I've known rivers:
Ancient, dusky rivers.

My soul has grown deep like the rivers.

[1921, 1926]

The Weary Blues

LANGSTON HUGHES

Droning a drowsy syncopated tune,
Rocking back and forth to a mellow croon,
   I heard a Negro play.
Down on Lenox Avenue the other night
By the pale dull pallor of an old gas light   5
   He did a lazy sway. . . .
   He did a lazy sway. . . .
To the tune o' those Weary Blues.
With his ebony hands on each ivory key
He made that poor piano moan with melody.   10
   O Blues!
Swaying to and fro on his rickety stool
He played that sad raggy tune like a musical fool.
   Sweet Blues!
Coming from a black man's soul.   15
   O Blues!
In a deep song voice with a melancholy tone
I heard that Negro sing, that old piano moan—
   "Ain't got nobody in all this world,
      Ain't got nobody but ma self.   20
      I's gwine to quit ma frownin'
      And put ma troubles on the shelf."

Thump, thump, thump, went his foot on the floor.
He played a few chords then he sang some more—
   "I got the Weary Blues   25
      And I can't be satisfied.
      Got the Weary Blues
      And can't be satisfied—

I ain't happy no mo'
   And I wish that I had died."   *30*
And far into the night he crooned that tune.
The stars went out and so did the moon.
The singer stopped playing and went to bed
While the Weary Blues echoed through his head.
He slept like a rock or a man that's dead.   *35*

[1925]

Dream Boogie

LANGSTON HUGHES

Good morning, daddy!
Ain't you heard
The boogie-woogie rumble
Of a dream deferred?

Listen closely: 5
You'll hear their feet
Beating out and beating out a—

*You think
It's a happy beat?*

Listen to it closely: 10
Ain't you heard
something underneath
like a–

What did I say?

Sure,   15
I'm happy!
Take it away!

*Hey, pop!
Re-bop!
Mop!*   20

Y-e-a-h!

[1951]

John Keats
[1795–1821]

JOHN KEATS'S *father kept a London livery stable—not a very auspicious beginning for the Romantic poet of the sublimely beautiful. His father died when he
was nine, and when he was fifteen, he lost his mother to tuberculosis. His brother
died of the same disease a few years later, and it took Keats, too, at age twenty-
six. Tuberculosis was common in the early 1800s, and was especially prevelant
among those who lived in London's smoggy interior. Despite these challenges, and
his early death, Keats produced a large volume of memorable poetry.*

*He attended school at Enfield, but in 1810 was apprenticed to a surgeon. The
medical profession did not have the status that it has today, and this change was
not a social improvement for the young Keats. Despite his removal from school,
he read and fell in love with Edmund Spenser's* Faerie Queen, *and even as he finished his apprenticeship and began work in a London hospital, his heart and
imagination were with Spenser's world of elves and knights. He met all the
Romantic writers, including Percy Byssche Shelley and Samuel Taylor Coleridge,
and became friends with Leigh Hunt, editor of* The Examiner, *which published
some of his early sonnets. Keats dedicated his first volume of poems to Hunt in
1817. His first long poem,* Endymion, *appeared in 1818, but his friendship with
Hunt, who was on the outs with the London critics, drew criticism of the poem.
Keats was hurt, but continued to write, despite Shelley's later argument in*
Adonais *that the critics had killed Keats with their reviews. At the same time he
fell hopelessly in love with Fanny Brawne, whose social position would not allow
her to marry a stable-boy-turned-physician, whatever poetic talents he possessed.
These losses seemed to fuel his poetic passion. In 1819, he published* The Eve of
St. Agnes, *arguably the signature poem of the sensuous and fanciful wing of the
Romantic movement. This poem tells the story of a young knight who brings
beautiful food to his lady's chamber, and appears to her as if in a dream to persuade her to run away with him, which she does. His next two poems,* La Belle
Dame sans Merci (The Beautiful Woman Without Mercy), *a poem about a
witch, and* Lamia, *a poem about a woman who can become a snake, followed in
1820.* Isabella, or The Pot of Basil, *followed, a tale taken from Boccaccio's*
Decameron *about a woman who plants her unfaithful lover's head in a pot of
herbs. His last poem, the unfinished* Hyperion, *recounts a classical myth, and
throughout the last years of his life, he wrote the sonnets that have become the
jewels of the Romantic movement.*

On First Looking into Chapman's Homer[1]

JOHN KEATS

Much have I traveled in the realms of gold,
    And many goodly states and kingdoms seen;
    Round many western islands have I been
Which bards in fealty[2] to Apollo[3] hold.
Oft of one wide expanse had I been told   5
    That deep-browed Homer ruled as his demesne,[4]
    Yet did I never breathe its pure serene
Till I heard Chapman speak out loud and bold.
Then felt I like some watcher of the skies
    When a new planet swims into his ken;   10
Or like stout Cortez[5] when with eagle eyes
    He stared at the Pacific—and all his men
Looked at each other with a wild surmise—
    Silent, upon a peak in Darien.[6]

[1816]

---

[1]Keats recounts the excitement he felt reading George Chapman's Elizabethan translations of *The Iliad* and *The Odyssey*.

[2]Loyalty

[3]The god of the sun and of poetry.

[4]Domain

[5]Not, unfortunately, the first Spaniard to see the Pacific; Keats goofed.

[6]Isthmus of Panama.

First published in London's *The Examiner,* Dec. 1, 1816.

Ode to a Nightingale

JOHN KEATS

I

My heart aches, and a drowsy numbness pains
   My sense, as though of hemlock[1] I had drunk,
Or emptied some dull opiate to the drains
   One minute past, and Lethe-wards[2] had sunk:
'Tis not through envy of thy happy lot,   *5*
   But being too happy in thine happiness—
      That thou, light-wingèd Dryad[3] of the trees,
        In some melodious plot
   Of beechen green, and shadows numberless,
      Singest of summer in full-throated ease.   *10*

II

O, for a draught of vintage! that hath been
   Cooled a long age in the deep-delved earth,
Tasting of Flora[4] and the country green,
   Dance, and Provençal song, and sunburnt mirth!
O for a beaker full of the warm South,   *15*
   Full of the true, the blushful Hippocrene,[5]
      With beaded bubbles winking at the brim,
        And purple-stainèd mouth;
   That I might drink, and leave the world unseen,
      And with thee fade away into the forest dim.   *20*

---

[1] Poison

[2] Lethe, river of forgetfulness in Greek mythic Hades.

[3] Wood nymph

[4] Flower goddess

[5] Fountain of the muses.

First published in *Annals of the Fine Arts* in July, 1819. Republished in *John Keats, Lamia, Isabella, The Eve of St. Agnes, and Other Poems* in 1820.

III

Fade far away, dissolve, and quite forget
    What thou, among the leaves hast never known,
The weariness, the fever, and the fret
    Here, where men sit and hear each other groan;
Where palsy shakes a few, sad, last gray hairs,   *25*
      Where youth grows pale, and specter-thin, and dies,
        Where but to think is to be full of sorrow
          And leaden-eyed despairs,
      Where Beauty cannot keep her lustrous eyes;
        Or new Love pine at them beyond tomorrow.   *30*

IV

Away! away! for I will fly to thee,
    Not charioted by Bacchus and his pards,[6]
But on the viewless wings of Poesy,
    Though the dull brain perplexes and retards:
Already with thee! tender is the night,   *35*
      And haply the Queen-Moon is on her throne,
        Clustered around by all her starry Fays;
          But here there is no light,
    Save what from heaven is with the breezes blown
      Through verdurous glooms and winding mossy ways.   *40*

V

I cannot see what flowers are at my feet,
    Nor what soft incense hangs upon the boughs,
But, in embalmed[7] darkness, guess each sweet
    Wherewith the seasonable month endows
The grass, the thicket, and the fruit-tree wild;   *45*
      What hawthorn, and the pastoral eglantine;
        Fast fading violets covered up in leaves;
          And mid-May's eldest child,
    The coming musk-rose, full of dewy wine,
      The murmurous haunt of flies on summer eves.   *50*

---

[6]God of wine, whose chariot was drawn by leopards.

[7]Wrapped in sweet scent.

VI

Darkling I listen; and for many a time
  I have been half in love with easeful Death,
Called him soft names in many a musèd rhyme,
  To take into the air my quiet breath;
Now more than ever seems it rich to die,   55
  To cease upon the midnight with no pain,
    While thou art pouring forth thy soul abroad
      In such an ecstasy!
  Still wouldst thou sing, and I have ears in vain—
    To thy high requiem become a sod.   60

VII

Thou wast not born for death, immortal Bird!
  No hungry generations tread thee down;
The voice I hear this passing night was heard
  In ancient days by emperor and clown:
Perhaps the selfsame song that found a path   65
  Through the sad heart of Ruth[8] when, sick for home,
    She stood in tears amid the alien corn:
      The same that oft-times hath
  Charmed magic casements, opening on the foam
    Of perilous seas, in faery lands forlorn.   70

VIII

Forlorn! the very word is like a bell
  To toll me back from thee to my sole self!
Adieu! the fancy cannot cheat so well
  As she is famed to do, deceiving elf.
Adieu! adieu! thy plaintive anthem fades   75
  Past the near meadows, over the still stream,
    Up the hill side; and now 'tis buried deep
      In the next valley-glades:
  Was it a vision, or a waking dream?
    Fled is that music:—Do I wake or sleep?   80

[1819]

---

[8]The Book of Ruth in the Bible tells of a young woman far from home.

Ode on a Grecian Urn

JOHN KEATS

I

Thou still unravished bride of quietness,
  Thou foster-child of silence and slow time,
Sylvan[1] historian, who canst thus express
  A flowery tale more sweetly than our rhyme:
What leaf-fringed legend haunts about thy shape   5
  Of deities or mortals, or of both,
    In Tempe or the dales of Arcady?
  What men or gods are these? What maidens loth?
What mad pursuit? What struggle to escape?
    What pipes and timbrels? What wild ecstasy?   10

II

Heard melodies are sweet, but those unheard
  Are sweeter; therefore, ye soft pipes, play on;
Not to the sensual ear, but, more endeared,
  Pipe to the spirit ditties of no tone:
Fair youth, beneath the trees, thou canst not leave   15
  Thy song, nor ever can those trees be bare;
    Bold Lover, never, never canst thou kiss,
Though winning near the goal—yet, do not grieve;
  She cannot fade, though thou hast not thy bliss,
    For ever wilt thou love, and she be fair!   20

---

[1]Of the woodland.

First published in *Annals of the Fine Arts,* December, 1819. Reprinted with minor changes in *John Keats, Lamia, Isabella, The Eve of St. Agnes, and Other Poems* in 1820.

III

Ah, happy, happy boughs! that cannot shed
   Your leaves, nor ever bid the Spring adieu;
And, happy melodist, unwearièd,
   For ever piping songs for ever new;
More happy love! more happy, happy love!   25
   For ever warm and still to be enjoyed,
      For ever panting, and for ever young—
All breathing human passion far above,
   That leaves a heart high-sorrowful and cloyed,
      A burning forehead, and a parching tongue.   30

IV

Who are these coming to the sacrifice?
   To what green altar, O mysterious priest,
Lead'st thou that heifer lowing at the skies,
   And all her silken flanks with garlands dressed?
What little town by river or sea shore,   35
   Or mountain-built with peaceful citadel,
      Is emptied of this folk, this pious morn?
And, little town, thy streets for evermore
   Will silent be; and not a soul to tell
      Why thou art desolate, can e'er return.   40

V

O Attic[2] shape! Fair attitude! with brede
   Of marble men and maidens overwrought,
With forest branches and the trodden weed;
   Thou, silent form, dost tease us out of thought
As doth eternity: Cold Pastoral!   45
   When old age shall this generation waste,
      Thou shalt remain, in midst of other woe
Than ours, a friend to man, to whom thou say'st,
   'Beauty is truth, truth beauty,—that is all
      Ye know on earth, and all ye need to know.'   50

[1819]

---

[2]Grecian

Christopher Marlowe
[1564–1593]

CHRISTOPHER MARLOWE *was born to a Canterbury shoemaker in 1564—the exact year as William Shakespeare. Both men became celebrated poets and playwrights, but Marlowe was the predecessor because his brilliant literary career was established at the time of his tragic death, when Shakespeare's was only beginning.*

Marlowe received a scholarship to the prestigious King's School and then another to Corpus Christi College, at the University of Cambridge, where he matriculated in 1580. Around this time he became involved with the secret service organized by Sir Francis Walsingham to protect Queen Elizabeth I, primarily from Catholics conspiring to overthrow her Protestant regime. Despite tantalizing evidence discovered and debated by recent scholarship, it is not known precisely what Marlowe's spywork involved, though it may have included a trip to Rheims, a center of Catholic intrigue on the Continent. Marlowe's long absences from university raised suspicions with college officials that he was secretly a Catholic convert and his master's degree was withheld. In an extraordinary move, the Queen's Privy Council intervened with a letter to the university, to allow him to receive his degree, in 1587, "because it was not Her Majesty's pleasure that anyone employed, as he had been, in matters touching the benefit of his country, should be defamed by those that are ignorant in th' affairs he went about."

Marlowe's six short years on the literary and intellectual cutting edge in London came to an end at an inn where he was fatally stabbed in the company of three men who, like him, had ties to the world of double agents and con men. Court records discovered in 1925 indicate that he was involved in a dispute over the "reckoning" of the bill, but speculation continues as to whether the true reason was a matter of political intrigue.

As a student Marlowe had already written verse translations from the classical Latin poets Lucan and Ovid and, before leaving Cambridge, he wrote a hugely successful play that revolutionized the London stage, Tamburlaine. *Its protagonist, a fourteenth century Mongol of humble birth who rose to conquer much of Asia, embodies boundless human ambition and articulates it in blank verse of unprecedented dramatic power. This play, among others, most notably the intellectually daring* Doctor Faustus, *served as a school for later Elizabethan dramatists. Marlowe also left an unfinished narrative poem in iambic pentameter couplets,* Hero and Leander, *which is an original, erotic version of a classical myth.*

—Curtis Gruenler, *Hope College*

The Passionate Shepherd to His Love

CHRISTOPHER MARLOWE

Come live with me and be my love,
And we will all the pleasures prove
That valleys, groves, hills, and fields,
Woods, or steepy mountain yields.

And we will sit upon the rocks,   5
Seeing the shepherds feed their flocks,
By shallow rivers to whose falls
Melodious birds sing madrigals.

And I will make thee beds of roses
And a thousand fragrant posies.   10
A cap of flowers, and a kirtle
Embroidered all with leaves of myrtle.

A gown made of the finest wool
Which from our pretty lambs we pull;
Fair lined slippers for the cold,   15
With buckles of the purest gold;

A belt of straw and ivy buds,
With coral clasps and amber studs:
And if these pleasures may thee move,
Come live with me, and be my love.   20

The shepherd swains shall dance and sing
For thy delight each May morning:
If these delights thy mind may move,
Then live with me and be my love.

[c.1599]

First published in *The Passionate Pilgrim* in 1599. Reprinted in *England's Helicon* in 1600.

Andrew Marvell
[1621–1678]

ANDREW MARVELL *was born in England, in the region of Yorkshire, as the son of a reverend. He began his studies at Trinity College in Cambridge at the age of twelve, but eventually abandoned his formal studies after his father died in a drowning accident. By sixteen he had already published two poems, one written in Latin and the other in Greek, in a Cambridge anthology. While still in his twenties, he traveled throughout Europe—learning French, Spanish, Italian, and Dutch in the process. He worked as a tutor and was for a time the secretary to the poet John Milton. In 1660 he was elected to Parliament under Oliver Cromwell during a period of much political upheaval in England. Marvell turned out to be an astute politician, pamphleteer, and a severe critic of the English parliament and the court system. He wrote poems and satires, many of them related to the political topics of the period. Some of his best known of these poems include "Upon Appleton House," the* Mower *series, and "The Garden." No collection of Marvell's poetry was published until three years after his sudden death of a fever, although a few individual poems appeared during his lifetime. His more famous poems, however, were published after his death. Marvell is remembered for his sharp political satire and his poetic lyricism. He wrote in the neoclassical tradition, a period in which writers sought to imitate the lessons from the classical period—aesthetic discipline and perfection. "To His Coy Mistress" is perhaps his best-known poem. It is a supreme example of a* carpe diem *lyric, a poem that explores how time acts upon physical beauty and sexual desire.*

To His Coy Mistress

ANDREW MARVELL

Had we but world enough, and time,
This coyness, lady, were no crime.
We would sit down, and think which way
To walk, and pass our long love's day.
Thou by the Indian Ganges' side   5
Shouldst rubies find: I by the tide
Of Humber would complain. I would
Love you ten years before the Flood,
And you should if you please refuse
Till the conversion of the Jews.   10
My vegetable love should grow
Vaster than empires, and more slow;
An hundred years should go to praise
Thine eyes, and on thy forehead gaze;
Two hundred to adore each breast,   15
But thirty thousand to the rest.
An age at least to every part,
And the last age should show your heart.
For, lady, you deserve this state;
Nor would I love at lower rate.   20
     But at my back I always hear
Time's wingéd chariot hurrying near;
And yonder all before us lie
Deserts of vast eternity.
Thy beauty shall no more be found,   25
Nor, in thy marble vault, shall sound
My echoing song; then worms shall try
That long preserved virginity,
And your quaint honor turn to dust,
And into ashes all my lust: 30

First published in *Miscellaneous Poems* in 1681.

The grave's a fine and private place,
But none, I think, do there embrace.
    Now therefore, while the youthful hue
Sits on thy skin like morning dew,
And while thy willing soul transpires   35
At every pore with instant fires,
Now let us sport us while we may,
And now, like am'rous birds of prey,
Rather at once our time devour
Than languish in his slow-chapped pow'r.   40
Let us roll all our strength and all
Our sweetness up into one ball,
And tear our pleasures with rough strife
Thorough the iron gates of life.
Thus, though we cannot make our sun   45
Stand still, yet we will make him run.

[1681]

Edgar Allan Poe
[1809–1849]

The son of traveling actors, EDGAR ALLAN POE *was probably abandoned by his father shortly after his birth. In any case, his father died in 1810, and his mother continued to act, moving frequently with her children until 1811, when she too died, leaving Poe and his siblings destitute. Poe was adopted by the family of John and Frances Allan, and at his baptism assumed his benefactor's name. Despite this early gesture of connectedness, Poe's relationship with the Allans was fractious, especially after Poe began attending the University of Virginia in 1836. Here Poe was known both for his writing and also for his gambling and drinking. His repeated, abusive pleas for money caused John Allan to cut him off periodically. After one such incident Poe left the university and joined the army. During his service he published his first book of poetry,* Tamerlane and Other Poems *(1827). His second,* Al Aaraaf, *was published in 1829. In 1830, through Allan's influence, Poe was awarded an appointment to West Point, but he was soon expelled. Among cadets the legend still circulates that he forced this himself by showing up naked for morning formation, but it is more likely that drinking and gambling lay at the heart of the matter. In any event, this disgrace seems to have been fortuitous, because at this time Poe began to devote himself to writing, publishing several stories and winning a fiction contest in 1832.*

In 1833 he became editor of the Southern Literary Messenger, *one of several important literary posts he would fill in his life. In 1839 he became editor of* Burton's Gentleman's Magazine; *in 1840 editor of* Graham's; *and in 1845 editor of the* Broadway Journal. *He published a great deal of his own poetry and fiction in these journals, as well as numerous reviews (many of them quite strident), and in this way had a significant impact on literary trends and tastes. However, despite the fact that he continued to be awarded editorial positions, the same kind of behavior that resulted in his dismissal from West Point—drinking, gambling, and a disinclination to bow to authority—led him regularly into conflict with his employers. And although he published his work regularly, he was never far from poverty. He also had a tendency to pick literary fights, and was most famously dismissive of the New England transcendentalists. Some speculate that this kind of controversy may have been a ploy to sell magazines.*

Although his writing career was relatively brief and his habits were self-destructive, Poe managed to amass an impressive canon before his death in 1849. In addition to such works as "Ligeia" (1838); "The Fall of the House of Usher" (1839); Tales of the Grotesque and Arabesque *(1840); and the popular "The Raven" (1844); Poe is credited with the invention of the detective story. His character C. Auguste Dupin from "The Murders in the Rue Morgue"; "The Mystery of Marie Roget"; and "The Purloined Letter" served as type for Sherlock Holmes and countless other detectives. In these and other stories Poe demonstrates an obsession with the dark side of human psychology. Many of his tales explore a concept he labeled "the spirit of perverseness . . . the unfathomable longing of the soul to vex itself." This phenomenon can be seen in stories such as "The Black Cat" and "The Tell-Tale Heart," in which seemingly rational characters are drawn to commit ghastly crimes for reasons they cannot explain. While his last years were clouded by the death of his wife from tuberculosis in 1846, he seemed on the road to recovery when, in 1849, he stopped in Baltimore on his way to Philadelphia and was found on the street four days later, unconscious and near death. The exact cause of his death on October 7 remains a mystery.*

—David L. G. Arnold, *University of Wisconsin, Stevens Point*

Annabel Lee

EDGAR ALLAN POE

It was many and many a year ago,
   In a kingdom by the sea,
That a maiden there lived whom you may know
   By the name of Annabel Lee;
And this maiden she lived with no other thought   5
   Than to love and be loved by me.
I was a child and *she* was a child,
   In this kingdom by the sea,
But we loved with a love that was more than love—
   I and my Annabel Lee—   10
With a love that the wingéd seraphs of Heaven
   Coveted her and me.

And this was the reason that, long ago,
   In this kingdom by the sea,
A wind blew out of a cloud, chilling   15
   My beautiful Annabel Lee;
So that her highborn kinsmen came
   And bore her away from me,
To shut her up in a sepulchre
   In this kingdom by the sea.   20

The angels, not half so happy in Heaven,
   Went envying her and me:—
Yes!—that was the reason (as all men know,
   In this kingdom by the sea)
That the wind came out of the cloud by night,   25
   Chilling and killing my Annabel Lee.

First published in 1849.

But our love it was stronger by far than the love
    Of those who were older than we—
    Of many far wiser than we—
And neither the angels in Heaven above,   *30*
    Nor the demons down under the sea,
Can ever dissever my soul from the soul
    Of the beautiful Annabel Lee:—

For the moon never beams, without bringing me dreams
    Of the beautiful Annabel Lee;   *35*
And the stars never rise, but I feel the bright eyes
    Of the beautiful Annabel Lee:
And so, all the night-tide, I lie down by the side
    Of my darling—my darling—my life and my bride,
    In the sepulchre there by the sea—   *40*
    In her tomb by the sounding sea.

[1849]

The Raven

EDGAR ALLAN POE

Once upon a midnight dreary, while I pondered, weak and
   weary,
Over many a quaint and curious volume of forgotten lore—
While I nodded, nearly napping, suddenly there came a tapping,
As of some one gently rapping, rapping at my chamber door.
"'Tis some visiter," I muttered, "tapping at my chamber door—   5
       Only this and nothing more."

Ah, distinctly I remember it was in the bleak December;
And each separate dying ember wrought its ghost upon the floor.
Eagerly I wished the morrow;—vainly I had sought to borrow
From my books surcease of sorrow—sorrow for the lost
   Lenore—   10
For the rare and radiant maiden whom the angels name
   Lenore—
       Nameless *here* for evermore.

And the silken, sad, uncertain rustling of each purple curtain
Thrilled me—filled me with fantastic terrors never felt before;
So that now, to still the beating of my heart, I stood repeating   15
"'Tis some visiter entreating entrance at my chamber door—
Some late visiter entreating entrance at my chamber door;—
       This it is and nothing more."

Presently my soul grew stronger; hesitating then no longer,
"Sir," said I, "or Madam, truly your forgiveness I implore;   20
But the fact is I was napping, and so gently you came rapping,
And so faintly you came tapping, tapping at my chamber door,
That I scarce was sure I heard you"—here I opened wide the
   door;——
       Darkness there and nothing more.

Deep into that darkness peering, long I stood there wondering,
    fearing,   25
Doubting, dreaming dreams no mortal ever dared to dream
    before;
But the silence was unbroken, and the stillness gave no token,
And the only word there spoken was the whispered word,
    "Lenore?"
This I whispered, and an echo murmured back the word,
    "Lenore!"
                  Merely this and nothing more.   30

Back into the chamber turning, all my soul within me burning,
Soon again I heard a tapping somewhat louder than before.
"Surely," said I, "surely that is something at my window lattice;
Let me see, then, what thereat is, and this mystery explore—
Let my heart be still a moment and this mystery explore;—   35
                'Tis the wind and nothing more!"

Open here I flung the shutter, when, with many a flirt and
    flutter,
In there stepped a stately Raven of the saintly days of yore;
Not the least obeisance made he; not a minute stopped or
    stayed he;
But, with mien of lord or lady, perched above my chamber
    door—   40
Perched upon a bust of Pallas[1] just above my chamber door—
                Perched, and sat, and nothing more.

Then this ebony bird beguiling my sad fancy into smiling,
By the grave and stern decorum of the countenance it wore,
"Though thy crest be shorn and shaven, thou," I said, "art sure no
    craven,   45
Ghastly grim and ancient Raven wandering from the Nightly
    shore—
Tell me what thy lordly name is on the Night's Plutonian shore!"[2]
                Quoth the Raven "Nevermore."

---

[1] Pallas: Pallas Athene, Greek goddess of wisdom, arts, and war.
[2] Poe's speaker here associates the raven with Pluto, Roman god of death and the underworld.

Much I marvelled this ungainly fowl to hear discourse so plainly,
Though its answer little meaning—little relevancy bore;   *50*
For we cannot help agreeing that no living human being
Ever yet was blessed with seeing bird above his chamber door—
Bird or beast upon the sculptured bust above his chamber door,
        With such name as "Nevermore."

But the Raven, sitting lonely on the placid bust, spoke only   *55*
That one word, as if his soul in that one word he did outpour.
Nothing farther then he uttered—not a feather then he
    fluttered—
Till I scarcely more than muttered "Other friends have flown
    before—
On the morrow *he* will leave me, as my Hopes have flown
    before."
        Then the bird said "Nevermore."   *60*

Startled at the stillness broken by reply so aptly spoken,
"Doubtless," said I, "what it utters is its only stock and store
Caught from some unhappy master whom unmerciful Disaster
Followed fast and followed faster till his songs one burden
    bore—
Till the dirges of his Hope that melancholy burden bore   *65*
        Of 'Never—nevermore.'"

But the Raven still beguiling my sad fancy into smiling,
Straight I wheeled a cushioned seat in front of bird, and bust
    and door;
Then, upon the velvet sinking, I betook myself to linking
Fancy unto fancy, thinking what this ominous bird of yore—   *70*
What this grim, ungainly, ghastly, gaunt, and ominous bird of
    yore
        Meant in croaking "Nevermore."

This I sat engaged in guessing, but no syllable expressing
To the fowl whose fiery eyes now burned into my bosom's core;
This and more I sat divining, with my head at ease reclining   *75*
On the cushion's velvet lining that the lamp-light gloated o'er,
But whose velvet-violet lining with the lamp-light gloating o'er,
        She shall press, ah, nevermore!

Then, methought, the air grew denser, perfumed from an unseen
censer
Swung by seraphim[3] whose foot-falls tinkled on the tufted
floor.   *80*
"Wretch," I cried, "thy God hath lent thee—by these angels he
hath sent thee
Respite—respite and nepenthe[4] from thy memories of Lenore;
Quaff, oh quaff this kind nepenthe and forget this lost Lenore!"
      Quoth the Raven "Nevermore."

"Prophet!" said I, "thing of evil!—prophet still, if bird or
devil!—   *85*
Whether Tempter sent, or whether tempest tossed thee here
ashore,
Desolate yet all undaunted, on this desert land enchanted—
On this home by Horror haunted—tell me truly, I implore—
Is there—*is* there balm in Gilead?[5]—tell me—tell me, I implore!"
      Quoth the Raven "Nevermore."   *90*

"Prophet!" said I, "thing of evil!—prophet still, if bird or devil!
By that Heaven that bends above us—by that God we both
adore—
Tell this soul with sorrow laden if, within the distant Aidenn,[6]
It shall clasp a sainted maiden whom the angels name Lenore—
Clasp a rare and radiant maiden whom the angels name
Lenore."   *95*
      Quoth the Raven "Nevermore."

"Be that word our sign of parting, bird or fiend!" I shrieked,
upstarting—
"Get thee back into the tempest and the Night's Plutonian shore!
Leave no black plume as a token of that lie thy soul hath spoken!
Leave my loneliness unbroken!—quit the bust above my door!   *100*
Take thy beak from out my heart, and take thy form from off my
door!"
      Quoth the Raven "Nevermore."

---

[3] Seraphim: in Judeo-Christian tradition, seraphim are the highest order of angels; these beings are known to inspire prophecy.
[4] Nepenthe: an ancient potion reputed to cure grief and sorrow.
[5] In the Hebrew Bible, the "balm of Gilead" is a healing ointment suggestive of God's power to restore the soul.
[6] Aidenn: this is an alternate spelling for the biblical Garden of Eden.

And the Raven, never flitting, still is sitting, *still* is sitting
On the pallid bust of Pallas just above my chamber door;
And his eyes have all the seeming of a demon's that is dreaming,   *105*
And the lamp-light o'er him streaming throws his shadow on the
   floor;
And my soul from out that shadow that lies floating on the floor
               Shall be lifted—nevermore!

                                                    [1845]

Ezra Pound
[1885–1972]

EZRA POUND *was a poet, translator, critic, essayist, editor, and mentor to many of the great writers of the twentieth century. He also created literary movements, and his most famous statement about art, "make it new", captured what Pound believed about how literature should reflect the conditions of modern society. Accordingly, many give him credit for having originated modern poetry, freeing it from the attitudes of the previous era.*

Pound was born in Idaho but soon moved with his parents to Philadelphia. When he was sixteen he entered the University of Pennsylvania. Two years later he transferred to Hamilton College where he studied several languages, particularly Italian and Spanish. His interest in languages would have considerable bearing on the texture of his poetry and his ideas about translating literary works into English. For a brief time he taught college in the United States, but in 1907 left for Europe, first settling in England and later in Italy.

His first book of poems, A Lume Spento, *was published in Italy in 1908. In 1912, Pound started a movement in poetry, called Imagism. His imagist manifesto stated that poetry should be free of sentimentality, be direct, concise, and musically varied. That movement resulted in the publication of an anthology of imagist poetry titled* Des Imagists *(1914). By 1915, his interests turned to translating Chinese poetry. He published his first translations that year in the volume,* Cathay. *In 1917 he began work on his epic poem, the* Cantos, *which he continued to expand throughout his life. It was published, along with a collection of his translations, in 1953. This work, with its nonnarrative structure, symbolism, and allusions to politics, history, and culture, is considered by many to be a major example of the principles of twentieth century Modernism.*

Pound's influence on literature cannot be understated. In his own work, and with his support of poets such as T. S. Eliot and William Carlos Williams, and novelists such as James Joyce and Earnest Hemingway, he changed the face of literature. His early interest in world literature put him ahead of his time, as witnessed today by the increasing focus on writers from non-English-speaking cultures.

In a Station of the Metro

EZRA POUND

The apparition of these faces in the crowd;
Petals on a wet, black bough.

[1913]

First published in *Poetry: A Magazine of Verse* in April, 1913.

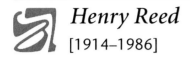

Henry Reed

[1914–1986]

Born in Birmingham, England several months before the outbreak of World War I, HENRY REED *came of age in the years prior to and during World War II. Having earned a master's degree from the University of Birmingham in 1937, Reed worked as a journalist and teacher before enlisting in the British Army in 1941. In 1942 he left the service to join the British Foreign Office, where he remained until the war's end in 1945. From that time until his death, Reed published poetry and criticism in a wide range of periodicals, including the* New Yorker, The Nation, Time, *and* Newsweek. *During his lifetime Reed published two collections of poetry,* A Map of Verona: Poems *(1946) and* Lessons of War *(1970); a posthumous volume,* Collected Poems, *was edited with an introduction by the poet Jon Stallworthy in 1991. In addition to his poetry and criticism, Reed also translated the work of French writer Honoré de Balzac and Italian writers Dino Buzzati and Ugo Betti.*

It was for his radio plays, however, that Reed was best known. From 1947 to 1971 he wrote or adapted almost forty plays, including Herman Melville's Moby Dick *(1947) and the original works* Noises On *(1947);* The Streets of Pompeii *(1952);* Don Juan in Love *(1956); and* Summertime *(1969). The Streets of Pompeii, a verse play, was lauded for its lyrical evocation of ancient Rome through a contemporary perspective, and was awarded an Italia Prize in Palermo. Reed also adapted his poetry for radio; in 1960 five of his poems were broadcast in a program titled* The Complete Lessons of War, *with Reed himself sharing the reading. The program ends with a son returning from war only to find that his father has died, and lies "crumpled in that small grave"; with his home now gone, the soldier has no choice but to return to the army.*

Reed wrote little after 1971, but one of his more famous poems, "Naming of Parts," was adapted for film in 1972. The poem, a deceptively simple account of a military training exercise, employs flower images to underscore the destructive nature of warfare. In 1971 the British Broadcasting Company published two collections of his radio scripts: The Streets of Pompeii, and Other Plays for Radio *and* Hilda Tablet and Others. *According to London critic Douglas Cleverdon, Reed's poetic radio plays can be compared to the novels of acclaimed English writer Evelyn Waugh for "their satirical wit, their compassion, and their impeccable style." Reed's notable work in radio was acknowledged in 1979, with the first Pye Golden Award for Radio from the Society of Authors.*

Naming of Parts

HENRY REED

Today we have naming of parts. Yesterday,
We had daily cleaning. And tomorrow morning,
We shall have what to do after firing. But today,
Today we have naming of parts. Japonica[1]
Glistens like coral in all of the neighboring gardens,   5
       And today we have naming of parts.

This is the lower sling swivel. And this
Is the upper sling swivel, whose use you will see,
When you are given your slings. And this is the piling swivel,
Which in your case you have not got. The branches   10
Hold in the gardens their silent, eloquent gestures,
       Which in our case we have not got.

This is the safety-catch, which is always released
With an easy flick of the thumb. And please do not let me
See anyone using his finger. You can do it quite easy   15
If you have any strength in your thumb. The blossoms
Are fragile and motionless, never letting anyone see
       Any of them using their finger.

And this you can see is the bolt. The purpose of this
Is to open the breech, as you see. We can slide it   20
Rapidly backwards and forwards: we call this
Easing the spring. And rapidly backwards and forwards
The early bees are assaulting and fumbling the flowers:
       They call it easing the Spring.

---

[1]Japanese quince

Reprinted from *A Map of Verona,* by permission John Tyderman.

They call it easing the Spring: it is perfectly easy   25
If you have any strength in your thumb: like the bolt,
And the breech, and the cocking-piece, and the point of balance,
Which in our case we have not got; and the almond-blossom
Silent in all of the gardens and the bees going backwards and
       forwards,
      For today we have naming of parts.   *30*

[1946]

Edwin Arlington Robinson
[1869–1935]

EDWIN ARLINGTON ROBINSON *was born in Head Tide, Maine into a family whose wealth came from the timber industry, though the national depression of the 1890s left his family virtually penniless. Though Robinson attended Harvard, he left after only two years of study due to his family's declining fortune and the deaths of his father in 1892 and his mother in 1896. He began writing by the age of eleven and was, as a high school student, the youngest member of the poetry society in the town of Gardiner, where his family had moved shortly after his birth. Robinson's first two books were published during these years*—The Torrent and the Night Before *(1896) and* The Children of the Night *(1897). Though the first book received some good reviews, the second did not. After its publication, Robinson moved to New York to live in Greenwich Village where he worked at temporary jobs until the publication of* Captain Craig *in 1902, which drew the attention of Theodore Roosevelt, then the president. Roosevelt arranged for Robinson to work in a secure government job. Robinson dedicated his next volume,* The Town down the River *(1909) to Roosevelt, and this began his most productive phase. Robinson wrote an Arthurian series,* Merlin *(1917),* Lancelot *(1920), and* Tristram *(1927), and won the Pulitzer Prize three times: the first time in 1921 for his* Collected Poems, *the second for* The Man Who Died Twice *(1924), and the third for* Tristram. The Man against the Sky *(1916) was described by Amy Lowell as powerful and dynamic. Robinson continuously wrote and published throughout his life. By the time he died, Robinson had published twenty volumes of poetry. His later volumes of narrative verse included* Dionysus in Doubt *(1925),* Matthias at the Door *(1931), and* King Jasper *(1953). He is best known for formal verse in traditional forms, with an intense psychological focus. Opposed to the Puritanism of his day, which he saw as repressive, Robinson was critical of the kind of materialism that conspired against average citizens.*

Richard Cory

EDWIN ARLINGTON ROBINSON

Whenever Richard Cory went down town,
We people on the pavement looked at him:
He was a gentleman from sole to crown,
Clean favored, and imperially slim.

And he was always quietly arrayed,   5
And he was always human when he talked;
But still he fluttered pulses when he said,
"Good-morning," and he glittered when he walked.

And he was rich—yes, richer than a king—
And admirably schooled in every grace: 10
In fine, we thought that he was everything
To make us wish that we were in his place.

So on we worked, and waited for the light,
And went without the meat, and cursed the bread;
And Richard Cory, one calm summer night,   15
Went home and put a bullet through his head.

[1897]

First published in *The Children of the Night: A Book of Poems* by Edward Arlington Robinson, in 1897.

Carl Sandburg
[1878–1967]

CARL SANDBURG *was born in Illinois, the son of Swedish immigrants. His father worked in the railroad yards. As one of seven children, Sandburg attended elementary school, but dropped out of school at the age of thirteen to help support his family. He spent some months at nineteen tramping on a freight train, after which he served in the infantry in the Spanish American War. It was after this that he enrolled at Lombard College, where he began to write poetry at the encouragement of his teacher Philip Wright, himself a poet. Wright published four small books of Sandburg's poetry.*

Sandburg worked as a journalist for much of his adult life, with his life as a poet intertwined with his journalistic work. Many of the publications he worked for, especially early on, were associated with the socialist movement, and this can be seen as the influence of his early life—the son of a worker, a sometime tramp—in both his journalism and in his poetry. Sandburg esteemed the vernacular, rough-hewn language of workers and ordinary people. This very quality in his writing made him a figure of controversy when his first works were published in the modernist little magazine Poetry. *His first book by a major publisher,* Chicago Poems *(1916) focuses on urban life; his second,* Cornhuskers *(1918), focuses on American rural life. Though Sandburg continued to write poetry after these first two books, the most important writing he did was a multi-volume biography of Abraham Lincoln, which appeared from 1926 through 1939. Sandburg's interest in vernacular culture led him to a lifelong interest in American folksongs, which he collected and published as* The American Songbag *in 1927; this compilation contained the words and music to 280 songs and ballads from American history. This collection, perhaps shows another of the motives for Sandburg's work—a democratic celebration of the song of America.*

Chicago

CARL SANDBURG

Hog Butcher for the World,
Tool Maker, Stacker of Wheat,
Player with Railroads and the Nation's Freight Handler;
Stormy, husky, brawling,
City of the Big Shoulders: 5

They tell me you are wicked and I believe them, for I have seen
    your painted women under the gas lamps luring the farm
    boys.
And they tell me you are crooked and I answer: Yes, it is true I
    have seen the gunman kill and go free to kill again.
And they tell me you are brutal and my reply is: On the faces of
    women and children I have seen the marks of wanton hunger.
And having answered so I turn once more to those who sneer at
    this my city, and I give them back the sneer and say to them:
Come and show me another city with lifted head singing so
    proud to be alive and coarse and strong and cunning.   10
Flinging magnetic curses amid the toil of piling job on job, here
    is a tall bold slugger set vivid against the little soft cities;
Fierce as a dog with tongue lapping for action, cunning as a
    savage pitted against the wilderness,
        Bareheaded,
        Shoveling,
        Wrecking,   15
        Planning,
        Building, breaking, rebuilding,
Under the smoke, dust all over his mouth, laughing with white
    teeth,
Under the terrible burden of destiny laughing as a young man
    laughs,

First published in *Poetry* in 1914. Later collected in Sandburg's *Chicago Poems* in 1916.

Laughing even as an ignorant fighter laughs who has never
    lost a battle,   *20*
Bragging and laughing that under his wrist is the pulse, and
    under his ribs the heart of the people,
                Laughing!
Laughing, the stormy, husky, brawling laughter of Youth, half-
    naked, sweating, proud to be Hog Butcher, Tool Maker,
    Stacker of Wheat, Player with Railroads and Freight Handler
    to the Nation.

                                                  [1914]

William Shakespeare
[1564–1616]

WILLIAM SHAKESPEARE *was born in Stratford-upon-Avon, the son of a glove-maker and wool dealer. Though his father, John, held some status in the city, at some point the family lost its position and thus, though his eldest son William attended Stratford Grammar School and may have had hopes of attending university, he did not. When Shakespeare was eighteen years old, he married Anne Hathaway and had three children before his twenty-first birthday. By the early 1590s he was established in London as an actor and a playwright, as well as the part-owner and manager of a theater company. He was a prolific writer, having written (or, in a couple of cases, co-written) at the time of his death thirty-eight plays and several volumes of poetry—*The Sonnets *(1609),* Venus and Adonis *(1593), and* The Rape of Lucrece *(1593).*

Perhaps the most pored-over of all authors, Shakespeare fascinates in part because of the lack of detail known about his life. However, a good deal is discernable about the social milieu surrounding his life and work. By the time Shakespeare emerged as an actor and a playwright in the theater scene in London of the early 1590s, he must have spent some time as an apprentice actor, and tried his hand at playwriting. Theater-going at that time spanned all social classes. His earliest plays draw heavily on classical sources and models, suggesting something about his early education. Playwriting at that time was probably considered more a professional skill than an art. When theaters were shut down because of the plague (1592–1593), he wrote his narrative poems, probably dedicated to the Earl of Southampton, a patron. When Shakespeare retired to Stratford-upon-Avon, he had seen to the publication of the poems, though not his plays. Plays at that time were written for a fee, with the rights retained by production companies. Shakespeare owned a share of the theater company, which had Lord Chamberlain as its patron and was under the royal sponsorship of King James. The company built the Globe Theater, where many of the plays were produced. He was buried in the same parish church where he was baptized. Not until seven years after his death were most of the plays collected and published by two of his partners.

The sonnets have a special place in the Shakespeare oeuvre. They are still considered models of the form, and are part of a vibrant sonnet-writing tradition in the Renaissance. The kind of sonnet Shakespeare—and other Renaissance writers such as Sir Thomas Wyatt, Henry Howard, Earl of Surrey, Edmund Spenser, and Sir Philip Sidney—wrote is often called the Elizabethan or Shakespearean sonnet. Differing from the Italian or Petrarchan sonnet, the

Elizabethan sonnet was organized in quatrains, with a concluding couplet. (*The Petrarchan sonnet had an octave and a sestet.*) Typically, the quatrains created an argument of examples, with each set of four lines offering an instance or amplification of the poem's central idea.

My Mistress' Eyes are Nothing Like the Sun

WILLIAM SHAKESPEARE

My mistress' eyes are nothing like the sun;
Coral is far more red than her lips' red;
If snow be white, why then her breasts are dun;
If hairs be wires, black wires grow on her head.
I have seen roses damasked red and white,   5
But no such roses see I in her cheeks;
And in some perfumes is there more delight
Than in the breath that from my mistress reeks.
I love to hear her speak, yet well I know
That music hath a far more pleasing sound;   10
I grant I never saw a goddess go:
My mistress, when she walks, treads on the ground.
   And yet, by heaven, I think my love as rare
   As any she belied with false compare.

[1609]

First published in the 1609 *Shake-speares sonnets.*

Shall I Compare Thee to a Summer's Day?

WILLIAM SHAKESPEARE

Shall I compare thee to a summer's day?
Thou art more lovely and more temperate.
Rough winds do shake the darling buds of May,
And summer's lease hath all too short a date.
Sometime too hot the eye of heaven shines,   5
And often is his gold complexion dimmed;
And every fair from fair sometimes declines,
By chance, or nature's changing course, untrimmed.
But thy eternal summer shall not fade,
Nor lose possession of that fair thou ow'st;   10
Nor shall death brag thou wand'rest in his shade,
When in eternal lines to time thou grow'st.
   So long as men can breathe or eyes can see,
   So long lives this, and this gives life to thee.

[1609]

First published in the 1609 *Shake-speares sonnets.*

Let Me Not to the Marriage of True Minds

WILLIAM SHAKESPEARE

Let me not to the marriage of true minds
Admit impediments; love is not love
Which alters when it alteration finds,
Or bends with the remover to remove.
O, no, it is an ever-fixèd mark[1]   5
That looks on tempests and is never shaken;
It is the star[2] to every wand'ring bark,[3]
Whose worth's unknown, although his height be taken.
Love's not Time's fool, though rosy lips and cheeks
Within his bending sickle's compass[4] come;   10
Love alters not with his brief hours and weeks
But bears it out even to the edge of doom.[5]
   If this be error and upon me proved,
   I never writ, nor no man ever loved.

[1609]

---

[1]Lighthouse

[2]North Star, which guided sailors.

[3]Boat

[4]Range

[5]Death or, more generally, doomsday.

First published in the 1609 *Shake-speares sonnets.*

When, in Disgrace with Fortune and Men's Eyes

WILLIAM SHAKESPEARE

When, in disgrace with Fortune and men's eyes,
I all alone beweep my outcast state,
And trouble deaf heaven with my bootless cries,
And look upon myself and curse my fate,
Wishing me like to one more rich in hope,   5
Featured like him, like him with friends possessed,
Desiring this man's art, and that man's scope,
With what I most enjoy contented least,
Yet in these thoughts myself almost despising,
Haply I think on thee, and then my state,   10
Like to the lark at break of day arising
From sullen earth, sings hymns at heaven's gate;
   For thy sweet love rememb'red such wealth brings
   That then I scorn to change my state with kings.

[1609]

First published in the 1609 *Shake-speares sonnets*.

Jonathan Swift
[1667–1745]

Jonathan Swift's epitaph, which he wrote himself, reads
> Swift sailed into his rest;
> Savage indignation there
> Cannot lacerate his breast.
> Imitate him if you dare,
> World-besotted traveler; he
> Served human liberty.

In this epitaph, a translation from the Latin by W. B. Yeats, perhaps the expression "savage indignation" most captures the significance of Swift's life and writings. He was a true satirist in that he used humor and wit to critique humanity and its institutions for the purpose of holding people accountable for society's imperfections and in order to improve social conditions. At various times Swift used pseudonyms or published works anonymously to enhance his ends, such as with Gulliver's Travels *(1726) and* A Modest Proposal *(1729). By not using his actual name, readers of these great works were convinced of their authenticity. That is, for the satire to have its intended effect, readers had to accept the reality of Lemuel Gulliver's experiences. Further, they had to believe that the "modest" proposal of breeding infants as food for the wealthy was made in all sincerity— that the author of the pamphlet was an actual person. This famous essay was motivated by Swift's despair over England's mute response to the latest famine in Ireland. It was an unflinching indictment of England's policies toward Ireland.*

Swift was born in Dublin, received a degree from Trinity College in 1686 and furthered his studies at Oxford University, from which he earned a master of arts degree in 1692. In 1694 he returned to Ireland and in the following year was ordained in the Church of Ireland (Anglican), and eventually became Dean of St. Patrick's Cathedral. In 1704 Swift anonymously published A Tale of a Tub, *a satire on religious debates. Soon after, Swift published* The Battle of the Books *and* The Mechanical Operation of the Spirit. *The series of satirical pamphlets on church issues,* An Argument Against Abolishing Christianity, *appeared in 1708. Swift became the editor of the newspaper* The Examiner *siding with the Tories, (outlaw Irish), against the Whig party that supported English parliamentary rights. However, the Whigs gained power after the death of Queen Anne, which fueled Swift's sense of injustice experienced by the Irish people. By the time of* The Drapier's Letters *(1724), Swift was extremely popular in Ireland, having also donated much of his earnings to the establishment of St. Patrick's Hospital. Swift continued to resist English authority in* A Short View of the State of Ireland *(1728). By 1735 Swift's Ménière's disease became more pronounced, causing him bouts of dizziness and nausea. His memory was already beginning to fail, possibly due to Alzheimer's disease. Senility had set in by 1735 and eventually, after a stroke, he could no longer be deemed responsible to conduct his own affairs. When he died, Ireland mourned his passing.*

A Description of the Morning

JONATHAN SWIFT

Now hardly here and there an hackney-coach,
Appearing, showed the ruddy morn's approach.
Now Betty from her master's bed had flown
And softly stole to discompose her own.
The slipshod 'prentice from his master's door   5
Had pared the dirt, and sprinkled round the floor.
Now Moll had whirled her mop with dextrous airs,
Prepared to scrub the entry and the stairs.
The youth with broomy stumps began to trace
The kennel-edge, where wheels had worn the place.   10
The small-coal man was heard with cadence deep
Till drowned in shriller notes of chimneysweep,
Duns at his lordship's gate began to meet,
And Brickdust Moll had screamed through half the street.
The turnkey now his flock returning sees,   15
Duly let out a-nights to steal for fees;
The watchful bailiffs take their silent stands;
And schoolboys lag with satchels in their hands.

[1709]

First published in 1709.

Alfred, Lord Tennyson
[1809–1892]

ALFRED TENNYSON'S *life spans most of the years of Queen Victoria's reign. He was born in a Lincolnshire rectory into a talented and literate family, the fourth child and one of eight sons and four daughters. All the children were brought up as intellectuals. Tennyson's publication of poetry included the works of his two brothers, Frederick and Charles* (Poems by Two Brothers, *1827). Tennyson looked the part of a poet, tall and slender with an elegant head, and he was quickly adopted by the artistic circle at school. At Trinity College, Cambridge, he became a member of the poets' club, The Apostles, where he met Arthur Henry Hallam, whose early death was to shape both Tennyson's temperament and his poetry. Before that event, however, Tennyson won the Chancellor's prize for a poem titled* Timbuctoo *and saw his first volume of poetry published in 1830,* Poems, Chiefly Lyrical. *His second volume appeared in 1832. In 1833, Hallam, by then engaged to Tennyson's sister, Emily, died in Vienna. Tennyson began his poem on faith and doubt,* In Memoriam, *that was eventually to make him famous. He worked on the poem for seventeen years. At the same time, he worked on* Idylls of the King, *a long work retelling the tales of King Arthur from Malory but molded into the Victorian mindset. In 1842, he published* Poems, *which included* Ulysses *and* Morte D'Arthur. *In 1847, his popular satire on women's place in the world,* Princess, *appeared. These were difficult times for Tennyson, despite the success of the latest poems. Then in 1850 he married Emily Sellwood and finally published* In Memoriam. *That year he was chosen to succeed Wordsworth as Poet Laureate. A long formal poem,* Ode on the Death of the Duke of Wellington *(1852) preceded* Maud *(1855), a romantic tale of love and death, followed by* Enoch Arden *and* Northern Farmer *(1964). He dedicated a new edition of* Idylls *to the memory of Queen Victoria's beloved husband Prince Albert, who had died in 1861, and became a great favorite of the queen. In 1884, he became Lord Tennyson and published* Becket, *a successful drama. In his last years, he wrote apace, publishing* Tiresias and Other Poems *in 1885,* Locksley Hall Sixty Years After *in 1886,* Demeter and Other Poems *in 1889, and* The Death of Oenone *in 1892, published just after his death. Assessments of Tennyson's work was, in turn, criticized and then praised in the past century. During most of the twentieth century, he was thought to be too ornate for most readers, but in time his poetic talent and his ability to bring sound and light to life were honored. Those who love a talented wordsmith and those who love a mythic vision of ancient England love Tennyson.*

The Eagle

ALFRED, LORD TENNYSON

He clasps the crag with crooked hands;
Close to the sun in lonely lands,
Ringed with the azure world, he stands.

The wrinkled sea beneath him crawls;
He watches from his mountain walls,   5
And like a thunderbolt he falls.

[1851]

First published in *Poems of Alfred Tennyson* in 1851.

Ulysses[1]

ALFRED, LORD TENNYSON

It little profits that an idle king,
By this still hearth, among these barren crags,
Matched with an agèd wife, I mete and dole
Unequal laws unto a savage race
That hoard, and sleep, and feed, and know not me.   *5*
I cannot rest from travel; I will drink
Life to the lees. All times I have enjoyed
Greatly, have suffered greatly, both with those
That loved me, and alone; on shore, and when
Through scudding drifts the rainy Hyades[2]   *10*
Vexed the dim sea. I am become a name;
For always roaming with a hungry heart
Much have I seen and known—cities of men
And manners, climates, councils, governments,
Myself not least, but honored of them all—   *15*
And drunk delight of battle with my peers,
Far on the ringing plains of windy Troy.
I am a part of all that I have met;
Yet all experience is an arch wherethrough
Gleams that untraveled world whose margin fades   *20*
Forever and forever when I move.
How dull it is to pause, to make an end,
To rust unburnished, not to shine in use!
As though to breathe were life! Life piled on life
Were all too little, and of one to me   *25*
Little remains; but every hour is saved

---

[1]Ulysses was the hero of the Trojan war. He left his wife Penelope, who wove a cloth to avoid her suitors, and then he returned to her and his son Telemachus after the war.

[2]Hyades was Atlas's daughters who became the stars.

First published in *English Idyls and Other Poems* in 1842.

From that eternal silence, something more,
A bringer of new things; and vile it were
For some three suns to store and hoard myself,
And this grey spirit yearning in desire   30
To follow knowledge like a sinking star,
Beyond the utmost bound of human thought.
    This is my son, mine own Telemachus,
To whom I leave the scepter and the isle—
Well-loved of me, discerning to fulfill   35
This labor, by slow prudence to make mild
A rugged people, and through soft degrees
Subdue them to the useful and the good.
Most blameless is he, centered in the sphere
Of common duties, decent not to fail   40
In offices of tenderness, and pay
Meet adoration to my household gods,
When I am gone. He works his work, I mine.
    There lies the port; the vessel puffs her sail;
There gloom the dark, broad seas. My mariners,   45
Souls that have toiled, and wrought, and thought with me—
That ever with a frolic welcome took
The thunder and the sunshine, and opposed
Free hearts, free foreheads—you and I are old;
Old age hath yet his honor and his toil.   50
Death closes all; but something ere the end,
Some work of noble note, may yet be done,
Not unbecoming men that strove with Gods.
The lights begin to twinkle from the rocks;
The long day wanes; the low moon climbs; the deep   55
Moans round with many voices. Come, my friends,
'Tis not too late to seek a newer world.
Push off, and sitting well in order smite
The sounding furrows; for my purpose holds
To sail beyond the sunset, and the baths   60
Of all the western stars, until I die.
It may be that the gulfs will wash us down;
It may be we shall touch the Happy Isles,
And see the great Achilles, whom we knew.
Though much is taken, much abides; and though   65
We are not now that strength which in old days

Moved earth and heaven, that which we are, we are—
One equal temper of heroic hearts,
Made weak by time and fate, but strong in will
To strive, to seek, to find, and not to yield.   70

[1833]

Phillis Wheatley
[1753?–1784]

PHILLIS WHEATLEY *was brought as a small child to Boston on a slave ship. A Fulani child, she had come from Senegal in West Africa. A tailor, John Wheatley, purchased her in 1761 as a companion for his wife, Susannah. Boston had none of the Southern laws against teaching a slave to read so Phillis was able to learn easily in this religious and very literate household. She mastered English in sixteen months and was able to read the Bible with ease at an age that would have been impressive for a native English speaker. Her eagerness to learn led to her mastery of mythology, classical languages, and English verse. By age thirteen she was writing compositions such as "To the University of Cambridge in New England." This essay still has relevance because Wheatley wrote about the circumstances that enable one person to receive a good education while another does not. Not only did she study at home, but she also studied with the pastor of the Old North Church, the Reverend Dr. Richard Sewall, for whom she wrote an elegy at his death. She also wrote an elegy for the evangelist George Whitefield titled "On the Death of the Rev. Mr. George Whitefield." This elegy was her first publication (1770).*

She quickly became well known as a prodigy and began writing letters to famous Christian writers and to members of the Transatlantic abolitionist network. At about the same time she became ill and was sent to England with Wheatley's son Nathaniel for her health. There she met the Countess of Huntingdon, Sebina Hastings, a woman with whom she had exchanged letters. Hastings became Wheatley's patron, a form of support that brought Wheatley's book, Poems on Various Subjects, Religious and Moral *(1773) to the public eye. Wheatley quickly became not only famous but an example of proof that an African could be both learned and talented in letters. In 1772 the Somerset Decision in England could have freed her, but John Wheatley persuaded her to come home to be with his dying wife on the promise of manumission. She did come back to Boston and was rewarded with her freedom. She married John Peters in 1778 and worked on a second book. The book was never published though many of the poems have been recovered from other publications such as magazines and newspapers. Her later life was plagued by illness and the death of her two children. Her work stayed in front of the public eye thanks to abolitionists and African-American women's literary societies. She has received much critical interest in recent years, and the poems for her second book have become objects of archival treasure hunts.*

On Being Brought from Africa to America

PHILLIS WHEATLEY

'Twas mercy brought me from my *Pagan*[1] land,
Taught my benighted soul to understand
That there's a God, that there's a *Saviour* too:
Once I redemption neither sought nor knew.
Some view our sable race with scornful eye,   5
"Their colour is a diabolic die."
Remember, *Christians*, *Negros*, black as *Cain*,
May be refin'd, and join th'angelic train.

[1773]

---

[1] The peoples of Senegal were animists.

From *Poems on Various Subjects, Religious and Moral* (1773).

Walt Whitman
[1819–1892]

WALT WHITMAN *was born in New York to Walter Whitman, a housebuilder, and Louisa Van Velsor. Both his parents descended from early settlers of Long Island. In Whitman's early childhood, his parents moved to Brooklyn, where he attended public school. As an adolescent, he worked as an office boy and learned the printing trade at the* Patriot *and* Star *newspapers in Brooklyn. He worked as a printer until 1836 until a fire destroyed much of the printing district, and he then took up school teaching on Long Island. In 1838 he founded a weekly newspaper,* Long-Islander, *which he published and edited. During this period, he wrote poetry and literary prose.*

During the 1840s, Whitman worked for various newspapers as an editor, writer, and compositor, while he continued to write in various genres, including a novel, stories, sketches, and poetry. He briefly edited a New Orleans newspaper in 1848, the Daily Crescent, *though the job was short-lived (he resigned just months after he arrived). He traveled back to Brooklyn via the Mississippi, the Great Lakes, and the Hudson River. Around this time, he wrote and published several poems that later appeared in the first edition of* Leaves of Grass. *Much of that work, however, existed only as fragments until it was collected and published in 1855. The first edition was 795 copies, and consisted of twelve untitled poems and a preface. A subsequent edition the next year contained thirty-three poems. Whitman added to and altered* Leaves of Grass *many times—in 1860, 1867, 1870, 1876, 1881, and 1891.*

The book achieved recognition almost immediately. Ralph Waldo Emerson sent Whitman a letter shortly after the book's publication, saying, "I greet you at the beginning of a great career." Many literary and other public figures hailed the work, and his writing was published in various well-known periodicals such as Harper's Magazine, Galaxy, *and* The Radical. *William Michael Rossetti published a selection of Whitman's work in London under the title* Poems of Walt Whitman *in 1868, which brought him to the attention of the literary lights of England, including Tennyson and Swinburne.*

During the Civil War, Whitman worked as a freelance journalist and as a visitor—a "wound-dresser"—in different hospitals. After the war, he worked in various government offices, and was fired from at least one of those positions, in part because some of the poems in Leaves of Grass *were considered obscene. In later years, his health was not good, though he continued writing, lecturing on diverse topics including Thomas Paine and Abraham Lincoln, and editing his own work. In 1884, he purchased a small house—a "little old shanty of my own"—on Mickle Street in Camden, New Jersey. Friends and admirers helped him financially and otherwise. Active as a writer and lecturer till nearly the end of his life, Whitman died in 1892 and was buried in the Harleigh Cemetery.*

Whitman is one of the great original poets, certainly of America but almost as certainly of all writers in English. His work is marked by the long exclamatory line, the oratorical, hortatory power of his voice, and the democratic inclusiveness of his subjects. In the preface to the first edition of Leaves of Grass, *Whitman wrote, "The messages of great poets to each man and woman are, Come to us on equal terms, Only then can you understand us, We are no better than you, What we enclose you enclose, What we enjoy you may enjoy. Did you suppose there could be only one Supreme?" In his every gesture as a poet, Whitman's ardor, and the genuineness of this invitation, reach out afresh to the reader.*

A Noiseless Patient Spider

WALT WHITMAN

A noiseless patient spider,
I mark'd where on a little promontory it stood isolated,
Mark'd how to explore the vacant vast surrounding,
It launch'd forth filament, filament, filament, out of itself,
Ever unreeling them, ever tirelessly speeding them.   5

And you O my soul where you stand,
Surrounded, detached, in measureless oceans of space,
Ceaselessly musing, venturing, throwing, seeking the spheres
    to connect them,
Till the bridge you will need be form'd, till the ductile
    anchor hold,
Till the gossamer thread you fling catch somewhere, O my
    soul.   10

[1868]

First composed for and published in the London *Broadway Magazine* in October of 1868.

I Hear America Singing

WALT WHITMAN

I hear America singing, the varied carols I hear,
Those of mechanics, each one singing his as it should be
    blithe and strong,
The carpenter singing his as he measures his plank or beam,
The mason singing his as he makes ready for work, or leaves
    off work,
The boatman singing what belongs to him in his boat, the deckhand
    singing on the steamboat deck,   5
The shoemaker singing as he sits on his bench, the hatter
    singing as he stands,
The wood-cutter's song, the ploughboy's on his way in the
    morning, or at noon intermission or at sundown,
The delicious singing of the mother, or of the young wife at
    work, or of the girl sewing or washing,
Each singing what belongs to him or her and to none else,
The day what belongs to the day—at night the party of
    young fellows, robust, friendly,   10
Singing with open mouths their strong melodious songs.

[1860]

From *Leaves of Grass*, 1867.

When I Heard the Learn'd Astronomer

WALT WHITMAN

When I heard the learn'd astronomer,
When the proofs, the figures, were ranged in columns
    before me,
When I was shown the charts and diagrams, to add, divide,
    and measure them,
When I sitting heard the astronomer where he lectured with
    much applause in the lecture-room,
How soon unaccountable I became tired and sick,   5
Till rising and gliding out I wander'd off by myself,
In the mystical moist night-air, and from time to time,
Look'd up in perfect silence at the stars.

[1865]

First published in *Drum-Taps* in 1865 and reprinted in the 1867 *Leaves of Grass*.

William Wordsworth
[1770–1850]

Born in Cockermouth, Cumberland, a country village, WILLIAM WORDSWORTH *was the child of an attorney who was well educated and wealthy. He sent his son to Cambridge in 1787 at the age of seventeen. Wordsworth excelled at school but took time off to travel to Switzerland and northern Italy and then on to France. In France he became excited about the French Revolution and met the philosopher Jean-Jacques Rousseau, whose ideas about nature and humanity greatly influenced the young poet. He lived in France during the turbulent year of 1792, fathering a child, Caroline, with Annette Vallon. He wrote romantically about the affair in later years but seems to have decided after a second visit in 1802 to end the relationship. He married his sister Dorothy's friend Mary Hutchinson shortly thereafter and settled in Grasmere in the Lake Country. In the meantime, around 1795, he met and became extremely close to Samuel Taylor Coleridge. From 1795 to 1798, in quiet Somersetshire, the two men created what was to become the touchstone work for the Romantic movement, the* Lyrical Ballads, *followed by its famous Preface in 1800. This work contains the most famous of Wordsworth's and Coleridge's poems as well as Wordsworth's clear statement of their literary values and beliefs. At first light this work was not well received because it was both revolutionary (not a good thing to be so closely after the American Revolution) in that it supported the rights of the common person and was religiously challenging. Wordsworth propounded a love of nature so strong that it could be said to look almost pagan. Needless to say, opinion changed over the centuries, and the work is now considered one of literary history's most important milestones. Some literary historians set the date of 1798 as the great change in the direction of British literature.*

After a trip to Germany with Coleridge and Coleridge's wife, Wordsworth settled at Rydal Mount near Lake Windermere, where he spent the rest of his life in peace and serenity. As the years passed, he became more and more conservative, rejecting the French Revolution with the advent of Napoleon and returning to the church of England. In 1813 he became distributor of stamps, a conservative governmental office, having completely joined the conservatives and turned away from Romantic ideals. During his last years, in 1843 he became Poet Laureate and held the post until his death. His most famous works include the Lucy poems, Tintern Abbey, *and the* Ode on Intimations of Immortality, *all written in his youth. He is also known for his two autobiographical poems,* The Prelude *and* The Excursion, *both of which were included in a longer unfinished work,* The Recluse.

London, 1802

WILLIAM WORDSWORTH

Milton![1] thou shouldst be living at this hour:
England hath need of thee: she is a fen
Of stagnant waters: altar, sword, and pen,
Fireside, the heroic wealth of hall and bower,
Have forfeited their ancient English dower   5
Of inward happiness. We are selfish men:
Oh! raise us up, return to us again;
And give us manners, virtue, freedom, power.
Thy soul was like a Star, and dwelt apart:
Thou hadst a voice whose sound was like the sea,   10
Pure as the naked heavens, majestic, free;
So didst thou travel on life's common way
In cheerful godliness; and yet thy heart
The lowliest duties on herself did lay.

[1802; 1807]

---

[1]John Milton (1608–1674) wrote great religious poetry (*Paradise Lost*) but also powerful political
tracts on literary and political freedom.

Composed in 1802. First published in *Poems in Two Volumes* in 1807.

William Butler Yeats
[1865–1939]

Like many of the upper class in Ireland, WILLIAM BUTLER YEATS *came from an Anglo-Irish background. His father was a noted artist, a portrait painter, and member of the Royal Hibernian Academy. Yeats was born near Dublin, attended school in both London and Dublin, and university at Dublin University. There he began to publish poems and articles in the* Dublin University Review. *By 1888 he moved to London and was initiated into the Rhymers' Club. In 1889 his first volume of verse appeared,* The Wanderings of Oisin and Other Poems. *His early work owes much to the pre-Raphaelites, to the Romantic poets Percy Bysshe Shelley and William Blake, and even to his father's painting. In these early years he helped organize Irish literary societies in both London and Dublin, as well as the Irish Literary Theater, later the Abbey Theater. In his youth he fell in love with a political activist and writer, Maude Gonne, with whom he worked but never married. Many of his most poignant poems are written to and about her. In 1895* Poems *appeared, the first of his lyric volumes, and a collection of prose legends and tales (*The Secret Rose) *followed in 1897. In 1899 another lyric volume,* The Wind among the Reeds *appeared. These lyric poems express much of the Celtic psyche and has a certain elfin charm, always with a touch of melancholy for the age of magic that has passed. At the same time, he was making his mark on the theater with* The Countess Cathleen *(1892) and* The Land of Heart's Desire *(1894). Many more volumes of poetry followed including* The Green Helmet and Other Poems *(1910),* Michael Robartes and the Dancer, *and* Reveries over Childhood and Youth *(1915), but in the 1920s he burst forth into greater public awareness. He became a senator in the new Irish Free State in 1922; in 1923 he received the Noble Prize for Literature, followed by his autobiographical* A Vision *and his greatest poetic work,* The Tower *(1928).*

Yeats's poetry and drama reflect his interest in Irish history and Irish politics, as well as his love for the beauty of the Irish landscape. He was also concerned with the tumult of the early twentieth century, often speaking as a prophet about the war that was to come in the middle of the century, though he did not live to see it. In 1918 he wrote a piece called Per Amica Silentia Lunae *(Friend of the Silent Moon), a volume of philosophical essays that suggested the later interests of his life. He was always a kind of mystic, and in later life he became more and more interested in magic, astrology, and a complex philosophy called Theosophy. The* Silentia Lunae *categorizes humanity according to the phases of the moon, an interest that was a part of the thinking of Jungians and other psychological and philosophical thinkers of the time. Whatever the influences on his thinking, he continued to express the plaintive feelings that are distinctly Irish. Yeats was buried first at Roquebrune but his body was later moved to County Sligo.*

The Second Coming

WILLIAM BUTLER YEATS

Turning and turning in the widening gyre   *1*
The falcon cannot hear the falconer;
Things fall apart; the center cannot hold;
Mere anarchy is loosed upon the world,
The blood-dimmed tide is loosed, and everywhere   *5*
The ceremony of innocence is drowned;
The best lack all conviction, while the worst
Are full of passionate intensity.
Surely some revelation is at hand;
Surely the Second Coming is at hand.   *10*
The Second Coming! Hardly are those words out
When a vast image out of *Spiritus Mundi*
Troubles my sight: somewhere in sands of the desert
A shape with lion body and the head of a man,
A gaze blank and pitiless as the sun,   *15*
Is moving its slow thighs, while all about it
Reel shadows of the indignant desert birds.
The darkness drops again; but now I know
That twenty centuries of stony sleep
Were vexed to nightmare by a rocking cradle,   *20*
And what rough beast, its hour come round at last,
Slouches toward Bethlehem to be born?

[1921]

Composed in 1921.

Sailing to Byzantium[1]

WILLIAM BUTLER YEATS

That is no country for old men. The young
In one another's arms, birds in the trees
—Those dying generations—at their song,
The salmon-falls, the mackerel-crowded seas,
Fish, flesh, or fowl, commend all summer long   5
Whatever is begotten, born, and dies.
Caught in that sensual music all neglect
Monuments of unaging intellect.

An aged man is but a paltry thing,
A tattered coat upon a stick, unless   10
Soul clap its hands and sing, and louder sing
For every tatter in its mortal dress,
Nor is there singing school but studying
Monuments of its own magnificence;
And therefore I have sailed the seas and come   15
To the holy city of Byzantium.

O sages standing in God's holy fire
As in the gold mosaic of a wall,
Come from the holy fire, perne in a gyre[2],
And be the singing-masters of my soul.   20
Consume my heart away; sick with desire
And fastened to a dying animal
It knows not what it is; and gather me
Into the artifice of eternity.

---

[1]Byzantium was the capitol of the Byzantine empire, now Istanbul, Turkey, but Yeats means a holy
city in the hereafter or in the imagination.

[2]Perne in a gyre: Yeats frequently used this image of a spiral to indicate spiritual descent or ascent.

Composed in 1917.

Once out of nature I shall never take 25
My bodily form from any natural thing,
But such a form as Grecian goldsmiths make
Of hammered gold and gold enameling
To keep a drowsy Emperor awake;
Or set upon a golden bough to sing 30
To lords and ladies of Byzantium
Of what is past, or passing, or to come.

[1927]

Section II: What Is Fiction?

Aesop

[sixth century B.C.E.]

This nearly mythical Greek story teller is thought to have been the slave of the historian Herodotus. AESOP is said to have lived on the island of Samos, where he was eventually freed. But all of this history is clouded in myth and mystery and there are various tales about the possible real person. Other versions of Aesop's life place him in connection with pre-Grecian rulers Solon and Croesus (senator and king of Greek city states, c. 560 B.C.E.) and portray him as an adventurer and trickster. The tales then wend their way through literary history first by way of Fabius, a second century B.C.E. Roman who was acquainted with Greek folktales. Regardless of the specifics, this Aesop was the source of the earliest medieval versions of the tales. Later, Phaerus in the first century C.E., a freed slave of Caesar Augustus, the first emperor of Rome, recorded the tales. His work is the source of many of the versions of the stories that circulated throughout Western Europe in the Middle Ages. Later, Panodes Maximus (c. 1260–1330 C.E.), a Byzantian scholar and monk, produced the Greek Anthology, *a prose account of the fables. Still later, French writer Jean de LaFontaine (1621–1695) completed his masterpiece,* Fables Choisies, Mises en Vers *(Choice Fables in Verse). This work comprised twelve books including 230 fables from Aesop. The tales are about beasts acting as humans, but this version clearly emphasizes satire of French society and humorous social commentary. The work appeared in thirty-seven editions, the best-known of which are "The Fox and the Grapes" and "The Tortoise and the Hare." From these versions the fables were translated throughout the world and appear in many versions in children's books.*

The Fox and the Grapes

AESOP

A FOX LOOKED AND beheld the grapes that grew upon a huge vine, the which grapes he much desired for to eat them. And when he saw that none he might get, he turned his sorrow into joy, and said, "These grapes are sour, and if I had some I would not eat them."

He is wise which faineth not to desire the thing the which he may not have.

[SIXTH CENTURY B.C.E.]

"The Fox and the Grapes" is among the most famous fable by the writer known as Aesop. Most of Aesop's work were preserved over time through translations by Babrius, Phaedrus, Planudes Maximus, and La Fontaine.

Sandra Cisneros
[1954–   ]

One of the most popular and critically acclaimed Latina writers of the past twenty years, SANDRA CISNEROS *has created a body of work that clearly reflects her cultural background. As she says in a* New York Times *interview: "I am a woman and I am a Latina. Those are the things that make my writing distinctive. Those are the things that give my writing power. They are the things that give it sabor [flavor], the things that give it picante [spice]."*

Born in Chicago in 1954 to a Mexican father and a Chicana mother, Cisneros spent much of her childhood moving from the United States to Mexico and back. The sense of displacement she felt as a result of these frequent moves was offset by the tight control exercised by her father and six brothers. Her desire for stability and control over her own life led her to read avidly and to write poems and stories even as a child. Her writing ability earned her admission to the prestigious University of Iowa Writers Workshop, an experience that revealed to her the vast difference between her life and that of her classmates. She says she knew nothing of the suburban houses and gardens about which they wrote; her experience was of "third-floor flats" in economically depressed and ethnically segregated Chicago neighborhoods. It was at Iowa that the metaphor of the house came to represent to Cisneros a freedom and independence that she never enjoyed as a child.

After earning a master of fine arts degree from Iowa, Cisneros went on to teach in high school and college and to write—first poetry and later fiction. Her first collection of poetry, Bad Boys, *was published in 1980, followed in 1983 by the fiction collection* The House on Mango Street. *Other work followed, including the poetry collection* My Wicked Wicked Ways *(1987) and the fiction collection* Woman Hollering Creek *(1991). Her most recent novel,* Caramelo *(2002), intersperses lyrics and prose with extensive footnotes on family and Mexican history. Cisneros has won a number of literary prizes, including the Before Columbus Foundation American Book Award for* The House on Mango Street, *the PEN Center West Best Fiction Award for* Woman Hollering Creek, *and a MacArthur Foundation grant.*

Cisneros believes that a good deal of her intensity comes from the influence of her mother, whom she describes as "a fierce woman who was brave enough to raise her daughter in a nontraditional way, who fought for my right to be a person of letters." Calling her work "fiercely political," Cisneros writes about gender, culture, and class. In her work she focuses on people whose lives have been marginalized, whose "stories don't get told—my mother's stories, my students" stories, the stories of women in the neighborhood, the stories of all of those people who don't have the ability to document their lives." Cisneros currently lives—to the chagrin of many of her neighbors—in a bright purple house in the historic King William neighborhood in San Antonio. She remains, as she stated in a biographical sketch for The House on Mango Street, *"nobody's mother and nobody's wife."*

The House on Mango Street

SANDRA CISNEROS

WE DIDN'T ALWAYS LIVE on Mango Street. Before that we lived on Loomis on the third floor, and before that we lived on Keeler. Before Keeler it was Paulina, and before that I can't remember. But what I remember most is moving a lot. Each time it seemed there'd be one more of us. By the time we got to Mango Street we were six—Mama, Papa, Carlos, Kiki, my sister Nenny and me.

The house on Mango Street is ours, and we don't have to pay rent to anybody, or share the yard with the people downstairs, or be careful not to make too much noise, and there isn't a landlord banging on the ceiling with a broom. But even so, it's not the house we'd thought we'd get.

We had to leave the flat on Loomis quick. The water pipes broke and the landlord wouldn't fix them because the house was too old. We had to leave fast. We were using the washroom next door and carrying water over in empty milk gallons. That's why Mama and Papa looked for a house, and that's why we moved into the house on Mango Street, far away, on the other side of town.

They always told us that one day we would move into a house, a real house that would be ours for always so we wouldn't have to move each year. And our house would have running water and pipes that worked. And inside it would have real stairs, not hallway stairs, but stairs inside like the houses on TV. And we'd have a basement and at least three washrooms so when we took a bath we wouldn't have to tell everybody. Our house would be white with trees around it, a great big yard and grass growing without a fence. This was the house Papa talked about when he held a lottery ticket and this was the house Mama dreamed up in the stories she told us before we went to bed.

But the house on Mango Street is not the way they told it at all. It's small and red with tight steps in front and windows so small you'd think they were holding their breath. Bricks are crumbling in places, and the front door is so swollen you have to push hard to get in. There is no front yard, only four little elms the city planted by the curb. Out back is a small garage for the car we don't own yet and a small yard that looks smaller between the two buildings on either side. There are stairs in our house, but they're ordinary hallway stairs, and the house has only one washroom. Everybody has to share a bedroom—Mama and Papa, Carlos and Kiki, me and Nenny.

Once when we were living on Loomis, a nun from my school passed by and saw me playing out front. The laundromat downstairs had been boarded up because it had been robbed two days before and the owner had painted on the wood YES WE'RE OPEN so as not to lose business.

Where do you live? she asked.

There, I said pointing up to the third floor.

You live *there?*

There. I had to look to where she pointed—the third floor, the paint peeling, wooden bars Papa had nailed on the windows so we wouldn't fall out. You live *there?* The way she said it made me feel like nothing. *There.* I lived *there.* I nodded.

I knew then I had to have a house. A real house. One I could point to. But this isn't it. The house on Mango Street isn't it. For the time being, Mama says. Temporary, says Papa. But I know how those things go.

[1983]

Stephen Crane
[1871–1900]

The fourteenth child of a Methodist preacher and a temperance crusader, STEPHEN CRANE *amassed an exceptional body of experience—and produced an impressive canon of writing—in his short life. Crane was born in Newark, New Jersey, and settled in Port Jervis, New York, when he was seven. There he led an active outdoor life and aspired to become a soldier, spending the years between 1888 and 1890 at Claverack College, a military prep school. He left this rigid life in 1890 and enrolled in the engineering program at Lafayette College in Pennsylvania, but departed after only a term, transferring to Syracuse University. By this time his intentions to become a writer had solidified and, in addition to playing baseball, he wrote short stories and worked as a correspondent for the* New York Tribune. *He moved to New York City, still without taking a degree, and devoted himself to observing life, particularly the struggles of the poor in New York's notorious Bowery and other slums. These experiences lead to the publication in 1893 of his first novel:* Maggie, a Girl of the Streets, *whose graphic descriptions of conditions in which New York's poor survived constitute an early example of the genre that would become know as naturalism. However, the book was so disturbing that Crane was unable to find a publisher, and had to print it at his own expense.*

Following this inauspicious beginning Crane published, in 1895, The Red Badge of Courage. *This account of the thoughts and emotions of a naïve young soldier after a Civil War battle, written by an author with no direct experience of war himself was a success, and led to the reissue of* Maggie, *as well as a series of assignments as a war correspondent. In this capacity Crane traveled to Greece, Mexico, and the American Southwest. During the winter of 1896, he survived the foundering of a ship running guns to Cuba. This experience became the basis for his story "The Open Boat" and its journalistic counterpart, "Stephen Crane's Own Story," both published in 1897. Ironically, it was experiences like this, which lay at the heart of Crane's vigorous writing, that lead to his death. His health ruined during his travels as a correspondent, he retired to a German sanitarium to recuperate from a fever and died in 1900 from tuberculosis.*

Though regarded primarily as one of America's first naturalist writers, Crane could also be lighthearted, as his early sketches of upstate New York and his 1898 parody of Westerns, "The Bride Comes to Yellow Sky," demonstrate. In "The Blue Hotel" (1898) this sense of satire begins to merge with the graphic violence of naturalism and assumes an almost Sartrian sense of existential absurdity. But it is chiefly as the author of grim, unflinching portraits of squalor and depravity like Maggie *and* The Monster *(1899) that Crane is remembered. Perhaps the most* condensed impression of this worldview can be found in his poems, the first volume of which, The Black Riders, was published in 1895. Here, in brief and often terrifying snippets of free verse, Crane paints a world devoid of the comforts offered by the Christianity to which both of his parents were devoted—a world in which humans have no agency and in which fate laughs grimly or, worse, ignores mankind completely.

—David L. G. Arnold, *University of Wisconsin, Stevens Point*

The Open Boat

STEPHEN CRANE

*A TALE INTENDED TO BE AFTER THE FACT BEING THE
EXPERIENCE OF FOUR MEN FROM THE SUNK STEAMER
COMMODORE[1]*

I

NONE OF THEM KNEW the color of the sky. Their eyes glanced level, and were fastened upon the waves that swept toward them. These waves were of the hue of slate, save for the tops, which were of foaming white, and all of the men knew the colors of the sea. The horizon narrowed and widened, and dipped and rose, and at all times its edge was jagged with waves that seemed thrust up in points like rocks.

Many a man ought to have a bath-tub larger than the boat which here rode upon the sea. These waves were most wrongfully and barbarously abrupt and tall, and each froth-top was a problem in small boat navigation.

The cook squatted in the bottom and looked with both eyes at the six inches of gunwale which separated him from the ocean. His sleeves were rolled over his fat forearms, and the two flaps of his unbuttoned vest dangled as he bent to bail out the boat. Often he said: "Gawd! That was a narrow clip." As he remarked it he invariably gazed eastward over the broken sea.

The oiler,[2] steering with one of the two oars in the boat, sometimes raised himself suddenly to keep clear of water that swirled in over the stern. It was a thin little oar and it seemed often ready to snap.

The correspondent, pulling at the other oar, watched the waves and wondered why he was there.

---

[1] On January 1, 1897, the tugboat *Commodore* sailed from Jacksonville, Florida, laden with munitions for Cubans fighting the Spanish. The ship sank the next morning, leaving Stephen Crane and three other survivors adrift in a small boat; they reached Daytona Beach, Florida, on January 3, after spending thirty hours at sea. Crane based "The Open Boat" on this incident.

[2] Seaman whose job is to oil machinery in the ship's engine room.

First published in *Scribner's Magazine*, June 1897. Reprinted in *The Open Boat & Other Stories* in 1898.

The injured captain, lying in the bow, was at this time buried in that profound dejection and indifference which comes, temporarily at least, to even the bravest and most enduring when, willy nilly, the firm fails, the army loses, the ship goes down. The mind of the master of a vessel is rooted deep in the timbers of her, though he command for a day or a decade, and this captain had on him the stern impression of a scene in the grays of dawn of seven turned faces, and later a stump of a top-mast with a white ball on it that slashed to and fro at the waves, went low and lower, and down. Thereafter there was something strange in his voice. Although steady, it was deep with mourning, and of a quality beyond oration or tears.

"Keep'er a little more south, Billie," said he.

" 'A little more south,' sir," said the oiler in the stern.

A seat in this boat was not unlike a seat upon a bucking broncho, and, by the same token, a broncho is not much smaller. The craft pranced and reared, and plunged like an animal. As each wave came, and she rose for it, she seemed like a horse making at a fence outrageously high. The manner of her scramble over these walls of water is a mystic thing, and, moreover, at the top of them were ordinarily these problems in white water, the foam racing down from the summit of each wave, requiring a new leap, and a leap from the air. Then, after scornfully bumping a crest, she would slide, and race, and splash down a long incline and arrive bobbing and nodding in front of the next menace.

A singular disadvantage of the sea lies in the fact that after successfully surmounting one wave you discover that there is another behind it just as important and just as nervously anxious to do something effective in the way of swamping boats. In a ten-foot dingey one can get an idea of the resources of the sea in the line of waves that is not probable to the average experience, which is never at sea in a dingey. As each slaty wall of water approached, it shut all else from the view of the men in the boat, and it was not difficult to imagine that this particular wave was the final outburst of the ocean, the last effort of the grim water. There was a terrible grace in the move of the waves, and they came in silence, save for the snarling of the crests.

In the wan light, the faces of the men must have been gray. Their eyes must have glinted in strange ways as they gazed steadily astern. Viewed from a balcony, the whole thing would doubtlessly have been weirdly picturesque. But the men in the boat had no time to see it, and if they had had leisure there were other things to occupy their minds. The sun swung steadily up the sky, and they knew it was broad day because the color of the sea changed from slate to emerald-green, streaked with amber lights, and the foam was like tumbling snow. The process of the breaking day was unknown to them. They were aware only of this effect upon the color of the waves that rolled toward them.

STEPHEN CRANE 🔊 *The Open Boat*

In disjointed sentences the cook and the correspondent argued as to the difference between a life-saving station and a house of refuge. The cook had said: "There's a house of refuge just north of the Mosquito Inlet Light, and as soon as they see us, they'll come off in their boat and pick us up."

"As soon as who see us?" said the correspondent.

"The crew," said the cook.

"Houses of refuge don't have crews," said the correspondent. "As I understand them, they are only places where clothes and grub are stored for the benefit of shipwrecked people. They don't carry crews."

"Oh, yes, they do," said the cook.

"No, they don't," said the correspondent.

"Well, we're not there yet, anyhow," said the oiler, in the stern.

"Well," said the cook, "perhaps it's not a house of refuge that I'm thinking of as being near Mosquito Inlet Light. Perhaps it's a life-saving station."

"We're not there yet," said the oiler, in the stern.

II

As the boat bounced from the top of each wave, the wind tore through the hair of the hatless men, and as the craft plopped her stern down again the spray slashed past them. The crest of each of these waves was a hill, from the top of which the men surveyed, for a moment, a broad tumultuous expanse; shining and wind-riven. It was probably splendid. It was probably glorious, this play of the free sea, wild with lights of emerald and white and amber.

"Bully good thing it's an on-shore wind," said the cook. "If not, where would we be? Wouldn't have a show."

"That's right," said the correspondent.

The busy oiler nodded his assent.

Then the captain, in the bow, chuckled in a way that expressed humor, contempt, tragedy, all in one. "Do you think we've got much of a show, now, boys?" said he.

Whereupon the three were silent, save for a trifle of hemming and hawing. To express any particular optimism at this time they felt to be childish and stupid, but they all doubtless possessed this sense of the situation in their mind. A young man thinks doggedly at such times. On the other hand, the ethics of their condition was decidedly against any open suggestion of hopelessness. So they were silent.

"Oh, well," said the captain, soothing his children, "we'll get ashore all right."

But there was that in his tone which made them think, so the oiler quoth: "Yes! If this wind holds!"

The cook was bailing: "Yes! If we don't catch hell in the surf."

Canton flannel gulls[3] flew near and far. Sometimes they sat down on the sea, near patches of brown sea-weed that rolled over the waves with a movement like carpets on a line in a gale. The birds sat comfortably in groups, and they were envied by some in the dingey, for the wrath of the sea was no more to them than it was to a covey of prairie chickens a thousand miles inland. Often they came very close and stared at the men with black beadlike eyes. At these times they were uncanny and sinister in their unblinking scrutiny, and the men hooted angrily at them, telling them to be gone. One came, and evidently decided to alight on the top of the captain's head. The bird flew parallel to the boat and did not circle, but made short sidelong jumps in the air in chicken-fashion. His black eyes were wistfully fixed upon the captain's head. "Ugly brute," said the oiler to the bird. "You look as if you were made with a jack-knife." The cook and the correspondent swore darkly at the creature. The captain naturally wished to knock it away with the end of the heavy painter,[4] but he did not dare do it, because anything resembling an emphatic gesture would have capsized this freighted boat, and so with his open hand, the captain gently and carefully waved the gull away. After it had been discouraged from the pursuit the captain breathed easier on account of his hair, and others breathed easier because the bird struck their minds at this time as being somehow grewsome and ominous.

In the meantime the oiler and the correspondent rowed. And also they rowed.

They sat together in the same seat, and each rowed an oar. Then the oiler took both oars; then the correspondent took both oars; then the oiler; then the correspondent. They rowed and they rowed. The very ticklish part of the business was when the time came for the reclining one in the stern to take his turn at the oars. By the very last star of truth, it is easier to steal eggs from under a hen than it was to change seats in the dingey. First the man in the stern slid his hand along the thwart and moved with care, as if he were of Sèvres.[5] Then the man in the rowing seat slid his hand along the other thwart. It was all done with the most extraordinary care. As the two sidled past each other, the whole party kept watchful eyes on the coming wave, and the captain cried: "Look out now! Steady there!"

The brown mats of sea-weed that appeared from time to time were like islands, bits of earth. They were travelling, apparently, neither one way nor the

---

[3]Seagulls visually associated with a thick cotton fabric, "Canton flannel."

[4]In nautical terminology, a "painter" is a mooring rope at the boat's bow.

[5]Fine, fragile china named for the French city where it is manufactured.

other. They were, to all intents, stationary. They informed the men in the boat that it was making progress slowly toward the land.

The captain, rearing cautiously in the bow, after the dingey soared on a great swell, said that he had seen the lighthouse at Mosquito Inlet. Presently the cook remarked that he had seen it. The correspondent was at the oars, then, and for some reason he too wished to look at the lighthouse, but his back was toward the far shore and the waves were important, and for some time he could not seize an opportunity to turn his head. But at last there came a wave more gentle than the others, and when at the crest of it he swiftly scoured the western horizon.

"See it?" said the captain.

"No," said the correspondent, slowly, I didn't see anything."

"Look again," said the captain. He pointed. "It's exactly in that direction."

At the top of another wave, the correspondent did as he was bid, and this time his eyes chanced on a small still thing on the edge of the swaying horizon. It was precisely like the point of a pin. It took an anxious eye to find a lighthouse so tiny.

"Think we'll make it, captain?"

"If this wind holds and the boat don't swamp, we can't do much else," said the captain.

The little boat, lifted by each towering sea, and splashed viciously by the crests, made progress that in the absence of seaweed was not apparent to those in her. She seemed just a wee thing wallowing, miraculously, top-up, at the mercy of five oceans. Occasionally, a great spread of water, like white flames, swarmed into her.

"Bail her, cook," said the captain, serenely.

"All right, captain," said the cheerful cook.

III

It would be difficult to describe the subtle brotherhood of men that was here established on the seas. No one said that it was so. No one mentioned it. But it dwelt in the boat, and each man felt it warm him. They were a captain, an oiler, a cook, and a correspondent, and they were friends, friends in a more curiously ironbound degree than may be common. The hurt captain, lying against the waterjar in the bow, spoke always in a low voice and calmly, but he could never command a more ready and swiftly obedient crew than the motley three of the dingey. It was more than a mere recognition of what was best for the common safety. There was surely in it a quality that was personal and heartfelt. And after this devotion to the commander of the boat there was this comradeship that the correspondent, for instance, who had been taught to be cynical of men, knew even at the time was the best experience of his life. But no one said that it was so. No one mentioned it.

"I wish we had a sail," remarked the captain. "We might try my overcoat on the end of an oar and give you two boys a chance to rest." So the cook and the correspondent held the mast and spread wide the overcoat. The oiler steered, and the little boat made good way with her new rig. Sometimes the oiler had to scull sharply to keep a sea from breaking into the boat, but otherwise sailing was a success.

Meanwhile the light-house had been growing slowly larger. It had now almost assumed color, and appeared like a little gray shadow on the sky. The man at the oars could not be prevented from turning his head rather often to try for a glimpse of this little gray shadow.

At last, from the top of each wave the men in the tossing boat could see land. Even as the light-house was an upright shadow on the sky, this land seemed but a long black shadow on the sea. It certainly was thinner than paper. "We must be about opposite New Smyrna," said the cook, who had coasted this shore often in schooners. "Captain, by the way, I believe they abandoned that life-saving station there about a year ago."

"Did they?" said the captain.

The wind slowly died away. The cook and the correspondent were not now obliged to slave in order to hold high the oar. But the waves continued their old impetuous swooping at the dingey, and the little craft, no longer under way, struggled woundily over them. The oiler or the correspondent took the oars again.

Shipwrecks are *apropos* of nothing. If men could only train for them and have them occur when the men had reached pink condition, there would be less drowning at sea. Of the four in the dingey none had slept any time worth mentioning for two days and two nights previous to embarking in the dingey, and in the excitement of clambering about the deck of a foundering ship they had also forgotten to eat heartily.

For these reasons, and for others, neither the oiler nor the correspondent was fond of rowing at this time. The correspondent wondered ingenuously how in the name of all that was sane could there be people who thought it amusing to row a boat. It was not an amusement; it was a diabolical punishment, and even a genius of mental aberrations could never conclude that it was anything but a horror to the muscles and a crime against the back. He mentioned to the boat in general how the amusement of rowing struck him, and the weary-faced oiler smiled in full sympathy. Previously to the foundering, by the way, the oiler had worked doublewatch in the engine-room of the ship.

"Take her easy, now, boys," said the captain. "Don't spend yourselves. If we have to run a surf you'll need all your strength, because we'll sure have to swim for it. Take your time."

Slowly the land arose from the sea. From a black line it became a line of black and a line of white, trees, and sand. Finally, the captain said that he could make out a house on the shore. "That's the house of refuge, sure," said the cook. "They'll see us before long, and come out after us."

The distant light-house reared high. "The keeper ought to be able to make us out now, if he's looking through a glass," said the captain. "He'll notify the life-saving people."

"None of those other boats could have got ashore to give word of the wreck," said the oiler, in a low voice. "Else the life-boat would be out hunting us."

Slowly and beautifully the land loomed out of the sea. The wind came again. It had veered from the northeast to the southeast. Finally, a new sound struck the ears of the men in the boat. It was the low thunder of the surf on the shore. "We'll never be able to make the light-house now," said the captain. "Swing her head a little more north, Billie," said the captain.

" 'A little more north,' sir," said the oiler.

Whereupon the little boat turned her nose once more down the wind, and all but the oarsman watched the shore grow. Under the influence of this expansion doubt and direful apprehension was leaving the minds of the men. The management of the boat was still most absorbing, but it could not prevent a quiet cheerfulness. In an hour, perhaps, they would be ashore.

Their back-bones had become thoroughly used to balancing in the boat and they now rode this wild colt of a dingey like circus men. The correspondent thought that he had been drenched to the skin, but happening to feel in the top pocket of his coat, he found therein eight cigars. Four of them were soaked with sea-water; four were perfectly scatheless. After a search, somebody produced three dry matches, and thereupon the four waifs rode in their little boat, and with an assurance of an impending rescue shining in their eyes, puffed at the big cigars and judged well and ill of all men. Everybody took a drink of water.

IV

"Cook," remarked the captain, "there don't seem to be any signs of life about your house of refuge."

"No," replied the cook. "Funny they don't see us!"

A broad stretch of lowly coast lay before the eyes of the men. It was of low dunes topped with dark vegetation. The roar of the surf was plain, and sometimes they could see the white lip of a wave as it spun up the beach. A tiny house was blocked out black upon the sky. Southward, the slim light-house lifted its little gray length.

Tide, wind, and waves were swinging the dingey northward. "Funny they don't see us," said the men.

The surf's roar was here dulled, but its tone was, nevertheless, thunderous and mighty. As the boat swam over the great rollers, the men sat listening to this roar.

"We'll swamp sure," said everybody.

It is fair to say here that there was not a life-saving station within twenty miles in either direction, but the men did not know this fact and in consequence they made dark and opprobrious remarks concerning the eyesight of the nation's life-savers. Four scowling men sat in the dingey and surpassed records in the invention of epithets.

"Funny they don't see us."

The light-heartedness of a former time had completely faded. To their sharpened minds it was easy to conjure pictures of all kinds of incompetency and blindness and, indeed, cowardice. There was the shore of the populous land, and it was bitter and bitter to them that from it came no sign.

"Well," said the captain, ultimately, "I suppose we'll have to make a try for ourselves. If we stay out here too long, we'll none of us have strength left to swim after the boat swamps."

And so the oiler, who was at the oars, turned the boat straight for the shore. There was a sudden tightening of muscles. There was some thinking.

"If we don't all get ashore—" said the captain. "If we don't all get ashore, I suppose you fellows know where to send news of my finish?"

They then briefly exchanged some addresses and admonitions. As for the reflections of the men, there was a great deal of rage in them. Perchance they might be formulated thus: "If I am going to be drowned—if I am going to be drowned—if I am going to be drowned, why, in the name of the seven mad gods who rule the sea, was I allowed to come thus far and contemplate sand and trees? Was I brought here merely to have my nose dragged away as I was about to nibble the sacred cheese of life? It is preposterous. If this old ninny-woman, Fate, cannot do better than this, she should be deprived of the management of men's fortunes. She is an old hen who knows not her intention. If she has decided to drown me, why did she not do it in the beginning and save me all this trouble. The whole affair is absurd. . . . But, no, she cannot mean to drown me. She dare not drown me. She cannot drown me. Not after all this work." Afterward the man might have had an impulse to shake his fist at the clouds: "Just you drown me, now, and then hear what I call you!"

The billows that came at this time were more formidable. They seemed always just about to break and roll over the little boat in a turmoil of foam. There was a preparatory and long growl in the speech of them. No mind unused to the sea would have concluded that the dingey could ascend these sheer heights in time. The shore was still afar. The oiler was a wily surfman. "Boys," he said, swiftly, "she won't live three minutes more and we're too far out to swim. Shall I take her to sea again, captain?"

"Yes! Go ahead!" said the captain.

This oiler, by a series of quick miracles, and fast and steady oarsmanship, turned the boat in the middle of the surf and took her safely to sea again.

There was a considerable silence as the boat bumped over the furrowed sea to deeper water. Then somebody in gloom spoke. "Well, anyhow, they must have seen us from the shore by now."

The gulls went in slanting flight up the wind toward the gray desolate east. A squall, marked by dingy clouds, and clouds brick-red, like smoke from a burning building, appeared from the southeast.

"What do you think of those life-saving people? Ain't they peaches?"

"Funny they haven't seen us."

"Maybe they think we're out here for sport! Maybe they think we're fishin'. Maybe they think we're damned fools."

It was a long afternoon. A changed tide tried to force them southward, but wind and wave said northward. Far ahead, where coast-line, sea, and sky formed their mighty angle, there were little dots which seemed to indicate a city on the shore.

"St. Augustine?"

The captain shook his head. "Too near Mosquito Inlet."

And the oiler rowed, and then the correspondent rowed. Then the oiler rowed. It was a weary business. The human back can become the seat of more aches and pains than are registered in books for the composite anatomy of a regiment. It is a limited area, but it can become the theatre of innumerable muscular conflicts, tangles, wrenches, knots, and other comforts.

"Did you ever like to row, Billie?" asked the correspondent.

"No," said the oiler. "Hang it."

When one exchanged the rowing-seat for a place in the bottom of the boat, he suffered a bodily depression that caused him to be careless of everything save an obligation to wiggle one finger. There was cold sea-water swashing to and fro in the boat, and he lay in it. His head, pillowed on a thwart, was within an inch of the swirl of a wave crest, and sometimes a particularly obstreperous sea came in-board and drenched him once more. But these matters did not annoy him. It is almost certain that if the boat had capsized he would have tumbled comfortably out upon the ocean as if he felt sure that it was a great soft mattress.

"Look! There's a man on the shore!"

"Where?"

"There! See 'im? See 'im?"

"Yes, sure! He's walking along."

"Now he's stopped. Look! He's facing us!"

"He's waving at us!"

"So he is! By thunder!"

"Ah, now, we're all right! Now we're all right! There'll be a boat out here for us in half an hour."

"He's going on. He's running. He's going up to that house there."

The remote beach seemed lower than the sea, and it required a searching glance to discern the little black figure. The captain saw a floating stick and they rowed to it. A bath-towel was by some weird chance in the boat, and, tying this on the stick, the captain waved it. The oarsman did not dare turn his head, so he was obliged to ask questions.

"What's he doing now?"

"He's standing still again. He's looking, I think. . . . There he goes again. Toward the house. . . . Now he's stopped again."

"Is he waving at us?"

"No, not now! he was, though."

"Look! There comes another man!"

"He's running."

"Look at him go, would you."

"Why, he's on a bicycle. Now he's met the other man. They're both waving at us. Look!"

"There comes something up the beach."

"What the devil is that thing?"

"Why, it looks like a boat."

"Why, certainly it's a boat."

"No, it's on wheels."

"Yes, so it is. Well, that must be the life-boat. They drag them along shore on a wagon.

"That's the life-boat, sure."

"No, by—, it's—it's an omnibus."

"I tell you it's a life-boat."

"It is not! It's an omnibus. I can see it plain. See? One of these big hotel omnibuses."

"By thunder, you're right. It's an omnibus, sure as fate. What do you suppose they are doing with an omnibus? Maybe they are going around collecting the life-crew, hey?"

"That's it, likely. Look! There's a fellow waving a little black flag. He's standing on the steps of the omnibus. There come those other two fellows. Now they're all talking together. Look at the fellow with the flag. Maybe he ain't waving it."

"That ain't a flag, is it? That's his coat. Why, certainly, that's his coat."

"So it is. It's his coat. He's taken it off and is waving it around his head. But would you look at him swing it."

"Oh, say, there isn't any life-saving station there. That's just a winter resort hotel omnibus that has brought over some of the boarders to see us drown."

"What's that idiot with the coat mean? What's he signaling, anyhow?"

"It looks as if he were trying to tell us to go north. There must be a life-saving station up there."

"No! He thinks we're fishing. Just giving us a merry hand. See? Ah, there, Willie."

"Well, I wish I could make something out of those signals. What do you suppose he means?"

"He don't mean anything. He's just playing."

"Well, if he'd just signal us to try the surf again, or to go to sea and wait, or go north, or go south, or go to hell—there would be some reason in it. But look at him. He just stands there and keeps his coat revolving like a wheel. The ass!"

"There come more people."

"Now there's quite a mob. Look! Isn't that a boat?"

"Where? Oh, I see where you mean. No, that's no boat."

"That fellow is still waving his coat."

"He must think we like to see him do that. Why don't he quit it. It don't mean anything."

"I don't know. I think he is trying to make us go north. It must be that there's a life-saving station there somewhere."

"Say, he ain't tired yet. Look at 'im wave."

"Wonder how long he can keep that up. He's been revolving his coat ever since he caught sight of us. He's an idiot. Why aren't they getting men to bring a boat out. A fishing boat—one of those big yawls—could come out here all right. Why don't he do something?"

"Oh, it's all right, now."

"They'll have a boat out here for us in less than no time, now that they've seen us."

A faint yellow tone came into the sky over the low land. The shadows on the sea slowly deepened. The wind bore coldness with it, and the men began to shiver.

"Holy smoke!" said one, allowing his voice to express his impious mood, "if we keep on monkeying out here! If we've got to flounder out here all night!"

"Oh, we'll never have to stay here all night! Don't you worry. They've seen us now, and it won't be long before they'll come chasing out after us."

The shore grew dusky. The man waving a coat blended gradually into this gloom, and it swallowed in the same manner the omnibus and the group of people. The spray, when it dashed uproariously over the side, made the voyagers shrink and swear like men who were being branded.

"I'd like to catch the chump who waved the coat. I feel like soaking him one, just for luck."

"Why? What did he do?"

"Oh, nothing, but then he seemed so damned cheerful."

In the meantime the oiler rowed, and then the correspondent rowed, and then the oiler rowed. Gray-faced and bowed forward, they mechanically, turn by turn, plied the leaden oars. The form of the light-house had vanished from the southern horizon, but finally a pale star appeared, just lifting from the sea. The streaked saffron in the west passed before the all-merging darkness, and the sea to the east was black. The land had vanished, and was expressed only by the low and drear thunder of the surf.

"If I am going to be drowned—if I am going to be drowned—if I am going to be drowned, why, in the name of the seven mad gods, who rule the sea, was I allowed to come thus far and contemplate sand and trees? Was I brought here merely to have my nose dragged away as I was about to nibble the sacred cheese of life?"

The patient captain, drooped over the water-jar, was sometimes obliged to speak to the oarsman.

"Keep her head up! Keep her head up!"

" 'Keep her head up,' sir." The voices were weary and low.

This was surely a quiet evening. All save the oarsman lay heavily and listlessly in the boat's bottom. As for him, his eyes were just capable of noting the tall black waves that swept forward in a most sinister silence, save for an occasional subdued growl of a crest.

The cook's head was on a thwart, and he looked without interest at the water under his nose. He was deep in other scenes. Finally he spoke. "Billie," he murmured, dreamfully, "what kind of pie do you like best?"

V

"Pie," said the oiler and the correspondent, agitatedly. "Don't talk about those things, blast you!"

"Well," said the cook, "I was just thinking about ham sandwiches, and—"

A night on the sea in an open boat is a long night. As darkness settled finally, the shine of the light, lifting from the sea in the south, changed to full gold. On the northern horizon a new light appeared, a small bluish gleam on the edge of the waters. These two lights were the furniture of the world. Otherwise there was nothing but waves.

Two men huddled in the stern, and distances were so magnificent in the dingey that the rower was enabled to keep his feet partly warmed by thrusting them under his companions. Their legs indeed extended far under the rowing-seat until they touched the feet of the captain forward. Sometimes, despite the efforts of the tired oarsman, a wave came piling into the boat, an icy wave of the night, and the chilling water soaked them anew. They would twist their bodies for a moment and groan, and sleep the dead sleep once more, while the water in the boat gurgled about them as the craft rocked.

The plan of the oiler and the correspondent was for one to row until he lost the ability, and then arouse the other from his sea-water couch in the bottom of the boat.

The oiler plied the oars until his head drooped forward, and the overpowering sleep blinded him. And he rowed yet afterward. Then he touched a man in the bottom of the boat, and called his name. "Will you spell me for a little while?" he said, meekly.

"Sure, Billie," said the correspondent, awakening and dragging himself to a sitting position. They exchanged places carefully, and the oiler, cuddling down in the sea-water at the cook's side, seemed to go to sleep instantly.

The particular violence of the sea had ceased. The waves came without snarling. The obligation of the man at the oars was to keep the boat headed so that the tilt of the rollers would not capsize her, and to preserve her from filling when the crests rushed past. The black waves were silent and hard to be seen in the darkness. Often one was almost upon the boat before the oarsman was aware.

In a low voice the correspondent addressed the captain. He was not sure that the captain was awake, although this iron man seemed to be always awake. "Captain, shall I keep her making for that light north, sir?"

The same steady voice answered him. "Yes. Keep it about two points off the port bow."

The cook had tied a life-belt around himself in order to get even the warmth which this clumsy cork contrivance could donate, and he seemed almost stove-like when a rower, whose teeth invariably chattered wildly as soon as he ceased his labor, dropped down to sleep.

The correspondent, as he rowed, looked down at the two men sleeping under foot. The cook's arm was around the oiler's shoulders, and, with their fragmentary clothing and haggard faces, they were the babes of the sea, a grotesque rendering of the old babes in the wood.

Later he must have grown stupid at his work, for suddenly there was a growling of water, and a crest came with a roar and a swash into the boat, and it was a wonder that it did not set the cook afloat in his life-belt. The cook continued to sleep, but the oiler sat up, blinking his eyes and shaking with the new cold.

"Oh, I'm awful sorry, Billie," said the correspondent, contritely.

"That's all right, old boy," said the oiler, and lay down again and was asleep.

Presently it seemed that even the captain dozed, and the correspondent thought that he was the one man afloat on all the oceans. The wind had a voice as it came over the waves, and it was sadder than the end.

There was a long, loud swishing astern of the boat, and a gleaming trail of phosphorescence, like blue flame, was furrowed on the black waters. It might have been made by a monstrous knife.

Then there came a stillness, while the correspondent breathed with the open mouth and looked at the sea.

Suddenly there was another swish and another long flash of bluish light, and this time it was alongside the boat, and might almost have been reached with an oar. The correspondent saw an enormous fin speed like a shadow through the water, hurling the crystalline spray and leaving the long glowing trail.

The correspondent looked over his shoulder at the captain. His face was hidden, and he seemed to be asleep. He looked at the babes of the sea. They certainly were asleep. So, being bereft of sympathy, he leaned a little way to one side and swore softly into the sea.

But the thing did not then leave the vicinity of the boat. Ahead or astern, on one side or the other, at intervals long or short, fled the long sparkling streak, and there was to be heard the whiroo of the dark fin. The speed and power of the thing was greatly to be admired. It cut the water like a gigantic and keen projectile.

The presence of this biding thing did not affect the man with the same horror that it would if he had been a picnicker. He simply looked at the sea dully and swore in an undertone.

Nevertheless, it is true that he did not wish to be alone with the thing. He wished one of his companions to awaken by chance and keep him company with it. But the captain hung motionless over the water-jar and the oiler and the cook in the bottom of the boat were plunged in slumber.

VI

"If I am going to be drowned—if I am going to be drowned—if I am going to be drowned, why, in the name of the seven mad gods, who rule the sea, was I allowed to come thus far and contemplate sand and trees?"

During this dismal night, it may be remarked that a man would conclude that it was really the intention of the seven mad gods to drown him, despite the abominable injustice of it. For it was certainly an abominable injustice to drown a man who had worked so hard, so hard. The man felt it would be a crime most unnatural. Other people had drowned at sea since galleys swarmed with painted sails, but still—

When it occurs to a man that nature does not regard him as important, and that she feels she would not maim the universe by disposing of him, he at first wishes to throw bricks at the temple, and he hates deeply the fact that there are no bricks and no temples. Any visible expression of nature would surely be pelleted with his jeers.

Then, if there be no tangible thing to hoot he feels, perhaps, the desire to confront a personification and indulge in pleas, bowed to one knee, and with hands supplicant, saying: "Yes, but I love myself."

A high cold star on a winter's night is the word he feels that she says to him. Thereafter he knows the pathos of his situation.

The men in the dingey had not discussed these matters, but each had, no doubt, reflected upon them in silence and according to his mind. There was seldom any expression upon their faces save the general one of complete weariness. Speech was devoted to the business of the boat.

To chime the notes of his emotion, a verse mysteriously entered the correspondent's head. He had even forgotten that he had forgotten this verse, but it suddenly was in his mind.

> A soldier of the Legion lay dying in Algiers,
> There was lack of woman's nursing, there was dearth of woman's
> tears;
> But a comrade stood beside him, and he took that comrade's hand
> And he said: "I shall never see my own, my native land."[6]

In his childhood, the correspondent had been made acquainted with the fact that a soldier of the Legion lay dying in Algiers, but he had never regarded the fact as important. Myriads of his school-fellows had informed him of the soldier's plight, but the dinning had naturally ended by making him perfectly indifferent. He had never considered it his affair that a soldier of the Legion lay dying in Algiers, nor had it appeared to him as a matter for sorrow. It was less to him than breaking of a pencil's point.

Now, however, it quaintly came to him as a human, living thing. It was no longer merely a picture of a few throes in the breast of a poet, meanwhile

---

[6]The narrator somewhat edits these lines from Caroline E. S. Norton's poem "Bingen on the Rhine" (1883).

drinking tea and warming his feet at the grate; it was an actuality—stern, mournful, and fine.

The correspondent plainly saw the soldier. He lay on the sand with his feet out straight and still. While his pale left hand was upon his chest in an attempt to thwart the going of his life, the blood came between his fingers. In the far Algerian distance, a city of low square forms was set against a sky that was faint with the last sunset hues. The correspondent, plying the oars and dreaming of the slow and slower movements of the lips of the soldier, was moved by a profound and perfectly impersonal comprehension. He was sorry for the soldier of the Legion who lay dying in Algiers.

The thing which had followed the boat and waited had evidently grown bored at the delay. There was no longer to be heard the slash of the cutwater, and there was no longer the flame of the long trail. The light in the north still glimmered, but it was apparently no nearer to the boat. Sometimes the boom of the surf rang in the correspondent's ears, and he turned the craft seaward then and rowed harder. Southward, someone had evidently built a watch-fire on the beach. It was too low and too far to be seen, but it made a shimmering, roseate reflection upon the bluff back of it, and this could be discerned from the boat. The wind came stronger, and sometimes a wave suddenly raged out like a mountain-cat and there was to be seen the sheen and sparkle of a broken crest.

The captain, in the bow, moved on his water-jar and sat erect. "Pretty long night," he observed to the correspondent. He looked at the shore. "Those life-saving people take their time."

"Did you see that shark playing around?"

"Yes, I saw him. He was a big fellow, all right."

"Wish I had known you were awake."

Later the correspondent spoke into the bottom of the boat.

"Billie!" There was a slow and gradual disentanglement. "Billie, will you spell me?"

"Sure," said the oiler.

As soon as the correspondent touched the cold comfortable sea-water in the bottom of the boat, and had huddled close to the cook's life-belt he was deep in sleep, despite the fact that his teeth played all the popular airs. This sleep was so good to him that it was but a moment before he heard a voice call his name in a tone that demonstrated the last stages of exhaustion. "Will you spell me?"

"Sure, Billie."

The light in the north had mysteriously vanished, but the correspondent took his course from the wide-awake captain.

Later in the night they took the boat farther out to sea, and the captain directed the cook to take one oar at the stern and keep the boat facing the seas.

He was to call out if he should hear the thunder of the surf. This plan enabled the oiler and the correspondent to get respite together. "We'll give those boys a chance to get into shape again," said the captain. They curled down and, after a few preliminary chatterings and trembles, slept once more the dead sleep. Neither knew they had bequeathed to the cook the company of another shark, or perhaps the same shark.

As the boat caroused on the waves, spray occasionally bumped over the side and gave them a fresh soaking, but this had no power to break their repose. The ominous slash of the wind and the water affected them as it would have affected mummies.

"Boys," said the cook, with the notes of every reluctance in his voice, "she's drifted in pretty close. I guess one of you had better take her to sea again." The correspondent, aroused, heard the crash of the toppled crests.

As he was rowing, the captain gave him some whiskey and water, and this steadied the chills out of him. "If I ever get ashore and anybody shows me even a photograph of an oar—"

At last there was a short conversation.

"Billie. . . . Billie, will you spell me?"

"Sure," said the oiler.

VII

When the correspondent again opened his eyes, the sea and the sky were each of the gray hue of the dawning. Later, carmine and gold was painted upon the waters. The morning appeared finally, in its splendor, with a sky of pure blue, and the sunlight flamed on the tips of the waves.

On the distant dunes were set many little black cottages, and a tall white windmill reared above them. No man, nor dog, nor bicycle appeared on the beach. The cottages might have formed a deserted village.

The voyagers scanned the shore. A conference was held in the boat. "Well," said the captain, "if no help is coming, we might better try to run through the surf right away. If we stay out here much longer we will be too weak to do anything for ourselves at all." The others silently acquiesced in this reasoning. The boat was headed for the beach. The correspondent wondered if none ever ascended the tall wind-tower, and if then they never looked seaward. This tower was a giant, standing with its back to the plight of the ants. It represented in a degree, to the correspondent, the serenity of nature amid the struggles of the individual—nature in the wind, and nature in the vision of men. She did not seem cruel to him then, nor beneficent, nor treacherous, nor wise. But she was indifferent, flatly indifferent. It is, perhaps, plausible that a man in this situation, impressed with the unconcern of the universe, should see the innumerable flaws of his life and have them taste wickedly in his mind and wish for another chance. A distinction between right and wrong seems absurdly clear to him, then, in this new ignorance of the grave-edge, and he understands that if he were given another opportunity he would mend his conduct and his words, and be better and brighter during an introduction, or at a tea.

"Now, boys," said the captain, "she is going to swamp sure. All we can do is to work her in as far as possible, and then when she swamps, pile out and scramble for the beach. Keep cool now and don't jump until she swamps sure."

The oiler took the oars. Over his shoulders he scanned the surf. "Captain," he said, "I think I'd better bring her about, and keep her head-on to the seas and back her in."

"All right, Billie," said the captain. "Back her in." The oiler swung the boat then and, seated in the stern, the cook and the correspondent were obliged to look over their shoulders to contemplate the lonely and indifferent shore.

The monstrous inshore rollers heaved the boat high until the men were again enabled to see the white sheets of water scudding up the slanted beach. "We won't get in very close," said the captain. Each time a man could wrest his attention from the rollers, he turned his glance toward the shore, and in the expression of the eyes during this contemplation there was a singular quality. The correspondent, observing the others, knew that they were not afraid, but the full meaning of their glances was shrouded.

As for himself, he was too tired to grapple fundamentally with the fact. He tried to coerce his mind into thinking of it, but the mind was dominated at this time by the muscles, and the muscles said they did not care. It merely occurred to him that if he should drown it would be a shame.

There were no hurried words, no pallor, no plain agitation. The men simply looked at the shore. "Now, remember to get well clear of the boat when you jump," said the captain.

Seaward the crest of a roller suddenly fell with a thunderous crash, and the long white comber came roaring down upon the boat.

"Steady now," said the captain. The men were silent. They turned their eyes from the shore to the comber and waited. The boat slid up the incline, leaped at the furious top, bounced over it, and swung down the long back of the waves. Some water had been shipped and the cook bailed it out.

But the next crest crashed also. The tumbling boiling flood of white water caught the boat and whirled it almost perpendicular. Water swarmed in from all sides. The correspondent had his hands on the gunwale at this time, and when the water entered at that place he swiftly withdrew his fingers, as if he objected to wetting them.

The little boat, drunken with this weight of water, reeled and snuggled deeper into the sea.

"Bail her out, cook! Bail her out," said the captain.

"All right, captain," said the cook.

"Now, boys, the next one will do for us, sure," said the oiler. "Mind to jump clear of the boat."

The third wave moved forward, huge, furious, implacable. It fairly swallowed the dingey, and almost simultaneously the men tumbled into the sea. A piece of life-belt had lain in the bottom of the boat, and as the correspondent went overboard he held this to his chest with his left hand.

The January water was icy, and he reflected immediately that it was colder than he had expected to find it off the coast of Florida. This appeared to his dazed mind as a fact important enough to be noted at the time. The coldness of the water was sad; it was tragic. This fact was somehow mixed and confused with his opinion of his own situation that it seemed almost a proper reason for tears. The water was cold.

When he came to the surface he was conscious of little but the noisy water. Afterward he saw his companions in the sea. The oiler was ahead in the race. He was swimming strongly and rapidly. Off to the correspondent's left, the cook's great white and corked back bulged out of the water, and in the rear the captain was hanging with his one good hand to the keel of the overturned dingey.

There is a certain immovable quality to a shore, and the correspondent wondered at it amid the confusion of the sea.

It seemed also very attractive, but the correspondent knew that it was a long journey, and he paddled leisurely. The piece of life-preserver lay under him, and sometimes he whirled down the incline of a wave as if he were on a hand-sled.

But finally he arrived at a place in the sea where travel was beset with difficulty. He did not pause swimming to inquire what manner of current had caught him, but there his progress ceased. The shore was set before him like a bit of scenery on a stage, and he looked at it and understood with his eyes each detail of it.

As the cook passed, much farther to the left, the captain was calling to him, "Turn over on your back, cook! Turn over on your back and use the oar."

"All right, sir." The cook turned on his back, and, paddling with an oar, went ahead as if he were a canoe.

Presently the boat also passed to the left of the correspondent with the captain clinging with one hand to the keel. He would have appeared like a man raising himself to look over a board fence, if it were not for the extraordinary gymnastics of the boat. The correspondent marvelled that the captain could still hold to it.

They passed on, nearer to shore—the oiler, the cook, the captain—and following them went the water-jar, bouncing gayly over the seas.

The correspondent remained in the grip of this strange new enemy—a current. The shore, with its white slope of sand and its green bluff, topped with little silent cottages, was spread like a picture before him. It was very near to him then, but he was impressed as one who in a gallery looks at a scene from Brittany or Algiers.

He thought: "I am going to drown? Can it be possible? Can it be possible? Can it be possible?" Perhaps an individual must consider his own death to be the final phenomenon of nature.

But later a wave perhaps whirled him out of this small deadly current, for he found suddenly that he could again make progress toward the shore. Later still, he was aware that the captain, clinging with one hand to the keel of the dingey, had his face turned away from the shore and toward him, and was calling his name. "Come to the boat! Come to the boat!"

In his struggle to reach the captain and the boat, he reflected that when one gets properly wearied, drowning must really be a comfortable arrangement, a cessation of hostilities accompanied by a large degree of relief, and he was glad of it, for the main thing in his mind for some moments had been horror of the temporary agony. He did not wish to be hurt.

Presently he saw a man running along the shore. He was undressing with most remarkable speed. Coat, trousers, shirt, everything flew magically off him.

"Come to the boat," called the captain.

"All right, captain." As the correspondent paddled, he saw the captain let himself down to bottom and leave the boat. Then the correspondent performed his one little marvel of the voyage. A large wave caught him and flung him with ease and supreme speed completely over the boat and far beyond it. It struck him even then as an event in gymnastics, and a true miracle of the sea. An overturned boat in the surf is not a plaything to a swimming man.

The correspondent arrived in water that reached only to his waist, but his condition did not enable him to stand for more than a moment. Each wave knocked him into a heap, and the under-tow pulled at him.

Then he saw the man who had been running and undressing, and undressing and running, come bounding into the water. He dragged ashore the cook, and then waded toward the captain, but the captain waved him away, and sent him to the correspondent. He was naked, naked as a tree in winter, but a halo was about his head, and he shone like a saint. He gave a strong pull, and a long drag, and a bully heave at the correspondent's hand. The correspondent, schooled in the minor formulae, said: "Thanks, old man." But suddenly the man cried: "What's that?" He pointed a swift finger. The correspondent said: "Go."

In the shallows, face downward, lay the oiler. His forehead touched sand that was periodically, between each wave, clear of the sea.

The correspondent did not know all that transpired afterward. When he achieved safe ground he fell, striking the sand with each particular part of his body. It was as if he had dropped from a roof, but the thud was grateful to him.

It seems that instantly the beach was populated with men with blankets, clothes, and flasks, and women with coffee-pots and all the remedies sacred to their minds. The welcome of the land to the men from the sea was warm and generous, but a still and dripping shape was carried slowly up the beach, and the land's welcome for it could only be the different and sinister hospitality of the grave.

When it came night, the white waves paced to and fro in the moonlight, and the wind brought the sound of the great sea's voice to the men on shore, and they felt that they could then be interpreters.

[1897]

William Faulkner

[1897–1962]

Born in New Albany, Mississippi, WILLIAM CUTHBERT FALKNER *(The writer added the "u" to his name as a young man) moved with his family to Oxford, Mississippi in 1902, where his father worked as a livery stable owner, a hardware store owner, and finally as a business manager at the University of Mississippi. Although the presence of the university in this otherwise small, nondescript southern town likely influenced Faulkner's decision to become a writer, it is more probable that he looked to his paternal grandfather, William Clark Falkner (1825–1889), as a source of inspiration. A writer and a figure out of antebellum mythology, the Old Colonel, as the family referred to him, lead a life of almost cartoonish violence and bravado, stories of which filled the young Faulkner with wonder. With some modifications, this larger-than-life figure made his way into Faulkner's fiction as Colonel John Sartoris, a recurrent character in Faulkner's fiction.*

Faulkner's relationships with both his parents also enhanced and compli-cated his literary aspirations. While his mother was devoted to reading and cul-ture, his father was immersed in the masculine world of horses, whisky, and physical violence. These parental influences are evident in a body of fiction that is both dizzyingly intellectual and insistently physical. Though he demonstrated early precociousness at school, he was drifting away by the eighth grade, and he never managed to take a degree at the local university. In 1918 he volunteered for and was rejected by the Army Air Corps because of his diminutive size. Not to be cheated out of the opportunity to relive the martial grandeur of his grandfather, he traveled to Toronto and enlisted in the RAF in July 1918, only to have World War I end before he could complete his training. He returned to Oxford in December of that year sporting an RAF captain's uniform, a phony limp, and a story about being shot down over enemy lines in France. Though no one in Oxford much believed him, he carried an obsession with World War I that stayed with him from his first novel, Soldier's Pay *(1926), through the late work* A Fable *(1954), both of which focus on the hollowness and hypocrisy that sometimes over-shadow the heroics of war.*

Faulkner's literary career can be considered in terms of three phases. Throughout the early 1920s, Faulkner wrote a series of unsuccessful works—a collection of poetry titled the The Marble Faun *(1924) and the early novels* Soldier's Pay, Mosquitoes *(1927), and* Flags in the Dust *(published in 1929 as* Sartoris*). This period is also marked by transience and uncertainty, as Faulkner moved to New York, New Orleans, and back to Oxford. He studied briefly at the University of Mississippi, served for a time as the university's postmaster, and* *worked at odd jobs about the town of Oxford. Despite its flaws,* Flags in the Dust *represents Faulkner's first attempt to use the history of his family and his region as a source for his art. The novel therefore heralds the second, mature phase of his career. Faulkner gained critical acclaim with* The Sound and the Fury *(1929), the story of a disintegrating Southern family told through the modernist techniques of stream-of-consciousness narration and multiple, fragmented points of view. In 1930, the noteworthy Faulkner then became somewhat notorious with the publication of* Sanctuary, *a lurid potboiler about bootlegging, prostitution, and rape. In the same year, Faulkner completed yet another important novel,* As I Lay Dying. *Here again presented through the distracted comments of several narrators (including a purported lunatic, a traumatized young boy, and a delusional religious zealot), this harrowing tale treats a poor rural family who struggle to carry their dead mother to a cemetery many miles away. In this story, the language of the rural South becomes a kind of mythological poetry. This burst of creative activity launched the major period of Faulkner's career, eleven or twelve years that saw the publication of* Light in August *(1932),* Absalom, Absalom! *(1935),* The Unvanquished *(1938),* The Wild Palms *(1939), and* Go Down, Moses *(1942). During this time Faulkner also wrote short stories and worked in Hollywood as a screenwriter, an occupation he loathed. His near destitution would only begin to abate in 1948, when he was paid $50,000 by MGM for the film rights to his 1948 novel* Intruder in the Dust *and when, in 1949, he received the Nobel Prize for Literature. The third and final phase of Faulkner's career is characterized by a mellowing of his artistic vision, as is evident in his final novel,* The Rievers *(1962). In his later years, Faulkner assumed the role of "elder man of letters." He traveled to Japan as a kind of literary ambassador, served as a writer-in-residence at the University of Virginia, and addressed cadets at West Point, where his son-in-law had gone to school. He also weighed in on the racial controversies of the time, but his comments seemed to anger equally those on all sides of the debate. As he aged, Faulkner's health suffered from his heavy drinking and from several falls sustained while riding horses. It is suspected that one of these falls landed him in the hospital on July 5, 1962, where he died of a heart attack the next day.*

Critical reception of Faulkner's work ranged from prudish dismissal to adulation, but today he is widely regarded as the best American writer of the twentieth century. During the eighties and nineties many critics began to question this status, given the apparent racism and misogyny that color Faulkner's canon. This debate is ongoing, but what remains unimpeachable, besides the explosive beauty of his experiments with language and style, and with the form of the novel itself, is his quiet confidence in the perseverance of the human soul.

—David L. G. Arnold, *University of Wisconsin, Stevens Point*

Barn Burning

WILLIAM FAULKNER

THE STORE IN WHICH the Justice of the Peace's court was sitting smelled of cheese. The boy, crouched on his nail keg at the back of the crowded room, knew he smelled cheese, and more: from where he sat he could see the ranked shelves close-packed with the solid, squat, dynamic shapes of tin cans whose labels his stomach read, not from the lettering which meant nothing to his mind but from the scarlet devils and the silver curve of fish—this, the cheese which he knew he smelled and the hermetic[1] meat which his intestines believed he smelled coming in intermittent gusts momentary and brief between the other constant one, the smell and sense just a little of fear because mostly of despair and grief, the old fierce pull of blood. He could not see the table where the Justice sat and before which his father and his father's enemy (*our enemy* he thought in that despair; *ourn! mine and hisn both! He's my father!*) stood, but he could hear them, the two of them that is, because his father had said no word yet:

"But what proof have you, Mr. Harris?"

"I told you. The hog got into my corn. I caught it up and sent it back to him. He had no fence that would hold it. I told him so, warned him. The next time I put the hog in my pen. When he came to get it I gave him enough wire to patch up his pen. The next time I put the hog up and kept it. I rode down to his house and saw the wire I gave him still rolled on to the spool in his yard. I told him he could have the hog when he paid me a dollar pound fee.[2] That evening a nigger came with the dollar and got the hog. He was a strange nigger. He said, 'He say to tell you wood and hay kin burn.' I said, 'What?' 'That whut he say to tell you,' the nigger said. 'Wood and hay kin burn.' That night my barn burned. I got the stock out but I lost the barn."

"Where is the nigger? Have you got him?"

"He was a strange nigger, I tell you. I don't know what became of him."

"But that's not proof. Don't you see that's not proof?"

---

[1] Tinned or canned.

[2] A payment for feeding and housing the animal in question.

"Get that boy up here. He knows." For a moment the boy thought too that the man meant his older brother until Harris said, "Not him. The little one. The boy," and, crouching, small for his age, small and wiry like his father, in patched and faded jeans even too small for him, with straight, uncombed, brown hair and eyes gray and wild as storm scud, he saw the men between himself and the table part and become a lane of grim faces, at the end of which he saw the Justice, a shabby, collarless, graying man in spectacles, beckoning him. He felt no floor under his bare feet; he seemed to walk beneath the palpable weight of the grim turning faces. His father, stiff in his black Sunday coat donned not for the trial but for the moving, did not even look at him. *He aims for me to lie,* he thought, again with that frantic grief and despair. *And I will have to do hit.*

"What's your name, boy?" the Justice said.

"Colonel Sartoris Snopes,"[3] the boy whispered.

"Hey?" the Justice said. "Talk louder. Colonel Sartoris? I reckon anybody named for Colonel Sartoris in this country can't help but tell the truth, can they?" The boy said nothing. *Enemy! Enemy!* he thought; for a moment he could not even see, could not see that the Justice's face was kindly nor discern that his voice was troubled when he spoke to the man named Harris: "Do you want me to question this boy?" But he could hear, and during those subsequent long seconds while there was absolutely no sound in the crowded little room save that of quiet and intent breathing it was as if he had swung outward at the end of a grape vine, over a ravine, and at the top of the swing had been caught in a prolonged instant of mesmerized gravity, weightless in time.

"No!" Harris said violently, explosively. "Damnation! Send him out of here!" Now time, the fluid world, rushed beneath him again, the voices coming to him again through the smell of cheese and sealed meat, the fear and despair and the old grief of blood:

"This case is closed. I can't find against you, Snopes, but I can give you advice. Leave this country and don't come back to it."

His father spoke for the first time, his voice cold and harsh, level, without emphasis: "I aim to. I don't figure to stay in a country among people who . . ." he said something unprintable and vile, addressed to no one.

"That'll do," the Justice said. "Take your wagon and get out of this country before dark. Case dismissed."

His father turned, and he followed the stiff black coat, the wiry figure walking a little stiffly from where a Confederate provost's man's musket ball had taken him in the heel on a stolen horse thirty years ago, followed the two

---

[3]Born to the poor Snopes family, the boy has been named for a prominent citizen of Jefferson, a Confederate veteran of the Civil War.

backs now, since his older brother had appeared from somewhere in the crowd, no taller than the father but thicker, chewing tobacco steadily, between the two lines of grim-faced men and out of the store and across the worn gallery and down the sagging steps and among the dogs and half-grown boys in the mild May dust, where as he passed a voice hissed:

"Barn burner!"

Again he could not see, whirling; there was a face in a red haze, moonlike, bigger than the full moon, the owner of it half again his size, he leaping in the red haze toward the face, feeling no blow, feeling no shock when his head struck the earth, scrabbling up and leaping again, feeling no blow this time either and tasting no blood, scrabbling up to see the other boy in full flight and himself already leaping into pursuit as his father's hand jerked him back, the harsh, cold voice speaking above him: "Go get in the wagon."

It stood in a grove of locusts and mulberries across the road. His two hulking sisters in their Sunday dresses and his mother and her sister in calico and sunbonnets were already in it, sitting on and among the sorry residue of the dozen and more movings which even the boy could remember—the battered stove, the broken beds and chairs, the clock inlaid with mother-of-pearl, which would not run, stopped at some fourteen minutes past two o'clock of a dead and forgotten day and time, which had been his mother's dowry. She was crying, though when she saw him she drew her sleeve across her face and began to descend from the wagon. "Get back," the father said.

"He's hurt. I got to get some water and wash his . . ."

"Get back in the wagon," his father said. He got in too, over the tail-gate. His father mounted to the seat where the older brother already sat and struck the gaunt mules two savage blows with the peeled willow, but without heat. It was not even sadistic; it was exactly that same quality which in later years would cause his descendants to over-run the engine before putting a motor car into motion, striking and reining back in the same movement. The wagon went on, the store with its quiet crowd of grimly watching men dropped behind; a curve in the road hid it. *Forever* he thought. *Maybe he's done satisfied now, now that he has . . .* stopping himself, not to say it aloud even to himself. His mother's hand touched his shoulder.

"Does hit hurt?" she said.

"Naw," he said. "Hit don't hurt. Lemme be."

"Can't you wipe some of the blood off before hit dries?"

"I'll wash to-night," he said. "Lemme be, I tell you."

The wagon went on. He did not know where they were going. None of them ever did or ever asked, because it was always somewhere, always a house of sorts waiting for them a day or two days or even three days away. Likely his father had already arranged to make a crop on another farm before he . . . Again he had to stop himself. He (the father) always did. There was something about his wolflike independence and even courage when the advantage was at least neutral which impressed strangers, as if they got from his latent ravening ferocity not so much a sense of dependability as a feeling that his ferocious conviction in the rightness of his own actions would be of advantage to all whose interest lay with his.

That night they camped, in a grove of oaks and beeches where a spring ran. The nights were still cool and they had a fire against it, of a rail lifted from a nearby fence and cut into lengths—a small fire, neat, niggard almost, a shrewd fire; such fires were his father's habit and custom always, even in freezing weather. Older, the boy might have remarked this and wondered why not a big one; why should not a man who had not only seen the waste and extravagance of war, but who had in his blood an inherent voracious prodigality with material not his own, have burned everything in sight? Then he might have gone a step farther and thought that that was the reason: that niggard blaze was the living fruit of nights passed during those four years in the woods hiding from all men, blue or gray, with his strings of horses (captured horses, he called them). And older still, he might have divined the true reason: that the element of fire spoke to some deep mainspring of his father's being, as the element of steel or of powder spoke to other men, as the one weapon for the preservation of integrity, else breath were not worth the breathing, and hence to be regarded with respect and used with discretion.

But he did not think this now and he had seen those same niggard blazes all his life. He merely ate his supper beside it and was already half asleep over his iron plate when his father called him, and once more he followed the stiff back, the stiff and ruthless limp, up the slope and on to the starlit road where, turning, he could see his father against the stars but without face or depth—a shape black, flat, and bloodless as though cut from tin in the iron folds of the frockcoat which had not been made for him, the voice harsh like tin and without heat like tin:

"You were fixing to tell them. You would have told him." He didn't answer. His father struck him with the flat of his hand on the side of the head, hard but without heat, exactly as he had struck the two mules at the store, exactly as he would strike either of them with any stick in order to kill a horse fly, his voice still without heat or anger: "You're getting to be a man. You got to learn. You got to learn to stick to your own blood or you ain't going to have any blood to stick to you. Do you think either of them, any man there this morning, would? Don't you know all they wanted was a chance to get at me because they knew I had them beat? Eh?" Later, twenty years later, he was to tell himself, "If I had said they wanted only truth, justice, he would have hit me again." But now he said nothing. He was not crying. He just stood there. "Answer me," his father said.

"Yes," he whispered. His father turned.

"Get on to bed. We'll be there tomorrow."

To-morrow they were there. In the early afternoon the wagon stopped before a paintless two-room house identical almost with the dozen others it had stopped before even in the boy's ten years, and again, as on the other dozen occasions, his mother and aunt got down and began to unload the wagon, although his two sisters and his father and brother had not moved.

"Likely hit ain't fitten for hawgs," one of the sisters said.

"Nevertheless, fit it will and you'll hog it and like it," his father said. "Get out of them chairs and help your Ma unload."

The two sisters got down, big, bovine, in a flutter of cheap ribbons; one of them drew from the jumbled wagon bed a battered lantern, the other a worn broom. His father handed the reins to the older son and began to climb stiffly over the wheel. "When they get unloaded, take the team to the barn and feed them." Then he said, and at first the boy thought he was still speaking to his brother: "Come with me."

"Me?" he said.

"Yes," his father said. "You."

"Abner," his mother said. His father paused and looked back—the harsh level stare beneath the shaggy, graying, irascible brows.

"I reckon I'll have a word with the man that aims to begin to-morrow owning me body and soul for the next eight months."

They went back up the road. A week ago—or before last night, that is—he would have asked where they were going, but not now. His father had struck him before last night but never before had he paused afterward to explain why; it was as if the blow and the following calm, outrageous voice still rang, repercussed, divulging nothing to him save the terrible handicap of being young, the light weight of his few years, just heavy enough to prevent his soaring free of the world as it seemed to be ordered but not heavy enough to keep him footed solid in it, to resist it and try to change the course of its events.

Presently he could see the grove of oaks and cedars and the other flowering trees and shrubs where the house would be, though not the house yet. They walked beside a fence massed with honeysuckle and Cherokee roses and came to a gate swinging open between two brick pillars, and now, beyond a sweep of drive, he saw the house for the first time and at that instant he forgot his father and the terror and despair both, and even when he remembered his father again (who had not stopped) the terror and despair did not return. Because, for all the twelve movings, they had sojourned until now in a poor country, a land of small farms and fields and houses, and he had never seen a house like this before. *Hit's big as a courthouse* he thought quietly, with a surge of peace and joy whose reason he could not have thought into words, being too young for that: *They are safe from him. People whose lives are a part of this peace and dignity are beyond his touch, he no more to them than a buzzing wasp: capable of stinging for a little moment but that's all; the spell of this peace and dignity rendering even the barns and stable and cribs which belong to it impervious to the puny flames he might contrive* . . . this, the peace and joy, ebbing for an instant, as he looked again at the stiff black back, the stiff and implacable limp of the figure which was not dwarfed by the house, for the reason that it had never looked big anywhere and which now, against the serene columned backdrop, had more than ever that impervious quality of something cut ruthlessly from tin, depthless, as though, sidewise to the sun, it would cast no shadow. Watching him, the boy remarked the absolutely undeviating course which his father held and saw the stiff foot come squarely down in a pile of fresh droppings where a horse had stood in the drive and which his father could have avoided by a simple change of stride. But it ebbed only for a moment, though he could not have thought this into words either, walking on in the spell of the house, which he could ever want but without envy, without sorrow, certainly never with that ravening and jealous rage which unknown to him walked in the ironlike black coat before him: *Maybe he will feel it too. Maybe it will even change him now from what maybe he couldn't help but be.*

They crossed the portico. Now he could hear his father's stiff foot as it came down on the boards with clocklike finality, a sound out of all proportion to the displacement of the body it bore and which was not dwarfed either by the white door before it, as though it had attained to a sort of vicious and ravening minimum not to be dwarfed by anything—the flat, wide, black hat, the formal coat of broadcloth which had once been black but which had now that friction-glazed greenish cast of the bodies of old house flies, the lifted sleeve which was too large, the lifted hand like a curled claw. The door opened so promptly that the boy knew the Negro must have been watching them all the time, an old man with neat grizzled hair, in a linen jacket, who stood barring the door with his body, saying, "Wipe yo foots, white man, fo you come in here. Major ain't home nohow."

"Get out of my way, nigger," his father said, without heat too, flinging the door back and the Negro also and entering, his hat still on his head. And now the boy saw the prints of the stiff foot on the doorjamb and saw them appear on the pale rug behind the machinelike deliberation of the foot which seemed to bear (or transmit) twice the weight which the body compassed. The Negro was shouting "Miss Lula! Miss Lula!" somewhere behind them, then the boy, deluged as though by a warm wave by a suave turn of carpeted stair and a pendant glitter of chandeliers and a mute gleam of gold frames, heard the swift feet and saw her too, a lady—perhaps he had never seen her like before either—in a gray, smooth gown with lace at the throat and an apron tied at the waist and the sleeves turned back, wiping cake or biscuit dough from her hands with a towel as she came up the hall, looking not at his father at all but at the tracks on the blond rug with an expression of incredulous amazement.

"I tried," the Negro cried. "I tole him to . . ."

"Will you please go away?" she said in a shaking voice. "Major de Spain is not at home. Will you please go away?"

His father had not spoken again. He did not speak again. He did not even look at her. He just stood stiff in the center of the rug, in his hat, the shaggy iron-gray brows twitching slightly above the pebble-colored eyes as he appeared to examine the house with brief deliberation. Then with the same deliberation he turned; the boy watched him pivot on the good leg and saw the stiff foot drag round the arc of the turning, leaving a final long and fading smear. His father never looked at it, he never once looked down at the rug. The Negro held the door. It closed behind them, upon the hysteric and indistinguishable woman-wail. His father stopped at the top of the steps and scraped his boot clean on the edge of it. At the gate he stopped again. He stood for a moment, planted stiffly on the stiff foot, looking back at the house. "Pretty and white, ain't it?" he said. "That's sweat. Nigger sweat. Maybe it ain't white enough yet to suit him. Maybe he wants to mix some white sweat with it."

Two hours later the boy was chopping wood behind the house within which his mother and aunt and the two sisters (the mother and aunt, not the two girls, he knew that; even at this distance and muffled by walls the flat loud voices of the two girls emanated an incorrigible idle inertia) were setting up the stove to prepare a meal, when he heard the hooves and saw the linen-clad man on a fine sorrel mare, whom he recognized even before he saw the rolled rug in front of the Negro youth following on a fat bay carriage horse—a suffused, angry face vanishing, still at full gallop, beyond the corner of the house where his father and brother were sitting in the two tilted chairs; and a moment later, almost before he could have put the axe down, he heard the hooves again and watched the sorrel mare go back out of the yard, already galloping again. Then his father began to shout one of the sisters' names, who presently emerged backward from the kitchen door dragging the rolled rug along the ground by one end while the other sister walked behind it.

"If you ain't going to tote, go on and set up the wash pot," the first said.

"You, Sarty!" the second shouted. "Set up the wash pot!" His father appeared at the door, framed against that shabbiness, as he had been against that other bland perfection, impervious to either, the mother's anxious face at his shoulder.

"Go on," the father said. "Pick it up." The two sisters stooped, broad, lethargic; stooping, they presented an incredible expanse of pale cloth and a flutter of tawdry ribbons.

"If I thought enough of a rug to have to git hit all the way from France I wouldn't keep hit where folks coming in would have to tromp on hit," the first said. They raised the rug.

"Abner," the mother said. "Let me do it."

"You go back and git dinner," his father said. "I'll tend to this."

From the woodpile through the rest of the afternoon the boy watched them, the rug spread flat in the dust beside the bubbling wash-pot, the two sisters stooping over it with that profound and lethargic reluctance, while the father stood over them in turn, implacable and grim, driving them though never raising his voice again. He could smell the harsh homemade lye they were using; he saw his mother come to the door once and look toward them with an expression not anxious now but very like despair; he saw his father turn, and he fell to with the axe and saw from the corner of his eye his father raise from the ground a flattish fragment of field stone and examine it and return to the pot, and this time his mother actually spoke: "Abner. Abner. Please don't. Please, Abner."

Then he was done too. It was dusk; the whippoorwills had already begun. He could smell coffee from the room where they would presently eat the cold food remaining from the mid-afternoon meal, though when he entered the house he realized they were having coffee again probably because there was a fire on the hearth, before which the rug now lay spread over the backs of the two chairs. The tracks of his father's foot were gone. Where they had been were now long, water-cloudy scoriations resembling the sporadic course of a lilliputian[4] mowing machine.

It still hung there while they ate the cold food and then went to bed, scattered without order or claim up and down the two rooms, his mother in one bed, where his father would later lie, the older brother in the other, himself, the aunt, and the two sisters on pallets on the floor. But his father was not in bed yet. The last thing the boy remembered was the depthless, harsh silhouette of the hat and coat bending over the rug and it seemed to him that he had not even closed his eyes when the silhouette was standing over him, the fire almost dead behind it, the stiff foot prodding him awake. "Catch up the mule," his father said.

When he returned with the mule his father was standing in the black door, the rolled rug over his shoulder. "Ain't you going to ride?" he said.

"No. Give me your foot."

He bent his knee into his father's hand, the wiry, surprising power flowed smoothly, rising, he rising with it, on to the mule's bare back (they had owned

---

[4]An allusion to the six-inch tall people of Lilliput in Jonathan Swift's *Gulliver's Travels* (1726).

a saddle once; the boy could remember it though not when or where) and with the same effortlessness his father swung the rug up in front of him. Now in the starlight they retraced the afternoon's path, up the dusty road rife with honeysuckle, through the gate and up the black tunnel of the drive to the lightless house, where he sat on the mule and felt the rough warp of the rug drag across his thighs and vanish.

"Don't you want me to help?" he whispered. His father did not answer and now he heard again that stiff foot striking the hollow portico with that wooden and clocklike deliberation, that outrageous overstatement of the weight it carried. The rug, hunched, not flung (the boy could tell that even in the darkness) from his father's shoulder struck the angle of wall and floor with a sound unbelievably loud, thunderous, then the foot again, unhurried and enormous; a light came on in the house and the boy sat, tense, breathing steadily and quietly and just a little fast, though the foot itself did not increase its beat at all, descending the steps now; now the boy could see him.

"Don't you want to ride now?" he whispered. "We kin both ride now," the light within the house altering now, flaring up and sinking. *He's coming down the stairs now*, he thought. He had already ridden the mule up beside the horse block; presently his father was up behind him and he doubled the reins over and slashed the mule across the neck, but before the animal could begin to trot the hard, thin arm came round him, the hard, knotted hand jerking the mule back to a walk.

In the first red rays of the sun they were in the lot, putting plow gear on the mules. This time the sorrel mare was in the lot before he heard it at all, the rider collarless and even bareheaded, trembling, speaking in a shaking voice as the woman in the house had done, his father merely looking up once before stooping again to the hame he was buckling, so that the man on the mare spoke to his stooping back:

"You must realize you have ruined that rug. Wasn't there anybody here, any of your women . . ." he ceased, shaking, the boy watching him, the older brother leaning now in the stable door, chewing, blinking slowly and steadily at nothing apparently. "It cost a hundred dollars. But you never had a hundred dollars. You never will. So I'm going to charge you twenty bushels of corn against your crop. I'll add it in your contract and when you come to the commissary you can sign it. That won't keep Mrs. de Spain quiet but maybe it will teach you to wipe your feet off before you enter her house again."

Then he was gone. The boy looked at his father, who still had not spoken or even looked up again, who was now adjusting the logger-head in the hame.[5]

---

[5]On a plow, the logger-head is an iron piece by which trace-chains are hooked to the hames, the curved bars that attach to the horse-collar.

"Pap," he said. His father looked at him—the inscrutable face, the shaggy brows beneath which the gray eyes glinted coldly. Suddenly the boy went toward him, fast, stopping as suddenly. "You done the best you could!" he cried. "If he wanted hit done different why didn't he wait and tell you how? He won't git no twenty bushels! He won't git none! We'll gether hit and hide hit! I kin watch . . ."

"Did you put the cutter back in that straight stock[6] like I told you?"

"No, sir," he said.

"Then go do it."

That was Wednesday. During the rest of that week he worked steadily, at what was within his scope and some which was beyond it, with an industry that did not need to be driven nor even commanded twice; he had this from his mother, with the difference that some at least of what he did he liked to do, such as splitting wood with the half-size axe which his mother and aunt had earned, or saved money somehow, to present him with at Christmas. In company with the two older women (and on one afternoon, even one of the sisters), he built pens for the shoat and the cow which were a part of his father's contract with the landlord, and one afternoon, his father being absent, gone somewhere on one of the mules, he went to the field.

They were running a middle buster now, his brother holding the plow straight while he handled the reins, and walking beside the straining mule, the rich black soil shearing cool and damp against his bare ankles, he thought *Maybe this is the end of it. Maybe even that twenty bushels that seems hard to have to pay for just a rug will be a cheap price for him to stop forever and always from being what he used to be;* thinking, dreaming now, so that his brother had to speak sharply to him to mind the mule: *Maybe he even won't collect the twenty bushels. May be it will all add up and balance and vanish—corn, rug, fire; the terror and grief, the being pulled two ways like between two teams of horses— gone, done with for ever and ever.*

Then it was Saturday; he looked up from beneath the mule he was harnessing and saw his father in the black coat and hat. "Not that," his father said. "The wagon gear." And then, two hours later, sitting in the wagon bed behind his father and brother on the seat, the wagon accomplished a final curve, and he saw the weathered paintless store with its tattered tobacco- and patent-medicine posters and the tethered wagons and saddle animals below the gallery. He mounted the gnawed steps behind his father and brother, and there again was the lane of quiet, watching faces for the three of them to walk through. He saw the man in spectacles sitting at the plank table and he did not need to be told this was a Justice of the Peace; he sent one glare of fierce, exul-

---

[6]The plow's blade and frame, respectively.

tant, partisan defiance at the man in collar and cravat now, whom he had seen but twice before in his life, and that on a galloping horse, who now wore on his face an expression not of rage but of amazed unbelief which the boy could not have known was at the incredible circumstance of being sued by one of his own tenants, and came and stood against his father and cried at the Justice: "He ain't done it! He ain't burnt . . ."

"Go back to the wagon," his father said.

"Burnt?" the Justice said. "Do I understand this rug was burned too?"

"Does anybody here claim it was?" his father said. "Go back to the wagon." But he did not, he merely retreated to the rear of the room, crowded as that other had been, but not to sit down this time, instead, to stand pressing among the motionless bodies, listening to the voices:

"And you claim twenty bushels of corn is too high for the damage you did to the rug?"

"He brought the rug to me and said he wanted the tracks washed out of it. I washed the tracks out and took the rug back to him."

"But you didn't carry the rug back to him in the same condition it was in before you made the tracks on it."

His father did not answer, and now for perhaps half a minute there was no sound at all save that of breathing, the faint, steady suspiration of complete and intent listening.

"You decline to answer that, Mr. Snopes?" Again his father did not answer. "I'm going to find against you, Mr. Snopes. I'm going to find that you were responsible for the injury to Major de Spain's rug and hold you liable for it. But twenty bushels of corn seems a little high for a man in your circumstances to have to pay. Major de Spain claims it cost a hundred dollars. October corn will be worth about fifty cents. I figure that if Major de Spain can stand a ninety-five dollar loss on something he paid cash for, you can stand a five-dollar loss you haven't earned yet. I hold you in damages to Major de Spain to the amount of ten bushels of corn over and above your contract with him, to be paid to him out of your crop at gathering time. Court adjourned."

It had taken no time hardly, the morning was but half begun. He thought they would return home and perhaps back to the field, since they were late, far behind all other farmers. But instead his father passed on behind the wagon, merely indicating with his hand for the older brother to follow with it, and crossed the road toward the blacksmith shop opposite, pressing on after his father, overtaking him, speaking, whispering up at the harsh, calm face beneath the weathered hat: "He won't git no ten bushels neither. He won't git one. We'll . . ." until his father glanced for an instant down at him, the face absolutely calm, the grizzled eyebrows tangled above the cold eyes, the voice almost pleasant, almost gentle:

"You think so? Well, we'll wait till October anyway."

The matter of the wagon—the setting of a spoke or two and the tightening of the tires—did not take long either, the business of the tires accomplished by driving the wagon into the spring branch behind the shop and letting it stand there, the mules nuzzling into the water from time to time, and the boy on the seat with the idle reins, looking up the slope and through the sooty tunnel of the shed where the slow hammer rang and where his father sat on an upended cypress bolt, easily, either talking or listening, still sitting there when the boy brought the dripping wagon up out of the branch and halted it before the door.

"Take them on to the shade and hitch," his father said. He did so and returned. His father and the smith and a third man squatting on his heels inside the door were talking, about crops and animals; the boy, squatting too in the ammoniac dust and hoof-parings and scales of rust, heard his father tell a long and unhurried story out of the time before the birth of the older brother even when he had been a professional horsetrader. And then his father came up beside him where he stood before a tattered last year's circus poster on the other side of the store, gazing rapt and quiet at the scarlet horses, the incredible poisings and convolutions of tulle and tights and the painted leers of comedians, and said, "It's time to eat."

But not at home. Squatting beside his brother against the front wall, he watched his father emerge from the store and produce from a paper sack a segment of cheese and divide it carefully and deliberately into three with his pocket knife and produce crackers from the same sack. They all three squatted on the gallery and ate, slowly, without talking; then in the store again, they drank from a tin dipper tepid water smelling of the cedar bucket and of living beech trees. And still they did not go home. It was a horse lot this time, a tall rail fence upon and along which men stood and sat and out of which one by one horses were led, to be walked and trotted and then cantered back and forth along the road while the slow swapping and buying went on and the sun began to slant westward, they—the three of them—watching and listening, the older brother with his muddy eyes and his steady, inevitable tobacco, the father commenting now and then on certain of the animals, to no one in particular.

It was after sundown when they reached home. They ate supper by lamplight, then, sitting on the doorstep, the boy watched the night fully accomplish, listening to the whippoorwills and the frogs, when he heard his mother's voice: "Abner! No! No! Oh, God. Oh, God. Abner!" and he rose, whirled, and saw the altered light through the door where a candle stub now burned in a bottle neck on the table and his father, still in the hat and coat, at once formal and burlesque as though dressed carefully for some shabby and ceremonial violence, emptying the reservoir of the lamp back into the five-gallon kerosene can from which it had been filled, while the mother tugged at his arm until he shifted the lamp to the other hand and flung her back, not savagely or viciously, just hard, into the wall, her hands flung out against the wall for balance, her mouth open and in her face the same quality of hopeless despair as had been in her voice. Then his father saw him standing in the door.

"Go to the barn and get that can of oil we were oiling the wagon with," he said. The boy did not move. Then he could speak.

"What . . ." he cried. "What are you . . ."

"Go get that oil," his father said. "Go."

Then he was moving, running, outside the house, toward the stable: this the old habit, the old blood which he had not been permitted to choose for himself, which had been bequeathed him willy nilly and which had run for so long (and who knew where, battening on what of outrage and savagery and lust) before it came to him. *I could keep on*, he thought. *I could run on and on and never look back, never need to see his face again. Only I can't. I can't*, the rusted can in his hand now, the liquid sploshing in it as he ran back to the house and into it, into the sound of his mother's weeping in the next room, and handed the can to his father.

"Ain't you going to even send a nigger?" he cried. "At least you sent a nigger before!"

This time his father didn't strike him. The hand came even faster than the blow had, the same hand which had set the can on the table with almost excruciating care flashing from the can toward him too quick for him to follow it, gripping him by the back of his shirt and on to tiptoe before he had seen it quit the can, the face stooping at him in breathless and frozen ferocity, the cold, dead voice speaking over him to the older brother who leaned against the table, chewing with that steady, curious, sidewise motion of cows:

"Empty the can into the big one and go on. I'll catch up with you."

"Better tie him up to the bedpost," the brother said.

"Do like I told you," the father said. Then the boy was moving, his bunched shirt and the hard, bony hand between his shoulder-blades, his toes just touching the floor, across the room and into the other one, past the sisters sitting with spread heavy thighs in the two chairs over the cold hearth, and to where his mother and aunt sat side by side on the bed, the aunt's arms about his mother's shoulders.

"Hold him," the father said. The aunt made a startled movement. "Not you," the father said. "Lennie. Take hold of him. I want to see you do it." His mother took him by the wrist. "You'll hold him better than that. If he gets loose don't you know what he is going to do? He will go up yonder." He jerked his head toward the road. "Maybe I'd better tie him."

"I'll hold him," his mother whispered.

"See you do then." Then his father was gone, the stiff foot heavy and measured upon the boards, ceasing at last.

Then he began to struggle. His mother caught him in both arms, he jerking and wrenching at them. He would be stronger in the end, he knew that. But he had no time to wait for it. "Lemme go!" he cried. "I don't want to have to hit you!"

"Let him go!" the aunt said. "If he don't go, before God, I am going up there myself!"

"Don't you see I can't?" his mother cried. "Sarty! Sarty! No! No! Help me, Lizzie!"

Then he was free. His aunt grasped at him but it was too late. He whirled, running, his mother stumbled forward on to her knees behind him, crying to the nearer sister: "Catch him, Net! Catch him!" But that was too late too, the sister (the sisters were twins, born at the same time, yet either of them now gave the impression of being, encompassing as much living meat and volume and weight as any other two of the family) not yet having begun to rise from the chair, her head, face, alone merely turned, presenting to him in the flying instant an astonishing expanse of young female features untroubled by any surprise even, wearing only an expression of bovine interest. Then he was out of the room, out of the house, in the mild dust of the starlit road and the heavy rifeness of honeysuckle, the pale ribbon unspooling with terrific slowness under his running feet, reaching the gate at last and turning in, running, his heart and lungs drumming, on up the drive toward the lighted house, the lighted door. He did not knock, he burst in, sobbing for breath, incapable for the moment of speech; he saw the astonished face of the Negro in the linen jacket without knowing when the Negro had appeared.

"De Spain!" he cried, panted. "Where's . . ." then he saw the white man too emerging from a white door down the hall. "Barn!" he cried. "Barn!"

"What?" the white man said. "Barn?"

"Yes!" the boy cried. "Barn!"

"Catch him!" the white man shouted.

But it was too late this time too. The Negro grasped his shirt, but the entire sleeve, rotten with washing, carried away, and he was out that door too and in the drive again, and had actually never ceased to run even while he was screaming into the white man's face.

Behind him the white man was shouting, "My horse! Fetch my horse!" and he thought for an instant of cutting across the park and climbing the fence into the road, but he did not know the park nor how high the vine-massed fence might be and he dared not risk it. So he ran on down the drive, blood and breath roaring; presently he was in the road again though he could not see it. He could not hear either: the galloping mare was almost upon him before he heard her, and even then he held his course, as if the very urgency of his wild grief and need must in a moment more find him wings, waiting until the ultimate instant to hurl himself aside and into the weed-choked roadside ditch as the horse thundered past and on, for an instant in furious silhouette against the stars, the tranquil early summer night sky which, even before the shape of the horse and rider vanished, stained abruptly and violently upward: a long, swirling roar incredible and soundless, blotting the stars, and he springing up and into the road again, running again, knowing it was too late yet still running even after he heard the shot and, an instant later, two shots, pausing now without knowing he had ceased to run, crying "Pap! Pap!", running again before he knew he had begun to run, stumbling, tripping over something and scrabbling up again without ceasing to run, looking backward over his shoulder at the glare as he got up, running on among the invisible trees, panting, sobbing, "Father! Father!"

At midnight he was sitting on the crest of a hill. He did not know it was midnight and he did not know how far he had come. But there was no glare behind him now and he sat now, his back toward what he had called home for four days anyhow, his face toward the dark woods which he would enter when breath was strong again, small, shaking steadily in the chill darkness, hugging himself into the remainder of his thin, rotten shirt, the grief and despair now no longer terror and fear but just grief and despair. *Father. My father*, he thought. "He was brave!" he cried suddenly, aloud but not loud, no more than a whisper: "He was! He was in the war! He was in Colonel Sartoris' cav'ry!" not knowing that his father had gone to that war a private in the fine old European sense, wearing no uniform, admitting the authority of and giving fidelity to no man or army or flag, going to war as Malbrouck himself did: for booty—it meant nothing and less than nothing to him if it were enemy booty or his own.

The slow constellations wheeled on. It would be dawn and then sun-up after a while and he would be hungry. But that would be to-morrow and now he was only cold, and walking would cure that. His breathing was easier now and he decided to get up and go on, and then he found that he had been asleep because he knew it was almost dawn, the night almost over. He could tell that from the whippoorwills. They were everywhere now among the dark trees below him, constant and inflectioned and ceaseless, so that, as the instant for giving over to the day birds drew nearer and nearer, there was no interval at all between them. He got up. He was a little stiff, but walking would cure that too as it would the cold, and soon there would be the sun. He went on down the hill, toward the dark woods within which the liquid silver voices of the birds called unceasing—the rapid and urgent beating of the urgent and quiring heart of the late spring night. He did not look back.

[1939]

192

A Rose for Emily

WILLIAM FAULKNER

I

WHEN MISS EMILY GRIERSON DIED, our whole town went to her funeral: the men through a sort of respectful affection for a fallen monument, the women mostly out of curiosity to see the inside of her house, which no one save an old manservant—a combined gardener and cook—had seen in at least ten years.

It was a big, squarish frame house that had once been white, decorated with cupolas and spires and scrolled balconies in the heavily lightsome style of the seventies, set on what had once been our most select street. But garages and cotton gins had encroached and obliterated even the august names of that neighborhood; only Miss Emily's house was left, lifting its stubborn and coquettish decay above the cotton wagons and the gasoline pumps—an eyesore among eyesores. And now Miss Emily had gone to join the representatives of those august names where they lay in the cedar-bemused cemetery among the ranked and anonymous graves of Union and Confederate soldiers who fell at the battle of Jefferson.

Alive, Miss Emily had been a tradition, a duty, and a care; a sort of hereditary obligation upon the town, dating from that day in 1894 when Colonel Sartoris, the mayor—he who fathered the edict that no Negro woman should appear on the streets without an apron—remitted her taxes, the dispensation dating from the death of her father on into perpetuity. Not that Miss Emily would have accepted charity. Colonel Sartoris invented an involved tale to the effect that Miss Emily's father had loaned money to the town, which the town, as a matter of business, preferred this way of repaying. Only a man of Colonel Sartoris' generation and thought could have invented it, and only a woman could have believed it.

When the next generation, with its more modern ideas, became mayors and aldermen, this arrangement created some little dissatisfaction. On the first of the year they mailed her a tax notice. February came, and there was no

Reprinted from *The Collected Short Stories of William Faulkner*, by permission of Lee Caplin.

reply. They wrote her a formal letter, asking her to call at the sheriff's office at her convenience. A week later the mayor wrote her himself, offering to call or to send his car for her, and received in reply a note on paper of an archaic shape, in a thin, flowing calligraphy in faded ink, to the effect that she no longer went out at all. The tax notice was also enclosed, without comment.

They called a special meeting of the Board of Aldermen. A deputation waited upon her, knocked at the door through which no visitor had passed since she ceased giving china-painting lessons eight or ten years earlier. They were admitted by the old Negro into a dim hall from which a staircase mounted into still more shadow. It smelled of dust and disuse—a close, dank smell. The Negro led them into the parlor. It was furnished in heavy, leather-covered furniture. When the Negro opened the blinds of one window, a faint dust rose sluggishly about their thighs, spinning with slow motes in the single sun-ray. On a tarnished gilt easel before the fireplace stood a crayon portrait of Miss Emily's father.

They rose when she entered—a small, fat woman in black, with a thin gold chain descending to her waist and vanishing into her belt, leaning on an ebony cane with a tarnished gold head. Her skeleton was small and spare; perhaps that was why what would have been merely plumpness in another was obesity in her. She looked bloated, like a body long submerged in motionless water, and of that pallid hue. Her eyes, lost in the fatty ridges of her face, looked like two small pieces of coal pressed into a lump of dough as they moved from one face to another while the visitors stated their errand.

She did not ask them to sit. She just stood in the door and listened quietly until the spokesman came to a stumbling halt. Then they could hear the invisible watch ticking at the end of the gold chain.

Her voice was dry and cold. "I have no taxes in Jefferson. Colonel Sartoris explained it to me. Perhaps one of you can gain access to the city records and satisfy yourselves."

"But we have. We are the city authorities, Miss Emily. Didn't you get a notice from the sheriff, signed by him?"

"I received a paper, yes," Miss Emily said. "Perhaps he considers himself the sheriff. . . . I have no taxes in Jefferson."

"But there is nothing on the books to show that, you see. We must go by the—"

"See Colonel Sartoris. I have no taxes in Jefferson."

"But, Miss Emily—"

"See Colonel Sartoris." (Colonel Sartoris had been dead almost ten years.) "I have no taxes in Jefferson. Tobe!" The Negro appeared. "Show these gentlemen out."

II

So she vanquished them, horse and foot, just as she had vanquished their fathers thirty years before about the smell. That was two years after her father's death and a short time after her sweetheart—the one we believed would marry her—had deserted her. After her father's death she went out very little; after her sweetheart went away, people hardly saw her at all. A few of the ladies had the temerity to call, but were not received, and the only sign of life about the place was the Negro man—a young man then—going in and out with a market basket.

"Just as if a man—any man—could keep a kitchen properly," the ladies said, so they were not surprised when the smell developed. It was another link between the gross, teeming world and the high and mighty Griersons.

A neighbor, a woman, complained to the mayor, Judge Stevens, eighty years old.

"But what will you have me do about it, madam?" he said.

"Why, send her word to stop it," the woman said. "Isn't there a law?"

"I'm sure that won't be necessary," Judge Stevens said. "It's probably just a snake or a rat that nigger of hers killed in the yard. I'll speak to him about it."

The next day he received two more complaints, one from a man who came in diffident deprecation. "We really must do something about it, Judge. I'd be the last one in the world to bother Miss Emily, but we've got to do something." That night the Board of Aldermen met—three graybeards and one younger man, a member of the rising generation.

"It's simple enough," he said. "Send her word to have her place cleaned up. Give her a certain time to do it in, and if she don't . . ."

"Dammit, sir," Judge Stevens said, "will you accuse a lady to her face of smelling bad?"

So the next night, after midnight, four men crossed Miss Emily's lawn and slunk about the house like burglars, sniffing along the base of the brickwork and at the cellar openings while one of them performed a regular sowing motion with his hand out of a sack slung from his shoulder. They broke open the cellar door and sprinkled lime there, and in all the outbuildings. As they recrossed the lawn, a window that had been dark was lighted and Miss Emily sat in it, the light behind her, and her upright torso motionless as that of an idol. They crept quietly across the lawn and into the shadow of the locusts that lined the street. After a week or two the smell went away.

That was when people had begun to feel sorry for her. People in our town remembering how old lady Wyatt, her great-aunt, had gone completely crazy at last, believed that the Griersons held themselves a little too high for what they really were. None of the young men were quite good enough for Miss Emily and such. We had long thought of them as a tableau: Miss Emily a slender figure in white in the background, her father a spraddled silhouette in the foreground, his back to her and clutching a horsewhip, the two of them framed by the backflung front door. So when she got to be thirty and was still single, we were not pleased exactly, but vindicated; even with insanity in the family she wouldn't have turned down all of her chances if they had really materialized.

When her father died, it got about that the house was all that was left to her; and in a way, people were glad. At last they could pity Miss Emily. Being left alone, and a pauper, she had become humanized. Now she too would know the old thrill and the old despair of a penny more or less.

The day after his death all the ladies prepared to call at the house and offer condolence and aid, as is our custom. Miss Emily met them at the door, dressed as usual and with no trace of grief on her face. She told them that her father was not dead. She did that for three days, with the ministers calling on her, and the doctors trying to persuade her to let them dispose of the body. Just as they were about to resort to law and force, she broke down, and they buried her father quickly.

We did not say she was crazy then. We believed she had to do that. We remembered all the young men her father had driven away, and we knew that with nothing left, she would have to cling to that which had robbed her, as people will.

III

She was sick for a long time. When we saw her again, her hair was cut short, making her look like a girl, with a vague resemblance to those angels in colored church windows—sort of tragic and serene.

The town had just let the contracts for paving the sidewalks, and in the summer after her father's death they began to work. The construction company came with niggers and mules and machinery, and a foreman named Homer Barron, a Yankee—a big, dark, ready man, with a big voice and eyes lighter than his face. The little boys would follow in groups to hear him cuss the niggers, and the niggers singing in time to the rise and fall of picks. Pretty soon he knew everybody in town. Whenever you heard a lot of laughing anywhere about the square, Homer Barron would be in the center of the group. Presently we began to see him and Miss Emily on Sunday afternoons driving in the yellow-wheeled buggy and the matched team of bays from the livery stable.

At first we were glad that Miss Emily would have an interest, because the ladies all said, "Of course a Grierson would not think seriously of a Northerner, a day laborer." But there were still others, older people, who said that even grief could not cause a real lady to forget *noblesse oblige*—without calling it *noblesse oblige*. They just said, "Poor Emily. Her kinsfolk should come to her." She had some kin in Alabama; but years ago her father had fallen out with them over the estate of old lady Wyatt, the crazy woman, and there was no communication between the two families. They had not even been represented at the funeral.

And as soon as the old people said, "Poor Emily," the whispering began. "Do you suppose it's really so?" they said to one another. "Of course it is. What else could . . ." This behind their hands; rustling of craned silk and satin behind jalousies closed upon the sun of Sunday afternoon as the thin, swift clop-clop-clop of the matched team passed: "Poor Emily."

She carried her head high enough—even when we believed that she was fallen. It was as if she demanded more than ever the recognition of her dignity as the last Grierson; as if it had wanted that touch of earthliness to reaffirm her imperviousness. Like when she bought the rat poison, the arsenic. That was over a year after they had begun to say "Poor Emily," and while the two female cousins were visiting her.

"I want some poison," she said to the druggist. She was over thirty then, still a slight woman, though thinner than usual, with cold, haughty black eyes in a face the flesh of which was strained across the temples and about the eye-sockets as you imagine a lighthouse-keeper's face ought to look. "I want some poison," she said.

"Yes, Miss Emily. What kind? For rats and such? I'd recom—"

"I want the best you have. I don't care what kind."

The druggist named several. "They'll kill anything up to an elephant. But what you want is—"

"Arsenic," Miss Emily said. "Is that a good one?"

"Is . . . arsenic? Yes ma'am. But what you want—"

"I want arsenic."

The druggist looked down at her. She looked back at him, erect, her face like a strained flag. "Why, of course," the druggist said. "If that's what you want. But the law requires you to tell what you are going to use it for."

Miss Emily just stared at him, her head tilted back in order to look him eye for eye, until he looked away and went and got the arsenic and wrapped it up. The Negro delivery boy brought her the package; the druggist didn't come back. When she opened the package at home there was written on the box, under the skull and bones: "For rats."

IV

So the next day we all said, "She will kill herself"; and we said it would be the best thing. When she had first begun to be seen with Homer Barron, we had said, "She will marry him." Then we said, "She will persuade him yet," because Homer himself had remarked—he liked men, and it was known that he drank with the younger men in the Elk's Club—that he was not a marrying man. Later we said, "Poor Emily," behind the jalousies as they passed on Sunday afternoon in the glittering buggy, Miss Emily with her head high and Homer Barron with his hat cocked and a cigar in his teeth, reins and whip in a yellow glove.

Then some of the ladies began to say that it was a disgrace to the town and a bad example to the young people. The men did not want to interfere, but at last the ladies forced the Baptist minister—Miss Emily's people were Episcopal—to call upon her. He would never divulge what happened during that interview, but he refused to go back again. The next Sunday they again drove about the streets and the following day the minister's wife wrote to Miss Emily's relations in Alabama.

So she had blood-kin under her roof again and we sat back to watch developments. At first nothing happened. Then we were sure that they had to be married. We learned that Miss Emily had been to the jeweler's and ordered a man's toilet set in silver, with the letters H.B. on each piece. Two days later we learned that she had bought a complete outfit of men's clothing, including a nightshirt, and we said "They are married." We were really glad. We were glad because the two female cousins were even more Grierson than Miss Emily had ever been.

So we were surprised when Homer Barron—the streets had been finished some time since—was gone. We were a little disappointed that there was not a public blowing-off, but we believed that he had gone on to prepare for Miss Emily's coming, or to give a chance to get rid of the cousins. (By that time it was a cabal, and we were all Miss Emily's allies to help circumvent the cousins.) Sure enough, after another week they departed. And, as we had expected all along, within three days Homer Barron was back in town. A neighbor saw the Negro man admit him at the kitchen door at dusk one evening.

And that was the last we saw of Homer Barron. And of Miss Emily for some time. The Negro man went in and out with the market basket, but the front door remained closed. Now and then we would see her at a window for a moment, as the men did that night when they sprinkled the lime, but for almost six months she did not appear on the streets. Then we knew that this was to be expected too; as if that quality of her father which had thwarted her woman's life so many times had been too virulent and too furious to die.

When we next saw Miss Emily, she had grown fat and her hair was turning gray. During the next few years it grew grayer and grayer until it attained an even pepper-and-salt iron-gray, when it ceased turning. Up to the day of her death at seventy-four it was still that vigorous iron-gray, like the hair of an active man.

From that time on her front door remained closed, save for a period of six or seven years, when she was about forty, during which she gave lessons in china-painting. She fitted up a studio in one of the downstairs rooms, where the daughters and granddaughters of Colonel Sartoris' contemporaries were sent to her with the same regularity and in the same spirit that they were sent on Sundays with a twenty-five cent piece for the collection plate. Meanwhile her taxes had been remitted.

Then the newer generation became the backbone and the spirit of the town, and the painting pupils grew up and fell away and did not send their children to her with boxes of color and tedious brushes and pictures cut from the ladies' magazines. The front door closed upon the last one and remained closed for good. When the town got free postal delivery Miss Emily alone refused to let them fasten the metal numbers above her door and attach a mailbox to it. She would not listen to them.

Daily, monthly, yearly we watched the Negro grow grayer and more stooped, going in and out with the market basket. Each December we sent her a tax notice, which would be returned by the post office a week later, unclaimed. Now and then we would see her in one of the downstairs windows—she had evidently shut up the top floor of the house—like the carven torso of an idol in a niche, looking or not looking at us, we could never tell which. Thus she passed from generation to generation—dear, inescapable, impervious, tranquil, and perverse.

And so she died. Fell ill in the house filled with dust and shadows, with only a doddering Negro man to wait on her. We did not even know she was sick; we had long since given up trying to get any information from the Negro. He talked to no one, probably not even to her, for his voice had grown harsh and rusty, as if from disuse.

She died in one of the downstairs rooms, in a heavy walnut bed with a curtain, her gray head propped on a pillow yellow and moldy with age and lack of sunlight.

V

The Negro met the first of the ladies at the front door and let them in, with their hushed, sibilant voices and their quick, curious glances, and then he disappeared. He walked right through the house and out the back and was not seen again.

The two female cousins came at once. They held the funeral on the second day, with the town coming to look at Miss Emily beneath a mass of bought flowers, with the crayon face of her father musing profoundly above the bier and the ladies sibilant and macabre; and the very old men—some in their brushed Confederate uniforms—on the porch and the lawn, talking of Miss Emily as if she had been a contemporary of theirs, believing that they had danced with her and courted her perhaps, confusing time with its mathematical progression, as the old do, to whom all the past is not a diminishing road, but, instead, a huge meadow which no winter ever quite touches, divided from them now by the narrow bottleneck of the most recent decade of years.

Already we knew that there was one room in the region above the stairs which no one had seen in forty years, and which would have to be forced. They waited until Miss Emily was decently in the ground before they opened it.

The violence of breaking down the door seemed to fill this room with pervading dust. A thin, acrid pall as of the tomb seemed to lie everywhere upon this room decked and furnished as for a bridal: upon the valance curtains of faded rose color, upon the rose-shaded lights, upon the dressing table, upon the delicate array of crystal and the man's toilet things backed with tarnished silver, silver so tarnished that the monogram was obscured. Among them lay a collar and tie, as if they had just been removed, which, lifted, left upon the surface a pale crescent in the dust. Upon a chair hung the suit, carefully folded; beneath it the two mute shoes and the discarded socks.

The man himself lay in the bed.

For a long while we just stood there, looking down at the profound and fleshless grin. The body had aparently once lain in the attitude of an embrace, but now the long sleep that outlasts love, that conquers even the grimace of love, had cuckolded him. What was left of him, rotted beneath what was left of the nightshirt, had become inextricable from the bed in which he lay; and upon him and upon the pillow beside him lay that even coating of the patient and biding dust.

Then we noticed that in the second pillow was the indentation of a head. One of us lifted something from it, and leaning forward, that faint and invisible dust dry and acrid in the nostrils, we saw a long strand of iron-gray hair.

[1930]

Charlotte Perkins Gilman
[1860–1935]

Born in Hartford, Connecticut to a branch of the famous New England Beecher family, CHARLOTTE PERKINS GILMAN grew up in near poverty after her father abandoned the family. Her sense of independence may well have been fostered by her encounters with great-aunt Harriet Beecher Stowe, author of the abolitionist novel Uncle Tom's Cabin; and feminist/suffragist great-aunts Catherine Beecher and Isabella Beecher Hooker. Despite a childhood pledge to retain her independence by remaining single, Gilman married at twenty-three, had a child a year later, and immediately plunged into depression. The treatment prescribed by the highly respected nerve specialist S. Weir Mitchell was for her to avoid writing and intellectual activity of any kind, and this only served to deepen her depression. She divorced her husband and took her mother and daughter to California. There Gilman resumed writing and lecturing on women's rights, and eventually married a cousin, George Gilman, in 1900.

The year 1894 found Gilman in San Francisco, where she helped to organize the California Women's Congresses of 1894–1895; she and social reformer Jane Addams cofounded the Women's Peace Party in 1895. Her activism on behalf of women's rights took her to cities and towns throughout the United States and England. She argued that women were not biologically inferior to men, but rather had been conditioned to behave subserviently. "Women are human beings as much as men, by nature; and as women, are even more sympathetic with human processes," she argued. "To develop human life in its true powers we need fully equal citizenship for women." Toward that end, Gilman advocated communal living in which women could leave household duties and childcare to trained domestic workers, and then participate fully in the public sphere.

In 1935, a year after her husband's death and with a diagnosis of breast cancer, Gilman committed suicide, explaining her choice in the most rational terms: "When one is assured of unavoidable and imminent death, it is the simplest of human rights to choose a quick and easy death in place of a slow and horrible one."

Gilman was a prolific writer, and published a highly acclaimed exploration of women's status in Women and Economics (1898) and a thoughtful, witty feminist-utopian novel in Herland (1915). She also published the magazine The Forerunner, for which she was the sole contributor, from 1910 to 1916; and wrote several novels, a poetry collection, and over two hundred short stories. "The Yellow Wallpaper," published in 1892 in New England Magazine, after a rejection from the Atlantic Monthly, draws from her experience with the common *treatment of depression in women at the turn of the century. Carrie Chapman Catt, one of the most revered pioneers of the women's rights movement, called Charlotte Perkins Gilman, "the most original and challenging mind the movement produced." That sentiment was echoed by contemporary feminists in 1994, when Gilman was inducted into the National Women's Hall of Fame in Seneca Falls, New York.*

The Yellow Wall-Paper

CHARLOTTE PERKINS GILMAN

It is very seldom that mere ordinary people like John and myself secure halls for the summer.

A colonial mansion, a hereditary estate, I would say a haunted house, and reach the height of romantic felicity—but that would be asking too much of fate!

Still I will proudly declare that there is something queer about it.

Else, why should it be let so cheaply? And why have stood so long untenanted?

John laughs at me, of course, but one expects that in marriage.

John is practical in the extreme. He has no patience with faith, an intense horror of superstition, and he scoffs openly at any talk of things not to be felt and seen and put down in figures.

John is a physician, and *perhaps*—(I would not say it to a living soul, of course, but this is dead paper and a great relief to my mind—) *perhaps* that is one reason I do not get well faster.

You see he does not believe I am sick!

And what can one do?

If a physician of high standing, and one's own husband, assures friends and relatives that there is really nothing the matter with one but temporary nervous depression—a slight hysterical tendency—what is one to do?

My brother is also a physician, and also of high standing, and he says the same thing.

So I take phosphates or phosphites—whichever it is, and tonics, and journeys, and air, and exercise, and am absolutely forbidden to "work" until I am well again.

Personally, I disagree with their ideas.

Personally, I believe that congenial work, with excitement and change, would do me good.

But what is one to do?

I did write for a while in spite of them; but it *does* exhaust me a good deal—having to be so sly about it, or else meet with heavy opposition.

First published in *New England Magazine*, August 1892.

I sometimes fancy that in my condition if I had less opposition and more society and stimulus—but John says the very worst thing I can do is to think about my condition, and I confess it always makes me feel bad.

So I will let it alone and talk about the house.

The most beautiful place! It is quite alone, standing well back from the road, quite three miles from the village. It makes me think of English places that you read about, for there are hedges and walls and gates that lock, and lots of separate little houses for the gardeners and people.

There is a *delicious* garden! I never saw such a garden—large and shady, full of box-bordered paths, and lined with long grape-covered arbors with seats under them.

There were greenhouses, too, but they are all broken now.

There was some legal trouble, I believe, something about the heirs and coheirs; anyhow, the place has been empty for years.

That spoils my ghostliness, I am afraid, but I don't care—there is something strange about the house—I can feel it.

I even said so to John one moonlight evening, but he said what I felt was a *draught*, and shut the window.

I get unreasonably angry with John sometimes. I'm sure I never used to be so sensitive. I think it is due to this nervous condition.

But John says if I feel so, I shall neglect proper self-control; so I take pains to control myself—before him, at least, and that makes me very tired.

I don't like our room a bit. I wanted one downstairs that opened on the piazza and had roses all over the window, and such pretty old-fashioned chintz hangings! but John would not hear of it.

He said there was only one window and not room for two beds, and no near room for him if he took another.

He is very careful and loving, and hardly lets me stir without special direction.

I have a schedule prescription for each hour in the day; he takes all care from me, and so I feel basely ungrateful not to value it more.

He said we came here solely on my account, that I was to have perfect rest and all the air I could get. "Your exercise depends on your strength, my dear," said he, "and your food somewhat on your appetite; but air you can absorb all the time." So we took the nursery at the top of the house.

It is a big, airy room, the whole floor nearly, with windows that look all ways, and air and sunshine galore. It was nursery first and then playroom and gymnasium, I should judge; for the windows are barred for little children, and there are rings and things in the walls.

The paint and paper look as if a boys' school had used it. It is stripped off—the paper—in great patches all around the head of my bed, about as far as I can reach, and in a great place on the other side of the room low down. I never saw a worse paper in my life.

One of those sprawling flamboyant patterns committing every artistic sin.

It is dull enough to confuse the eye in following, pronounced enough to constantly irritate and provoke study, and when you follow the lame uncertain curves for a little distance they suddenly commit suicide—plunge off at outrageous angles, destroy themselves in unheard of contradictions.

The color is repellant, almost revolting; a smouldering unclean yellow, strangely faded by the slow-turning sunlight.

It is a dull yet lurid orange in some places, a sickly sulphur tint in others.

No wonder the children hated it! I should hate it myself if I had to live in this room long.

There comes John, and I must put this away,—he hates to have me write a word.

We have been here two weeks, and I haven't felt like writing before, since that first day.

I am sitting by the window now, up in this atrocious nursery, and there is nothing to hinder my writing as much as I please, save lack of strength.

John is away all day, and even some nights when his cases are serious.

I am glad my case is not serious!

But these nervous troubles are dreadfully depressing.

John does not know how much I really suffer. He knows there is no *reason* to suffer, and that satisfies him.

Of course it is only nervousness. It does weigh on me so not to do my duty in any way!

I meant to be such a help to John, such a real rest and comfort, and here I am a comparative burden already!

Nobody would believe what an effort it is to do what little I am able,—to dress and entertain, and order things.

It is fortunate Mary is so good with the baby. Such a dear baby!

And yet I *cannot* be with him, it makes me so nervous.

I suppose John never was nervous in his life. He laughs at me so about this wall-paper!

At first he meant to repaper the room, but afterwards he said that I was letting it get the better of me, and that nothing was worse for a nervous patient than to give way to such fancies.

He said that after the wall-paper was changed it would be the heavy bedstead, and then the barred windows, and then that gate at the head of the stairs, and so on.

"You know the place is doing you good," he said, "and really, dear, I don't care to renovate the house just for a three months' rental."

"Then do let us go downstairs," I said, "there are such pretty rooms there."

Then he took me in his arms and called me a blessed little goose, and said he would go down cellar, if I wished, and have it whitewashed into the bargain.

But he is right enough about the beds and windows and things.

It is an airy and comfortable room as any one need wish, and, of course, I would not be so silly as to make him uncomfortable just for a whim.

I'm really getting quite fond of the big room, all but that horrid paper.

Out of one window I can see the garden, those mysterious deep-shaded arbors, the riotous old-fashioned flowers, and bushes and gnarly trees.

Out of another I get a lovely view of the bay and a little private wharf belonging to the estate. There is a beautiful shaded lane that runs down there from the house. I always fancy I see people walking in these numerous paths and arbors, but John has cautioned me not to give way to fancy in the least. He says that with my imaginative power and habit of story-making, a nervous weakness like mine is sure to lead to all manner of excited fancies, and that I ought to use my will and good sense to check the tendency. So I try.

I think sometimes that if I were only well enough to write a little it would relieve the press of ideas and rest me.

But I find I get pretty tired when I try.

It is so discouraging not to have any advice and companionship about my work. When I get really well, John says we will ask cousin Henry and Julia down for a long visit; but he says he would as soon put fireworks in my pillow-case as to let me have those stimulating people about now.

I wish I could get well faster.

But I must not think about that. This paper looks to me as if it *knew* what a vicious influence it had!

There is a recurrent spot where the pattern lolls like a broken neck and two bulbous eyes stare at you upside down.

I get positively angry with the impertinence of it and the everlastingness. Up and down and sideways they crawl, and those absurd, unblinking eyes are everywhere. There is one place where two breadths didn't match, and the eyes go all up and down the line, one a little higher than the other.

I never saw so much expression in an inanimate thing before, and we all know how much expression they have! I used to lie awake as a child and get more entertainment and terror out of blank walls and plain furniture than most children could find in a toy-store.

I remember what a kindly wink the knobs of our big, old bureau used to have, and there was one chair that always seemed like a strong friend.

I used to feel that if any of the other things looked too fierce I could always hop into that chair and be safe.

The furniture in this room is no worse than inharmonious, however, for we had to bring it all from downstairs. I suppose when this was used as a play-room they had to take the nursery things out, and no wonder! I never saw such ravages as the children have made here.

The wall-paper, as I said before, is torn off in spots, and it sticketh closer than a brother—they must have had perseverance as well as hatred.

Then the floor is scratched and gouged and splintered, the plaster itself is dug out here and there, and this great heavy bed which is all we found in the room, looks as if it had been through the wars.

But I don't mind it a bit—only the paper.

There comes John's sister. Such a dear girl as she is, and so careful of me! I must not let her find me writing.

She is a perfect and enthusiastic housekeeper, and hopes for no better profession. I verily believe she thinks it is the writing which made me sick!

But I can write when she is out, and see her a long way off from these windows.

There is one that commands the road, a lovely shaded winding road, and one that just looks off over the country. A lovely country, too, full of great elms and velvet meadows.

This wall-paper has a kind of subpattern in a different shade, a particularly irritating one, for you can only see it in certain lights, and not clearly then.

But in the places where it isn't faded and where the sun is just so—I can see a strange, provoking, formless sort of figure, that seems to skulk about behind that silly and conspicuous front design.

There's sister on the stairs!

Well, the Fourth of July is over! The people are all gone and I am tired out. John thought it might do me good to see a little company, so we just had mother and Nellie and the children down for a week.

Of course I didn't do a thing. Jennie sees to everything now.

But it tired me all the same.

John says if I don't pick up faster he shall send me to Weir Mitchell[1] in the fall.

But I don't want to go there at all. I had a friend who was in his hands once, and she says he is just like John and my brother, only more so!

Besides, it is such an undertaking to go so far.

---

[1] Dr. S. Weir Mitchell (1829–1914), physician famous for his "rest cures" for "hysterical" women. Mitchell treated Gilman for a time.

I don't feel as if it was worth while to turn my hand over for anything, and I'm getting dreadfully fretful and querulous.

I cry at nothing, and cry most of the time.

Of course I don't when John is here, or anybody else, but when I am alone.

And I am alone a good deal just now. John is kept in town very often by serious cases, and Jennie is good and lets me alone when I want her to.

So I walk a little in the garden or down that lovely lane, sit on the porch under the roses, and lie down up here a good deal.

I'm getting really fond of the room in spite of the wall-paper. Perhaps *because* of the wall-paper.

It dwells in my mind so!

I lie here on this great immovable bed—it is nailed down, I believe—and follow that pattern about by the hour. It is as good as gymnastics, I assure you. I start, we'll say, at the bottom, down in the corner over there where it has not been touched, and I determine for the thousandth time that I *will* follow that pointless pattern to some sort of a conclusion.

I know a little of the principle of design, and I know this thing was not arranged on any laws of radiation, or alternation, or repetition, or symmetry, or anything else that I ever heard of.

It is repeated, of course, by the breadths, but not otherwise.

Looked at in one way each breadth stands alone, the bloated curves and flourishes—a kind of "debased Romanesque" with *delirium tremens*—go waddling up and down in isolated columns of fatuity.

But, on the other hand, they connect diagonally, and the sprawling outlines run off in great slanting waves of optic horror, like a lot of wallowing seaweeds in full chase.

The whole thing goes horizontally, too, at least it seems so, and I exhaust myself in trying to distinguish the order of its going in that direction.

They have used a horizontal breadth for a frieze, and that adds wonderfully to the confusion.

There is one end of the room where it is almost intact, and there, when the crosslights fade and the low sun shines directly upon it, I can almost fancy radiation after all,—the interminable grotesques seem to form around a common centre and rush off in headlong plunges of equal distraction.

It makes me tired to follow it. I will take a nap I guess.

I don't know why I should write this.

I don't want to.

I don't feel able.

And I know John would think it absurd. But I *must* say what I feel and think in some way—it is such a relief!

But the effort is getting to be greater than the relief.

Half the time now I am awfully lazy, and lie down ever so much.

John says I mustn't lose my strength, and has me take cod liver oil and lots of tonics and things, to say nothing of ale and wine and rare meat.

Dear John! He loves me very dearly, and hates to have me sick. I tried to have a real earnest reasonable talk with him the other day, and tell him how I wish he would let me go and make a visit to Cousin Henry and Julia.

But he said I wasn't able to go, nor able to stand it after I got there; and I did not make out a very good case for myself, for I was crying before I had finished.

It is getting to be a great effort for me to think straight. Just this nervous weakness I suppose.

And dear John gathered me up in his arms, and just carried me upstairs and laid me on the bed, and sat by me and read to me till it tired my head.

He said I was his darling and his comfort and all he had, and that I must take care of myself for his sake, and keep well.

He says no one but myself can help me out of it, that I must use my will and self-control and not let any silly fancies run away with me.

There's one comfort, the baby is well and happy, and does not have to occupy this nursery with the horrid wall-paper.

If we had not used it, that blessed child would have! What a fortunate escape! Why, I wouldn't have a child of mine, an impressionable little thing, live in such a room for worlds.

I never thought of it before, but it is lucky that John kept me here after all, I can stand it so much easier than a baby, you see.

Of course I never mention it to them any more—I am too wise,—but I keep watch of it all the same.

There are things in that paper that nobody knows but me, or ever will.

Behind that outside pattern the dim shapes get clearer every day.

It is always the same shape, only very numerous.

And it is like a woman stooping down and creeping about behind that pattern. I don't like it a bit. I wonder—I begin to think—I wish John would take me away from here!

It is so hard to talk with John about my case, because he is so wise, and because he loves me so.

But I tried it last night.

It was moonlight. The moon shines in all around just as the sun does.

I hate to see it sometimes, it creeps so slowly, and always comes in by one window or another.

John was asleep and I hated to waken him, so I kept still and watched the moonlight on that undulating wall-paper till I felt creepy.

The faint figure behind seemed to shake the pattern, just as if she wanted to get out.

I got up softly and went to feel and see if the paper *did* move, and when I came back John was awake.

"What is it, little girl?" he said. "Don't go walking about like that—you'll get cold."

I thought it was a good time to talk, so I told him that I really was not gaining here, and that I wished he would take me away.

"Why, darling!" said he, "our lease will be up in three weeks, and I can't see how to leave before.

"The repairs are not done at home, and I cannot possibly leave town just now. Of course if you were in any danger, I could and would, but you really are better, dear, whether you can see it or not. I am a doctor, dear, and I know. You are gaining flesh and color, your appetite is better, I feel really much easier about you."

"I don't weigh a bit more," said I, "nor as much; and my appetite may be better in the evening when you are here, but it is worse in the morning when you are away!"

"Bless her little heart!" said he with a big hug, "she shall be as sick as she pleases! But now let's improve the shining hours by going to sleep, and talk about it in the morning!"

"And you won't go away?" I asked gloomily.

"Why, how can I, dear? It is only three weeks more and then we will take a nice little trip of a few days while Jennie is getting the house ready. Really dear you are better!"

"Better in body perhaps—" I began, and stopped short, for he sat up straight and looked at me with such a stern, reproachful look that I could not say another word.

"My darling," said he, "I beg of you, for my sake and for our child's sake, as well as for your own, that you will never for one instant let that idea enter your mind! There is nothing so dangerous, so fascinating, to a temperament like yours. It is a false and foolish fancy. Can you not trust me as a physician when I tell you so?"

So of course I said no more on that score, and we went to sleep before long. He thought I was asleep first, but I wasn't, and lay there for hours trying to decide whether that front pattern and the back pattern really did move together or separately.

On a pattern like this, by daylight, there is a lack of sequence, a defiance of law, that is a constant irritant to a normal mind.

The color is hideous enough, and unreliable enough, and infuriating enough, but the pattern is torturing.

You think you have mastered it, but just as you get well underway in following, it turns a back-somersault and there you are. It slaps you in the face, knocks you down, and tramples upon you. It is like a bad dream.

The outside pattern is a florid arabesque, reminding one of a fungus. If you can imagine a toadstool in joints, an interminable string of toadstools, budding and sprouting in endless convolutions—why, that is something like it.

That is, sometimes!

There is one marked peculiarity about this paper, a thing nobody seems to notice but myself, and that is that it changes as the light changes.

When the sun shoots in through the east window—I always watch for that first long, straight ray—it changes so quickly that I never can quite believe it.

That is why I watch it always.

By moonlight—the moon shines in all night when there is a moon—I wouldn't know it was the same paper.

At night in any kind of light, in twilight, candlelight, lamplight, and worst of all by moonlight, it becomes bars! The outside pattern I mean, and the woman behind it is as plain as can be.

I didn't realize for a long time what the thing was that showed behind, that dim sub-pattern, but now I am quite sure it is a woman.

By daylight she is subdued, quiet. I fancy it is the pattern that keeps her so still. It is so puzzling. It keeps me quiet by the hour.

I lie down ever so much now. John says it is good for me, and to sleep all I can.

Indeed he started the habit by making me lie down for an hour after each meal.

It is a very bad habit I am convinced, for you see I don't sleep.

And that cultivates deceit, for I don't tell them I'm awake—O no!

The fact is I am getting a little afraid of John.

He seems very queer sometimes, and even Jennie has an inexplicable look.

It strikes me occasionally, just as a scientific hypothesis,—that perhaps it is the paper!

I have watched John when he did not know I was looking, and come into the room suddenly on the most innocent excuses, and I've caught him several times *looking at the paper!* And Jennie too. I caught Jennie with her hand on it once.

She didn't know I was in the room, and when I asked her in a quiet, a very quiet voice, with the most restrained manner possible, what she was doing with the paper—she turned around as if she had been caught stealing, and looked quite angry—asked me why I should frighten her so!

Then she said that the paper stained everything it touched, that she had found yellow smooches on all my clothes and John's, and she wished we would be more careful!

Did not that sound innocent? But I know she was studying that pattern, and I am determined that nobody shall find it out but myself!

Life is very much more exciting now than it used to be. You see I have something more to expect, to look forward to, to watch. I really do eat better, and am more quiet than I was.

John is so pleased to see me improve! He laughed a little the other day, and said I seemed to be flourishing in spite of my wall-paper.

I turned it off with a laugh. I had no intention of telling him it was *because* of the wall-paper—he would make fun of me. He might even want to take me away.

I don't want to leave now until I have found it out. There is a week more, and I think that will be enough.

I'm feeling ever so much better! I don't sleep much at night, for it is so interesting to watch developments; but I sleep a good deal in the daytime.

In the daytime it is tiresome and perplexing.

There are always new shoots on the fungus, and new shades of yellow all over it. I cannot keep count of them, though I have tried conscientiously.

It is the strangest yellow, that wall-paper! It makes me think of all the yellow things I ever saw—not beautiful ones like buttercups, but old foul, bad yellow things.

But there is something else about that paper—the smell! I noticed it the moment we came into the room, but with so much air and sun it was not bad. Now we have had a week of fog and rain, and whether the windows are open or not, the smell is here.

It creeps all over the house.

I find it hovering in the dining-room, skulking in the parlor, hiding in the hall, lying in wait for me on the stairs.

It gets into my hair.

Even when I go to ride, if I turn my head suddenly and surprise it—there is that smell!

Such a peculiar odor, too! I have spent hours in trying to analyze it, to find what it smelled like.

It is not bad—at first, and very gentle, but quite the subtlest, most enduring odor I ever met.

In this damp weather it is awful, I wake up in the night and find it hanging over me.

It used to disturb me at first. I thought seriously of burning the house—to reach the smell.

But now I am used to it. The only thing I can think of that it is like is the *color* of the paper! A yellow smell.

There is a very funny mark on this wall, low down, near the mopboard. A streak that runs round the room. It goes behind every piece of furniture, except the bed, a long, straight, even *smooch*, as if it had been rubbed over and over.

I wonder how it was done and who did it, and what they did it for. Round and round and round—round and round and round—it makes me dizzy!

I really have discovered something at last.

Through watching so much at night, when it changes so, I have finally found out.

The front pattern *does* move—and no wonder! The woman behind shakes it!

Sometimes I think there are a great many women behind, and sometimes only one, and she crawls around fast, and her crawling shakes it all over.

Then in the very bright spots she keeps still, and in the very shady spots she just takes hold of the bars and shakes them hard.

And she is all the time trying to climb through. But nobody could climb through that pattern—it strangles so; I think that is why it has so many heads.

They get through, and then the pattern strangles them off and turns them upside down, and makes their eyes white!

If those heads were covered or taken off it would not be half so bad.

I think that woman gets out in the daytime!

And I'll tell you why—privately—I've seen her!

I can see her out of every one of my windows!

It is the same woman, I know, for she is always creeping, and most women do not creep by daylight.

I see her in that long shaded lane, creeping up and down. I see her in those dark grape arbors, creeping all around the garden.

I see her on that long road under the trees, creeping along, and when a carriage comes she hides under the blackberry vines.

I don't blame her a bit. It must be very humiliating to be caught creeping by daylight!

I always lock the door when I creep by daylight. I can't do it at night, for I know John would suspect something at once.

And John is so queer now, that I don't want to irritate him. I wish he would take another room! Besides, I don't want anybody to get that woman out at night but myself.

I often wonder if I could see her out of all the windows at once.

But, turn as fast as I can, I can only see out of one at one time.

And though I always see her, she *may* be able to creep faster than I can turn!

I have watched her sometimes away off in the open country, creeping as fast as a cloud shadow in a high wind.

If only that top pattern could be gotten off from the under one! I mean to try it, little by little.

I have found out another funny thing, but I shan't tell it this time! It does not do to trust people too much.

There are only two more days to get this paper off, and I believe John is beginning to notice. I don't like the look in his eyes.

And I heard him ask Jennie a lot of professional questions about me. She had a very good report to give.

She said I slept a good deal in the daytime.

John knows I don't sleep very well at night, for all I'm so quiet!

He asked me all sorts of questions, too, and pretended to be very loving and kind.

As if I couldn't see through him!

Still, I don't wonder he acts so, sleeping under this paper for three months.

It only interests me, but I feel sure John and Jennie are secretly affected by it.

Hurrah! This is the last day, but it is enough. John is to stay in town over night, and won't be out until this evening.

Jennie wanted to sleep with me—the sly thing! but I told her I should undoubtedly rest better for a night all alone.

That was clever, for really I wasn't alone a bit! As soon as it was moonlight and that poor thing began to crawl and shake the pattern, I got up and ran to help her.

I pulled and she shook, I shook and she pulled, and before morning we had peeled off yards of that paper.

A strip about as high as my head and half around the room.

And then when the sun came and that awful pattern began to laugh at me, I declared I would finish it to-day!

We go away to-morrow, and they are moving all my furniture down again to leave things as they were before.

Jennie looked at the wall in amazement, but I told her merrily that I did it out of pure spite at the vicious thing.

She laughed and said she wouldn't mind doing it herself, but I must not get tired.

How she betrayed herself that time!

But I am here, and no person touches this paper but me,—not *alive*!

She tried to get me out of the room—it was too patent! But I said it was so quiet and empty and clean now that I believed I would lie down again and sleep all I could; and not to wake me even for dinner—I would call when I woke.

So now she is gone, and the servants are gone, and the things are gone, and there is nothing left but that great bedstead nailed down, with the canvas mattress we found on it.

We shall sleep downstairs to-night, and take the boat home to-morrow.

I quite enjoy the room, now it is bare again.

How those children did tear about here!

This bedstead is fairly gnawed!

But I must get to work.

I have locked the door and thrown the key down into the front path.

I don't want to go out, and I don't want to have anybody come in, till John comes.

I want to astonish him.

I've got a rope up here that even Jennie did not find. If that woman does get out, and tries to get away, I can tie her!

But I forgot I could not reach far without anything to stand on!

This bed will *not* move!

I tried to lift and push it until I was lame, and then I got so angry I bit off a little piece at one corner—but it hurt my teeth.

Then I peeled off all the paper I could reach standing on the floor. It sticks horribly and the pattern just enjoys it! All those strangled heads and bulbous eyes and waddling fungus growths just shriek with derision!

I am getting angry enough to do something desperate. To jump out of the window would be admirable exercise, but the bars are too strong even to try.

Besides I wouldn't do it. Of course not. I know well enough that a step like that is improper and might be misconstrued.

I don't like to *look* out of the windows even—there are so many of those creeping women, and they creep so fast.

I wonder if they all come out of that wall-paper as I did?

But I am securely fastened now by my well-hidden rope—you don't get *me* out in the road there!

I suppose I shall have to get back behind the pattern when it comes night, and that is hard!

It is so pleasant to be out in this great room and creep around as I please!

I don't want to go outside. I won't, even if Jennie asks me to.

For outside you have to creep on the ground, and everything is green instead of yellow.

But here I can creep smoothly on the floor, and my shoulder just fits in that long smooch around the wall, so I cannot lose my way.

Why there's John at the door!

It is no use, young man, you can't open it!

How he does call and pound!

Now he's crying for an axe.

It would be a shame to break down that beautiful door!

"John dear!" said I in the gentlest voice, "the key is down by the front steps, under a plantain leaf!"

That silenced him for a few moments.

Then he said—very quietly indeed, "Open the door, my darling!"

"I can't," said I. "The key is down by the front door under a plantain leaf!"

And then I said it again, several times, very gently and slowly, and said it so often that he had to go and see, and he got it of course, and came in. He stopped short by the door.

"What is the matter?" he cried. "For God's sake, what are you doing!"

I kept on creeping just the same, but I looked at him over my shoulder.

"I've got out at last," said I, "in spite of you and Jane. And I've pulled off most of the paper, so you can't put me back!"

Now why should that man have fainted? But he did, and right across my path by the wall, so that I had to creep over him every time!

[1892]

Nathaniel Hawthorne
[1804–1864]

No writer's work has been more informed by the ghosts of the past than NATHANIEL HAWTHORNE'S. *He was born on Independence Day, 1804, in Salem, Massachusetts, to a family whose ancestors included a judge who persecuted Quakers, and another who played a key role in the Salem witchcraft trials. An acute awareness of his Puritan past would later lead to the complex explorations of sin and guilt found in his short stories and novels: As critic Alfred Kazin remarked, "Hawthorne's great subject was, indeed, the sense of guilt that is perhaps the most enduring theme in the moral history of the West—guilt that is the secret tie that binds us to others and to our own past."*

His position as a major literary figure was slow in coming, however. After graduating from Bowdoin College in Maine (where his classmates included poet Henry Wadsworth Longfellow and future U.S. President Franklin Pierce), he spent the next twelve years at his mother's house in Salem. During this time, he earned little income, lived in relative isolation, and immersed himself in literature and New England history. In 1828 he anonymously published the historical novel Fanshawe, *a work he would later go to great lengths to repudiate (always the harshest critic of his own work, he retrieved and destroyed as many copies of the novel as he could find). He struggled to find a publisher for a collection of his stories until 1836, when old friend Horatio Bridge helped him publish* Twice-told Tales. *Named after a line in Shakespeare's* King John, *the book featured several of Hawthorne's most enduring stories, including "The Maypole of Merry Mount" and "The Minister's Black Veil."*

Despite his success, Hawthorne still found it hard to make a living from writing. In order to support himself, and to earn money for his impending marriage (to Sophia Peabody in 1842), he spent the next couple of years working as a salt and coal measurer in the Boston Custom House. He also lived for a time at the experimental utopian community Brook Farm in West Roxbury, Massachusetts—an experience that provided the plot for his novel The Blithedale Romance *(1852). Hawthorne also published several more collections of short stories, including* Mosses from an Old Manse *in 1846. However, it was his novel* The Scarlet Letter *(1850) that secured his place in American letters. The story of Hester Prynne, a woman condemned by her community for bearing a child out of wedlock, the novel created a literary sensation in both the United States and England, and has since become one of the classics of literature.*

Hawthorne's other novels are The House of the Seven Gables *(1851), a work whose biographical elements include a family curse, and* The Marble Faun *(1860). He also penned the campaign biography* The Life of Franklin Pierce

(1852), an endeavor that his old Bowdoin classmate rewarded with a consulship at Liverpool, England. This position finally earned Hawthorne a measure of financial security for his later years in Concord, Massachusetts, when his creative abilities were on the decline. He died, most likely from a brain tumor, while visiting Pierce in Plymouth, New Hampshire, in 1864. He left behind a legacy of some of the most psychologically penetrating stories and novels in all of American fiction.

—Mark Lovely, *Merrimack College*

Young Goodman Brown

NATHANIEL HAWTHORNE

YOUNG GOODMAN BROWN CAME forth, at sunset, into the street of Salem village, but put his head back, after crossing the threshold, to exchange a parting kiss with his young wife.[1] And Faith, as the wife was aptly named, thrust her own pretty head into the street, letting the wind play with the pink ribbons of her cap, while she called to Goodman Brown.

"Dearest heart," whispered she, softly and rather sadly, when her lips were close to his ear, "pr'y thee, put off your journey until sunrise, and sleep in your own bed to-night. A lone woman is troubled with such dreams and such thoughts, that she's afeard of herself, sometimes. Pray, tarry with me this night, dear husband, of all nights in the year!"

"My love and my Faith," replied young Goodman Brown, "of all nights in the year, this one night must I tarry away from thee. My journey, as thou callest it, forth and back again, must needs be done 'twixt now and sunrise. What, my sweet, pretty wife, dost thou doubt me already, and we but three months married!"

"Then, God bless you!" said Faith, with the pink ribbons, "and may you find all well when you come back."

"Amen!" cried Goodman Brown. "Say thy prayers, dear Faith, and go to bed at dusk, and no harm will come to thee."

So they parted; and the young man pursued his way, until, being about to turn the corner by the meeting-house, he looked back, and saw the head of Faith still peeping after him, with a melancholy air, in spite of her pink ribbons.

"Poor little Faith!" thought he, for his heart smote him. "What a wretch am I, to leave her on such an errand! She talks of dreams, too. Methought, as she spoke, there was trouble in her face, as if a dream had warned her what work is to be done to-night. But, no, no! 'twould kill her to think it. Well; she's a blessed angel on earth; and after this one night, I'll cling to her skirts and follow her to Heaven."

---

[1] "Goodman" and "Goodwife" (short form "Goody") were typical forms of address for common people in colonial New England.

First published in the *New England Magazine* in April, 1835. Collected in *Mosses from an Old Manse* in 1846.

With this excellent resolve for the future, Goodman Brown felt himself justified in making more haste on his present evil purpose. He had taken a dreary road, darkened by all the gloomiest trees of the forest, which barely stood aside to let the narrow path creep through, and closed immediately behind. It was all as lonely as could be; and there is this peculiarity in such a solitude, that the traveller knows not who may be concealed by the innumerable trunks and the thick boughs overhead; so that, with lonely footsteps, he may yet be passing through an unseen multitude.

"There may be a devilish Indian behind every tree," said Goodman Brown, to himself; and he glanced fearfully behind him, as he added, "What if the devil himself should be at my very elbow!"

His head being turned back, he passed a crook of the road, and looking forward again, beheld the figure of a man, in grave and decent attire, seated at the foot of an old tree. He arose, at Goodman Brown's approach, and walked onward, side by side with him.

"You are late, Goodman Brown," said he. "The clock of the Old South[2] was striking as I came through Boston; and that is full fifteen minutes agone."

"Faith kept me back awhile," replied the young man, with a tremor in his voice, caused by the sudden appearance of his companion, though not wholly unexpected.

It was now deep dusk in the forest, and deepest in that part of it where these two were journeying. As nearly as could be discerned, the second traveller was about fifty years old, apparently in the same rank of life as Goodman Brown, and bearing a considerable resemblance to him, though perhaps more in expression than features. Still, they might have been taken for father and son. And yet, though the elder person was as simply clad as the younger, and as simple in manner too, he had an indescribable air of one who knew the world, and would not have felt abashed at the governor's dinner-table, or in King William's court, were it possible that his affairs should call him thither. But the only thing about him, that could be fixed upon as remarkable, was his staff, which bore the likeness of a great black snake, so curiously wrought, that it might almost be seen to twist and wriggle itself, like a living serpent. This, of course, must have been an ocular deception, assisted by the uncertain light.

"Come, Goodman Brown!" cried his fellow-traveller, "this is a dull pace for the beginning of a journey. Take my staff, if you are so soon weary."

"Friend," said the other, exchanging his slow pace for a full stop, "having kept covenant by meeting thee here, it is my purpose now to return whence I came. I have scruples, touching the matter thou wot'st[3] of.

---

[2]The Old South Church in Boston, near Salem village.

[3]Knowest

"Sayest thou so?" replied he of the serpent, smiling apart. "Let us walk on, nevertheless, reasoning as we go, and if I convince thee not, thou shalt turn back. We are but a little way in the forest, yet."

"Too far, too far!" exclaimed the goodman, unconsciously resuming his walk. "My father never went into the woods on such an errand, nor his father before him. We have been a race of honest men and good Christians, since the days of the martyrs.[4] And shall I be the first of the name of Brown, that ever took this path, and kept—"

"Such company, thou wouldst say," observed the elder person, interpreting his pause. "Well said, Goodman Brown! I have been as well acquainted with your family as with ever a one among the Puritans; and that's no trifle to say. I helped your grandfather, the constable, when he lashed the Quaker woman so smartly through the streets of Salem. And it was I that brought your father a pitch-pine knot, kindled at my own hearth, to set fire to an Indian village, in King Philip's war.[5] They were my good friends, both; and many a pleasant walk have we had along this path, and returned merrily after midnight. I would fain be friends with you, for their sake."

"If it be as thou sayest," replied Goodman Brown, "I marvel they never spoke of these matters. Or, verily, I marvel not, seeing that the least rumor of the sort would have driven them from New-England. We are a people of prayer, and good works, to boot, and abide no such wickedness."

"Wickedness or not," said the traveller with the twisted staff, "I have a very general acquaintance here in New-England. The deacons of many a church have drunk the communion wine with me; the selectmen, of divers towns, make me their chairman; and a majority of the Great and General Court[6] are firm supporters of my interest. The governor and I, too—but these are state-secrets."

"Can this be so!" cried Goodman Brown, with a stare of amazement at his undisturbed companion. "Howbeit, I have nothing to do with the governor and council; they have their own ways, and are no rule for a simple husbandman,[7] like me. But, were I to go on with thee, how should I meet the eye of that good old man, our minister, at Salem village? Oh, his voice would make me tremble, both Sabbath-day and lecture-day!"[8]

---

[4]Reference to the hundreds of Protestants executed between 1553 and 1558, during the reign of Roman Catholic Queen Mary I (1516–1558), who was known as Bloody Mary.

[5]Public whipping was a punishment for unrepentant Quakers, according to a 1661 Massachusetts law. Wampanoag chief Metacom, known as King Philip, led New England Indians in the King Philip's War against English colonists in 1675 and 1676,

[6]The legislative body of the Massachusetts Bay colony.

[7]Common man

[8]A mid-week day when attendance at a sermon was required.

Thus far, the elder traveller had listened with due gravity, but now burst into a fit of irrepressible mirth, shaking himself so violently, that his snake-like staff actually seemed to wriggle in sympathy.

"Ha! ha! ha!" shouted he, again and again; then composing himself, "Well, go on, Goodman Brown, go on; but pr'y thee, don't kill me with laughing!"

"Well, then, to end the matter at once," said Goodman Brown, considerably nettled, "there is my wife, Faith. It would break her dear little heart; and I'd rather break my own!"

"Nay, if that be the case," answered the other, "e'en go thy ways, Goodman Brown. I would not, for twenty old women like the one hobbling before us, that Faith should come to any harm."

As he spoke, he pointed his staff at a female figure on the path, in whom Goodman Brown recognized a very pious and exemplary dame, who had taught him his catechism, in youth, and was still his moral and spiritual adviser, jointly with the minister and Deacon Gookin.

"A marvel, truly, that Goody Cloyse[9] should be so far in the wilderness, at night-fall!" said he. "But, with your leave, friend, I shall take a cut through the woods, until we have left this Christian woman behind. Being a stranger to you, she might ask whom I was consorting with, and whither I was going."

"Be it so," said his fellow-traveller. "Betake you to the woods, and let me keep the path."

Accordingly, the young man turned aside, but took care to watch his companion, who advanced softly along the road, until he had come within a staff's length of the old dame. She, meanwhile, was making the best of her way, with singular speed for so aged a woman, and mumbling some indistinct words, a prayer, doubtless, as she went. The traveller put forth his staff, and touched her withered neck with what seemed the serpent's tail.

"The devil!" screamed the pious old lady.

"Then Goody Cloyse knows her old friend?" observed the traveller, confronting her, and leaning on his writhing stick.

"Ah, forsooth, and is it your worship, indeed?" cried the good dame. "Yea, truly is it, and in the very image of my old gossip, Goodman Brown, the grandfather of the silly fellow that now is. But—would your worship believe it?—my broomstick hath strangely disappeared, stolen, as I suspect, by that unhanged witch, Goody Cory,[10] and that, too, when I was all anointed with the juice of smallage and cinque-foil and wolf's-bane—"[11]

---

[9]Sarah Cloyse was one of the women sentence to death for witchcraft in 1692; she was not executed.

[10]Martha Corey was hanged as a witch in 1692.

[11]Plants thought to be used by witches.

"Mingled with fine wheat and the fat of a new-born babe," said the shape of old Goodman Brown.

"Ah, your worship knows the receipt," cried the old lady, cackling aloud. "So, as I was saying, being all ready for the meeting, and no horse to ride on, I made up my mind to foot it; for they tell me, there is a nice young man to be taken into communion to-night. But now your good worship will lend me your arm, and we shall be there in a twinkling."

"That can hardly be," answered her friend. "I may not spare you my arm, Goody Cloyse, but here is my staff, if you will."

So saying, he threw it down at her feet, where, perhaps, it assumed life, being one of the rods which its owner had formerly lent to the Egyptian Magi.[12] Of this fact, however, Goodman Brown could not take cognizance. He had cast up his eyes in astonishment, and looking down again, beheld neither Goody Cloyse nor the serpentine staff, but his fellow-traveller alone, who waited for him as calmly as if nothing had happened.

"That old woman taught me my catechism!" said the young man; and there was a world of meaning in this simple comment.

They continued to walk onward, while the elder traveller exhorted his companion to make good speed and persevere in the path, discoursing so aptly, that his arguments seemed rather to spring up in the bosom of his auditor, than to be suggested by himself. As they went, he plucked a branch of maple, to serve for a walking-stick, and began to strip it of the twigs and little boughs, which were wet with evening dew. The moment his fingers touched them, they became strangely withered and dried up, as with a week's sunshine. Thus the pair proceeded, at a good free pace, until suddenly, in a gloomy hollow of the road, Goodman Brown sat himself down on the stump of a tree, and refused to go any farther.

"Friend," said he, stubbornly, "my mind is made up. Not another step will I budge on this errand. What if a wretched old woman do choose to go to the devil, when I thought she was going to Heaven! Is that any reason why I should quit my dear Faith, and go after her?"

"You will think better of this, by-and-by," said his acquaintance, composedly. "Sit here and rest yourself awhile; and when you feel like moving again, there is my staff to help you along."

Without more words, he threw his companion the maple stick, and was as speedily out of sight, as if he had vanished into the deepening gloom. The young man sat a few moments, by the road-side, applauding himself greatly, and thinking with how clear a conscience he should meet the minister, in his morning-walk, nor shrink from the eye of good old Deacon Gookin. And

---

[12]In the Book of Exodus (7:9–12), Egyptian priests transform their rods into serpents.

what calm sleep would be his, that very night, which was to have been spent so wickedly, but purely and sweetly now, in the arms of Faith! Amidst these pleasant and praiseworthy meditations, Goodman Brown heard the tramp of horses along the road, and deemed it advisable to conceal himself within the verge of the forest, conscious of the guilty purpose that had brought him thither, though now so happily turned from it.

On came the hoof-tramps and the voices of the riders, two grave old voices, conversing soberly as they drew near. These mingled sounds appeared to pass along the road, within a few yards of the young man's hiding-place; but owing, doubtless, to the depth of the gloom, at that particular spot, neither the travellers nor their steeds were visible. Though their figures brushed the small boughs by the way-side, it could not be seen that they intercepted, even for a moment, the faint gleam from the strip of bright sky, athwart which they must have passed. Goodman Brown alternately crouched and stood on tip-toe, pulling aside the branches, and thrusting forth his head as far as he durst, without discerning so much as a shadow. It vexed him the more, because he could have sworn, were such a thing possible, that he recognized the voices of the minister and Deacon Gookin, jogging along quietly, as they were wont to do, when bound to some ordination or ecclesiastical council. While yet within hearing, one of the riders stopped to pluck a switch.

"Of the two, reverend Sir," said the voice like the deacon's, "I had rather miss an ordination-dinner than to-night's meeting. They tell me that some of our community are to be here from Falmouth and beyond, and others from Connecticut and Rhode-Island; besides several of the Indian powows,[13] who, after their fashion, know almost as much deviltry as the best of us. Moreover, there is a goodly young woman to be taken into communion."

"Mighty well, Deacon Gookin!" replied the solemn old tones of the minister. "Spur up, or we shall be late. Nothing can be done, you know, until I get on the ground."

The hoofs clattered again, and the voices, talking so strangely in the empty air, passed on through the forest, where no church had ever been gathered, nor solitary Christian prayed. Whither, then, could these holy men be journeying, so deep into the heathen wilderness? Young Goodman Brown caught hold of a tree, for support, being ready to sink down on the ground, faint and over-burthened with the heavy sickness of his heart. He looked up to the sky, doubting whether there really was a Heaven above him. Yet, there was the blue arch, and the stars brightening in it.

"With Heaven above, and Faith below, I will yet stand firm against the devil!" cried Goodman Brown.

---

[13]Medicine men

While he still gazed upward, into the deep arch of the firmament, and had lifted his hands to pray, a cloud, though no wind was stirring, hurried across the zenith, and hid the brightening stars. The blue sky was still visible, except directly overhead, where this black mass of cloud was sweeping swiftly northward. Aloft in the air, as if from the depths of the cloud, came a confused and doubtful sound of voices. Once, the listener fancied that he could distinguish the accents of town's-people of his own, men and women, both pious and ungodly, many of whom he had met at the communion-table, and had seen others rioting at the tavern. The next moment, so indistinct were the sounds, he doubted whether he had heard aught but the murmur of the old forest, whispering without a wind. Then came a stronger swell of those familiar tones, heard daily in the sunshine, at Salem village, but never, until now, from a cloud of night. There was one voice, of a young woman, uttering lamentations, yet with an uncertain sorrow, and entreating for some favor, which, perhaps, it would grieve her to obtain. And all the unseen multitude, both saints and sinners, seemed to encourage her onward.

"Faith!" shouted Goodman Brown, in a voice of agony and desperation; and the echoes of the forest mocked him, crying—"Faith! Faith!" as if bewildered wretches were seeking her, all through the wilderness.

The cry of grief, rage, and terror, was yet piercing the night, when the unhappy husband held his breath for a response. There was a scream, drowned immediately in a louder murmur of voices, fading into far-off laughter, as the dark cloud swept away, leaving the clear and silent sky above Goodman Brown. But something fluttered lightly down through the air, and caught on the branch of a tree. The young man seized it, and beheld a pink ribbon.

"My Faith is gone!" cried he, after one stupefied moment. "There is no good on earth; and sin is but a name. Come, devil! for to thee is this world given."

And maddened with despair, so that he laughed loud and long, did Goodman Brown grasp his staff and set forth again, at such a rate, that he seemed to fly along the forest-path, rather than to walk or run. The road grew wilder and drearier, and more faintly traced, and vanished at length, leaving him in the heart of the dark wilderness, still rushing onward, with the instinct that guides mortal man to evil. The whole forest was peopled with frightful sounds; the creaking of the trees, the howling of wild beasts, and the yell of Indians; while, sometimes, the wind tolled like a distant church-bell, and sometimes gave a broad roar around the traveller, as if all Nature were laughing him to scorn. But he was himself the chief horror of the scene, and shrank not from its other horrors.

"Ha! ha! ha!" roared Goodman Brown, when the wind laughed at him. "Let us hear which will laugh loudest! Think not to frighten me with your deviltry! Come witch, come wizard, come Indian powow, come devil himself! and here comes Goodman Brown. You may as well fear him as he fear you!"

In truth, all through the haunted forest, there could be nothing more frightful than the figure of Goodman Brown. On he flew, among the black pines, brandishing his staff with frenzied gestures, now giving vent to an inspiration of horrid blasphemy, and now shouting forth such laughter, as set all the echoes of the forest laughing like demons around him. The fiend in his own shape is less hideous, than when he rages in the breast of man. Thus sped the demoniac on his course, until, quivering among the trees, he saw a red light before him, as when the felled trunks and branches of a clearing have been set on fire, and throw up their lurid blaze against the sky, at the hour of midnight. He paused, in a lull of the tempest that had driven him onward, and heard the swell of what seemed a hymn, rolling solemnly from a distance, with the weight of many voices. He knew the tune; it was a familiar one in the choir of the village meeting-house. The verse died heavily away, and was lengthened by a chorus, not of human voices, but of all the sounds of the benighted wilderness, pealing in awful harmony together. Goodman Brown cried out; and his cry was lost to his own ear, by its unison with the cry of the desert.

In the interval of silence, he stole forward, until the light glared full upon his eyes. At one extremity of an open space, hemmed in by the dark wall of the forest, arose a rock, bearing some rude, natural resemblance either to an altar or a pulpit, and surrounded by four blazing pines, their tops aflame, their stems untouched, like candles at an evening meeting. The mass of foliage, that had overgrown the summit of the rock, was all on fire, blazing high into the night, and fitfully illuminating the whole field. Each pendent twig and leafy festoon was in a blaze. As the red light arose and fell, a numerous congregation alternately shone forth, then disappeared in shadow, and again grew, as it were, out of the darkness, peopling the heart of the solitary woods at once.

"A grave and dark-clad company!" quoth Goodman Brown.

In truth, they were such. Among them, quivering to-and-fro, between gloom and splendor, appeared faces that would be seen, next day, at the council-board of the province, and others which, Sabbath after Sabbath, looked devoutly heavenward, and benignantly over the crowded pews, from the holiest pulpits in the land. Some affirm, that the lady of the governor was there. At least, there were high dames well known to her, and wives of honored husbands, and widows, a great multitude, and ancient maidens, all of excellent repute, and fair young girls, who trembled, lest their mothers should espy them. Either the sudden gleams of light, flashing over the obscure field, bedazzled Goodman Brown, or he recognized a score of the churchmembers of Salem village, famous for their especial sanctity. Good old Deacon Gookin had arrived, and waited at the skirts of that venerable saint, his revered pastor.

But, irreverently consorting with these grave, reputable, and pious people, these elders of the church, these chaste dames and dewy virgins, there were men of dissolute lives and women of spotted fame, wretches given over to all mean and filthy vice, and suspected even of horrid crimes. It was strange to see, that the good shrank not from the wicked, nor were the sinners abashed by the saints. Scattered, also, among their palefaced enemies, were the Indian priests, or powows, who had often scared their native forest with more hideous incantations than any known to English witchcraft.

"But, where is Faith?" thought Goodman Brown; and, as hope came into his heart, he trembled.

Another verse of the hymn arose, a slow and mournful strain, such as the pious love, but joined to words which expressed all that our nature can conceive of sin, and darkly hinted at far more. Unfathomable to mere mortals is the lore of fiends. Verse after verse was sung, and still the chorus of the desert swelled between, like the deepest tone of a mighty organ. And, with the final peal of that dreadful anthem, there came a sound, as if the roaring wind, the rushing streams, the howling beasts, and every other voice of the unconverted wilderness, were mingling and according with the voice of guilty man, in homage to the prince of all. The four blazing pines threw up a loftier flame, and obscurely discovered shapes and visages of horror on the smokewreaths, above the impious assembly. At the same moment, the fire on the rock shot redly forth, and formed a glowing arch above its base, where now appeared a figure. With reverence be it spoken, the figure bore no slight similitude, both in garb and manner, to some grave divine of the New-England churches.

"Bring forth the converts!" cried a voice, that echoed through the field and rolled into the forest.

At the word, Goodman Brown stept forth from the shadow of the trees, and approached the congregation, with whom he felt a loathful brotherhood, by the sympathy of all that was wicked in his heart. He could have well nigh sworn, that the shape of his own dead father beckoned him to advance, looking downward from a smoke-wreath, while a woman, with dim features of despair, threw out her hand to warn him back. Was it his mother? But he had no power to retreat one step, nor to resist, even in thought, when the minister and good old Deacon Gookin seized his arms, and led him to the blazing rock. Thither came also the slender form of a veiled female, led between Goody Cloyse, that pious teacher of the catechism, and Martha Carrier,[14] who had received the devil's promise to be queen of hell. A rampant hag was she! And there stood the proselytes, beneath the canopy of fire.

---

[14]Hanged as a witch in 1692.

"Welcome, my children," said the dark figure, "to the communion of your race! Ye have found, thus young, your nature and your destiny. My children, look behind you!"

They turned; and flashing forth, as it were, in a sheet of flame, the fiend-worshippers were seen; the smile of welcome gleamed darkly on every visage.

"There," resumed the sable form, "are all whom ye have reverenced from youth. Ye deemed them holier than yourselves, and shrank from your own sin, contrasting it with their lives of righteousness, and prayerful aspirations heavenward. Yet, here are they all, in my worshipping assembly! This night it shall be granted you to know their secret deeds; how hoary-bearded elders of the church have whispered wanton words to the young maids of their households; how many a woman, eager for widow's weeds, has given her husband a drink at bedtime, and let him sleep his last sleep in her bosom; how beardless youths have made haste to inherit their fathers' wealth; and how fair damsels—blush not, sweet ones!—have dug little graves in the garden, and bidden me, the sole guest, to an infant's funeral. By the sympathy of your human hearts for sin, ye shall scent out all the places—whether in church, bed-chamber, street, field, or forest—where crime has been committed, and shall exult to behold the whole earth one stain of guilt, one mighty blood-spot. Far more than this! It shall be yours to penetrate, in every bosom, the deep mystery of sin, the fountain of all wicked arts, and which inexhaustibly supplies more evil impulses than human power—than my power, at its utmost!—can make manifest in deeds. And now, my children, look upon each other."

They did so; and, by the blaze of the hell-kindled torches, the wretched man beheld his Faith, and the wife her husband, trembling before that unhallowed altar.

"Lo! there ye stand, my children," said the figure, in a deep and solemn tone, almost sad, with its despairing awfulness, as if his once angelic nature could yet mourn for our miserable race. "Depending upon one another's hearts, ye had still hoped, that virtue were not all a dream. Now are ye undeceived! Evil is the nature of mankind. Evil must be your only happiness. Welcome, again, my children, to the communion of your race!"

"Welcome!" repeated the fiend-worshippers, in one cry of despair and triumph.

And there they stood, the only pair, as it seemed, who were yet hesitating on the verge of wickedness, in this dark world. A basin was hollowed, naturally, in the rock. Did it contain water, reddened by the lurid light? or was it blood? or, perchance, a liquid flame? Herein did the Shape of Evil dip his hand, and prepare to lay the mark of baptism upon their foreheads, that they might be partakers of the mystery of sin, more conscious of the secret guilt of others, both in deed and thought, than they could now be of their own. The husband cast one look at his pale wife, and Faith at him. What polluted wretches would the next glance shew them to each other, shuddering alike at what they disclosed and what they saw!

"Faith! Faith!" cried the husband. "Look up to Heaven, and resist the Wicked One!"

Whether Faith obeyed, he knew not. Hardly had he spoken, when he found himself amid calm night and solitude, listening to a roar of the wind, which died heavily away through the forest. He staggered against the rock and felt it chill and damp, while a hanging twig, that had been all on fire, besprinkled his cheek with the coldest dew.

The next morning, young Goodman Brown came slowly into the street of Salem village, staring around him like a bewildered man. The good old minister was taking a walk along the grave-yard, to get an appetite for breakfast and meditate his sermon, and bestowed a blessing, as he passed, on Goodman Brown. He shrank from the venerable saint, as if to avoid an anathema. Old Deacon Gookin was at domestic worship, and the holy words of his prayer were heard through the open window. "What God doth the wizard pray to?" quoth Goodman Brown. Goody Cloyse, that excellent old Christian, stood in the early sunshine, at her own lattice, catechising a little girl, who had brought her a pint of morning's milk. Goodman Brown snatched away the child, as from the grasp of the fiend himself. Turning the corner by the meeting-house, he spied the head of Faith, with the pink ribbons, gazing anxiously forth, and bursting into such joy at sight of him, that she skipt along the street, and almost kissed her husband before the whole village. But, Goodman Brown looked sternly and sadly into her face, and passed on without a greeting.

Had Goodman Brown fallen asleep in the forest, and only dreamed a wild dream of a witch-meeting?

Be it so, if you will. But, alas! it was a dream of evil omen for young Goodman Brown. A stern, a sad, a darkly meditative, a distrustful, if not a desperate man, did he become, from the night of that fearful dream. On the Sabbath-day, when the congregation were singing a holy psalm, he could not listen, because an anthem of sin rushed loudly upon his ear, and drowned all the blessed strain. When the minister spoke from the pulpit, with power and fervid eloquence, and, with his hand on the open Bible, of the sacred truths of our religion, and of saint-like lives and triumphant deaths, and of future bliss or misery unutterable, then did Goodman Brown turn pale, dreading, lest the roof should thunder down upon the gray blasphemer and his hearers. Often, awakening suddenly at midnight, he shrank from the bosom of Faith, and at morning or eventide, when the family knelt down at prayer, he scowled, and muttered to himself, and gazed sternly at his wife, and turned away. And when he had lived long, and was borne to his grave, a hoary corpse, followed by Faith, an aged woman, and children and grand-children, a goodly procession, besides neighbors, not a few, they carved no hopeful verse upon his tombstone; for his dying hour was gloom.

[1835]

The Minister's Black Veil

NATHANIEL HAWTHORNE

A Parable[1]

THE SEXTON STOOD IN the porch of Milford meeting-house, pulling lustily at the bell-rope. The old people of the village came stooping along the street. Children, with bright faces, tript merrily beside their parents, or mimicked a graver gait, in the conscious dignity of their Sunday clothes. Spruce bachelors looked sidelong at the pretty maidens, and fancied that the Sabbath sunshine made them prettier than on weekdays. When the throng had mostly streamed into the porch, the sexton began to toll the bell, keeping his eye on the Reverend Mr. Hooper's door. The first glimpse of the clergyman's figure was the signal for the bell to cease its summons.

"But what has good Parson Hooper got upon his face?" cried the sexton in astonishment.

All within hearing immediately turned about, and beheld the semblance of Mr. Hooper, pacing slowly his meditative way towards the meeting-house. With one accord they started, expressing more wonder than if some strange minister were coming to dust the cushions of Mr. Hooper's pulpit.

"Are you sure it is our parson?" inquired Goodman Gray of the sexton.

"Of a certainty it is good Mr. Hooper," replied the sexton. "He was to have exchanged pulpits with Parson Shute of Westbury; but Parson Shute sent to excuse himself yesterday, being to preach a funeral sermon."

The cause of so much amazement may appear sufficiently slight. Mr. Hooper, a gentlemanly person of about thirty, though still a bachelor, was dressed with due clerical neatness, as if a careful wife had starched his band, and brushed the weekly dust from his Sunday's garb. There was but one thing

---

[1]"Another clergyman in New England, Mr. Joseph Moody, of York, Maine, who died about eighty years since, made himself remarkable by the same eccentricity that is here related of the Reverend Mr. Hooper. In his case, however, the symbol had a different import. In early life he had accidentally killed a beloved friend; and from that day till the hour of his own death, he hid his face from men."[Hawthorne's note]

First published in *The Token* in 1836. Collected in *Twice-told Tales* in 1837.

remarkable in his appearance. Swathed about his forehead, and hanging down over his face, so low as to be shaken by his breath, Mr. Hooper had on a black veil. On a nearer view, it seemed to consist of two folds of crape, which entirely concealed his features, except the mouth and chin, but probably did not intercept his sight, farther than to give a darkened aspect to all living and inanimate things. With this gloomy shade before him, good Mr. Hooper walked onward, at a slow and quiet pace, stooping somewhat and looking on the ground, as is customary with abstracted men, yet nodding kindly to those of his parishioners who still waited on the meeting-house steps. But so wonder-struck were they, that his greeting hardly met with a return.

"I can't really feel as if good Mr. Hooper's face was behind that piece of crape," said the sexton.

"I don't like it," muttered an old woman, as she hobbled into the meeting-house. "He has changed himself into something awful, only by hiding his face."

"Our parson has gone mad!" cried Goodman Gray, following him across the threshold.

A rumor of some unaccountable phenomenon had preceded Mr. Hooper into the meeting-house, and set all the congregation astir. Few could refrain from twisting their heads towards the door; many stood upright, and turned directly about; while several little boys clambered upon the seats, and came down again with a terrible racket. There was a general bustle, a rustling of the women's gowns and shuffling of the men's feet, greatly at variance with that hushed repose which should attend the entrance of the minister. But Mr. Hooper appeared not to notice the perturbation of his people. He entered with an almost noiseless step, bent his head mildly to the pews on each side, and bowed as he passed his oldest parishioner, a white-haired great-grandsire, who occupied an arm-chair in the centre of the aisle. It was strange to observe, how slowly this venerable man became conscious of something singular in the appearance of his pastor. He seemed not fully to partake of the prevailing wonder, till Mr. Hooper had ascended the stairs, and showed himself in the pulpit, face to face with his congregation, except for the black veil. That mysterious emblem was never once withdrawn. It shook with his measured breath as he gave out the psalm; it threw its obscurity between him and the holy page, as he read the Scriptures; and while he prayed, the veil lay heavily on his uplifted countenance. Did he seek to hide it from the dread Being whom he was addressing?

Such was the effect of this simple piece of crape, that more than one woman of delicate nerves was forced to leave the meeting-house. Yet perhaps the pale-faced congregation was almost as fearful a sight to the minister, as his black veil to them.

Mr. Hooper had the reputation of a good preacher, but not an energetic one: he strove to win his people heavenward, by mild persuasive influences, rather than to drive them thither, by the thunders of the Word. The sermon which he now delivered, was marked by the same characteristics of style and manner, as the general series of his pulpit oratory. But there was something, either in the sentiment of the discourse itself, or in the imagination of the auditors, which made it greatly the most powerful effort that they had ever heard from their pastor's lips. It was tinged, rather more darkly than usual, with the gentle gloom of Mr. Hooper's temperament. The subject had reference to secret sin, and those sad mysteries which we hide from our nearest and dearest, and would fain conceal from our own consciousness, even forgetting that the Omniscient can detect them. A subtle power was breathed into his words. Each member of the congregation, the most innocent girl, and the man of hardened breast, felt as if the preacher had crept upon them, behind his awful veil, and discovered their boarded iniquity of deed or thought. Many spread their clasped hands on their bosoms. There was nothing terrible in what Mr. Hooper said; at least, no violence; and yet, with every tremor of his melancholy voice, the hearers quaked. An unsought pathos came hand in hand with awe. So sensible were the audience of some unwonted attribute in their minister, that they longed for a breath of wind to blow aside the veil, almost believing that a stranger's visage would be discovered; though the form, gesture, and voice were those of Mr. Hooper.

At the close of the services, the people hurried out with indecorous confusion, eager to communicate their pent-up amazement, and conscious of lighter spirits, the moment they lost sight of the black veil. Some gathered in little circles, huddled closely together, with their mouths all whispering in the centre; some went homeward alone, wrapt in silent meditation; some talked loudly, and profaned the Sabbath-day with ostentatious laughter. A few shook their sagacious heads, intimating that they could penetrate the mystery; while one or two affirmed that there was no mystery at all, but only that Mr. Hooper's eyes were so weakened by the midnight lamp, as to require a shade. After a brief interval, forth came good Mr. Hooper also, in the rear of his flock. Turning his veiled face from one group to another, he paid due reverence to the hoary heads, saluted the middle-aged with kind dignity, as their friend and spiritual guide, greeted the young with mingled authority and love, and laid his hands on the little children's heads to bless them. Such was always his custom on the Sabbath-day. Strange and bewildered looks repaid him for his courtesy. None, as on former occasions, aspired to the honor of walking by their pastor's side. Old Squire Saunders, doubtless by an accidental lapse of memory, neglected to invite Mr. Hooper to his table, where the good clergyman had been wont to bless the food, almost every Sunday since his settlement. He returned, therefore, to the parsonage, and, at the moment of closing the door, was observed to look back upon the people, all of whom had their eyes fixed upon the minister. A sad smile gleamed faintly from beneath the black veil, and flickered about his mouth, glimmering as he disappeared.

"How strange," said a lady, "that a simple black veil, such as any woman might wear on her bonnet, should become such a terrible thing on Mr. Hooper's face!"

"Something must surely be amiss with Mr. Hooper's intellects," observed her husband, the physician of the village. "But the strangest part of the affair is the effect of this vagary, even on a sober-minded man like myself. The black veil, though it covers only our pastor's face, throws its influence over his whole person, and makes him ghost-like from head to foot. Do you not feel it so?"

"Truly do I," replied the lady; "and I would not be alone with him for the world. I wonder he is not afraid to be alone with himself!"

"Men sometimes are so," said her husband.

The afternoon service was attended with similar circumstances. At its conclusion, the bell tolled for the funeral of a young lady. The relatives and friends were assembled in the house, and the more distant acquaintances stood about the door, speaking of the good qualities of the deceased, when their talk was interrupted by the appearance of Mr. Hooper, still covered with his black veil. It was now an appropriate emblem. The clergyman stepped into the room where the corpse was laid, and bent over the coffin, to take a last farewell of his deceased parishioner. As he stooped, the veil hung straight down from his forehead, so that, if her eye-lids had not been closed for ever, the dead maiden might have seen his face. Could Mr. Hooper be fearful of her glance, that he so hastily caught back the black veil? A person, who watched the interview between the dead and living, scrupled not to affirm, that, at the instant when the clergyman's features were disclosed, the corpse had slightly shuddered, rustling the shroud and muslin cap, though the countenance retained the composure of death. A superstitious old woman was the only witness of this prodigy. From the coffin, Mr. Hooper passed into the chamber of the mourners, and thence to the head of the staircase, to make the funeral prayer. It was a tender and heart-dissolving prayer, full of sorrow, yet so imbued with celestial hopes, that the music of a heavenly harp, swept by the fingers of the dead, seemed faintly to be heard among the saddest accents of the minister. The people trembled, though they but darkly understood him, when he prayed that they, and himself, and all of mortal race, might be ready, as he trusted this young maiden had been, for the dreadful hour that should snatch the veil from their faces. The bearers went heavily forth, and the mourners followed, saddening all the street, with the dead before them, and Mr. Hooper in his black veil behind.

"Why do you look back?" said one in the procession to his partner.

"I had a fancy," replied she, "that the minister and the maiden's spirit were walking hand in hand."

"And so had I, at the same moment," said the other.

That night, the handsomest couple in Milford village were to be joined in wedlock. Though reckoned a melancholy man, Mr. Hooper had a placid cheerfulness for such occasions, which often excited a sympathetic smile, where livelier merriment would have been thrown away. There was no quality of his disposition which made him more beloved than this. The company at the wedding awaited his arrival with impatience, trusting that the strange awe, which had gathered over him throughout the day, would now be dispelled. But such was not the result. When Mr. Hooper came, the first thing that their eyes rested on was the same horrible black veil, which had added deeper gloom to the funeral, and could portend nothing but evil to the wedding. Such was its immediate effect on the guests, that a cloud seemed to have rolled duskily from beneath the black crape, and dimmed the light of the candles. The bridal pair stood up before the minister. But the bride's cold fingers quivered in the tremulous hand of the bridegroom, and her deathlike paleness caused a whisper, that the maiden who had been buried a few hours before, was come from her grave to be married. If ever another wedding were so dismal, it was that famous one, where they tolled the wedding-knell[2]. After performing the ceremony, Mr. Hooper raised a glass of wine to his lips, wishing happiness to the new-married couple, in a strain of mild pleasantry that ought to have brightened the features of the guests, like a cheerful gleam from the hearth. At that instant, catching a glimpse of his figure in the looking-glass, the black veil involved his own spirit in the horror with which it overwhelmed all others. His frame shuddered—his lips grew white—he spilt the untasted wine upon the carpet—and rushed forth into the darkness. For the Earth, too, had on her Black Veil.

The next day, the whole village of Milford talked of little else than Parson Hooper's black veil. That, and the mystery concealed behind it, supplied a topic for discussion between acquaintances meeting in the street, and good women gossiping at their open windows. It was the first item of news that the tavern-keeper told to his guests. The children babbled of it on their way to school. One imitative little imp covered his face with an old black handkerchief, thereby so affrighting his playmates, that the panic seized himself, and he well nigh lost his wits by his own waggery.

It was remarkable, that, of all the busy-bodies and impertinent people in the parish, not one ventured to put the plain question to Mr. Hooper,

---

[2]A reference to Hawthorne's story "The Wedding-Knell," published in the same year as "The Minister's Black Veil."

wherefore he did this thing. Hitherto, whenever there appeared the slightest call for such interference, he had never lacked advisers, nor shown himself averse to be guided by their judgment. If he erred at all, it was by so painful a degree of self-distrust, that even the mildest censure would lead him to consider an indifferent action as a crime. Yet, though so well acquainted with this amiable weakness, no individual among his parishioners chose to make the black veil a subject of friendly remonstrance. There was a feeling of dread, neither plainly confessed nor carefully concealed, which caused each to shift the responsibility upon another, till at length it was found expedient to send a deputation of the church, in order to deal with Mr. Hooper about the mystery, before it should grow into a scandal. Never did an embassy so ill discharge its duties. The minister received them with friendly courtesy, but became silent, after they were seated, leaving to his visiters the whole burthen of introducing their important business. The topic, it might be supposed, was obvious enough. There was the black veil, swathed round Mr. Hooper's forehead, and concealing every feature above his placid mouth, on which, at times, they could perceive the glimmering of a melancholy smile. But that piece of crape, to their imagination, seemed to hang down before his heart, the symbol of a fearful secret between him and them. Were the veil but cast aside, they might speak freely of it, but not, till then. Thus they sat a considerable time, speechless, confused, and shrinking uneasily from Mr. Hooper's eye, which they felt to be fixed upon them with an invisible glance. Finally, the deputies returned abashed to their constituents, pronouncing the matter too weighty to be handled, except by a council of the churches, if, indeed, it might not require a general synod.

But there was one person in the village, unappalled by the awe with which the black veil had impressed all beside herself. When the deputies returned without an explanation, or even venturing to demand one, she, with the calm energy of her character, determined to chase away the strange cloud that appeared to be settling round Mr. Hooper, every moment more darkly than before. As his plighted wife, it should be her privilege to know what the black veil concealed. At the minister's first visit, therefore, she entered upon the subject, with a direct simplicity, which made the task easier both for him and her. After he had seated himself, she fixed her eyes steadfastly upon the veil, but could discern nothing of the dreadful gloom that had so overawed the multitude: it was but a double fold of crape, hanging down from his forehead to his mouth, and slightly stirring with his breath.

"No," said she aloud, and smiling, "there is nothing terrible in this piece of crape, except that it hides a face which I am always glad to look upon. Come, good sir, let the sun shine from behind the cloud. First lay aside your black veil: then tell me why you put it on."

Mr. Hooper's smile glimmered faintly.

"There is an hour to come," said he, "when all of us shall cast aside our veils. Take it not amiss, beloved friend, if I wear this piece of crape till then."

"Your words are a mystery too," returned the young lady. "Take away the veil from them, at least."

"Elizabeth, I will," said he, "so far as my vow may suffer me. Know, then, this veil is a type and a symbol, and I am bound to wear it ever, both in light and darkness, in solitude and before the gaze of multitudes, and as with strangers, so with my familiar friends. No mortal eye will see it withdrawn. This dismal shade must separate me from the world: even you, Elizabeth, can never come behind it!"

"What grievous affliction hath befallen you," she earnestly inquired, "that you should thus darken your eyes for ever?"

"If it be a sign of mourning," replied Mr. Hooper, "I, perhaps, like most other mortals, have sorrows dark enough to be typified by a black veil."

"But what if the world will not believe that it is the type of an innocent sorrow?" urged Elizabeth. "Beloved and respected as you are, there may be whispers, that you hide your face under the consciousness of secret sin. For the sake of your holy office, do away this scandal!"

The color rose into her cheeks, as she intimated the nature of the rumors that were already abroad in the village. But Mr. Hooper's mildness did not forsake him. He even smiled again—that same sad smile, which always appeared like a faint glimmering of light, proceeding from the obscurity beneath the veil.

"If I hide my face for sorrow, there is cause enough," he merely replied; "and if I cover it for secret sin, what mortal might not do the same?"

And with this gentle, but unconquerable obstinacy, did he resist all her entreaties. At length Elizabeth sat silent. For a few moments she appeared lost in thought, considering, probably, what new methods might be tried, to withdraw her lover from so dark a fantasy, which, if it had no other meaning, was perhaps a symptom of mental disease. Though of a firmer character than his own, the tears rolled down her cheeks. But, in an instant, as it were, a new feeling took the place of sorrow: her eyes were fixed insensibly on the black veil, when, like a sudden twilight in the air, its terrors fell around her. She arose, and stood trembling before him.

"And do you feel it then at last?" said he mournfully.

She made no reply, but covered her eyes with her hand, and turned to leave the room. He rushed forward and caught her arm.

"Have patience with me, Elizabeth!" cried he passionately. "Do not desert me, though this veil must be between us here on earth. Be mine, and hereafter there shall be no veil over my face, no darkness between our souls! It is but a mortal veil—it is not for eternity! Oh! you know not how lonely I am, and how frightened to be alone behind my black veil. Do not leave me in this miserable obscurity for ever!"

"Lift the veil but once, and look me in the face," said she.

"Never! It cannot be!" replied Mr. Hooper.

"Then, farewell!" said Elizabeth.

She withdrew her arm from his grasp, and slowly departed, pausing at the door, to give one long, shuddering gaze, that seemed almost to penetrate the mystery of the black veil. But, even amid his grief, Mr. Hooper smiled to think that only a material emblem had separated him from happiness, though the horrors which it shadowed forth, must be drawn darkly between the fondest of lovers.

From that time no attempts were made to remove Mr. Hooper's black veil, or, by a direct appeal, to discover the secret which it was supposed to hide. By persons who claimed a superiority to popular prejudice, it was reckoned merely an eccentric whim, such as often mingles with the sober actions of men otherwise rational, and tinges them all with its own semblance of insanity. But with the multitude, good Mr. Hooper was irreparably a bugbear. He could not walk the streets with any peace of mind, so conscious was he that the gentle and timid would turn aside to avoid him, and that others would make it a point of hardihood to throw themselves in his way. The impertinence of the latter class compelled him to give up his customary walk, at sunset, to the burial ground; for when he leaned pensively over the gate, there would always be faces behind the grave-stones, peeping at his black veil. A fable went the rounds, that the stare of the dead people drove him thence. It grieved him, to the very depth of his kind heart, to observe how the children fled from his approach, breaking up their merriest sports, while his melancholy figure was yet afar off. Their instinctive dread caused him to feel, more strongly than aught else, that a preternatural horror was interwoven with the threads of the black crape. In truth, his own antipathy to the veil was known to be so great, that he never willingly passed before a mirror, nor stooped to drink at a still fountain, lest, in its peaceful bosom, he should be affrighted by himself. This was what gave plausibility to the whispers, that Mr. Hooper's conscience tortured him for some great crime, too horrible to be entirely concealed, or otherwise than so obscurely intimated. Thus, from beneath the black veil, there rolled a cloud into the sunshine, an ambiguity of sin or sorrow, which enveloped the poor minister, so that love or sympathy could never reach him. It was said, that ghost and fiend consorted with him there. With self-shudderings and outward terrors, he walked continually in its shadow, groping darkly within his own soul, or gazing through a medium that saddened the whole world. Even the lawless wind, it was believed, respected his dreadful secret, and never blew aside the veil. But still good Mr. Hooper sadly smiled, at the pale visages of the worldly throng as he passed by.

Among all its bad influences, the black veil had the one desirable effect, of making its wearer a very efficient clergyman. By the aid of his mysterious emblem—for there was no other apparent cause—he became a man of awful power, over souls that were in agony for sin. His converts always regarded him with a dread peculiar to themselves, affirming, though but figuratively, that, before he brought them to celestial light, they had been with him behind the black veil. Its gloom, indeed, enabled him to sympathize with all dark affections. Dying sinners cried aloud for Mr. Hooper, and would not yield their breath till he appeared; though ever, as he stooped to whisper consolation, they shuddered at the veiled face so near their own. Such were the terrors of the black veil, even when Death had bared his visage! Strangers came long distances to attend service at his church, with the mere idle purpose of gazing at his figure, because it was forbidden them to behold his face. But many were made to quake ere they departed! Once, during Governor Belcher's administration, Mr. Hooper was appointed to preach the election sermon.[3] Covered with his black veil, he stood before the chief magistrate, the council, and the representatives, and wrought so deep an impression, that the legislative measures of that year, were characterized by all the gloom and piety of our earliest ancestral sway.

In this manner Mr. Hooper spent a long life, irreproachable in outward act, yet shrouded in dismal suspicions; kind and loving, though unloved, and dimly feared; a man apart from men, shunned in their health and joy, but ever summoned to their aid in mortal anguish. As years wore on, shedding their snows above his sable veil, he acquired a name throughout the New-England churches, and they called him Father Hooper. Nearly all his parishioners, who were of mature age when he was settled, had been borne away by many a funeral: he had one congregation in the church, and a more crowded one in the church-yard; and having wrought so late into the evening, and done his work so well, it was now good Father Hooper's turn to rest.

Several persons were visible by the shaded candlelight, in the death-chamber of the old clergyman. Natural connections he had none. But there was the decorously grave, though unmoved physician, seeking only to mitigate the last pangs of the patient whom he could not save. There were the deacons, and other eminently pious members of his church. There, also, was the Reverend Mr. Clark, of Westbury, a young and zealous divine, who had ridden

---

[3]Jonathan Belcher (1681–1757) served as governor of Massachusestts and New Hampshire from 1730 to 1741. At the time it was considered an honor for a clergyman to be selected to preach the election sermon on inauguration day.

in haste to pray by the bed-side of the expiring minister. There was the nurse, no hired handmaiden of death, but one whose calm affection had endured thus long, in secresy, in solitude, amid the chill of age, and would not perish, even at the dying hour. Who, but Elizabeth! And there lay the hoary head of good Father Hooper upon the death-pillow, with the black veil still swathed about his brow and reaching down over his face, so that each more difficult gasp of his faint breath caused it to stir. All through life that piece of crape had hung between him and the world: it had separated him from cheerful brotherhood and woman's love, and kept him in that saddest of all prisons, his own heart; and still it lay upon his face, as if to deepen the gloom of his darksome chamber, and shade him from the sunshine of eternity.

For some time previous, his mind had been confused, wavering doubtfully between the past and the present, and hovering forward, as it were, at intervals, into the indistinctness of the world to come. There had been feverish turns, which tossed him from side to side, and wore away what little strength he had. But in his most convulsive struggles, and in the wildest vagaries of his intellect, when no other thought retained its sober influence, he still showed an awful solicitude lest the black veil should slip aside. Even if his bewildered soul could have forgotten, there was a faithful woman at his pillow, who, with averted eyes, would have covered that aged face, which she had last beheld in the comeliness of manhood. At length the death-stricken old man lay quietly in the torpor of mental and bodily exhaustion, with an imperceptible pulse, and breath that grew fainter and fainter, except when a long, deep, and irregular inspiration seemed to prelude the flight of his spirit.

The minister of Westbury approached the bedside.

"Venerable Father Hooper," said he, "the moment of your release is at hand. Are you ready for the lifting of the veil, that shuts in time from eternity?"

Father Hooper at first replied merely by a feeble motion of his head; then, apprehensive, perhaps, that his meaning might be doubtful, he exerted himself to speak.

"Yea," said he, in faint accents, "my soul hath a patient weariness until that veil be lifted."

"And is it fitting," resumed the Reverend Mr. Clark, "that a man so given to prayer, of such a blameless example, holy in deed and thought, so far as mortal judgment may pronounce; is it fitting that a father in the church should leave a shadow on his memory, that may seem to blacken a life so pure? I pray you, my venerable brother, let not this thing be! Suffer us to be gladdened by your triumphant aspect, as you go to your reward. Before the veil of eternity be lifted, let me cast aside this black veil from your face!"

And thus speaking, the Reverend Mr. Clark bent forward to reveal the mystery of so many years. But, exerting a sudden energy, that made all the beholders stand aghast, Father Hooper snatched both his hands from beneath the bed-clothes, and pressed them strongly on the black veil, resolute to struggle, if the minister of Westbury would contend with a dying man.

"Never!" cried the veiled clergyman. "On earth, never!"

"Dark old man!" exclaimed the affrighted minister, "with what horrible crime upon your soul are you now passing to the judgment?"

Father Hooper's breath heaved; it rattled in his throat; but, with a mighty effort, grasping forward with his hands, he caught hold of life, and held it back till he should speak. He even raised himself in bed; and there he sat, shivering with the arms of death around him, while the black veil hung down, awful, at that last moment, in the gathered terrors of a life-time. And yet the faint, sad smile, so often there, now seemed to glimmer from its obscurity, and linger on Father Hooper's lips.

"Why do you tremble at me alone?" cried he, turning his veiled face round the circle of pale spectators. "Tremble also at each other! Have men avoided me, and women shown no pity, and children screamed and fled, only for my black veil? What, but the mystery which it obscurely typifies, has made this piece of crape so awful? When the friend shows his inmost heart to his friend; the lover to his best-beloved; when man does not vainly shrink from the eye of his Creator, loathsomely treasuring up the secret of his sin; then deem me a monster, for the symbol beneath which I have lived, and die! I look around me, and, lo! on every visage a Black Veil!"

While his auditors shrank from one another, in mutual affright, Father Hooper fell back upon his pillow, a veiled corpse, with a faint smile lingering on the lips. Still veiled, they laid him in his coffin, and a veiled corpse they bore him to the grave. The grass of many years has sprung up and withered on that grave, the burial-stone is moss-grown, and good Mr. Hooper's face is dust; but awful is still the thought, that it mouldered beneath the Black Veil!

[1836]

Rappaccini's Daughter

NATHANIEL HAWTHORNE

WE DO NOT REMEMBER to have seen any translated specimens of the productions of M. de l'Aubépine—a fact the less to be wondered at, as his very name is unknown to many of his own countrymen as well as to the student of foreign literature. As a writer, he seems to occupy an unfortunate position between the Transcendentalists (who, under one name or another, have their share in all the current literature of the world) and the great body of pen-and-ink men who address the intellect and sympathies of the multitude. If not too refined, at all events too remote, too shadowy, and unsubstanial in his modes of development to suit the taste of the latter class, and yet too popular to satisfy the spiritual or metaphysical requisitions of the former, he must necessarily find himself without an audience, except here and there an individual or possibly an isolated clique. His writings, to do them justice, are not altogether destitute of fancy and originality; they might have won him greater reputation but for an inveterate love of allegory, which is apt to invest his plots and characters with the aspect of scenery and people in the clouds, and to steal away the human warmth out of his conceptions. His fictions are sometimes historical, sometimes of the present day, and sometimes, so far as can be discovered, have little or no reference either to time or space. In any case, he generally contents himself with a very slight embroidery of outward manners—the faintest possible counterfeit of real life,—and endeavors to create an interest by some less obvious peculiarity of the subject. Occasionally a breath of Nature, a raindrop of pathos and tenderness, or a gleam of humor, will find its way into the midst of his fantastic imagery, and make us feel as if, after all, we were yet within the limits of our native earth. We will only add to this very cursory notice that M. de l'Aubépine's productions, if the reader chance to take them in precisely the proper point of view, may amuse a leisure hour as well as those of a brighter man; if otherwise, they can hardly fail to look excessively like nonsense.

Our author is voluminous; he continues to write and publish with as much praiseworthy and indefatigable prolixity as if his efforts were crowned with the brilliant success that so justly attends those of Eugene Sue. His first appearance was by a collection of stories in a long series of volumes entitled

---

First published in *The United States Magazine* and *Democratic Review* in December, 1844. Collected in *Mosses from an Old Manse* in 1846.

"Contes deux fois racontées." The titles of some of his more recent works (we quote from memory) are as follows: "Le Voyage Céleste à Chemin de Fer," 3 tom., 1838; "Le nouveau Père Adam et la nouvelle Mère Eve," 2 tom., 1839; "Roderic; ou le Serpent a l'estomac," 2 tom., 1840; "Le Culte du Feu," a folio volume of ponderous research into the religion and ritual of the old Persian Ghebers, published in 1841; "La Soirée du Chateau en Espagne," 1 tom., 8vo, 1842; and "L'Artiste du Beau; ou le Papillon Mécanique," 5 tom., 4to, 1843. Our somewhat wearisome perusal of this startling catalogue of volumes has left behind it a certain personal affection and sympathy, though by no means admiration, for M. de l'Aubépine; and we would fain do the little in our power towards introducing him favorably to the American public. The ensuing tale is a translation of his "Beatrice; ou la Belle Empoisonneuse," recently published in "La Revue Anti-Aristocratique." This journal, edited by the Comte de Bearhaven, has for some years past led the defense of liberal principles and popular rights with faithfulness and ability worthy of all praise.[1]

A young man, named Giovanni Guasconti, came, very long ago, from the more southern region of Italy, to pursue his studies at the University of Padua. Giovanni, who had but a scanty supply of gold ducats in his pocket, took lodgings in a high and gloomy chamber of an old edifice which looked not unworthy to have been the palace of a Paduan noble, and which, in fact, exhibited over its entrance the armorial bearings of a family long since extinct. The young stranger, who was not unstudied in the great poem of his country, recollected that one of the ancestors of this family, and perhaps an occupant of this very mansion, had been pictured by Dante as a partaker of the immortal agonies of his Inferno.[2] These reminiscences and associations, together with the tendency to heartbreak natural to a young man for the first time out of his native sphere, caused Giovanni to sigh heavily as he looked around the desolate and ill-furnished apartment.

"Holy Virgin, signor!" cried old Dame Lisabetta, who, won by the youth's remarkable beauty of person, was kindly endeavoring to give the chamber a habitable air, "what a sigh was that to come out of a young man's heart! Do

---

[1] In this introduction, Hawthorne pokes fun at himself. "Aubepine" is the French word for "hawthorn," and the titles listed are French translations of Hawthorne's own work, including "Twice-told Tales"; "The Celestial Rail-Road"; "The New Adam and Eve"; "Egotism, or The Bosom Serpent"; "The Cult of Fire"; "Evening in a Spanish Castle"; and "The Artist of the Beautiful, or The Mechanical Butterfly." The story "Beatrice, or the Beautiful Poisoner" is supposed to have appeared in the fictional *The Anti-Aristocratic Review*, edited by the fictional Compte de Bearhaven.

[2] In "The Inferno," the first of *The Divine Comedy* by Italian poet Dante Alighieri (1265–1321), various historical figures from medieval Italy endure the horrors of Hell. The figure who leads Dante from Hell, through Purgatory, and finally into Heaven is named Beatrice.

you find this old mansion gloomy? For the love of Heaven, then, put your head out of the window, and you will see as bright sunshine as you have left in Naples."

Guasconti mechanically did as the old woman advised, but could not quite agree with her that the Paduan sunshine was as cheerful as that of southern Italy. Such as it was, however, it fell upon a garden beneath the window and expended its fostering influences on a variety of plants, which seemed to have been cultivated with exceeding care.

"Does this garden belong to the house?" asked Giovanni.

"Heaven forbid, signor, unless it were fruitful of better pot herbs than any that grow there now," answered old Lisabetta. "No; that garden is cultivated by the own hands of Signor Giacomo Rappaccini, the famous doctor, who, I warrant him, has been heard of as far as Naples. It is said that he distils these plants into medicines that are as potent as a charm. Oftentimes you may see the signor doctor at work, and perchance the signora, his daughter, too, gathering the strange flowers that grow in the garden."

The old woman had now done what she could for the aspect of the chamber; and, commending the young man to the protection of the saints, took her departure.

Giovanni still found no better occupation than to look down into the garden beneath his window. From its appearance, he judged it to be one of those botanic gardens which were of earlier date in Padua than elsewhere in Italy or in the world. Or, not improbably, it might once have been the pleasure-place of an opulent family; for there was the ruin of a marble fountain in the center, sculptured with rare art, but so wofully shattered that it was impossible to trace the original design from the chaos of remaining fragments. The water, however, continued to gush and sparkle into the sunbeams as cheerfully as ever. A little gurgling sound ascended to the young man's window, and made him feel as if the fountain were an immortal spirit that sung its song unceasingly and without heeding the vicissitudes around it, while one century imbodied it in marble and another scattered the perishable garniture on the soil. All about the pool into which the water subsided grew various plants, that seemed to require a plentiful supply of moisture for the nourishment of gigantic leaves, and in some instances, flowers gorgeously magnificent. There was one shrub in particular, set in a marble vase in the midst of the pool, that bore a profusion of purple blossoms, each of which had the lustre and richness of a gem; and the whole together made a show so resplendent that it seemed enough to illuminate the garden, even had there been no sunshine. Every portion of the soil was peopled with plants and herbs, which, if less beautiful, still bore tokens of assiduous care, as if all had their individual virtues, known to the scientific mind that fostered them. Some were placed in urns, rich with old carving, and others in common garden pots; some crept serpent-like along the ground or climbed on high, using whatever means of ascent was offered them. One plant had wreathed itself round a statue of Vertumnus,[3] which was thus quite veiled and shrouded in a drapery of hanging foliage, so happily arranged that it might have served a sculptor for a study.

While Giovanni stood at the window he heard a rustling behind a screen of leaves, and became aware that a person was at work in the garden. His figure soon emerged into view, and showed itself to be that of no common laborer, but a tall, emaciated, sallow, and sickly-looking man, dressed in a scholar's garb of black. He was beyond the middle term of life, with gray hair, a thin, gray beard, and a face singularly marked with intellect and cultivation, but which could never, even in his more youthful days, have expressed much warmth of heart.

Nothing could exceed the intentness with which this scientific gardener examined every shrub which grew in his path: it seemed as if he was looking into their inmost nature, making observations in regard to their creative essence, and discovering why one leaf grew in this shape and another in that, and wherefore such and such flowers differed among themselves in hue and perfume. Nevertheless, in spite of this deep intelligence on his part, there was no approach to intimacy between himself and these vegetable existences. On the contrary, he avoided their actual touch or the direct inhaling of their odors with a caution that impressed Giovanni most disagreeably; for the man's demeanor was that of one walking among malignant influences, such as savage beasts, or deadly snakes, or evil spirits, which, should he allow them one moment of license, would wreak upon him some terrible fatality. It was strangely frightful to the young man's imagination to see this air of insecurity in a person cultivating a garden, that most simple and innocent of human toils, and which had been alike the joy and labor of the unfallen parents of the race. Was this garden, then, the Eden of the present world? And this man, with such a perception of harm in what his own hands caused to grow,—was he the Adam?

The distrustful gardener, while plucking away the dead leaves or pruning the too luxuriant growth of the shrubs, defended his hands with a pair of thick gloves. Nor were these his only armor. When, in his walk through the garden, he came to the magnificent plant that hung its purple gems beside the marble fountain, he placed a kind of mask over his mouth and nostrils, as if all this beauty did but conceal a deadlier malice; but, finding his task still too dangerous, he drew back, removed the mask, and called loudly, but in the infirm voice of a person affected with inward disease,—

---

[3]Roman god of seasons and patron of gardens.

"Beatrice! Beatrice!"

"Here am I, my father. What would you?" cried a rich and youthful voice from the window of the opposite house—a voice as rich as a tropical sunset, and which made Giovanni, though he knew not why, think of deep hues of purple or crimson and of perfumes heavily delectable. "Are you in the garden?"

"Yes, Beatrice," answered the gardener, "and I need your help."

Soon there emerged from under a sculptured portal the figure of a young girl, arrayed with as much richness of taste as the most splendid of the flowers, beautiful as the day, and with a bloom so deep and vivid that one shade more would have been too much. She looked redundant with life, health, and energy; all of which attributes were bound down and compressed, as it were, and girdled tensely, in their luxuriance, by her virgin zone. Yet Giovanni's fancy must have grown morbid while he looked down into the garden; for the impression which the fair stranger made upon him was as if here were another flower, the human sister of those vegetable ones, as beautiful as they, more beautiful than the richest of them, but still to be touched only with a glove, nor to be approached without a mask. As Beatrice came down the garden path, it was observable that she handled and inhaled the odor of several of the plants which her father had most sedulously avoided.

"Here, Beatrice," said the latter, "see how many needful offices require to be done to our chief treasure. Yet, shattered as I am, my life might pay the penalty of approaching it so closely as circumstances demand. Henceforth, I fear, this plant must be consigned to your sole charge."

"And gladly will I undertake it," cried again the rich tones of the young lady, as she bent towards the magnificent plant and opened her arms as if to embrace it. "Yes, my sister, my splendor, it shall be Beatrice's task to nurse and serve thee; and thou shalt reward her with thy kisses and perfumed breath, which to her is as the breath of life."

Then, with all the tenderness in her manner that was so strikingly expressed in her words, she busied herself with such attentions as the plant seemed to require; and Giovanni, at his lofty window, rubbed his eyes and almost doubted whether it were a girl tending her favorite flower, or one sister performing the duties of affection to another. The scene soon terminated. Whether Dr. Rappaccini had finished his labors in the garden, or that his watchful eye had caught the stranger's face, he now took his daughter's arm and retired. Night was already closing in; oppressive exhalations seemed to proceed from the plants and steal upward past the open window; and Giovanni, closing the lattice, went to his couch and dreamed of a rich flower and beautiful girl. Flower and maiden were different, and yet the same, and fraught with some strange peril in either shape.

But there is an influence in the light of morning that tends to rectify whatever errors of fancy, or even of judgment, we may have incurred during the sun's decline, or among the shadows of the night, or in the less wholesome glow of moonshine. Giovanni's first movement, on starting from sleep, was to throw open the window and gaze down into the garden which his dreams had made so fertile of mysteries. He was surprised and a little ashamed to find how real and matter-of-fact an affair it proved to be, in the first rays of the sun which gilded the dew-drops that hung upon leaf and blossom, and, while giving a brighter beauty to each rare flower, brought everything within the limits of ordinary experience. The young man rejoiced that, in the heart of the barren city, he had the privilege of overlooking this spot of lovely and luxuriant vegetation. It would serve, he said to himself, as a symbolic language to keep him in communion with Nature. Neither the sickly and thoughtworn Dr. Giacomo Rappaccini, it is true, nor his brilliant daughter, were now visible; so that Giovanni could not determine how much of the singularity which he attributed to both was due to their own qualities and how much to his wonder-working fancy; but he was inclined to take a most rational view of the whole matter.

In the course of the day he paid his respects to Signor Pietro Baglioni, professor of medicine in the university, a physician of eminent repute to whom Giovanni had brought a letter of introduction. The professor was an elderly personage, apparently of genial nature, and habits that might almost be called jovial. He kept the young man to dinner, and made himself very agreeable by the freedom and liveliness of his conversation, especially when warmed by a flask or two of Tuscan wine. Giovanni, conceiving that men of science, inhabitants of the same city, must needs be on familiar terms with one another, took an opportunity to mention the name of Dr. Rappaccini. But the professor did not respond with so much cordiality as he had anticipated.

"Ill would it become a teacher of the divine art of medicine," said Professor Pietro Baglioni, in answer to a question of Giovanni, "to withhold due and well-considered praise of a physician so eminently skilled as Rappaccini; but, on the other hand, I should answer it but scantily to my conscience were I to permit a worthy youth like yourself, Signor Giovanni, the son of an ancient friend, to imbibe erroneous ideas respecting a man who might hereafter chance to hold your life and death in his hands. The truth is, our worshipful Dr. Rappaccini has as much science as any member of the faculty—with perhaps one single exception—in Padua, or all Italy; but there are certain grave objections to his professional character."

"And what are they?" asked the young man.

"Has my friend Giovanni any disease of body or heart, that he is so inquisitive about physicians?" said the professor, with a smile. "But as for Rappaccini, it is said of him—and I, who know the man well, can answer for its truth—that he cares infinitely more for science than for mankind. His patients are interesting to him only as subjects for some new experiment. He would sacrifice human life, his own among the rest, or whatever else was dearest to him, for the sake of adding so much as a grain of mustard seed to the great heap of his accumulated knowledge."

"Methinks he is an awful man indeed," remarked Guasconti, mentally recalling the cold and purely intellectual aspect of Rappaccini. "And yet, worshipful professor, is it not a noble spirit? Are there many men capable of so spiritual a love of science?"

"God forbid," answered the professor, somewhat testily; "at least, unless they take sounder views of the healing art than those adopted by Rappaccini. It is his theory that all medicinal virtues are comprised within those substances which we term vegetable poisons. These he cultivates with his own hands, and is said even to have produced new varieties of poison, more horribly deleterious than Nature, without the assistance of this learned person, would ever have plagued the world withal. That the signor doctor does less mischief than might be expected with such dangerous substances is undeniable. Now and then, it must be owned, he has effected, or seemed to effect, a marvellous cure; but, to tell you my private mind, Signor Giovanni, he should receive little credit for such instances of success—they being probably the work of chance,—but should be held strictly accountable for his failures, which may justly be considered his own work."

The youth might have taken Baglioni's opinions with many grains of allowance had he known that there was a professional warfare of long continuance between him and Dr. Rappaccini, in which the latter was generally thought to have gained the advantage. If the reader be inclined to judge for himself, we refer him to certain black-letter tracts on both sides, preserved in the medical department of the University of Padua.

"I know not, most learned professor," returned Giovanni, after musing on what had been said of Rappaccini's exclusive zeal for science,—"I know not how dearly this physician may love his art; but surely there is one object more dear to him. He has a daughter."

"Aha!" cried the professor, with a laugh. "So now our friend Giovanni's secret is out. You have heard of this daughter, whom all the young men in Padua are wild about, though not half a dozen have ever had the good hap to see her face. I know little of the Signora Beatrice save that Rappaccini is said to have instructed her deeply in his science, and that, young and beautiful as fame reports her, she is already qualified to fill a professor's chair. Perchance her father destines her for mine! Other absurd rumors there be, not worth talking about or listening to. So now, Signor Giovanni, drink off your glass of lachryma."

Guasconti returned to his lodgings somewhat heated with the wine he had quaffed, and which caused his brain to swim with strange fantasies in reference to Dr. Rappaccini and the beautiful Beatrice. On his way, happening to pass by a florist's, he bought a fresh bouquet of flowers.

Ascending to his chamber, he seated himself near the window, but within the shadow thrown by the depth of the wall, so that he could look down into the garden with little risk of being discovered. All beneath his eye was a solitude. The strange plants were basking in the sunshine, and now and then nodding gently to one another, as if in acknowledgment of sympathy and kindred. In the midst, by the shattered fountain, grew the magnificent shrub, with its purple gems clustering all over it; they glowed in the air, and gleamed back again out of the depths of the pool, which thus seemed to overflow with colored radiance from the rich reflection that was steeped in it. At first, as we have said, the garden was a solitude. Soon, however,—as Giovanni had half hoped, half feared, would be the case,—a figure appeared beneath the antique sculptured portal, and came down between the rows of plants, inhaling their various perfumes as if she were one of those beings of old classic fable that lived upon sweet odors. On again beholding Beatrice, the young man was even startled to perceive how much her beauty exceeded his recollection of it; so brilliant, so vivid, was its character, that she glowed amid the sunlight, and, as Giovanni whispered to himself, positively illuminated the more shadowy intervals of the garden path. Her face being now more revealed than on the former occasion, he was struck by its expression of simplicity and sweetness,—qualities that had not entered into his idea of her character, and which made him ask anew what manner of mortal she might be. Nor did he fail again to observe, or imagine, an analogy between the beautiful girl and the gorgeous shrub that hung its gemlike flowers over the fountain,—a resemblance which Beatrice seemed to have indulged a fantastic humor in heightening, both by the arrangement of her dress and the selection of its hues.

Approaching the shrub, she threw open her arms, as with a passionate ardor, and drew its branches into an intimate embrace—so intimate that her features were hidden in its leafy bosom and her glistening ringlets all intermingled with the flowers.

"Give me thy breath, my sister," exclaimed Beatrice; "for I am faint with common air. And give me this flower of thine, which I separate with gentlest fingers from the stem and place it close beside my heart."

With these words the beautiful daughter of Rappaccini plucked one of the richest blossoms of the shrub, and was about to fasten it in her bosom. But now, unless Giovanni's draughts of wine had bewildered his senses, a singular incident occurred. A small orange-colored reptile, of the lizard or chameleon species, chanced to be creeping along the path, just at the feet of Beatrice. It appeared to

Giovanni,—but, at the distance from which he gazed, he could scarcely have seen anything so minute,—it appeared to him, however, that a drop or two of moisture from the broken stem of the flower descended upon the lizard's head. For an instant the reptile contorted itself violently, and then lay motionless in the sunshine. Beatrice observed this remarkable phenomenon, and crossed herself, sadly, but without surprise; nor did she therefore hesitate to arrange the fatal flower in her bosom. There it blushed, and almost glimmered with the dazzling effect of a precious stone, adding to her dress and aspect the one appropriate charm which nothing else in the world could have supplied. But Giovanni, out of the shadow of his window, bent forward and shrank back, and murmured and trembled.

"Am I awake? Have I my senses?" said he to himself. "What is this being? Beautiful shall I call her, or inexpressibly terrible?"

Beatrice now strayed carelessly through the garden, approaching closer beneath Giovanni's window, so that he was compelled to thrust his head quite out of its concealment in order to gratify the intense and painful curiosity which she excited. At this moment there came a beautiful insect over the garden wall; it had, perhaps, wandered through the city, and found no flowers or verdure among those antique haunts of men until the heavy perfumes of Dr. Rappaccini's shrubs had lured it from afar. Without alighting on the flowers, this winged brightness seemed to be attracted by Beatrice, and lingered in the air and fluttered about her head. Now, here it could not be but that Giovanni Guasconti's eyes deceived him. Be that as it might, he fancied that, while Beatrice was gazing at the insect with childish delight, it grew faint and fell at her feet; its bright wings shivered; it was dead—from no cause that he could discern, unless it were the atmosphere of her breath. Again Beatrice crossed herself and sighed heavily as she bent over the dead insect.

An impulsive movement of Giovanni drew her eyes to the window. There she beheld the beautiful head of the young man—rather a Grecian than an Italian head, with fair, regular features, and a glistening of gold among his ringlets—gazing down upon her like a being that hovered in mid air. Scarcely knowing what he did, Giovanni threw down the bouquet which he had hitherto held in his hand.

"Signora," said he, "there are pure and healthful flowers. Wear them for the sake of Giovanni Guasconti."

"Thanks, signor," replied Beatrice, with her rich voice, that came forth as it were like a gush of music, and with a mirthful expression half childish and half woman-like. "I accept your gift, and would fain recompense it with this precious purple flower; but if I toss it into the air it will not reach you. So Signor Guasconti must even content himself with my thanks."

She lifted the bouquet from the ground, and then, as if inwardly ashamed at having stepped aside from her maidenly reserve to respond to a stranger's greeting, passed swiftly homeward through the garden. But few as the moments were, it seemed to Giovanni, when she was on the point of vanishing beneath the sculptured portal, that his beautiful bouquet was already beginning to wither in her grasp. It was an idle thought; there could be no possibility of distinguishing a faded flower from a fresh one at so great a distance.

For many days after this incident the young man avoided the window that looked into Dr. Rappaccini's garden, as if something ugly and monstrous would have blasted his eyesight had he been betrayed into a glance. He felt conscious of having put himself, to a certain extent, within the influence of an unintelligible power by the communication which he had opened with Beatrice. The wisest course would have been, if his heart were in any real danger, to quit his lodgings and Padua itself at once; the next wiser, to have accustomed himself, as far as possible, to the familiar and daylight view of Beatrice—thus bringing her rigidly and systematically within the limits of ordinary experience. Least of all, while avoiding her sight, ought Giovanni to have remained so near this extraordinary being that the proximity and possibility even of intercourse should give a kind of substance and reality to the wild vagaries which his imagination ran riot continually in producing. Guasconti had not a deep heart—or, at all events, its depths were not sounded now; but he had a quick fancy, and an ardent southern temperament, which rose every instant to a higher fever pitch. Whether or no Beatrice possessed those terrible attributes, that fatal breath, the affinity with those so beautiful and deadly flowers which were indicated by what Giovanni had witnessed, she had at least instilled a fierce and subtle poison into his system. It was not love, although her rich beauty was a madness to him; nor horror, even while he fancied her spirit to be imbued with the same baneful essence that seemed to pervade her physical frame; but a wild offspring of both love and horror that had each parent in it, and burned like one and shivered like the other. Giovanni knew not what to dread; still less did he know what to hope; yet hope and dread kept a continual warfare in his breast, alternately vanquishing one another and starting up afresh to renew the contest. Blessed are all simple emotions, be they dark or bright! It is the lurid intermixture of the two that produces the illuminating blaze of the infernal regions.

Sometimes he endeavored to assuage the fever of his spirit by a rapid walk through the streets of Padua or beyond its gates: his footsteps kept time with the throbbings of his brain, so that the walk was apt to accelerate itself to a race. One day he found himself arrested; his arm was seized by a portly personage, who had turned back on recognizing the young man and expended much breath in overtaking him.

"Signor Giovanni! Stay, my young friend!" cried he. "Have you forgotten me? That might well be the case if I were as much altered as yourself."

It was Baglioni, whom Giovanni had avoided ever since their first meeting, from a doubt that the professor's sagacity would look too deeply into his secrets. Endeavoring to recover himself, he stared forth wildly from his inner world into the outer one and spoke like a man in a dream.

"Yes; I am Giovanni Guasconti. You are Professor Pietro Baglioni. Now let me pass!"

"Not yet, not yet, Signor Giovanni Guasconti," said the professor, smiling, but at the same time scrutinizing the youth with an earnest glance. "What! did I grow up side by side with your father? and shall his son pass me like a stranger in these old streets of Padua? Stand still, Signor Giovanni; for we must have a word or two before we part."

"Speedily, then, most worshipful professor, speedily," said Giovanni, with feverish impatience. "Does not your worship see that I am in haste?"

Now, while he was speaking there came a man in black along the street, stooping and moving feebly like a person in inferior health. His face was all overspread with a most sickly and sallow hue, but yet so pervaded with an expression of piercing and active intellect that an observer might easily have overlooked the merely physical attributes and have seen only this wonderful energy. As he passed, this person exchanged a cold and distant salutation with Baglioni, but fixed his eyes upon Giovanni with an intentness that seemed to bring out whatever was within him worthy of notice. Nevertheless, there was a peculiar quietness in the look, as if taking merely a speculative, not a human interest, in the young man.

"It is Dr. Rappaccini!" whispered the professor when the stranger had passed. "Has he ever seen your face before?"

"Not that I know," answered Giovanni, starting at the name.

"He *has* seen you! he must have seen you!" said Baglioni, hastily. "For some purpose or other, this man of science is making a study of you. I know that look of his! It is the same that coldly illuminates his face as he bends over a bird, a mouse, or a butterfly, which, in pursuance of some experiment, he has killed by the perfume of a flower; a look as deep as Nature itself, but without Nature's warmth of love. Signor Giovanni, I will stake my life upon it, you are the subject of one of Rappaccini's experiments!"

"Will you make a fool of me?" cried Giovanni, passionately. "*That*, signor professor, were an untoward experiment."

"Patience! patience!" replied the imperturbable professor. "I tell thee, my poor Giovanni, that Rappaccini has a scientific interest in thee. Thou hast fallen into fearful hands! And the Signora Beatrice,—what part does she act in this mystery?"

But Guasconti, finding Baglioni's pertinacity intolerable, here broke away, and was gone before the professor could again seize his arm. He looked after the young man intently and shook his head.

"This must not be," said Baglioni to himself "The youth is the son of my old friend, and shall not come to any harm from which the arcana of medical science can preserve him. Besides, it is too insufferable an impertinence in Rappaccini, thus to snatch the lad out of my own hands, as I may say, and make use of him for his infernal experiments. This daughter of his! It shall be looked to. Perchance, most learned Rappaccini, I may foil you where you little dream of it!"

Meanwhile Giovanni had pursued a circuitous route, and at length found himself at the door of his lodgings. As he crossed the threshold he was met by old Lisabetta, who smirked and smiled, and was evidently desirous to attract his attention; vainly, however, as the ebullition of his feelings had momentarily subsided into a cold and dull vacuity. He turned his eyes full upon the withered face that was puckering itself into a smile, but seemed to behold it not. The old dame, therefore, laid her grasp upon his cloak.

"Signor! signor!" whispered she, still with a smile over the whole breadth of her visage, so that it looked not unlike a grotesque carving in wood, darkened by centuries. "Listen, signor! There is a private entrance into the garden!"

"What do you say?" exclaimed Giovanni, turning quickly about, as if an inanimate thing should start into feverish life. "A private entrance into Dr. Rappaccini's garden?"

"Hush! hush! not so loud!" whispered Lisabetta, putting her hand over his mouth. "Yes; into the worshipful doctor's garden, where you may see all his fine shrubbery. Many a young man in Padua would give gold to be admitted among those flowers."

Giovanni put a piece of gold into her hand.

"Show me the way," said he.

A surmise, probably excited by his conversation with Baglioni, crossed his mind, that this interposition of old Lisabetta might perchance be connected with the intrigue, whatever were its nature, in which the professor seemed to suppose that Dr. Rappaccini was involving him. But such a suspicion, though it disturbed Giovanni, was inadequate to restrain him. The instant that he was aware of the possibility of approaching Beatrice, it seemed an absolute necessity of his existence to do so. It mattered not whether she were angel or demon; he was irrevocably within her sphere, and must obey the law that whirled him onward, in ever-lessening circles, towards a result which he did not attempt to foreshadow; and yet, strange to say, there came across him a sudden doubt whether this intense interest on his part were not delusory; whether it were really of so deep and positive a nature as to justify him in now thrusting himself into an incalculable position; whether it were not merely the fantasy of a young man's brain, only slightly or not at all connected with his heart.

He paused, hesitated, turned half about, but again went on. His withered guide led him along several obscure passages, and finally undid a door, through which, as it was opened, there came the sight and sound of rustling leaves, with the broken sunshine glimmering among them. Giovanni stepped forth, and, forcing himself through the entanglement of a shrub that wreathed its tendrils over the hidden entrance, stood beneath his own window in the open area of Dr. Rappaccini's garden.

How often is it the case that, when impossibilities have come to pass and dreams have condensed their misty substance into tangible realities, we find ourselves calm, and even coldly self-possessed, amid circumstances which it would have been a delirium of joy or agony to anticipate! Fate delights to thwart us thus. Passion will choose his own time to rush upon the scene, and lingers sluggishly behind when an appropriate adjustment of events would seem to summon his appearance. So was it now with Giovanni. Day after day his pulses had throbbed with feverish blood at the improbable idea of an interview with Beatrice, and of standing with her, face to face, in this very garden, basking in the Oriental sunshine of her beauty, and snatching from her full gaze the mystery which he deemed the riddle of his own existence. But now there was a singular and untimely equanimity within his breast. He threw a glance around the garden to discover if Beatrice or her father were present, and, perceiving that he was alone, began a critical observation of the plants.

The aspect of one and all of them dissatisfied him; their gorgeousness seemed fierce, passionate, and even unnatural. There was hardly an individual shrub which a wanderer, straying by himself through a forest, would not have been startled to find growing wild, as if an unearthly face had glared at him out of the thicket. Several also would have shocked a delicate instinct by an appearance of artificialness indicating that there had been such commixture, and, as it were, adultery, of various vegetable species, that the production was no longer of God's making, but the monstrous offspring of man's depraved fancy, glowing with only an evil mockery of beauty. They were probably the result of experiment, which in one or two cases had succeeded in mingling plants individually lovely into a compound possessing the questionable and ominous character that distinguished the whole growth of the garden. In fine, Giovanni recognized but two or three plants in the collection, and those of a kind that he well knew to be poisonous. While busy with these contemplations he heard the rustling of a silken garment, and, turning, beheld Beatrice emerging from beneath the sculptured portal.

Giovanni had not considered with himself what should be his deportment; whether he should apologize for his intrusion into the garden, or assume that he was there with the privity at least, if not by the desire, of Dr. Rappaccini or his daughter; but Beatrice's manner placed him at his ease, though leaving him still in doubt by what agency he had gained admittance. She came lightly along the path and met him near the broken fountain. There was surprise in her face, but brightened by a simple and kind expression of pleasure.

"You are a connoisseur in flowers, signor," said Beatrice, with a smile, alluding to the bouquet which he had flung her from the window. "It is no marvel, therefore, if the sight of my father's rare collection has tempted you to take a nearer view. If he were here, he could tell you many strange and interesting facts as to the nature and habits of these shrubs; for he has spent a lifetime in such studies, and this garden is his world."

"And yourself, lady," observed Giovanni, "if fame says true,—you likewise are deeply skilled in the virtues indicated by these rich blossoms and these spicy perfumes. Would you deign to be my instructress, I should prove an apter scholar than if taught by Signor Rappaccini himself."

"Are there such idle rumors?" asked Beatrice, with the music of a pleasant laugh. "Do people say that I am skilled in my father's science of plants? What a jest is there! No; though I have grown up among these flowers, I know no more of them than their hues and perfume; and sometimes methinks I would fain rid myself of even that small knowledge. There are many flowers here, and those not the least brilliant, that shock and offend me when they meet my eye. But pray, signor, do not believe these stories about my science. Believe nothing of me save what you see with your own eyes."

"And must I believe all that I have seen with my own eyes?" asked Giovanni, pointedly, while the recollection of former scenes made him shrink. "No, signora; you demand too little of me. Bid me believe nothing save what comes from your own lips."

It would appear that Beatrice understood him. There came a deep flush to her cheek; but she looked full into Giovanni's eyes, and responded to his gaze of uneasy suspicion with a queenlike haughtiness.

"I do so bid you, signor," she replied. "Forget whatever you may have fancied in regard to me. If true to the outward senses, still it may be false in its essence; but the words of Beatrice Rappaccini's lips are true from the depths of the heart outward. Those you may believe."

A fervor glowed in her whole aspect and beamed upon Giovanni's consciousness like the light of truth itself; but while she spoke there was a fragrance in the atmosphere around her, rich and delightful, though evanescent, yet which the young man, from an indefinable reluctance, scarcely dared to draw into his lungs. It might be the odor of the flowers. Could it be Beatrice's breath which thus embalmed her words with a strange richness, as if by steeping them in her heart? A faintness passed like a shadow over Giovanni and flitted away; he seemed to gaze through the beautiful girl's eyes into her transparent soul, and felt no more doubt or fear.

The tinge of passion that had colored Beatrice's manner vanished; she became gay, and appeared to derive a pure delight from her communion with the youth not unlike what the maiden of a lonely island might have felt conversing with a voyager from the civilized world. Evidently her experience of life had been confined within the limits of that garden. She talked now about matters as simple as the daylight or summer clouds, and now asked questions in reference to the city, or Giovanni's distant home, his friends, his mother, and his sisters—questions indicating such seclusion, and such lack of familiarity with modes and forms, that Giovanni responded as if to an infant. Her spirit gushed out before him like a fresh rill that was just catching its first glimpse of the sunlight and wondering at the reflections of earth and sky which were flung into its bosom. There came thoughts, too, from a deep source, and fantasies of a gemlike brilliancy, as if diamonds and rubies sparkled upward among the bubbles of the fountain. Ever and anon there gleamed across the young man's mind a sense of wonder that he should be walking side by side with the being who had so wrought upon his imagination, whom he had idealized in such hues of terror, in whom he had positively witnessed such manifestations of dreadful attributes,—that he should be conversing with Beatrice like a brother, and should find her so human and so maidenlike. But such reflections were only momentary; the effect of her character was too real not to make itself familiar at once.

In this free intercourse they had strayed through the garden, and now, after many turns among its avenues, were come to the shattered fountain, beside which grew the magnificent shrub, with its treasury of glowing blossoms. A fragrance was diffused from it which Giovanni recognized as identical with that which he had attributed to Beatrice's breath, but incomparably more powerful. As her eyes fell upon it, Giovanni beheld her press her hand to her bosom as if her heart were throbbing suddenly and painfully.

"For the first time in my life" murmured she, addressing the shrub, "I had forgotten thee."

"I remember, signora," said Giovanni, "that you once promised to reward me with one of these living gems for the bouquet which I had the happy boldness to fling to your feet. Permit me now to pluck it as a memorial of this interview."

He made a step towards the shrub with extended hand; but Beatrice darted forward, uttering a shriek that went through his heart like a dagger. She caught his hand and drew it back with the whole force of her slender figure. Giovanni felt her touch thrilling through his fibres.

"Touch it not!" exclaimed she, in a voice of agony. "Not for thy life! It is fatal!"

Then, hiding her face, she fled from him and vanished beneath the sculptured portal. As Giovanni followed her with his eyes, he beheld the emaciated figure and pale intelligence of Dr. Rappaccini, who had been watching the scene, he knew not how long, within the shadow of the entrance.

No sooner was Guasconti alone in his chamber than the image of Beatrice came back to his passionate musings, invested with all the witchery that had been gathering around it ever since his first glimpse of her, and now likewise imbued with a tender warmth of girlish womanhood. She was human; her nature was endowed with all gentle and feminine qualities; she was worthiest to be worshipped; she was capable, surely, on her part, of the height and hero-ism of love. Those tokens which he had hitherto considered as proofs of a frightful peculiarity in her physical and moral system were now either forgot-ten, or, by the subtle sophistry of passion transmitted into a golden crown of enchantment, rendering Beatrice the more admirable by so much as she was the more unique. Whatever had looked ugly was now beautiful; or, if inca-pable of such a change, it stole away and hid itself among those shapeless half ideas which throng the dim region beyond the daylight of our perfect con-sciousness. Thus did he spend the night, nor fell asleep until the dawn had begun to awake the slumbering flowers in Dr. Rappaccini's garden, whither Giovanni's dreams doubtless led him. Up rose the sun in his due season, and, flinging his beams upon the young man's eyelids, awoke him to a sense of pain. When thoroughly aroused, he became sensible of a burning and tingling agony in his hand—in his right hand—the very hand which Beattrice had grasped in her own when he was on the point of plucking one of the gemlike flowers. On the back of that hand there was now a purple print like that of four small fingers, and the likeness of a slender thumb upon his wrist.

Oh, how stubbornly does love,—or even that cunning semblance of love which flourishes in the imagination, but strikes no depth of root into the heart,—how stubbornly does it hold its faith until the moment comes when it is doomed to vanish into thin mist! Giovanni wrapped a handkerchief about his hand and wondered what evil thing had stung him, and soon forgot his pain in a reverie of Beatrice.

After the first interview, a second was in the inevitable course of what we call fate. A third; a fourth; and a meeting with Beatrice in the garden was no longer an incident in Giovanni's daily life, but the whole space in which he might be said to live; for the anticipation and memory of that ecstatic hour made up the remainder. Nor was it otherwise with the daughter of Rappaccini. She watched for the youth's appearance, and flew to his side with confidence as unreserved as if they had been playmates from early infancy—as if they were such playmates still. If, by any unwonted chance, he failed to come at the appointed moment, she stood beneath the window and sent up the rich sweetness of her tones to float around him in his chamber and echo and reverberate throughout his heart: "Giovanni! Giovanni! Why tarriest thou? Come down!" And down he hastened into that Eden of poisonous flowers.

But, with all this intimate familiarity, there was still a reserve in Beatrice's demeanor, so rigidly and invariably sustained that the idea of infringing it scarcely occurred to his imagination. By all appreciable signs, they loved; they had looked love with eyes that conveyed the holy secret from the depths of one soul into the depths of the other, as if it were too sacred to be whispered by the way; they had even spoken love in those gushes of passion when their spirits darted forth in articulated breath like tongues of long-hidden flame; and yet there had been no seal of lips, no clasp of hands, nor any slightest caress such as love claims and hallows. He had never touched one of the gleaming ringlets of her hair; her garment—so marked was the physical barrier between them—had never been waved against him by a breeze. On the few occasions when Giovanni had seemed tempted to overstep the limit, Beatrice grew so sad, so stern, and withal wore such a look of desolate separation, shuddering at itself, that not a spoken word was requisite to repel him. At such times he was startled at the horrible suspicions that rose, monster-like, out of the caverns of his heart and stared him in the face; his love grew thin and faint as the morning mist, his doubts alone had substance. But, when Beatrice's face brightened again after the momentary shadow, she was transformed at once from the mysterious, questionable being whom he had watched with so much awe and horror; she was now the beautiful and unsophisticated girl whom he felt that his spirit knew with a certainty beyond all other knowledge.

A considerable time had now passed since Giovanni's last meeting with Baglioni. One morning, however, he was disagreeably surprised by a visit from the professor, whom he had scarcely thought of for whole weeks, and would willingly have forgotten still longer. Given up as he had long been to a pervading excitement, he could tolerate no companions except upon condition of their perfect sympathy with his present state of feeling. Such sympathy was not to be expected from Professor Baglioni.

The visitor chatted carelessly for a few moments about the gossip of the city and the university, and then took up another topic.

"I have been reading an old classic author lately," said he, "and met with a story that strangely interested me. Possibly you may remember it. It is of an Indian prince, who sent a beautiful woman as a present to Alexander the Great. She was as lovely as the dawn and gorgeous as the sunset; but what especially distinguished her was a certain rich perfume in her breath—richer than a garden of Persian roses. Alexander, as was natural to a youthful conqueror, fell in love at first sight with this magnificent stranger; but a certain sage physician, happening to be present, discovered a terrible secret in regard to her."

"And what was that?" asked Giovanni, turning his eyes downward to avoid those of the professor.

"That this lovely woman," continued Baglioni, with emphasis, "had been nourished with poisons from her birth upward, until her whole nature was so imbued with them that she herself had become the deadliest poison in existence. Poison was her element of life. With that rich perfume of her breath she blasted the very air. Her love would have been poison—her embrace death. Is not this a marvellous tale?"

"A childish fable," answered Giovanni, nervously starting from his chair. "I marvel how your worship finds time to read such nonsense among your graver studies."

"By the by," said the professor, looking uneasily about him, "what singular fragrance is this in your apartment? Is it the perfume of your gloves? It is faint, but delicious; and yet, after all, by no means agreeable. Were I to breathe it long, methinks it would make me ill. It is like the breath of a flower; but I see no flowers in the chamber."

"Nor are there any," replied Giovanni, who had turned pale as the professor spoke; "nor, I think, is there any fragrance except in your worship's imagination. Odors, being a sort of element combined of the sensual and the spiritual, are apt to deceive us in this manner. The recollection of a perfume, the bare idea of it, may easily be mistaken for a present reality."

"Ay; but my sober imagination does not often play such tricks," said Baglioni; "and, were I to fancy any kind of odor, it would be that of some vile apothecary drug, wherewith my fingers are likely enough to be imbued. Our worshipful friend Rappaccini, as I have heard, tinctures his medicaments with odors richer than those of Araby. Doubtless, likewise, the fair and learned Signora Beatrice would minister to her patients with draughts as sweet as a maiden's breath; but woe to him that sips them!"

Giovanni's face evinced many contending emotions. The tone in which the professor alluded to the pure and lovely daughter of Rappaccini was a torture to his soul; and yet the intimation of a view of her character, opposite to his own, gave instantaneous distinctness to a thousand dim suspicions, which now grinned at him like so many demons. But he strove hard to quell them and to respond to Baglioni with a true lover's perfect faith.

"Signor professor," said he, "you were my father's friend; perchance, too, it is your purpose to act a friendly part towards his son. I would fain feel nothing towards you save respect and deference; but I pray you to observe, signor, that there is one subject on which we must not speak. You know not the Signora Beatrice. You cannot, therefore, estimate the wrong—the blasphemy, I may even say—that is offered to her character by a light or injurious word."

"Giovanni! My poor Giovanni!" answered the professor, with a calm expression of pity, "I know this wretched girl far better than yourself. You shall hear the truth in respect to the poisoner Rappaccini and his poisonous daughter; yes, poisonous as she is beautiful. Listen; for, even should you do violence to my gray hairs, it shall not silence me. That old fable of the Indian woman has become a truth by the deep and deadly science of Rappaccini and in the person of the lovely Beatrice."

Giovanni groaned and hid his face.

"Her father," continued Baglioni, "was not restrained by natural affection from offering up his child in this horrible manner as the victim of his insane zeal for science; for, let us do him justice, he is as true a man of science as ever distilled his own heart in an alembic. What, then, will be your fate? Beyond a doubt you are selected as the material of some new experiment. Perhaps the result is to be death; perhaps a fate more awful still. Rappaccini, with what he calls the interest of science before his eyes, will hesitate at nothing."

"It is a dream," muttered Giovanni to himself; "surely it is a dream."

"But," resumed the professor, "be of good cheer, son of my friend. It is not yet too late for the rescue. Possibly we may even succeed in bringing back this miserable child within the limits of ordinary nature, from which her father's madness has estranged her. Behold this little silver vase! It was wrought by the hands of the renowned Benvenuto Cellini, and is well worthy to be a love gift to the fairest dame in Italy. But its contents are invaluable. One little sip of this antidote would have rendered the most virulent poisons of the Borgias[4] innocuous. Doubt not that it will be as efficacious against those of Rappaccini. Bestow the vase, and the precious liquid within it, on your Beatrice, and hopefully await the result."

Baglioni laid a small, exquisitely wrought silver vial on the table and withdrew, leaving what he had said to produce its effect upon the young man's mind.

"We will thwart Rappaccini yet," thought he, chuckling to himself, as he descended the stairs; "but, let us confess the truth of him, he is a wonderful man—a wonderful man indeed; a vile empiric, however, in his practice, and therefore not to be tolerated by those who respect the good old rules of the medical profession."

Throughout Giovanni's whole acquaintance with Beatrice, he had occasionally, as we have said, been haunted by dark surmises as to her character; yet so thoroughly had she made herself felt by him as a simple, natural, most affectionate, and guileless creature, that the image now held up by Professor

---

[4]Notorious family in Renaissance Italy, rumored to have murdered many of their victims with poison.

Baglioni looked as strange and incredible as if it were not in accordance with his own original conception. True, there were ugly recollections connected with his first glimpses of the beautiful girl; he could not quite forget the bouquet that withered in her grasp, and the insect that perished amid the sunny air, by no ostensible agency save the fragrance of her breath. These incidents, however, dissolving in the pure light of her character, had no longer the efficacy of facts, but were acknowledged as mistaken fantasies, by whatever testimony of the senses they might appear to be substantiated. There is something truer and more real than what we can see with the eyes and touch with the finger. On such better evidence had Giovanni founded his confidence in Beatrice, though rather by the necessary force of her high attributes than by any deep and generous faith on his part. But now his spirit was incapable of sustaining itself at the height to which the early enthusiasm of passion had exalted it; he fell down, grovelling among earthly doubts, and defiled therewith the pure whiteness of Beatrice's image. Not that he gave her up; he did but distrust. He resolved to institute some decisive test that should satisfy him, once for all, whether there were those dreadful peculiarities in her physical nature which could not be supposed to exist without some corresponding monstrosity of soul. His eyes, gazing down afar, might have deceived him as to the lizard, the insect, and the flowers; but if he could witness, at the distance of a few paces, the sudden blight of one fresh and healthful flower in Beatrice's hand, there would be room for no further question. With this idea he hastened to the florist's and purchased a bouquet that was still gemmed with the morning dew-drops.

It was now the customary hour of his daily interview with Beatrice. Before descending into the garden, Giovanni failed not to look at his figure in the mirror—a vanity to be expected in a beautiful young man, yet, as displaying itself at that troubled and feverish moment, the token of a certain shallowness of feeling and insincerity of character. He did gaze, however, and said to himself that his features had never before possessed so rich a grace, nor his eyes such vivacity, nor his cheeks so warm a hue of superabundant life.

"At least," thought he, "her poison has not yet insinuated itself into my system. I am no flower to perish in her grasp."

With that thought he turned his eyes on the bouquet, which he had never once laid aside from his hand. A thrill of indefinable horror shot through his frame on perceiving that those dewy flowers were already beginning to droop; they wore the aspect of things that had been fresh and lovely yesterday. Giovanni grew white as marble, and stood motionless before the mirror, staring at his own reflection there as at the likeness of something frightful. He remembered Baglioni's remark about the fragrance that seemed to pervade the chamber. It must have been the poison in his breath! Then he shuddered—shuddered at himself. Recovering from his stupor, he began to watch with curious eye a spider that was busily at work hanging its web from the antique cornice of the apartment, crossing and recrossing the artful system of interwoven lines—as vigorous and active a spider as ever dangled from an old ceiling. Giovanni bent towards the insect, and emitted a deep, long breath. The spider suddenly ceased its toil; the web vibrated with a tremor originating in the body of the small artisan. Again Giovanni sent forth a breath, deeper, longer, and imbued with a venomous feeling out of his heart: he knew not whether he were wicked, or only desperate. The spider made a convulsive gripe with his limbs and hung dead across the window.

"Accursed! accursed!" muttered Giovanni, addressing himself. "Hast thou grown so poisonous that this deadly insect perishes by thy breath?"

At that moment a rich, sweet voice came floating up from the garden.

"Giovanni! Giovanni! It is past the hour! Why tarriest thou? Come down!"

"Yes," muttered Giovanni again. "She is the only being whom my breath may not slay! Would that it might!"

He rushed down, and in an instant was standing before the bright and loving eyes of Beatrice. A moment ago his wrath and despair had been so fierce that he could have desired nothing so much as to wither her by a glance; but with her actual presence there came influences which had too real an existence to be at once shaken off: recollections of the delicate and benign power of her feminine nature, which had so often enveloped him in a religious calm; recollections of many a holy and passionate outgush of her heart, when the pure fountain had been unsealed from its depths and made visible in its transparency to his mental eye; recollections which, had Giovanni known how to estimate them, would have assured him that all this ugly mystery was but an earthly illusion, and that, whatever mist of evil might seem to have gathered over her, the real Beatrice was a heavenly angel. Incapable as he was of such high faith, still her presence had not utterly lost its magic. Giovanni's rage was quelled into an aspect of sullen insensibility. Beatrice, with a quick spiritual sense, immediately felt that there was a gulf of blackness between them which neither he nor she could pass. They walked on together, sad and silent, and came thus to the marble fountain and to its pool of water on the ground, in the midst of which grew the shrub that bore gem-like blossoms. Giovanni was affrighted at the eager enjoyment—the appetite, as it were—with which he found himself inhaling the fragrance of the flowers.

"Beatrice," asked he, abruptly, "whence came this shrub?"

"My father created it," answered she, with simplicity.

"Created it! Created it!" repeated Giovanni. "What mean you, Beatrice?"

"He is a man fearfully acquainted with the secrets of Nature," replied Beatrice; "and, at the hour when I first drew breath, this plant sprang from the soil, the offspring of his science, of his intellect, while I was but his earthly child. Approach it not!" continued she, observing with terror that Giovanni was drawing nearer to the shrub. "It has qualities that you little dream of. But I, dearest Giovanni,—I grew up and blossomed with the plant and was nourished with its breath. It was my sister, and I loved it with a human affection; for, alas!—hast thou not suspected it?—there was an awful doom."

Here Giovanni frowned so darkly upon her that Beatrice paused and trembled. But her faith in his tenderness reassured her, and made her blush that she had doubted for an instant.

"There was an awful doom," she continued, "the effect of my father's fatal love of science, which estranged me from all society of my kind. Until Heaven sent thee, dearest Giovanni, oh, how lonely was thy poor Beatrice!"

"Was it a hard doom?" asked Giovanni, fixing his eyes upon her.

"Only of late have I known how hard it was," answered she, tenderly. "Oh, yes; but my heart was torpid, and therefore quiet."

Giovanni's rage broke forth from his sullen gloom like a lightning flash out of a dark cloud.

"Accursed one!" cried he, with venomous scorn and anger. "And, finding thy solitude wearisome, thou hast severed me likewise from all the warmth of life and enticed me into thy region of unspeakable horror!"

"Giovanni!" exclaimed Beatrice, turning her large bright eyes upon his face. The force of his words had not found its way into her mind; she was merely thunderstruck.

"Yes, poisonous thing!" repeated Giovanni, beside himself with passion. "Thou hast done it! Thou hast blasted me! Thou hast filled my veins with poison! Thou hast made me as hateful, as ugly, as loathsome and deadly a creature as thyself—a world's wonder of hideous monstrosity! Now, if our breath be happily as fatal to ourselves as to all others, let us join our lips in one kiss of unutterable hatred, and so die!"

"What has befallen me?" murmured Beatrice, with a low moan out of her heart. "Holy Virgin, pity me, a poor heart-broken child!"

"Thou,—dost thou pray?" cried Giovanni, still with the same fiendish scorn. "Thy very prayers, as they come from thy lips, taint the atmosphere with death. Yes, yes; let us pray! Let us to church and dip our fingers in the holy water at the portal! They that come after us will perish as by a pestilence! Let us sign crosses in the air! It will be scattering curses abroad in the likeness of holy symbols!"

"Giovanni," said Beatrice, calmly, for her grief was beyond passion, "why dost thou join thyself with me thus in those terrible words? I, it is true, am the horrible thing thou namest me. But thou,—what hast thou to do, save with one other shudder at my hideous misery to go forth out of the garden and mingle with thy race, and forget there ever crawled on earth such a monster as poor Beatrice?"

"Dost thou pretend ignorance?" asked Giovanni, scowling upon "Behold! this power have I gained from the pure daughter of Rappaccini."

There was a swarm of summer insects flitting through the air in search of the food promised by the flower odors of the fatal garden. They circled round her.

Giovanni's head, and were evidently attracted towards him by the same influence which had drawn them for an instant within the sphere of several of the shrubs. He sent forth a breath among them, and smiled bitterly at Beatrice as at least a score of the insects fell dead upon the ground.

"I see it! I see it!" shrieked Beatrice. "It is my father's fatal science! No, no, Giovanni; it was not I! Never! Never! I dreamed only to love thee and be with thee a little time, and so to let thee pass away, leaving but thine image in mine heart; for, Giovanni, believe it, though my body be nourished with poison, my spirit is God's creature, and craves love as its daily food. But my father,—he has united us in this fearful sympathy. Yes; spurn me, tread upon me, kill me! Oh, what is death after such words as thine? But it was not I. Not for a world of bliss would I have done it."

Giovanni's passion had exhausted itself in its outburst from his lips. There now came across him a sense, mournful, and not without tenderness, of the intimate and peculiar relationship between Beatrice and himself. They stood, as it were, in an utter solitude, which would be made none the less solitary by the densest throng of human life. Ought not, then, the desert of humanity around them to press this insulated pair closer together? If they should be cruel to one another, who was there to be kind to them? Besides, thought Giovanni, might there not still be a hope of his returning within the limits of ordinary nature, and leading Beatrice, the redeemed Beatrice, by the hand? O, weak, and selfish, and unworthy spirit, that could dream of an earthly union and earthly happiness as possible, after such deep love had been so bitterly wronged as was Beatrice's love by Giovanni's blighting words! No, no; there could be no such hope. She must pass heavily, with that broken heart, across the borders of Time—she must bathe her hurts in some font of paradise, and forget her grief in the light of immortality, and *there* be well.

But Giovanni did not know it.

"Dear Beatrice," said he, approaching her, while she shrank away as always at his approach, but now with a different impulse, "dearest Beatrice our fate is not yet so desperate. Behold! There is a medicine, potent, as a wise physician has assured me, and almost divine in its efficacy. It is composed of ingredients the most opposite to those by which thy awful father has brought this calamity upon thee and me. It is distilled of blessed herbs. Shall we not quaff it together, and thus be purified from evil?"

"Give it me!" said Beatrice, extending her hand to receive the little silver vial which Giovanni took from his bosom. She added, with a peculiar emphasis, "I will drink; but do thou await the result."

She put Baglioni's antidote to her lips; and, at the same moment, the figure of Rappaccini emerged from the portal and came slowly towards the marble fountain. As he drew near, the pale man of science seemed to gaze with a triumphant expression at the beautiful youth and maiden, as might an artist who should spend his life in achieving a picture or a group of statuary and finally be satisfied with his success. He paused; his bent form grew erect with conscious power; he spread out his hands over them in the attitude of a father imploring a blessing upon his children; but those were the same hands that had thrown poison into the stream of their lives. Giovanni trembled. Beatrice shuddered nervously, and pressed her hand upon her heart.

"My daughter," said Rappaccini, "thou art no longer lonely in the world. Pluck one of those precious gems from thy sister shrub and bid thy bridegroom wear it in his bosom. It will not harm him now. My science and the sympathy between thee and him have so wrought within his system that he now stands apart from common men, as thou dost, daughter of my pride and triumph, from ordinary women. Pass on, then, through the world, most dear to one another and dreadful to all besides!"

"My father," said Beatrice, feebly,—and still as she spoke she kept her hand upon her heart,—"wherefore didst thou inflict this miserable doom upon thy child?"

"Miserable!" exclaimed Rappaccini. "What mean you, foolish girl? Dost thou deem it misery to be endowed with marvellous gifts against which no power nor strength could avail an enemy—misery, to be able to quell the mightiest with a breath—misery, to be as terrible as thou art beautiful? Wouldst thou, then, have preferred the condition of a weak woman, exposed to all evil and capable of none?"

"I would fain have been loved, not feared," murmured Beatrice, sinking down upon the ground. "But now it matters not. I am going, father, where the evil which thou hast striven to mingle with my being will pass away like a dream—like the fragrance of these poisonous flowers, which will no longer taint my breath among the flowers of Eden. Farewell, Giovanni! Thy words of hatred are like lead within my heart; but they, too, will fall away as I ascend. Oh, was there not, from the first, more poison in thy nature than in mine?"

To Beatrice,—so radically had her earthly part been wrought upon by Rappaccini's skill,—as poison had been life, so the powerful antidote was death; and thus the poor victim of man's ingenuity and of thwarted nature, and of the fatality that attends all such efforts of perverted wisdom, perished there, at the feet of her father and Giovanni. Just at that moment Professor Pietro Baglioni looked forth from the window, and called loudly, in a tone of triumph mixed with horror, to the thunderstricken man of science—

"Rappaccini! Rappaccini! And is *this* the upshot of your experiment!"

[1917]

Ernest Hemingway

[1899–1961]

ERNEST HEMINGWAY *was born in Oak Park, Illinois. His father was a devoted naturalist who shared his outdoor pursuits with his family during summers spent in rural Michigan. His mother was a professional-level musician, who followed the Victorian practice of dressing all toddlers in feminine clothing. This has fueled speculation regarding Hemingway's hatred of her; their problems stemmed more directly from their similar strong, artistic personalities. Although he is often accused of misogyny, most critics now say that he was questioning gender roles, and subtly critiquing their artificiality. In his writing, Hemingway displaced his sympathy for his female characters and his awe at their innate power onto the natural world.*

Hemingway first worked as a reporter for the Kansas City Star. *At the outbreak of World War I he volunteered for the ambulance service (he never served as a combatant with any army), was stationed in Italy, and was wounded at the front. During convalescence, he fell in love with his nurse, on whom he later modeled Catherine in* A Farewell to Arms *(1929). He returned to the United States a celebrity—the first American wounded in the war. After the war, he lived briefly in Chicago, where he met his first wife, Hadley Richardson, and the writer Sherwood Anderson, on whose advice the couple moved to Paris. There he met Gertrude Stein, who strongly influenced his early style, and F. Scott Fitzgerald. Still a journalist, he strove for literary publication, but a suitcase containing almost all of his work was randomly stolen. He overcame subsequent writer's block by deliberately crafting single sentences and paragraphs. Critics cite these efforts as the formation of his concise early style. These paragraphs became the "chapters" between short stories in his first major work,* In Our Time *(1925). He achieved early critical success with* The Sun Also Rises *(1926). Critics were stymied by his 1930s work, especially* Death in the Afternoon *(1931), an allegory for the conflict between aesthetics and capitalism, but disguised as a bullfighting encyclopedia. Critics celebrated his return to a form they understood with* For Whom the Bell Tolls *(1940), his greatest mature novel, set during the Spanish Civil War, (which he had covered in the 1930s, predicting the spread of fascism and the advent of World War II). After covering the war in Europe, he began several ambitious projects that occupied the rest of his life. Dismissed as a has-been in the reviews for* Across the River and Into the Trees *(1950), he stunned the world with* The Old Man and the Sea *(1952). This novel drew on his fear instilled by two near-fatal plane crashes, and it earned the Nobel Prize in 1954. He published no more literature in his lifetime; much work appeared posthumously, including* A Moveable Feast *(1964) and* The Garden of Eden *(1986).*

In the two plane crashes, Hemingway suffered severe internal injuries and a skull fracture, but it was weeks before he received adequate medical care. He sought interim pain management through alcohol; his drinking, which had never had any impact on his writing, became a spiraling problem. He came under government scrutiny for his uncanny perception of political and ideological trends, especially in Cuba, where he had lived since 1939. Always prone to depression, and finally unable to write due to memory loss exacerbated by electro-shock therapy, Hemingway ended his life with a shotgun in Idaho on July 2, 1961.

—Hillary Justice, *Illinois State University*

Hills Like White Elephants

ERNEST HEMINGWAY

THE HILLS ACROSS THE valley of the Ebro[1] were long and white. On this side there was no shade and no trees and the station was between two lines of rails in the sun. Close against the side of the station there was the warm shadow of the building and a curtain, made of strings of bamboo beads, hung across the open door into the bar, to keep out flies. The American and the girl with him sat at a table in the shade, outside the building. It was very hot and the express from Barcelona would come in forty minutes. It stopped at this junction for two minutes and went on to Madrid.

"What should we drink?" the girl asked. She had taken off her hat and put it on the table.

"It's pretty hot," the man said.

"Let's drink beer."

"Dos cervezas," the man said into the curtain.

"Big ones?" a woman asked from the doorway.

"Yes. Two big ones."

The woman brought two glasses of beer and two felt pads. She put the felt pads and the beer glasses on the table and looked at the man and the girl. The girl was looking off at the line of hills. They were white in the sun and the country was brown and dry.

"They look like white elephants," she said.

"I've never seen one," the man drank his beer.

"No, you wouldn't have."

"I might have," the man said. "Just because you say I wouldn't have doesn't prove anything."

The girl looked at the bead curtain. "They've painted something on it," she said. "What does it say?"

"Anis del Toro. It's a drink."

"Could we try it?"

---

[1]River in northern Spain.

Reprinted from *Men Without Women*, by permission of Simon & Schuster.

The man called "Listen" through the curtain. The woman came out from the bar.

"Four reales."[2]

"We want two Anis del Toro."

"With water?"

"Do you want it with water?"

"I don't know," the girl said. "Is it good with water?"

"It's all right."

"You want them with water?" asked the woman.

"Yes, with water."

"It tastes like licorice," the girl said and put the glass down.

"That's the way with everything."

"Yes," said the girl. "Everything tastes of licorice. Especially all the things you've waited so long for, like absinthe."

"Oh, cut it out."

"You started it," the girl said. "I was being amused. I was having a fine time."

"Well, let's try and have a fine time."

"All right. I was trying. I said the mountains looked like white elephants. Wasn't that bright?"

"That was bright."

"I wanted to try this new drink. That's all we do, isn't it—look at things and try new drinks?"

"I guess so."

The girl looked across at the hills.

"They're lovely hills," she said. "They don't really look like white elephants. I just meant the coloring of their skin through the trees."

"Should we have another drink?"

"All right."

The warm wind blew the bead curtain against the table.

"The beer's nice and cool," the man said.

"It's lovely," the girl said.

"It's really an awfully simple operation, Jig," the man said. "It's not really an operation at all."

The girl looked at the ground the table legs rested on.

"I know you wouldn't mind it, Jig. It's really not anything. It's just to let the air in."

The girl did not say anything.

---

[2]Spanish coins

"I'll go with you and I'll stay with you all the time. They just let the air in and then it's all perfectly natural."

"Then what will we do afterward?"

"We'll be fine afterward. Just like we were before."

"What makes you think so?"

"That's the only thing that bothers us. It's the only thing that's made us unhappy."

The girl looked at the bead curtain, put her hand out and took hold of two of the strings of beads.

"And you think then we'll be all right and be happy."

"I know we will. You don't have to be afraid. I've known lots of people that have done it."

"So have I," said the girl. "And afterward they were all so happy."

"Well," the man said, "if you don't want to you don't have to. I wouldn't have you do it if you didn't want to. But I know it's perfectly simple."

"And you really want to?"

"I think it's the best thing to do. But I don't want you to do it if you don't really want to."

"And if I do it you'll be happy and things will be like they were and you'll love me?"

"I love you now. You know I love you."

"I know. But if I do it, then it will be nice again if I say things are like white elephants, and you'll like it?"

"I'll love it. I love it now but I just can't think about it. You know how I get when I worry."

"If I do it you won't ever worry?"

"I won't worry about that because it's perfectly simple."

"Then I'll do it. Because I don't care about me."

"What do you mean?"

"I don't care about me."

"Well, I care about you."

"Oh, yes. But I don't care about me. And I'll do it and then everything will be fine."

"I don't want you to do it if you feel that way."

The girl stood up and walked to the end of the station. Across, on the other side, were fields of grain and trees along the banks of the Ebro. Far away, beyond the river, were mountains. The shadow of a cloud moved across the field of grain and she saw the river through the trees.

"And we could have all this," she said. "And we could have everything and every day we make it more impossible."

"What did you say?"

"I said we could have everything."

"We can have everything."

"No, we can't."

"We can have the whole world."

"No, we can't."

"We can go everywhere."

"No, we can't. It isn't ours any more."

"It's ours."

"No, it isn't. And once they take it away, you never get it back."

"But they haven't taken it away."

"We'll wait and see."

"Come on back in the shade," he said. "You mustn't feel that way."

"I don't feel any way," the girl said. "I just know things."

"I don't want you to do anything that you don't want to do—"

"Nor that isn't good for me," she said. "I know. Could we have another beer?"

"All right. But you've got to realize—"

"I realize," the girl said. "Can't we maybe stop talking?"

They sat down at the table and the girl looked across at the hills on the dry side of the valley and the man looked at her and at the table.

"You've got to realize," he said, "that I don't want you to do it if you don't want to. I'm perfectly willing to go through with it if it means anything to you."

"Doesn't it mean anything to you? We could get along."

"Of course it does. But I don't want anybody but you. I don't want any one else. And I know it's perfectly simple."

"Yes, you know it's perfectly simple."

"It's all right for you to say that, but I do know it."

"Would you do something for me now?"

"I'd do anything for you."

"Would you please please please please please please please stop talking?"

He did not say anything but looked at the bags against the wall of the station.

There were labels on them from all the hotels where they had spent nights.

"But I don't want you to," he said, "I don't care anything about it."

"I'll scream," the girl said.

The woman came out through the curtains with two glasses of beer and put them down on the damp felt pads. "The train comes in five minutes," she said.

"What did she say?" asked the girl.

"That the train is coming in five minutes."

The girl smiled brightly at the woman, to thank her.

"I'd better take the bags over to the other side of the station," the man said. She smiled at him.

"All right. Then come back and we'll finish the beer."

He picked up the two heavy bags and carried them around the station to the other tracks. He looked up the tracks but could not see the train. Coming back, he walked through the barroom, where people waiting for the train were drinking. He drank an Anis at the bar and looked at the people. They were all waiting reasonably for the train. He went out through the bead curtain. She was sitting at the table and smiled at him.

"Do you feel better?" he asked.

"I feel fine," she said. "There's nothing wrong with me. I feel fine."

[1927]

Shirley Jackson
[1919–1965]

At once a doting mother who wrote humorous accounts of her family life and a self-described witch who penned incisive studies of psychologic aberration and unsettling tales of the supernatural, SHIRLEY JACKSON *explored the unstable boundary between domesticity and horror. Considered one of the finest American fiction writers of the 1950s and 1960s, Jackson is now best known for the widely anthologized short story "The Lottery" (1948).*

Jackson was born in 1919 in San Francisco, the first child of an affluent and conservative family. During childhood and adolescence and well into adulthood, this unruly and overweight daughter struggled against her mother Geraldine's firmly held standards of propriety and femininity. As she resisted the conventions of class and gender, Jackson developed her gift of seeing beneath the decorous surface of middle-class life into its vicious core. In the sunny and seemingly placid northern California suburb of Burlingame, where she attended high school and began writing poetry and short stories, Jackson discerned her neighbors' intolerance and cruelty—traits that later characterized the suburbanites of her fiction.

In 1933 Jackson's family moved to Rochester, New York. After attending the University of Rochester from 1934 to 1936, Jackson withdrew from school and spent a year at home, writing a thousand words a day. In 1937 she entered Syracuse University, where she edited the campus humor magazine, won second prize in a poetry contest, and founded the literary magazine Spectre. *She married the magazine's managing editor, Stanley Edgar Hyman, immediately after her graduation in 1940. The couple moved to New York City, where Jackson held a variety of unsatisfying jobs while continuing to write. In 1941 her experience selling books at Macy's formed the basis for "My Life with R. H. Macy," published in the* New Republic. *This success was followed by the birth of her first child and the publication of many stories in the* New Yorker. *Her reputation as a writer of short fiction grew, and in 1944 "Come Dance with Me in Ireland" was the first of her four stories chosen for* Best American Short Stories.

Jackson's family continued to grow, and her body of writing continued to expand after she moved to North Bennington, Vermont. She had three more children and published short stories, novels, family chronicles, a one-act play, a children's book, and a nonfictional account of witchcraft in Salem. Her works were made into plays, films, and television shows. "The Lottery" appeared as a short play, a television drama, a radio show, an opera, and a ballet. The family chronicles Life Among the Savages *(1953) and* Raising Demons *(1957) were bestsellers, and Jackson's popular success was matched by critical acclaim for her short fiction and novels alike. These latter include* The Road Through the Wall *(1948), a look at the dark side of suburban life inspired by Jackson's years in Burlingame;* Hangsaman *(1951) and* The Bird's Nest *(1954), two penetrating depictions of mental illness; and* The Sundial *(1958), a Gothic fantasy about the end of the world. Jackson's last two novels,* The Haunting of Hill House *(1959) and* We Have Always Lived in the Castle *(1962), are her best. At once chilling and tender, these haunted-house stories transcend their genre, portraying the often-strained relationship between mother and daughter with consummate sympathy and skill. Three years after* We Have Always Lived in the Castle *appeared on the bestseller list and was named one of the year's best novels by* Time *magazine, Shirley Jackson died of heart failure on August 8, 1965.*

—Jamil Musstafa, *Lewis University*

The Lottery

SHIRLEY JACKSON

THE MORNING OF JUNE 27TH was clear and sunny, with the fresh warmth of a full-summer day; the flowers were blossoming profusely and the grass was richly green. The people of the village began to gather in the square, between the post office and the bank, around ten o'clock; in some towns there were so many people that the lottery took two days and had to be started on June 26th, but in this village, where there were only about three hundred people, the whole lottery took less than two hours, so it could begin at ten o'clock in the morning and still be through in time to allow the villagers to get home for noon dinner.

The children assembled first, of course. School was recently over for the summer, and the feeling of liberty sat uneasily on most of them; they tended to gather together quietly for a while before they broke into boisterous play, and their talk was still of the classroom and the teacher, of books and reprimands. Bobby Martin had already stuffed his pockets full of stones, and the other boys soon followed his example, selecting the smoothest and roundest stones; Bobby and Harry Jones and Dickie Delacroix—the villagers pronounced this name "Dellacroy"—eventually made a great pile of stones in one corner of the square and guarded it against the raids of the other boys. The girls stood aside, talking among themselves, looking over their shoulders at the boys, and the very small children rolled in the dust or clung to the hands of their older brothers or sisters.

Soon the men began to gather, surveying their own children, speaking of planting and rain, tractors and taxes. They stood together, away from the pile of stones in the corner, and their jokes were quiet and they smiled rather than laughed. The women, wearing faded house dresses and sweaters, came shortly after their menfolk. They greeted one another and exchanged bits of gossip as they went to join their husbands. Soon the women, standing by their husbands, began to call to their children, and the children came reluctantly, having to be called four or five times. Bobby Martin ducked under his mother's grasping hand and ran, laughing, back to the pile of stones. His father spoke up sharply, and Bobby came quickly and took his place between his father and his oldest brother.

The lottery was conducted—as were the square dances, the teenage club, the Halloween program—by Mr. Summers, who had time and energy to devote to civic activities. He was a round-faced, jovial man and he ran the coal business, and people were sorry for him, because he had no children and his wife was a scold. When he arrived in the square, carrying the black wooden box, there was a murmur of conversation among the villagers, and he waved and called, "Little late today, folks." The postmaster, Mr. Graves, followed him, carrying a three-legged stool, and the stool was put in the center of the square and Mr. Summers set the black box down on it. The villagers kept their distance, leaving a space between themselves and the stool, and when Mr. Summers said, "Some of you fellows want to give me a hand?" there was a hesitation before two men, Mr. Martin and his oldest son, Baxter, came forward to hold the box steady on the stool while Mr. Summers stirred up the papers inside it.

The original paraphernalia for the lottery had been lost long ago, and the black box now resting on the stool had been put into use even before Old Man Warner, the oldest man in town, was born. Mr. Summers spoke frequently to the villagers about making a new box, but no one liked to upset even as much tradition as was represented by the black box. There was a story that the present box had been made with some pieces of the box that had preceded it, the one that had been constructed when the first people settled down to make a village here. Every year, after the lottery, Mr. Summers began talking again about a new box, but every year the subject was allowed to fade off without anything's being done. The black box grew shabbier each year; by now it was no longer completely black but splintered badly along one side to show the original wood color, and in some places faded or stained.

Mr. Martin and his oldest son, Baxter, held the black box securely on the stool until Mr. Summers had stirred the papers thoroughly with his hand. Because so much of the ritual had been forgotten or discarded, Mr. Summers had been successful in having slips of paper substituted for the chips of wood that had been used for generations. Chips of wood, Mr. Summers had argued, had been all very well when the village was tiny, but now that the population was more than three hundred and likely to keep on growing, it was necessary to use something that would fit more easily into the black box. The night before the lottery, Mr. Summers and Mr. Graves made up the slips of paper and put them in the box, and it was then taken to the safe of Mr. Summers' coal company and locked up until Mr. Summers was ready to take it to the square next morning. The rest of the year, the box was put away, sometimes one place, sometimes another; it had spent one year in Mr. Graves's barn and another year underfoot in the post office, and sometimes it was set on a shelf in the Martin grocery and left there.

There was a great deal of fussing to be done before Mr. Summers declared the lottery open. There were the lists to make up—of heads of families, heads of households in each family, members of each household in each family. There was the proper swearing-in of Mr. Summers by the postmaster, as the official of the lottery; at one time, some people remembered, there had been a recital of some sort, performed by the official of the lottery, a perfunctory, tuneless chant that had been rattled off duly each year; some people believed that the official of the lottery used to stand just so when he said or sang it, others believed that he was supposed to walk among the people, but years and years ago this part of the ritual had been allowed to lapse. There had been, also, a ritual salute, which the official of the lottery had had to use in addressing each person who came up to draw from the box, but this also had changed with time, until now it was felt necessary only for the official to speak to each person approaching. Mr. Summers was very good at all this; in his clean white shirt and blue jeans, with one hand resting carelessly on the black box, he seemed very proper and important as he talked interminably to Mr. Graves and the Martins.

Just as Mr. Summers finally left off talking and turned to the assembled villagers, Mrs. Hutchinson came hurriedly along the path to the square, her sweater thrown over her shoulders, and slid into place in the back of the crowd. "Clean forgot what day it was," she said to Mrs. Delacroix, who stood next to her, and they both laughed softly. "Thought my old man was out back stacking wood," Mrs. Hutchinson went on, "and then I looked out the window and the kids were gone, and then I remembered it was the twentyseventh and came a-running." She dried her hands on her apron, and Mrs. Delacroix said, "You're in time, though. They're still talking away up there."

Mrs. Hutchinson craned her neck to see through the crowd and found her husband and children standing near the front. She tapped Mrs. Delacroix on the arm as a farewell and began to make her way through the crowd. The people separated good-humoredly to let her through; two or three people said, in voices just loud enough to be heard across the crowd, "Here comes your Missus, Hutchinson," and "Bill, she made it after all." Mrs. Hutchinson reached her husband, and Mr. Summers, who had been waiting, said cheerfully, "Thought we were going to have to get on without you, Tessie." Mrs. Hutchinson said, grinning, "Wouldn't have me leave m'dishes in the sink, now, would you, Joe?" and soft laughter ran through the crowd as the people stirred back into position after Mrs. Hutchinson's arrival.

"Well, now," Mr. Summers said soberly, "guess we better get started, get this over with, so's we can go back to work. Anybody ain't here?"

"Dunbar," several people said. "Dunbar, Dunbar."

Mr. Summers consulted his list. "Clyde Dunbar," he said. "That's right. He's broke his leg, hasn't he? Who's drawing for him?"

"Me, I guess," a woman said, and Mr. Summers turned to look at her. "Wife draws for her husband," Mr. Summers said. "Don't you have a grown boy to do it for you, Janey?" Although Mr. Summers and everyone else in the village knew the answer perfectly well, it was the business of the official of the lottery to ask such questions formally. Mr. Summers waited with an expression of polite interest while Mrs. Dunbar answered.

"Horace's not but sixteen yet," Mrs. Dunbar said regretfully. "Guess I gotta fill in for the old man this year."

"Right," Mr. Summers said. He made a note on the list he was holding. Then he asked, "Watson boy drawing this year?"

A tall boy in the crowd raised his hand. "Here," he said. "I'm drawing for m'mother and me." He blinked his eyes nervously and ducked his head as several voices in the crowd said things like "Good fellow, Jack," and "Glad to see your mother's got a man to do it."

"Well," Mr. Summers said, "guess that's everyone. Old Man Warner make it?"

"Here," a voice said, and Mr. Summers nodded.

A sudden hush fell on the crowd as Mr. Summers cleared his throat and looked at the list. "All ready?" he called. "Now, I'll read the names—heads of families first—and the men come up and take a paper out of the box. Keep the paper folded in your hand without looking at it until everyone has had a turn. Everything clear?"

The people had done it so many times that they only half listened to the directions; most of them were quiet, wetting their lips, not looking around. Then Mr. Summers raised one hand high and said, "Adams." A man disengaged himself from the crowd and came forward. "Hi, Steve," Mr. Summers said, and Mr. Adams said, "Hi, Joe." They grinned at one another humorlessly and nervously. Then Mr. Adams reached into the black box and took out a folded paper. He held it firmly by one corner as he turned and went hastily back to his place in the crowd, where he stood a little apart from his family, not looking down at his hand.

"Allen," Mr. Summers said. "Anderson . . . Bentham."

"Seems like there's no time at all between lotteries any more," Mrs. Delacroix said to Mrs. Graves in the back row. "Seems like we got through with the last one only last week."

"Time sure goes fast," Mrs. Graves said.

"Clark . . . Delacroix."

"There goes my old man," Mrs. Delacroix said. She held her breath while her husband went forward.

"Dunbar," Mr. Summers said, and Mrs. Dunbar went steadily to the box while one of the women said, "Go on, Janey," and another said, "There she goes."

"We're next," Mrs. Graves said. She watched while Mr. Graves came around from the side of the box, greeted Mr. Summers gravely, and selected a slip of paper from the box. By now, all through the crowd there were men holding the small folded papers in their large hands, turning them over and over nervously. Mrs. Dunbar and her two sons stood together, Mrs. Dunbar holding the slip of paper.

"Harburt . . . Hutchinson."

"Get up there, Bill," Mrs. Hutchinson said, and the people near her laughed.

"Jones."

"They do say," Mr. Adams said to Old Man Warner, who stood next to him, "that over in the north village they're talking of giving up the lottery."

Old Man Warner snorted. "Pack of crazy fools," he said. "Listening to the young folks, nothing's good enough for *them*. Next thing you know, they'll be wanting to go back to living in caves, nobody work any more, live *that* way for a while. Used to be a saying about 'Lottery in June, corn be heavy soon.' First thing you know, we'd all be eating stewed chickweed and acorns. There's *always* been a lottery," he added petulantly. "Bad enough to see young Joe Summers up there joking with everybody."

"Some places have already quit lotteries," Mrs. Adams said.

"Nothing but trouble in *that*," Old Man Warner said stoutly. "Pack of young fools."

"Martin." And Bobby Martin watched his father go forward. "Overdyke . . . Percy."

"I wish they'd hurry," Mrs. Dunbar said to her older son. "I wish they'd hurry."

"They're almost through," her son said.

"You get ready to run tell Dad," Mrs. Dunbar said.

Mr. Summers called his own name and then stepped forward precisely and selected a slip from the box. Then he called, "Warner."

"Seventy-seventh year I been in the lottery," Old Man Warner said as he went through the crowd. "Seventy-seventh time."

"Watson." The tall boy came awkwardly through the crowd. Someone said, "Don't be nervous, Jack," and Mr. Summers said, "Take your time, son."

"Zanini."

After that, there was a long pause, a breathless pause, until Mr. Summers, holding his slip of paper in the air, said, "All right, fellows." For a minute, no one moved, and then all the slips of paper were opened. Suddenly, all the women began to speak at once, saying, "Who is it?" "Who's got it?" "Is it the Dunbars?" "Is it the Watsons?" Then the voices began to say, "It's Hutchinson. It's Bill," "Bill Hutchinson's got it."

"Go tell your father," Mrs. Dunbar said to her older son.

People began to look around to see the Hutchinsons. Bill Hutchinson was standing quiet, staring down at the paper in his hand. Suddenly, Tessie Hutchinson shouted to Mr. Summers, "You didn't give him time enough to take any paper he wanted. I saw you. It wasn't fair."

"Be a good sport, Tessie," Mrs. Delacroix called, and Mrs. Graves said, "All of us took the same chance."

"Shut up, Tessie," Bill Hutchinson said.

"Well, everyone," Mr. Summers said, "that was done pretty fast, and now we've got to be hurrying a little more to get done in time." He consulted his next list. "Bill," he said, "you draw for the Hutchinson family. You got any other households in the Hutchinsons?"

"There's Don and Eva," Mrs. Hutchinson yelled. "Make them take their chance!"

"Daughters draw with their husbands' families, Tessie," Mr. Summers said gently. "You know that as well as anyone else."

"It wasn't *fair*," Tessie said.

"I guess not, Joe," Bill Hutchinson said regretfully. "My daughter draws with her husband's family, that's only fair. And I've got no other family except the kids."

"Then, as far as drawing for families is concerned, it's you." Mr. Summers said in explanation, "and as far as drawing for households is concerned, that's you, too. Right?"

"Right," Bill Hutchinson said.

"How many kids, Bill?" Mr. Summers asked formally.

"Three," Bill Hutchinson said. "There's Bill, Jr., and Nancy, and little Dave. And Tessie and me."

"All right, then," Mr. Summers said. "Harry, you got their tickets back?"

Mr. Graves nodded and held up the slips of paper. "Put them in the box, then," Mr. Summers directed. "Take Bill's and put it in."

"I think we ought to start over," Mrs. Hutchinson said, as quietly as she could. "I tell you it wasn't *fair*. You didn't give him time enough to choose. *Every*body saw that."

Mr. Graves had selected the five slips and put them in the box, and he dropped all the papers but those onto the ground, where the breeze caught them and lifted them off.

"Listen, everybody," Mrs. Hutchinson was saying to the people around her.

"Ready, Bill?" Mr. Summers asked, and Bill Hutchinson, with one quick glance around at his wife and children, nodded.

"Remember," Mr. Summers said, "take the slips and keep them folded until each person has taken one. Harry, you help little Dave." Mr. Graves took the hand of the little boy, who came willingly with him up to the box. "Take a paper out of the box, Davy," Mr. Summers said. Davy put his hand into the box and laughed. "Take just *one* paper," Mr. Summers said. "Harry, you hold it for him." Mr. Graves took the child's hand and removed the folded paper from the tight fist and held it while little Dave stood next to him and looked up at him wonderingly.

"Nancy next," Mr. Summers said. Nancy was twelve, and her school friends breathed heavily as she went forward, switching her skirt, and took a slip daintily from the box. "Bill, Jr.," Mr. Summers said, and Billy, his face red and his feet over-large, nearly knocked the box over as he got a paper out. "Tessie," Mr. Summers said. She hesitated for a minute, looking around defiantly, and then set her lips and went up to the box. She snatched a paper out and held it behind her.

"Bill," Mr. Summers said, and Bill Hutchinson reached into the box and felt around, bringing his hand out at last with the slip of paper in it.

The crowd was quiet. A girl whispered, "I hope it's not Nancy," and the sound of the whisper reached the edges of the crowd.

"It's not the way it used to be," Old Man Warner said clearly. "People ain't the way they used to be."

"All right," Mr. Summers said. "Open the papers. Harry, you open little Dave's."

Mr. Graves opened the slip of paper and there was a general sigh through the crowd as he held it up and everyone could see that it was blank. Nancy and Bill, Jr., opened theirs at the same time, and both beamed and laughed, turning around to the crowd and holding their slips of paper above their heads.

"Tessie," Mr. Summers said. There was a pause, and then Mr. Summers looked at Bill Hutchinson, and Bill unfolded his paper and showed it. It was blank.

"It's Tessie," Mr. Summers said, and his voice was hushed. "Show us her paper, Bill."

Bill Hutchinson went over to his wife and forced the slip of paper out of her hand. It had a black spot on it, the black spot Mr. Summers had made the night before with the heavy pencil in the coal-company office. Bill Hutchinson held it up, and there was a stir in the crowd.

"All right, folks," Mr. Summers said. "Let's finish quickly."

Although the villagers had forgotten the ritual and lost the original black box, they still remembered to use stones. The pile of stones the boys had made earlier was ready; there were stones on the ground with the blowing scraps of paper that had come out of the box. Mrs. Delacroix selected a stone so large she had to pick it up with both hands and turned, to Mrs. Dunbar. "Come on," she said. "Hurry up."

Mrs. Dunbar had small stones in both hands, and she said, gasping for breath, "I can't run at all. You'll have to go ahead and I'll catch up with you."

The children had stones already, and someone gave little Davy Hutchinson a few pebbles.

Tessie Hutchinson was in the center of a cleared space by now, and she held her hands out desperately as the villagers moved in on her. "It isn't fair," she said. A stone hit her on the side of the head.

Old Man Warner was saying, "Come on, come on, everyone." Steve Adams was in the front of the crowd of villagers, with Mrs. Graves beside him.

"It isn't fair, it isn't right," Mrs. Hutchinson screamed, and then they were upon her.

[1949]

Sarah Orne Jewett
[1849–1909]

SARAH ORNE JEWETT'S *familiarity with books and nature, as well as with the people she would meet while accompanying her obstetrician father on his rounds, contributed to the richly detailed prose she would later write about her native New England. Born to Theodore and Caroline (Perry) Jewett in South Berwick, Maine, Jewett grew up in a literate and literary household. Her father, who was also a medical professor at Bowdoin College, urged his young daughter to immerse herself in his library. She read widely in literature and theology, science and philosophy. Her education extended to the outdoors as well, where she often walked as therapy to treat persistent childhood rheumatoid arthritis. One of her earliest influences was Harriet Beecher Stowe, whose 1862 novel* The Pearl of Orr's Island *was set in rural coastal Maine. This work is considered to be one of the first examples of what would become Jewett's preferred genre: local color, a literary form that captures the essence of a region through careful attention to setting, history, and dialect.*

After graduating from Berwick Academy in 1866, Jewett began submitting stories and sketches about coastal Maine to several magazines, including the prestigious Atlantic Monthly. *The magazine's editor, novelist William Dean Howells, encouraged Jewett to publish a collection of her stories, resulting in the 1877 publication of* Deephaven. *In the decades that followed, Jewett published well over a hundred stories and sketches, five novels (two of them for an audience of girls), and a number of children's stories. Her stories and novels for adults explored the changing social landscape of coastal Maine after the Civil War, featuring largely female and often elderly characters who quietly adapted to the encroachment of industrialization on their way of life. Equally threatening to many of these characters was the science of men, as evidenced by the affable ornithologist in one of her most famous stories, "A White Heron," whose association with nature consists of killing, stuffing, and collecting birds.*

In the 1870s, having established her reputation as a leading regional writer, Jewett became a part of a literary circle centered on James Fields, publisher of the Atlantic, *and his wife Annie, a childhood friend of Jewett's. After Fields's death in 1881, the two women became intimate companions, with Jewett dividing her time between Boston and Maine and traveling through Europe with Annie. During this period Jewett published some of her most notable work, including the* The Country Doctor *and* The Mate of the Daylight, *and* Friends Ashore *in 1884,* Strangers and Wayfarers *in 1890,* The Queen's Twin, *and* Other Stories *in 1899, and* The Tory Lover *in 1901. By far the most critically acclaimed work of this period, indeed of her career, was the 1896 episodic novel* The Country of the Pointed Firs. *In this novel, the inhabitants of the fictional Dunnet Landing are viewed through the keen but sympathetic eyes of a summer visitor, a woman writer whose sketches of the townspeople portray their everyday travails in mythic terms. Jewett wrote little after being seriously injured in a carriage accident in 1902, but her stature among American regional writers had been long established by that time.*

A White Heron

SARAH ORNE JEWETT

I

THE WOODS WERE already filled with shadows one June evening, just before eight o'clock, though a bright sunset still glimmered faintly among the trunks of the trees. A little girl was driving home her cow, a plodding, dilatory, provoking creature in her behavior, but a valued companion for all that. They were going away from whatever light there was, and striking deep into the woods, but their feet were familiar with the path, and it was no matter whether their eyes could see it or not.

There was hardly a night the summer through when the old cow could be found waiting at the pasture bars; on the contrary, it was her greatest pleasure to hide herself away among the huckleberry bushes, and though she wore a loud bell she had made the discovery that if one stood perfectly still it would not ring. So Sylvia had to hunt for her until she found her, and call Co'! Co'! with never an answering Moo, until her childish patience was quite spent. If the creature had not given good milk and plenty of it, the case would have seemed very different to her owners. Besides, Sylvia had all the time there was, and very little use to make of it. Sometimes in pleasant weather it was a consolation to look upon the cow's pranks as an intelligent attempt to play hide and seek, and as the child had no playmates she lent herself to this amusement with a good deal of zest. Though this chase had been so long that the wary animal herself had given an unusual signal of her whereabouts, Sylvia had only laughed when she came upon Mistress Moolly at the swampside, and urged her affectionately homeward with a twig of birch leaves. The old cow was not inclined to wander farther, she even turned in the right direction for once as they left the pasture, and stepped along the road at a good pace. She was quite ready to be milked now, and seldom stopped to browse. Sylvia wondered what her grandmother would say because they were so late. It was a great while since she had left home at half-past five o'clock, but everybody knew the difficulty of making this errand a short one. Mrs. Tilley had chased the hornéd torment too many summer evenings herself to blame any one else for lingering, and was only thankful as she waited that she had Sylvia, nowadays, to give such valuable assistance. The good woman suspected that Sylvia loitered occasionally on her own account; there never was such a child for straying about out-of-doors since the world was made! Everybody said that it was a good change for a little maid who had tried to grow for eight years in a crowded manufacturing town, but, as for Sylvia herself, it seemed as if she never had been alive at all before she came to live at the farm. She thought often with wistful compassion of a wretched geranium that belonged to a town neighbor.

"'Afraid of folks,'" old Mrs. Tilley said to herself, with a smile, after she had made the unlikely choice of Sylvia from her daughter's houseful of children, and was returning to the farm. "'Afraid of folks,' they said! I guess she won't be troubled no great with 'em up to the old place!" When they reached the door of the lonely house and stopped to unlock it, and the cat came to purr loudly, and rub against them, a deserted pussy, indeed, but fat with young robins, Sylvia whispered that this was a beautiful place to live in, and she never should wish to go home.

The companions followed the shady woodroad, the cow taking slow steps and the child very fast ones. The cow stopped long at the brook to drink, as if the pasture were not half a swamp, and Sylvia stood still and waited, letting her bare feet cool themselves in the shoal water, while the great twilight moths struck softly against her. She waded on through the brook as the cow moved away, and listened to the thrushes with a heart that beat fast with pleasure. There was a stirring in the great boughs overhead. They were full of little birds and beasts that seemed to be wide awake, and going about their world, or else saying good-night to each other in sleepy twitters. Sylvia herself felt sleepy as she walked along. However, it was not much farther to the house, and the air was soft and sweet. She was not often in the woods so late as this, and it made her feel as if she were a part of the gray shadows and the moving leaves. She was just thinking how long it seemed since she first came to the farm a year ago, and wondering if everything went on in the noisy town just the same as when she was there; the thought of the great red-faced boy who used to chase and frighten her made her hurry along the path to escape from the shadow of the trees.

Suddenly this little woods-girl is horror-stricken to hear a clear whistle not very far away. Not a bird's-whistle, which would have a sort of friendliness, but a boy's whistle, determined, and somewhat aggressive. Sylvia left the cow to whatever sad fate might await her, and stepped discreetly aside into the bushes, but she was just too late. The enemy had discovered her, and called out in a very cheerful and persuasive tone, "Halloa, little girl, how far is it to the road?" and trembling Sylvia answered almost inaudibly, "A good ways."

She did not dare to look boldly at the tall young man, who carried a gun over his shoulder, but she came out of her bush and again followed the cow, while he walked alongside.

"I have been hunting for some birds," the stranger said kindly, "and I have lost my way, and need a friend very much. Don't be afraid," he added gallantly. "Speak up and tell me what your name is, and whether you think I can spend the night at your house, and go out gunning early in the morning."

Sylvia was more alarmed than before. Would not her grandmother consider her much to blame? But who could have foreseen such an accident as this? It did not seem to be her fault, and she hung her head as if the stem of it were broken, but managed to answer "Sylvy," with much effort when her companion again asked her name.

Mrs. Tilley was standing in the doorway when the trio came into view. The cow gave a loud moo by way of explanation.

"Yes, you'd better speak up for yourself, you old trial! Where'd she tucked herself away this time, Sylvy?" But Sylvia kept an awed silence; she knew by instinct that her grandmother did not comprehend the gravity of the situation. She must be mistaking the stranger for one of the farmer-lads of the region.

The young man stood his gun beside the door, and dropped a lumpy game-bag beside it; then he bade Mrs. Tilley good-evening, and repeated his wayfarer's story, and asked if he could have a night's lodging.

"Put me anywhere you like," he said. "I must be off early in the morning, before day; but I am very hungry, indeed. You can give me some milk at any rate, that's plain."

"Dear sakes, yes," responded the hostess, whose long slumbering hospitality seemed to be easily awakened. "You might fare better if you went out to the main road a mile or so, but you're welcome to what we've got. I'll milk right off, and you make yourself at home. You can sleep on husks or feathers," she proffered graciously. "I raised them all myself. There's good pasturing for geese just below here towards the ma'sh. Now step round and set a plate for the gentleman, Sylvy!" And Sylvia promptly stepped. She was glad to have something to do, and she was hungry herself.

It was a surprise to find so clean and comfortable a little dwelling in this New England wilderness. The young man had known the horrors of its most primitive housekeeping, and the dreary squalor of that level of society which does not rebel at the companionship of hens. This was the best thrift of an old-fashioned farmstead, though on such a small scale that it seemed like a hermitage. He listened eagerly to the old woman's quaint talk, he watched Sylvia's pale face and shining gray eyes with ever growing enthusiasm, and insisted that this was the best supper he had eaten for a month, and afterward the new-made friends sat down in the door-way together while the moon came up.

Soon it would be berry-time, and Sylvia was a great help at picking. The cow was a good milker, though a plaguy thing to keep track of, the hostess gossiped frankly, adding presently that she had buried four children, so Sylvia's mother, and a son (who might be dead) in California were all the children she had left. "Dan, my boy, was a great hand to go gunning," she explained sadly. "I never wanted for pa'tridges or gray squer'ls while he was to home. He's been a great wand'rer, I expect, and he's no hand to write letters. There, I don't blame him, I'd ha' seen the world myself if it had been so I could."

"Sylvy takes after him," the grandmother continued affectionately, after a minute's pause. "There ain't a foot o' ground she don't know her way over, and the wild creatures counts her one o' themselves. Squer'ls she'll tame to come an' feed right out o' her hands, and all sorts o' birds. Last winter she got the jay-birds to bangeing[1] here, and I believe she'd 'a' scanted herself of her own meals to have plenty to throw out amongst 'em, if I had n't kep' watch. Anything but crows, I tell her, I'm willin' to help support—though Dan he had a tamed one o' them that did seem to have reason same as folks. It was round here a good spell after he went away. Dan an' his father they did n't hitch,—but he never held up his head ag'in after Dan had dared him an' gone off."

The guest did not notice this hint of family sorrows in his eager interest in something else.

"So Sylvy knows all about birds, does she?" he exclaimed, as he looked round at the little girl who sat, very demure but increasingly sleepy, in the moonlight. "I am making a collection of birds myself. I have been at it ever since I was a boy." (Mrs. Tilley smiled.) "There are two or three very rare ones I have been hunting for these five years. I mean to get them on my own ground if they can be found."

"Do you cage 'em up?" asked Mrs. Tilley doubtfully, in response to this enthusiastic announcement.

"Oh no, they're stuffed and preserved, dozens and dozens of them," said the ornithologist, "and I have shot or snared every one myself. I caught a glimpse of a white heron a few miles from here on Saturday, and I have followed it in this direction. They have never been found in this district at all. The little white heron, it is," and he turned again to look at Sylvia with the hope of discovering that the rare bird was one of her acquaintances.

But Sylvia was watching a hop-toad in the narrow footpath.

"You would know the heron if you saw it," the stranger continued eagerly. "A queer tall white bird with soft feathers and long thin legs. And it would have a nest perhaps in the top of a high tree, made of sticks, something like a hawk's nest."

Sylvia's heart gave a wild beat; she knew that strange white bird, and had once stolen softly near where it stood in some bright green swamp grass, away over at the other side of the woods. There was an open place where the sunshine always seemed strangely yellow and hot, where tall, nodding rushes grew,

---

[1] *bangeing*: regionalism for congregating informally, hanging around

and her grandmother had warned her that she might sink in the soft black mud underneath and never be heard of more. Not far beyond were the salt marshes just this side the sea itself, which Sylvia wondered and dreamed much about, but never had seen, whose great voice could sometimes be heard above the noise of the woods on stormy nights.

"I can't think of anything I should like so much as to find that heron's nest," the handsome stranger was saying. "I would give ten dollars to anybody who could show it to me," he added desperately, "and I mean to spend my whole vacation hunting for it if need be. Perhaps it was only migrating, or had been chased out of its own region by some bird of prey."

Mrs. Tilley gave amazed attention to all this, but Sylvia still watched the toad, not divining, as she might have done at some calmer time, that the creature wished to get to its hole under the door-step, and was much hindered by the unusual spectators at that hour of the evening. No amount of thought, that night, could decide how many wished-for treasures the ten dollars, so lightly spoken of, would buy.

The next day the young sportsman hovered about the woods, and Sylvia kept him company, having lost her first fear of the friendly lad, who proved to be most kind and sympathetic. He told her many things about the birds and what they knew and where they lived and what they did with themselves. And he gave her a jackknife, which she thought as great a treasure as if she were a desert-islander. All day long he did not once make her troubled or afraid except when he brought down some unsuspecting singing creature from its bough. Sylvia would have liked him vastly better without his gun; she could not understand why he killed the very birds he seemed to like so much. But as the day waned, Sylvia still watched the young man with loving admiration. She had never seen anybody so charming and delightful; the woman's heart, asleep in the child, was vaguely thrilled by a dream of love. Some premonition of that great power stirred and swayed these young creatures who traversed the solemn woodlands with soft-footed silent care. They stopped to listen to a bird's song; they pressed forward again eagerly, parting the branches—speaking to each other rarely and in whispers; the young man going first and Sylvia following, fascinated, a few steps behind, with her gray eyes dark with excitement.

She grieved because the longed-for white heron was elusive, but she did not lead the guest, she only followed, and there was no such thing as speaking first. The sound of her own unquestioned voice would have terrified her—it was hard enough to answer yes or no when there was need of that. At last evening began to fall, and they drove the cow home together, and Sylvia smiled with pleasure when they came to the place where she heard the whistle and was afraid only the night before.

II

Half a mile from home, at the farther edge of the woods, where the land was highest, a great pine-tree stood, the last of its generation. Whether it was left for a boundary mark, or for what reason, no one could say; the wood-choppers who had felled its mates were dead and gone long ago, and a whole forest of sturdy trees, pines and oaks and maples, had grown again. But the stately head of this old pine towered above them all and made a landmark for sea and shore miles and miles away. Sylvia knew it well. She had always believed that whoever climbed to the top of it could see the ocean; and the little girl had often laid her hand on the great rough trunk and looked up wistfully at those dark boughs that the wind always stirred, no matter how hot and still the air might be below. Now she thought of the tree with a new excitement, for why, if one climbed it at break of day could not one see all the world, and easily discover from whence the white heron flew, and mark the place, and find the hidden nest?

What a spirit of adventure, what wild ambition! What fancied triumph and delight and glory for the later morning when she could make known the secret! It was almost too real and too great for the childish heart to bear.

All night the door of the little house stood open and the whippoorwills came and sang upon the very step. The young sportsman and his old hostess were sound asleep, but Sylvia's great design kept her broad awake and watching. She forgot to think of sleep. The short summer night seemed as long as the winter darkness, and at last when the whippoorwills ceased, and she was afraid the morning would after all come too soon, she stole out of the house and followed the pasture path through the woods, hastening toward the open ground beyond, listening with a sense of comfort and companionship to the drowsy twitter of a half-awakened bird, whose perch she had jarred in passing. Alas, if the great wave of human interest which flooded for the first time this dull little life should sweep away the satisfactions of an existence heart to heart with nature and the dumb life of the forest!

There was the huge tree asleep yet in the paling moonlight, and small and silly Sylvia began with utmost bravery to mount to the top of it, with tingling, eager blood coursing the channels of her whole frame, with her bare feet and fingers, that pinched and held like bird's claws to the monstrous ladder reaching up, up, almost to the sky itself. First she must mount the white oak tree that grew alongside, where she was almost lost among the dark branches and the green leaves heavy and wet with dew; a bird fluttered off its nest, and a red squirrel ran to and fro and scolded pettishly at the harmless housebreaker. Sylvia felt her way easily. She had often climbed there, and knew that higher still one of the oak's upper branches chafed against the pine trunk, just where its lower boughs were set close together. There, when she made the dangerous pass from one tree to the other, the great enterprise would really begin.

She crept out along the swaying oak limb at last, and took the daring step across into the old pine-tree. The way was harder than she thought; she must reach far and hold fast, the sharp dry twigs caught and held her and scratched her like angry talons, the pitch made her thin little fingers clumsy and stiff as she went round and round the tree's great stem, higher and higher upward. The sparrows and robins in the woods below were beginning to wake and twitter to the dawn, yet it seemed much lighter there aloft in the pine-tree, and the child knew she must hurry if her project were to be of any use.

The tree seemed to lengthen itself out as she went up, and to reach farther and farther upward. It was like a great main-mast to the voyaging earth; it must truly have been amazed that morning through all its ponderous frame as it felt this determined spark of human spirit wending its way from higher branch to branch. Who knows how steadily the least twigs held themselves to advantage this light, weak creature on her way! The old pine must have loved his new dependent. More than all the hawks, and bats, and moths, and even the sweet voiced thrushes, was the brave, beating heart of the solitary gray-eyed child. And the tree stood still and frowned away the winds that June morning while the dawn grew bright in the east.

Sylvia's face was like a pale star, if one had seen it from the ground, when the last thorny bough was past, and she stood trembling and tired but wholly triumphant, high in the treetop. Yes, there was the sea with the dawning sun making a golden dazzle over it, and toward that glorious east flew two hawks with slow-moving pinions. How low they looked in the air from that height when one had only seen them before far up, and dark against the blue sky. Their gray feathers were as soft as moths; they seemed only a little way from the tree, and Sylvia felt as if she too could go flying away among the clouds. Westward, the woodlands and farms reached miles and miles into the distance; here and there were church steeples, and white villages, truly it was a vast and awesome world!

The birds sang louder and louder. At last the sun came up bewilderingly bright. Sylvia could see the white sails of ships out at sea, and the clouds that were purple and rose-colored and yellow at first began to fade away. Where was the white heron's nest in the sea of green branches, and was this wonderful sight and pageant of the world the only reward for having climbed to such a giddy height? Now look down again, Sylvia, where the green marsh is set among the shining birches and dark hemlocks; there where you saw the white heron once you will see him again; look, look! a white spot of him like a single floating feather comes up from the dead hemlock and grows larger, and rises, and comes close at last, and goes by the landmark pine with steady sweep of wing and outstretched slender neck and crested head. And wait! wait! do not move a foot or a finger, little girl, do not send an arrow of light and consciousness from your two eager eyes, for the heron has perched on a pine bough not far beyond yours, and cries back to his mate on the nest and plumes his feathers for the new day!

The child gives a long sigh a minute later when a company of shouting cat-birds comes also to the tree, and vexed by their fluttering and lawlessness the solemn heron goes away. She knows his secret now, the wild, light, slender bird that floats and wavers, and goes back like an arrow presently to his home in the green world beneath. Then Sylvia, well satisfied, makes her perilous way down again, not daring to look far below the branch she stands on, ready to cry sometimes because her fingers ache and her lamed feet slip. Wondering over and over again what the stranger would say to her, and what he would think when she told him how to find his way straight to the heron's nest.

"Sylvy, Sylvy!" called the busy old grandmother again and again, but nobody answered, and the small husk bed was empty and Sylvia had disappeared.

The guest waked from a dream, and remembering his day's pleasure hurried to dress himself that might it sooner begin. He was sure from the way the shy little girl looked once or twice yesterday that she had at least seen the white heron, and now she must really be made to tell. Here she comes now, paler than ever, and her worn old frock is torn and tattered, and smeared with pine pitch. The grandmother and the sportsman stand in the door together and question her, and the splendid moment has come to speak of the dead hemlock-tree by the green marsh.

But Sylvia does not speak after all, though the old grandmother fretfully rebukes her, and the young man's kind, appealing eyes are looking straight in her own. He can make them rich with money; he has promised it, and they are poor now. He is so well worth making happy, and he waits to hear the story she can tell.

No, she must keep silence! What is it that suddenly forbids her and makes her dumb? Has she been nine years growing and now, when the great world for the first time puts out a hand to her, must she thrust it aside for a bird's sake? The murmur of the pine's green branches is in her ears, she remembers how the white heron came flying through the golden air and how they watched the sea and the morning together, and Sylvia cannot speak; she cannot tell the heron's secret and give its life away.

Dear loyalty, that suffered a sharp pang as the guest went away disappointed later in the day, that could have served and followed him and loved him as a dog loves! Many a night Sylvia heard the echo of his whistle haunting the pasture path as she came home with the loitering cow. She forgot even her sorrow at the sharp report of his gun and the sight of thrushes and sparrows dropping silent to the ground, their songs hushed and their pretty feathers stained and wet with blood. Were the birds better friends than their hunter might have been,—who can tell? Whatever treasures were lost to her, woodlands and summer-time, remember! Bring your gifts and graces and tell your secrets to this lonely country child!

James Joyce
[1882–1941]

JAMES JOYCE *was born at Rathgar outside of Dublin, Ireland. Joyce's father was musical and charming but given to losing money, or at least not keeping it. Joyce's young life was spent watching the family fortunes dwindle. The combination of a charming but unreliable father and a strong and demanding mother may have set the scenes for much of his later writing. Joyce attended boarding school where he suffered the abuses of Jesuit discipline as it was practiced in the late 1800s. In his first novel,* A Portrait of the Artist as a Young Man, *he describes beatings and verbal abuse. Joyce joined the Faculty of Arts in University College, Dublin, but soon found that he was meant for the life in early twentieth century Paris. In Ireland Joyce spent time with such notable writers as William Butler Yeats and developed a strong interest in the Irish independence movement though he never actually participated in the rebellion. Joyce's collection of short stories,* Dubliners, *is a kind of farewell to Ireland, since the portraits that he draws in these tales all suggest a kind of moral and political paralysis in the Irish mind. Joyce sympathized with his countrymen but was unable to find interest or energy in joining their battles with the British.*

After his mother's death in 1902, Joyce and his lover Nora Barnacle departed for Paris and Europe permanently. They became the parents of a son and daughter and did eventually marry in 1931, despite Joyce's objections to formal marriage. Joyce taught in Switzerland, but the Paris appeal was always strong. The American poet Ezra Pound encouraged Joyce in his writing and acted as coach and editor as well as literary supporter. Joyce spent most of the rest of his life working on his two major works, Ulysses *and* Finnegans Wake. *The American courts fought over the pornographic nature of* Ulysses, *the case having elicited the famous quotation by a judge that he "knew pornography when he saw it."* Ulysses *would hardly be considered shocking by twenty-first century MTV standards, but in its day the novel was controversial.*

In the meantime, Joyce's eyesight deteriorated, but he continued to write, supported by patrons, or people who were willing to give money to important artists to encourage their writing. Harriet Weaver, a wealthy woman who supported the Joyces for most of Joyce's writing life, was willing to continue to offer patronage even when his works were threatened by American disapproval. Both wars caused the Joyces to move to neutral Switzerland. Joyce lived in Switzerland during World War I and went there again as World War II threatened. It was there that he died during the war. He is now thought of as one of the greatest writers of the twentieth century. His contributions to the changes in the way that novels and stories tell about life began what was to become a postmodern way of writing despite the modernist centrality of Joyce's attitudes and artistic temperament.

Araby

JAMES JOYCE

NORTH RICHMOND STREET, being blind, was a quiet street except at the hour when the Christian Brothers' School set the boys free. An uninhabited house of two storeys stood at the blind end, detached from its neighbours in a square ground. The other houses of the street, conscious of decent lives within them, gazed at one another with brown imperturbable faces.

The former tenant of our house, a priest, had died in the back drawing room. Air, musty from having long been enclosed, hung in all the rooms, and the waste room behind the kitchen was littered with old useless papers. Among these I found a few paper-covered books, the pages of which were curled and damp: *The Abbott,* by Walter Scott, *The Devout Communicant* and *The Memoirs of Vidocq.* I liked the last best because its leaves were yellow. The wild garden behind the house contained a central apple-tree and a few straggling bushes under one of which I found the late tenant's rusty bicycle-pump. He had been a very charitable priest; in his will he had left all his money to institutions and the furniture of his house to his sister.

When the short days of winter came dusk fell before we had well eaten our dinners. When we met in the street the houses had grown sombre. The space of sky above us was the colour of ever-changing violet and towards it the lamps of the street lifted their feeble lanterns. The cold air stung us and we played till our bodies glowed. Our shouts echoed in the silent street. The career of our play brought us through the dark muddy lanes behind the houses where we ran the gauntlet of the rough tribes from the cottages, to the back doors of the dark dripping gardens where odours arose from the ashpits, to the dark odorous stables where a coachman smoothed and combed the horse or shook music from the buckled harness. When we returned to the street light from the kitchen windows had filled the areas. If my uncle was seen turning the corner we hid in the shadow until we had seen him safely housed. Or if Mangan's sister came out on the doorstep to call her brother in to his tea we watched her from our shadow peer up and down the street. We waited to see whether she would remain or go in and, if she remained, we left our shadow and walked up to Mangan's steps resignedly. She was waiting for us, her figure defined by the light from the half-opened door. Her brother always teased her before he obeyed and I stood by the railings looking at her. Her dress swung as she moved her body and the soft rope of her hair tossed from side to side.

Every morning I lay on the floor in the front parlor watching her door. The blind was pulled down within an inch of the sash so that I could not be seen. When she came out on the doorstep my heart leaped. I ran to the hall, seized my books and followed her. I kept her brown figure always in my eye and, when we came near the point at which our ways diverged, I quickened my pace and passed her. This happened morning after morning. I had never spoken to her, except for a few casual words, and yet her name was like a summons to all my foolish blood.

Her image accompanied me even in places the most hostile to romance. On Saturday evenings when my aunt went marketing I had to go to carry some of the parcels. We walked through the flaring street, jostled by drunken men and bargaining women, amid the curses of labourers, the shrill litanies of shop-boys who stood on guard by the barrels of pigs' cheeks, the nasal chanting of street singers, who sang a *come-all-you* about O'Donovan Rossa, or a ballad about the troubles in our native land. These noises converged in a single sensation of life for me: I imagined that I bore my chalice safely through the throng of foes. Her name sprang to my lips at moments in strange prayers and praises which I myself did not understand. My eyes were often full of tears (I could not tell why) and at times a flood from my heart seemed to pour itself out into my bosom. I thought little of the future. I did not know whether I would ever speak to her or not or, if I spoke to her, how I could tell her of my confused adoration. But my body was like a harp and her words and gestures were like fingers running upon the wires.

One evening I went into the back drawing-room in which the priest had died. It was a dark rainy evening and there was no sound in the house. Through one of the broken panes I heard the rain impinge upon the earth, the fine incessant needles of water playing in the sodden beds. Some distant lamp or lighted window gleamed below me. I was thankful that I could see so little. All my senses seemed to desire to veil themselves and, feeling that I was about to slip from them, I pressed the palms of my hands together until they trembled, murmuring: "*O love! O love!*" many times.

At last she spoke to me. When she addressed the first words to me I was so confused that I did not know what to answer. She asked me was I going to *Araby.* I forget whether I answered yes or no. It would be a splendid bazaar, she said; she would love to go.

—And why can't you? I asked.

While she spoke she turned a silver bracelet round and round her wrist. She could not go, she said, because there would be a retreat that week in her convent. Her brother and two other boys were fighting for their caps and I was alone at the railings. She held one of the spikes, bowing her head towards me. The light from the lamp opposite our door caught the white curve of her neck, lit up her hair that rested there and, falling, lit up the hand upon the railing. It fell over one side of her dress and caught the white border of a petticoat, just visible as she stood at ease.

—It's well for you, she said.

—If I go, I said, I will bring you something.

What innumerable follies laid waste my waking and sleeping thoughts after that evening! I wished to annihilate the tedious intervening days. I chafed against the work of school. At night in my bedroom and by day in the classroom her image came between me and the page I strove to read. The syllables of the word *Araby* were called to me through the silence in which my soul luxuriated and cast an Eastern enchantment over me. I asked for leave to go to the bazaar on Saturday night. My aunt was surprised and hoped it was not some Freemason affair. I answered few questions in class. I watched my master's face pass from amiability to sternness; he hoped I was not beginning to idle. I could not call my wandering thoughts together. I had hardly any patience with the serious work of life which, now that it stood between me and my desire, seemed to me child's play, ugly monotonous child's play.

On Saturday morning I reminded my uncle that I wished to go to the bazaar in the evening. He was fussing at the hallstand, looking for the hatbrush, and answered me curtly:

—Yes, boy, I know.

As he was in the hall I could not go into the front parlour and lie at the window. I left the house in bad humour and walked slowly towards the school. The air was pitilessly raw and already my heart misgave me.

When I came home to dinner my uncle had not yet been home. Still, it was early. I sat staring at the clock for some time and, when its ticking began to irritate me, I left the room. I mounted the staircase and gained the upper part of the house. The high cold empty gloomy rooms liberated me and I went from room to room singing. From the front window I saw my companions playing below in the street. Their cries reached me weakened and indistinct and, leaning my forehead against the cool glass, I looked over at the dark house where she lived. I may have stood there for an hour, seeing nothing but the brown-clad figure cast by my imagination, touched discreetly by the lamplight at the curved neck, at the hand upon the railing and at the border below the dress.

When I came downstairs again I found Mrs. Mercer sitting at the fire. She was an old garrulous woman, a pawnbroker's widow, who collected used stamps for some pious purpose. I had to endure the gossip of the tea-table. The meal was prolonged beyond an hour and still my uncle did not come. Mrs. Mercer stood up to go: she was sorry she couldn't wait any longer, but it was after eight o'clock and she did not like to be out late, as the night air was bad for her. When she had gone I began to walk up and down the room, clenching my fists. My aunt said:

—I'm afraid you may put off your bazaar for this night of Our Lord.

At nine o'clock I heard my uncle's latchkey in the halldoor. I heard him talking to himself and heard the hallstand rocking when it had received the weight of his overcoat. I could interpret these signs. When he was midway through his dinner I asked him to give me the money to go to the bazaar. He had forgotten.

—The people are in bed and after their first sleep now, he said.

I did not smile. My aunt said to him energetically:

—Can't you give him the money and let him go? You've kept him late enough as it is.

My uncle said he was very sorry he had forgotten. He said he believed in the old saying: "All work and no play makes Jack a dull boy." He asked me where I was going and, when I had told him a second time he asked me did I know *The Arab's Farewell to his Steed.* When I left the kitchen he was about to recite the opening lines of the piece to my aunt.

I held a florin tightly in my hand as I strode down Buckingham Street towards the station. The sight of the streets thronged with buyers and glaring with gas recalled to me the purpose of my journey. I took my seat in a third-class carriage of a deserted train. After an intolerable delay the train moved out of the station slowly. It crept onward among ruinous houses and over the twinkling river. At Westland Row Station a crowd of people pressed to the carriage doors; but the porters moved them back, saying that it was a special train for the bazaar. I remained alone in the bare carriage. In a few minutes the train drew up beside an improvised wooden platform. I passed out on to the road and saw by the lighted dial of a clock that it was ten minutes to ten. In front of me was a large building which displayed the magical name.

I could not find any sixpenny entrance and, fearing that the bazaar would be closed, I passed in quickly through a turnstile, handing a shilling to a weary-looking man. I found myself in a big hall girdled at half its height by a gallery. Nearly all the stalls were closed and the greater part of the hall was in darkness. I recognized a silence like that which pervades a church after a service. I walked into the centre of the bazaar timidly. A few people were gathered about the stalls which were still open. Before a curtain, over which the words *Café Chantant* were written in coloured lamps, two men were counting money on a salver. I listened to the fall of the coins.

Remembering with difficulty why I had come I went over to one of the stalls and examined porcelain vases and flowered tea-sets. At the door of the stall a young lady was talking and laughing with two young gentlemen. I remarked their English accents and listened vaguely to their conversation.

—O, I never said such a thing!

—O, but you did!

—O, but I didn't!

—Didn't she say that?

—Yes I heard her.

—O, there's a . . . fib!

Observing me the young lady came over and asked me did I wish to buy anything. The tone in her voice was not encouraging; she seemed to have spoken to me out of a sense of duty. I looked humbly at the great jars that stood like eastern guards at either side of the dark entrance to the stall and murmured:

—No, thank you.

The young lady changed the position of one of the vases and went back to the two young men. They began to talk of the same subject. Once or twice the young lady glanced at me over her shoulder.

I lingered before her stall, though I knew my stay was useless, to make my interest in her wares seem the more real. Then I turned away slowly and walked down the middle of the bazaar. I allowed the two pennies to fall against the sixpence in my pocket. I heard a voice call from one end of the gallery that the light was out. The upper part of the hall was now completely dark.

Gazing up into the darkness I saw myself as a creature driven and derided by vanity; and my eyes burned with anguish and anger.

[1914]

D. H. Lawrence

[1885-1930]

D. H. LAWRENCE *was born David Herbert in a coal town in the dusty industrial area of England. Eastwood, Nottinghamshire, was on its way downhill as a source of coal, but Lawrence's father managed to work the mines until his retirement. Lawrence's mother was particularly attached to this fourth child, for by this time her husband had become one of the hard-drinking, hard-working miners who supported their families financially but not necessarily emotionally. Lawrence became his mother's favorite and, because of illness, did not find his way into the mines. Instead, he became an outstanding student at the local Board school, was enrolled at Nottingham High School, and then became a teacher at Nottingham University College. His first novel,* The White Peacock *(1911), was published shortly after the death of his mother. In 1912 he began an affair with Frieda Weekley, the German wife of a fellow professor. Meanwhile, his next novel,* Sons and Lovers *(1913), which is an autobiographical account of his relationship with his possessive mother and with the various young women who passed through his life, was quickly followed by the novel* The Rainbow *(1915). Its successor,* Women in Love *(1920), caused a scandal for its intimate account of two women's lives. The novels are now critically acclaimed, but were considered outrageous at the time of their publication.*

Lawrence and Frieda traveled the world, but returned to Europe in 1925 when he fell seriously ill. He finished Aaron's Rod *(1922),* Kangaroo *(1923), and* The Plumed Serpent *(1926) as his illness progressed. These novels portray his understanding of the lives of those Europeans who wander through other countries looking for meaning in their own lives. In* Serpent, *a white woman of a certain age wanders among the various cults of Mexico, experiencing life in a world to which she can never belong. The novel is fascinating in that a male author attempts to portray not only the inner life of a woman but that of an older woman, and one who leads a totally different life from his. The novel does not totally succeed, but it certainly tantalizes. Two years before his death, he published the novel that he thought was his best,* Lady Chatterley's Lover *(1928), a work that shocked and scandalized some British readers and most American readers when it appeared. In it, a noblewoman has a love affair with her gardener, an affair that Lawrence attempts to portray with sympathy, but in his efforts to write realistic love scenes, he offends those with delicate sensibilities and amuses those of more raucous temperament. Laughter destroys any intended romance for the modern reader of the novel. Still it was a wild and rebellious text at its time and is still interesting for the same reason as* The Plumed Serpent: *A male attempts to enter the consciousness of a female protagonist, with some surprising effects. Lawrence was also a prolific poet, publishing seven volumes containing hundreds of poems in his lifetime.*

🦁 🦁 🦁

The Horse-Dealer's Daughter

D. H. LAWRENCE

"WELL, MABEL, AND WHAT are you going to do with yourself?" asked Joe, with foolish flippancy. He felt quite safe himself. Without listening for an answer, he turned aside, worked a grain of tobacco to the tip of his tongue, and spat it out. He did not care about anything, since he felt safe himself.

The three brothers and the sister sat round the desolate breakfast-table, attempting some sort of desultory consultation. The morning's post had given the final tap to the family fortunes, and all was over. The dreary dining-room itself, with its heavy mahogany furniture, looked as if it were waiting to be done away with.

But the consultation amounted to nothing. There was a strange air of ineffectuality about the three men, as they sprawled at table, smoking and reflecting vaguely on their own condition. The girl was alone, a rather short, sullen-looking young woman of twenty-seven. She did not share the same life as her brothers. She would have been good-looking, save for the impassive fixity of her face, "bull-dog," as her brothers called it.

There was a confused tramping of horses' feet outside. The three men all sprawled round in their chairs, to watch. Beyond the dark holly-bushes that separated the strip of lawn from the high road, they could see a cavalcade of shire horses swinging out of their own yard, being taken for exercise. This was the last time. These were the last horses that would go through their hands. The young men watched with critical, callous look. They were all frightened at the collapse of their lives, and the sense of disaster in which they were involved left them no inner freedom.

Yet they were three fine, well-set fellows enough. Joe, the eldest, was a man of thirty-three, broad and handsome in a hot, flushed way. His face was red, he twisted his black moustache over a thick finger, his eyes were shallow and restless. He had a sensual way of uncovering his teeth when he laughed, and his bearing was stupid. Now he watched the horses with a glazed look of helplessness in his eyes, a certain stupor of downfall.

The great draft-horses swung past. They were tied head to tail, four of them, and they heaved along to where a lane branched off from the high road,

---

First published in 1933.

planting their great hoofs floutingly in the fine black mud, swinging their great rounded haunches sumptuously, and trotting a few sudden steps as they were led into the lane, round the corner. Every moment showed a massive, slumbrous strength, and a stupidity which held them in subjection. The groom at the head looked back, jerking the leading rope. And the cavalcade moved out of sight up the lane, the tail of the last horse, bobbed up tight and stiff, held out taut from the swinging great haunches as they rocked behind the hedges in a motion like sleep.

Joe watched with glazed, hopeless eyes. The horses were almost like his own body to him. He felt he was done for now. Luckily he was engaged to a woman as old as himself, and therefore her father, who was steward of a neighboring estate, would provide him with a job. He would marry and go into harness. His life was over, he would be a subject animal now.

He turned uneasily aside, the retreating steps of the horses echoing in his ears. Then, with foolish restlessness, he reached for the scraps of bacon-rind from the plates, and, making a faint whistling sound, flung them to the terrier that lay against the fender. He watched the dog swallow them, and waited till the creature looked into his eyes. Then a faint grin came on his face, and in a high, foolish voice he said.

"You won't get much more bacon, shall you little b—?"

The dog faintly and dismally wagged its tail, then lowered its haunches, circled round, and lay down again.

There was another helpless silence at the table. Joe sprawled uneasily in his seat, not willing to go till the family conclave was dissolved. Fred Henry, the second brother, was erect, clean-limbed, alert. He had watched the passing of the horses with more *sang-froid*. If he was an animal, like Joe, he was an animal which controls, not one which is controlled. He was master of any horse, and he carried himself with a well-tempered air of mastery. But he was not master of the situations of life. He pushed his coarse brown moustache upwards, off his lip, and glanced irritably at his sister, who sat impassive and inscrutable.

"You'll go and stop with Lucy for a bit, shan't you?" he asked. The girl did not answer.

"I don't see what else you can do," persisted Fred Henry.

"Go as a skivvy," Joe interpolated laconically.

The girl did not move a muscle.

"If I was her, I should go in for training for a nurse," said Malcolm, the youngest of them all. He was the baby of the family, a young man of twenty-two, with a fresh, jaunty *museau*.

But Mabel did not take any notice of him. They had talked to her and round her for so many years, that she hardly heard them at all.

The marble clock on the mantelpiece softly chimed the half-hour, the dog rose uneasily from the hearthrug and looked at the party at the breakfast-table. But still they sat on in ineffectual conclave.

"Oh all right," said Joe suddenly, *a propos* of nothing. "I'll get a move on."

He pushed back his chair, straddled his knees with a downward jerk, to get them free, in horsey fashion, and went to the fire. Still he did not go out of the room, he was curious to know what the others would do or say. He began to *charge* his pipe, looking down at the dog and saying, in a high, affected voice:

"Going wi' me? Going wi' me are ter? Tha'rt goin' further than tha counts on just now, dost hear?"

The dog faintly wagged its tail, the man stuck out his jaw and covered his pipe with his hands, and puffed intently, losing himself in the tobacco, looking down all the while at the dog, with an absent brown eye. The dog looked up at him in mournful distrust. Joe stood with his knees stuck out, in real horsey fashion.

"Have you had a letter from Lucy?" Fred Henry asked of his sister.

"Last week," came the neutral reply.

"And what does she say?"

There was no answer.

"Does she *ask* you to go and stop there?" Fred Henry asked of his sister.

"She says I can if I like."

"Well, then, you'd better. Tell her you'll come on Monday."

This was received in silence.

"That's what you'll do then, is it?" said Fred Henry, in some exasperation.

But she made no answer. There was a silence of futility and irritation in the room. Malcolm grinned fatuously.

"You'll have to make up your mind between now and next Wednesday," said Joe loudly, "or else find yourself lodgings on the curbstone."

The face of the young woman darkened, but she sat on immutable.

"Here's Jack Fergusson!" exclaimed Malcolm, who was looking aimlessly out the window.

"Where?" exclaimed Joe loudly.

"Just gone past."

"Coming in?"

Malcolm craned his neck to see the gate.

"Yes," he said.

There was a silence. Mabel sat on like one condemned, at the head of the table. Then a whistle was heard from the kitchen. The dog got up and barked sharply. Joe opened the door and shouted:

"Come on."

After a moment, a young man entered. He was muffled up in overcoat and a purple woollen scarf, and his tweed cap, which he did not remove, was pulled down on his head. He was of medium height, his face was rather long and pale, his eyes looked tired.

"Hallo, Jack! Well, Jack!" exclaimed Malcolm and Joe. Fred Henry merely said "Jack!"

"What's doing?" asked the newcomer, evidently addressing Fred Henry.

"Same. We've got to be out by Wednesday.—Got a cold?"

"I have—got it bad, too."

"Why don't you stop in?"

"*Me* stop in? When I can't stand on my legs, perhaps I shall have a chance." The young man spoke huskily. He had a slight Scotch accent.

"It's a knock-out, isn't it," said Joe boisterously, "if a doctor goes round croaking with a cold. Looks bad for the patients, doesn't it?"

The young doctor looked at him slowly.

"Anything the matter with *you*, then?" he asked sarcastically.

"Not as I know of. Damn your eyes, I hope not. Why?"

"I thought you were very concerned about the patients, wondered if you might be one yourself."

"Damn it, no, I've never been patient to no flaming doctor, and hope I never shall be," returned Joe.

At this point Mabel rose from the table, and they all seemed to become aware of her existence. She began putting the dishes together. The young doctor looked at her, but did not address her. He had not greeted her. She went out of the room with the tray, her face impassive and unchanged.

"When are you off then, all of you?" asked the doctor.

"I'm catching the eleven-forty," replied Malcolm. "Are you goin' down wi' th' trap, Joe?"

"Yes, you young b—, I've told you I'm going down wi' th' trap, haven't I?"

"We'd better be getting her in then.—So long, Jack, if I don't see you before I go," said Malcolm, shaking hands.

He went out, followed by Joe, who seemed to have his tail between his legs.

"Well, this is the devil's own," exclaimed the doctor when he was left alone with Fred Henry. "Going before Wednesday, are you?"

"That's the orders," replied the other.

Where, to Northampton?'

"That's it."

"The devil!" exclaimed Fergusson with quiet chagrin.

And there was silence between the two.

"All settled up, are you," asked Fergusson.

"About."

There was another pause.

"Well, I shall miss yer, Freddy boy," said the young doctor.

"And I shall miss thee, Jack," returned the other.

"Miss you like Hell," mused the doctor.

Fred Henry turned aside. There was nothing to say. Mabel came in again, to finish clearing the table.

"What are *you* going to do then, Miss Pervin?" asked Fergusson. "Going to your sister's are you?"

Mabel looked at him with her steady, dangerous eyes, that always made him uncomfortable, unsettling his superficial ease.

"No," she said.

"Well, what in the name of fortune *are* you going to do? Say what you *mean* to do," cried Fred Henry with futile intensity.

But she only averted her head and continued her work. She folded the white tablecloth, and put on the chenille cloth.

"The sulkiest bitch that ever trod!" muttered her brother.

But she finished her task with perfectly impassive face, the young doctor watching her interestedly all the while. Then she went out.

Fred Henry stared after her, clenching his lips, his blue eyes fixing in sharp antagonism, as he made a grimace of sour exasperation.

"You could bray her into bits, and that's all you'd get out of her," he said in a small, narrowed tone.

The doctor smiled faintly.

"What's she *going* to do then?" he asked.

"Strike me if *I* know!" returned the other.

There was a pause. Then the doctor stirred.

"I'll be seeing you to-night, shall I?" he said to his friend.

"Ay—where's it to be? Are we going over to Jessdale?"

"I don't know. I've got such a cold on me. I'll come round to the Moon and Stars, anyway."

"Let Lizzie and May miss their night for once, eh?"

"That's it—if I feel as I do now."

"All's one—"

The two young men went through the passage and down to the back door together. The house was large, but it was servantless now, and desolate. At the back was a small bricked house-yard, and beyond that a big square, gravelled fine and red, and having stables on two sides. Sloping, dank, winter-dark fields stretched away on the open sides.

But the stables were empty. Joseph Pervin, the father of the family, had been a man of no education, who had become a fairly large horse-dealer. The stables had been full of horses, there was a great turmoil and come-and-go of horses and of dealers and grooms. Then the kitchen was full of servants. But of late things had declined. The old man had married a second time, to retrieve his fortunes. Now he was dead and everything was gone to the dogs, there was nothing but debt and threatening.

For months Mabel had been servantless in the big house, keeping the home together in penury for her ineffectual brothers. She had kept house for ten years. But previously it was with unstinted means. Then, however brutal and coarse everything was, the sense of money had kept her proud, confident. The men might be foul-mouthed, the women in the kitchen might have bad reputations, her brothers might have illegitimate children. But so long as there was money, the girl felt herself established, and brutally proud, reserved.

No company came to the house, save dealers and coarse men. Mabel had not associates of her own sex, after her sister went away. But she did not mind. She went regularly to church, she attended to her father. And she lived in the memory of her mother, who had died when she was fourteen, and whom she had loved. She had loved her father too, in a different way, depending upon him, and feeling secure in him, until at the age of fifty-four he married again. And then she had set hard against him. Now he had died and left them all hopelessly in debt.

She had suffered badly during the period of poverty. Nothing, however, could shake the curious sullen, animal pride that dominated each member of the family. Now, for Mabel, the end had come. Still she would not cast about her. She would follow her own way just the same. She would always hold the keys of her own situation. Mindless and persistent, she endured from day to day. Why should she think? Why should she answer anybody? It was enough that this was the end, and there was no way out. She need not pass anymore darkly along the main street of the small town, avoiding every eye. She need not demean herself anymore, going into the shops and buying the cheapest food. This was at the end. She thought of nobody, not even herself. Mindless and persistent, she seemed in a sort of ecstasy to be coming nearer to her fulfillment, her own glorification, approaching her dead mother, who was glorified.

In the afternoon she took a little bag, with shears and sponge and a small scrubbing brush, and went out. It was a grey, wintry day, with saddened, dark-green fields and an atmosphere blackened by the smoke of foundries not far off. She went quickly, darkly along the causeway, heeding nobody, through the town to the churchyard.

There she always felt secure, as if no one could see her, although as a matter of fact she was exposed to the stare of everyone who passed along under the churchyard wall. Nevertheless, once under the shadow of the great looming church, among the graves, she felt immune from the world, reserved within the thick churchyard wall as in another country.

Carefully she clipped the grass from the grave, and arranged the pinky-white small chrysanthemums in the tin cross. When this was done, she took an empty jar from a neighboring grave, brought water, and carefully, most scrupulously sponged the marble head stone and the coping-stone.

It gave her sincere satisfaction to do this. She felt in immediate contact with the world of her mother. She took minute pains, went through the work in a state bordering on pure happiness, as if in performing this task she came into a subtle, intimate connection with her mother. For the life she followed here in the world was far less real than the world of death she inherited from her mother.

The doctor's house was just by the church. Fergusson, being a mere hired assistant, was slave to the countryside. As he hurried now to attend to the out-patients in the surgery, glancing across the graveyard with his quick eye he saw the girl at her task at the grave. She seemed so intent and remote, it was like looking into another world. Some mystical element was touched in him. He slowed down as he walked, watching her as if spellbound.

She lifted her eyes, feeling him looking. Their eyes met. And each looked away again at once, each feeling in some way found out by the other. He lifted his cap and passed on down the road. There remained distinct in his consciousness, like a vision, the memory of her face, lifted from the tombstone in the churchyard, and looking at him with slow, large, portentous eyes. It *was* portentous, her face. It seemed to mesmerize him. There was a heavy power in her eyes which laid hold of his whole being, as if he had drunk some powerful drug. He had been feeling weak and done before. Now the life came back into him, he felt delivered from his own fretted, daily self.

He finished his duties at the surgery as quickly as might be, hastily filling up the bottles of the waiting people with cheap drugs. Then, in perpetual haste, he set off again to visit several cases in another part of his round before tea-time. At all times he preferred to walk, if he could, but particularly when he was not well. He fancied the motion restored him.

The afternoon was falling. It was grey, deadened, and wintry, with a slow, moist, heavy coldness sinking in and deadening all the faculties. But why should he think or notice? He hastily climbed the hill and turned across the dark-green fields, following the black cinder-track. In the distance, across a shallow dip in the country, the small town was clustered like smoldering ash, a tower, a spire, a heap of low, raw, extinct houses. And on the nearest fringe of the town, sloping into the dip, was Oldmeadow, the Pervins' house. He could see the stables and the outbuildings distinctly, as they lay towards him on the slope. Well, he would not go there many more times! Another resource would be lost to him, another place gone: the only company he cared for in the alien, ugly little town, he was losing. Nothing but work, drudgery, constant hastening from dwelling to dwelling among the colliers and the iron-workers. It wore him out, but at the same time he had a craving for it. It was a stimulant to him to be in the homes of the working people, moving, as it were, through the innermost body of their life. His nerves were excited and gratified. He could come so near, into the very lives of the rough, inarticulate, powerfully emotional men and women. He grumbled, he said he hated the hellish hole. But as a matter of fact it excited him, the contact with the rough, strongly-feeling people was a stimulant applied direct to his nerves.

Below Oldmeadow, in the green, shallow, soddened hollows of fields, lay a square deep pond. Roving across the landscape, the doctor's quick eye detected a figure in black passing through the gates of the field, down towards the pond. He looked again. It would be Mabel Pervin. His mind suddenly became alive and attentive.

Why was she going down there? He pulled up on the path on the slope above, and stood staring. He could just make sure of the small black figure moving in the hollow of the failing day. He seemed to see her in the midst of such obscurity, that he was like a clairvoyant, seeing rather with the mind's eye than with ordinary sight. Yet he could see her positively enough, whilst he kept his eye attentive. He felt, if he looked away from her, in the thick, ugly, falling dusk, he would lose her altogether.

He followed her minutely as she moved, direct and intent, like something transmitted rather than stirring in voluntary activity, straight down the field towards the pond. There she stood on the bank for a moment. She never raised her head. Then she waded slowly into the water.

He stood motionless as the small black figure walked slowly and deliberately towards the center of the pond, very slowly, gradually moving deeper into the motionless water, and still moving forward as the water got up to her breast. Then he could see her no more in the dusk of the dead afternoon.

"There!" he exclaimed. "Would you believe it?"

And he hastened straight down, running over the wet, soddened fields, pushing through the hedges, down into the depression of callous wintry obscurity. It took him several minutes to come to the pond. He stood on the bank, breathing heavily. He could see nothing. His eyes seemed to penetrate the dead water. Yes, perhaps that was the dark shadow of her black clothing beneath the surface of the water.

He slowly ventured into the pond. The bottom was deep, soft clay; he sank in, and the water clasped dead cold round his legs. As he stirred he could smell the cold rotten clay that fouled up into the water. It was objectionable in his lungs. Still, repelled and yet not heeding, he moved deeper into the pond. The cold water rose over his thighs, over his loins, upon his abdomen. The lower part of his body was all sunk in the hideous cold element. And the bottom was so deeply soft and uncertain, he was afraid of pitching with his mouth underneath. He could not swim, and was afraid.

He crouched a little, spreading his hands under the water and moving them round, trying to feel for her. The dead cold pond swayed upon his chest. He moved again, a little deeper, and again, with his hands underneath, he felt all around under the water. And he touched her clothing. But it evaded his fingers. He made a desperate effort to grasp it.

And so doing he lost his balance and went under, horribly, suffocating in the foul, earthy water, struggling madly for a few moments. At last, after what seemed an eternity, he got his footing, rose again into the air and looked around. He gasped, and he knew he was in the world. Then he looked at the water. She had risen near him. He grasped her clothing, and, drawing her nearer, turned to take his way to land again.

He went very slowly, carefully, absorbed in the slow progress. He rose higher, climbing out of the pond. The water was now only about his legs; he was thankful, full of relief to be out of the clutches of the pond. He lifted her and staggered on to the bank, out of the horror of wet grey day.

He laid her down on the bank. She was quite unconscious and running with water. He made the water come from her mouth, he worked to restore her. He did not have to work very long before he could feel the breathing begin again in her, she was breathing naturally. He worked a little longer. He could feel her live beneath his hands, she was coming back. He wiped her face, wrapped her in his overcoat, looked round into the dim, dark-grey world, then lifted her and staggered down the bank and across the fields.

It seemed an unthinkably long way, and his burden so heavy he felt he would never get to the house. But at last he was in the stable-yard, and then in the house-yard. He opened the door and went into the house. In the kitchen he laid her down on the hearthrug, and called. The house was empty. But the fire was burning in the grate.

Then again he kneeled to attend to her. She was breathing regularly, her eyes were wide open and as if conscious, but there seemed something missing in her look. She was conscious in herself, but unconscious of her surroundings.

He ran upstairs, took blankets from a bed, and put them before the fire to warm. Then he removed her saturated, earthy-smelling clothing, rubbed her dry with a towel, and wrapped her naked in the blankets. Then he went into the dining-room to look for spirits. There was a little whisky. He drank a gulp himself, and put some into her mouth.

The effect was instantaneous. She looked full into his face, as if she had been seeing him for some time, yet had only just become conscious of him.

"Dr. Fergusson?" she said.

"What?" he answered.

He was divesting himself of his coat, intending to find some dry clothing upstairs. He could not bear the smell of the dead, clayey water, and he was mortally afraid of his own health.

"What did I do?" she asked.

"Walked into the pond." He replied. He had begun to shudder like one sick, and could hardly attend to her. Her eyes remained full on him; he seemed to be going dark in his mind, looking back at her helplessly. The shuddering became quieter in him, his life came back in him, dark and unknowing, but strong again.

"Was I out of my mind?" she asked, while her eyes were fixed on him all the time.

"Maybe, for the moment," he replied. He felt quiet, because his strength had come back. The strange fretful strain had left him.

"Am I out of my mind now?" she asked.

"Are you?" he reflected a moment. "No," he answered truthfully, "I don't see that you are." He turned his face aside. He was afraid, now, because he felt dazed, and felt dimly that her power was stronger than his, in this issue. And she continued to look at him fixedly all the time. "Can you tell me where I shall find some dry things to put on?" he asked.

"Did you dive into the pond for me?" she asked.

"No," he answered. "I walked in. But I went in overhead as well."

There was silence for a moment. He hesitated. He very much wanted to go upstairs to get into dry clothing. But there was another desire in him. And she seemed to hold him. His will seemed to have gone to sleep, and left him, standing there slack before her. But he felt warm inside himself. He did not shudder at all, though his clothes were sodden on him.

"Why did you?" she asked.

"Because I didn't want you to do such a foolish thing," he said.

"It wasn't foolish," she said, still gazing at him as she lay on the floor, with a sofa cushion under her head. "It was the right thing to do. *I* knew best, then."

"I'll go and shift these wet things," he said. But still he had not the power to move out of her presence, until she sent him. It was as if she had the life of his body in her hands, and he could not extricate himself. Or perhaps he did not want to.

Suddenly she sat up. Then she became aware of her own immediate condition. She felt the blankets about her, she knew her own limbs. For a moment it seemed as if her reason were going. She looked round, with wild eye, as if seeking something. He stood still with fear. She saw her clothing lying scattered.

"Who undressed me?" she asked, her eyes resting full and inevitable on his face.

"I did," he replied, "to bring you round."

For some moments she sat and gazed at him awfully, her lips parted.

"Do you love me then?" she asked.

He only stood and stared at her fascinated. His soul seemed to melt.

She shuffled forward on her knees, and put her arms round him, round his legs, as he stood there, pressing her breasts against his knees and thighs, clutching him with strange, convulsive certainty, pressing his thighs against her, drawing him to her face, her throat, as she looked up at him with flaring, humble eyes of transfiguration, triumphant in first possession.

"You love me," she murmured, in strange transport, yearning and triumphant and confident. "You love me. I know you love me, I know."

And she was passionately kissing his knees through the wet clothing, passionately and indiscriminately kissing his knees, his legs, as if unaware of everything.

He looked down at the tangled wet hair, the wild, bare, animal shoulders. He was amazed, bewildered, and afraid. He had never thought of loving her. He had never wanted to love her. When he rescued her and restored her, he was a doctor and she was a patient. He had had no single personal thought of her. Nay, this introduction of the personal element was very distasteful to him, a violation of his professional honor. It was horrible to have her there embracing his knees. It was horrible. He revolted from it violently. And yet—and yet—he had not the power to break away.

She looked at him again, with the same supplication of powerful love, and that same transcendent, frightening light of triumph. In view of the delicate flame which seemed to come from her face like a light, he was powerless. And yet he had never intended to love her. He had never intended. And something stubborn in him could not give way.

"You love me," she repeated, in a murmur of deep, rhapsodic assurance. "You love me."

Her hands were drawing him, drawing him down to her. He was afraid, even a little horrified. For he had really no intention of loving her. Yet her hands were drawing him towards her. He put out his hand quickly to steady himself, and grasped her bare shoulder. A flame seemed to burn the hand that grasped her soft shoulder. He had no intention of loving her; his whole will was against his yielding. It was horrible—And yet wonderful was the touch of her shoulder, beautiful the shining of her face. Was she perhaps mad? He had a horror of yielding to her. Yet something in him ached also.

He had been staring away at the door, away from her. But his hand remained on her shoulder. She had gone suddenly very still. He looked down at her. Her eyes were now wide with fear, with doubt, the light was dying from her face, a shadow of terrible greyness was returning. He could not bear the touch of her eyes' question upon him, and the look of death behind the question.

With an inward groan he gave way, and let his heart yield towards her. A sudden gentle smile came on his face. And her eyes, which never left his face, slowly, slowly filled with tears. He watched the strange water rise in her eyes, like some slow fountain coming up. And his heart seemed to burn and melt in his breast.

He could not bear to look at her anymore. He dropped on his knees and caught her head with his arm and pressed her face against his throat. She was very still. His heart, which seemed to have broken, was burning with a kind of agony in his breast. And he felt her slow, hot tears wetting his throat. But he could not move.

He felt the hot tears wet his neck and the hollows of his neck, and he remained motionless, suspended through one of man's eternities. Only now it had become indispensable to him to have her face pressed close to him, he could never let her go again. He could never let her head go away from the close clutch of his arm. He wanted to remain like that forever, with his heart hurting him in a pain that was also life to him. Without knowing, he was looking down on her damp, soft brown hair.

Then, as it were suddenly, he smelt the horrid stagnant smell of that water. And at the same moment she drew away from him and looked at him. Her eyes were wistful and unfathomable. He was afraid of them, and he fell to kissing her, not knowing what he was doing. He wanted her eyes not to have that terrible wistful, unfathomable look.

When she turned her face to him again, a faint delicate flush was glowing, and there was again dawning that terrible shining of joy in her eyes, which really terrified him, and yet which he now wanted to see, because he feared the look of doubt still more.

"You love me?" she said, rather faltering.

"Yes." The word cost him a painful effort. Not because it wasn't true. But because it was too newly true, the *saying* seemed to tear open again his newly-torn heart. And he hardly wanted it to be true, even now.

She lifted her face to him, and he bent forward and kissed her on the mouth, gently, with the one kiss that is an eternal pledge. And as he kissed her his heart strained again in his breast. He never intended to love her. But now it was over. He had crossed over the gulf to her, and all that he had left behind had shrivelled and become void.

After the kiss, her eyes again slowly filled with tears. She sat still, away from him, with her face dropped aside, and her hands folded in her lap. The tears fell very slowly. There was complete silence. He too sat there motionless and silent on the hearthrug. The strange pain of his heart that was broken seemed to consume him. That he should love her! That this was love! That he should be ripped open in this way!—him, a doctor!—How they would all jeer if they knew!—it was agony to him to think they might know.

In the curious naked pain of the thought he looked again to her. She was sitting there drooped into a muse. He saw a tear fall, and his heart flared hot. He saw for the first time that one of her shoulders was quite uncovered, one arm bare, he could see one of her small breasts; dimly, because it had become almost dark in the room.

"Why are you crying?" he asked in an altered voice.

She looked up at him, and behind her tears the consciousness of her situation for the first time brought a dark look of shame to her eyes.

"I'm not crying, really," she said, watching him half-frightened.

He reached his hand, and softly closed in on her bare arm.

"I love you! I love you!" he said in a soft, low, vibrating voice, unlike himself.

She shrank, and dropped her head. The soft, penetrating grip of his hand on her arm distressed her. She looked up at him.

"I want to go," she said, "I want to go and get you some dry things."

"Why?" he said. "I'm all right."

"But I want to go," she said. "And I want you to change your things."

He released her arm, and she wrapped herself in the blanket, looking at him rather frightened. And still she did not rise.

"Kiss me," she said wistfully.

He kissed her, but briefly, half in anger.

Then, after a second, she rose nervously, all mixed up in the blanket. He watched her in her confusion, as she tried to extricate herself and wrap herself up so that she could walk. He watched her relentlessly, as she knew. And as she went, the blanket trailing, and as he saw a glimpse of her feet and her white leg, he tried to remember her as she was when he had wrapped her in the blanket. But he didn't want to remember, because she had been nothing to him then, and his nature revolted from remembering what she was when she was nothing to him.

A tumbling, muffled noise from within the dark house startled him. Then he heard her voice:—"There are clothes." He rose and went to the foot of the stairs, and gathered up the garments she had thrown down. Then he came back to the fire, to rub himself down and dress. He grinned at his own appearance when he had finished.

The fire was sinking, so he put on coal. The house was not quite dark, save for the light of a street-lamp that shone in faintly from beyond the holly trees. He lit the gas with matches he found on the mantelpiece. Then he emptied the pockets of his own clothes, and threw all his wet things in a heap into the scullery. After which he gathered up her sodden clothes, gently, and put them in a separate heap on the copper-top in the scullery.

It was six o'clock on the clock. His own watched had stopped. He ought to go back to the surgery. He waited, and still she did not come down. So he went to the foot of the stairs and called:

"I shall have to go."

Almost immediately he heard her coming down. She had on her best dress of black voile, and her hair was tidy, but still damp. She looked at him—and, in spite of herself, smiled.

"I don't like you in those clothes," she said.

"Do I look a sight?" he answered.

They were shy of one another.

"I'll make you some tea," she said.

"No, I must go."

"Must you?" And she looked at him again with the wide, strained, doubtful eyes. And again, from the pain of his breast, he knew how he loved her. He went and bent to kiss her, gently, passionately, with his heart's painful kiss.

"And my hair smells so horrible," she murmured in distraction. "And I'm so awful, I'm so awful! Oh, no, I'm too awful," and she broke into bitter, heartbroken sobbing. "You can't want to love me, I'm horrible."

"Don't be silly, don't be silly," he said, trying to comfort her, kissing her, holding her in his arms. "I want you, I want to marry you; we're going to be married, quickly, quickly—tomorrow if I can."

But she only sobbed terribly, and cried.

"No, I want you, I want you," was all he answered, blindly, with that terrible intonation which frightened her almost more than her horror lest he should *not* want her.

[1922]

The King James Bible
[1611]

The Bible is the most authoritative text in the Judeo-Christian tradition, and is regarded as divinely inspired, even today, by more conservative elements within Christianity and Judaism. It is divided into two large parts: the Jewish Scriptures, known to Christians as the Old Testament; and the New Testament, containing twenty-seven books recognized as authoritative by Christians but not by Jews. In addition to the thirty-nine books of the Old Testament recognized by Protestant Christianity and by normative Judaism are another fifteen books or parts of books that were handed down with the ancient Greek version of the Jewish Scriptures, known as the Septuagint. Most of these are accepted as canonical by the Roman Catholic Church and are referred to in its tradition as the "deuterocanonical" books.

The Old Testament contains a great variety of writings including myths, legends, legal codes, chronicles, edifying stories, poetry, prophecy, and wisdom literature. The original texts were compiled at various times between the twelfth and the second centuries B.C.E. Almost all of them were written in classical Hebrew, except for a few short passages in Aramaic. The canon of the Hebrew scriptures (the so-called Massoretic text) was only established by Palestinian Jews toward the end of the first century C.E. and has remained substantially unchanged since that time. Greek Christians, however, made use of the Septuagint text, while Roman Catholic Christians in the Middle Ages used the Latin translation of St. Jerome (C. 342–420 C.E.) based on the Hebrew. Since the Reformation the customary practice in Protestant countries is to use vernacular translations based on the original Hebrew text.

In the first generations following the death of Christ (29/30 C.E.), Christians continued to use the Jewish Scriptures as sacred writings, interpreting them in the light of the teachings of Jesus and the apostle Paul. Gradually they assembled a body of their own writings, believed to be of apostolic origin. These were written in Greek during a seventy-five-year period between about 50 and 125 C.E. The first attested use of the expression "New Testament," however, comes in the writings of Tertullian around 200 C.E., and the first serious attempts by the Church to define the canon of the New Testament date only from the late fourth century C.E. The New Testament includes four early accounts of the life and teachings of Christ (the Gospels), a historical account of the early missions of the Church (the Acts of the Apostles); letters of various apostles; and a book for prophecies (Revelation) attributed to the apostle John. The letters of the apostle Paul are particularly significant statements of early Christian theology, and all the apostolic epistles contain instructions concerning morality and Church discipline.

Martin Luther first translated the Bible into the common language of the people in the 1500s. His German translation is still widely used. In the early 1600s King James of England commissioned an English translation that is still widely acclaimed as the most beautiful poetry and prose version of the text. The modern era has seen translations into hundreds of languages, and both scholarly and popular translations into English. Reading preferences depend on the purposes of the reader, but the King James is still the version most often used for aesthetic purposes.

The Parable of the Prodigal Son

THE KING JAMES BIBLE

AND HE SAID. A certain man had two sons: And the younger of them said to his father, Father, give me the portion of goods that falleth to me. And he divided unto them his living. And not many days after the younger son gathered all together, and took his journey into a far country, and there wasted his substance with riotous living. And when he had spent all, there arose a mighty famine in that land; and he began to be in want. And he went and joined himself to a citizen of that country; and he sent him into his fields to feed swine. And he would fain have filled his belly with the husks that the swine did eat: and no man gave unto him. And when he came to himself, he said, How many hired servants of my father's have bread enough and to spare, and I perish with hunger! I will arise and go to my father, and will say unto him, Father I have sinned against heaven, and before thee, And am no more worthy to be called thy son; make me as one of thy hired servants. And he arose, and came to his father. But when he was yet a great way off, his father saw him, and had compassion, and ran, and fell on his neck, and kissed him. And the son said unto him, Father I have sinned against heaven, and in thy sight, and am no more worthy to be called thy son. But the father said to his servants, Bring forth the best robe, and put it on him; and put a ring on his hand, and shoes on his feet: And bring hither the fatted calf, and kill it; and let us eat, and be merry: For this my son was dead, and is alive again; he was lost, and is found. And they began to be merry. Now his elder son was in the field: and he came and drew nigh to the house, he heard music and dancing. And he called one of the servants, and asked what these things meant. And he said unto him, Thy brother is come; and thy father hath killed the fatted calf, because he hath received him safe and sound. And he was angry, and would not go in: therefore came his father out, and entreated him. And he answering said to his father, Lo, these many years do I serve thee, neither transgressed I at any time thy commandment; and yet thou never gavest me a kid, that I might make merry with my friends: But as soon as this thy son was come, which hath devoured thy living with harlots, thou hast killed for him the fatted calf. And he said unto him, Son thou art

---

The King James Bible was first printed in 1611.

318

ever with me, and all that I have is thine. It was meet that we should make merry, and be glad: for this thy brother was dead, and is alive again; and was lost, and is found.

[1611]

Joyce Carol Oates
[1938–   ]

JOYCE CAROL OATES *numbers among the most prolific authors in U.S. literary history; since the 1968 publication of her first volume of short stories,* By the North Gate, *Oates has published at least one book or has had at least one play produced every single year—and frequently more than one. All told, in just over forty years, she has published forty novels under her own name, another eight novels under the pseudonym Rosamund Smith, twenty-six volumes of short fiction, fifteen volumes of poetry, eleven volumes of essays and other nonfiction, five books for children and young adults, and somewhere around twenty plays. The tremendous quantity of her writing alone is worth noting, but what makes Oates a remarkable writer is the range of her interests and styles; she is equally successful at domestic novels and at horror fiction, at crime stories and at the gothic romance. Much of her writing bears a thread of subterranean, and at times overt, violence; as she has told an interviewer, "I am a chronicler of the American experience. We have been historically a nation prone to violence, and it would be unreal to ignore this fact. What intrigues me is the response to violence: its aftermath in the private lives of women and children in particular."*

Joyce Carol Oates was born in rural Lockport, New York, and spent much of her time growing up on her grandparents' farm. She began writing at an extremely early age, completing her first novel at age fifteen; the publisher she submitted it too, however, felt that it was too dark for young adult readers. Oates attended Syracuse University, from which she graduated in 1960, and received a master's degree from University of Wisconsin in 1961. She married that same year, and she and her husband, Raymond Joseph Smith, moved to Detroit, where Oates taught at the University of Detroit from 1961 to 1967. She was a member of the faculty of the University of Windsor, in Ontario, Canada, from 1967 to 1978, and became a writer-in-residence at Princeton University in 1978, where she remains today as the Roger S. Berlind Distinguished Professor in the Humanities. That she has combined teaching with writing, and done each so successfully, is a stunning accomplishment, one that few writers can claim. Oates has, in addition, won a plethora of prizes, including three O. Henry Awards; the Rosenthal Award of the National Institute of Arts and Letters; the National Book Award; the O. Henry Special Award for Continuing Achievement, twice; the Elmer Holmed Bobst Award for Lifetime Achievement in Fiction; the Bram Stoker Lifetime Achievement Award for horror fiction; and too many others to enumerate.

Among her many novels, to name only a few, are them *(1969), a story of racial tension, political violence, and urban upheaval set in Detroit in the middle decades of the twentieth century;* Because It Is Bitter, and Because It Is My Heart

(1990), which explores racial segregation and violence in the late 1950s; Black Water *(1992), a fictionalized updating of the story of Senator Ted Kennedy's car accident at Chappaquiddick that left the young woman he was with dead;* Foxfire *(1993), which traces the bonds among members of a girl gang, and the damage such bonds cause;* We Were the Mulvaneys *(1996), the story of a family's downfall in the wake of sexual violence; and* Blonde *(2000), a fictional retelling of the life of Marilyn Monroe. Oates's most recent publications include* Black Girl/White Girl *(2006) and* The Gravedigger's Daughter *(2007). What links these disparate texts is their similar concern, as Oates has pointed out, with "the moral and social conditions of my generation." Her explorations of these conditions resonate with millions of readers, and continue to draw more readers in each year, with each new publication.*

Where Are You Going, Where Have You Been?

JOYCE CAROL OATES

HER NAME WAS CONNIE. She was fifteen and she had a quick nervous giggling habit of craning her neck to glance into mirrors, or checking other people's faces to make sure her own was all right. Her mother, who noticed everything and knew everything and who hadn't much reason any longer to look at her own face, always scolded Connie about it. "Stop gawking at yourself, who are you? You think you're so pretty?" she would say. Connie would raise her eyebrows at these familiar complaints and look right through her mother, into a shadowy vision of herself as she was right at that moment: she knew she was pretty and that was everything. Her mother had been pretty once too, if you could believe those old snapshots in the album, but now her looks were gone and that was why she was always after Connie.

"Why don't you keep your room clean like your sister? How've you got your hair fixed—what the hell stinks? Hair spray? You don't see your sister using that junk."

Her sister June was twenty-four and still lived at home. She was a secretary in the high school Connie attended, and if that wasn't bad enough—with her in the same building—she was so plain and chunky and steady that Connie had to hear her praised all the time by her mother and her mother's sisters. June did this, June did that, she saved money and helped clean the house and cooked and Connie couldn't do a thing, her mind was all filled with trashy daydreams. Their father was away at work most of the time and when he came home he wanted supper and he read the newspaper at supper and after supper he went to bed. He didn't bother talking much to them, but around his bent head Connie's mother kept picking at her until Connie wished her mother was dead and she herself was dead and it was all over. "She makes me want to throw up sometimes," she complained to her friends. She had a high, breathless, amused voice which made everything she said sound a little forced, whether it was sincere or not.

There was one good thing: June went places with girl friends of hers, girls who were just as plain and steady as she, and so when Connie wanted to do that her mother had no objections. The father of Connie's best girl friend drove the girls the three miles to town and left them off at a shopping plaza, so that they could walk through the stores or go to a movie, and when he came to pick them up again at eleven he never bothered to ask what they had done.

They must have been familiar sights, walking around that shopping plaza in their shorts and flat ballerina slippers that always scuffed the sidewalk, with charm bracelets jingling on their thin wrists; they would lean together to whisper and laugh secretly if someone passed by who amused or interested them. Connie had long dark blond hair that drew anyone's eye to it, and she wore part of it pulled up on her head and puffed out and the rest of it she let fall down her back. She wore a pullover jersey blouse that looked one way when she was at home and another way when she was away from home. Everything about her had two sides to it, one for home and one for anywhere that was not home: her walk that could be childlike and bobbing, or languid enough to make anyone think she was hearing music in her head, her mouth which was pale and smirking most of the time, but bright and pink on these evenings out, her laugh which was cynical and drawling at home—"Ha, ha, very funny"—but high-pitched and nervous anywhere else, like the jingling of the charms on her bracelet.

Sometimes they did go shopping or to a movie, but sometimes they went across the highway, ducking fast across the busy road, to a drive-in restaurant where older kids hung out. The restaurant was shaped like a big bottle, though squatter than a real bottle, and on its cap was a revolving figure of a grinning boy who held a hamburger aloft. One night in mid-summer they ran across, breathless with daring, and right away someone leaned out a car window and invited them over, but it was just a boy from high school they didn't like. It made them feel good to be able to ignore him. They went up through the maze of parked and cruising cars to the bright-lit, fly-infested restaurant, their faces pleased and expectant as if they were entering a sacred building that loomed out of the night to give them what haven and what blessing they yearned for. They sat at the counter and crossed their legs at the ankles, their thin shoulders rigid with excitement, and listened to the music that made everything so good: the music was always in the background like music at a church service, it was something to depend upon.

A boy named Eddie came in to talk with them. He sat backwards on his stool, turning himself jerkily around in semi-circles and then stopping and turning again, and after a while he asked Connie if she would like something to eat. She said she did and so she tapped her friend's arm on her way out— her friend pulled her face up into a brave droll look—and Connie said she would meet her at eleven, across the way. "I just hate to leave her like that," Connie said earnestly, but the boy said that she wouldn't be alone for long. So they went out to his car and on the way Connie couldn't help but let her eyes wander over the windshields and faces all around her, her face gleaming with a joy that had nothing to do with Eddie or even this place; it might have been the music. She drew her shoulders up and sucked in her breath with the pure pleasure of being alive, and just at that moment she happened to glance at a face just a few feet from hers. It was a boy with shaggy black hair, in a convertible jalopy painted gold. He stared at her and then his lips widened into a grin. Connie slit her eyes at him and turned away, but she couldn't help glancing back and there he was still watching her. He wagged a finger and laughed and said, "Gonna get you, baby," and Connie turned away again without Eddie noticing anything.

She spent three hours with him, at the restaurant where they ate hamburgers and drank Cokes in wax cups that were always sweating, and then down an alley a mile or so away, and when he left her off at five to eleven only the movie house was still open at the plaza. Her girl friend was there, talking with a boy. When Connie came up the two girls smiled at each other and Connie said, "How was the movie?" and the girl said, "You should know." They rode off with the girl's father, sleepy and pleased, and Connie couldn't help but look at the darkened shopping plaza with its big empty parking lot and its signs that were faded and ghostly now, and over at the drive-in restaurant where cars were still circling tirelessly. She couldn't hear the music at this distance.

Next morning June asked her how the movie was and Connie said, "So-so."

She and that girl and occasionally another girl went out several times a week that way, and the rest of the time Connie spent around the house—it was summer vacation—getting in her mother's way and thinking, dreaming, about the boys she met. But all the boys fell back and dissolved into a single face that was not even a face, but an idea, a feeling, mixed up with the urgent insistent pounding of the music and the humid night air of July. Connie's mother kept dragging her back to the daylight by finding things for her to do or saying, suddenly, "What's this about the Pettinger girl?"

And Connie would say nervously, "Oh, her. That dope." She always drew thick clear lines between herself and such girls, and her mother was simple and kindly enough to believe her. Her mother was so simple, Connie thought, that it was maybe cruel to fool her so much. Her mother went scuffling around the house in old bedroom slippers and complained over the telephone to one sister about the other, then the other called up and the two of them complained about the third one. If June's name was mentioned her mother's tone was approving, and if Connie's name was mentioned it was disapproving. This did not really mean she disliked Connie and actually Connie thought that her mother preferred her to June because she was prettier, but the two of them kept up a pretense of exasperation, a sense that they were tugging and struggling over something of little value to either of them. Sometimes, over coffee, they were almost friends, but something would come up—some vexation that was like a fly buzzing suddenly around their heads—and their faces went hard with contempt.

One Sunday Connie got up at eleven—none of them bothered with church—and washed her hair so that it could dry all day long, in the sun. Her parents and sister were going to a barbecue at an aunt's house and Connie said no, she wasn't interested, rolling her eyes to let her mother know just what she thought of it. "Stay home alone then," her mother said sharply. Connie sat out back in a lawn chair and watched them drive away, her father quiet and bald, hunched around so that he could back the car out, her mother with a look that was still angry and not at all softened through the windshield, and in the back seat poor old June all dressed up as if she didn't know what a barbecue was, with all the running yelling kids and the flies. Connie sat with her eyes closed in the sun, dreaming and dazed with the warmth about her as if this were a kind of love, the caresses of love, and her mind slipped over onto thoughts of the boy she had been with the night before and how nice he had been, how sweet it always was, not the way someone like June would suppose but sweet, gentle, the way it was in movies and promised in songs; and when she opened her eyes she hardly knew where she was, the back yard ran off into weeds and a fence-line of trees and behind it the sky was perfectly blue and still. The asbestos "ranch house" that was now three years old startled her—it looked small. She shook her head as if to get awake.

It was too hot. She went inside the house and turned on the radio to drown out the quiet. She sat on the edge of her bed, barefoot, and listened for an hour and a half to a program called XYZ Sunday Jamboree, record after record of hard, fast, shrieking songs she sang along with, interspersed by exclamations from "Bobby King": "An' look here you girls at Napoleon's—Son and Charley want you to pay real close attention to this song coming up!"

And Connie paid close attention herself, bathed in a glow of slowpulsed joy that seemed to rise mysteriously out of the music itself and lay languidly about the airless little room, breathed in and breathed out with each gentle rise and fall of her chest.

After a while she heard a car coming up the drive. She sat up at once, startled, because it couldn't be her father so soon. The gravel kept crunching all the way in from the road—the driveway was long—and Connie ran to the window. It was a car she didn't know. It was an open jalopy, painted a bright gold that caught the sunlight opaquely. Her heart began to pound and her fingers snatched at her hair, checking it, and she whispered "Christ. Christ," wondering how bad she looked. The car came to a stop at the side door and the horn sounded four short taps as if this were a signal Connie knew.

She went into the kitchen and approached the door slowly, then hung out the screen door, her bare toes curling down off the step. There were two boys in the car and now she recognized the driver: he had shaggy, shabby black hair that looked crazy as a wig and he was grinning at her.

"I ain't late, am I?" he said.

"Who the hell do you think you are?" Connie said.

"Toldja I'd be out, didn't I?"

"I don't even know who you are."

She spoke sullenly, careful to show no interest or pleasure, and he spoke in a fast bright monotone. Connie looked past him to the other boy, taking her time. He had fair brown hair, with a lock that fell onto his forehead. His sideburns gave him a fierce, embarrassed look, but so far he hadn't even bothered to glance at her. Both boys wore sunglasses. The driver's glasses were metallic and mirrored everything in miniature.

"You wanta come for a ride?" he said.

Connie smirked and let her hair fall loose over one shoulder.

"Don'tcha like my car? New paint job," he said. "Hey."

"What?"

"You're cute."

She pretended to fidget, chasing flies away from the door.

"Don'tcha believe me, or what?" he said.

"Look, I don't even know who you are," Connie said in disgust.

"Hey, Ellie's got a radio, see. Mine's broke down." He lifted his friend's arm and showed her the little transistor the boy was holding, and now Connie began to hear the music. It was the same program that was playing inside the house.

"Bobby King?" she said.

"I listen to him all the time. I think he's great."

"He's kind of great," Connie said reluctantly.

"Listen, that guy's great. He knows where the action is."

Connie blushed a little, because the glasses made it impossible for her to see just what this boy was looking at. She couldn't decide if she liked him or if he was just a jerk, and so she dawdled in the doorway and wouldn't come down or go back inside. She said, "What's all that stuff painted on your car?"

"Can'tcha read it?" He opened the door very carefully, as if he was afraid it might fall off. He slid out just as carefully, planting his feet firmly on the ground, the tiny metallic world in his glasses slowing down like gelatine hardening and in the midst of it Connie's bright green blouse. "This here is my name, to begin with," he said. ARNOLD FRIEND was written in tarlike black letters on the side, with a drawing of a round grinning face that reminded Connie of a pumpkin, except it wore sunglasses. "I wanta introduce myself, I'm Arnold Friend and that's my real name and I'm gonna be your friend, honey, and inside the car's Ellie Oscar, he's kinda shy." Ellie brought his transistor radio up to his shoulder and balanced it there. "Now these numbers are a secret code, honey," Arnold Friend explained. He read off the numbers 33, 19, 17 and raised his eyebrows at her to see what she thought of that, but she didn't think much of it. The left rear fender had been smashed and around it was written, on the gleaming gold background: DONE BY CRAZY WOMAN DRIVER. Connie had to laugh at that. Arnold Friend was pleased at her laughter and looked up at her. "Around the other side's a lot more—you wanta come and see them?"

"No."

"Why not?"

"Why should I?"

"Don'tcha wanta see what's on the car? Don'tcha wanta go for a ride?"

"I don't know."

"Why not?"

"I got things to do."

"Like what?"

"Things."

He laughed as if she had said something funny. He slapped his thighs. He was standing in a strange way, leaning back against the car as if he were balancing himself. He wasn't tall, only an inch or so taller than she would be if she came down to him. Connie liked the way he was dressed, which was the way all of them dressed: tight faded jeans stuffed into black, scuffed boots, a belt that pulled his waist in and showed how lean he was, and a white pullover shirt that was a little soiled and showed the hard small muscles of his arms and shoulders. He looked as if he probably did hard work, lifting and carrying things. Even his neck looked muscular. And his face was a familiar face, somehow: the jaw and chin and cheeks slightly darkened, because he hadn't shaved for a day or two, and the nose long and hawklike, sniffing as if she were a treat he was going to gobble up and it was all a joke.

"Connie, you ain't telling the truth. This is your day set aside for a ride with me and you know it," he said, still laughing. The way he straightened and recovered from his fit of laughing showed that it had been all fake.

"How do you know what my name is?" she said suspiciously.

"It's Connie."

"Maybe and maybe not."

"I know my Connie," he said, wagging his finger. Now she remembered him even better, back at the restaurant, and her cheeks warmed at the thought of how she sucked in her breath just at the moment she passed him—how she must have looked to him. And he had remembered her. "Ellie and I come out here especially for you," he said. "Ellie can sit in back. How about it?"

"Where?"

"Where what?"

"Where're we going?"

He looked at her. He took off the sunglasses and she saw how pale the skin around his eyes was, like holes that were not in shadow but instead in light. His eyes were chips of broken glass that catch the light in an amiable way. He smiled. It was as if the idea of going for a ride somewhere, to some place, was a new idea to him.

"Just for a ride, Connie sweetheart."

"I never said my name was Connie," she said.

"But I know what it is. I know your name and all about you, lots of things," Arnold Friend said. He had not moved yet but stood still leaning back against the side of his jalopy. "I took a special interest in you, such a pretty girl, and found out all about you like I know your parents and sister are gone somewheres and I know where and how long they're going to be gone, and I know who you were with last night, and your best girl friend's name is Betty. Right?"

He spoke in a simple lilting voice, exactly as if he were reciting the words to a song. His smile assured her that everything was fine. In the car Ellie turned up the volume on his radio and did not bother to look around at them.

"Ellie can sit in the back seat," Arnold Friend said. He indicated his friend with a casual jerk of his chin, as if Ellie did not count and she should not bother with him.

"How'd you find out all that stuff?" Connie said.

"Listen: Betty Schultz and Tony Fitch and Jimmy Pettinger and Nancy Pettinger," he said, in a chant. "Raymond Stanely and Bob Hutter—"

"Do you know all those kids?"

"I know everybody."

"Look, you're kidding. You're not from around here."

"Sure."

"But—how come we never saw you before?"

"Sure you saw me before," he said. He looked down at his boots, as if he were a little offended. "You just don't remember."

"I guess I'd remember you," Connie said.

"Yeah?" He looked up at this, beaming. He was pleased. He began to mark time with the music from Ellie's radio, tapping his fists lightly together. Connie looked away from his smile to the car, which was painted so bright it almost hurt her eyes to look at it. She looked at that name, ARNOLD FRIEND. And up at the front fender was an expression that was familiar—MAN THE FLYING SAUCERS. It was an expression kids had used the year before, but didn't use this year. She looked at it for a while as if the words meant something to her that she did not yet know.

"What're you thinking about? Huh?" Arnold Friend demanded. "Not worried about your hair blowing around in the car, are you?"

"No.

"Think I maybe can't drive good?"

"How do I know?"

"You're a hard girl to handle. How come?" he said. "Don't you know I'm your friend? Didn't you see me put my sign in the air when you walked by?"

"What sign?"

"My sign." And he drew an X in the air, leaning out toward her. They were maybe ten feet apart. After his hand fell back to his side the X was still in the air, almost visible. Connie let the screen door close and stood perfectly still inside it, listening to the music from her radio and the boy's blend together. She stared at Arnold Friend. He stood there so stiffly relaxed, pretending to be relaxed, with one hand idly on the door handle as if he were keeping himself up that way and had no intention of ever moving again. She recognized most things about him, the tight jeans that showed his thighs and buttocks and the greasy leather boots and the tight shirt, and even that slippery friendly smile of his, that sleepy dreamy smile that all the boys used to get across ideas they didn't want to put into words. She recognized all this and also the singsong way he talked, slightly mocking, kidding, but serious and a little melancholy, and she recognized the way he tapped one fist against the other in homage to the perpetual music behind him. But all these things did not come together.

She said suddenly, "Hey, how old are you?"

His smile faded. She could see then that he wasn't a kid, he was much older—thirty, maybe more. At this knowledge her heart began to pound faster.

"That's a crazy thing to ask. Can'tcha see I'm your own age?"

"Like hell you are."

"Or maybe a coupla years older, I'm eighteen."

"Eighteen?" she said doubtfully.

He grinned to reassure her and lines appeared at the corners of his mouth. His teeth were big and white. He grinned so broadly his eyes became slits and she saw how thick the lashes were, thick and black as if painted with a black tarlike material. Then he seemed to become embarrassed abruptly, and looked over his shoulder at Ellie. "*Him*, he's crazy," he said. "Ain't he a riot, he's a nut, a real character." Ellie was still listening to the music. His sunglasses told nothing about what he was thinking. He wore a bright orange shirt unbuttoned halfway to show his chest, which was a pale, bluish chest and not muscular like Arnold Friend's. His shirt collar was turned up all around and the very tips of the collar pointed out past his chin as if they were protecting him.

He was pressing the transistor radio up against his ear and sat there in a kind of daze, right in the sun.

"He's kinda strange," Connie said.

"Hey, she says you're kinda strange! Kinda strange!" Arnold Friend cried. He pounded on the car to get Ellie's attention. Ellie turned for the first time and Connie saw with shock that he wasn't a kid either—he had a fair, hairless face, cheeks reddened slightly as if the veins grew too close to the surface of his skin, the face of a forty-year-old baby. Connie felt a wave of dizziness rise in her at this sight and she stared at him as if waiting for something to change the shock of the moment, make it all right again. Ellie's lips kept shaping words, mumbling along with the words blasting in his ear.

"Maybe you two better go away," Connie said faintly.

"What? How come?" Arnold Friend cried. "We come out here to take you for a ride. It's Sunday." He had the voice of the man on the radio now. It was the same voice, Connie thought. "Don'tcha know it's Sunday all day and honey, no matter who you were with last night today you're with Arnold Friend and don't you forget it!—Maybe you better step out here," he said, and this last was in a different voice. It was a little flatter, as if the heat was finally getting to him.

"No. I got things to do."

"Hey."

"You two better leave."

"We ain't leaving until you come with us."

"Like hell I am—"

"Connie, don't fool around with me. I mean, I mean, don't fool *around*," he said, shaking his head. He laughed incredulously. He placed his sunglasses on top of his head, carefully, as if he were indeed wearing a wig, and brought the stems down behind his ears. Connie stared at him, another wave of dizziness and fear rising in her so that for a moment he wasn't even in focus but was just a blur, standing there against his gold car, and she had the idea that he had driven up the driveway all right but had come from nowhere before that and belonged nowhere and that everything about him and even about the music that was so familiar to her was only half real.

"If my father comes and sees you—"

"He ain't coming. He's at a barbecue."

"How do you know that?"

"Aunt Tillie's. Right now they're—uh—they're drinking. Sitting around," he said vaguely, squinting as if he were staring all the way to town and over to Aunt Tillie's backyard. Then the vision seemed to get clear and he nodded energetically. "Yeah. Sitting around. There's your sister in a blue dress, huh? And high heels, the poor sad bitch—nothing like you, sweetheart! And your mother's helping some fat woman with the corn, they're cleaning the corn—husking the corn—"

"What fat woman?" Connie cried.

"How do I know what fat woman. I don't know every goddam fat woman in the world!" Arnold Friend laughed.

"Oh, that's Mrs. Hornby. . . . Who invited her?" Connie said. She felt a little light-headed. Her breath was coming quickly.

"She's too fat. I don't like them fat. I like them the way you are, honey," he said, smiling sleepily at her. They stared at each other for a while, through the screen door. He said softly, "Now what you're going to do is this: you're going to come out that door. You're going to sit up front with me and Ellie's going to sit in the back, the hell with Ellie, right? This isn't Ellie's date. You're my date. I'm your lover, honey."

"What? You're crazy—"

"Yes, I'm your lover. You don't know what that is but you will," he said. "I know that too. I know all about you. But look: it's real nice and you couldn't ask for nobody better than me, or more polite. I always keep my word. I'll tell you how it is, I'm always nice at first, the first time. I'll hold you so tight you won't think you have to try to get away or pretend anything because you'll know you can't. And I'll come inside you where it's all secret and you'll give in to me and you'll love me—"

"Shut up! You're crazy!" Connie said. She backed away from the door. She put her hands against her ears as if she'd heard something terrible, something not meant for her. "People don't talk like that, you're crazy," she muttered. Her heart was almost too big now for her chest and its pumping made sweat break out all over her. She looked out to see Arnold Friend pause and then take a step toward the porch lurching. He almost fell. But, like a clever drunken man, he managed to catch his balance. He wobbled in his high boots and grabbed hold of one of the porch posts.

"Honey?" he said. "You still listening?"

"Get the hell out of here!"

"Be nice, honey. Listen."

"I'm going to call the police—"

He wobbled again and out of the side of his mouth came a fast spat curse, an aside not meant for her to hear. But even this "Christ!" sounded forced. Then he began to smile again. She watched this smile come, awkward as if he were smiling from inside a mask. His whole face was a mask, she thought wildly, tanned down onto his throat but then running out as if he had plastered make-up on his face but had forgotten about his throat.

"Honey—? Listen, here's how it is. I always tell the truth and I promise you this: I ain't coming in that house after you."

"You better not! I'm going to call the police if you—if you don't—"

"Honey," he said, talking right through her voice, "honey, I'm not coming in there but you are coming out here. You know why?"

She was panting. The kitchen looked like a place she had never seen before, some room she had run inside but which wasn't good enough, wasn't going to help her. The kitchen window had never had a curtain, after three years, and there were dishes in the sink for her to do—probably—and if you ran your hand across the table you'd probably feel something sticky there.

"You listening, honey? Hey?"

"—going to call the police—"

"Soon as you touch the phone I don't need to keep my promise and can come inside. You won't want that."

She rushed forward and tried to lock the door. Her fingers were shaking. "But why lock it," Arnold Friend said gently, talking right into her face. "It's just a screen door. It's just nothing." One of his boots was at a strange angle, as if his foot wasn't in it. It pointed out to the left, bent at the ankle. "I mean, anybody can break through a screen door and glass and wood and iron or anything else if he needs to, anybody at all and specially Arnold Friend. If the place got lit up with a fire honey you'd come running out into my arms, right into my arms and safe at home—like you knew I was your lover and'd stopped fooling around. I don't mind a nice shy girl but I don't like no fooling around." Part of those words were spoken with a slight rhythmic lilt, and Connie somehow recognized them—the echo of a song from last year, about a girl rushing into her boy friend's arms and coming home again—

Connie stood barefoot on the linoleum floor, staring at him. "What do you want?" she whispered.

"I want you," he said.

"What?"

"Seen you that night and thought, that's the one, yes sir. I never needed to look any more."

"But my father's coming back. He's coming to get me. I had to wash my hair first—" She spoke in a dry, rapid voice, hardly raising it for him to hear.

"No, your daddy is not coming and yes, you had to wash your hair and you washed it for me. It's nice and shining and all for me, I thank you, sweetheart," he said, with a mock bow, but again he almost lost his balance. He had to bend and adjust his boots. Evidently his feet did not go all the way down; the boots must have been stuffed with something so that he would seem taller. Connie stared out at him and behind him Ellie in the car, who seemed to be looking off toward Connie's right, into nothing. This Ellie said, pulling the words out of the air one after another as if he were just discovering them, "You want me to pull out the phone?"

"Shut your mouth and keep it shut," Arnold Friend said, his face red from bending over or maybe from embarrassment because Connie had seen his boots. "This ain't none of your business."

"What—what are you doing? What do you want?" Connie said. "If I call the police they'll get you, they'll arrest you—"

"Promise was not to come in unless you touch that phone, and I'll keep that promise," he said. He resumed his erect position and tried to force his shoulders back. He sounded like a hero in a movie, declaring something important. He spoke too loudly and it was as if he were speaking to someone behind Connie. "I ain't made plans for coming in that house where I don't belong but just for you to come out to me, the way you should. Don't you know who I am?"

"You're crazy," she whispered. She backed away from the door but did not want to go into another part of the house, as if this would give him permission to come through the door. "What do you. . . . You're crazy, you . . ."

"Huh? What're you saying, honey?"

Her eyes darted everywhere in the kitchen. She could not remember what it was, this room.

"This is how it is, honey: you come out and we'll drive away, have a nice ride. But if you don't come out we're gonna wait till your people come home and then they're all going to get it."

"You want that telephone pulled out?" Ellie said. He held the radio away from his ear and grimaced, as if without the radio the air was too much for him.

"I toldja shut up, Ellie," Arnold Friend said, "you're deaf, get a hearing aid, right? Fix yourself up. This little girl's no trouble and's gonna be nice to me, so Ellie keep to yourself, this ain't your date—right? Don't hem in on me. Don't hog. Don't crush. Don't bird dog. Don't trail me," he said in a rapid meaningless voice, as if he were running through all the expressions he'd learned but was no longer sure which one of them was in style, then rushing on to new ones, making them up with his eyes closed, "Don't crawl under my fence, don't squeeze in my chipmunk hole, don't sniff my glue, suck my pop-sicle, keep your own greasy fingers on yourself!" He shaded his eyes and peered in at Connie, who was backed against the kitchen table. "Don't mind him honey he's just a creep. He's a dope. Right? I'm the boy for you and like I said you come out here nice like a lady and give me your hand, and nobody else gets hurt, I mean, your nice old bald-headed daddy and your mummy and your sister in her high heels. Because listen: why bring them in this?"

"Leave me alone," Connie whispered.

"Hey, you know that old woman down the road, the one with the chickens and stuff—you know her?"

"She's dead!"

"Dead? What? You know her?" Arnold Friend said.

"She's dead—"

"Don't you like her?"

"She's dead—she's—she isn't here any more—"

"But don't you like her, I mean, you got something against her? Some grudge or something?" Then his voice dipped as if he were conscious of a rudeness. He touched the sunglasses perched on top of his head as if to make sure they were still there. "Now you be a good girl."

"What are you going to do?"

"Just two things, or maybe three," Arnold Friend said. "But I promise it won't last long and you'll like me that way you get to like people you're close to. You will. It's all over for you here, so come on out. You don't want your people in any trouble, do you?"

She turned and bumped against a chair or something, hurting her leg, but she ran into the back room and picked up the telephone. Something roared in her ear, a tiny roaring, and she was so sick with fear that she could do nothing but listen to it—the telephone was clammy and very heavy and her fingers groped down to the dial but were too weak to touch it. She began to scream into the phone, into the roaring. She cried out, she cried for her mother, she felt her breath start jerking back and forth in her lungs as if it were something Arnold Friend were stabbing her with again and again with no tenderness. A noisy sorrowful wailing rose all about her and she was locked inside it the way she was locked inside the house.

After a while she could hear again. She was sitting on the floor with her wet back against the wall.

Arnold Friend was saying from the door, "That's a good girl. Put the phone back."

She kicked the phone away from her.

"No, honey. Pick it up. Put it back right."

She picked it up and put it back. The dial tone stopped.

"That's a good girl. Now you come outside."

She was hollow with what had been fear, but what was now just an emptiness. All that screaming had blasted it out of her. She sat, one leg cramped under her, and deep inside her brain was something like a pinpoint of light that kept going and would not let her relax. She thought, I'm not going to see my mother again. She thought, I'm not going to sleep in my bed again. Her bright green blouse was all wet.

Arnold Friend said, in a gentle-loud voice that was like a stage voice, "The place where you came from ain't there any more, and where you had in mind to go is cancelled out. This place you are now—inside your daddy's house—is nothing but a cardboard box I can knock down any time. You know that and always did know it. You hear me?"

334

She thought, I have got to think. I have to know what to do.

"We'll go out to a nice field, out in the country here where it smells so nice and it's sunny," Arnold Friend said. "I'll have my arms around you so you won't need to try to get away and I'll show you what love is like, what it does. The hell with this house! It looks solid all right," he said. He ran a fingernail down the screen and the noise did not make Connie shiver, as it would have the day before. "Now put your hand on your heart, honey. Feel that? That feels solid too but we know better, be nice to me, be sweet like you can because what else is there for a girl like you but to be sweet and pretty and give in?— and get away before her people come back?"

She felt her pounding heart. Her hand seemed to enclose it. She thought for the first time in her life that it was nothing that was hers, that belonged to her, but just a pounding, living thing inside this body that wasn't really hers either.

"You don't want them to get hurt," Arnold Friend went on. "Now get up, honey. Get up all by yourself."

She stood.

"Now turn this way. That's right. Come over here to me—Ellie, put that away, didn't I tell you? You dope. You miserable creepy dope," Arnold Friend said. His words were not angry but only part of an incantation. The incantation was kindly. "Now come out through the kitchen to me honey and let's see a smile, try it, you're a brave sweet little girl and now they're eating corn and hotdogs cooked to bursting over an outdoor fire, and they don't know one thing about you and never did and honey you're better than them because not a one of them would have done this for you."

Connie felt the linoleum under her feet; it was cool. She brushed her hair back out of her eyes. Arnold Friend let go of the post tentatively and opened his arms for her, his elbows pointing in toward each other and his wrists limp, to show that this was an embarrassed embrace and a little mocking, he didn't want to make her self-conscious.

She put out her hand against the screen. She watched herself push the door slowly open as if she were safe back somewhere in the other doorway, watching this body and this head of long hair moving out into the sunlight where Arnold Friend waited.

"My sweet little blue-eyed girl," he said, in a half-sung sigh that had nothing to do with her brown eyes but was taken up just the same by the vast sun-lit reaches of the land behind him and on all sides of him, so much land that Connie had never seen before and did not recognize except to know that she was going to it.

[1970]

335

The Cask of Amontillado

EDGAR ALLAN POE

THE THOUSAND INJURIES OF Fortunato I had borne as I best could; but when he ventured upon insult, I vowed revenge. You, who so well know the nature of my soul, will not suppose, however, that I gave utterance to a threat. *At length* I would be avenged; this was a point definitely settled—but the very definitiveness with which it was resolved, precluded the idea of risk. I must not only punish, but punish with impunity. A wrong is unredressed when retribution overtakes its redresser. It is equally unredressed when the avenger fails to make himself felt as such to him who has done the wrong.

It must be understood, that neither by word nor deed had I given Fortunato cause to doubt my good-will. I continued, as was my wont, to smile in his face, and he did not perceive that my smile *now* was at the thought of his immolation.

He had a weak point—this Fortunato—although in other regards he was a man to be respected and even feared. He prided himself on his connoisseurship in wine. Few Italians have the true virtuoso[1] spirit. For the most part their enthusiasm is adopted to suit the time and opportunity—to practice imposture upon the British and Austrian *millionaires*. In painting and gemmary, Fortunato, like his countrymen, was quack[2]—but in the matter of old wines he was sincere. In this respect I did not differ from him materially: I was skilful in the Italian vintages myself, and bought largely whenever I could.

It was about dusk, one evening during the supreme madness of the carnival season, that I encountered my friend. He accosted me with excessive warmth, for he had been drinking much. The man wore motley[3]. He had on a tight-fitting parti-striped dress, and his head was surmounted by the conical cap and bells. I was so pleased to see him, that I thought I should never have done wringing his hand.

---

[1] A learned devotee

[2] An imposter, poseur

[3] A multi-colored costume, particularly that worn by a jester.

First published in 1846.

I said to him: "My dear Fortunato, you are luckily met. How remarkably well you are looking to-day! But I have received a pipe[4] of what passes for Amontillado[5], and I have my doubts."

"How?" said he. "Amontillado? A pipe? Impossible! And in the middle of the carnival!"

"I have my doubts," I replied; "and I was silly enough to pay the full Amontillado price without consulting you in the matter. You were not to be found, and I was fearful of losing a bargain."

"Amontillado!"

"I have my doubts."

"Amontillado!"

"And I must satisfy them."

"Amontillado!"

"As you are engaged, I am on my way to Luchesi. If any one has a critical turn it is he: He will tell me—"

"Luchesi cannot tell Amontillado from Sherry."

"And yet some fools will have it that his taste is a match for your own."

"Come, let us go."

"Whither?"

"To your vaults."

"My friend, no; I will not impose upon your good nature. I perceive you have an engagement. Luchesi—"

"I have no engagement;—come."

"My friend, no. It is not the engagement, but the severe cold with which I perceive you are afflicted. The vaults are insufferably damp. They are encrusted with nitre."[6]

"Let us go, nevertheless. The cold is merely nothing. Amontillado! You have been imposed upon. And as for Luchesi, he cannot distinguish Sherry from Amontillado."

Thus speaking, Fortunato possessed himself of my arm. Putting on a mask of black silk, and drawing a *roquelaire*[7] closely about my person, I suffered him to hurry me to my palazzo.

There were no attendants at home; they had absconded to make merry in honor of the time. I had told them that I should not return until the morning, and had given them explicit orders not to stir from the house. These orders

---

[4]A wine cask.

[5]A light sherry produced in the Spanish town of Montilla.

[6]Salt peter (potassium nitrate).

[7]A knee-length cloak.

were sufficient, I well knew, to insure their immediate disappearance, one and all, as soon as my back was turned.

I took from their sconces two flambeaux[8], and giving one to Fortunato, bowed him through several suites of rooms to the archway that led into the vaults. I passed down a long and winding staircase, requesting him to be cautious as he followed. We came at length to the foot of the descent, and stood together upon the damp ground of the catacombs of the Montresors.

The gait of my friend was unsteady, and the bells upon his cap jingled as he strode.

"The pipe?" said he.

"It is farther on," said I; "but observe the white web-work which gleams from these cavern walls."

He turned towards me, and looked into my eyes with two filmy orbs that distilled the rheum of intoxication.

"Nitre?" he asked, at length.

"Nitre," I replied. "How long have you had that cough?"

"Ugh! ugh! ugh!—ugh! ugh! ugh!—ugh! ugh! ugh!—ugh! ugh! ugh!— ugh! ugh! ugh!"

My poor friend found it impossible to reply for many minutes.

"It is nothing," he said, at last.

"Come," I said, with decision, "we will go back; your health is precious. You are rich, respected, admired, beloved; you are happy, as once I was. You are a man to be missed. For me it is no matter. We will go back; you will be ill, and I cannot be responsible. Besides there is Luchesi—"

"Enough," he said; "the cough is a mere nothing; it will not kill me. I shall not die of a cough."

"True—true," I replied; "and, indeed, I had no intention of alarming you unnecessarily; but you should use all proper caution. A draught of this Medoc[9] will defend us from the damps."

Here I knocked off the neck of a bottle which I drew from a long row of its fellows that lay upon the mould.

"Drink," I said, presenting him the wine.

He raised it to his lips with a leer. He paused and nodded to me familiarly, while his bells jingled.

"I drink," he said, "to the buried that repose around us."

"And I to your long life."

He again took my arm, and we proceeded.

---

[8]Torches

[9]A red wine named for the French region of its origin.

"These vaults," he said, "are extensive."

"The Montresors," I replied, "were a great and numerous family."

"I forget your arms."

"A huge human foot d'or, in a field azure; the foot crushes a serpent rampant whose fangs are imbedded in the heel."

"And the motto?"

"*Nemo me impune lacessit.*"[10]

"Good!" he said.

The wine sparkled in his eyes and the bells jingled. My own fancy grew warm with the Medoc. We had passed through long walls of piled bones, with casks and puncheons intermingling, into the inmost recesses of the catacombs. I paused again, and this time I made bold to seize Fortunato by an arm above the elbow.

"The nitre!" I said; "see, it increases. It hangs like moss upon the vaults. We are below the river's bed. The drops of moisture trickle among the bones. Come, we will go back ere it is too late. Your cough—"

"It is nothing," he said; "let us go on. But first, another draught of the Medoc."

I broke and reached him a flagon[11] of De Grâve[12]. He emptied it at a breath. His eyes flashed with a fierce light. He laughed and threw the bottle upward with a gesticulation I did not understand.

I looked at him in surprise. He repeated the movement—a grotesque one.

"You do not comprehend?" he said.

"Not I," I replied.

"Then you are not of the brotherhood."

"How?"

"You are not of the masons."

"Yes, yes," I said; "yes, yes."

"You? Impossible! A mason?"

"A mason," I replied.

"A sign," he said.

"It is this," I answered, producing a trowel from beneath the folds of my *roquelaire*.

"You jest," he exclaimed, recoiling a few paces. "But let us proceed to the Amontillado."

---

[10]Latin: "No one insults me with impunity." Such mottos are often inscribed in the coat of arms (symbol originally borne on a shield or clothing) of European aristocratic families.

[11]A large wine bottle.

[12]A white wine from Bordeaux.

"Be it so," I said, replacing the tool beneath the cloak, and again offering him my arm. He leaned upon it heavily. We continued our route in search of the Amontillado. We passed through a range of low arches, descended, passed on, and descending again, arrived at a deep crypt, in which the foulness of the air caused our flambeaux rather to glow than flame.

At the most remote end of the crypt there appeared another less spacious. Its walls had been lined with human remains, piled to the vault overhead, in the fashion of the great catacombs of Paris. Three sides of this interior crypt were still ornamented in this manner. From the fourth the bones had been thrown down, and lay promiscuously upon the earth, forming at one point a mound of some size. Within the wall thus exposed by the displacing of the bones, we perceived a still interior recess, in depth about four feet, in width three, in height six or seven. It seemed to have been constructed for no especial use within itself, but formed merely the interval between two of the colossal supports of the roof of the catacombs, and was backed by one of their circumscribing walls of solid granite.

It was in vain that Fortunato, uplifting his dull torch, endeavored to pry into the depth of the recess. Its termination the feeble light did not enable us to see.

"Proceed," I said; "herein is the Amontillado. As for Luchesi—"

"He is an ignoramus," interrupted my friend, as he stepped unsteadily forward, while I followed immediately at his heels. In an instant he had reached the extremity of the niche, and finding his progress arrested by the rock, stood stupidly bewildered. A moment more and I had fettered him to the granite. In its surface were two iron staples, distant from each other about two feet, horizontally. From one of these depended a short chain, from the other a padlock. Throwing the links about his waist, it was but the work of a few seconds to secure it. He was too much astounded to resist. Withdrawing the key I stepped back from the recess.

"Pass your hand," I said, "over the wall; you cannot help feeling the nitre. Indeed, it is *very* damp. Once more let me *implore* you to return. No? Then I must positively leave you. But I must first render you all the little attentions in my power."

"The Amontillado!" ejaculated my friend, not yet recovered from his astonishment.

"True," I replied; "the Amontillado."

As I said these words I busied myself among the pile of bones of which I have before spoken. Throwing them aside, I soon uncovered a quantity of building stone and mortar. With these materials and with the aid of my trowel, I began vigorously to wall up the entrance of the niche.

I had scarcely laid the first tier of the masonry when I discovered that the intoxication of Fortunato had in a great measure worn off. The earliest indication I had of this was a low moaning cry from the depths of the recess. It was *not* the cry of a drunken man. There was then a long and obstinate silence. I laid the second tier, and the third, and the fourth; and then I heard the furious vibrations of the chain. The noise lasted for several minutes, during which, that I might hearken to it with the more satisfaction, I ceased my labors and sat down upon the bones. When at last the clanking subsided, I resumed the trowel, and finished without interruption the fifth, the sixth, and the seventh tier. The wall was now nearly upon a level with my breast. I again paused, and holding the flambeaux over the mason-work, threw a few feeble rays upon the figure within.

A succession of loud and shrill screams, bursting suddenly from the throat of the chained form, seemed to thrust me violently back. For a brief moment I hesitated—I trembled. Unsheathing my rapier, I began to grope with it about the recess; but the thought of an instant reassured me. I placed my hand upon the solid fabric of the catacombs, and felt satisfied. I reapproached the wall. I replied to the yells of him who clamoured. I re-echoed—I aided—I surpassed them in volume and in strength. I did this, and the clamourer grew still.

It was now midnight, and my task was drawing to a close. I had completed the eighth, the ninth and the tenth tier. I had finished a portion of the last and the eleventh; there remained but a single stone to be fitted and plastered in. I struggled with its weight; I placed it partially in its destined position. But now there came from out the niche a low laugh that erected the hairs upon my head. It was succeeded by a sad voice, which I had difficulty in recognizing as that of the noble Fortunato. The voice said—

"Ha! ha! ha!—he! he!—a very good joke indeed—an excellent jest. We will have many a rich laugh about it at the palazzo—he! he! he!—over our wine—he! he! he!"

"The Amontillado!" I said.

"He! ha! he!—he! he! he!—yes, the Amontillado. But is it not getting late? Will not they be awaiting us at the palazzo, the Lady Fortunato and the rest? Let us be gone."

"Yes," I said, "let us be gone."

"*For the love of God, Montresor!*"

"Yes," I said, "for the love of God."

But to these words I hearkened in vain for a reply. I grew impatient. I called aloud:

"Fortunato!"

No answer. I called again:

"Fortunato!"

No answer still. I thrust a torch through the remaining aperture and let it fall within. There came forth in return only a tingling of the bells. My heart grew sick—on account of the dampness of the catacombs. I hastened to make an end of my labour. I forced the last stone into its position; I plastered it up. Against the new masonry I reerected the old rampart of bones. For the half of a century no mortal has disturbed them. *In pace requiescat!*[13]

[1850]

---

[13]Latin: "Rest in peace."

The Fall of the House of Usher

EDGAR ALLAN POE

Son coeur est un luth suspendu;
Sitô qu'on le touche il résonne.
—DE BÉRANGER[1]

DURING THE WHOLE OF a dull, dark, and soundless day in the autumn of the year, when the clouds hung oppressively low in the heavens, I had been passing alone, on horseback, through a singularly dreary tract of country, and at length found myself, as the shades of the evening drew on, within view of the melancholy House of Usher. I know not how it was—but, with the first glimpse of the building, a sense of insufferable gloom pervaded my spirit. I say insufferable; for the feeling was unrelieved by any of that halfpleasurable, because poetic, sentiment, with which the mind usually receives even the sternest natural images of the desolate or terrible. I looked upon the scene before me—upon the mere house, and the simple landscape features of the domain—upon the bleak walls—upon the vacant eye-like windows—upon a few rank sedges—and upon a few white trunks of decayed trees—with an utter depression of soul which I can compare to no earthly sensation more properly than to the after-dream of the reveller upon opium—the bitter lapse into every-day life—the hideous dropping off of the veil. There was an iciness, a sinking, a sickening of the heart—an unredeemed dreariness of thought which no goading of the imagination could torture into aught of the sublime. What was it—I paused to think—what was it that so unnerved me in the contemplation of the House of Usher? It was a mystery all insoluble; nor could I grapple with the shadowy fancies that crowded upon me as I pondered. I was forced to fall back upon the unsatisfactory conclusion, that while, beyond doubt, there *are* combinations of very simple natural objects which have the

---

[1]"His heart is a suspended lute; / No sooner touched, it sounds." This is a slight misquotation of a poem titled "Le Rufus" by Pierre-Jean de Béranger (1780–1857).

First published in *Burton's Gentleman's Magazine* in September, 1839.

power of thus affecting us, still the analysis of this power lies among considerations beyond our depth. It was possible, I reflected, that a mere different arrangement of the particulars of the scene, of the details of the picture, would be sufficient to modify, or perhaps to annihilate its capacity for sorrowful impression; and, acting upon this idea, I reined my horse to the precipitous brink of a black and lurid tarn[2] that lay in unruffled lustre by the dwelling, and gazed down—but with a shudder even more thrilling than before—upon the remodelled and inverted images of the gray sedge, and the ghastly tree-stems, and the vacant and eye-like windows.

Nevertheless, in this mansion of gloom I now proposed to myself a sojourn of some weeks. Its proprietor, Roderick Usher, had been one of my boon companions in boyhood; but many years had elapsed since our last meeting. A letter, however, had lately reached me in a distant part of the country—a letter from him—which, in its wildly importunate nature, had admitted of no other than a personal reply. The MS.[3] gave evidence of nervous agitation. The writer spoke of acute bodily illness—of a mental disorder which oppressed him—and of an earnest desire to see me, as his best, and indeed his only personal friend, with a view of attempting, by the cheerfulness of my society, some alleviation of his malady. It was the manner in which all this, and much more, was said—it was the apparent *heart* that went with his request—which allowed me no room for hesitation; and I accordingly obeyed forthwith what I still considered a very singular summons.

Although, as boys, we had been even intimate associates, yet I really knew little of my friend. His reserve had been always excessive and habitual. I was aware, however, that his very ancient family had been noted, time out of mind, for a peculiar sensibility of temperament, displaying itself, through long ages, in many works of exalted art, and manifested, of late, in repeated deeds of munificent yet unobtrusive charity, as well as in a passionate devotion to the intricacies, perhaps even more than to the orthodox and easily recognizable beauties, of musical science. I had learned, too, the very remarkable fact, that the stem of the Usher race, all time-honoured as it was, had put forth, at no period, any enduring branch; in other words, that the entire family lay in the direct line of descent, and had always, with very trifling and very temporary variation, so lain. It was this deficiency, I considered, while running over in thought the perfect keeping of the character of the premises with the accredited character of the people, and while speculating upon the possible influence which the one, in the long lapse of centuries, might have exercised upon the

---

[2] A deep mountain lake formed by glaciers.

[3] Manuscript

other—it was this deficiency, perhaps of collateral issue, and the consequent undeviating transmission, from sire to son, of the patrimony with the name, which had, at length, so identified the two as to merge the original title of the estate in the quaint and equivocal appellation of the "House of Usher"—an appellation[4] which seemed to include, in the minds of the peasantry who used it, both the family and the family mansion.

I have said that the sole effect of my somewhat childish experiment—that of looking down within the tarn—had been to deepen the first singular impression. There can be no doubt that the consciousness of the rapid increase of my superstition—for why should I not so term it?—served mainly to accelerate the increase itself. Such, I have long known, is the paradoxical law of all sentiments having terror as a basis. And it might have been for this reason only, that, when I again uplifted my eyes to the house itself, from its image in the pool, there grew in my mind a strange fancy—a fancy so ridiculous, indeed, that I but mention it to show the vivid force of the sensations which oppressed me. I had so worked upon my imagination as really to believe that about the whole mansion and domain there hung an atmosphere peculiar to themselves and their immediate vicinity—an atmosphere which had no affinity with the air of heaven, but which had reeked up from the decayed trees, and the gray wall, and the silent tarn—a pestilent and mystic vapour, dull, sluggish, faintly discernible, and leaden-hued.

Shaking off from my spirit what *must* have been a dream, I scanned more narrowly the real aspect of the building. Its principal feature seemed to be that of an excessive antiquity. The discoloration of ages had been great. Minute fungi overspread the whole exterior, hanging in a fine tangled webwork from the eaves. Yet all this was apart from an extraordinary dilapidation. No portion of the masonry had fallen; and there appeared to be a wild inconsistency between its still perfect adaptation of parts, and the crumbling condition of the individual stones. In this there was much that reminded me of the specious[5] totality of old woodwork which has rotted for long years in some neglected vault, with no disturbance from the breath of the external air. Beyond this indication of extensive decay, however, the fabric gave little token of instability. Perhaps the eye of a scrutinizing observer might have discovered a barely perceptible fissure, which, extending from the roof of the building in front, made its way down the wall in a zigzag direction, until it became lost in the sullen waters of the tarn.

Noticing these things, I rode over a short causeway to the house. A servant in waiting took my horse, and I entered the Gothic archway of the hall. A valet,

---

[4]Name

[5]False, despite the appearance of plausibility.

of stealthy step, thence conducted me, in silence, through many dark and intricate passages in my progress to the *studio* of his master. Much that I encountered on the way contributed, I know not how, to heighten the vague sentiments of which I have already spoken. While the objects around me—while the carvings of the ceilings, the sombre tapestries of the walls, the ebon blackness of the floors, and the phantasmagoric armorial trophies which rattled as I strode, were but matters to which, or to such as which, I had been accustomed from my infancy—while I hesitated not to acknowledge how familiar was all this—I still wondered to find how unfamiliar were the fancies which ordinary images were stirring up. On one of the staircases, I met the physician of the family. His countenance, I thought, wore a mingled expression of low cunning and perplexity. He accosted me with trepidation and passed on. The valet now threw open a door and ushered me into the presence of his master.

The room in which I found myself was very large and lofty. The windows were long, narrow, and pointed, and at so vast a distance from the black oaken floor as to be altogether inaccessible from within. Feeble gleams of encrimsoned light made their way through the trellissed panes, and served to render sufficiently distinct the more prominent objects around; the eye, however, struggled in vain to reach the remoter angles of the chamber, or the recesses of the vaulted and fretted ceiling. Dark draperies hung upon the walls. The general furniture was profuse, comfortless, antique, and tattered. Many books and musical instruments lay scattered about, but failed to give any vitality to the scene. I felt that I breathed an atmosphere of sorrow. An air of stern, deep, and irredeemable gloom hung over and pervaded all.

Upon my entrance, Usher arose from a sofa on which he had been lying at full length, and greeted me with a vivacious warmth which had much in it, I at first thought of an overdone cordiality—of the constrained effort of the *ennuye*[6] man of the world. A glance, however, at his countenance convinced me of his perfect sincerity. We sat down; and for some moments, while he spoke not, I gazed upon him with a feeling half of pity, half of awe. Surely, man had never before so terribly altered, in so brief a period, as had Roderick Usher! It was with difficulty that I could bring myself to admit the identity of the wan being before me with the companion of my early boyhood. Yet the character of his face had been at all times remarkable. A cadaverousness of complexion; an eye large, liquid, and luminous beyond comparison; lips somewhat thin and very pallid, but of a surpassingly beautiful curve; a nose of a delicate Hebrew model, but with a breadth of nostril unusual in similar formations; a finely moulded chin, speaking, in its want of prominence, of a want

---

[6]Bored

of moral energy; hair of a more than web-like softness and tenuity; these features, with an inordinate expansion above the regions of the temple, made up altogether a countenance not easily to be forgotten. And now in the mere exaggeration of the prevailing character of these features, and of the expression they were wont to convey, lay so much of change that I doubted to whom I spoke. The now ghastly pallor of the skin, and the now miraculous lustre of the eye, above all things startled and even awed me. The silken hair, too, had been suffered to grow all unheeded, and as, in its wild gossamer texture, it floated rather than fell about the face, I could not, even with effort, connect its Arabesque[7] expression with any idea of simple humanity.

In the manner of my friend I was at once struck with an incoherence—an inconsistency; and I soon found this to arise from a series of feeble and futile struggles to overcome an habitual trepidancy—an excessive nervous agitation. For something of this nature I had indeed been prepared, no less by his letter, than by reminiscences of certain boyish traits, and by conclusions deducted from his peculiar physical conformation and temperament. His action was alternately vivacious and sullen. His voice varied rapidly from a tremulous indecision (when the animal spirits seemed utterly in abeyance) to that species of energetic concision—that abrupt, weighty, unhurried, and hollow-sounding enunciation—that leaden, self-balanced, and perfectly modulated guttural utterance, which may be observed in the lost drunkard, or the irreclaimable eater of opium, during the periods of his most intense excitement.

It was thus that he spoke of the object of my visit, of his earnest desire to see me, and of the solace he expected me to afford him. He entered, at some length, into what he conceived to be the nature of his malady. It was, he said, a constitutional and a family evil, and one for which he despaired to find a remedy—a mere nervous affection, he immediately added, which would undoubtedly soon pass off. It displayed itself in a host of unnatural sensations. Some of these, as he detailed them, interested and bewildered me; although, perhaps, the terms and the general manner of their narration had their weight. He suffered much from a morbid acuteness of the senses; the most insipid food was alone endurable; he could wear only garments of certain texture; the odours of all flowers were oppressive; his eyes were tortured by even a faint light; and there were but peculiar sounds, and these from stringed instruments, which did not inspire him with horror.

To an anomalous species of terror I found him a bounden slave. "I shall perish," said he, "I *must* perish in this deplorable folly. Thus, thus, and not otherwise, shall I be lost. I dread the events of the future, not in themselves, but

---

[7]Whether applied to music or decorative art, "arabesque" refers to an intricate ornamental motif.

in their results. I shudder at the thought of any, even the most trivial, incident, which may operate upon this intolerable agitation of soul. I have, indeed, no abhorrence of danger, except in its absolute effect—in terror. In this unnerved—in this pitiable condition—I feel that the period will sooner or later arrive when I must abandon life and reason together, in some struggle with the grim phantasm, FEAR."

I learned, moreover, at intervals, and through broken and equivocal hints, another singular feature of his mental condition. He was enchained by certain superstitious impressions in regard to the dwelling which he tenanted, and whence, for many years, he had never ventured forth—in regard to an influence whose supposititious force was conveyed in terms too shadowy here to be re-stated—an influence which some peculiarities in the mere form and substance of his family mansion had, by dint of long sufferance, he said, obtained over his spirit—an effect which the *physique* of the gray wall and turrets, and of the dim tarn into which they all looked down, had, at length, brought about upon the *morale* of his existence.

He admitted, however, although with hesitation, that much of the peculiar gloom which thus afflicted him could be traced to a more natural and far more palpable origin—to the severe and long-continued illness—indeed to the evidently approaching dissolution—of a tenderly beloved sister, his sole companion for long years, his last and only relative on earth. "Her decease," he said, with a bitterness which I can never forget, "would leave him (him the hopeless and the frail) the last of the ancient race of the Ushers." While he spoke, the lady Madeline (for so was she called) passed slowly through a remote portion of the apartment, and, without having noticed my presence, disappeared. I regarded her with an utter astonishment not unmingled with dread—and yet I found it impossible to account for such feelings: A sensation of stupor oppressed me, as my eyes followed her retreating steps. When a door, at length, closed upon her, my glance sought instinctively and eagerly the countenance of the brother—but he had buried his face in his hands, and I could only perceive that a far more than ordinary wanness had overspread the emaciated fingers through which trickled many passionate tears.

The disease of the lady Madeline had long baffled the skill of her physicians. A settled apathy, a gradual wasting away of the person, and frequent although transient affections of a partially cataleptical character[8] were the unusual diagnosis. Hitherto she had steadily borne up against the pressure of her malady, and had not betaken herself finally to bed; but on the closing in of the evening of my arrival at the house, she succumbed (as her brother told me at night with inexpressible agitation) to the prostrating power of the

---

[8]A trance-like state of suspended animation.

destroyer; and I learned that the glimpse I had obtained of her person would thus probably be the last I should obtain—that the lady, at least while living, would be seen by me no more.

For several days ensuing, her name was unmentioned by either Usher or myself: and during this period I was busied in earnest endeavours to alleviate the melancholy of my friend. We painted and read together, or I listened, as if in a dream, to the wild improvisations of his speaking guitar. And thus, as a closer and still closer intimacy admitted me more unreservedly into the recesses of his spirit, the more bitterly did I perceive the futility of all attempt at cheering a mind from which darkness, as if an inherent positive quality, poured forth upon all objects of the moral and physical universe in one unceasing radiation of gloom.

I shall ever bear about me a memory of the many solemn hours I thus spent alone with the master of the House of Usher. Yet I should fail in any attempt to convey an idea of the exact character of the studies, or of the occupations, in which he involved me, or led me the way. An excited and highly distempered ideality threw a sulphureous lustre over all. His long improvised dirges will ring forever in my ears. Among other things, I hold painfully in mind a certain singular perversion and amplification of the wild air of the last waltz of Von Weber.[9] From the paintings over which his elaborate fancy brooded, and which grew, touch by touch, into vagueness at which I shuddered the more thrillingly, because I shuddered knowing not why;—from these paintings (vivid as their images now are before me) I would in vain endeavour to educe more than a small portion which should lie within the compass of merely written words. By the utter simplicity, by the nakedness of his designs, he arrested and overawed attention. If ever mortal painted an idea, that mortal was Roderick Usher. For me at least—in the circumstances then surrounding me—there arose out of the pure abstractions which the hypochondriac[10] contrived to throw upon his canvas, an intensity of intolerable awe, no shadow of which I felt ever yet in the contemplation of the certainly glowing yet too concrete reveries of Fuseli.[11]

One of the phantasmagoric conceptions of my friend, partaking not so rigidly of the spirit of abstraction, may be shadowed forth, although feebly, in words. A small picture presented the interior of an immensely long and rectangular vault or tunnel, with low walls, smooth, white, and without interruption

---

[9]A person afflicted with melancholy.

[10]German composer Karl Maria von Weber (1786–1826).

[11]Swiss-English painter Henry Fuseli (1741–1825) was famous as an illustrator of Shakespeare and Milton as well as phantasmic paintings such as "The Nightmare" (1781).

or device. Certain accessory points of the design served well to convey the idea that this excavation lay at an exceeding depth below the surface of the earth. No outlet was observed in any portion of its vast extent, and no torch or other artificial source of light was discernible; yet a flood of intense rays rolled throughout, and bathed the whole in a ghastly and inappropriate splendour.

I have just spoken of that morbid condition of the auditory nerve which rendered all music intolerable to the sufferer, with the exception of certain effects of stringed instruments. It was, perhaps, the narrow limits to which he thus confined himself upon the guitar, which gave birth, in great measure, to the fantastic character of his performances. But the fervid *facility* of his *impromptus*[12] could not be so accounted for. They must have been, and were, in the notes, as well as in the words of his wild fantasias (for he not unfrequently accompanied himself with rhymed verbal improvisations), the result of that intense mental collectedness and concentration to which I have previously alluded as observable only in particular moments of the highest artificial excitement. The words of one of these rhapsodies I have easily remembered. I was, perhaps, the more forcibly impressed with it, as he gave it, because, in the under or mystic current of its meaning, I fancied that I perceived, and for the first time, a full consciousness on the part of Usher, of the tottering of his lofty reason upon her throne. The verses, which were entitled "The Haunted Palace," ran very nearly, if not accurately, thus:

I

In the greenest of our valleys,
   By good angels tenanted,
Once a fair and stately palace—
   Radiant palace—reared its head.
In the monarch Thought's dominion—
   It stood there!
Never seraph spread a pinion
   Over fabric half so fair.

II

Banners yellow, glorious, golden,
   On its roof did float and flow;
(This—all this—was in the olden
   Time long ago)

---

[12]An "impromptu" is a spontaneously composed musical piece.

And every gentle air that dallied,
   In that sweet day,
Along the ramparts plumed and pallid,
   A winged odour went away.

III

Wanderers in that happy valley
   Through two luminous windows saw
Spirits moving musically
   To a lute's well-tunèd law,
Round about a throne, where sitting
   (Porphyrogene!)[13]
In state his glory well befitting,
   The ruler of the realm was seen,

IV

And all with pearl and ruby glowing
   Was the fair palace door,
Through which came flowing, flowing, flowing
   And sparkling evermore,
A troop of Echoes whose sweet duty
   Was but to sing,
In voices of surpassing beauty,
   The wit and wisdom of their king.

V

But evil things, in robes of sorrow,
   Assailed the monarch's high estate;
(Ah, let us mourn, for never morrow
   Shall dawn upon him, desolate!)
And, round about his home, the glory
   That blushed and bloomed
Is but a dim-remembered story
   Of the old time entombed.

---

[13]Born to wear purple; i.e., into royalty.

VI

And travellers now within that valley,
    Through the red-litten[14] windows see
Vast forms that move fantastically
    To a discordant melody;
While, like a rapid ghastly river,
    Through the pale door,
A hideous throng rush out forever,
    And laugh—but smile no more.

I well remember that suggestions arising from this ballad, led us into a train of thought, wherein there became manifest an opinion of Usher's which I mention not so much on account of its novelty, (for other men[15] have thought thus,) as on account of the pertinacity with which he maintained it. This opinion, in its general form, was that of the sentience[16] of all vegetable things. But, in his disordered fancy, the idea had assumed a more daring character, and trespassed, under certain conditions, upon the kingdom of inorganization. I lack words to express the full extent, or the earnest *abandon* of his persuasion. The belief, however, was connected (as I have previously hinted) with the gray stones of the home of his forefathers. The conditions of the sentience had been here, he imagined, fulfilled in the method of collocation of these stones—in the order of their arrangement, as well as in that of the many *fungi* which overspread them, and of the decayed trees which stood around— above all, in the long undisturbed endurance of this arrangement, and in its reduplication in the still waters of the tarn. Its evidence—the evidence of the sentience—was to be seen, he said (and I here started as he spoke), in the gradual yet certain condensation of an atmosphere of their own about the waters and the walls. The result was discoverable, he added, in that silent yet importunate and terrible influence which for centuries had moulded the destinies of his family, and which made *him* what I now saw him—what he was. Such opinions need no comment, and I will make none.

Our books—the books which, for years, had formed no small portion of the mental existence of the invalid—were, as might be supposed, in strict keeping with his character of phantasm. We pored together over such works as the Ververt et Chartreuse of Gresset; the Belphegor of Machiavelli; the

---

[14]Red lighted

[15]Watson, Dr. Percival, Spallanzani, and especially the Bishop of Landaf.—See "Chemical Essays," vol. v. [Poe's note]

[16]Capability of feeling.

Heaven and Hell of Swedenborg; the Subterranean Voyage of Nicholas Klimm of Holberg; the Chiromancy of Robert Flud, of Jean D'Indaginé, and of De la Chambre; the Journey into the Blue Distance of Tieck; and the City of the Sun of Campanella. One favourite volume was a small octavo edition of the *Directorium Inquisitorum*, by the Dominican Eymeric de Gironne; and there were passages in Pomponius Mela, about the old African Satyrs and Ægipans,[17] over which Usher would sit dreaming for hours. His chief delight, however, was found in the perusal of an exceedingly rare and curious book in quarto Gothic—the manual of a forgotten church—the *Vigiliæ Mortuorum secundum Chorum Eccelesiæ Maguntinæ*.[18]

I could not help thinking of the wild ritual of this work, and of its probable influence upon the hypochondriac, when, one evening, having informed me abruptly that the lady Madeline was no more, he stated his intention of preserving her corpse for a fortnight,[19] (previously to its final interment,) in one of the numerous vaults within the main walls of the building. The worldly reason, however, assigned for this singular proceeding, was one which I did not feel at liberty to dispute. The brother had been led to his resolution (so he told me) by consideration of the unusual character of the malady of the deceased, of certain obtrusive and eager inquiries on the part of her medical men, and of the remote and exposed situation of the burial-ground of the family. I will not deny that when I called to mind the sinister countenance of the person whom I met upon the staircase, on the day of my arrival at the house, I had no desire to oppose what I regarded as at best but a harmless, and by no means an unnatural, precaution.

At the request of Usher, I personally aided him in the arrangements for the temporary entombment. The body having been encoffined, we two alone bore it to its rest. The vault in which we placed it (and which had been so long unopened that our torches, half smothered in its oppressive atmosphere, gave us little opportunity for investigation) was small, damp, and entirely without means of admission for light; lying, at great depth, immediately beneath that portion of the building in which was my own sleeping apartment. It had been used, apparently, in remote feudal times, for the worst purposes of a donjon-keep,[20] and, in later days, as a place of deposit for powder, or some other highly combustible substance, as a portion of its floor, and the whole interior

---

[17]In Greek mythology, satyrs and aegipans are half-man/half-goat creatures related to Pan and known for aggressive sexuality.

[18]These titles share a preoccupation with Gothic, utopian, and/or supernatural themes.

[19]Two weeks

[20]The main tower of a castle.

of a long archway through which we reached it, were carefully sheathed with copper. The door, of massive iron, had been, also, similarly protected. Its immense weight caused an unusually sharp grating sound, as it moved upon its hinges.

Having deposited our mournful burden upon tressels within this region of horror, we partially turned aside the yet unscrewed lid of the coffin, and looked upon the face of the tenant. A striking similitude between the brother and sister now first arrested my attention; and Usher, divining, perhaps, my thoughts, murmured out some few words from which I learned that the deceased and himself had been twins, and that sympathies of a scarcely intelligible nature had always existed between them. Our glances, however, rested not long upon the dead—for we could not regard her unawed. The disease which had thus entombed the lady in the maturity of youth, had left, as usual in all maladies of a strictly cataleptical character, the mockery of a faint blush upon the bosom and the face, and that suspiciously lingering smile upon the lip which is so terrible in death. We replaced and screwed down the lid, and, having secured the door of iron, made our way, with toil, into the scarcely less gloomy apartments of the upper portion of the house.

And now, some days of bitter grief having elapsed, an observable change came over the features of the mental disorder of my friend. His ordinary manner had vanished. His ordinary occupations were neglected or forgotten. He roamed from chamber to chamber with hurried, unequal, and objectless step. The pallor of his countenance had assumed, if possible, a more ghastly hue—but the luminousness of his eye had utterly gone out. The once occasional huskiness of his tone was heard no more; and a tremulous quaver, as if of extreme terror, habitually characterized his utterance. There were times, indeed, when I thought his unceasingly agitated mind was labouring with some oppressive secret, to divulge which he struggled for the necessary courage. At times, again, I was obliged to resolve all into the mere inexplicable vagaries of madness, for I beheld him gazing upon vacancy for long hours, in an attitude of the profoundest attention, as if listening to some imaginary sound. It was no wonder that his condition terrified—that it infected me. I felt creeping upon me, by slow yet certain degrees, the wild influences of his own fantastic yet impressive superstitions.

It was, especially, upon retiring to bed late in the night of the seventh or eighth day after the placing of the lady Madeline within the donjon, that I experienced the full power of such feelings. Sleep came not near my couch—while the hours waned and waned away. I struggled to reason off the nervousness which had dominion over me. I endeavoured to believe that much, if not all of what I felt, was due to the bewildering influence of the gloomy furniture of the room—of the dark and tattered draperies, which, tortured into motion by the breath of a rising tempest, swayed fitfully to and fro upon the walls, and rustled uneasily about the decorations of the bed. But my efforts were fruitless. An irrepressible tremour gradually pervaded my frame; and, at length, there sat upon my very heart an incubus[21] of utterly causeless alarm. Shaking this off with a gasp and a struggle, I uplifted myself upon the pillows, and, peering earnestly within the intense darkness of the chamber, hearkened—I know not why, except that an instinctive spirit prompted me—to certain low and indefinite sounds which came, through the pauses of the storm, at long intervals, I knew not whence. Overpowered by an intense sentiment of horror, unaccountable yet unendurable, I threw on my clothes with haste, (for I felt that I should sleep no more during the night) and endeavoured to arouse myself from the pitiable condition into which I had fallen, by pacing rapidly to and fro through the apartment.

I had taken but few turns in this manner, when a light step on an adjoining staircase arrested my attention. I presently recognised it as that of Usher. In an instant afterward he rapped, with a gentle touch, at my door, and entered, bearing a lamp. His countenance was, as usual, cadaverously wan—but, moreover, there was a species of mad hilarity in his eyes—an evidently restrained *hysteria* in his whole demeanour. His air appalled me—but anything was preferable to the solitude which I had so long endured, and I even welcomed his presence as a relief.

"And you have not seen it?" he said abruptly, after having stared about him for some moments in silence—"you have not then seen it?—but, stay! you shall." Thus speaking, and having carefully shaded his lamp, he hurried to one of the casements, and threw it freely open to the storm.

The impetuous fury of the entering gust nearly lifted us from our feet. It was, indeed, a tempestuous yet sternly beautiful night, and one wildly singular in its terror and its beauty. A whirlwind had apparently collected its force in our vicinity; for there were frequent and violent alterations in the direction of the wind; and the exceeding density of the clouds (which hung so low as to press upon the turrets of the house) did not prevent our perceiving the life-like velocity with which they flew careering from all points against each other, without passing away into the distance. I say that even their exceeding density did not prevent our perceiving this—yet we had no glimpse of the moon or stars—nor was there any flashing forth of the lightning. But the under surfaces of the huge masses of agitated vapour, as well as all terrestrial objects immediately around us, were glowing in the unnatural light of a faintly luminous and distinctly visible gaseous exhalation which hung about and enshrouded the mansion.

---

[21]This term variously refers to a sexually aggressive male demon (one who violates female sleepers) or an opressive nightmare.

"You must not—you shall not behold this!" said I, shudderingly, to Usher, as I led him, with a gentlè violence, from the window to a seat. "These appearances, which bewilder you, are merely electrical phenomena not uncommon—or it may be that they have their ghastly origin in the rank miasma of the tarn. Let us close this casement;—the air is chilling and dangerous to your frame. Here is one of your favourite romances. I will read, and you shall listen;—and so we will pass away this terrible night together."

The antique volume which I had taken up was the "Mad Trist" of Sir Launcelot Canning, but I had called it a favourite of Usher's more in sad jest than in earnest; for, in truth, there is little in its uncouth and unimaginative prolixity[22] which could have had interest for the lofty and spiritual ideality of my friend. It was, however, the only book immediately at hand; and I indulged a vague hope that the excitement which now agitated the hypochondriac, might find relief (for the history of mental disorder is full of similar anomalies) even in the extremeness of the folly which I could read. Could I have judged, indeed, by the wild overstrained air of vivacity with which he hearkened, or apparently hearkened, to the words of the tale, I might well have congratulated myself upon the success of my design.

I had arrived at that well-known portion of the story where Ethelred, the hero of the Trist, having sought in vain for peaceable admission into the dwelling of the hermit, proceeds to make good an entrance by force. Here, it will be remembered, the words of the narrative run thus:

"And Ethelred, who was by nature of a doughty heart, and who was now mighty withal, on account of the powerfulness of the wine which he had drunken, waited no longer to hold parley with the hermit, who, in sooth, was of an obstinate and maliceful turn, but, feeling the rain upon his shoulders, and fearing the rising of the tempest, uplifted his mace outright, and, with blows, made quickly room in the plankings of the door for his gauntleted hand; and now pulling therewith sturdily, he so cracked, and ripped, and tore all asunder, that the noise of the dry and hollow-sounding wood alarmed and reverberated throughout the forest."

At the termination of this sentence I started and, for a moment, paused; for it appeared to me (although I at once concluded that my excited fancy had deceived me)—it appeared to me that, from some very remote portion of the mansion, there came, indistinctly, to my ears, what might have been, in its exact similarity of character, the echo (but a stifled and dull one certainly) of the very cracking and ripping sound which Sir Launcelot had so particularly described. It was, beyond doubt, the coincidence alone which had arrested my attention; for, amid the rattling of the sashes of the casements, and the

---

[22]Tediouslý long and verbose.

ordinary commingled noises of the still increasing storm, the sound, in itself, had nothing, surely, which should have interested or disturbed me. I continued the story:

"But the good champion Ethelred, now entering within the door, was sore enraged and amazed to perceive no signal of the maliceful hermit; but, in the stead thereof, a dragon of a scaly and prodigious demeanour, and of a fiery tongue, which sate in guard before a palace of gold, with a floor of silver; and upon the wall there hung a shield of shining brass with this legend enwritten—

Who entereth herein, a conqueror hath bin;
Who slayeth the dragon, the shield he shall win.

And Ethelred uplifted his mace, and struck upon the head of the dragon, which fell before him, and gave up his pesty breath, with a shriek so horrid and harsh, and withal so piercing, that Ethelred had fain to close his ears with his hands against the dreadful noise of it, the like whereof was never before heard."

Here again I paused abruptly, and now with a feeling of wild amazement—for there could be no doubt whatever that, in this instance, I did actually hear (although from what direction it proceeded I found it impossible to say) a low and apparently distant, but harsh, protracted, and most unusual screaming or grating sound—the exact counterpart of what my fancy had already conjured up for the dragon's unnatural shriek as described by the romancer.

Oppressed, as I certainly was, upon the occurrence of the second and most extraordinary coincidence, by a thousand conflicting sensations, in which wonder and extreme terror were predominant, I still retained sufficient presence of mind to avoid exciting, by any observation, the sensitive nervousness of my companion. I was by no means certain that he had noticed the sounds in question; although, assuredly, a strange alteration had, during the last few minutes, taken place in his demeanour. From a position fronting my own, he had gradually brought round his chair, so as to sit with his face to the door of the chamber; and thus I could but partially perceive his features, although I saw that his lips trembled as if he were murmuring inaudibly. His head had dropped upon his breast—yet I knew that he was not asleep, from the wide and rigid opening of the eye as I caught a glance of it in profile. The motion of his body, too, was at variance with this idea—for he rocked from side to side with a gentle yet constant and uniform sway. Having rapidly taken notice of all this, I resumed the narrative of Sir Launcelot, which thus proceeded:

"And now, the champion, having escaped from the terrible fury of the dragon, bethinking himself of the brazen shield, and of the breaking up of the enchantment which was upon it, removed the carcass from out of the way before him, and approached valorously over the silver pavement of the castle to where the shield was upon the wall; which in sooth tarried not for his full coming, but fell down at his feet upon the silver floor, with a mighty great and terrible ringing sound."

No sooner had these syllables passed my lips, than—as if a shield of brass had indeed, at the moment, fallen heavily upon a floor of silver—I became aware of a distinct, hollow, metallic, and clangorous, yet apparently muffled reverberation. Completely unnerved, I leaped to my feet; but the measured rocking movement of Usher was undisturbed. I rushed to the chair in which he sat. His eyes were bent fixedly before him, and throughout his whole countenance there reigned a stony rigidity. But, as I placed my hand upon his shoulder, there came a strong shudder over his whole person; a sickly smile quivered about his lips; and I saw that he spoke in a low, hurried, and gibbering murmur, as if unconscious of my presence. Bending closely over him, I at length drank in the hideous import of his words.

"Not hear it?—yes, I hear it, and *have* heard it. Long—long—long—many minutes, many hours, many days, have I heard it—yet I dared not—oh, pity me, miserable wretch that I am!—I dared not—I *dared* not speak! *We have put her living in the tomb!* Said I not that my senses were acute? I *now* tell you that I heard her first feeble movements in the hollow coffin. I heard them—many, many days ago—yet I dared not—I *dared not speak!* And now—to-night—Ethelred—ha! ha!—the breaking of the hermit's door, and the death-cry of the dragon, and the clangour of the shield!—say, rather, the rending of her coffin, and the grating of the iron hinges of her prison, and her struggles within the coppered archway of the vault! Oh whither shall I fly? Will she not be here anon? Is she not hurrying to upbraid me for my haste? Have I not heard her footsteps on the stair? Do I not distinguish that heavy and horrible beating of her heart? MADMAN!"—here he sprang furiously to his feet, and shrieked out his syllables, as if in the effort he were giving up his soul—"MADMAN! I TELL YOU THAT SHE NOW STANDS WITHOUT THE DOOR!"

As if in the superhuman energy of his utterance there had been found the potency of a spell—the huge antique panels to which the speaker pointed threw slowly back, upon the instant, their ponderous and ebony jaws. It was the work of the rushing gust—but then without those doors there DID stand the lofty and enshrouded figure of the lady Madeline of Usher. There was blood upon her white robes, and the evidence of some bitter struggle upon every portion of her emaciated frame. For a moment she remained trembling and reeling to and fro upon the threshold, then, with a low moaning cry, fell heavily inward upon the person of her brother, and in her violent and now final death-agonies, bore him to the floor a corpse, and a victim to the terrors he had anticipated.

From that chamber, and from that mansion, I fled aghast. The storm was still abroad in all its wrath as I found myself crossing the old causeway. Suddenly there shot along the path a wild light, and I turned to see whence a gleam so unusual could have issued; for the vast house and its shadows were alone behind me. The radiance was that of the full, setting, and blood-red moon, which now shone vividly through that once barely discernible fissure, of which I have before spoken as extending from the roof of the building, in a zigzag direction, to the base. While I gazed, this fissure rapidly widened— there came a fierce breath of the whirlwind—the entire orb of the satellite burst at once upon my sight—my brain reeled as I saw the mighty walls rushing asunder—there was a long tumultuous shouting sound like the voice of a thousand waters—and the deep and dank tarn at my feet closed sullenly and silently over the fragments of the "HOUSE OF USHER."

[1839]

🦜 🦜 🦜

The Masque of the Red Death

EDGAR ALLAN POE

THE "RED DEATH" HAD long devastated the country. No pestilence had ever been so fatal, or so hideous. Blood was its Avatar[1] and its seal—the redness and the horror of blood. There were sharp pains, and sudden dizziness, and then profuse bleeding at the pores, with dissolution. The scarlet stains upon the body and especially upon the face of the victim, were the pest ban which shut him out from the aid and from the sympathy of his fellow-men. And the whole seizure, progress and termination of the disease, were the incidents of half an hour.

But the Prince Prospero[2] was happy and dauntless and sagacious. When his dominions were half depopulated, he summoned to his presence a thousand hale and light-hearted friends from among the knights and dames of his court, and with these retired to the deep seclusion of one of his castellated abbeys. This was an extensive and magnificent structure, the creation of the prince's own eccentric yet august taste. A strong and lofty wall girdled it in. This wall had gates of iron. The courtiers, having entered, brought furnaces and massy hammers and welded the bolts. They resolved to leave means neither of ingress or egress to the sudden impulses of despair or of frenzy from within. The abbey was amply provisioned. With such precautions the courtiers might bid defiance to contagion. The external world could take care of itself. In the meantime it was folly to grieve, or to think. The prince had provided all the appliances of pleasure. There were buffoons, there were improvisatori,[3] there were ballet-dancers, there were musicians, there was Beauty, there was wine. All these and security were within. Without was the "Red Death."

It was toward the close of the fifth or sixth month of his seclusion, and while the pestilence raged most furiously abroad, that the Prince Prospero

[1]Hindu incarnation of a god.

[2]A character from Shakespeare's *The Tempest* (1611).

[3]An improvisatori composes music spontaneously, "on the spot."

First published in *Graham's Magazine* in May, 1842.

entertained his thousand friends at a masked ball of the most unusual magnificence.

It was a voluptuous scene, that masquerade. But first let me tell of the rooms in which it was held. There were seven—an imperial suite. In many palaces, however, such suites form a long and straight vista, while the folding doors slide back nearly to the walls on either hand, so that the view of the whole extent is scarcely impeded. Here the case was very different; as might have been expected from the duke's love of the *bizarre*. The apartments were so irregularly disposed that the vision embraced but little more than one at a time. There was a sharp turn at every twenty or thirty yards, and at each turn a novel effect. To the right and left, in the middle of each wall, a tall and narrow Gothic window looked out upon a closed corridor which pursued the windings of the suite. These windows were of stained glass whose color varied in accordance with the prevailing hue of the decorations of the chamber into which it opened. That at the eastern extremity was hung, for example, in blue—and vividly blue were its windows. The second chamber was purple in its ornaments and tapestries and here the panes were purple. The third was green throughout, and so were the casements. The fourth was furnished and lighted with orange—the fifth with white—the sixth with violet. The seventh apartment was closely shrouded in black velvet tapestries that hung all over the ceiling and down the walls, falling in heavy folds upon a carpet of the same material and hue. But in this chamber only, the color of the windows failed to correspond with the decorations. The panes here were scarlet—a deep blood color. Now in no one of the seven apartments was there any lamp or candelabrum, amid the profusion of golden ornaments that lay scattered to and fro or depended from the roof. There was no light of any kind emanating from lamp or candle within the suite of chambers. But in the corridors that followed the suite, there stood, opposite to each window, a heavy tripod, bearing a brazier of fire that projected its rays through the tinted glass and so glaringly illumined the room. And thus were produced a multitude of gaudy and fantastic appearances. But in the western or black chamber the effect of the firelight that streamed upon the dark hangings through the blood-tinted panes, was ghastly in the extreme, and produced so wild a look upon the countenances of those who entered, that there were few of the company bold enough to set foot within its precincts at all.

It was in this apartment, also, that there stood against the western wall, a gigantic clock of ebony. Its pendulum swung to and fro with a dull, heavy, monotonous clang; and when the minute-hand made the circuit of the face, and the hour was to be stricken, there came from the brazen lungs of the clock a sound which was clear and loud and deep and exceedingly musical, but of so peculiar a note and emphasis that, at each lapse of an hour, the musicians of the orchestra were constrained to pause, momentarily, in their performance, to hearken to the sound; and thus the waltzers perforce ceased their evolutions; and there was a brief disconcert of the whole gay company; and, while the chimes of the clock yet rang, it was observed that the giddiest grew pale, and the more aged and sedate passed their hands over their brows as if in confused reverie or meditation. But when the echoes had fully ceased, a light laughter at once pervaded the assembly; the musicians looked at each other and smiled as if at their own nervousness and folly, and made whispering vows, each to the other, that the next chiming of the clock should produce in them no similar emotion; and then, after the lapse of sixty minutes, (which embrace three thousand and six hundred seconds of the Time that flies,) there came yet another chiming of the clock, and then were the same disconcert and tremulousness and meditation as before.

But, in spite of these things, it was a gay and magnificent revel. The tastes of the duke were peculiar. He had a fine eye for colors and effects. He disregarded the *decora*[4] of mere fashion. His plans were bold and fiery, and his conceptions glowed with barbaric lustre. There are some who would have thought him mad. His followers felt that he was not. It was necessary to hear and see and touch him to be *sure* that he was not.

He had directed, in great part, the moveable embellishments of the seven chambers, upon occasion of this great *fête*, and it was his own guiding taste which had given character to the masqueraders. Be sure they were grotesque. There were much glare and glitter and piquancy and phantasm—much of what has been since seen in "Hernani." There were arabesque figures with unsuited limbs and appointments. There were delirious fancies such as the madman fashions. There was much of the beautiful, much of the wanton, much of the *bizarre*, something of the terrible, and not a little of that which might have excited disgust. To and fro in the seven chambers there stalked, in fact, a multitude of dreams. And these—the dreams—writhed in and about, taking hue from the rooms, and causing the wild music of the orchestra to seem as the echo of their steps. And, anon, there strikes the ebony clock which stands in the hall of the velvet. And then, for a moment, all is still, and all is silent save the voice of the clock. The dreams are stiff-frozen as they stand. But the echoes of the chime die away—they have endured but an instant—and a light, half-subdued laughter floats after them as they depart. And now again the music swells, and the dreams live, and writhe to and fro more merrily than

---

[4]Ornamentation

[5]Feast, festival

[6]1830 verse drama written by Victor Hugo (1802–1855).

ever, taking hue from the many-tinted windows through which stream the rays from the tripods. But to the chamber which lies most westwardly of the seven, there are now none of the maskers who venture; for the night is waning away; and there flows a ruddier light through the blood-colored panes; and the blackness of the sable drapery appals; and to him whose foot falls upon the sable carpet, there comes from the near clock of ebony a muffled peal more solemnly emphatic than any which reaches *their* ears who indulge in the more remote gaieties of the other apartments.

But these other apartments were densely crowded, and in them beat feverishly the heart of life. And the revel went whirlingly on, until at length there commenced the sounding of midnight upon the clock. And then the music ceased, as I have told; and the evolutions of the waltzers were quieted; and there was an uneasy cessation of all things as before. But now there were twelve strokes to be sounded by the bell of the clock; and thus it happened, perhaps, that more of thought crept, with more of time, into the meditations of the thoughtful among those who revelled. And thus, too, it happened, perhaps, that before the last echoes of the last chime had utterly sunk into silence, there were many individuals in the crowd who had found leisure to become aware of the presence of a masked figure which had arrested the attention of no single individual before. And the rumor of this new presence having spread itself whisperingly around, there arose at length from the whole company a buzz, or murmur, expressive of disapprobation and surprise—then, finally, of terror, of horror, and of disgust.

In an assembly of phantasms such as I have painted, it may well be supposed that no ordinary appearance could have excited such sensation. In truth the masquerade license of the night was nearly unlimited; but the figure in question had out-Heroded Herod,[7] and gone beyond the bounds of even the prince's indefinite decorum. There are chords in the hearts of the most reckless which cannot be touched without emotion. Even with the utterly lost, to whom life and death are equally jests, there are matters of which no jest can be made. The whole company, indeed, seemed now deeply to feel that in the costume and bearing of the stranger neither wit nor propriety existed. The figure was tall and gaunt, and shrouded from head to foot in the habiliments of the grave. The mask which concealed the visage was made so nearly to resemble the countenance of a stiffened corpse that the closest scrutiny must have had difficulty in detecting the cheat. And yet all this might have been endured, if not approved, by the mad revellers around. But the mummer[8] had gone so

---

[7]A reference to the notoriously violent Biblical King Herod; Shakespeare's Hamlet uses this phrase to describe over-acting.

[8]Masked actor

far as to assume the type of the Red Death. His vesture was dabbled in *blood*—and his broad brow, with all the features of the face, was besprinkled with the scarlet horror.

When the eyes of Prince Prospero fell upon this spectral image (which with a slow and solemn movement, as if more fully to sustain its *rôle*, stalked to and fro among the waltzers) he was seen to be convulsed, in the first moment with a strong shudder either of terror or distaste; but, in the next, his brow reddened with rage.

"Who dares?" he demanded hoarsely of the courtiers who stood near him—"who dares insult us with this blasphemous mockery? Seize him and unmask him—that we may know whom we have to hang at sunrise, from the battlements!"

It was in the eastern or blue chamber in which stood the Prince Prospero as he uttered these words. They rang throughout the seven rooms loudly and clearly—for the prince was a bold and robust man, and the music had become hushed at the waving of his hand.

It was in the blue room where stood the prince, with a group of pale courtiers by his side. At first, as he spoke, there was a slight rushing movement of this group in the direction of the intruder, who at the moment was also near at hand, and now, with deliberate and stately step, made closer approach to the speaker. But from a certain nameless awe with which the mad assumptions of the mummer had inspired the whole party, there were found none who put forth hand to seize him; so that, unimpeded, he passed within a yard of the prince's person; and, while the vast assembly, as if with one impulse, shrank from the centres of the rooms to the walls, he made his way uninterruptedly, but with the same solemn and measured step which had distinguished him from the first, through the blue chamber to the purple—through the purple to the green—through the green to the orange—through this again to the white—and even thence to the violet, ere a decided movement had been made to arrest him. It was then, however, that the Prince Prospero, maddening with rage and the shame of his own momentary cowardice, rushed hurriedly through the six chambers, while none followed him on account of a deadly terror that had seized upon all. He bore aloft a drawn dagger, and had approached, in rapid impetuosity, to within three or four feet of the retreating figure, when the latter, having attained the extremity of the velvet apartment, turned suddenly and confronted his pursuer. There was a sharp cry—and the dagger dropped gleaming upon the sable carpet, upon which, instantly afterwards, fell prostrate in death the Prince Prospero. Then, summoning the wild courage of despair, a throng of the revellers at once threw themselves into the black apartment, and, seizing the mummer, whose tall figure stood erect and motionless within the shadow of the ebony clock, gasped in unutterable horror at finding the grave-cerements[9] and corpse-like mask which they handled with so violent a rudeness, untenanted by any tangible form.

And now was acknowledged the presence of the Red Death. He had come like a thief in the night. And one by one dropped the revellers in the blood-bedewed halls of their revel, and died each in the despairing posture of his fall. And the life of the ebony clock went out with that of the last of the gay. And the flames of the tripods expired. And Darkness and Decay and the Red Death held illimitable dominion over all.

[1842]

---

[9]Shroud

John Updike
[1932–2009]

JOHN UPDIKE *was born and raised in Shillington, Pennsylvania, where his early academic success led to a scholarship to Harvard University. After graduating in 1954, Updike studied at the Ruskin School of Drawing and Fine Arts in Oxford, England, returning to the United States the following year to take a position on the staff of* The New Yorker, *where he worked under James Thurber for two years.*

The New Yorker *was also the venue for Updike's earliest publications, and he continued publishing fiction, poems, and essays in the magazine for decades after he left its staff. Updike is numbered among the most prolific contemporary writers, having published some fifty books. His second novel,* Rabbit, Run *(1960), inspired three sequels,* Rabbit Redux *(1972),* Rabbit is Rich *(1981), and* Rabbit at Rest, *(1990); each of the last two was awarded the Pulitzer Prize for fiction. Updike also received the Rosenthal Award from the National Institute of Arts and Letters (1959); the National Book Award in Fiction (1964); the O. Henry Prize (1967); the American Book Award (1982); the National Book Critics Circle Award for fiction (1982 and 1990); the National Arts Club Medal of Honor (1984); and both the National Medal of the Arts (1989) and the National Medal for the Humanities (2003).*

Among Updike's dozens of other notable publications include Bech: A Book *(1970), which introduced Henry Bech, a moderately successful Jewish-American novelist whom many read as Updike's fictional alter ego, and who returned in* Bech is Back *(1982) and* Bech at Bay *(1998). Updike's novel* The Witches of Eastwick *(1984) was adapted for a major motion picture starring Jack Nicholson. Many of his best short stories, such as "A&P," feature an eye for detail and an interest in sexuality and its repressions. These themes have characterized Updike's work throughout his career.*

For nearly five decades, Updike moved fluidly between multiple genres—novels, short stories, poetry, criticism, and other nonfiction—with equal grace. His realistic style, his masterful exploration of the conventions of prose narrative, and his attention to the nuances of life in postwar suburbia make Updike among the most beloved writers of the twentieth century.

A & P

JOHN UPDIKE

IN WALKS THESE THREE girls in nothing but bathing suits. I'm in the third check-out slot, with my back to the door, so I don't see them until they're over by the bread. The one that caught my eye first was the one in the plaid green two-piece. She was a chunky kid, with a good tan and a sweet broad soft-looking can with those two crescents of white just under it, where the sun never seems to hit, at the top of the backs of her legs. I stood there with my hand on a box of HiHo crackers trying to remember if I rang it up or not. I ring it up again and the customer starts giving me hell. She's one of these cash-register-watchers, a witch about fifty with rouge on her cheekbones and no eyebrows, and I know it made her day to trip me up. She'd been watching cash registers for fifty years and probably never seen a mistake before.

By the time I got her feathers smoothed and her goodies into a bag—she gives me a little snort in passing, if she'd been born at the right time they would have burned her over in Salem—by the time I get her on her way the girls had circled around the bread and were coming back, without a pushcart, back my way along the counters, in the aisle between the checkouts and the Special bins. They didn't even have shoes on. There was this chunky one, with the two-piece—it was bright green and the seams on the bra were still sharp and her belly was still pretty pale so I guessed she just got it (the suit)—there was this one, with one of those chubby berry-faces, the lips all bunched together under her nose, this one, and a tall one, with black hair that hadn't quite frizzed right, and one of these sunburns right across under the eyes, and a chin that was too long—you know, the kind of girl other girls think is very "striking" and "attractive" but never quite makes it, as they very well know, which is why they like her so much—and then the third one, that wasn't quite so tall. She was the queen. She kind of led them, the other two peeking around and making their shoulders round. She didn't look around, not this queen, she just walked straight on slowly, on these long white primadonna legs. She came down a little hard on her heels, as if she didn't walk in bare feet that much, putting down her heels and then letting the weight move along to her toes as if she was testing the floor with every step, putting a little deliberate extra action into it. You never know for sure how girls' minds work (do you really think it's a mind in there or just a little buzz like a bee in a glass jar?) but you got the idea she had talked the other two into coming in here with her, and now she was showing them how to do it, walk slow and hold yourself straight.

She had on a kind of dirty-pink—beige maybe, I don't know—bathing suit with a little nubble all over it and, what got me, the straps were down. They were off her shoulders looped loose around the cool tops of her arms, and I guess as a result the suit had slipped a little on her, so all around the top of the cloth there was this shining rim. If it hadn't been there you wouldn't have known there could have been anything whiter than those shoulders. With the straps pushed off, there was nothing between the top of the suit and the top of her head except just *her* this clean bare plane of the top of her chest down from the shoulder bones like a dented sheet of metal tilted in the light. I mean, it was more than pretty.

She had a sort of oaky hair that sun and salt had bleached, done up in a bun that was unravelling, and a kind of prim face. Walking into the A & P with your straps down, I suppose it's the only kind of face you *can* have. She held her head so high her neck, coming up out of those white shoulders, looked kind of stretched, but I didn't mind. The longer her neck was, the more of her there was.

She must have felt in the corner of her eye me and over my shoulder Stokesie in the second slot watching, but she didn't tip. Not this queen. She kept her eyes moving across the racks, and stopped, and turned so slow it made my stomach rub the inside of my apron, and buzzed to the other two, who kind of huddled against her for relief, and then they all three of them went up the cat-and-dog-food-breakfast-cereal-macaroni-rice-raisins-seasonings-spreads-spaghetti-soft-drinks-crackers-and-cookies aisle. From the third slot I look straight up this aisle to the meat counter, and I watched them all the way. The fat one with the tan sort of fumbled with the cookies, but on second thought she put the package back. The sheep pushing their carts down the aisle—the girls were walking against the usual traffic (not that we have one-way signs or anything)—were pretty hilarious. You could see them, when Queenie's white shoulders dawned on them, kind of jerk, or hop, or hiccup, but their eyes snapped back to their own baskets and on they pushed. I bet you could set off dynamite in an A & P and the people would by and large keep reaching and checking oatmeal off their lists and muttering "Let me see, there was a third thing, began with A, asparagus, no, ah, yes, applesauce!" or whatever it is they do mutter. But there was no doubt, this jiggled them. A few house-slaves in pin curlers even looked around after pushing their carts past to make sure what they had seen was correct.

You know, it's one thing to have a girl in a bathing suit down on the beach, where what with the glare nobody can look at each other much anyway, and another thing in the cool of the A & P, under the fluorescent lights, against all those stacked packages, with her feet paddling along naked over our checkerboard green-and-cream rubber-tile floor.

"Oh Daddy," Stokesie said beside me. "I feel so faint."

"Darling," I said. "Hold me tight." Stokesie's married, with two babies chalked up on his fuselage already, but as far as I can tell that's the only difference. He's twenty-two, and I was nineteen this April.

"Is it done?" he asks, the responsible married man finding his voice. I forgot to say he thinks he's going to be manager some sunny day, maybe in 1990 when it's called the Great Alexandrov and Petrooshki Tea Company or something.

What he meant was, our town is five miles from a beach, with a big summer colony out on the Point, but we're right in the middle of town, and the women generally put on a shirt or shorts or something before they get out of the car into the street. And anyway these are usually women with six children and varicose veins mapping their legs and nobody, including them, could care less. As I say, we're right in the middle of town, and if you stand at our front doors you can see two banks and the Congregational church and the newspaper store and three real-estate offices and about twenty-seven old freeloaders tearing up Central Street because the sewer broke again. It's not as if we're on the Cape; we're north of Boston and there's people in this town haven't seen the ocean for twenty years.

The girls had reached the meat counter and were asking McMahon something. He pointed, they pointed, and they shuffled out of sight behind a pyramid of Diet Delight peaches. All that was left for us to see was old McMahon patting his mouth and looking after them sizing up their joints. Poor kids, I began to feel sorry for them, they couldn't help it.

Now here comes the sad part of the story, at least my family says it's sad, but I don't think it's so sad myself. The store's pretty empty, it being Thursday afternoon, so there was nothing much to do except lean on the register and wait for the girls to show up again. The whole store was like a pinball machine and I didn't know which tunnel they'd come out of. After a while they come around out of the far aisle, around the light bulbs, records at discount of the Caribbean Six or Tony Martin Sings or some such gunk you wonder they waste wax on, six-packs of candy bars, and plastic toys done up in cellophane that fall apart when a kid looks at them anyway. Around they come, Queenie still leading the way, and holding a little gray jar in her hand. Slots Three through Seven are unmanned and I could see her wondering between Stokes and me, but Stokesie with his usual luck draws an old party in baggy gray pants who stumbles up with four giant cans of pineapple juice (what do these bums *do* with all that pineapple juice? I've often asked myself) so the girls come to me. Queenie puts down the jar and I take it into my fingers icy cold. Kingfish Fancy Herring Snacks in Pure Sour Cream: 49¢. Now her hands are empty, not a ring or a bracelet, bare as God made them, and I wonder where the money's coming from. Still with that prim look she lifts a folded dollar bill out of the hollow at the center of her nubbled pink top. The jar went heavy in my hand. Really, I thought that was so cute.

Then everybody's luck begins to run out. Lengel comes in from haggling with a truck full of cabbages on the lot and is about to scuttle into the door marked MANAGER behind which he hides all day when the girls touch his eye. Lengel's pretty dreary, teaches Sunday school and the rest, but he doesn't miss that much. He comes over and says, "Girls, this isn't the beach."

Queenie blushes, though maybe it's just a brush of sunburn I was noticing for the first time, now that she was so close. "My mother asked me to pick up a jar of herring snacks." Her voice kind of startled me, the way voices do when you see the people first, coming out so flat and dumb yet kind of tony, too, the way it ticked over "pick up" and "snacks." All of a sudden I slid right down her voice into her living room. Her father and the other men were standing around in ice-cream coats and bow ties and the women were in sandals picking up herring snacks on toothpicks off a big glass plate and they were all holding drinks the color of water with olives and sprigs of mint in them. When my parents have somebody over they get lemonade and if it's a real racy affair Schlitz in tall glasses with "They Do It Every Time" cartoons stencilled on.

"That's all right," Lengel said. "But this isn't the beach." His repeating this struck me as funny, as if it had just occurred to him, and he had been thinking all these years the A & P was a great big dune and he was the head lifeguard. He didn't like my smiling—as I say he doesn't miss much—but he concentrates on giving the girls that sad Sunday-school-superintendent stare.

Queenie's blush is no sunburn now, and the plump one in plaid, that I liked better from the back—a really sweet can—pipes up, "We weren't doing any shopping. We just came in for one thing."

"That makes no difference," Lengel tells her, and I could see from the way his eyes went that he hadn't noticed she was wearing a two-piece before. "We want you decently dressed when you come in here."

"We *are* decent," Queenie says suddenly, her lower lip pushing, getting sore now that she remembers her place, a place from which the crowd that runs the A & P must look pretty crummy. Fancy Herring Snacks flashed in her very blue eyes.

"Girls, I don't want to argue with you. After this come in here with your shoulders covered. It's our policy." He turns back. That's policy for you. Policy is what the kingpins want. What the others want is juvenile delinquency.

All this while, the customers had been showing up with their carts but, you know, sheep, seeing a scene, they had all bunched up on Stokesie, who shook open a paper bag as gently as peeling a peach, not wanting to miss a word. I could feel in the silence everybody getting nervous, most of all Lengel, who asks me, "Sammy, have you rung up their purchase?"

I thought and said "No" but it wasn't about that I was thinking. I go through the punches, 4, 9, GROC, TOT—it's more complicated than you think, and after you do it often enough, it begins to make a little song, that you hear words to, in my case "Hello (*bing*) there, you (*gung*) hap-py peepul (*splat*)"— the *splat* being the drawer flying out. I uncreased the bill, tenderly as you may imagine, it just having come from between the two smoothest scoops of vanilla I had ever known there were, and pass a half and a penny into her narrow pink palm, and nestle the herrings in a bag and twist its neck and hand it over, all the time thinking.

The girls, and who'd blame them, are in a hurry to get out, so I say "I quit" to Lengel quick enough for them to hear, hoping they'll stop and watch me, their unsuspected hero. They keep right on going, into the electric eye; the door flies open and they flicker across the lot to their car, Queenie and Plaid and Big Tall Goony-Goony (not that as raw material she was so bad), leaving me with Lengel and a kink in his eyebrow.

"Did you say something, Sammy?"

"I said I quit."

"I thought you did."

"You didn't have to embarrass them."

"It was they who were embarrassing us."

I started to say something that came out "Fiddle-de-doo." It's a saying of my grandmother's, and I know she would have been pleased.

"I don't think you know what you're saying." Lengel said.

"I know you don't," I said. "But I do." I pull the bow at the back of my apron and start shrugging it off my shoulders. A couple of customers that had been heading for my slot begin to knock against each other, like scared pigs in a chute.

Lengel sighs and begins to look very patient and old and gray. He's been a friend of my parents for years. "Sammy, you don't want to do this to your Mom and Dad," he tells me. It's true, I don't. But it seems to me that once you begin a gesture it's fatal not to go through with it. I fold the apron, "Sammy" stitched in red on the pocket, and put it on the counter, and drop the bow tie on top of it. The bow tie is theirs, if you've ever wondered. "You'll feel this for the rest of your life," Lengel says, and I know that's true, too, but remembering how he made that pretty girl blush makes me so scrunchy inside I punch the No Sale tab and the machine whirs "pee-pul" and the drawer splats out. One advantage to this scene taking place in summer, I can follow this up with a clean exit, there's no fumbling around getting your coat and galoshes, I just saunter into the electric eye in my white shirt that my mother ironed the night before, and the door heaves itself open, and outside the sunshine is skating around on the asphalt.

I look around for my girls, but they're gone, of course. There wasn't anybody but some young married screaming with her children about some candy they didn't get by the door of a powder-blue Falcon station wagon. Looking back in the big windows, over the bags of peat moss and aluminum lawn furniture stacked on the pavement, I could see Lengel in my place in the slot, checking the sheep through. His face was dark gray and his back stiff, as if he's just had an injection of iron, and my stomach kind of fell as I felt how hard the world was going to be to me hereafter.

[1961]

Section III: What Is Drama?

Lorraine Hansberry
[1930–1965]

"Young, gifted, and black." The playwright, activist, and essayist
LORRAINE HANSBERRY *used this phrase in a speech commending the winners of a writing contest sponsored by the United Negro College Fund, but this description also aptly captures her own short creative life, which ended tragically when she died of cancer at the age of thirty-four.*

Born in Chicago, Hansberry was the daughter of prominent intellectuals and activists, and the niece of a professor of African history at Howard University. In college, Hansberry studied art, and decided to become a writer after seeing a performance of a play by the Irish playwright Sean O'Casey. She took writing classes in New York City, where she encountered influential African-American intellectuals such as Paul Robeson, Langston Hughes, and W. E. B Du Bois, with whom she took a class on African history. Hansberry was also active in the American civil rights movement. Through this involvement, she met her husband Robert Nemiroff, a Jewish songwriter who, despite their divorce a year before her death, served as executor of her literary estate.

Hansberry's A Raisin in the Sun *was the first play by a black woman produced on Broadway, as well as distinguishing her as the first black, the fifth woman, and the youngest playwright to win the prestigious New York Drama Critics Circle Award for Best Play of the Year. The play takes its name from poem "Harlem (A Dream Deferred)," penned by the Harlem Renaissance poet Langston Hughes. This play was unique in its realist depiction of the Youngers, an African-American family seeking to achieve the American Dream. Their quest to move into a largely white neighborhood was informed partially by Hansberry's own experiences growing up in Woodlawn, a neighborhood on Chicago's south side.*

Since its premiere, A Raisin in the Sun *(1959) has been hugely successful with audiences. It was adapted into a popular 1961 film and a 1989 television drama. In 1973, Nemiroff helped tailor the play into a musical titled* Raisin, *which had a long and successful run and won the 1974 Tony Award for Best Musical. More recently, a 2004 Broadway revival of the play broke box office records, and earned Tony Awards for best actress and best supporting actress, as well as offering the well-publicized performance of the rapper Sean (P. Diddy) Combs. Despite its enduring popularity, the play has not been without critics. In the 1960s, African-American theater, such as that produced by members of the Black Arts Movement, sought to intervene politically and socially through more avant-garde dramatic forms; consequently, Hansberry's realism was seen by some as a political compromise.*

Hansberry's other work confirms her great promise cut short. Her play The Sign in Sidney Brustein's Window *(1964), a political drama set in Greenwich Village with a largely white cast, ran briefly on Broadway, and an adaptation of her writings, entitled* To Be Young, Gifted, and Black, *was produced off-Broadway in 1969. Three of her unpublished plays have also been collected as* Les Blancs: The Last Plays of Lorraine Hansberry *(1972).*

A Raisin in the Sun

LORRAINE HANSBERRY

What happens to a dream deferred?
Does it dry up
Like a raisin in the sun?
Or fester like a sore—
And then run?
Does it stink like rotten meat?
Or crust and sugar over—
Like a syrupy sweet?

Maybe it just sags
Like a heavy load.

Or does it explode?

—Langston Hughes

CHARACTERS

RUTH YOUNGER
TRAVIS YOUNGER
WALTER LEE YOUNGER (BROTHER)
BENEATHA YOUNGER
LENA YOUNGER (MAMA)
JOSEPH ASAGAI
GEORGE MURCHISON
KARL LINDNER
BOBO
MOVING MEN

The action of the play is set in Chicago's Southside, sometime between World War II and the present.

ACT ONE

ACT ONE

SCENE 1

The Younger living room would be a comfortable and well-ordered room if it were not for a number of indestructible contradictions to this state of being. Its furnishings are typical and undistinguished and their primary feature now is that they have clearly had to accommodate the living of too many people for too many years—and they are tired. Still, we can see that at some time, a time probably no longer remembered by the family (except perhaps for Mama), the furnishings of this room were actually selected with care and love and even hope—and brought to this apartment and arranged with taste and pride.

That was a long time ago. Now the once loved pattern of the couch upholstery has to fight to show itself from under acres of crocheted doilies and couch covers which have themselves finally come to be more important than the upholstery. And here a table or a chair has been moved to disguise the worn places in the carpet; but the carpet has fought back by showing its weariness, with depressing uniformity, elsewhere on its surface.

Weariness has, in fact, won in this room. Everything has been polished, washed, sat on, used, scrubbed too often. All pretenses but living itself have long since vanished from the very atmosphere of this room.

Moreover, a section of this room, for it is not really a room unto itself, though the landlord's lease would make it seem so, slopes backward to provide a small kitchen area, where the family prepares the meals that are eaten in the living room proper, which must also serve as dining room. The single window that has been provided for these "two" rooms is located in this kitchen area. The sole natural light the family may enjoy in the course of a day is only that which fights its way through this little window.

At left, a door leads to a bedroom which is shared by Mama and her daughter, Beneatha. At right, opposite, is a second room (which in the beginning of the life of this apartment was probably a breakfast room) which serves as a bedroom for Walter and his wife, Ruth.

TIME: *Sometime between World War II and the present.*

PLACE: *Chicago's Southside.*

At rise: It is morning dark in the living room. Travis is asleep on the make-down bed at center. An alarm clock sounds from within the bedroom at right, and presently Ruth enters from that room and closes the door behind her. She crosses sleepily toward the window. As she passes her sleeping son she reaches down and shakes him a little. At the window she raises the shade and a dusky Southside morning light comes in feebly. She fills a pot with water and puts it on to boil. She calls to the boy, between yawns, in a slightly muffled voice.

Ruth is about thirty. We can see that she was a pretty girl, even exceptionally so, but now it is apparent that life has been little that she expected, and disappointment has already begun to hang in her face. In a few years, before thirty-five even, she will be known among her people as a "settled woman."

She crosses to her son and gives him a good, final, rousing shake.

RUTH. Come on now, boy, it's seven thirty! *(Her son sits up at last, in a stupor of sleepiness)* I say hurry up. Travis! You ain't the only person in the world got to use a bathroom! *(The child, a sturdy, handsome little boy of ten or eleven, drags himself out of the bed and almost blindly takes his towels and "today's clothes" from drawers and a closet and goes out to the bathroom, which is in an outside hall and which is shared by another family or families on the same floor. Ruth crosses to the bedroom door at right and open it and calls in the her husband)* Walter Lee! . . . It's after seven thirty! Lemme see you do some walking up in there now! *(She waits)* You better get up from there, man! It's after seven thirty I tell you *(She waits again)* All right, you just go ahead and lay there and next thing you know Travis be finished and Mr. Johnson'll be in there and you'll be fussing and cussing round here like a mad man! And be late too! *(She waits, at the end of patience)* Walter Lee—it's time for you to get up!

(She waits another second and then starts to go into the bedroom, but is apparently satisfied that her husband has begun to get up. She stops, pulls the door to, and returns to the kitchen area. She wipes her face with a moist cloth and runs her fingers through her sleep-disheveled hair in a vain effort and ties an apron around her housecoat. The bedroom door at right opens and her husband stands in the doorway in his pajamas, which are rumpled and mismated. He is a lean, intense

*young man in his middle thirties, inclined to quick nervous movements and errat-
ic speech habits—and always in his voice there is a quality of indictment)*

WALTER. Is he out yet?

RUTH. What you mean *out*? He ain't hardly got in there good yet.

WALTER *(Wandering in, still more oriented to sleep than to a new day).* Well,
what was you doing all that yelling for if I can't even get in there yet?
(Stopping and thinking) Check coming today?

RUTH. They *said* Saturday and this is just Friday and I hopes to God you ain't
going to get up here first thing this morning and start talking to me 'bout
no money—'cause I 'bout don't want to hear it.

WALTER. Something the matter with you this morning?

RUTH. No—I'm just sleepy as the devil. What kind of eggs you want?

WALTER. Not scrambled. *(Ruth starts to scramble eggs)* Paper come? *(Ruth
points impatiently to the rolled up* Tribune *on the table, and he gets it and
spreads it out and vaguely reads the front page)* Set off another bomb yesterday.[1]

RUTH *(Maximum indifference).* Did they?

WALTER *(Looking up).* What's the matter with you?

RUTH. Ain't nothing the matter with me. And don't keep asking me that this
morning.

WALTER. Ain't nobody bothering you. *(Reading the news of the day absently
again)* Say Colonel McCormick is sick.[2]

RUTH *(Affecting tea-party interest).* Is he now? Poor thing.

WALTER *(Sighing and looking at his watch).* Oh, me. *(He waits)* Now what is
that boy doing in that bathroom all this time? He just going to have to
start getting up earlier. I can't be being late to work on account of him
fooling around in there.

RUTH *(Turning on him).* Oh, no he ain't going to be getting up no earlier no
such thing! It ain't his fault that he can't get to bed no earlier nights 'cause
he got a bunch of crazy good-for-nothing clowns sitting up running their
mouths in what is supposed to be his bedroom after ten o'clock at
night . . .

WALTER. That's what you mad about, ain't it? The things I want to talk about
with my friends just couldn't be important in your mind, could they?

*(He rises and finds a cigarette in her handbag on the table and crosses to the little
window and looks out, smoking and deeply enjoying this first one)*

---

[1]Reference to nuclear weapons testing.

[2]Robert Rutherford McCormick, publisher and editor in chief of the *Chicago Tribune* from 1925-
1955.

RUTH *(Almost matter of factly, a complaint too automatic to deserve emphasis)*. Why you always got to smoke before you eat in the morning?

WALTER *(At the window)*. Just look at 'em down there . . . Running and racing to work . . . *(He turns and faces his wife and watches her a moment at the stove, and then, suddenly)* You look young this morning, baby.

RUTH *(Indifferently)*. Yeah?

WALTER. Just for a second—stirring them eggs. It's gone now—just for a second it was—you looked real young again. *(Then, drily)* It's gone now— you look like yourself again.

RUTH. Man, if you don't shut up and leave me alone.

WALTER *(Looking out to the street again)*. First thing a man ought to learn in life is not to make love to no colored woman first thing in the morning. You all some evil people at eight o'clock in the morning.

(Travis appears in the hall doorway, almost fully dressed and quite wide awake now, his towels and pajamas across his shoulders. He opens the door and signals for his father to make the bathroom in a hurry)

TRAVIS *(Watching the bathroom)*. Daddy, come on! *(Walter gets his bathroom utensils and flies out to the bathroom)*

RUTH. Sit down and have your breakfast, Travis.

TRAVIS. Mama, this is Friday. *(Gleefully)* Check coming tomorrow, huh?

RUTH. You get your mind off money and eat your breakfast.

TRAVIS *(Eating)*. This is the morning we supposed to bring the fifty cents to school.

RUTH. Well, I ain't got no fifty cents this morning.

TRAVIS. Teacher say we have to.

RUTH. I don't care what teacher say. I ain't got it. Eat your breakfast, Travis.

TRAVIS. I *am* eating.

RUTH. Hush up now and just eat!

(The boy gives her an exasperated look for her lack of understanding, and eats grudgingly)

TRAVIS. You think grandmama would have it?

RUTH. No! And I want you to stop asking your grandmother for money, you hear me?

TRAVIS *(Outraged)*. Gaaaleee! I don't ask her, she just gimme it sometimes!

RUTH. Travis Willard Younger—I got too much on me this morning to be—

TRAVIS. Maybe Daddy—

RUTH. *Travis!*

(The boy hushes abruptly. They are both quiet and tense for several seconds)

TRAVIS *(Presently)*. Could I maybe go carry some groceries in front of the supermarket for a little while after school then?

RUTH. Just hush, I said. *(Travis jabs his spoon into his cereal bowl viciously, and rests his head in anger upon his fists)* If you through eating, you can get over there and make up your bed.

(The boy obeys stiffly and crosses the room, almost mechanically, to the bed and more or less carefully folds the covering. He carries the bedding into his mother's room and returns with his books and cap)

TRAVIS *(Sulking and standing apart from her unnaturally)*. I'm gone.

RUTH *(Looking up from the stove to inspect him automatically)*. Come here. *(He crosses to her and she studies his head)* If you don't take this comb and fix this here head, you better! *(Travis puts down his books with a great sigh of oppression, and crosses to the mirror. His mother mutters under her breath about his "slubbornness")* 'Bout to march out of here with that head looking just like chickens slept in it! I just don't know where you get your slubborn ways . . . And get your jacket, too. Looks chilly out this morning.

TRAVIS *(With conspicuously brushed hair and jacket)*. I'm gone.

RUTH. Get carfare and milk money—*(Waving one finger)*—and not a single penny for no caps,[3] you hear me?

TRAVIS *(With sullen politeness)*. Yes'm.

(He turns in outrage to leave. His mother watches after him as in his frustration he approaches the door almost comically. When she speaks to him, her voice has become a very gentle tease)

RUTH *(Mocking; as she thinks he would say it)*. Oh, Mama makes me so mad sometimes, I don't know what to do! *(She waits and continues to his back as he stands stock-still in front of the door)* I wouldn't kiss that woman good-bye for nothing in this world this morning! *(The boy finally turns around and rolls his eyes at her, knowing the mood has changed and he is vindicated; he does not, however, move toward her yet)* Not for nothing in this world! *(She finally laughs aloud at him and holds out her arms to him and we see that it is a way between them, very old and practiced. He crosses to her and allows her to embrace him warmly but keeps his face fixed with masculine rigidity. She holds him back from her presently and looks at him and runs her fingers over the features of his face. With utter gentleness—)* Now—whose little old angry man are you?

TRAVIS *(The masculinity and gruffness start to fade at last)*. Aw gaalee— Mama . . .

---

[3] Ammunition for a child's cap gun.

RUTH (*Mimicking*). Aw—gaaaaalleeeee, Mama! (*She pushes him, with rough playfulness and finality, toward the door*) Get on out of here or you going to be late.

TRAVIS (*In the face of love, new aggressiveness*). Mama, could I *please* go carry groceries?

RUTH. Honey, it's starting to get so cold evenings.

WALTER (*Coming in from the bathroom and drawing a make-believe gun from a make-believe holster and shooting at his son*). What is it he wants to do?

RUTH. Go carry groceries after school at the supermarket.

WALTER. Well, let him go . . .

TRAVIS (*Quickly, to the ally*). I *have* to—she won't gimme the fifty cents . . .

WALTER (*To his wife only*). Why not?

RUTH (*Simply, and with flavor*). 'Cause we don't have it.

WALTER (*To Ruth only*). What you tell the boy things like that for? (*Reaching down into his pants with a rather important gesture*) Here, son—

(*He hands the boy the coin, but his eyes are directed to his wife's. Travis takes the money happily*)

TRAVIS. Thanks, Daddy.

(*He starts out. Ruth watches both of them with murder in her eyes. Walter stands and stares back at her with defiance, and suddenly reaches into his pocket again on an afterthought*)

WALTER (*Without even looking at his son, still staring hard at his wife*). In fact, here's another fifty cents . . . Buy yourself some fruit today—or take a taxicab to school or something!

TRAVIS. Whoopee—

(*He leaps up and clasps his father around the middle with his legs, and they face each other in mutual appreciation; slowly Walter Lee peeks around the boy to catch the violent rays from his wife's eyes and draws his head back as if shot*)

WALTER. You better get down now—and get to school, man.

TRAVIS (*At the door*). O.K. Good-bye.

(*He exits*)

WALTER (*After him, pointing with pride*). That's my boy. (*She looks at him in disgust and turns back to her work*) You know what I was thinking 'bout in the bathroom this morning?

RUTH. No.

WALTER. How come you always try to be so pleasant!

RUTH. What is there to be pleasant 'bout!

WALTER. You want to know what I was thinking 'bout in the bathroom or not!

RUTH. I know what you thinking 'bout.

WALTER *(Ignoring her)*. 'Bout what me and Willy Harris was talking about last night.

RUTH *(Immediately—a refrain)*. Willy Harris is a good-for-nothing loud mouth.

WALTER. Anybody who talks to me has got to be a good-for-nothing loud mouth, ain't he? And what you know about who is just a good-for-nothing loud mouth? Charlie Atkins was just a "good-for-nothing loud mouth" too, wasn't he! When he wanted me to go in the dry-cleaning business with him. And now—he's grossing a hundred thousand a year. A hundred thousand dollars a year! You still call *him* a loud mouth!

RUTH *(Bitterly)*. Oh, Walter Lee . . .

(She folds her head on her arms over the table)

WALTER *(Rising and coming to her and standing over her)*. You tired, ain't you? Tired of everything. Me, the boy, the way we live—this beat-up hole—everything. Ain't you? *(She doesn't look up, doesn't answer)* So tired—moaning and groaning all the time, but you wouldn't do nothing to help, would you? You couldn't be on my side that long for nothing, could you?

RUTH. Walter, please leave me alone.

WALTER. A man needs for a woman to back him up . . .

RUTH. Walter—

WALTER. Mama would listen to you. You know she listen to you more than she do me and Bennie. She think more of you. All you have to do is just sit down with her when you drinking your coffee one morning and talking 'bout things like you do and—*(He sits down beside her and demonstrates graphically what he thinks her methods and tone should be)*—you just sip your coffee, see, and say easy like that you been thinking 'bout that deal Walter Lee is so interested in, 'bout the store and all, and sip some more coffee, like what you saying ain't really that important to you—And the next thing you know, she be listening good and asking you questions and when I come home—I can tell her the details. This ain't no fly-by-night proposition, baby. I mean we figured it out, me and Willy and Bobo.

RUTH *(With a frown)*. Bobo?

WALTER. Yeah. You see, this little liquor store we got in mind cost seventy-five thousand and we figured the initial investment on the place be 'bout thirty thousand, see. That be ten thousand each. Course, there's a couple of hundred you got to pay so's you don't spend your life just waiting for them clowns to let your license get approved—

RUTH. You mean graft?

WALTER (*Frowning impatiently*). Don't call it that. See there, that just goes to show you what women understand about the world. Baby, don't *nothing* happen for you in this world 'less you pay *somebody* off!

RUTH. Walter, leave me alone! (*She raises her head and stares at him vigorously— then says, more quietly*) Eat your eggs, they gonna be cold.

WALTER (*Straightening up from her and looking off*). That's it. There you are. Man say to his woman: I got me a dream. His woman say: Eat your eggs. (*Sadly, but gaining in power*) Man say: I got to take hold of this here world, baby! And a woman will say: Eat your eggs and go to work. (*Passionately now*) Man say: I got to change my life, I'm choking to death, baby! And his woman say—(*In utter anguish as he brings his fists down on his thighs*)—Your eggs is getting cold!

RUTH (*Softly*). Walter, that ain't none of our money.

WALTER (*Not listening at all or even looking at her*). This morning, I was lookin' in the mirror and thinking about it . . . I'm thirty-five years old; I been married eleven years and I got a boy who sleeps in the living room— (*Very, very quietly*)—and all I got to give him is stories about how rich white people live . . .

RUTH. Eat your eggs, Walter.

WALTER. *Damn my eggs . . . damn all the eggs that ever was!*

RUTH. Then go to work.

WALTER (*Looking up at her*). See—I'm trying to talk to you 'bout myself— (*Shaking his head with the repetition*)—and all you can say is eat them eggs and go to work.

RUTH (*Wearily*). Honey, you never say nothing new. I listen to you every day, every night and every morning, and you never say nothing new. (*Shrugging*) So you would rather *be* Mr. Arnold than be his chauffeur. So—I would *rather* be living in Buckingham Palace.

WALTER. That is just what is wrong with the colored woman in this world . . . Don't understand about building their men up and making 'em feel like they somebody. Like they can do something.

RUTH (*Drily, but to hurt*). There *are* colored men who do things.

WALTER. No thanks to the colored woman.

RUTH. Well, being a colored woman, I guess I can't help myself none.

(*She rises and gets the ironing board and sets it up and attacks a huge pile of rough-dried clothes, sprinkling them in preparation for the ironing and then rolling them into tight fat balls*)

WALTER *(Mumbling)*. We one group of men tied to a race of women with small minds.

(His sister Beneatha enters. She is about twenty, as slim and intense as her brother. She is not as pretty as her sister-in-law, but her lean, almost intellectual face has a handsomeness of its own. She wears a bright-red flannel nightie, and her thick hair stands wildly about her head. Her speech is a mixture of many things; it is different from the rest of the family's insofar as education has permeated her sense of English—and perhaps the Midwest rather than the South has finally—at last— won out in her inflection; but not altogether, because over all of it is a soft slurring and transformed use of vowels which is the decided influence of the Southside. She passes through the room without looking at either Ruth or Walter and goes to the outside door and looks, a little blindly, out to the bathroom. She sees that it has been lost to the Johnsons. She closes the door with a sleepy vengeance and crosses to the table and sits down a little defeated)

BENEATHA. I am going to start timing those people.

WALTER. You should get up earlier.

BENEATHA *(Her face in her hands. She is still fighting the urge to go back to bed)*. Really—would you suggest dawn? Where's the paper?

WALTER *(Pushing the paper across the table to her as he studies her almost clini- cally, as though he has never seen her before)*. You a horrible-looking chick at this hour.

BENEATHA *(Drily)*. Good morning, everybody.

WALTER *(Senselessly)*. How is school coming?

BENEATHA *(In the same spirit)*. Lovely. Lovely. And you know, biology is the greatest. *(Looking up at him)* I dissected something that looked just like you yesterday.

WALTER. I just wondered if you've made up your mind and everything.

BENEATHA *(Gaining in sharpness and impatience)*. And what did I answer yes- terday morning—and the day before that?

RUTH *(From the ironing board, like someone disinterested and old)*. Don't be so nasty, Bennie.

BENEATHA *(Still to her brother)*. And the day before that and the day before that!

WALTER *(Defensively)*. I'm interested in you. Something wrong with that? Ain't many girls who decide—

WALTER AND BENEATHA *(In unison)*.—"to be a doctor."

(Silence)

WALTER. Have we figured out yet just exactly how much medical school is going to cost?

RUTH. Walter Lee, why don't you leave that girl alone and get out of here to work?

BENEATHA (*Exits to the bathroom and bangs on the door*). Come on out of there, please!

(*She comes back into the room*)

WALTER (*Looking at his sister intently*). You know the check is coming tomorrow.

BENEATHA (*Turning on him with a sharpness all her own*). That money belongs to Mama, Walter, and it's for her to decide how she wants to use it. I don't care if she wants to buy a house or a rocket ship or just nail it up somewhere and look at it. It's hers. Not ours—*hers*.

WALTER (*Bitterly*). Now ain't that fine! You just got your mother's interest at heart, ain't you, girl? You such a nice girl—but if Mama got that money she can always take a few thousand and help you through school too—can't she?

BENEATHA. I have never asked anyone around here to do anything for me!

WALTER. No! And the line between asking and just accepting when the time comes is big and wide—ain't it!

BENEATHA (*With fury*). What do you want from me, Brother—that I quit school or just drop dead, which!

WALTER. I don't want nothing but for you to stop acting holy 'round here. Me and Ruth done made some sacrifices for you—why can't you do something for the family?

RUTH. Walter, don't be dragging me in it.

WALTER. You are in it—Don't you get up and go work in somebody's kitchen for the last three years to help put clothes on her back?

RUTH. Oh, Walter—that's not fair . . .

WALTER. It ain't that nobody expects you to get on your knees and say thank you, Brother; thank you, Ruth; thank you, Mama—and thank you, Travis, for wearing the same pair of shoes for two semesters—

BENEATHA (*Dropping to her knees*). Well—I *do*—all right?—thank everybody . . . and forgive me for ever wanting to be anything at all . . . forgive me, forgive me!

RUTH. Please stop it! Your mama'll hear you.

WALTER. Who the hell told you you had to be a doctor? If you so crazy 'bout messing 'round with sick people—then go be a nurse like other women—or just get married and be quiet . . .

BENEATHA. Well—you finally got it said . . . It took you three years but you finally got it said. Walter, give up; leave me alone—it's Mama's money.

WALTER. *He was my father, too!*

BENEATHA. So what? He was mine, too—and Travis' grandfather—but the insurance money belongs to Mama. Picking on me is not going to make her give it to you to invest in any liquor stores—*(Underbreath, dropping into a chair)*—and I for one say, God bless Mama for that!

WALTER *(To Ruth)*. See—did you hear? Did you hear!

RUTH. Honey, please go to work.

WALTER. Nobody in this house is ever going to understand me.

BENEATHA. Because you're a nut.

WALTER. Who's a nut?

BENEATHA. You—you are a nut. Thee is mad, boy.

WALTER *(Looking at his wife and his sister from the door, very sadly)*. The world's most backward race of people, and that's a fact.

BENEATHA *(Turning slowly in her chair)*. And then there are all those prophets who would lead us out of the wilderness—*(Walter slams out of the house)*—into the swamps!

RUTH. Bennie, why you always gotta be pickin' on your brother? Can't you be a little sweeter sometimes? *(Door opens. Walter walks in)*

WALTER *(To Ruth)*. I need some money for carfare.

RUTH *(Looks at him, then warms; teasing, but tenderly)*. Fifty cents? *(She goes to her bag and gets money)* Here, take a taxi.

(Walter exits. Mama enters. She is a woman in her early sixties, full-bodied and strong. She is one of those women of a certain grace and beauty who wear it so unobtrusively that it takes a while to notice. Her dark-brown face is surrounded by the total whiteness of her hair, and, being a woman who has adjusted to many things in life and overcome many more, her face is full of strength. She has, we can see, wit and faith of a kind that keep her eyes lit and full of interest and expectancy. She is, in a word, a beautiful woman. Her bearing is perhaps most like the noble bearing of the women of the Hereros of Southwest Africa[4]—rather as if she imagines that as she walks she still bears a basket or a vessel upon her head. Her speech, on the other hand, is as careless as her carriage is precise—she is inclined to slur everything—but her voice is perhaps not so much quiet as simply soft)

MAMA. Who that 'round here slamming doors at this hour?

(She crosses through the room, goes to the window, opens it, and brings in a feeble little plant growing doggedly in a small pot on the window sill. She feels the dirt and puts it back out)

RUTH. That was Walter Lee. He and Bennie was at it again.

---

[4]Major tribe of South-West Africa, now known as Namibia.

MAMA. My children and they tempers. Lord, if this little old plant don't get more sun than it's been getting it ain't never going to see spring again. *(She turns from the window)* What's the matter with you this morning, Ruth? You looks right peaked. You aiming to iron all them things? Leave some for me. I'll get to 'em this afternoon. Bennie honey, it's too drafty for you to be sitting 'round half dressed. Where's your robe?

BENEATHA. In the cleaners.

MAMA. Well, go get mine and put it on.

BENEATHA. I'm not cold, Mama, honest.

MAMA. I know—but you so thin . . .

BENEATHA *(Irritably)*. Mama, I'm not cold.

MAMA *(Seeing the make-down bed as Travis has left it)*. Lord have mercy, look at that poor bed. Bless his heart—he tries, don't he?

(She moves to the bed Travis has sloppily made up)

RUTH. No—he don't half try at all 'cause he knows you going to come along behind him and fix everything. That's just how come he don't know how to do nothing right now—you done spoiled that boy so.

MAMA. Well—he's a little boy. Ain't supposed to know 'bout housekeeping. My baby, that's what he is. What you fix for his breakfast this morning?

RUTH *(Angrily)*. I feed my son, Lena!

MAMA. I ain't meddling—*(Underbreath; busy-bodyish)* I just noticed all last week he had cold cereal, and when it starts getting this chilly in the fall a child ought to have some hot grits or something when he goes out in the cold—

RUTH *(Furious)*. I gave him hot oats—is that all right!

MAMA. I ain't meddling. *(Pause)* Put a lot of nice butter on it? *(Ruth shoots her an angry look and does not reply)* He likes lots of butter.

RUTH *(Exasperated)*. Lena—

MAMA *(To Beneatha. Mama is inclined to wander conversationally sometimes)*. What was you and your brother fussing 'bout this morning?

BENEATHA. It's not important, Mama.

(She gets up and goes to look out at the bathroom, which is apparently free, and she picks up her towels and rushes out)

MAMA. What was they fighting about?

RUTH. Now you know as well as I do.

MAMA *(Shaking her head)*. Brother still worrying hisself sick about that money?

RUTH. You know he is.

MAMA. You had breakfast?

RUTH. Some coffee.

MAMA. Girl you better start eating and looking after yourself better. You almost thin as Travis.

RUTH. Lena—

MAMA. Un-hunh?

RUTH. What are you going to do with it?

MAMA. Now don't you start, child. It's too early in the morning to be talking about money. It ain't Christian.

RUTH. It's just that he got his heart set on that store—

MAMA. You mean that liquor store that Willy Harris want him to invest in?

RUTH. Yes—

MAMA. We ain't no business people, Ruth. We just plain working folks.

RUTH. Ain't nobody business people till they go into business. Walter Lee say colored people ain't never going to start getting ahead till they start gambling on some different kinds of things in the world—investments and things.

MAMA. What done got into you, girl? Walter Lee done finally sold you on investing.

RUTH. No. Mama, something is happening between Walter and me. I don't know what it is—but he needs something—something I can't give him any more. He needs this chance, Lena.

MAMA *(Frowning deeply)*. But liquor, honey—

RUTH. Well—like Walter say—I spec people going to always be drinking themselves some liquor.

MAMA. Well—whether they drinks it or not ain't none of my business. But whether I go into business selling it to 'em *is,* and I don't want that on my ledger this late in life. *(Stopping suddenly and studying her daughter-in-law)* Ruth Younger, what's the matter with you today? You look like you could fall over right there.

RUTH. I'm tired.

MAMA. Then you better stay home from work today.

RUTH. I can't stay home. She'd be calling up the agency and screaming at them. "My girl didn't come in today—send me somebody! My girl didn't come in!" Oh, she just have a fit . . .

MAMA. Well, let her have it. I'll just call her up and say you got the flu—

RUTH *(Laughing)*. Why the flu?

MAMA. 'Cause it sounds respectable to 'em. Something white people get, too. They know 'bout the flu. Otherwise they think you been cut up or something when you tell 'em you sick.

RUTH. I got to go in. We need the money.

MAMA. Somebody would of thought my children done all but starved to death the way they talk about money here late. Child, we got a great big old check coming tomorrow.

RUTH *(Sincerely, but also self-righteously)*. Now that's your money. It ain't got nothing to do with me. We all feel like that—Walter and Bennie and me—even Travis.

MAMA *(Thoughtfully, and suddenly very far away)*. Ten thousand dollars—

RUTH. Sure is wonderful.

MAMA. Ten thousand dollars.

RUTH. You know what you should do, Miss Lena? You should take yourself a trip somewhere. To Europe or South America or someplace—

MAMA *(Throwing up her hands at the thought)*. Oh, child!

RUTH. I'm serious. Just pack up and leave! Go on away and enjoy yourself some. Forget about the family and have yourself a ball for once in your life—

MAMA *(Drily)*. You sound like I'm just about ready to die. Who'd go with me? What I look like wandering 'round Europe by myself?

RUTH. Shoot—these here rich white women do it all the time. They don't think nothing of packing up they suitcases and piling on one of them big steamships and—swoosh!—they gone, child.

MAMA. Something always told me I wasn't no rich white woman.

RUTH. Well—what are you going to do with it then?

MAMA. I ain't rightly decided. *(Thinking. She speaks now with emphasis)* Some of it got to be put away for Beneatha and her schoolin'—and ain't nothing going to touch that part of it. Nothing. *(She waits several seconds, trying to make up her mind about something, and looks at Ruth a little tentatively before going on)* Been thinking that we maybe could meet the notes on a little old two-story somewhere, with a yard where Travis could play in the summertime, if we use part of the insurance for a down payment and everybody kind of pitch in. I could maybe take on a little day work again, few days a week—

RUTH *(Studying her mother-in-law furtively and concentrating on her ironing, anxious to encourage without seeming to)*. Well, Lord knows, we've put enough rent into this here rat trap to pay for four houses by now . . .

MAMA *(Looking up at the words "rat trap" and then looking around and leaning back and sighing—in a suddenly reflective mood—)*. "Rat trap"—yes, that's all it is. *(Smiling)* I remember just as well the day me and Big Walter moved in here. Hadn't been married but two weeks and wasn't planning on living here no more than a year. *(She shakes her head at the dissolved dream)* We was going to set away, little by little, don't you know, and buy a little place out in Morgan park. We had even picked out the house.

(Chuckling a little) Looks right dumpy today. But Lord, child, you should know all the dreams I had 'bout buying that house and fixing it up and making me a little garden in the back—*(She waits and stops smiling)* And didn't none of it happen.

(Dropping her hands in a futile gesture)

RUTH *(Keeps her head down, ironing)*. Yes, life can be a barrel of disappointments, sometimes.

MAMA. Honey, Big Walter would come in here some nights back then and slump down on that couch there and just look at the rug, and look at me and look at the rug and then back at me—and I'd know he was down then . . . really down. *(After a second very long and thoughtful pause; she is seeing back to times that only she can see)* And then, Lord, when I lost that baby—little Claude—I almost thought I was going to lose Big Walter too. Oh, that man grieved hisself! He was one man to love his children.

RUTH. Ain't nothin' can tear at you like losin' your baby.

MAMA. I guess that's how come that man finally worked hisself to death like he done. Like he was fighting his own war with this here world that took his baby from him.

RUTH. He sure was a fine man, all right. I always liked Mr. Younger.

MAMA. Crazy 'bout his children! God knows there was plenty wrong with Walter Younger—hard-headed, mean, kind of wild with women—plenty wrong with him. But he sure loved his children. Always wanted them to have something—be something. That's where Brother gets all these notions, I reckon. Big Walter used to say, he'd get right wet in the eyes sometimes, lean his head back with the water standing in his eyes and say, "Seem like God didn't see fit to give the black man nothing but dreams—but He did give us children to make them dreams seem worth while." *(She smiles)* He could talk like that, don't you know.

RUTH. Yes, he sure could. He was a good man, Mr. Younger.

MAMA. Yes, a fine man—just couldn't never catch up with his dreams, that's all.

(Beneatha comes in, brushing her hair and looking up to the ceiling, where the sound of a vacuum cleaner has started up)

BENEATHA. What could be so dirty on that woman's rugs that she has to vacuum them every single day?

RUTH. I wish certain young women 'round here who I could name would take inspiration about certain rugs in a certain apartment I could also mention.

BENEATHA *(Shrugging).* How much cleaning can a house need, for Christ's sakes.

MAMA *(Not liking the Lord's name used thus).* Bennie!

RUTH. Just listen to her—just listen!

BENEATHA. Oh, God!

MAMA. If you use the Lord's name just one more time—

BENEATHA *(A bit of a whine).* Oh, Mama—

RUTH. Fresh—just fresh as salt, this girl!

BENEATHA *(Drily).* Well—if the salt loses its savor—

MAMA. Now that will do. I just ain't going to have you 'round here reciting the scriptures in vain—you hear me?

BENEATHA. How did I manage to get on everybody's wrong side by just walking into a room?

RUTH. If you weren't so fresh—

BENEATHA. Ruth, I'm twenty years old.

MAMA. What time you be home from school today?

BENEATHA. Kind of late. *(With enthusiasm)* Madeline is going to start my guitar lessons today.

(Mama and Ruth look up with the same expression)

MAMA. Your *what* kind of lessons?

BENEATHA. Guitar.

RUTH. Oh, Father!

MAMA. How come you done taken it in your mind to learn to play the guitar?

BENEATHA. I just want to, that's all.

MAMA *(Smiling).* Lord, child, don't you know what to do with yourself? How long it going to be before you get tired of this now—like you got tired of that little play-acting group you joined last year? *(Looking at Ruth)* And what was it the year before that?

RUTH. The horseback-riding club for which she bought that fifty-five-dollar riding habit that's been hanging in the closet ever since!

MAMA *(To Beneatha).* Why you got to flit so from one thing to another, baby?

BENEATHA *(Sharply).* I just want to learn to play the guitar. Is there anything wrong with that?

MAMA. Ain't nobody trying to stop you. I just wonders sometimes why you has to flit so from one thing to another all the time. You ain't never done nothing with all that camera equipment you brought home—

BENEATHA. I don't flit! I—I experiment with different forms of expression—

RUTH. Like riding a horse?

BENEATHA. —People have to express themselves one way or another.

MAMA. What is it you want to express?

BENEATHA *(Angrily)*. Me! *(Mama and Ruth look at each other and burst into raucous laughter)* Don't worry—I don't expect you to understand.

MAMA *(To change the subject)*. Who you going out with tomorrow night?

BENEATHA *(With displeasure)*. George Murchison again.

MAMA *(Pleased)*. Oh—you getting a little sweet on him?

RUTH. You ask me, this child ain't sweet on nobody but herself—*(Under-breath)* Express herself!

(They laugh)

BENEATHA. Oh—I like George all right, Mama. I mean I like him enough to go out with him and stuff, but—

RUTH *(For devilment)*. What does *and stuff* mean?

BENEATHA. Mind your own business.

MAMA. Stop picking at her now, Ruth. *(A thoughtful pause, and then a suspicious sudden look at her daughter as she turns in her chair for emphasis)* What *does* it mean?

BENEATHA *(Wearily)*. Oh, I just mean I couldn't ever really be serious about George. He's—he's so shallow.

RUTH. Shallow—what do you mean he's shallow? He's *Rich*!

MAMA. Hush, Ruth.

BENEATHA. I know he's rich. He knows he's rich, too.

RUTH. Well—what other qualities a man got to have to satisfy you, little girl?

BENEATHA. You wouldn't even begin to understand. Anybody who married Walter could not possibly understand.

MAMA *(Outraged)*. What kind of way is that to talk about your brother?

BENEATHA. Brother is a flip—let's face it.

MAMA *(To Ruth, helplessly)*. What's a flip?

RUTH *(Glad to add kindling)*. She's saying he's crazy.

BENEATHA. Not crazy. Brother isn't really crazy yet—he—he's an elaborate neurotic.

MAMA. Hush your mouth!

BENEATHA. As for George. Well. George looks good—he's got a beautiful car and he takes me to nice places and, as my sister-in-law says, he is probably the richest boy I will ever get to know and I even like him sometimes—but if the Youngers are sitting around waiting to see if their little Bennie is going to tie up the family with the Murchisons, they are wasting their time.

RUTH. You mean you wouldn't marry George Murchison if he asked you someday? That pretty, rich thing? Honey, I knew you was odd—

BENEATHA. No I would not marry him if all I felt for him was what I feel now. Besides, George's family wouldn't really like it.

MAMA. Why not?

BENEATHA. Oh, Mama—The Murchisons are honest-to-God-real-*live*-rich colored people, and the only people in the world who are more snobbish than rich white people are rich colored people. I thought everybody knew that. I've met Mrs. Murchison. She's a scene!

MAMA. You must not dislike people 'cause they well off, honey.

BENEATHA. Why not? It makes just as much sense as disliking people 'cause they are poor, and lots of people do that.

RUTH (*A wisdom-of-the-ages manner. To Mama*). Well, she'll get over some of this—

BENEATHA. Get over it? What are you talking about, Ruth? Listen, I'm going to be a doctor. I'm not worried about who I'm going to marry yet—if I ever get married.

MAMA AND RUTH. *If!*

MAMA. Now, Bennie—

BENEATHA. Oh, I probably will . . . but first I'm going to be a doctor, and George, for one, still thinks that's pretty funny. I couldn't be bothered with that. I am going to be a doctor and everybody around here better understand that!

MAMA (*Kindly*). 'Course you going to be a doctor, honey, God willing.

BENEATHA (*Drily*). God hasn't got a thing to do with it.

MAMA. Beneatha—that just wasn't necessary.

BENEATHA. Well—neither is God. I get sick of hearing about God.

MAMA. Beneatha!

BENEATHA. I mean it! I'm just tired of hearing about God all the time. What has He got to do with anything? Does he pay tuition?

MAMA. You 'bout to get your fresh little jaw slapped!

RUTH. That's just what she needs, all right!

BENEATHA. Why? Why can't I say what I want to around here, like everybody else?

MAMA. It don't sound nice for a young girl to say things like that—you wasn't brought up that way. Me and your father went to trouble to get you and Brother to church every Sunday.

BENEATHA. Mama, you don't understand. It's all a matter of ideas, and God is just one idea I don't accept. It's not important. I am not going out and be immoral or commit crimes because I don't believe in God. I don't even think about it. It's just that I get tired of Him getting credit for all the things the human race achieves through its own stubborn effort. There simply is no blasted God—there is only man and it is he who makes miracles!

(Mama absorbs this speech, studies her daughter and rises slowly and crosses to Beneatha and slaps her powerfully across the face. After, there is only silence and the daughter drops her eyes from her mother's face, and Mama is very tall before her)

MAMA. Now—you say after me, in my mother's house there is still God. *(There is a long pause and Beneatha stares at the floor wordlessly. Mama repeats the phrase with precision and cool emotion)* In my mother's house there is still God.

BENEATHA. In my mother's house there is still God.

(A long pause)

MAMA *(Walking away from Beneatha, too disturbed for triumphant posture. Stopping and turning back to her daughter).* There are some ideas we ain't going to have in this house. Not long as I am at the head of this family.

BENEATHA. Yes, ma'am.

(Mama walks out of the room)

RUTH *(Almost gently, with profound understanding).* You think you a woman, Bennie—but you still a little girl. What you did was childish—so you got treated like a child.

BENEATHA. I see. *(Quietly)* I also see that everybody thinks it's all right for Mama to be a tyrant. But all the tyranny in the world will never put a God in the heavens!

(She picks up her books and goes out)

RUTH *(Goes to Mama's door).* She said she was sorry.

MAMA *(Coming out, going to her plant).* They frightens me, Ruth. My children.

RUTH. You got good children, Lena. They just a little off sometimes—but they're good.

MAMA. No—there's something come down between me and them that don't let us understand each other and I don't know what it is. One done almost lost his mind thinking 'bout money all the time and the other done commence to talk about things I can't seem to understand in no form or fashion. What is it that's changing, Ruth?

RUTH *(Soothingly, older than her years).* Now . . . you taking it all too seriously. You just got strong-willed children and it takes a strong woman like you to keep 'em in hand.

MAMA *(Looking at her plant and sprinkling a little water on it).* They spirited all right, my children. Got to admit they got spirit—Bennie and Walter.

Like this little old plant that ain't never had enough sunshine or nothing—and look at it . . .

*(She has her back to Ruth, who has had to stop ironing and lean against
something and put the back of her hand to her forehead)*

RUTH *(Trying to keep Mama from noticing)*. You . . . sure . . . loves that little
old thing, don't you?

MAMA. Well, I always wanted me a garden like I used to see sometimes at the
back of the houses down home. This plant is close as I ever got to having
one. *(She looks out of the window as she replaces the plant)* Lord, ain't nothing as dreary as the view from this window on a dreary day, is there? Why
ain't you singing this morning, Ruth? Sing that "No Ways Tired." That
song always lifts me up so—*(She turns at last to see that* Ruth *has slipped
quietly into a chair, in a state of semiconsciousness)* Ruth! Ruth honey—
what's the matter with you . . . Ruth!

CURTAIN

SCENE 2

*It is the following morning; a Saturday morning, and house cleaning is in
progress at the Youngers. Furniture has been shoved hither and you and Mama is
giving the kitchen-area walls a washing down. Beneatha, in dungarees, with a
handkerchief tied around her face, is spraying insecticide into the cracks in the
walls. As they work, the radio is on and a Southside disk-jockey program is
inappropriately filling the house with a rather exotic saxophone blues. Travis, the
sole idle one, is leaning on his arms, looking out of the window.*

TRAVIS. Grandmama, that stuff Bennie is using smells awful. Can I go downstairs, please?

MAMA. Did you get all them chores done already? I ain't seen you doing much.

TRAVIS Yes'm—finished early. Where did Mama go this morning?

MAMA *(Looking at Beneatha)*. She had to go on a little errand.

TRAVIS. Where?

MAMA. To tend to her business.

TRAVIS. Can I go outside then?

MAMA. Oh, I guess so. You better stay right in front of the house,
though . . . and keep a good lookout for the postman.

TRAVIS. Yes'm. *(He starts out and decides to give his Aunt Beneatha a good swat
on the legs as he passes her)* Leave them poor little old cockroaches alone,
they ain't bothering you none.

(He runs as she swings the spray gun at him both viciously and playfully. Walter enters from the bedroom and goes to the phone)

MAMA. Look out there, girl, before you be spilling some of that stuff on that child!

TRAVIS *(Teasing)*. That's right—look out now!

(He exits)

BENEATHA *(Drily)*. I can't imagaine that it would hurt him—it has never hurt the roaches.

MAMA. Well, little boys' hides ain't as tough as Southside roaches.

WALTER *(Into phone)*. Hello—Let me talk to Willy Harris.

MAMA. You better get over there behind the bureau. I seen one marching out of there like Napoleon yesterday.

WALTER. Hello, Willy? It ain't come yet. It'll be here in a few minutes. Did the lawyer give you the papers?

BENEATHA. There's really only one way to get rid of them, Mama—

MAMA. How?

BENEATHA. Set fire to this building.

WALTER. Good. Good. I'll be right over.

BENEATHA. Where did Ruth go, Walter?

WALTER. I don't know.

(He exits abruptly)

BENEATHA. Mama, where did Ruth go?

MAMA *(Looking at her with meaning)*. To the doctor, I think.

BENEATHA. The doctor? What's the matter? *(They exchange glances)* You don't think—

MAMA *(With her sense of drama)*. Now I ain't saying what I think. But I ain't never been wrong 'bout a woman neither.

(The phone rings)

BENEATHA *(At the phone)*. Hay-lo . . . *(Pause, and a moment of recognition)* Well—when did you get back! . . . And how was it? . . . Of course I've missed you—in my way . . . This morning? No . . . house cleaning and all that and Mama hates it if I let people come over when the house is like this . . . You *have*? Well, that's different . . . What is it—Oh, what the hell, come on over . . . Right, see you then.

(She hangs up)

MAMA *(Who has listened vigorously, as is her habit)*. Who is that you inviting over here with this house looking like this? You ain't got the pride you was born with!

BENEATHA. Asagai doesn't care how houses look, Mama—he's an intellectual.

MAMA. *Who?*

BENEATHA. Asagai—Joseph Asagai. He's an African boy I met on campus. He's been studying in Canada all summer.

MAMA. What's his name?

BENEATHA. Asagai, Joseph. Ah-sah-guy . . . He's from Nigeria.

MAMA. Oh, that's the little country that was founded by slaves way back . . .

BENEATHA. No, Mama—that's Liberia.

MAMA. I don't think I never met no African before.

BENEATHA. Well, do me a favor and don't ask him a whole lot of ignorant questions about Africans. I mean, do they wear clothes and all that—

MAMA. Well, now, I guess if you think we so ignorant 'round here maybe you shouldn't bring your friends here—

BENEATHA. It's just that people ask such crazy things. All anyone seems to know about when it comes to Africa is Tarzan—

MAMA *(Indignantly)*. Why should I know anything about Africa?

BENEATHA. Why do you give money at church for the missionary work?

MAMA. Well, that's to help save people.

BENEATHA. You mean save them from *heathenism*—

MAMA *(Innocently)*. Yes.

BENEATHA. I'm afraid they need more salvation from the British and the French.

(Ruth comes in forlornly and pulls off her coat with dejection. They both turn to look at her)

RUTH *(Dispiritedly)*. Well, I guess from all the happy faces—everybody knows.

BENEATHA. You pregnant?

MAMA. Lord have mercy, I sure hope it's a little old girl. Travis ought to have a sister.

(Beneatha and Ruth give her a hopeless look for this grandmotherly enthusiasm)

BENEATHA. How far along are you?

RUTH. Two months.

BENEATHA. Did you mean to? I mean did you plan it or was it an accident?

MAMA. What do you know about planning or not planning?

BENEATHA. Oh, Mama.

RUTH *(Wearily)*. She's twenty years old, Lena.

BENEATHA. Did you plan it, Ruth?

RUTH. Mind your own business.

BENEATHA. It is my business—where is he going to live, on the *roof*? *(There is silence following the remark as the three women react to the sense of it)*

Gee—I didn't mean that, Ruth, honest. Gee, I don't feel like that at all. I—
I think it is wonderful.

RUTH *(Dully)*. Wonderful.

BENEATHA. Yes—really.

MAMA *(Looking at Ruth, worried)*. Doctor say everything going to be all right?

RUTH *(Far away)*. Yes—she says everything is going to be fine . . .

MAMA *(Immediately suspicious)*. "She"—What doctor you went to?

(Ruth folds over, near hysteria)

MAMA *(Worriedly hovering over Ruth)*. Ruth honey—what's the matter with
you—you sick?

*(Ruth has her fists clenched on her thighs and is fighting hard to suppress a
scream that seems to be rising in her)*

BENEATHA. What's the matter with her, Mama?

MAMA *(Working her fingers in Ruth's shoulder to relax her)* She be all right.
Women gets right depressed sometimes when they get her way. *(Speaking
softly, expertly, rapidly)* Now you just relax. That's right . . . just lean back,
don't think 'bout nothing at all . . . nothing at all—

RUTH. I'm all right . . .

*(The glassy-eyed look melts and then she collapses into a fit of heavy sobbing. The
bell rings)*

BENEATHA. Oh, my God—that must be Asagai.

MAMA *(To Ruth)* Come on now, honey. You need to lie down and rest
awhile . . . then have some nice hot food.

*(They exit, Ruth's weight on her mother-in-law. Beneatha, herself profoundly
disturbed, opens the door to admit a rather dramatic-looking young man with a
large package)*

ASAGAI. Hello, Alaiyo—

BENEATHA *(Holding the door open and regarding him with pleasure)*.
Hello . . . *(Long pause)* Well—come in. And please excuse everything. My
mother was very upset about my letting anyone come here with the place
like this.

ASAGAI *(Coming into the room)*. You look disturbed too . . . Is something
wrong?

BENEATHA *(Still at the door, absently)*. Yes . . . we've all got acute ghetto-itus.
(She smiles and comes toward him, finding a cigarette and sitting) So—sit
down! How was Canada?

ASAGAI *(A sophisticate)*. Canadian.

BENEATHA *(Looking at him)*. I'm very glad you are back.

ASAGAI *(Looking back at her in turn)*. Are you really?

BENEATHA. Yes—very.

ASAGAI. Why—you were quite glad when I went away. What happened?

BENEATHA. You went away.

ASAGAI. Ahhhhhhhh.

BENEATHA. Before—you wanted to be so serious before there was time.

ASAGAI. How much time must there be before one knows what one feels?

BENEATHA *(Stalling this particular conversation. Her hands pressed together, in a deliberately childish gesture)*. What did you bring me?

ASAGAI *(Handing her the package)*. Open it and see.

BENEATHA *(Eagerly opening the package and drawing out some records and the colorful robes of a Nigerian woman)*. Oh, Asagai! . . . You got them for me! . . . How beautiful . . . and the records too! *(She lifts out the robes and runs to the mirror with them and holds the drapery up in front of herself)*

ASAGAI *(Coming to her at the mirror)*. I shall have to teach you how to drape it properly. *(He flings the material about her for the moment and stands back to look at her)* Ah—*Oh-pay-gay-day, oh-gbah-mu-shay.* *(A Yoruba exclamation for admiration)* You wear it well . . . very well . . . mutilated hair and all.

BENEATHA *(Turning suddenly)*. My hair—what's wrong with my hair?

ASAGAI *(Shrugging)*. Were you born with it like that?

BENEATHA *(Reaching up to touch it)*. No . . . of course not.

(She looks back to the mirror, disturbed)

ASAGAI *(Smiling)*. How then?

BENEATHA. You know perfectly well how . . . as crinkly as yours . . . that's how.

ASAGAI. And it is ugly to you that way?

BENEATHA *(Quickly)*. Oh, no—not ugly . . . *(More slowly, apologetically)* But it's so hard to manage when it's, well—raw.

ASAGAI. And so to accommodate that—you mutilate it every week?

BENEATHA. It's not mutilation!

ASAGAI *(Laughing aloud at her seriousness)*. Oh . . . please! I am only teasing you because you are so very serious about these things. *(He stands back from her and folds his arms across his chest as he watches her pulling at her hair and frowning in the mirror)* Do you remember the first time you met me at school? . . . *(He laughs)* You came up to me and you said—and I thought you were the most serious little thing I had ever seen—you said: *(He imitates her)* "Mr. Asagai—I want very much to talk with you. About Africa. You see, Mr. Asagai, I am looking for my *identity!*"

(He laughs)

BENEATHA *(Turning to him, not laughing)*. Yes—

(Her face is quizzical, profoundly disturbed)

ASAGAI *(Still teasing and reaching out and taking her face in his hands and turning her profile to him)*. Well . . . it is true that this is not so much a profile of a Hollywood queen as perhaps a queen of the Nile—*(A mock dismissal of the importance of the question)* But what does it matter? Assimilationism is so popular in your country.

BENEATHA *(Wheeling, passionately, sharply)*. I am not an assimilationist!

ASAGAI *(The protest hangs in the room for a moment and Asagai studies her, his laughter fading)*. Such a serious one. *(There is a pause)* So—you like the robes? You must take excellent care of them—they are from my sister's personal wardrobe.

BENEATHA *(With incredulity)*. You—you sent all the way home—for me?

ASAGAI *(With charm)*. For you—I would do much more . . . Well, that is what I came for. I must go.

BENEATHA. Will you call me Monday?

ASAGAI. Yes . . . We have a great deal to talk about. I mean about identity and time and all that.

BENEATHA. Time?

ASAGAI. Yes. About how much time one needs to know what one feels.

BENEATHA. You never understood that there is more than one kind of feeling which can exist between a man and a woman—or, at least, there should be.

ASAGAI *(Shaking his head negatively but gently)*. No. Between a man and a woman there need be only one kind of feeling. I have that for you . . . Now even . . . right this moment . . .

BENEATHA. I know—and by itself—it won't do. I can find that anywhere.

ASAGAI. For a woman it should be enough.

BENEATHA. I know—because that's what it says in all the novels that men write. But it isn't. Go ahead and laugh—but I'm not interested in being someone's little episode in America or—*(With feminine vengeance)*— one of them! *(Asagai has burst into laughter again)* That's funny as hell, huh!

ASAGAI. It's just that every American girl I have known has said that to me. White—black—in this you are all the same. And the same speech, too!

BENEATHA *(Angrily)*. Yuk, yuk, yuk!

ASAGAI. It's how you can be sure that the world's most liberated women are not liberated at all. You all talk about it too much!

(Mama enters and is immediately all social charm because of the presence of a guest)

BENEATHA. Oh—Mama—this is Mr. Asagai.

MAMA. How do you do?

ASAGAI *(Total politeness to an elder)*. How do you do, Mrs. Younger. Please forgive me for coming at such an outrageous hour on a Saturday.

MAMA. Well, you are quite welcome. I just hope you understand that our house don't always look like this. *(Chatterish)* You must come again. I would love to hear all about—*(Not sure of the name)*—your country. I think it's so sad the way our American Negroes don't know nothing about Africa 'cept Tarzan and all that. And all that money they pour into these churches when they ought to be helping you people over there drive out them French and Englishmen done taken away your land.

(The mother flashes a slightly superior look at her daughter upon completion of the recitation)

ASAGAI *(Taken aback by this sudden and acutely unrelated expression of sympathy)*. Yes . . . yes . . .

MAMA *(Smiling at him suddenly and relaxing and looking him over)*. How many miles is it from here to where you come from?

ASAGAI. Many thousands.

MAMA *(Looking at him as she would Walter)*. I bet you don't half look after yourself, being away from your mama either. I spec you better come 'round here from time to time and get yourself some decent homecooked meals . . .

ASAGAI *(Moved)*. Thank you. Thank you very much. *(They are all quiet, then—)* Well . . . I must go, I will call you Monday, Alaiyo.

MAMA. What's that he call you?

ASAGAI. Oh—"Alaiyo." I hope you don't mind. It is what you would call a nickname, I think. It is a Yoruba word. I am a Yoruba.

MAMA *(Looking at Beneatha)*. I—I thought he was from—

ASAGAI *(Understanding)*. Nigeria is my country. Yoruba is my tribal origin—

BENEATHA. You didn't tell us what Alaiyo means . . . for all I know, you might be calling me Little Idiot or something . . .

ASAGAI. Well . . . let me see . . . I do not know how just to explain it . . . The sense of a thing can be so different when it changes languages.

BENEATHA. You're evading.

ASAGAI. No—really it is difficult . . . *(Thinking)* It means . . . it means One for Whom Bread—Food—Is Not Enough. *(He looks at her)* Is that all right?

BENEATHA *(Understanding, softly).* Thank you.

MAMA *(Looking from one to the other and not understanding any of it).* Well . . . that's nice . . . You must come see us again—Mr.—

ASAGAI. Ah-sah-guy . . .

MAMA. Yes . . . Do come again.

ASAGAI. Good-bye.

(He exits)

MAMA *(After him).* Lord, that's a pretty thing just went out here! *(Insinuatingly, to her daughter)* Yes, I guess I see why we done commence to get so interested in Africa 'round here. Missionaries my aunt Jenny!

(She exits)

BENEATHA. Oh, Mama! . . .

(She picks up the Nigerian dress and holds it up to her in front of the mirror again. She sets the headdress on haphazardly and then notices her hair again and clutches at it and then replaces the headdress and frowns at herself. Then she starts to wriggle in front of the mirror as she thinks a Nigerian woman might. Travis enters and regards her)

TRAVIS. You cracking up?

BENEATHA. Shut up.

(She pulls the headdress off and looks at herself in the mirror and clutches at her hair again and squinches her eyes as if trying to imagine something. Then, suddenly, she gets her raincoat and kerchief and hurriedly prepares for going out)

MAMA *(Coming back into the room).* She's resting now. Travis, baby, run next door and ask Miss Johnson to please let me have a little kitchen cleanser. This here can is empty as Jacob's kettle.[5]

TRAVIS. I just came in.

MAMA. Do as you told. *(He exits and she looks at her daughter)* Where you going?

BENEATHA *(Halting at the door).* To become a queen of the Nile!

(She exits in a breathless blaze of glory. Ruth appears in the bedroom doorway)

MAMA. Who told you to get up?

RUTH. Ain't nothing wrong with me to be lying in no bed for. Where did Bennie go?

---

[5]Possibly drawn from the parable in which Christ sits beside Jacob's well, asks a Samaritan woman to draw water for him, then informs her that he is the Messiah (John 4:1-26).

MAMA *(Drumming her fingers)*. Far as I could make out—to Egypt. *(Ruth just looks at her)* What time is it getting to?

RUTH. Ten twenty. And the mailman going to ring that bell this morning just like he done every morning for the last umpteen years.

(Travis comes in with the cleanser can)

TRAVIS. She say to tell you that she don't have much.

MAMA *(Angrily)*. Lord, some people I could name sure is tight-fisted! *(Directing her grandson)* Mark two cans of cleanser down on the list there. If she that hard up for kitchen cleanser, I sure don't want to forget to get her none!

RUTH. Lena—maybe the woman is just short on cleanser—

MAMA *(Not listening)*.—Much baking powder as she done borrowed from me all these years, she could of done gone into the baking business!

(The bell sounds suddenly and sharply and all three are stunned—serious and silent—mid-speech. In spite of all the other conversations and distractions of the morning, this is what they have been waiting for, even Travis, who looks helplessly from his mother to his grandmother. Ruth is the first to come to life again)

RUTH *(To Travis)*. Get down them steps, boy!

(Travis snaps to life and flies out to get the mail)

MAMA *(Her eyes wide, her hand to her breast)*. You mean it done really come?

RUTH *(Excited)*. Oh, Miss Lena!

MAMA *(Collecting herself)*. Well . . . I don't know what we all so excited about 'round here for. We known it was coming for months.

RUTH. That's a whole lot different from having it come and being able to hold it in your hands . . . a piece of paper worth ten thousand dollars . . . *(Travis bursts back into the room. He holds the envelope high above his head, like a little dancer, his face is radiant and he is breathless. He moves to his grandmother with sudden slow ceremony and puts the envelope into her hands. She accepts it, and then merely holds it and looks at it)* Come on! Open it . . . Lord have mercy, I wish Walter Lee was here!

TRAVIS. Open it, Grandmama!

MAMA *(Staring at it)*. Now you all be quiet. It's just a check.

RUTH. Open it . . .

MAMA *(Still staring at it)*. Now don't act silly . . . We ain't never been no people to act silly 'bout no money—

RUTH *(Swiftly)*. We ain't never had none before—open it!

(Mama finally makes a good strong tear and pulls out the thin blue slice of paper and inspects it closely. The boy and his mother study it raptly over Mama's shoulders)

MAMA. *Travis! (She is counting off with doubt).* Is that the right number of zeros.

TRAVIS. Yes'm . . . ten thousand dollars. Gaalee, Grandmama, you rich.

MAMA *(She holds the check away from her, still looking at it. Slowly her face sobers into a mask of unhappiness).* Ten thousand dollars. *(She hands it to Ruth)* Put it away somewhere, Ruth. *(She does not look at Ruth; her eyes seem to be seeing something somewhere very far off)* Ten thousand dollars they give you. Ten thousand dollars.

TRAVIS *(To his mother, sincerely).* What's the matter with Grandmama—don't she want to be rich?

RUTH *(Distractedly).* You go on out and play now, baby. *(Travis exits. Mama starts wiping dishes absently, humming intently to herself. Ruth turns to her, with kind exasperation)* You've gone and got yourself upset.

MAMA *(Not looking at her).* I spec if it wasn't for you all . . . I would just put that money away or give it to the church or something.

RUTH. Now what kind of talk is that. Mr. Younger would just be plain mad if he could hear you talking foolish like that.

MAMA *(Stopping and staring off).* Yes . . . he sure would. *(Sighing)* We got enough to do with that money, all right. *(She halts then, and turns and looks at her daughter-in-law hard; Ruth avoids her eyes and Mama wipes her hands with finality and starts to speak firmly to Ruth)* Where did you go today, girl?

RUTH. To the doctor.

MAMA *(Impatiently).* Now, Ruth . . . you know better than that. Old Doctor Jones is strange enough in his way but there ain't nothing 'bout him make somebody slip and call him "she"—like you done this morning.

RUTH. Well, that's what happened—my tongue slipped.

MAMA. You went to see that woman, didn't you?

RUTH *(Defensively, giving herself away).* What woman you talking about?

MAMA *(Angrily).* That woman who—

(Walter enters in great excitement)

WALTER. Did it come?

MAMA *(Quietly).* Can't you give people a Christian greeting before you start asking about money?

WALTER *(To Ruth).* Did it come? *(Ruth unfolds the check and lays it quietly before him, watching him intently with thoughts of her own. Walter sits down and grasps it close and counts off the zeros)* Ten thousand dollars—*(He turns suddenly, frantically to his mother and draws some papers out of his breast pocket)* Mama—look. Old Willy Harris put everything on paper—

MAMA. Son—I think you ought to talk to your wife . . . I'll go on out and leave you alone if you want—

WALTER. I can talk to her later—Mama, look—

MAMA. Son—

WALTER. WILL SOMEBODY PLEASE LISTEN TO ME TODAY!

MAMA *(Quietly)*. I don't 'low no yellin' in this house, Walter Lee, and you know it—*(Walter stares at them in frustration and starts to speak several times)* And there ain't going to be no investing in no liquor stores. I don't aim to have to speak on that again.

(A long pause)

WALTER. Oh—so you don't aim to have to speak on that again? So *you* have decided . . . *(Crumpling his papers)* Well, *you* tell that to my boy tonight when you put him to sleep on the living-room couch . . . *(Turning to Mama and speaking directly to her)* Yeah—and tell it to my wife, Mama, tomorrow when she has to go out of here to look after somebody else's kids. And tell it to *me,* Mama, every time we need a new pair of curtains and I have to watch *you* go out and work in somebody's kitchen. Yeah, you tell me then!

(Walter starts out)

RUTH. Where you going?

WALTER. I'm going out!

RUTH. Where?

WALTER. Just out of this house somewhere—

RUTH *(Getting her coat)*. I'll come too.

WALTER. I don't want you to come!

RUTH. I got something to talk to you about, Walter.

WALTER. That's too bad.

MAMA *(Still quietly)*. Walter Lee—*(She waits and he finally turns and looks at her)* Sit down.

WALTER. I'm a grown man, Mama.

MAMA. Ain't nobody said you wasn't grown. But you still in my house and my presence. And as long as you are—you'll talk to your wife civil. Now sit down.

RUTH *(Suddenly)*. Oh, let him go on out and drink himself to death! He makes me sick to my stomach! *(She flings her coat against him)*

WALTER *(Violently)*. And you turn mine too, baby! *(Ruth goes into their bedroom and slams the door behind her)* That was my greatest mistake—

MAMA *(Still quietly)*. Walter, what is the matter with you?

WALTER. Matter with me? Ain't nothing the matter with *me*!

MAMA. Yes there is. Something eating you up like a crazy man. Something more than me not giving you this money. The past few years I been watching it happen to you. You get all nervous acting and kind of wild in the eyes—*(Walter jumps up impatiently at her words)* I said sit there now, I'm talking to you!

WALTER. Mama—I don't need no nagging at me today.

MAMA. Seem like you getting to a place where you always tied up in some kind of knot about something. But if anybody ask you 'bout it you just yell at 'em and bust out the house and go out and drink somewheres. Walter Lee, people can't live with that. Ruth's a good, patient girl in her way—but you getting to be too much. Boy, don't make the mistake of driving that girl away from you.

WALTER. Why—what she do for me?

MAMA. She loves you.

WALTER. Mama—I'm going out. I want to go off somewhere and be by myself for a while.

MAMA. I'm sorry 'bout your liquor store, son. It just wasn't the thing for us to do. That's what I want to tell you about—

WALTER. I got to go out, Mama—

(He rises)

MAMA. It's dangerous, son.

WALTER. What's dangerous?

MAMA. When a man goes outside his home to look for peace.

WALTER *(Beseechingly)*. Then why can't there never be no peace in this house then?

MAMA. You done found it in some other house?

WALTER. No—there ain't no woman! Why do women always think there's a woman somewhere when a man gets restless. *(Coming to her)* Mama— Mama—I want so many things . . .

MAMA. Yes, son—

WALTER. I want so many things that they are driving me kind of crazy . . . Mama—look at me.

MAMA. I'm looking at you. You a good-looking boy. You got a job, a nice wife, a fine boy and—

WALTER. A job. *(Looks at her)* Mama, a job? I open and close car doors all day long. I drive a man around in his limousine and I say, "Yes, sir; no, sir; very good, sir; shall I take the Drive, sir?" Mama, that ain't no kind of job . . . that ain't nothing at all. *(Very quietly)* Mama, I don't know if I can make you understand.

MAMA. Understand what, baby?

WALTER *(Quietly)*. Sometimes it's like I can see the future stretched out in front of me—just plain as day. The future, Mama. Hanging over there at the edge of my days. Just waiting for me—a big, looming blank space—full of *nothing*. Just waiting for me. *(Pause)* Mama—sometimes when I'm downtown and I pass them cool, quiet-looking restaurants where them white boys are sitting back and talking 'bout things . . . sitting there turning deals worth millions of dollars . . . sometimes I see guys don't look much older than me—

MAMA. Son—how come you talk so much 'bout money?

WALTER *(With immense passion)*. Because it is life, Mama!

MAMA *(Quietly)*. Oh—*(Very quietly)* So now it's life. Money is life. Once upon a time freedom used to be life—now it's money. I guess the world really do change . . .

WALTER. No—it was always money, Mama. We just didn't know about it.

MAMA. No . . . something has changed. *(She looks at him)* You something new, boy. In my time we was worried about not being lynched and getting to the North if we could and how to stay alive and still have a pinch of dignity too . . . Now here come you and Beneatha—talking 'bout things we ain't never even thought about hardly, me and your daddy. You ain't satisfied or proud of nothing we done. I mean that you had a home; that we kept you out of trouble till you was grown; that you don't have to ride to work on the back of nobody's streetcar—You my children—but how different we done become.

WALTER. You just don't understand, Mama, you just don't understand.

MAMA. Son—do you know your wife is expecting another baby? *(Walter stands, stunned, and absorbs what his mother has said)* That's what she wanted to talk to you about. *(Walter sinks down into a chair)* This ain't for me to be telling—but you ought to know. *(She waits)* I think Ruth is thinking 'bout getting rid of that child.

WALTER *(Slowly understanding)*. No—no—Ruth wouldn't do that.

MAMA. When the world gets ugly enough—a woman will do anything for her family. The part that's already living.

WALTER. You don't know Ruth, Mama, if you think she would do that.

(Ruth opens the bedroom door and stands there a little limp)

RUTH *(Beaten)*. Yes I would too, Walter. *(Pause)* I gave her a five-dollar down payment.

(There is total silence as the man stares at his wife and the mother stares at her son)

MAMA *(Presently)*. Well—*(Tightly)* Well—son, I'm waiting to hear you say something . . . I'm waiting to hear how you be your father's son. Be the man he was . . . *(Pause)* Your wife say she going to destroy your child. And I'm waiting to hear you talk like him and say we a people who give children life, not who destroys them—*(She rises)* I'm waiting to see you stand up and look like your daddy and say we done give up one baby to poverty and that we ain't going to give up nary another one . . . I'm waiting.

WALTER. Ruth—

MAMA. If you a son of mine, tell her! *(Walter turns, looks at her and can say nothing. She continues, bitterly)* You . . . you are a disgrace to your father's memory. Somebody get me my hat.

CURTAIN

ACT TWO

SCENE 1

TIME: Later the same day.

At rise: Ruth is ironing again. She has the radio going. Presently Beneatha's bedroom door opens and Ruth's mouth falls and she puts down the iron in fascination.

RUTH. What have we got on tonight!

BENEATHA *(Emerging grandly from the doorway so that we can see her thoroughly robed in the costume Asagai brought)*. You are looking at what a well-dressed Nigerian woman wears—*(She parades for Ruth, her hair completely hidden by the headdress; she is coquettishly fanning herself with an ornate oriental fan, mistakenly more like Butterfly[6] than any Nigerian that ever was)* Isn't it beautiful? *(She promenades to the radio and, with an arrogant flourish, turns off the good loud blues that is playing)* Enough of this assimilationist junk! *(Ruth follows her with her eyes as she goes to the phonograph and puts on a record and turns and waits ceremoniously for the music to come up. Then, with a shout—)* OCOMOGOSIAY!

(Ruth jumps. The music comes up, a lovely Nigerian melody. Beneatha listens, enraptured, her eyes far away—"back to the past." She begins to dance. Ruth is dumfounded)

RUTH. What kind of dance is that?

BENEATHA. A folk dance.

---

[6]Title character of Giacomo Puccini's *Madame Butterfly* (1904), an Italian opera set in Japan.

RUTH *(Pearl Bailey).*[7] What kind of folks do that, honey?

BENEATHA. It's from Nigeria. It's a dance of welcome.

RUTH. Who you welcoming?

BENEATHA. The men back to the village.

RUTH. Where they been?

BENEATHA. How should I know—out hunting or something. Anyway, they are coming back now . . .

RUTH. Well, that's good.

BENEATHA *(With the record).*

Alundi, alundi
Alundi alunya
Jop pu a jeepua
Ang gu soooooooooo

Ai yai yae . . .
Ayehaye—alundi . . .

(Walter comes in during this performance; he has obviously been drinking. He leans against the door heavily and watches his sister, at first with distaste. Then his eyes look off—"back to the past"—as he lifts both his fists to the roof screaming)

WALTER. YEAH . . . AND ETHIOPIA STRETCH FORTH HER HANDS AGAIN! . . .

RUTH *(Drily, looking at him).* Yes—and Africa sure is claiming her own tonight. *(She gives them both up and starts ironing again)*

WALTER *(All in a drunken, dramatic shout).* Shut up! . . . I'm digging them drums . . . them drums move me! . . . *(He makes his weaving way to his wife's face and leans in close to her)* In my *heart of hearts—(He thumps his chest)*—I am much warrior!

RUTH *(Without even looking up).* In your heart of hearts you are much drunkard.

WALTER *(Coming away from her and starting to wander around the room, shouting)* Me and Jomo . . .[8] *(Intently, in his sister's face. She has stopped dancing to watch him in this unknown mood)* That's my man, Kenyatta. *(Shouting and thumping his chest)* FLAMING SPEAR! HOT DAMN! *(He is suddenly in possession of an imaginary spear and actively spearing enemies all over the*

---

[7]Popular African-American entertainer, known for her sly delivery.

[8]Jomo Kenyatta, African revolutionary and first president of independent Kenya.

room) OCOMOGOSIAY . . . THE LION IS WAKING . . . OWIMOWEH! *(He pulls his shirt open and leaps up on a table and gestures with his spear. The bell rings. Ruth goes to answer)*

BENEATHA *(To encourage Walter, thoroughly caught up with this side of him).* OCOMOGOSIAY, FLAMING SPEAR!

WALTER *(On the table, very far gone, his eyes pure glass sheets. He sees what we cannot, that he is a leader of his people, a great chief a descendant of Chaka, and that the hour to march has come).* Listen, my black brothers—

BENEATHA. OCOMOGOSIAY!

WALTER. —Do you hear the waters rushing against the shores of the coastlands—

BENEATHA. OCOMOGOSIAY!

WALTER. —Do you hear the screeching of the cocks in yonder hills beyond where the chiefs meet in council for the coming of the mighty war—

BENEATHA. OCOMOGOSIAY!

WALTER. —Do you hear the beating of the wings of the birds flying low over the mountains and the low places of our land—

(Ruth opens the door. George Murchison enters)

BENEATHA. OCOMOGOSIAY!

WALTER. —Do you hear the singing of the women, singing the war songs of our fathers to the babies in the great houses . . . singing the sweet war songs? OH, DO YOU HEAR, MY BLACK BROTHERS!

BENEATHA *(Completely gone).* We hear you, Flaming Spear—

WALTER. Telling us to prepare for the greatness of the time—*(To George)* Black Brother!

(He extends his hand for the fraternal clasp)

GEORGE. Black Brother, hell!

RUTH *(Having had enough, and embarrassed for the family).* Beneatha, you got company—what's the matter with you? Walter Lee Younger, get down off that table and stop acting like a fool . . .

(Walter comes down off the table suddenly and makes a quick exit to the bathroom)

RUTH. He's had a little to drink . . . I don't know what her excuse is.

GEORGE *(To Beneatha).* Look honey, we're going *to* the theatre—we're not going to be *in* it . . . so go change, huh?

RUTH. You expect this boy to go out with you looking like that?

BENEATHA *(Looking at George).* That's up to George. If he's ashamed of his heritage—

GEORGE. Oh, don't be so proud of yourself, Bennie—just because you look eccentric.

BENEATHA. How can something that's natural be eccentric?

GEORGE. That's what being eccentric means—being natural. Get dressed.

BENEATHA. I don't like that, George.

RUTH. Why must you and your brother make an argument out of everything people say?

BENEATHA. Because I hate assimilationist Negroes!

RUTH. Will somebody please tell me what assimila-whoever means!

GEORGE. Oh, it's just a college girl's way of calling people Uncle Toms[9]—but that isn't what it means at all.

RUTH. Well, what does it mean?

BENEATHA *(Cutting George off and staring at him as she replies to Ruth).* It means someone who is willing to give up his own culture and submerge himself completely in the dominant, and in this case, oppressive culture!

GEORGE. Oh, dear, dear, dear! Here we go! A lecture on the African past! On our Great West African Heritage! In one second we will hear all about the great Ashanti empires; the great Songhay civilizations; and the great sculpture of Bénin—and then some poetry in the Bantu—and the whole monologue will end with the word *heritage! (Nastily)* Let's face it, baby, your heritage is nothing but a bunch of raggedy-assed spirituals and some grass huts!

BENEATHA. Grass huts! (Ruth crosses to her and forcibly pushes her toward the bedroom) See there . . . you are standing there in your splendid ignorance talking about people who were the first to smelt iron on the face of the earth! *(Ruth is pushing her through the door)* The Ashanti were performing surgical operations when the English—*(Ruth pulls the door to, with Beneatha on the other side, and smiles graciously at George. Beneatha opens the door and shouts the end of the sentence defiantly at George)*—were still tatooing themselves with blue dragons . . . *(She goes back inside)*

RUTH. Have a seat, George. *(They both sit. Ruth folds her hands rather primly on her lap, determined to demonstrate the civilization of the family)* Warm, ain't it? I mean for September. *(Pause)* Just like they always say about Chicago weather: If it's too hot or cold for you, just wait a minute and it'll change. *(She smiles happily at this cliché of clichés)* Everybody say it's got to do with them bombs and things they keep setting off. *(Pause)* Would you like a nice cold beer?

GEORGE. No, thank you. I don't care for beer. *(He looks at his watch)* I hope she hurries up.

---

[9]Derogatory term for black people who join forces with white culture.

RUTH. What time is the show?

GEORGE. It's an eight-thirty curtain. That's just Chicago, though. In New York standard curtain time is eight forty.

(He is rather proud of this knowledge)

RUTH *(Properly appreciating it)*. You get to New York a lot?

GEORGE *(Offhand)*. Few times a year.

RUTH. Oh—that's nice. I've never been to New York.

(Walter enters. We feel he has relieved himself but the edge of unreality is still with him)

WALTER. New York ain't got nothing Chicago ain't. Just a bunch of hustling people all squeezed up together—being "Eastern."

(He turns his face into a screw of displeasure)

GEORGE. Oh—you've been?

WALTER. *Plenty* of times.

RUTH *(Shocked at the lie)*. Walter Lee Younger!

WALTER *(Staring her down)*. Plenty! *(Pause)* What we got to drink in this house? Why don't you offer this man some refreshment. *(To George)* They don't know how to entertain people in this house, man.

GEORGE. Thank you—I don't really care for anything.

WALTER *(Feeling his head; sobriety coming)*. Where's Mama?

RUTH. She ain't come back yet.

WALTER *(Looking Murchison over from head to toe, scrutinizing his carefully casual tweed sports jacket over cashmere V-neck sweater over soft eyelet shirt and tie, and soft slacks, finished off with white buckskin shoes)*. Why all you college boys wear them fairyish-looking white shoes?

RUTH. Walter Lee!

(George Murchison ignores the remark)

WALTER *(To Ruth)*. Well, they look crazy as hell—white shoes, cold as it is.

RUTH *(Crushed)*. You have to excuse him—

WALTER. No he don't! Excuse me for what? What you always excusing me for! I'll excuse myself when I needs to be excused! *(A pause)* They look as funny as them black knee socks Beneatha wears out of here all the time.

RUTH. It's the college *style*, Walter.

WALTER. Style, hell. She looks like she got burnt legs or something!

RUTH. Oh, Walter—

WALTER. *(An irritable mimic)* Oh, Walter! Oh, Walter! *(To Murchison)* How's your old man making out? I understand you all going to buy that big hotel on the Drive? (*He finds a beer in the refrigerator, wanders over to Murchison, sipping and wiping his lips with the back of his hand, and straddling a chair backwards to talk to the other man*) Shrewd move. Your old man is all right, man. (*Tapping his head and half winking for emphasis*) I mean he knows how to operate. I mean he thinks *big*, you know what I mean, I mean for a *home*, you know? But I think he's kind of running out of ideas now. I'd like to talk to him. Listen, man, I got some plans that could turn this city upside down. I mean I think like he does. *Big*. Invest big, gamble big, hell, lose *big* if you have to, you know what I mean. It's hard to find a man on this whole Southside who understands my kind of thinking—you dig? (*He scrutinizes Murchison again, drinks his beer, squints his eyes and leans in close, confidential, man to man*) Me and you ought to sit down and talk sometimes, man. Man, I got me some ideas . . .

MURCHISON. (*With boredom*). Yeah—sometimes we'll have to do that, Walter.

WALTER (*Understanding the indifference, and offended*). Yeah—well, when you get the time, man. I know you a busy little boy.

RUTH. Walter, please—

WALTER (*Bitterly, hurt*). I know ain't nothing in this world as busy as you colored college boys with your fraternity pins and white shoes . . .

RUTH (*Covering her face with humiliation*). Oh, Walter Lee—

WALTER. I see you all all the time—with the books tucked under your arms—going to your (*British A—a mimic*) "clahsses." And for what! What the hell you learning over there? Filling up your heads—(*Counting off on his fingers*)—with the sociology and the psychology—but they teaching you how to be a man? How to take over and run the world? They teaching you how to run a rubber plantation or a steel mill? Naw—just to talk proper and read books and wear white shoes . . .

GEORGE (*Looking at him with distaste, a little above it all*). You're all wacked up with bitterness, man.

WALTER (*Intently, almost quietly, between the teeth, glaring at the boy*). And you—ain't you bitter, man? Ain't you just about had it yet? Don't you see no stars gleaming that you can't reach out and grab? You happy?—You contented son-of-a-bitch—you happy? You got it made? Bitter? Man, I'm a volcano. Bitter? Here I am a giant—surrounded by ants! Ants who can't even understand what it is the giant is talking about.

RUTH (*Passionately and suddenly*). Oh, Walter—ain't you with nobody!

WALTER (*Violently*). No! 'Cause ain't nobody with me! Not even my own mother!

RUTH. Walter, that's a terrible thing to say!

(Beneatha enters, dressed for the evening in a cocktail dress and earrings)

GEORGE. Well—hey, you look great.

BENEATHA. Let's go, George. See you all later.

RUTH. Have a nice time.

GEORGE. Thanks. Good night. *(To Walter, sarcastically,)* Good night, Prometheus.[10]

(Beneatha and George exit)

WALTER *(To Ruth)*. Who is Prometheus?

RUTH. I don't know. Don't worry about it.

WALTER *(In fury, pointing after George)*. See there—they get to a point where they can't insult you man to man—they got to go talk about something ain't nobody never heard of!

RUTH. How do you know it was an insult? *(To humor him)* Maybe Prometheus is a nice fellow.

WALTER. Prometheus! I bet there ain't even no such thing! I bet that simple-minded clown—

RUTH. Walter—

(She stops what she is doing and looks at him)

WALTER *(Yelling)*. Don't start!

RUTH. Start what?

WALTER. Your nagging! Where was I? Who was I with? How much money did I spend?

RUTH *(Plaintively)*. Walter Lee—why don't we just try to talk about it . . .

WALTER *(Not listening)*. I been out talking with people who understand me. People who care about the things I got on my mind.

RUTH *(Wearily)*. I guess that means people like Willy Harris.

WALTER. Yes, people like Willy Harris.

RUTH *(With a sudden flash of impatience)*. Why don't you all just hurry up and go into the banking business and stop talking about it!

WALTER. Why? You want to know why? 'Cause we all tied up in a race of people that don't know how to do nothing but moan, pray and have babies!

(The line is too bitter even for him and he looks at her and sits down)

RUTH. Oh, Walter . . . *(Softly)* Honey, why can't you stop fighting me?

WALTER *(Without thinking)*. Who's fighting you? Who even cares about you?

---

[10]In Greek mythology, the god of fire who has come to be associated with defiance against tyrannical authority.

(This line begins the retardation of his mood)

RUTH. Well—*(She waits a long time, and then with resignation starts to put away her things)* I guess I might as well go on to bed . . . *(More or less to herself)* I don't know where we lost it . . . but we have . . . *(Then, to him)* I—I'm sorry about this new baby, Walter. I guess maybe I better go on and do what I started . . . I guess I just didn't realize how bad things was with us . . . I guess I just didn't really realize—*(She starts out to the bedroom and stops)* You want some hot milk?

WALTER. Hot milk?

RUTH. Yes—hot milk.

WALTER. Why hot milk?

RUTH. 'Cause after all that liquor you come home with you ought to have something hot in your stomach.

WALTER. I don't want no milk.

RUTH. You want some coffee then?

WALTER. No, I don't want no coffee. I don't want nothing hot to drink. *(Almost plaintively)* Why you always trying to give me something to eat?

RUTH *(Standing and looking at him helplessly)*. What else can I give you, Walter Lee Younger?

(She stands and looks at him and presently turns to go out again. He lifts his head and watches her going away from him in a new mood which began to emerge when he asked her "Who cares about you?")

WALTER. It's been rough, ain't it, baby? *(She hears and stops but does not turn around and he continues to her back)* I guess between two people there ain't never as much understood as folks generally thinks there is. I mean like between me and you—*(She turns to face him)* How we gets to the place where we scared to talk softness to each other. *(He waits, thinking hard himself)* Why you think it got to be like that? *(He is thoughtful, almost as a child would be)* Ruth, what is it gets into people ought to be close?

RUTH. I don't know, honey. I think about it a lot.

WALTER. On account of you and me, you mean? The way things are with us. The way something done come down between us.

RUTH. There ain't so much between us, Walter . . . Not when you come to me and try to talk to me. Try to be with me . . . a little even.

WALTER *(Total honesty)*. Sometimes . . . sometimes . . . I don't even know how to try.

RUTH. Walter—

WALTER. Yes?

RUTH *(Coming to him, gently and with misgiving, but coming to him).* Honey . . . life don't have to be like this. I mean sometimes people can do things so that things are better . . . You remember how we used to talk when Travis was born . . . about the way we were going to live . . . the kind of house . . . *(She is stroking his head)* Well, it's all starting to slip away from us . . .

(Mama enters, and Walter jumps up and shouts at her)

WALTER. Mama, where have you been?

MAMA. My—them steps is longer than they used to be. Whew! *(She sits down and ignores him)* How you feeling this evening, Ruth?

(Ruth shrugs, disturbed some at having been prematurely interrupted and watching her husband knowingly)

WALTER. Mama, where have you been all day?

MAMA *(Still ignoring him and leaning on the table and changing to more comfortable shoes).* Where's Travis?

RUTH. I let him go out earlier and he ain't come back yet. Boy, is he going to get it!

WALTER. Mama!

MAMA *(As if she has heard him for the first time).* Yes, son?

WALTER. Where did you go this afternoon?

MAMA. I went downtown to tend to some business that I had to tend to.

WALTER. What kind of business?

MAMA. You know better than to question me like a child, Brother.

WALTER *(Rising and bending over the table).* Where were you, Mama? *(Bringing his fists down and shouting)* Mama, you didn't go do something with that insurance money, something crazy?

(The front door opens slowly, interrupting him, and Travis peeks his head in, less than hopefully)

TRAVIS *(To his mother).* Mama, I—

RUTH. "Mama I" nothing! You're going to get it, boy! Get on in that bedroom and get yourself ready!

TRAVIS. But I—

MAMA. Why don't you all never let the child explain hisself.

RUTH. Keep out of it now, Lena.

(Mama clamps her lips together, and Ruth advances toward her son menacingly)

RUTH. A thousand times I have told you not to go off like that—

MAMA *(Holding out her arms to her grandson)*. Well—at least let me tell him something. I want him to be the first one to hear . . . Come here, Travis *(The boy obeys, gladly)* Travis—*(She takes him by the shoulder and looks into his face)*—you know that money we got in the mail this morning?

TRAVIS. Yes'm—

MAMA. Well—what you think your grandmama gone and done with that money?

TRAVIS. I don't know, Grandmama.

MAMA *(Putting her finger on his nose for emphasis)*. She went out and she bought you a house! *(The explosion comes from Walter at the end of the revelation and he jumps up and turns away from all of them in a fury. Mama continues, to Travis)* You glad about the house? It's going to be yours when you get to be a man.

TRAVIS. Yeah—I always wanted to live in a house.

MAMA. All right, gimme some sugar then—*(Travis puts his arms around her neck as she watches her son over the boy's shoulder. Then, to Travis, after the embrace)* Now when you say your prayers tonight, you thank God and your grandfather—'cause it was him who give you the house—in his way.

RUTH *(Taking the boy from Mama and pushing him toward the bedroom)*. Now you get out of here and get ready for your beating.

TRAVIS. Aw, Mama—

RUTH. Get on in there—*(Closing the door behind him and turning radiantly to her mother-in-law)* So you went and did it!

MAMA *(Quietly, looking at her son with pain)*. Yes, I did.

RUTH *(Raising both arms classically)*. Praise God! *(Looks at Walter a moment, who says nothing. She crosses rapidly to her husband)* Please, honey—let me be glad . . . you be glad too. *(She has laid her hands on his shoulders, but he shakes himself free of her roughly, without turning to face her)* Oh, Walter . . . a home . . . a home. *(She comes back to Mama)* Well—where is it? How big is it? How much it going to cost?

MAMA. Well—

RUTH. When we moving?

MAMA *(Smiling at her)*. First of the month.

RUTH *(Throwing back her head with jubilance)*. Praise God!

MAMA *(Tentatively, still looking at her son's back turned against her and Ruth)* It's—it's a nice house too . . . *(She cannot help speaking directly to him. An imploring quality in her voice, her manner, makes her almost like a girl now)* Three bedrooms—nice big one for you and Ruth . . . Me and Beneatha still have to share our room, but Travis have one of his own—and *(With*

417

difficulty) I figure if the—new baby—is a boy, we could get one of them doubledecker outfits . . . And there's a yard with a little patch of dirt where I could maybe get to grow me a few flowers . . . And a nice big basement . . .

RUTH. Walter honey, be glad—

MAMA (*Still to his back, fingering things on the table*). 'Course I don't want to make it sound fancier than it is . . . It's just a plain little old house—but it's made good and solid—and it will be *ours*. Walter Lee—it makes a difference in a man when he can walk on floors that belong to *him* . . .

RUTH. Where is it?

MAMA (*Frightened at this telling*). Well—well—it's out there in Clybourne Park—

(*Ruth's radiance fades abruptly, and Walter finally turns slowly to face his mother with incredulity and hostility*)

RUTH. Where?

MAMA (*Matter-of-factly*). Four o six Clybourne Street, Clybourne Park.

RUTH. Clybourne Park? Mama, there ain't no colored people living in Clybourne Park.

MAMA (*Almost idiotically*). Well, I guess there's going to be some now.

WALTER (*Bitterly*). So that's the peace and comfort you went out and bought for us today!

MAMA (*Raising her eves to meet his finally*). Son—I just tried to find the nicest place for the least amount of money for my family.

RUTH (*Trying to recover from the shock*). Well—well—'course I ain't one never been 'fraid of no crackers, mind you—but—well, wasn't there no other houses nowhere?

MAMA. Them houses they put up for colored in them areas way out all seem to cost twice as much as other houses. I did the best I could.

RUTH (*Struck senseless with the news, in its various degrees of goodness and trouble, she sits a moment, her fists propping her chin in thought, and then she starts to rise, bringing her fists down with vigor, the radiance spreading from cheek to cheek again*). Well—well!—All I can say is—if this is my time in life—my time—to say good-bye—(*And she builds with momentum as she starts to circle the room with exuberant, almost tearfully happy release*)—to these Goddamned cracking walls!—(*She pounds the walls*)—and these marching roaches!—(*She wipes at an imaginary army of marching roaches*)—and this cramped little closet which ain't now or never was no kitchen! . . . then I say it loud and good, Hallelujah! and goodbye misery . . . I don't never want to see your ugly face again! (*She laughs joyously, having practically destroyed the apartment, and flings her arms up and lets them come down happily, slowly, reflectively, over her abdomen, aware for the first time perhaps that the life therein pulses with happiness and not despair)* Lena?

MAMA *(Moved, watching her happiness).* Yes, honey?

RUTH *(Looking off).* Is there—is there a whole lot of sunlight?

MAMA *(Understanding).* Yes, child, there's a whole lot of sunlight.

(Long pause)

RUTH *(Collecting herself and going to the door of the room Travis is in).* Well— I guess I better see 'bout Travis. *(To Mama)* Lord, I sure don't feel like whipping nobody today!

(She exits)

MAMA *(The mother and son are left alone now and the mother waits a long time, considering deeply, before she speaks).* Son—you—you understand what I done, don't you? *(Walter is silent and sullen)* I—I just seen my family falling apart today . . . just falling to pieces in front of my eyes . . . We couldn't of gone on like we was today. We was going backwards 'stead of forwards—talking 'bout killing babies and wishing each other was dead . . . When it gets like that in life—you just got to do something different, push on out and do something bigger . . . *(She waits)* I wish you say something, son . . . I wish you'd say how deep inside you you think I done the right thing—

WALTER *(Crossing slowly to his bedroom door and finally turning there and speaking measuredly).* What you need me to say you done right for? *You* the head of this family. You run our lives like you want to. It was your money and you did what you wanted with it. So what you need for me to say it was all right for? *(Bitterly, to hurt her as deeply as he knows is possible)* So you butchered up a dream of mine—you—who always talking 'bout your children's dreams . . .

MAMA. Walter Lee—

(He just closes the door behind him. Mama sits alone, thinking heavily)

CURTAIN

SCENE 2

TIME: *Friday night. A few weeks later.*

At rise: *Packing crates mark the intention of the family to move. Beneatha and George come in, presumably from an evening out again.*

GEORGE. O.K. . . . O.K., whatever you say . . . *(They both sit on the couch. He tries to kiss her. She moves away)* Look, we've had a nice evening; let's not spoil it, huh?

(He again turns her head and tries to nuzzle in and she turns away from him, not with distaste but with momentary lack of interest; in a mood to pursue what they were talking about)

BENEATHA. I'm *trying* to talk to you.

GEORGE. We always talk.

BENEATHA. Yes—and I love to talk.

GEORGE *(Exasperated; rising)*. I know it and I don't mind it sometimes . . . I want you to cut it out, see—The moody stuff, I mean. I don't like it. You're a nice-looking girl . . . all over. That's all you need, honey, forget the atmosphere. Guys aren't going to go for the atmosphere—they're going to go for what they see. Be glad for that. Drop the Garbo routine.[11] It doesn't go with you. As for myself, I want a nice—*(Groping)*—simple *(Thoughtfully)*—sophisticated girl . . . not a poet—O.K.?

(She rebuffs him again and he starts to leave)

BENEATHA. Why are you angry?

GEORGE. Because this is stupid! I don't go out with you to discuss the nature of "quiet desperation" or to hear all about your thoughts—because the world will go on thinking what it thinks regardless—

BENEATHA. Then why read books? Why go to school?

GEORGE *(With artificial patience, counting on his fingers)*. It's simple. You read books—to learn facts—to get grades—to pass the course—to get a degree. That's all—it has nothing to do with thoughts.

(A long pause)

BENEATHA. I see. *(A longer pause as she looks at him)* Good night, George.

(George looks at her a little oddly, and starts to exit. He meets Mama coming in)

GEORGE. Oh—hello, Mrs. Younger.

MAMA. Hello, George, how you feeling?

GEORGE. Fine—fine, how are you?

MAMA. Oh, a little tired. You know them steps can get you after a day's work. You all have a nice time tonight?

GEORGE. Yes—a fine time. Well, good night.

---

[11]Greta Garbo, early film actress known for her silent intensity and mysteriousness.

MAMA. Good night. *(He exits. Mama closes the door behind her)* Hello, honey. What you sitting like that for?

BENEATHA. I'm just sitting.

MAMA. Didn't you have a nice time?

BENEATHA. No.

MAMA. No? What's the matter?

BENEATHA. Mama, George is a fool—honest. *(She rises)*

MAMA *(Hustling around unloading the packages she has entered with. She stops)*. Is he, baby?

BENEATHA. Yes.

(Beneatha makes up Travis' bed as she talks)

MAMA. You sure?

BENEATHA. Yes.

MAMA. Well—I guess you better not waste your time with no fools.

(Beneatha looks up at her mother, watching her put groceries in the refrigerator. Finally she gathers up her things and starts into the bedroom. At the door she stops and looks back at her mother)

BENEATHA. Mama—

MAMA. Yes, baby—

BENEATHA. Thank you.

MAMA. For what?

BENEATHA. For understanding me this time.

(She exits quickly and the mother stands, smiling a little, looking at the place where Beneatha just stood. Ruth enters)

RUTH. Now don't you fool with any of this stuff, Lena—

MAMA. Oh, I just thought I'd sort a few things out.

(The phone rings. Ruth answers)

RUTH *(At the phone)*. Hello—Just a minute. *(Goes to door)* Walter, it's Mrs. Arnold. *(Waits. Goes back to the phone. Tense)* Hello. Yes, this is his wife speaking . . . He's lying down now. Yes . . . well, he'll be in tomorrow. He's been very sick. Yes—I know we should have called, but we were so sure he'd be able to come in today. Yes—yes, I'm very sorry. Yes . . . Thank you very much. *(She hangs up. Walter is standing in the doorway of the bedroom behind her)* That was Mrs. Arnold.

WALTER *(Indifferently)*. Was it?

RUTH. She said if you don't come in tomorrow that they are getting a new man . . .

WALTER. Ain't that sad—ain't that crying sad.

RUTH. She said Mr. Arnold has had to take a cab for three days . . . Walter, you ain't been to work for three days! *(This is a revelation to her)* Where you been, Walter Lee Younger? *(Walter looks at her and starts to laugh)* You're going to lose your job.

WALTER. That's right . . .

RUTH. Oh, Walter, and with your mother working like a dog every day—

WALTER. That's sad too—Everything is sad.

MAMA. What you been doing for these three days, son?

WALTER. Mama—you don't know all the things a man what got leisure can find to do in this city . . . What's this—Friday night? Well—Wednesday I borrowed Willy Harris' car and I went for a drive . . . just me and myself and I drove and drove . . . Way out . . . way past South Chicago, and I parked the car and I sat and looked at the steel mills all day long. I just sat in the car and looked at them big black chimneys for hours. Then I drove back and I went to the Green Hat. *(Pause)* And Thursday—Thursday I borrowed the car again and I got in it and I pointed it the other way and I drove the other way—for hours—way, way up to Wisconsin, and I looked at the farms. I just drove and looked at the farms. Then I drove back and I went to the Green Hat. *(Pause)* And today—today I didn't get the car. Today I just walked. All over the Southside. And I looked at the Negroes and they looked at me and finally I just sat down on the curb at Thirty-ninth and South Parkway and I just sat there and watched the Negroes go by. And then I went to the Green Hat. You all sad? You all depressed? And you know where I am going right now—

(Ruth goes out quietly)

MAMA. Oh, Big Walter, is this the harvest of our days?

WALTER. You know what I like about the Green Hat? *(He turns the radio on and a steamy, deep blues pours into the room)* I like this little cat they got there who blows a sax . . . He blows. He talks to me. He ain't but 'bout five feet tall and he's got a conked head and his eyes is always closed and he's all music—

MAMA *(Rising and getting some papers out of her handbag)*. Walter—

WALTER. And there's this other guy who plays the piano . . . and they got a sound. I mean they can work on some music . . . They got the best little combo in the world in the Green Hat . . . You can just sit there and drink and listen to them three men play and you realize that don't nothing matter worth a damn, but just being there—

MAMA. I've helped do it to you, haven't I, son? Walter, I been wrong.

WALTER. Naw—you ain't never been wrong about nothing, Mama.

MAMA. Listen to me, now. I say I been wrong, son. That I been doing to you what the rest of the world been doing to you. *(She stops and he looks up slowly at her and she meets his eyes pleadingly)* Walter—what you ain't never understood is that I ain't got nothing, don't own nothing, ain't never really wanted nothing that wasn't for you. There ain't nothing as precious to me . . . There ain't nothing worth holding on to, money, dreams, nothing else—if it means—if it means it's going to destroy my boy. *(She puts her papers in front of him and he watches her without speaking or moving)* I paid the man thirty-five hundred dollars down on the house. That leaves sixty-five hundred dollars. Monday morning I want you to take this money and take three thousand dollars and put it in a savings account for Beneatha's medical schooling. The rest you put in a checking account—with your name on it. And from now on any penny that come out of it or that go in it is for you to look after. For you to decide. *(She drops her hands a little helplessly)* It ain't much, but it's all I got in the world and I'm putting it in your hands. I'm telling you to be the head of this family from now on like you supposed to be.

WALTER *(Stares at the money)*. You trust me like that, Mama?

MAMA. I ain't never stop trusting you. Like I ain't never stop loving you.

(She goes out, and Walter sits looking at the money on the table as the music continues in its idiom, pulsing in the room. Finally, in a decisive gesture, he gets up, and, in mingled joy and desperation, picks up the money. At the same moment, Travis enters for bed)

TRAVIS. What's the matter, Daddy? You drunk?

WALTER *(Sweetly, more sweetly than we have ever known him)*. No, Daddy ain't drunk. Daddy ain't going to never be drunk again . . .

TRAVIS. Well, good night, Daddy.

(The Father has come from behind the couch and leans over, embracing his son)

WALTER. Son, I feel like talking to you tonight.

TRAVIS. About what?

WALTER. Oh, about a lot of things. About you and what kind of man you going to be when you grow up. . . . Son—son, what do you want to be when you grow up?

TRAVIS. A bus driver.

WALTER *(Laughing a little)*. A what? Man, that ain't nothing to want to be!

TRAVIS. Why not?

WALTER. 'Cause, man—it ain't big enough—you know what I mean.

TRAVIS. I don't know then. I can't make up my mind. Sometimes Mama asks me that too. And sometimes when I tell her I just want to be like you—

she says she don't want me to be like that and sometimes she says she does. . . .

WALTER *(Gathering him up in his arms)*. You know what, Travis? In seven years you going to be seventeen years old. And things is going to be very different with us in seven years, Travis. . . . One day when you are seventeen I'll come home—home from my office downtown somewhere—

TRAVIS. You don't work in no office, Daddy.

WALTER. No—but after tonight. After what your daddy gonna do tonight, there's going to be offices—a whole lot of offices. . . .

TRAVIS. What you gonna do tonight, Daddy?

WALTER. You wouldn't understand yet, son, but your daddy's gonna make a transaction . . . a business transaction that's going to change our lives. . . . That's how come one day when you 'bout seventeen years old I'll come home and I'll be pretty tired, you know what I mean, after a day of conferences and secretaries getting things wrong the way they do . . . 'cause an executive's life is hell, man—*(The more he talks the farther away he gets)* And I'll pull the car up on the driveway . . . just a plain black Chrysler, I think, with white walls—no—black tires. More elegant. Rich people don't have to be flashy . . . though I'll have to get something a little sportier for Ruth—maybe a Cadillac convertible to do her shopping in . . . And I'll come up the steps to the house and the gardener will be clipping away at the hedges and he'll say, "Good evening, Mr. Younger." And I'll say, "Hello, Jefferson, how are you this evening?" And I'll go inside and Ruth will come downstairs and meet me at the door and we'll kiss each other and she'll take my arm and we'll go up to your room to see you sitting on the floor with the catalogues of all the great schools in America around you. . . . All the great schools in the world! And—and I'll say, all right son—it's your seventeenth birthday, what is it you've decided? . . . Just tell me where you want to go to school and you'll *go*. Just tell me, what it is you want to be—and you'll *be* it. . . . Whatever you want to be—Yessir! *(He holds his arms open for* Travis*)* You just name it, son . . . *(Travis leaps into them)* and I hand you the world!

(Walter's voice has risen in pitch and hysterical promise and on the last line he lifts Travis high)

(BLACKOUT)

SCENE 3

TIME: *Saturday, moving day, one week later.*

Before the curtain rises, Ruth's voice, a strident, dramatic church alto, cuts through the silence.

It is, in the darkness, a triumphant surge, a penetrating statement of expectation: "Oh, Lord, I don't feel no ways tired! Children, oh, glory hallelujah!"

As the curtain rises we see that Ruth is alone in the living room, finishing up the family's packing. It is moving day. She is nailing crates and tying cartons. Beneatha enters, carrying a guitar case, and watches her exuberant sister-in-law,

RUTH. Hey!

BENEATHA *(Putting away the case)*. Hi.

RUTH *(Pointing at a package)*. Honey—look in that package there and see what I found on sale this morning at the South Center. *(Ruth gets up and moves to the package and draws out some curtains)* Lookahere—hand-turned hems!

BENEATHA. How do you know the window size out there?

RUTH *(Who hadn't thought of that)*. Oh—Well, they bound to fit something in the whole house. Anyhow, they was too good a bargain to pass up. *(Ruth slaps her head, suddenly remembering something)* Oh, Bennie—I meant to put a special note on that carton over there. That's your mama's good china and she wants 'em to be very careful with it.

BENEATHA. I'll do it.

(Beneatha finds a piece of paper and starts to draw large letters on it)

RUTH. You know what I'm going to do soon as I get in that new house?

BENEATHA. What?

RUTH. Honey—I'm going to run me a tub of water up to here . . . *(With her fingers practically up to her nostrils)* And I'm going to get in it—and I am going to sit . . . and sit . . . and sit in that hot water and the first person who knocks to tell *me* to hurry up and come out—

BENEATHA. Gets shot at sunrise.

RUTH *(Laughing happily)*. You said it, sister! *(Noticing how large Beneatha is absentmindedly making the note)* Honey, they ain't going to read that from no airplane.

BENEATHA *(Laughing herself)*. I guess I always think things have more emphasis if they are big, somehow.

RUTH *(Looking up at her and smiling)*. You and your brother seem to have that as a philosophy of life. Lord, that man—done changed so 'round here. You know—you know what we did last night? Me and Walter Lee?

BENEATHA. What?

RUTH *(Smiling to herself)*. We went to the movies. *(Looking at Beneatha to see if she understands)* We went to the movies. You know the last time me and Walter went to the movies together?

BENEATHA. No.

RUTH. Me neither. That's how long it been. *(Smiling again)* But we went last night. The picture wasn't much good, but that didn't seem to matter. We went—and we held hands.

BENEATHA. Oh, Lord!

RUTH. We held hands—and you know what?

BENEATHA. What?

RUTH. When we come out of the show it was late and dark and all the stores and things was closed up . . . and it was kind of chilly and there wasn't many people on the streets . . . and we was still holding hands, me and Walter.

BENEATHA. You're killing me.

(Walter enters with a large package. His happiness is deep in him; he cannot keep still with his new-found exuberance. He is singing and wiggling and snapping his fingers. He puts his package in a corner and puts a phonograph record, which he has brought in with him, on the record player. As the music comes up he dances over to Ruth and tries to get her to dance with him. She gives in at last to his raunchiness and in a fit of giggling allows herself to be drawn into his mood and together they deliberately burlesque an old social dance of their youth)

BENEATHA *(Regarding them a long time as they dance, then drawing in her breath for a deeply exaggerated comment which she does not particularly mean)*. Talk about—olddddddddddd-fashionedddddddd—Negroes!

WALTER *(Stopping momentarily)*. What kind of Negroes?

(He says this in fun. He is not angry with her today, nor with anyone. He starts to dance with his wife again)

BENEATHA. Old-fashioned.

WALTER *(As he dances with Ruth)*. You know, when these *New Negroes* have their convention—*(Pointing at his sister)*—that is going to be the chairman of the Committee on Unending Agitation. *(He goes on dancing, then stops)* Race, race, race! . . . Girl, I do believe you are the first person in the history of the entire human race to successfully brainwash yourself. *(Beneatha breaks up and he goes on dancing. He stops again, enjoying his tease)* Damn, even the N double A C P[12] takes a holiday sometimes! *(Beneatha and Ruth laugh. He dances with Ruth some more and starts to laugh and stops and pantomimes someone over an operating table)* I can just see that chick someday looking down at some poor cat on an operating table before she starts to slice him, saying . . . *(Pulling his sleeves back*

---

[12]National Association for the Advancement of Colored People (NAACP), an organization that works to end segregation, discrimination, and other forms of racial oppression.

maliciously) "By the way, what are your views on civil rights down there? . . ."

(He laughs at her again and starts to dance happily. The bell sounds)

BENEATHA. Sticks and stones may break my bones but . . . words will never hurt me!

(Beneatha goes to the door and opens it as Walter and Ruth go on with the clowning. Beneatha is somewhat surprised to see a quiet-looking middle-aged white man in a business suit holding his hat and a briefcase in his hand and consulting a small piece of paper)

MAN. Uh—how do you do, miss. I am looking for a Mrs.—*(He looks at the slip of paper)* Mrs. Lena Younger?

BENEATHA *(Smoothing her hair with slight embarrassment).* Oh—yes, that's my mother. Excuse me. *(She closes the door and turns to quiet the other two)* Ruth! Brother! Somebody's here. *(Then she opens the door. The man casts a curious quick glance at all of them)* Uh—come in please.

MAN *(Coming in).* Thank you.

BENEATHA. My mother isn't here just now. Is it business?

MAN. Yes . . . well, of a sort.

WALTER *(Freely, the Man of the House).* Have a seat. I'm Mrs. Younger's son. I look after most of her business matters.

(Ruth and Beneatha exchange amused glances)

MAN *(Regarding Walter, and sitting).* Well—My name is Karl Lindner . . .

WALTER *(Stretching out his hand).* Walter Younger. This is my wife—*(Ruth nods politely)*—and my sister.

LINDNER. How do you do.

WALTER *(Amiably, as he sits himself easily on a chair, leaning with interest forward on his knees and looking expectantly into the newcomer's face).* What can we do for you, Mr. Lindner!

LINDNER *(Some minor shuffling of the hat and briefcase on his knees).* Well—I am a representative of the Clybourne Park Improvement Association—

WALTER *(Pointing).* Why don't you sit your things on the floor?

LINDNER. Oh—yes. Thank you. *(He slides the briefcase and hat under the chair)* And as I was saying—I am from the Clybourne Park Improvement Association and we have had it brought to our attention at the last meeting that you people—or at least your mother—has bought a piece of residential property at—*(He digs for the slip of paper again)*—four o six Clybourne Street . . .

WALTER. That's right. Care for something to drink? Ruth, get Mr. Lindner a beer.

LINDNER *(Upset for some reason)*. Oh—no, really. I mean thank you very much, but no thank you.

RUTH *(Innocently)*. Some coffee?

LINDNER. Thank you, nothing at all.

(Beneatha is watching the man carefully)

LINDNER. Well, I don't know how much you folks know about our organization. *(He is a gentle man; thoughtful and somewhat labored in his manner)* It is one of these community organizations set up to look after—oh, you know, things like block up-keep and special projects and we also have what we call our New Neighbors Orientation Committee . . .

BENEATHA *(Drily)*. Yes—and what do they do?

LINDNER *(Turning a little to her and then returning the main force to Walter)*. Well—it's what you might call a sort of welcoming committee, I guess. I mean they, we, I'm the chairman of the committee—go around and see the new people who move into the neighborhood and sort of give them the lowdown on the way we do things out in Clybourne Park.

BENEATHA *(With appreciation of the two meanings, which escape Ruth and Walter)*. Un-huh.

LINDNER. And we also have the category of what the association calls—*(He looks elsewhere)*—uh—special community problems . . .

BENEATHA. Yes—and what are some of those?

WALTER. Girl, let the man talk.

LINDNER *(With understated relief)*. Thank you. I would sort of like to explain this thing in my own way. I mean I want to explain to you in a certain way.

WALTER. Go ahead.

LINDNER. Yes. I'm going to try to get right to the point. I'm sure we'll all appreciate that in the long run.

BENEATHA. Yes.

WALTER. Be still now!

LINDNER. Well—

RUTH *(Still innocently)*. Would you like another chair—you don't look comfortable.

LINDNER *(More frustrated than annoyed)*. No, thank you very much. Please. Well—to get right to the point I—*(A great breath, and he is off at last)* I am sure you people must be aware of some of the incidents which have happened in various parts of the city when colored people have moved into certain areas—*(Beneatha exhales heavily and starts tossing a piece of fruit up and down in the air)* Well—because we have what I think is going to be a unique type of organization in American community life—not only do we deplore that kind of thing—but we are trying to do something about it. *(Beneatha stops tossing and turns with a new and quizzical interest to the man)* We feel—*(gaining confidence in his mission because of the interest in the faces of the people he is talking to)*—we feel that most of the trouble in this world, when you come right down to it—*(He hits his knee for emphasis)*—most of the trouble exists because people just don't sit down and talk to each other.

RUTH *(Nodding as she might in church, pleased with the remark)*. You can say that again, mister.

LINDNER *(More encouraged by such affirmation)*. That we don't try hard enough in this world to understand the other fellow's problem. The other guy's point of view.

RUTH. Now that's right.

(Beneatha and Walter merely watch and listen with genuine interest)

LINDNER. Yes—that's the way we feel out in Clybourne Park. And that's why I was elected to come here this afternoon and talk to you people. Friendly like, you know, the way people should talk to each other and see if we couldn't find some way to work this thing out. As I say, the whole business is a matter of *caring* about the other fellow. Anybody can see that you are a nice family of folks, hard working and honest I'm sure. *(Beneatha frowns slightly, quizzically, her head tilted regarding him)* Today everybody knows what it means to be on the outside of *something*. And of course, there is always somebody who is out to take the advantage of people who don't always understand.

WALTER. What do you mean?

LINDNER. Well—you see our community is made up of people who've worked hard as the dickens for years to build up that little community. They're not rich and fancy people; just hard-working, honest people who don't really have much but those little homes and a dream of the kind of community they want to raise their children in. Now, I don't say we are perfect and there is a lot wrong in some of the things they want. But you've got to admit that a man, right or wrong, has the right to want to have the neighborhood he lives in a certain kind of way. And at the moment the overwhelming majority of our people out there feel that people get along better, take more of a common interest in the life of the community, when they share a common background. I want you to believe me when I tell you that race prejudice simply doesn't enter into it. It is a matter of the people of Clybourne Park believing, rightly or wrongly, as I say, that for the happiness of all concerned that our Negro families are happier when they live in their *own* communities.

BENEATHA *(With a grand and bitter gesture)*. This, friends, is the Welcoming Committee!

WALTER *(Dumfounded, looking at Lindner)*. Is this what you came marching all the way over here to tell us?

LINDNER. Well, now we've been having a fine conversation. I hope you'll hear me all the way through.

WALTER *(Tightly)*. Go ahead, man.

LINDNER. You see—in the face of all things I have said, we are prepared to make your family a very generous offer . . .

BENEATHA. Thirty pieces and not a coin less![13]

WALTER. Yeah?

LINDNER *(Putting on his glasses and drawing a form out of the briefcase)*. Our association is prepared, through the collective effort of our people, to buy the house from you at a financial gain to your family.

RUTH. Lord have mercy, ain't this the living gall!

WALTER. All right, you through?

LINDNER. Well, I want to give you the exact terms of the financial arrangement—

WALTER. We don't want to hear no exact terms of no arrangements. I want to know if you got any more to tell us 'bout getting together?

LINDNER *(Taking off his glasses)*. Well—I don't suppose that you feel . . .

WALTER. Never mind how I feel—you got any more to say 'bout how people ought to sit down and talk to each other? . . . Get out of my house, man.

(He turns his back and walks to the door)

LINDNER *(Looking around at the hostile faces and reaching and assembling his hat and briefcase)*. Well—I don't understand why you people are reacting this way. What do you think you are going to gain by moving into a neighborhood where you just aren't wanted and where some elements—well—people can get awful worked up when they feel that their whole way of life and everything they've ever worked for is threatened.

WALTER. Get out.

LINDNER *(At the door, holding a small card)*. Well—I'm sorry it went like this.

WALTER. Get out.

LINDNER *(Almost sadly regarding Walter)*. You just can't force people to change their hearts, son.

---

[13]In the Bible, Judas received thirty pieces of silver for betraying Jesus.

(He turns and puts his card on a table and exits. Walter pushes the door to with stinging hatred, and stands looking at it. Ruth just sits and Beneatha just stands. They say nothing. Mama and Travis enter)

MAMA. Well—this all the packing got done since I left out of here this morning. I testify before God that my children got all the energy of the dead. What time the moving men due?
BENEATHA. Four o'clock. You had a caller, Mama.

(She is smiling, teasingly)

MAMA. Sure enough—who?
BENEATHA *(Her arms folded saucily)*. The Welcoming Committee.

(Walter and Ruth giggle)

MAMA *(Innocently)*. Who?
BENEATHA. The Welcoming Committee. They said they're sure going to be glad to see you when you get there.
WALTER *(Devilishly)*. Yeah, they said they can't hardly wait to see your face.

(Laughter)

MAMA *(Sensing their facetiousness)*. What's the matter with you all?
WALTER. Ain't nothing the matter with us. We just telling you 'bout the gentleman who came to see you this afternoon. From the Clybourne Park Improvement Association.
MAMA. What he want?
RUTH *(In the same mood as Beneatha and Walter)*. To welcome you, honey.
WALTER. He said they can't hardly wait. He said the one thing they don't have, that they just *dying* to have out there is a fine family of colored people! *(To Ruth and Beneatha)* Ain't that right!
RUTH AND BENEATHA *(Mockingly)*. Yeah! He left his card in case—

(They indicate the card, and Mama picks it up and throws it on the floor— understanding and looking off as she draws her chair up to the table on which she has put her plant and some sticks and some cord)

MAMA. Father, give us strength. *(Knowingly—and without fun)* Did he threaten us?
BENEATHA. Oh—Mama—they don't do it like that any more. He talked Brotherhood. He said everybody ought to learn how to sit down and hate each other with good Christian fellowship.

(She and Walter shake hands to ridicule the remark)

MAMA *(Sadly)*. Lord, protect us . . .

RUTH. You should hear the money those folks raised to buy the house from us. All we paid and then some.

BENEATHA. What they think we going to do—eat 'em?

RUTH. No, honey, marry 'em.

MAMA *(Shaking her head)*. Lord, Lord, Lord . . .

RUTH. Well—that's the way the crackers crumble. Joke.

BENEATHA *(Laughingly noticing what her mother is doing)*. Mama, what are you doing?

MAMA. Fixing my plant so it won't get hurt none on the way . . .

BENEATHA. Mama, you going to take *that* to the new house?

MAMA. Un-huh—

BENEATHA. That raggedy-looking old thing?

MAMA *(Stopping and looking at her)*. It expresses me.

RUTH *(With delight, to Beneatha)*. So there, Miss Thing!

(Walter comes to Mama suddenly and bends down behind her and squeezes her in his arms with all his strength. She is overwhelmed by the suddenness of it and, though delighted, her manner is like that of Ruth with Travis)

MAMA. Look out now, boy! You make me mess up my thing here!

WALTER *(His face lit, he slips down on his knees beside her, his arms still about her)*. Mama . . . you know what it means to climb up in the chariot?

MAMA *(Gruffly, very happy)*. Get on away from me now . . .

RUTH *(Near the gift-wrapped package, trying to catch Walter's eye)*. Psst—

WALTER. What the old song say, Mama . . .

RUTH. Walter—Now?

(She is pointing at the package)

WALTER *(Speaking the lines, sweetly, playfully, in his mother's face)*.

I got wings . . . you got wings . . .
All God's children got wings . . .

MAMA. Boy—get out of my face and do some work . . .

WALTER.

When I get to heaven gonna put on my wings,
Gonna fly all over God's heaven . . .

BENEATHA *(Teasingly, from across the room)*. Everybody talking 'bout heaven ain't going there!

WALTER *(To Ruth, who is carrying the box across to them)*. I don't know, you think we ought to give her that . . . Seems to me she ain't been very appreciative around here.

MAMA *(Eying the box, which is obviously a gift)*. What is that?

WALTER *(Taking it from Ruth and putting it on the table in front of Mama)*. Well—what you all think? Should we give it to her?

RUTH. Oh—she was pretty good today.

MAMA. I'll good you—

(She turns her eyes to the box again)

BENEATHA. Open it, Mama.

(She stands up, looks at it, turns and looks at all of them, and then presses her hands together and does not open the package)

WALTER *(Sweetly)*. Open it, Mama. It's for you. *(Mama looks in his eyes. It is the first present in her life without its being Christmas. Slowly she opens her package and lifts out, one by one, a brand-new sparkling set of gardening tools. Walter continues, prodding)* Ruth made up the note—read it . . .

MAMA *(Picking up the card and adjusting her glasses)*. "To our own Mrs. Miniver[14]—Love from Brother, Ruth and Beneatha." Ain't that lovely . . .

TRAVIS *(Tugging at his father's sleeve)*. Daddy, can I give her mine now?

WALTER. All right, son. *(Travis flies to get his gift)* Travis didn't want to go in with the rest of us, Mama. He got his own. *(Somewhat amused)* We don't know what it is . . .

TRAVIS *(Racing back in the room with a large hatbox and putting it in front of his grandmother)*. Here!

MAMA. Lord have mercy, baby. You done gone and bought your grandmother a hat?

TRAVIS *(Very proud)*. Open it!

(She does and lifts out an elaborate, but very elaborate, wide gardening hat, and all the adults break up at the sight of it)

RUTH. Travis, honey, what is that?

TRAVIS *(Who thinks it is beautiful and appropriate)*. It's a gardening hat! Like the ladies always have on in the magazines when they work in their gardens.

BENEATHA *(Giggling fiercely)*. Travis—we were trying to make Mama Mrs. Miniver—not Scarlett O'Hara!

---

[14]In the film *Mrs. Miniver* (1942), a middle class English housewife heroically endures the horrors of World War II.

433

MAMA *(Indignantly)*. What's the matter with you all! This here is a beautiful hat! *(Absurdly)* I always wanted me one just like it!

(She pops it on her head to prove it to her grandson, and the hat is ludicrous and considerably oversized)

RUTH. Hot dog! Go, Mama!

WALTER *(Doubled over with laughter)*. I'm sorry, Mama—but you look like you ready to go out and chop you some cotton sure enough!

(They all laugh except Mama, out of deference to Travis' feelings)

MAMA *(Gathering the boy up to her)* Bless your heart—this is the prettiest hat I ever owned—*(Walter, Ruth and Beneatha chime in—noisily, festively and insincerely congratulating Travis on his gift)* What are we all standing around here for? We ain't finished packin' yet. Bennie, you ain't packed one book.

(The bell rings)

BENEATHA. That couldn't be the movers . . . it's not hardly two good yet—

(Beneatha goes into her room. Mama starts for door)

WALTER *(Turning, stiffening)*. Wait—wait—I'll get it.

(He stands and looks at the door)

MAMA. You expecting company, son?

WALTER *(Just looking at the door)*. Yeah—yeah . . .

(Mama looks at Ruth, and they exchange innocent and unfrightened glances)

MAMA *(Not understanding)*. Well, let them in, son.

BENEATHA *(From her room)*. We need some more string.

MAMA. Travis—you run to the hardware and get me some string cord.

(Mama goes out and Walter turns and looks at Ruth. Travis goes to a dish for money)

RUTH. Why don't you answer the door, man?

WALTER *(Suddenly bounding across the floor to her)*. 'Cause sometimes it hard to let the future begin! *(Stooping down in her face)*

I got wings! You got wings!
All God's children got wings!

(He crosses to the door and throws it open. Standing there is a very slight little man in a not too prosperous business suit and with haunted frightened eyes

and a hat pulled down tightly, brim up, around his forehead. Travis passes between the men and exits. Walter leans deep in the man's face, still in his jubilance)

When I get to heaven gonna put on my wings,
Gonna fly all over God's heaven . . .

(The little man just stares at him)

Heaven—

(Suddenly he stops and looks past the little man into the empty hallway)

Where's Willy, man?

BOBO. He ain't with me.

WALTER *(Not disturbed)*. Oh—come on in. You know my wife.

BOBO *(Dumbly, taking off his hat)*. Yes—h'you, Miss Ruth.

RUTH *(Quietly, a mood apart from her husband already, seeing Bobo)*. Hello, Bobo.

WALTER. You right on time today . . . Right on time. That's the way! *(He slaps Bobo on his back)* Sit down . . . lemme hear.

(Ruth stands stiffly and quietly in back of them, as though somehow she senses death, her eyes fixed on her husband)

BOBO *(His frightened eyes on the floor, his hat in his hands)*. Could I please get a drink of water, before I tell you about it, Walter Lee?

(Walter does not take his eyes off the man. Ruth goes blindly to the tap and gets a glass of water and brings it to Bobo)

WALTER. There ain't nothing wrong, is there?

BOBO. Lemme tell you—

WALTER. Man—didn't nothing go wrong?

BOBO. Lemme tell you—Walter Lee. *(Looking at Ruth and talking to her more than to Walter)* You know how it was. I got to tell you how it was. I mean first I got to tell you how it was all the way . . . I mean about the money I put in, Walter Lee . . .

WALTER *(With taut agitation now)*. What about the money you put in?

BOBO. Well—it wasn't much as we told you—me and Willy—*(He stops)* I'm sorry, Walter. I got a bad feeling about it. I got a real bad feeling about it . . .

WALTER. Man, what you telling me about all this for? . . . Tell me what happened in Springfield . . .

BOBO. Springfield.

RUTH *(Like a dead woman)*. What was supposed to happen in Springfield?

BOBO *(To her)*. This deal that me and Walter went into with Willy—Me and Willy was going to go down to Springfield and spread some money 'round so's we wouldn't have to wait so long for the liquor license . . . That's what we were going to do. Everybody said that was the way you had to do, you understand, Miss Ruth?

WALTER. Man—what happened down there?

BOBO *(A pitiful man, near tears)*. I'm trying to tell you, Walter.

WALTER *(Screaming at him suddenly)*. THEN TELL ME, GODDAMMIT . . . WHAT'S THE MATTER WITH YOU?

BOBO. Man . . . I didn't go to no Springfield, yesterday.

WALTER *(Halted, life hanging in the moment)*. Why not?

BOBO *(The long way, the hard way to tell)*. 'Cause I didn't have no reasons to . . .

WALTER. Man, what are you talking about!

BOBO. I'm talking about the fact that when I got to the train station yesterday morning—eight o'clock like we planned . . . Man—*Willy didn't never show up.*

WALTER. Why . . . where was he . . . where is he?

BOBO. That's what I'm trying to tell you . . . I don't know . . . I waited six hours . . . I called his house . . . and I waited . . . six hours . . . I waited in that train station six hours . . . *(Breaking, into tears)* That was all the extra money I had in the world . . . *(Looking up at Walter with the tears running down his face)* Man, *Willy is gone.*

WALTER. Gone, what you mean Willy is gone? Gone where? You mean he went by himself. You mean he went off to Springfield by himself—to take care of getting the license—*(Turns and looks anxiously at Ruth)* You mean maybe he didn't want too many people in on the business down there? *(Looks to Ruth again, as before)* You know Willy got his own ways. *(Looks back to Bobo)* Maybe you was late yesterday and he just went on down there without you. Maybe—maybe—he's been callin' you at home tryin' to tell you what happened or something. Maybe—maybe—he just got sick. He's somewhere—he's got to be somewhere. We just got to find him—me and you got to find him. *(Grabs Bobo senselessly by the collar and starts to shake him)* We got to!

BOBO *(In sudden angry, frightened agony)*. What's the matter with you, Walter! *When a cat take off with your money he don't leave you no maps!*

WALTER *(Turning madly, as though he is looking for Willy in the very room)*. Willy! . . . Willy . . . don't do it . . . Please don't do it . . . Man, not with

436

that money . . . Man, please, not with that money . . . Oh, God . . . Don't let it be true . . . *(He is wandering around, crying out for Willy and looking for him or perhaps for help from God)* Man . . . I trusted you . . . Man, I put my life in your hands . . . *(He starts to crumple down on the floor as Ruth just covers her face in horror. Mama opens the door and comes into the room, with Beneatha behind her)* Man . . . *(He starts to pound the floor with his fists, sobbing wildly)* That money is made out of my father's flesh . . .

BOBO *(Standing over him helplessly)*. I'm sorry, Walter . . . *(Only Walter's sobs reply. Bobo puts on his hat)* I had my life staked on this deal, too . . .

(He exits)

MAMA *(To Walter)*. Son—*(She goes to him, bends down to him, talks to his bent head)* Son . . . Is it gone? Son, I gave you sixty-five hundred dollars. Is it gone? All of it? Beneatha's money too?

WALTER *(Lifting his head slowly)*. Mama . . . I never . . . went to the bank at all . . .

MAMA *(Not wanting to believe him)*. You mean . . . your sister's school money . . . you used that too . . . Walter?

WALTER. Yessss! . . . All of it . . . It's all gone.

(There is total silence. Ruth stands with her face covered with her hands; Beneatha leans forlornly against a wall, fingering a piece of red ribbon from the mother's gift. Mama stops and looks at her son without recognition and then, quite without thinking about it, starts to beat him senselessly in the face. Beneatha goes to them and stops it)

BENEATHA. Mama!

(Mama stops and looks at both of her children and rises slowly and wanders vaguely, aimlessly away from them)

MAMA. I seen . . . him . . . night after night . . . come in . . . and look at that rug . . . and then look at me . . . the red showing in his eyes . . . the veins moving in his head . . . I seen him grow thin and old before he was forty . . . working and working and working like somebody's old horse . . . killing himself . . . and you—you give it all away in a day . . .

BENEATHA. Mama—

MAMA. Oh, God . . . *(She looks up to Him)* Look down here—and show me the strength.

BENEATHA. Mama—

MAMA *(Folding over)*. Strength . . .

BENEATHA *(Plaintively)*. Mama . . .

MAMA. Strength!

CURTAIN

ACT THREE

An hour later

At curtain, there is a sullen light of gloom in the living room, gray light not unlike that which began the first scene of Act One. At left we can see Walter within his room, alone with himself. He is stretched out on the bed, his shirt out and open, his arms under his head. He does not smoke, he does not cry out, he merely lies there, looking up at the ceiling, much as if he were alone in the world.

In the living room Beneatha sits at the table, still surrounded by the now almost ominous packing crates. She sits looking off. We feel that this is a mood struck perhaps an hour before, and it lingers now, full of the empty sound of profound disappointment. We see on a line from her brother's bedroom the sameness of their attitudes. Presently the bell rings and Beneatha rises without ambition or interest in answering. It is Asagai, smiling broadly, striding into the room with energy and happy expectation and conversation.

ASAGAI. I came over . . . I had some free time. I thought I might help with the packing. Ah, I like the look of packing crates! A household in preparation for a journey! It depresses some people . . . but for me . . . it is another feeling. Something full of the flow of life, do you understand? Movement, progress . . . It makes me think of Africa.

BENEATHA. Africa!

ASAGAI. What kind of a mood is this? Have I told you how deeply you move me?

BENEATHA. He gave away the money, Asagai . . .

ASAGAI. Who gave away what money?

BENEATHA. The insurance money. My brother gave it away.

ASAGAI. Gave it away?

BENEATHA. He made an investment! With a man even Travis wouldn't have trusted.

ASAGAI. And it's gone?

BENEATHA. Gone!

ASAGAI. I'm very sorry . . . And you, now?

BENEATHA. Me? . . . Me? . . . Me I'm nothing . . . Me. When I was very small . . . we used to take our sleds out in the wintertime and the only hills we had were the ice-covered stone steps of some houses down the street. And we used to fill them in with snow and make them smooth

438

and slide down them all day . . . and it was very dangerous you know . . . far too steep . . . and sure enough one day a kid named Rufus came down too fast and hit the sidewalk . . . and we saw his face just split open right there in front of us . . . And I remember standing there looking at his bloody open face thinking that was the end of Rufus. But the ambulance came and they took him to the hospital and they fixed the broken bones and they sewed it all up . . . and the next time I saw Rufus he just had a little line down the middle of his face . . . I never got over that . . .

(Walter sits up, listening on the bed. Throughout this scene it is important that we feel his reaction at all times, that he visibly respond to the words of his sister and Asagai)

ASAGAI. What?

BENEATHA. That that was what one person could do for another, fix him up— sew up the problem, make him all right again. That was the most marvelous thing in the world . . . I wanted to do that. I always thought it was the one concrete thing in the world that a human being could do. Fix up the sick, you know—and make them whole again. This was truly being God . . .

ASAGAI. You wanted to be God?

BENEATHA. No—I wanted to cure. It used to be so important to me. I wanted to cure. It used to matter. I used to care. I mean about people and how their bodies hurt . . .

ASAGAI. And you've stopped caring?

BENEATHA. Yes—I think so.

ASAGAI. Why?

(Walter rises, goes to the door of his room and is about to open it, then stops and stands listening, leaning on the door jamb)

BENEATHA. Because it doesn't seem deep enough, close enough to what ails mankind—I mean this thing of sewing up bodies or administering drugs. Don't you understand? It was a child's reaction to the world. I thought that doctors had the secret to all the hurts. . . . That's the way a child sees things—or an idealist.

ASAGAI. Children see things very well sometimes—and idealists even better.

BENEATHA. I know that's what you think. Because you are still where I left off—you still care. This is what you see for the world, for Africa. You with the dreams of the future will patch up all Africa—you are going to cure the Great Sore of colonialism with Independence—

ASAGAI. Yes!

BENEATHA. Yes—and you think that one word is the penicillin of the human spirit: "Independence!" But then what?

ASAGAI. That will be the problem for another time. First we must get there.

BENEATHA. And where does it end?

ASAGAI. End? Who even spoke of an end? To life? To living?

BENEATHA. An end to misery!

ASAGAI *(Smiling)*. You sound like a French intellectual.

BENEATHA. No! I sound like a human being who just had her future taken right out of her hands! While I was sleeping in my bed in there, things were happening in this world that directly concerned me—and nobody asked me, consulted me—they just went out and did things—and changed my life. Don't you see there isn't any real progress, Asagai, there is only one large circle that we march in, around and around, each of us with our own little picture—in front of us—our own little mirage that we think is the future.

ASAGAI. That is the mistake.

BENEATHA. What?

ASAGAI. What you just said—about the circle. It isn't a circle—it's simply a long line—as in geometry, you know, one that reaches into infinity. And because we cannot see the end—we also cannot see how it changes. And it is very odd but those who see the changes are called "idealists"—and those who cannot, or refuse to think, they are the "realists." It is very strange, and amusing too, I think.

BENEATHA. You—you are almost religious.

ASAGAI. Yes . . . I think I have the religion of doing what is necessary in the world—and of worshipping man—because he is so marvelous, you see.

BENEATHA. Man is foul! And the human race deserves its misery!

ASAGAI. You see: *you* have become the religious one in the old sense. Already, and after such a small defeat, you are worshipping despair.

BENEATHA. From now on, I worship the truth—and the truth is that people are puny, small and selfish. . . .

ASAGAI. Truth? Why is it that you despairing ones always think that only you have the truth? I never thought to see *you* like that. You! Your brother made a stupid, childish mistake—and you are grateful to him. So that now you can give up the ailing human race on account of it. You talk about what good is struggle; what good is anything? Where are we all going? And why are we bothering?

BENEATHA. *And you cannot answer it!* All your talk and dreams about Africa and Independence. Independence and then what? What about all the crooks and petty thieves and just plain idiots who will come into power to steal and plunder the same as before—only now they will be black and do it in the name of the new Independence—You cannot answer that.

ASAGAI *(Shouting over her). I live the answer! (Pause)* In my village at home it is the exceptional man who can even read a newspaper ... or who ever *sees* a book at all. I will go home and much of what I will have to say will seem strange to the people of my village ... But I will teach and work and things will happen, slowly and swiftly. At times it will seem that nothing changes at all ... and then again ... the sudden dramatic events which make history leap into the future. And then quiet again. Retrogression even. Guns, murder, revolution. And I even will have moments when I wonder if the quiet was not better than all that death and hatred. But I will look about my village at the illiteracy and disease and ignorance and I will not wonder long. And perhaps ... perhaps I will be a great man ... I mean perhaps I will hold on to the substance of truth and find my way always with the right course ... and perhaps for it I will be butchered in my bed some night by the servants of empire ...

BENEATHA. *The martyr!*

ASAGAI. ... or perhaps I shall live to be a very old man, respected and esteemed in my new nation ... And perhaps I shall hold office and this is what I'm trying to tell you, Alaiyo; perhaps the things I believe now for my country will be wrong and outmoded, and I will not understand and do terrible things to have things my way or merely to keep my power. Don't you see that there will be young men and women, not British soldiers then, but my own black countrymen ... to step out of the shadows some evening and slit my then useless throat? Don't you see they have always been there ... that they always will be. And that such a thing as my own death will be an advance? They who might kill me even ... actually replenish me!

BENEATHA. Oh, Asagai, I know all that.

ASAGAI. Good! Then stop moaning and groaning and tell me what you plan to do.

BENEATHA. Do?

ASAGAI. I have a bit of a suggestion.

BENEATHA. What?

ASAGAI *(Rather quietly for him).* That when it is all over—that you come home with me—

BENEATHA *(Slapping herself on the forehead with exasperation born of misunderstanding).* Oh—Asagai—at this moment you decide to be romantic!

ASAGAI *(Quickly understanding the misunderstanding).* My dear, young creature of the New World—I do not mean across the city—I mean across the ocean; home—to Africa.

BENEATHA *(Slowly understanding and turning to him with murmured amazement).* To—to Nigeria?

ASAGAI. Yes! . . . *(Smiling and lifting his arms playfully)* Three hundred years later the African Prince rose up out of the seas and swept the maiden back across the middle passage[15] over which her ancestors had come—

BENEATHA *(Unable to play).* Nigeria?

ASAGAI. Nigeria. Home. *(Coming to her with genuine romantic flippancy)* I will show you our mountains and our stars; and give you cool drinks from gourds and teach you the old songs and the ways of our people—and, in time, we will pretend that—*(Very softly)*—you have only been away for a day—

(She turns her back to him, thinking. He swings her around and takes her full in his arms in a long embrace which proceeds to passion)

BENEATHA *(Pulling away).* You're getting me all mixed up—

ASAGAI. Why?

BENEATHA. Too many things—too many things have happened today. I must sit down and think. I don't know what I feel about anything right this minute.

(She promptly sits down and props her chin on her fist)

ASAGAI *(Charmed).* All right, I shall leave you. No—don't get up. *(Touching her, gently, sweetly)* Just sit awhile and think . . . Never be afraid to sit awhile and think. *(He goes to door and looks at her)* How often I have looked at you and said, "Ah—so this is what the New World hath finally wrought . . ."

(He exits. Beneatha sits on alone. Presently Walter enters from his room and starts to rummage through things, feverishly looking for something. She looks up and turns in her seat)

BENEATHA *(Hissingly).* Yes—just look at what the New World hath wrought! . . . Just look! *(She gestures with bitter disgust)* There he is! *Monsieur le petit bourgeois noir*[16]—himself! There he is—Symbol of a Rising Class! Entrepreneur! Titan of the system! *(Walter ignores her completely and continues frantically and destructively looking for something and hurling things to floor and tearing things out of their place in his search. Beneatha ignores the eccentricity of his actions and goes on with the*

---

[15]Passage of the Atlantic Ocean through which African slaves were transported to America.

[16]*Monsieur le petit bourgeois noir* (French): Mr. Black Middle Class.

monologue of insult) Did you dream of yachts on Lake Michigan, Brother? Did you see yourself on that Great Day sitting down at the Conference Table, surrounded by all the mighty bald-headed men in America? All halted, waiting, breathless, waiting for your pronouncements on industry? Waiting for you—Chairman of the Board? *(Walter finds what he is looking for—a small piece of white paper—and pushes it in his pocket and puts on his coat and rushes out without ever having looked at her. She shouts after him)* I look at you and I see the final triumph of stupidity in the world!

(The door slams and she returns to just sitting again. Ruth comes quickly out of Mama's room)

RUTH. Who was that?

BENEATHA. Your husband.

RUTH. Where did he go?

BENEATHA. Who knows—maybe he has an appointment at U.S. Steel.

RUTH *(Anxiously, with frightened eyes).* You didn't say nothing bad to him, did you?

BENEATHA. Bad? Say anything bad to him? No—I told him he was a sweet boy and full of dreams and everything is strictly peachy keen, as the ofay[17] kids say!

(Mama enters from her bedroom. She is lost, vague, trying to catch hold, to make some sense of her former command of the world, but it still eludes her. A sense of waste overwhelms her gait; a measure of apology rides on her shoulders. She goes to her plant, which has remained on the table, looks at it, picks it up and takes it to the window sill and sits it outside, and she stands and looks at it a long moment. Then she closes the window, straightens her body with effort and turns around to her children)

MAMA. Well—ain't it a mess in here, though? *(A false cheerfulness, a beginning of something).* I guess we all better stop moping around and get some work done. All this unpacking and everything we got to do. *(Ruth raises her head slowly in response to the sense of the line; and Beneatha in similar manner turns very slowly to look at her mother)* One of you all better call the moving people and tell 'em not to come.

RUTH. Tell 'em not to come?

MAMA. Of course, baby. Ain't no need in 'em coming all the way here and having to go back. They charges for that too. *(She sits down, fingers to her brow, thinking)* Lord, ever since I was a little girl, I always remembers

---

[17]Slang for white.

people saying, "Lena—Lena Eggleston, you aims too high all the time. You needs to slow down and see life a little more like it is. Just slow down some." That's what they always used to say down home—"Lord, that Lena Eggleston is a high-minded thing. She'll get her due one day!"

RUTH. No, Lena . . .

MAMA. Me and Big Walter just didn't never learn right.

RUTH. Lena, no! We gotta go. Bennie—tell her . . . *(She rises and crosses to Beneatha with her arms outstretched. Beneatha doesn't respond)* Tell her we can still move . . . the notes ain't but a hundred and twenty-five a month. We got four grown people in this house—we can work . . .

MAMA *(To herself)*. Just aimed too high all the time—

RUTH *(Turning and going to Mama fast—the words pouring out with urgency and desperation)*. Lena—I'll work . . . I'll work twenty hours a day in all the kitchens in Chicago . . . I'll strap my baby on my back if I have to and scrub all the floors in America and wash all the sheets in America if I have to—but we got to move . . . We got to get out of here . . .

(Mama reaches out absently and pats Ruth's hand)

MAMA. No—I sees things differently now. Been thinking 'bout some of the things we could do to fix this place up some. I seen a second-hand bureau over on Maxwell Street just the other day that could fit right there. *(She points to where the new furniture might go. Ruth wanders away from her)* Would need some new handles on it and then a little varnish and then it look like something brand-new. And—we can put up them new curtains in the kitchen . . . Why this place be looking fine. Cheer us all up so that we forget trouble ever came . . . *(To Ruth)* And you could get some nice screens to put up in your room round the baby's bassinet . . . *(She looks at both of them, pleadingly)* Sometimes you just got to know when to give up some things . . . and hold on to what you got.

(Walter enters from the outside, looking spent and leaning against the door, his coat hanging from him)

MAMA. Where you been, son?

WALTER *(Breathing hard)*. Made a call.

MAMA. To who, son?

WALTER. To The Man.

MAMA. What man, baby?

WALTER. The Man, Mama. Don't you know who The Man is?

RUTH. Walter Lee?

WALTER. *The Man.* Like the guys in the streets say—The Man. Captain Boss— Mistuh Charley . . . Old Captain Please Mr. Bossman . . .

BENEATHA *(Suddenly)*. Lindner!

WALTER. That's right! That's good. I told him to come right over.

BENEATHA *(Fiercely, understanding)*. For what? What do you want to see him for!

WALTER *(Looking at his sister)*. We going to do business with him.

MAMA. What you talking 'bout, son?

WALTER. Talking 'bout life, Mama. You all always telling me to see life like it is. Well—I laid in there on my back today . . . and I figured it out. Life just like it is. Who gets and who don't get. *(He sits down with his coat on and laughs)* Mama, you know it's all divided up. Life is. Sure enough. Between the takers and the "tooken." *(He laughs)* I've figured it out finally. *(He looks around at them)* Yeah. Some of us always getting "tooken." *(He laughs)* People like Willy Harris, they don't never get "tooken." And you know why the rest of us do? 'Cause we all mixed up. Mixed up bad. We get to looking 'round for the right and the wrong; and we worry about it and cry about it and stay up nights trying to figure out 'bout the wrong and the right of things all the time . . . And all the time, man, them takers is out there operating, just taking and taking. Willy Harris? Shoot—Willy Harris don't even count. He don't even count in the big scheme of things. But I'll say one thing for old Willy Harris . . . he's taught me something. He's taught me to keep my eye on what counts in this world. Yeah—*(Shouting out a little)* Thanks, Willy!

RUTH. What did you call that man for, Walter Lee?

WALTER. Called him to tell him to come on over to the show. Gonna put on a show for the man. Just what he wants to see. You see, Mama, the man came here today and he told us that them people out there where you want us to move—well they so upset they willing to pay us not to move out there. *(He laughs again)* And—and oh, Mama—you would of been proud of the way me and Ruth and Bennie acted. We told him to get out . . . Lord have mercy! We told the man to get out. Oh, we was some proud folks this afternoon, yeah. *(He lights a cigarette)* We were still full of that old-time stuff . . .

RUTH *(Coming toward him slowly)*. You talking 'bout taking them people's money to keep us from moving in that house?

WALTER. I ain't just talking 'bout it, baby—I'm telling you that's what's going to happen.

BENEATHA. Oh, God! Where is the bottom! Where is the real honest-to-God bottom so he can't go any farther!

WALTER. See—that's the old stuff. You and that boy that was here today. You all want everybody to carry a flag and a spear and sing some marching songs, huh? You wanna spend your life looking into things and trying to find the right and the wrong part, huh? Yeah. You know what's going to happen to that boy someday—he'll find himself sitting in a dungeon, locked in forever—and the takers will have the key! Forget it, baby! There ain't no causes—there ain't nothing but taking in this world, and he who takes most is smartest—and it don't make a damn bit of difference *how*.

MAMA. You making something inside me cry, son. Some awful pain inside me.

WALTER. Don't cry, Mama. Understand. That white man is going to walk in that door able to write checks for more money than we ever had. It's important to him and I'm going to help him . . . I'm going to put on the show, Mama.

MAMA. Son—I come from five generations of people who was slaves and sharecroppers—but ain't nobody in my family never let nobody pay 'em no money that was a way of telling us we wasn't fit to walk the earth. We ain't never been that poor. *(Raising her eves and looking at him)* We ain't never been that dead inside.

BENEATHA. Well—we are dead now. All the talk about dreams and sunlight that goes on in this house. All dead.

WALTER. What's the matter with you all! I didn't make this world! It was give to me this way! Hell, yes, I want me some yachts someday! Yes, I want to hang some real pearls 'round my wife's neck. Ain't she supposed to wear no pearls? Somebody tell me—tell me, who decides which women is suppose to wear pearls in this world. I tell you I am a *man*—and I think my wife should wear some pearls in this world!

(This last line hangs a good while and Walter begins to move about the room. The word "Man" has penetrated his consciousness; he mumbles it to himself repeatedly between strange agitated pauses as he moves about)

MAMA. Baby, how you going to feel on the inside?

WALTER. Fine! . . . Going to feel fine . . . a man . . .

MAMA. You won't have nothing left then, Walter Lee.

WALTER *(Coming to her)*. I'm going to feel fine, Mama. I'm going to look that son-of-a-bitch in the eyes and say—*(He falters)*—and say, "All right, Mr. Lindner—*(He falters even more)*—that's your neighborhood out there. You got the right to keep it like you want. You got the right to have it like you want. Just write the check and—the house is yours." And, and I am going to say—*(His voice almost breaks)* And you—you people just put the money in my hand and you won't have to live next to this bunch of stinking niggers! . . . *(He straightens up and moves away from his mother, walking around the room)* Maybe—maybe I'll just get down on my black knees . . . *(He does so; Ruth and Bennie and Mama watch him in frozen horror)* Captain, Mistuh, Bossman. *(He starts crying)* A-hee-hee-hee! *(Wringing his hands in profoundly anguished imitation)* Yasssssuh! Great White Father, just gi' ussen de money, fo' God's sake, and we's ain't gwine come out deh and dirty up yo' white folks neighborhood . . .

(He breaks down completely; then gets up and goes into the bedroom)

BENEATHA. That is not a man. That is nothing but a toothless rat.

MAMA. Yes—death done come in this here house. *(She is nodding, slowly, reflectively)* Done come walking in my house. On the lips of my children. You what supposed to be my beginning again. You—what supposed to be my harvest. *(To Beneatha)* You—you mourning your brother?

BENEATHA. He's no brother of mine.

MAMA. What you say?

BENEATHA. I said that that individual in that room is no brother of mine.

MAMA. That's what I thought you said. You feeling like you better than he is today? *(Beneatha does not answer)* Yes? What you tell him a minute ago? That he wasn't a man? Yes? You give him up for me? You done wrote his epitaph too—like the rest of the world? Well, who give you the privilege?

BENEATHA. Be on my side for once! You saw what he just did, Mama! You saw him—down on his knees. Wasn't it you who taught me—to despise any man who would do that. Do what he's going to do.

MAMA. Yes—I taught you that. Me and your daddy. But I thought I taught you something else too . . . I thought I taught you to love him.

BENEATHA. Love him? There is nothing left to love.

MAMA. There is always something left to love. And if you ain't learned that, you ain't learned nothing. *(Looking at her)* Have you cried for that boy today? I don't mean for yourself and for the family 'cause we lost the money. I mean for him; what he been through and what it done to him. Child, when do you think is the time to love somebody the most; when they done good and made things easy for everybody? Well then, you ain't through learning—because that ain't the time at all. It's when he's at his lowest and can't believe in hisself 'cause the world done whipped him so. When you starts measuring somebody, measure him right, child, measure him right. Make sure you done taken into account what hills and valleys he come through before he got to wherever he is.

(Travis bursts into the room at the end of the speech, leaving the door open)

TRAVIS. Grandmama—the moving men are downstairs! The truck just pulled up.

MAMA *(Turning and looking at him).* Are they, baby? They downstairs?

(She sighs and sits. Lindner appears in the doorway. He peers in and knocks lightly, to gain attention, and comes in. All turn to look at him)

LINDNER *(Hat and briefcase in hand)*. Uh—hello . . . *(Ruth crosses mechanically to the bedroom door and opens it and lets it swing open freely and slowly as the lights come up on* Walter *within, still in his coat, sitting at the far corner of the room. He looks up and out through the room to Lindner)*
RUTH. He's here.

(A long minute passes and Walter slowly gets up)

LINDNER *(Coming to the table with efficiency, putting his briefcase on the table and starting to unfold papers and unscrew fountain pens)*. Well, I certainly was glad to hear from you people. *(Walter has begun the trek out of the room, slowly and awkwardly, rather like a small boy, passing the back of his sleeve across his mouth from time to time)* Life can really be so much simpler than people let it be most of the time. Well—with whom do I negotiate? You, Mrs. Younger, or your son here? *(Mama sits with her hands folded on her lap and her eyes closed as Walter advances. Travis goes close to Lindner and looks at the papers curiously)* Just some official papers, sonny.
RUTH. Travis, you go downstairs.
MAMA *(Opening her eyes and looking into Walter's)*. No. Travis, you stay right here. And you make him understand what you doing, Walter Lee. You teach him good. Like Willy Harris taught you. You show where our five generations done come to. Go ahead, son—
WALTER *(Looks down into his boy's eyes. Travis grins at him merrily and Walter draws him beside him with his arm lightly around his shoulders)*. Well, Mr. Lindner *(Beneatha turns away)* We called you—*(There is a profound, simple groping quality in his speech)*—because, well, me and my family *(He looks around and shifts from one foot to the other)* Well—we are very plain people . . .
LINDNER. Yes—
WALTER. I mean—I have worked as a chauffeur most of my life—and my wife here, she does domestic work in people's kitchens. So does my mother. I mean—we are plain people . . .
LINDER. Yes, Mr. Younger—
WALTER *(Really like a small boy, looking down at his shoes and then up at the man)*. And—uh—well, my father, well, he was a laborer most of his life.
LINDNER *(Absolutely confused)*. Uh, yes—
WALTER *(Looking down at his toes once again)*. My father almost beat a man to death once because this man called him a bad name or something, you know what I mean?

LINDNER. No, I'm afraid I don't.

WALTER *(Finally straightening up)*. Well, what I mean is that we come from people who had a lot of pride. I mean—we are very proud people. And that's my sister over there and she's going to be a doctor—and we are very proud—

LINDNER. Well—I am sure that is very nice, but—

WALTER *(Starting to cry and facing the man eye to eye)*. What I am telling you is that we called you over here to tell you that we are very proud and that this is—this is my son, who makes the sixth generation of our family in this country, and that we have all thought about your offer and we have decided to move into our house because my father—my father—he earned it. *(Mama has her eyes closed and is rocking back and forth as though she were in church, with her head nodding the amen yes)* We don't want to make no trouble for nobody or fight no causes—but we will try to be good neighbors. That's all we got to say. *(He looks the man absolutely in the eyes)* We don't want your money.

(He turns and walks away from the man)

LINDNER *(Looking around at all of them)*. I take it then that you have decided to occupy.

BENEATHA. That's what the man said.

LINDNER *(To Mama in her reverie)*. Then I would like to appeal to you, Mrs. Younger. You are older and wiser and understand things better I am sure . . .

MAMA *(Rising)*. I am afraid you don't understand. My son said we was going to move and there ain't nothing left for me to say. *(Shaking her head with double meaning)* You know how these young folks is nowadays, mister. Can't do a thing with 'em. Good-bye.

LINDNER *(Folding up his materials)*. Well—if you are that final about it . . . There is nothing left for me to say. *(He finishes. He is almost ignored by the family, who are concentrating on Walter Lee. At the door Lindner halts and looks around)* I sure hope you people know what you're doing.

(He shakes his head and exits)

RUTH *(Looking around and coming to life)*. Well, for God's sake—if the moving men are here—LET'S GET THE HELL OUT OF HERE!

MAMA *(Into action)*. Ain't it the truth! Look at all this here mess. Ruth, put Travis' good jacket on him . . . Walter Lee, fix your tie and tuck your shirt in, you look just like somebody's hoodlum. Lord have mercy, where is my plant? *(She flies to get it amid the general bustling of the family, who are deliberately trying to ignore the nobility of the past moment)* You all start on down . . . Travis child, don't go empty-handed . . . Ruth, where did I put that box with my skillets in it? I want to be in charge of it myself . . . I'm going to make us the biggest dinner we ever ate tonight . . . Beneatha, what's the matter with them stockings? Pull them things up, girl . . .

(The family starts to file out as two moving men appear and begin to carry out the heavier pieces of furniture, bumping into the family as they move about)

BENEATHA. Mama, Asagai—asked me to marry him today and go to Africa—
MAMA *(In the middle of her getting-ready activity)*. He did? You ain't old enough to marry nobody—*(Seeing the moving men lifting one of her chairs precariously)* Darling, that ain't no bale of cotton, please handle it so we can sit in it again. I had that chair twenty-five years . . .

(The movers sigh with exasperation and go on with their work)

BENEATHA *(Girlishly and unreasonably trying to pursue the conversation)*. To go to Africa, Mama—be a doctor in Africa . . .
MAMA *(Distracted)*. Yes, baby—
WALTER. Africa! What he want you to go to Africa for?
BENEATHA. To practice there . . .
WALTER. Girl, if you don't get all them silly ideas out your head! You better marry yourself a man with some loot . . .
BENEATHA *(Angrily, precisely as in the first scene of the play)*. What have you got to do with who I marry!
WALTER. Plenty. Now I think George Murchison—

(He and Beneatha go out yelling at each other vigorously; Beneatha is heard saying that she would not marry George Murchison if he were Adam and she were Eve, etc. The anger is loud and real till their voices diminish. Ruth stands at the door and turns to Mama and smiles knowingly)

MAMA *(Fixing her hat at last)*. Yeah—they something all right, my children . . .
RUTH. Yeah—they're something. Let's go, Lena.
MAMA *(Stalling, starting to look around at the house)*. Yes—I'm coming. Ruth—
RUTH. Yes?
MAMA *(Quietly, woman to woman)*. He finally come into his manhood today, didn't he? Kind of like a rainbow after the rain . . .
RUTH *(Biting her lip lest her own pride explode in front of Mama)*. Yes, Lena.

(Walter's voice calls for them raucously)

MAMA *(Waving Ruth out vaguely)*. All right, honey—go on down. I be down directly.

(Ruth hesitates, then exits. Mama stands, at last alone in the living room, her plant on the table before her as the lights start to come down. She looks around at all the walls and ceilings and suddenly, despite herself, while the children call below, a great heaving thing rises in her and she puts her fist to her mouth, takes a final desperate look, pulls her coat about her, pats her hat and goes out. The lights dim down. The door opens and she comes back in, grabs her plant, and goes out for the last time)

CURTAIN

[1959]

Henrik Ibsen
[1828–1906]

The playwright HENRIK IBSEN *was born into a provincial Norwegian family. As a young man, he studied medicine but soon began working as a stage manager at a local theater. While serving as the artistic director for the National Theater in Oslo, he wrote his first plays. Unfortunately, he met with little early success in his homeland. Consequently, he moved to Italy and to Germany, where he lived for twenty-seven years.*

During his early career, Ibsen wrote verse plays based on Norwegian myth and history, including Brand *(1866) and* Peer Gynt *(1867). He soon turned his attention to contemporary social problems and to dramatic realism. Dramatic realism endeavors to portray onstage an accurate representation of everyday life. These plays depict the details of contemporary existence through their dialogue, setting, and costumes; in doing so, they seek to produce the illusion of objectivity for their audiences. Created in opposition to the well-made play and to the popular melodrama, realism resisted the simple cause-and-effect plot structure and the sentimentality of those popular dramatic forms.*

Ibsen's three-act realist drama A Doll's House *(1879) addresses the "woman problem." As women became increasingly public and political during the nineteenth century, society grappled with the radical transformation of feminine roles—and with its consequent effects on the private sphere of the home. A Doll's House engages with these concerns by staging the marriage of Torvald and Nora Helmer in which the patronizing Torvald treats his wife Nora like a mindless child. This fictional marriage asked audiences to think critically about the oppressive roles to which women are confined. When Nora discovers her husband is a hypocrite, she leaves him, slamming the door in the final act of the play. Nineteenth century audiences, shocked by this conclusion, were challenged to speculate on Nora's fate. Audiences and readers are still intrigued by what happens to Nora once she leaves her home. (In a satirical sketch, the English comedy troupe Monty Python hypothesized that Nora walked out of the door . . . only to be met on the other side by a marching band, which promptly ran over her.)*

Like A Doll's House, *much of Ibsen's later work tackled social problems and the individuals affected by them. The plays—many of which continue to be produced regularly—include* An Enemy of the People *(1882);* The Wild Duck *(1884);* Hedda Gabler *(1890); and* The Master Builder *(1892). During the late nineteenth and early twentieth centuries, Ibsen's drama actively contributed to social debate. His critiques of society moved beyond the realm of the strictly artistic; they powerfully influenced society and politics. In fact, the term "Ibsenism" became a catchphrase for the critique of society, even as the playwright himself avoided politics. Notably, the content of these plays was frequently shocking and often bravely tackled subjects once taboo on the stage. For instance, Ghosts (1881) critiqued religious values and addressed frankly the issue of venereal disease.*

Ibsen has had a profound and enduring effect on modern drama. His contemporaries rapidly embraced his dramatic innovations, and his work was quickly translated and produced throughout Europe and the United States. He died in Norway in 1906.

A Doll's House

HENRIK IBSEN

DRAMATIS PERSONÆ

TORVALD HELMER.
NORA,   his wife.
DR. RANK.
MRS. LINDE.
NILS KROGSTAD.
THE HELMER'S THREE YOUNG CHILDREN.
ANNE,   their nurse.
A HOUSEMAID.
A PORTER.

SCENE

The action takes place in HELMER'S *house.*

ACT I

SCENE—*A room furnished comfortably and tastefully but not extravagantly. At the back a door to the right leads to the entrance hall; another to the left leads to* HELMER'S *study. Between the doors stands a piano. In the middle of the left-hand wall is a door and beyond a window. Near the window are a round table, armchairs and a small sofa. In the right-hand wall, at the farther end, another door; and on the same side, nearer the footlights, a stove, two easy chairs and a rocking chair; between the stove and the door a small table. Engravings on the walls; a cabinet with china and other small objects; a small bookcase with well-bound books. The floors are carpeted, and a fire burns in the stove. It is winter.*

A bell rings in the hall; shortly afterward the door is heard to open. Enter NORA, *humming a tune and in high spirits. She is in outdoor dress and carries a number of parcels; these she lays on the table to the right. She leaves the outer door open after her, and through it is seen a* PORTER *who is carrying a Christmas tree and a basket, which he gives to the* MAID *who has opened the door.*

NORA. Hide the Christmas tree carefully, Helen. Be sure the children do not see it till this evening, when it is dressed. (*To the* PORTER, *taking out her purse.*) How much?

POR. Sixpence.

NORA. There is a shilling. No, keep the change. (*The* PORTER *thanks her and goes out.* NORA *shuts the door. She is laughing to herself as she takes off her hat and coat. She takes a packet of macaroons from her pocket and eats one or two, then goes cautiously to her husband's door and listens.*) Yes, he is in. (*Still humming, she goes to the table on the right.*)

HEL. (*calls out from his room*). Is that my little lark twittering out there?

NORA (*busy opening some of the parcels*). Yes, it is!

HEL. Is it my little squirrel bustling about?

NORA. Yes!

HEL. When did my squirrel come home?

NORA. Just now. (*Puts the bag of macaroons into her pocket and wipes her mouth.*) Come in here, Torvald, and see what I have bought.

HEL. Don't disturb me. (*A little later he opens the door and looks into the room, pen in hand.*) Bought, did you say? All these things? Has my little spend-thrift been wasting money again?

NORA. Yes, but, Torvald, this year we really can let ourselves go a little. This is the first Christmas that we have not needed to economize.

HEL. Still, you know, we can't spend money recklessly.

NORA. Yes, Torvald, we may be a wee bit more reckless now, mayn't we? Just a tiny wee bit! You are going to have a big salary and earn lots and lots of money.

HEL. Yes, after the new year; but then it will be a whole quarter before the salary is due.

NORA. Pooh! We can borrow till then.

HEL. Nora! (*Goes up to her and takes her playfully by the ear.*) The same little featherhead! Suppose, now, that I borrowed fifty pounds today and you spent it all in the Christmas week and then on New Year's Eve a slate fell on my head and killed me and——

NORA (*putting her hands over his mouth*). Oh! don't say such horrid things.

HEL. Still, suppose that happened,—what then?

NORA. If that were to happen, I don't suppose I should care whether I owed money or not.

HEL. Yes, but what about the people who had lent it?

NORA. They? Who would bother about them? I should not know who they were.

HEL. That is like a woman! But seriously, Nora, you know what I think about that. No debt, no borrowing. There can be no freedom or beauty about a home life that depends on borrowing and debt. We two have kept bravely on the straight road so far, and we will go on the same way for the short time longer that there need be any struggle.

NORA (*moving toward the stove*). As you please, Torvald.

HEL. (*following her*). Come, come, my little skylark must not droop her wings. What is this! Is my little squirrel out of temper? (*Taking out his purse.*) Nora, what do you think I have got here?

NORA (*turning round quickly*). Money!

HEL. There you are. (*Gives her some money.*) Do you think I don't know what a lot is wanted for housekeeping at Christmas time?

NORA (*counting*). Ten shillings—a pound—two pounds! Thank you, thank you, Torvald; that will keep me going for a long time.

HEL. Indeed it must.

NORA. Yes, yes, it will. But come here and let me show you what I have bought. And all so cheap! Look, here is a new suit for Ivar and a sword, and a horse and a trumpet for Bob, and a doll and dolly's bedstead for Emmy—they are very plain, but anyway she will soon break them in pieces. And here are dress lengths and handkerchiefs for the maids; old Anne ought really to have something better.

HEL. And what is in this parcel?

NORA (*crying out*). No, no! You mustn't see that till this evening.

HEL. Very well. But now tell me, you extravagant little person, what would you like for yourself?

NORA. For myself? Oh, I am sure I don't want anything.

HEL. Yes, but you must. Tell me something reasonable that you would particularly like to have.

NORA. No, I really can't think of anything—unless, Torvald——

HEL. Well?

NORA (*playing with his coat buttons and without raising her eyes to his*). If you really want to give me something, you might—you might——

HEL. Well, out with it!

NORA (*speaking quickly*). You might give me money, Torvald. Only just as much as you can afford; and then one of these days I will buy something with it.

HEL. But, Nora——

NORA. Oh, do! dear Torvald; please, please do! Then I will wrap it up in beautiful gilt paper and hang it on the Christmas tree. Wouldn't that be fun?

HEL. What are little people called that are always wasting money?

NORA. Spendthrifts—I know. Let us do as I suggest, Torvald, and then I shall have time to think what I am most in want of. That is a very sensible plan, isn't it?

HEL. (*smiling*). Indeed it is—that is to say, if you were really to save out of the money I give you and then really buy something for yourself. But if you spend it all on the housekeeping and any number of unnecessary things, then I merely have to pay up again.

NORA. Oh, but, Torvald——

HEL. You can't deny it, my dear little Nora. (*Puts his arm around her waist.*) It's a sweet little spendthrift, but she uses up a deal of money. One would hardly believe how expensive such little persons are!

NORA. It's a shame to say that. I do really save all I can.

HEL. (*laughing*). That's very true—all you can. But you can't save anything!

NORA (*smiling quietly and happily*). You haven't any idea how many expenses we skylarks and squirrels have, Torvald.

HEL. You are an odd little soul. Very like your father. You always find some new way of wheedling money out of me, and as soon as you have got it it seems to melt in your hands. You never know where it has gone. Still, one must take you as you are. It is in the blood; for indeed it is true that you can inherit these things, Nora.

NORA. Ah, I wish I had inherited many of Papa's qualities.

HEL. And I would not wish you to be anything but just what you are, my sweet little skylark. But, do you know, it strikes me that you are looking rather—what shall I say?—rather uneasy today.

NORA. Do I?

HEL. You do, really. Look straight at me.

NORA (*looks at him*). Well?

HEL. (*wagging his finger at her*). Hasn't Miss Sweet Tooth been breaking rules in town today?

NORA. No; what makes you think that?

HEL. Hasn't she paid a visit to the confectioner's?

NORA. No, I assure you, Torvald——

HEL. Not been nibbling sweets?

NORA. No, certainly not.

HEL. Not even taken a bite at a macaroon or two?

NORA. No, Torvald, I assure you, really——

HEL. There, there, of course I was only joking.

NORA (*going to the table on the right*). I should not think of going against your wishes.

HEL. No, I am sure of that; besides, you gave me your word. (*Going up to her.*) Keep your little Christmas secrets to yourself, my darling. They will all be revealed tonight when the Christmas tree is lit, no doubt.

NORA. Did you remember to invite Doctor Rank?

HEL. No. But there is no need; as a matter of course he will come to dinner with us. However, I will ask him when he comes in this morning. I have ordered some good wine. Nora, you can't think how I am looking forward to this evening.

NORA. So am I! And how the children will enjoy themselves, Torvald!

HEL. It is splendid to feel that one has a perfectly safe appointment and a big enough income. It's delightful to think of, isn't it?

NORA. It's wonderful!

HEL. Do you remember last Christmas? For a full three weeks before hand you shut yourself up every evening till long after midnight, making ornaments for the Christmas tree and all the other fine things that were to be a surprise to us. It was the dullest three weeks I ever spent!

NORA. I didn't find it dull.

HEL. (*smiling*). But there was precious little result, Nora.

NORA. Oh, you shouldn't tease me about that again. How could I help the cat's going in and tearing everything to pieces?

HEL. Of course you couldn't, poor little girl. You had the best of intentions to please us all, and that's the main thing. But it is a good thing that our hard times are over.

NORA. Yes, it is really wonderful.

HEL. This time I needn't sit here and be dull all alone and you needn't ruin your dear eyes and your pretty little hands——

NORA (*clapping her hands*). No, Torvald, I needn't any longer, need I! It's wonderfully lovely to hear you say so! (*Taking his arm.*) Now I will tell you how I have been thinking we ought to arrange things, Torvald. As soon as Christmas is over——(*A bell rings in the hall.*) There's the bell. (*She tidies the room a little.*) There's someone at the door. What a nuisance!

HEL. If it is a caller, remember I am not at home.

MAID (*in the doorway*). A lady to see you, ma'am—a stranger.

NORA. Ask her to come in.

MAID (*to* HELMER). The doctor came at the same time, sir.

HEL. Did he go straight into my room?

MAID. Yes sir.

(HELMER *goes into his room. The* MAID *ushers in* MRS. LINDE, *who is in traveling dress, and shuts the door.*)

MRS. L. (*in a dejected and timid voice*). How do you do, Nora?

NORA (*doubtfully*). How do you do——

MRS. L. You don't recognize me, I suppose.

NORA. No, I don't know—yes, to be sure, I seem to——(*Suddenly.*) Yes! Christine! Is it really you?

MRS. L. Yes, it is I.

NORA. Christine! To think of my not recognizing you! And yet how could I? (*In a gentle voice.*) How you have altered, Christine!

MRS. L. Yes, I have indeed. In nine, ten long years——

NORA. Is it so long since we met? I suppose it is. The last eight years have been a happy time for me, I can tell you. And so now you have come into the town and have taken this long journey in winter—that was plucky of you.

MRS. L. I arrived by steamer this morning.

NORA. To have some fun at Christmas time, of course. How delightful! We will have such fun together! But take off your things. You are not cold, I hope. (*Helps her.*) Now we will sit down by the stove and be cozy. No, take this armchair; I will sit here in the rocking chair. (*Takes her hands.*) Now you look like your old self again; it was only the first moment——You are a little paler, Christine, and perhaps a little thinner.

MRS. L. And much, much older, Nora.

NORA. Perhaps a little older; very, very little; certainly not much. (*Stops suddenly and speaks seriously*). What a thoughtless creature I am, chattering away like this. My poor, dear Christine, do forgive me.

MRS. L. What do you mean, Nora?

NORA (*gently*). Poor Christine, you are a widow.

MRS. L. Yes; it is three years ago now.

NORA. Yes, I knew; I saw it in the papers. I assure you, Christine, I meant ever so often to write to you at the time, but I always put it off and something always prevented me.

MRS. L. I quite understand, dear.

NORA. It was very bad of me, Christine. Poor thing, how you must have suffered. And he left you nothing?

MRS. L. No.

NORA. And no children?

MRS. L. No.

NORA. Nothing at all, then?

MRS. L. Not even any sorrow or grief to live upon.

NORA (*looking incredulously at her*). But, Christine, is that possible?

MRS. L. (*smiles sadly and strokes her hair*). It sometimes happens, Nora.

NORA. So you are quite alone. How dreadfully sad that must be. I have three lovely children. You can't see them just now, for they are out with their nurse. But now you must tell me all about it.

MRS. L. No, no; I want to hear about you.

NORA. No, you must begin. I mustn't be selfish today; today I must only think of your affairs. But there is one thing I must tell you. Do you know we have just had a great piece of good luck?

MRS. L. No, what is it?

NORA. Just fancy, my husband has been made manager of the bank!

MRS. L. Your husband? What good luck!

NORA. Yes, tremendous! A barrister's profession is such an uncertain thing, especially if he won't undertake unsavory cases; and naturally Torvald has never been willing to do that, and I quite agree with him. You may imagine how pleased we are! He is to take up his work in the bank at the new year, and then he will have a big salary and lots of commissions. For the future we can live quite differently—we can do just as we like. I feel so relieved and so happy, Christine! It will be splendid to have heaps of money and not need to have any anxiety, won't it?

MRS. L. Yes, anyhow I think it would be delightful to have what one needs.

NORA. No, not only what one needs but heaps and heaps of money.

MRS. L. (*smiling*). Nora, Nora, haven't you learned sense yet? In our schooldays you were a great spendthrift.

NORA (*laughing*). Yes, that is what Torvald says now. (*Wags her finger at her.*) But "Nora, Nora" is not so silly as you think. We have not been in a position for me to waste money. We have both had to work.

MRS. L. You too?

NORA. Yes; odds and ends, needlework, crochet work, embroidery and that kind of thing. (*Dropping her voice.*) And other things as well. You know Torvald left his office when we were married? There was no prospect of promotion there, and he had to try and earn more than before. But during the first year he overworked himself dreadfully. You see, he had to make money every way he could; and he worked early and late; but he couldn't stand it and fell dreadfully ill, and the doctors said it was necessary for him to go south.

MRS. L. You spent a whole year in Italy, didn't you?

NORA. Yes. It was no easy matter to get away, I can tell you. It was just after Ivar was born; but naturally we had to go. It was a wonderfully beautiful journey, and it saved Torvald's life. But it cost a tremendous lot of money, Christine.

MRS. L. So I should think.

NORA. It cost about two hundred and fifty pounds. That's a lot, isn't it?

MRS. L. Yes, and in emergencies like that it is lucky to have the money.

NORA. I ought to tell you that we had it from Papa.

MRS. L. Oh, I see. It was just about that time that he died, wasn't it?

NORA. Yes; and, just think of it, I couldn't go and nurse him. I was expecting little Ivar's birth every day and I had my poor sick Torvald to look after. My dear, kind father—I never saw him again, Christine. That was the saddest time I have known since our marriage.

MRS. L. I know how fond you were of him. And then you went off to Italy?

NORA. Yes; you see, we had money then, and the doctors insisted on our going, so we started a month later.

MRS. L. And your husband came back quite well?

NORA. As sound as a bell!

MRS. L. But—the doctor?

NORA. What doctor?

MRS. L. I thought your maid said the gentleman who arrived here just as I did was the doctor.

NORA. Yes, that was Doctor Rank, but he doesn't come here professionally. He is our greatest friend and comes in at least once every day. No, Torvald has not had an hour's illness since then, and our children are strong and healthy and so am I. (*Jumps up and claps her hands.*) Christine! Christine! It's good to be alive and happy! But how horrid of me; I am talking of nothing but my own affairs. (*Sits on a stool near her and rests her arms on her knees.*) You mustn't be angry with me. Tell me, is it really true that you did not love your husband? Why did you marry him?

MRS. L. My mother was alive then and was bedridden and helpless, and I had to provide for my two younger brothers; so I did not think I was justified in refusing his offer.

NORA. No, perhaps you were quite right. He was rich at that time, then?

MRS. L. I believe he was quite well off. But his business was a precarious one, and when he died it all went to pieces and there was nothing left.

NORA. And then?

MRS. L. Well, I had to turn my hand to anything I could find—first a small shop, then a small school and so on. The last three years have seemed like one long working day, with no rest. Now it is at an end, Nora. My poor mother needs me no more, for she is gone; and the boys do not need me either; they have got situations and can shift for themselves.

NORA. What a relief you must feel it.

MRS. L. No indeed; I only feel my life unspeakably empty. No one to live for any more. (*Gets up restlessly.*) That was why I could not stand the life in my little backwater any longer. I hope it may be easier here to find something which will busy me and occupy my thoughts. If only I could have the good luck to get some regular work—office work of some kind——

NORA. But, Christine, that is so frightfully tiring, and you look tired out now. You had far better go away to some watering place.

MRS. L. (*walking to the window*). I have no father to give me money for a journey, Nora.

NORA (*rising*). Oh, don't be angry with me.

MRS. L. (*going up to her*). It is you that must not be angry with me, dear. The worst of a position like mine is that it makes one so bitter. No one to work for and yet obliged to be always on the lookout for chances. One must live, and so one becomes selfish. When you told me of the happy turn your fortunes have taken—you will hardly believe it—I was delighted not so much on your account as on my own.

NORA. How do you mean? Oh, I understand. You mean that perhaps Torvald could get you something to do.

MRS. L. Yes, that was what I was thinking of.

NORA. He must, Christine. Just leave it to me; I will broach the subject very cleverly—I will think of something that will please him very much. It will make me so happy to be of some use to you.

MRS. L. How kind you are, Nora, to be so anxious to help me! It is doubly kind in you, for you know so little of the burdens and troubles of life.

NORA. I? I know so little of them?

MRS. L. (*smiling*). My dear! Small household cares and that sort of thing! You are a child, Nora.

NORA (*tosses her head and crosses the stage*). You ought not to be so superior.

MRS. L. No?

NORA. You are just like the others. They all think that I am incapable of anything really serious——

MRS. L. Come, come.

NORA. —that I have gone through nothing in this world of cares.

MRS. L. But, my dear Nora, you have just told me all your troubles.

NORA. Pooh!—those were trifles. (*Lowering her voice.*) I have not told you the important thing.

MRS. L. The important thing? What do you mean?

NORA. You look down upon me altogether, Christine—but you ought not to. You are proud, aren't you, of having worked so hard and so long for your mother?

MRS. L. Indeed, I don't look down on anyone. But it is true that I am both proud and glad to think that I was privileged to make the end of my mother's life almost free from care.

NORA. And you are proud to think of what you have done for your brothers.

MRS. L. I think I have the right to be.

NORA. I think so too. But now listen to this; I too have something to be proud and glad of.

MRS. L. I have no doubt you have. But what do you refer to?

NORA. Speak low. Suppose Torvald were to hear! He mustn't on any account—no one in the world must know, Christine, except you.

MRS. L. But what is it?

NORA. Come here. (*Pulls her down on the sofa beside her.*) Now I will show you that I too have something to be proud and glad of. It was I who saved Torvald's life.

MRS. L. "Saved"? How?

NORA. I told you about our trip to Italy. Torvald would never have recovered if he had not gone there.

MRS. L. Yes, but your father gave you the necessary funds.

NORA (*smiling*). Yes, that is what Torvald and the others think, but——

MRS. L. But——

NORA. Papa didn't give us a shilling. It was I who procured the money.

MRS. L. You? All that large sum?

NORA. Two hundred and fifty pounds. What do you think of that?

MRS. L. But, Nora, how could you possibly do it? Did you win a prize in the lottery?

NORA (*contemptuously*). In the lottery? There would have been no credit in that.

MRS. L. But where did you get it from, then?

NORA (*humming and smiling with an air of mystery*). Hm, hm! Aha!

MRS. L. Because you couldn't have borrowed it.

NORA. Couldn't I? Why not?

MRS. L. No, a wife cannot borrow without her husband's consent.

NORA (*tossing her head*). Oh, if it is a wife who has any head for business—a wife who has the wit to be a little bit clever——

MRS. L. I don't understand it at all, Nora.

NORA. There is no need you should. I never said I had borrowed the money. I may have got it some other way. (*Lies back on the sofa.*) Perhaps I got it from some other admirers. When anyone is as attractive as I am——

MRS. L. You are a mad creature.

NORA. Now you know you're full of curiosity, Christine.

MRS. L. Listen to me, Nora dear. Haven't you been a little bit imprudent?

NORA (*sits up straight*). Is it imprudent to save your husband's life?

MRS. L. It seems to me imprudent, without his knowledge, to——

NORA. But it was absolutely necessary that he should not know! My goodness, can't you understand that? It was necessary he should have no idea what a dangerous condition he was in. It was to me that the doctors came and said that his life was in danger and that the only thing to save him was to live in the south. Do you suppose I didn't try, first of all, to get what I wanted as if it were for myself? I told him how much I should love to travel abroad like other young wives; I tried tears and entreaties with him; I told him that he ought to remember the condition I was in and that he ought to be kind and indulgent to me; I even hinted that he might raise a loan. That nearly made him angry, Christine. He said I was thoughtless and that it was his duty as my husband not to indulge me in my whims and caprices—as I believe he called them. Very well, I thought, you must be saved—and that was how I came to devise a way out of the difficulty.

MRS. L. And did your husband never get to know from your father that the money had not come from him?

NORA. No, never. Papa died just at that time. I had meant to let him into the secret and beg him never to reveal it. But he was so ill then—alas, there never was any need to tell him.

MRS. L. And since then have you never told your secret to your husband?

NORA. Good heavens, no! How could you think so? A man who has such strong opinions about these things! And besides, how painful and humiliating it would be for Torvald, with his manly independence, to know that he owed me anything! It would upset our mutual relations altogether; our beautiful happy home would no longer be what it is now.

MRS. L. Do you mean never to tell him about it?

NORA (*meditatively and with a half-smile*). Yes—someday, perhaps, after many years, when I am no longer as nice looking as I am now. Don't laugh at me! I mean, of course, when Torvald is no longer as devoted to me as he is now; when my dancing and dressing-up and reciting have palled on him; then it may be a good thing to have something in reserve——(*Breaking off.*) What nonsense! That time will never come. Now what do you think of my great secret, Christine? Do you still think I am of no use? I can tell you, too, that this affair has caused me a lot of worry. It has been by no means easy for me to meet my engagements punctually. I may tell you that there is something that is called, in business, quarterly interest and another thing called payment in installments, and it is always so dreadfully difficult to manage them. I have had to save a little here and there, where I could, you understand. I have not been able to put aside much from my housekeeping money, for Torvald must have a good table. I couldn't let my children be shabbily dressed; I have felt obliged to use up all he gave me for them, the sweet little darlings!

MRS. L. So it has all had to come out of your own necessaries of life, poor Nora?

NORA. Of course. Besides, I was the one responsible for it. Whenever Torvald has given me money for new dresses and such things I have never spent more than half of it; I have always bought the simplest and cheapest things. Thank heaven any clothes look well on me, and so Torvald has never noticed it. But it was often very hard on me, Christine—because it is delightful to be really well dressed, isn't it?

MRS. L. Quite so.

NORA. Well, then I have found other ways of earning money. Last winter I was lucky enough to get a lot of copying to do, so I locked myself up and sat writing every evening until quite late at night. Many a time I was desperately tired, but all the same it was a tremendous pleasure to sit there working and earning money. It was like being a man.

MRS. L. How much have you been able to pay off in that way?

NORA. I can't tell you exactly. You see, it is very difficult to keep an account of a business matter of that kind. I only know that I have paid every penny that I could scrape together. Many a time I was at my wits' end. (*Smiles.*) Then I used to sit here and imagine that a rich old gentleman had fallen in love with me——

MRS. L. What! Who was it?

NORA. Be quiet!—that he had died and that when his will was opened it contained, written in big letters, the instruction: "The lovely Mrs. Nora Helmer is to have all I possess paid over to her at once in cash."

MRS. L. But, my dear Nora—who could the man be?

NORA. Good gracious, can't you understand? There was no old gentleman at all; it was only something that I used to sit here and imagine, when I couldn't think of any way of procuring money. But it's all the same now; the tiresome old person can stay where he is as far as I am concerned; I don't care about him or his will either, for I am free from care now. (*Jumps up.*) My goodness, it's delightful to think of, Christine! Free from care! To be able to be free from care, quite free from care; to be able to play and romp with the children; to be able to keep the house beautifully and have everything just as Torvald likes it! And, think of it, soon the spring will come and the big blue sky! Perhaps we shall be able to take a little trip—perhaps I shall see the sea again! Oh, it's a wonderful thing to be alive and be happy. (*A bell is heard in the hall.*)

MRS. L. (*rising*). There is the bell; perhaps I had better go.

NORA. No, don't go; no one will come in here; it is sure to be for Torvald.

SERVANT (*at the hall door*). Excuse me, ma'am—there is a gentleman to see the master, and as the doctor is with him——

NORA. Who is it?

KROG. (*at the door*). It is I, Mrs. Helmer. (MRS. LINDE *starts, trembles and turns to the window.*)

NORA (*takes a step toward him and speaks in a strained, low voice*). You? What is it? What do you want to see my husband about?

KROG. Bank business—in a way. I have a small post in the bank, and I hear your husband is to be our chief now.

NORA. Then it is——

KROG. Nothing but dry business matters, Mrs. Helmer; absolutely nothing else.

NORA. Be so good as to go into the study then. (*She bows indifferently to him and shuts the door into the hall, then comes back and makes up the fire in the stove.*)

MRS. L. Nora—who was that man?

NORA. A lawyer of the name of Krogstad.

MRS. L. Then it really was he.

NORA. Do you know the man?

MRS. L. I used to—many years ago. At one time he was a solicitor's clerk in our town.

NORA. Yes, he was.

MRS. L. He is greatly altered.

NORA. He made a very unhappy marriage.

MRS. L. He is a widower now, isn't he?

NORA. With several children. There now, it is burning up. (*Shuts the door of the stove and moves the rocking chair aside.*)

MRS. L. They say he carries on various kinds of business.

NORA. Really! Perhaps he does; I don't know anything about it. But don't let us think of business; it is so tiresome.

DR. RANK (*comes out of* HELMER'S *study. Before he shuts the door he calls to him*). No, my dear fellow, I won't disturb you; I would rather go in to your wife for a little while. (*Shuts the door and sees* MRS. LINDE.) I beg your pardon; I am afraid I am disturbing you too.

NORA. No, not at all. (*Introducing him.*) Doctor Rank, Mrs. Linde.

RANK. I have often heard Mrs. Linde's name mentioned here. I think I passed you on the stairs when I arrived, Mrs. Linde?

MRS. L. Yes, I go up very slowly; I can't manage stairs well.

RANK. Ah! Some slight internal weakness?

MRS. L. No, the fact is I have been overworking myself.

RANK. Nothing more than that? Then I suppose you have come to town to amuse yourself with our entertainments?

MRS. L. I have come to look for work.

RANK. Is that a good cure for overwork?

MRS. L. One must live, Doctor Rank.

RANK. Yes, the general opinion seems to be that it is necessary.

NORA. Look here, Doctor Rank—you know you want to live.

RANK. Certainly. However wretched I may feel, I want to prolong the agony as long as possible. All my patients are like that. And so are those who are morally diseased; one of them, and a bad case too, is at this very moment with Helmer——

MRS. L. (*sadly*). Ah!

NORA. Whom do you mean?

RANK. A lawyer of the name of Krogstad, a fellow you don't know at all. He suffers from a diseased moral character, Mrs. Helmer, but even he began talking of its being highly important that he should live.

NORA. Did he? What did he want to speak to Torvald about?

RANK. I have no idea; I only heard that it was something about the bank.

NORA. I didn't know this—what's his name?—Krogstad had anything to do with the bank.

RANK. Yes, he has some sort of appointment there. (*To* MRS. LINDE.) I don't know whether you find also in your part of the world that there are certain people who go zealously snuffing about to smell out moral corruption and, as soon as they have found some, put the person concerned into some lucrative position where they can keep their eye on him. Healthy natures are left out in the cold.

MRS. L. Still I think the sick are those who most need taking care of.

RANK (*shrugging his shoulders*). Yes, there you are. That is the sentiment that is turning society into a sick house.

(NORA, *who has been absorbed in her thoughts, breaks out into smothered laughter and claps her hands.*)

RANK. Why do you laugh at that? Have you any notion what society really is?

NORA. What do I care about tiresome society? I am laughing at something quite different, something extremely amusing. Tell me, Doctor Rank, are all the people who are employed in the bank dependent on Torvald now?

RANK. Is that what you find so extremely amusing?

NORA (*smiling and humming*). That's my affair! (*Walking about the room.*) It's perfectly glorious to think that we have—that Torvald has so much power over so many people. (*Takes the packet from her pocket.*) Doctor Rank, what do you say to a macaroon?

RANK. What, macaroons? I thought they were forbidden here.

NORA. Yes, but these are some Christine gave me.

MRS. L. What! I?

NORA. Oh well, don't be alarmed! You couldn't know that Torvald had forbidden them. I must tell you that he is afraid they will spoil my teeth. But, bah!—once in a way——That's so, isn't it, Doctor Rank? By your leave! (*Puts a macaroon into his mouth.*) You must have one too, Christine. And I shall have one, just a little one—or at most two. (*Walking about.*) I am tremendously happy. There is just one thing in the world now that I should dearly love to do.

RANK. Well, what is that?

NORA. It's something I should dearly love to say if Torvald could hear me.

RANK. Well, why can't you say it?

NORA. No, I daren't; it's so shocking.

MRS. L. Shocking?

RANK. Well, I should not advise you to say it. Still, with us you might. What is it you would so much like to say if Torvald could hear you?

NORA. I should just love to say—Well, I'm damned!

RANK. Are you mad?

MRS. L. Nora dear!

RANK. Say it, here he is!

NORA (*hiding the packet*). Hush! Hush! Hush!

(HELMER *comes out of his room with his coat over his arm and his hat in his hand.*)

NORA. Well, Torvald dear, have you got rid of him?

HEL. Yes, he has just gone.

NORA. Let me introduce you—this is Christine, who has come to town.

HEL. Christine? Excuse me, but I don't know——

NORA. Mrs. Linde, dear; Christine Linde.

HEL. Of course. A school friend of my wife's, I presume?

MRS. L. Yes, we have known each other since then.

NORA. And just think, she has taken a long journey in order to see you.

HEL. What do you mean?

MRS. L. No, really, I——

NORA. Christine is tremendously clever at bookkeeping, and she is frightfully anxious to work under some clever man, so as to perfect herself——

HEL. Very sensible, Mrs. Linde.

NORA. And when she heard you had been appointed manager of the bank—the news was telegraphed, you know—she traveled here as quick as she could. Torvald, I am sure you will be able to do something for Christine, for my sake, won't you?

HEL. Well, it is not altogether impossible. I presume you are a widow, Mrs. Linde?

MRS. L. Yes.

HEL. And have had some experience of bookkeeping?

MRS. L. Yes, a fair amount.

HEL. Ah well, it's very likely I may be able to find something for you.

NORA (*clapping her hands*). What did I tell you?

HEL. You have just come at a fortunate moment, Mrs. Linde.

MRS. L. How am I to thank you?

HEL. There is no need. (*Puts on his coat.*) But today you must excuse me——

RANK. Wait a minute; I will come with you. (*Brings his fur coat from the hall and warms it at the fire.*)

NORA. Don't be long away, Torvald dear.

HEL. About an hour, not more.

NORA. Are you going too, Christine?

MRS. L. (*putting on her cloak*). Yes, I must go and look for a room.

HEL. Oh well, then, we can walk down the street together.

NORA (*helping her*). What a pity it is we are so short of space here; I am afraid it is impossible for us——

MRS. L. Please don't think of it! Good-by, Nora dear, and many thanks.

NORA. Good-by for the present. Of course you will come back this evening. And you too, Doctor Rank. What do you say? If you are well enough? Oh, you must be! Wrap yourself up well. (*They go to the door all talking together. Children's voices are heard on the staircase.*)

NORA. There they are. There they are! (*She runs to open the door. The* NURSE *comes in with the children.*) Come in! Come in! (*Stoops and kisses them.*) Oh, you sweet blessings! Look at them, Christine! Aren't they darlings?

RANK. Don't let us stand here in the draught.

HEL. Come along, Mrs. Linde; the place will only be bearable for a mother now!

(RANK, HELMER *and* MRS. LINDE *go downstairs. The* NURSE *comes forward with the children;* NORA *shuts the hall door.*)

NORA. How fresh and well you look! Such red cheeks!—like apples and roses. (*The children all talk at once while she speaks to them.*) Have you had great fun? That's splendid! What, you pulled both Emmy and Bob along on the sledge? Both at once? That *was* good. You are a clever boy, Ivar. Let me take her for a little, Anne. My sweet little baby doll! (*Takes the baby from the* MAID *and dances it up and down.*) Yes, yes, Mother will dance with Bob too. What! Have you been snowballing? I wish I had been there too! No, no, I will take their things off, Anne; please let me do it, it is such fun. Go in now, you look half frozen. There is some hot coffee for you on the stove.

(*The* NURSE *goes into the room on the left.* NORA *takes off the children's things and throws them about while they all talk to her at once.*)

NORA. *Really!* Did a big dog run after you? But it didn't bite you? No, dogs don't bite nice little dolly children. You mustn't look at the parcels, Ivar. What are they? Ah, I daresay you would like to know. No, no—it's something nasty! Come, let us have a game! What shall we play at? Hide and seek? Yes, we'll play hide and seek. Bob shall hide first. Must I hide? Very well, I'll hide first. (*She and the children laugh and shout and romp in and out of the room; at last* NORA *hides under the table; the children rush in and look for her but do not see her; they hear her smothered laughter, run to the table, lift up the cloth and find her. Shouts of laughter. She crawls forward and pretends to frighten them. Fresh laughter. Meanwhile there has been a knock at the hall door but none of them has noticed it. The door is half opened and* KROGSTAD *appears. He waits a little; the game goes on.*)

KROG. Excuse me, Mrs. Helmer.

NORA (*with a stifled cry turns round and gets up onto her knees*). Ah! What do you want?

KROG. Excuse me, the outer door was ajar; I suppose someone forgot to shut it.

NORA (*rising*). My husband is out, Mr. Krogstad.

KROG. I know that.

NORA. What do you want here then?

KROG. A word with you.

NORA. With me? (*To the children, gently.*) Go in to Nurse. What? No, the strange man won't do Mother any harm. When he has gone we will have another game. (*She takes the children into the room on the left and shuts the door after them.*) You want to speak to me?

KROG. Yes, I do.

NORA. Today? It is not the first of the month yet.

KROG. No, it is Christmas Eve, and it will depend on yourself what sort of a Christmas you will spend.

NORA. What do you want? Today it is absolutely impossible for me——

KROG. We won't talk about that till later on. This is something different. I presume you can give me a moment?

NORA. Yes—yes, I can—although——

KROG. Good. I was in Olsen's Restaurant and saw your husband going down the street——

NORA. Yes?

KROG. With a lady.

NORA. What then?

KROG. May I make so bold as to ask if it was a Mrs. Linde?

NORA. It was.

KROG. Just arrived in town?

NORA. Yes, today.

KROG. She is a great friend of yours, isn't she?

NORA. She is. But I don't see——

KROG. I knew her too, once upon a time.

NORA. I am aware of that.

KROG. Are you? So you know all about it; I thought as much. Then I can ask you, without beating about the bush—is Mrs. Linde to have an appointment in the bank?

NORA. What right have you to question me, Mr. Krogstad? You, one of my husband's subordinates! But since you ask, you shall know. Yes, Mrs. Linde *is* to have an appointment. And it was I who pleaded her cause, Mr. Krogstad, let me tell you that.

KROG. I was right in what I thought then.

NORA (*walking up and down the stage*). Sometimes one has a tiny little bit of influence, I should hope. Because one is a woman it does not necessarily follow that——When anyone is in a subordinate position, Mr. Krogstad, they should really be careful to avoid offending anyone who—who——

KROG. Who has influence?

NORA. Exactly.

KROG. (*changing his tone*). Mrs. Helmer, you will be so good as to use your influence on my behalf.

NORA. What? What do you mean?

KROG. You will be so kind as to see that I am allowed to keep my subordinate position in the bank.

NORA. What do you mean by that? Who proposes to take your post away from you?

KROG. Oh, there is no necessity to keep up the pretense of ignorance. I can quite understand that your friend is not very anxious to expose herself to the chance of rubbing shoulders with me, and I quite understand, too, whom I have to thank for being turned off.

NORA. But I assure you——

KROG. Very likely; but, to come to the point, the time has come when I should advise you to use your influence to prevent that.

NORA. But, Mr. Krogstad, I *have* no influence.

KROG. Haven't you? I thought you said yourself just now——

NORA. Naturally I did not mean you to put that construction on it. I! What should make you think I have any influence of that kind with my husband?

KROG. Oh, I have known your husband from our student days. I don't suppose he is any more unassailable than other husbands.

NORA. If you speak slightingly of my husband, I shall turn you out of the house.

KROG. You are bold, Mrs. Helmer.

NORA. I am not afraid of you any longer. As soon as the New Year comes I shall in a very short time be free of the whole thing.

KROG. (*controlling himself*). Listen to me, Mrs. Helmer. If necessary, I am prepared to fight for my small post in the bank as if I were fighting for my life.

NORA. So it seems.

KROG. It is not only for the sake of the money; indeed, that weighs least with me in the matter. There is another reason—well, I may as well tell you. My position is this. I daresay you know, like everybody else, that once, many years ago, I was guilty of an indiscretion.

NORA. I think I have heard something of the kind.

KROG. The matter never came into court, but every way seemed to be closed to me after that. So I took to the business that you know of. I had to do something; and, honestly, I don't think I've been one of the worst. But now I must cut myself free from all that. My sons are growing up; for their sake I must try and win back as much respect as I can in the town. This post in the bank was like the first step up for me—and now your husband is going to kick me downstairs again into the mud.

NORA. But you must believe me, Mr. Krogstad; it is not in my power to help you at all.

KROG. Then it is because you haven't the will, but I have means to compel you.

NORA. You don't mean that you will tell my husband that I owe you money?

KROG. Hm! Suppose I were to tell him?

NORA. It would be perfectly infamous of you. (*Sobbing.*) To think of his learning my secret, which has been my joy and pride, in such an ugly, clumsy way—that he should learn it from you! And it would put me in a horribly disagreeable position.

KROG. Only disagreeable?

NORA (*impetuously*). Well, do it then!—and it will be the worse for you. My husband will see for himself what a blackguard you are, and you certainly won't keep your post then.

KROG. I asked you if it was only a disagreeable scene at home that you were afraid of?

NORA. If my husband does get to know of it, of course he will at once pay you what is still owing, and we shall have nothing more to do with you.

KROG. (*coming a step nearer*). Listen to me, Mrs. Helmer. Either you have a very bad memory or you know very little of business. I shall be obliged to remind you of a few details.

NORA. What do you mean?

KROG. When your husband was ill you came to me to borrow two hundred and fifty pounds.

NORA. I didn't know anyone else to go to.

KROG. I promised to get you that amount——

NORA. Yes, and you did so.

KROG. I promised to get you that amount on certain conditions. Your mind was so taken up with your husband's illness and you were so anxious to get the money for your journey that you seem to have paid no attention to the conditions of our bargain. Therefore it will not be amiss if I remind you of them. Now I promised to get the money on the security of a bond which I drew up.

NORA. Yes, and which I signed.

KROG. Good. But below your signature there were a few lines constituting your father a surety for the money; those lines your father should have signed.

NORA. Should? He did sign them.

KROG. I had left the date blank; that is to say your father should himself have inserted the date on which he signed the paper. Do you remember that?

NORA. Yes, I think I remember.

KROG. Then I gave you the bond to send by post to your father. Is that not so?

NORA. Yes.

KROG. And you naturally did so at once, because five or six days afterward you brought me the bond with your father's signature. And then I gave you the money.

NORA. Well, haven't I been paying it off regularly?

KROG. Fairly so, yes. But—to come back to the matter in hand—that must have been a very trying time for you, Mrs. Helmer?

NORA. It was, indeed.

KROG. Your father was very ill, wasn't he?

NORA. He was very near his end.

KROG. And died soon afterward?

NORA. Yes.

KROG. Tell me, Mrs. Helmer, can you by any chance remember what day your father died?—on what day of the month, I mean.

NORA. Papa died on the twenty-ninth of September.

KROG. That is correct; I have ascertained it for myself. And, as that is so, there is a discrepancy (*taking a paper from his pocket*) which I cannot account for.

NORA. What discrepancy? I don't know——

KROG. The discrepancy consists, Mrs. Helmer, in the fact that your father signed this bond three days after his death.

NORA. What do you mean? I don't understand.

KROG. Your father died on the twenty-ninth of September. But look here; your father has dated his signature the second of October. It is a discrepancy, isn't it? (NORA *is silent.*) Can you explain it to me? (NORA *is still silent.*) It is a remarkable thing, too, that the words "second of October," as well as the year, are not written in your father's handwriting but in one that I think I know. Well, of course it can be explained; your father may have forgotten to date his signature and someone else may have dated it haphazard before they knew of his death. There is no harm in that. It all depends on the signature of the name, and *that* is genuine, I suppose, Mrs. Helmer? It was your father himself who signed his name here?

NORA (*after a short pause, throws her head up and looks defiantly at him*). No, it was not. It was I that wrote Papa's name.

KROG. Are you aware that is a dangerous confession?

NORA. In what way? You shall have your money soon.

KROG. Let me ask you a question: why did you not send the paper to your father?

NORA. It was impossible; Papa was so ill. If I had asked him for his signature, I should have had to tell him what the money was to be used for; and when he was so ill himself I couldn't tell him that my husband's life was in danger—it was impossible.

KROG. It would have been better for you if you had given up your trip abroad.

NORA. No, that was impossible. That trip was to save my husband's life; I couldn't give that up.

KROG. But did it never occur to you that you were committing a fraud on me?

NORA. I couldn't take that into account; I didn't trouble myself about you at all. I couldn't bear you because you put so many heartless difficulties in my way although you knew what a dangerous condition my husband was in.

KROG. Mrs. Helmer, you evidently do not realize clearly what it is that you have been guilty of. But I can assure you that my one false step, which lost me all my reputation, was nothing more or nothing worse than what you have done.

NORA. You? Do you ask me to believe that you were brave enough to run a risk to save your wife's life?

KROG. The law cares nothing about motives.

NORA. Then it must be a very foolish law.

KROG. Foolish or not, it is the law by which you will be judged if I produce this paper in court.

NORA. I don't believe it. Is a daughter not to be allowed to spare her dying father anxiety and care? Is a wife not to be allowed to save her husband's life? I don't know much about law, but I am certain that there must be laws permitting such things as that. Have you no knowledge of such laws—you who are a lawyer? You must be a very poor lawyer, Mr. Krogstad.

KROG. Maybe. But matters of business—such business as you and I have had together—do you think I don't understand that? Very well. Do as you please. But let me tell you this—if I lose my position a second time, you shall lose yours with me. (*He bows and goes out through the hall.*)

NORA (*appears buried in thought for a short time, then tosses her head*). Nonsense! Trying to frighten me like that! I am not so silly as he thinks. (*Begins to busy herself putting the children's things in order.*) And yet—— No, it's impossible! I did it for love's sake.

THE CHILDREN (*in the doorway on the left*). Mother, the stranger man has gone out through the gate.

NORA. Yes, dears, I know. But don't tell anyone about the stranger man. Do you hear? Not even Papa.

CHILDREN. No, Mother; but will you come and play again?

NORA. No, no—not now.

CHILDREN. But, Mother, you promised us.

NORA. Yes, but I can't now. Run away in; I have such a lot to do. Run away in, my sweet little darlings. (*She gets them into the room by degrees and shuts the door on them, then sits down on the sofa, takes up a piece of needlework and sews a few stitches but soon stops.*) No! (*Throws down the work, gets up, goes to the hall door and calls out.*) Helen! bring the tree in. (*Goes to the table on the left, opens a drawer and stops again.*) No, no! It is quite impossible!

MAID (*coming in with the tree*). Where shall I put it, ma'am?

NORA. Here, in the middle of the floor.

MAID. Shall I get you anything else?

NORA. No, thank you. I have all I want.

(*Exit* MAID.)

NORA (*begins dressing the tree*). A candle here—and flowers here—— The horrible man! It's all nonsense—there's nothing wrong. The tree shall be splendid! I will do everything I can think of to please you, Torvald! I will sing for you, dance for you—— (HELMER *comes in with some papers under his arm.*) Oh, are you back already?

HEL. Yes. Has anyone been here?

NORA. Here? No.

HEL. That is strange. I saw Krogstad going out of the gate.

NORA. Did you? Oh yes, I forgot, Krogstad was here for a moment.

HEL. Nora, I can see from your manner that he has been here begging you to say a good word for him.

NORA. Yes.

HEL. And you were to appear to do it of your own accord; you were to conceal from me the fact of his having been here; didn't he beg that of you too?

NORA. Yes, Torvald, but——

HEL. Nora, Nora, and you would be a party to that sort of thing? To have any talk with a man like that and give him any sort of promise? And to tell me a lie into the bargain?

NORA. A lie?

HEL. Didn't you tell me no one had been here? (*Shakes his finger at her.*) My little songbird must never do that again. A songbird must have a clean beak to chirp with—no false notes! (*Puts his arm around her waist.*) That is so, isn't it? Yes, I am sure it is. (*Lets her go.*) We will say no more about it. (*Sits down by the stove.*) How warm and snug it is here! (*Turns over his papers.*)

NORA (*after a short pause during which she busies herself with the Christmas tree*). Torvald!

HEL. Yes.

NORA. I am looking forward tremendously to the fancy-dress ball at the Stenborgs' the day after tomorrow.

HEL. And I am tremendously curious to see what you are going to surprise me with.

NORA. It was very silly of me to want to do that.

HEL. What do you mean?

NORA. I can't hit upon anything that will do; everything I think of seems so silly and insignificant.

HEL. Does my little Nora acknowledge that at last?

NORA (*standing behind his chair with her arms on the back of it*). Are you very busy, Torvald?

HEL. Well——

NORA. What are all those papers?

HEL. Bank business.

NORA. Already?

HEL. I have got authority from the retiring manager to undertake the necessary changes in the staff and in the rearrangement of the work, and I must make use of the Christmas week for that, so as to have everything in order for the new year.

NORA. Then that was why this poor Krogstad——

HEL. Hm!

NORA (*leans against the back of his chair and strokes his hair*). If you hadn't been so busy, I should have asked you a tremendously big favor, Torvald.

HEL. What is that? Tell me.

NORA. There is no one has such good taste as you. And I do so want to look nice at the fancy-dress ball. Torvald, couldn't you take me in hand and decide what I shall go as and what sort of a dress I shall wear?

HEL. Aha! So my obstinate little woman is obliged to get someone to come to her rescue?

NORA. Yes, Torvald, I can't get along a bit without your help.

HEL. Very well, I will think it over; we shall manage to hit upon something.

NORA. That is nice of you. (*Goes to the Christmas tree. A short pause.*) How pretty the red flowers look! But tell me, was it really something very bad that this Krogstad was guilty of?

HEL. He forged someone's name. Have you any idea what that means?

NORA. Isn't it possible that he was driven to do it by necessity?

HEL. Yes; or, as in so many cases, by imprudence. I am not so heartless as to condemn a man altogether because of a single false step of that kind.

NORA. No, you wouldn't, would you, Torvald?

HEL. Many a man has been able to retrieve his character if he has openly confessed his fault and taken his punishment.

NORA. Punishment?

HEL. But Krogstad did nothing of that sort; he got himself out of it by a cunning trick, and that is why he has gone under altogether.

NORA. But do you think it would——

HEL. Just think how a guilty man like that has to lie and play the hypocrite with everyone, how he has to wear a mask in the presence of those near and dear to him, even before his own wife and children. And about the children—that is the most terrible part of it all, Nora.

NORA. How?

HEL. Because such an atmosphere of lies infects and poisons the whole life of a home. Each breath the children take in such a house is full of the germs of evil.

NORA (*coming nearer him*). Are you sure of that?

HEL. My dear, I have often seen it in the course of my life as a lawyer. Almost everyone who has gone to the bad early in life has had a deceitful mother.

NORA. Why do you only say—mother?

HEL. It seems most commonly to be the mother's influence, though naturally a bad father's would have the same result. Every lawyer is familiar with the fact. This Krogstad, now, has been persistently poisoning his own children with lies and dissimulation; that is why I say he has lost all moral character. (*Holds out his hands to her.*) That is why my sweet little Nora must promise me not to plead his cause. Give me your hand on it. Come, come, what is this? Give me your hand. There now, that's settled. I assure you it would be quite impossible for me to work with him; I literally feel physically ill when I am in the company of such people.

NORA (*takes her hand out of his and goes to the opposite side of the Christmas tree*). How hot it is in here, and I have such a lot to do.

HEL. (*getting up and putting his papers in order*). Yes, and I must try and read through some of these before dinner, and I must think about your costume too. And it is just possible I may have something ready in gold paper to hang up on the tree. (*Puts his hand on her head.*) My precious little singing bird! (*He goes into his room and shuts the door after him.*)

NORA (*after a pause, whispers*). No, no—it isn't true. It's impossible; it must be impossible.

(*The* NURSE *opens the door on the left.*)

NURSE. The little ones are begging so hard to be allowed to come in to Mamma.

NORA. No, no, no! Don't let them come in to me! You stay with them, Anne.

NURSE. Very well, ma'am. (*Shuts the door.*)

NORA (*pale with terror*). Deprave my little children? Poison my home? (*A short pause. Then she tosses her head.*) It's not true. It can't possibly be true.

ACT II

THE SAME SCENE—*The Christmas tree is in the corner by the piano, stripped of its ornaments and with burned-down candle ends on its disheveled branches.* NORA'S *cloak and hat are lying on the sofa. She is alone in the room, walking about uneasily. She stops by the sofa and takes up her cloak.*

NORA (*drops the cloak*). Someone is coming now. (*Goes to the door and listens.*) No—it is no one. Of course no one will come today, Christmas Day—nor tomorrow either. But perhaps—— (*Opens the door and looks out.*) No, nothing in the letter box; it is quite empty. (*Comes forward.*) What rubbish! Of course he can't be in earnest about it. Such a thing couldn't happen; it is impossible—I have three little children.

(*Enter the* NURSE *from the room on the left, carrying a big cardboard box.*)

NURSE. At last I have found the box with the fancy dress.

NORA. Thanks; put it on the table.

NURSE (*in doing so*). But it is very much in want of mending.

NORA. I should like to tear it into a hundred thousand pieces.

NURSE. What an idea! It can easily be put in order—just a little patience.

NORA. Yes, I will go and get Mrs. Linde to come and help me with it.

NURSE. What, out again? In this horrible weather? You will catch cold, ma'am, and make yourself ill.

NORA. Well, worse than that might happen. How are the children?

NURSE. The poor little souls are playing with their Christmas presents, but——

NORA. Do they ask much for me?

NURSE. You see, they are so accustomed to having their mamma with them.

NORA. Yes—but, Nurse, I shall not be able to be so much with them now as I was before.

NURSE. Oh well, young children easily get accustomed to anything.

NORA. Do you think so? Do you think they would forget their mother if she went away altogether?

NURSE. Good heavens!—went away altogether?

NORA. Nurse, I want you to tell me something I have often wondered about— how could you have the heart to put your own child out among strangers?

NURSE. I was obliged to if I wanted to be little Nora's nurse.

NORA. Yes, but how could you be willing to do it?

NURSE. What, when I was going to get such a good place by it? A poor girl who has got into trouble should be glad to. Besides, that wicked man did- n't do a single thing for me.

NORA. But I suppose your daughter has quite forgotten you.

NURSE. No, indeed she hasn't. She wrote to me when she was confirmed and when she was married.

NORA (*putting her arms round her neck*). Dear old Anne, you were a good mother to me when I was little.

NURSE. Little Nora, poor dear, had no other mother but me.

NORA. And if my little ones had no other mother, I am sure you would—— What nonsense I am talking! (*Opens the box.*) Go in to them. Now I must—— You will see tomorrow how charming I shall look.

NURSE. I am sure there will be no one at the ball so charming as you, ma'am. (*Goes into the room on the left.*)

NORA (*begins to unpack the box but soon pushes it away from her*). If only I dared go out. If only no one would come. If only I could be sure nothing would happen here in the meantime. Stuff and nonsense! No one will come. Only I mustn't think about it. I will brush my muff. What lovely, lovely gloves! Out of my thoughts, out of my thoughts! One, two, three, four, five, six—— (*Screams.*) Ah! there is someone coming. (*Makes a movement toward the door but stands irresolute.*)

(*Enter* MRS. LINDE *from the hall, where she has taken off her cloak and hat.*)

NORA. Oh, it's you, Christine. There is no one else out there, is there? How good of you to come!

MRS. L. I heard you were up asking for me.

NORA. Yes, I was passing by. As a matter of fact, it is something you could help me with. Let us sit down here on the sofa. Look here. Tomorrow evening there is to be a fancy-dress ball at the Stenborgs', who live above us, and Torvald wants me to go as a Neapolitan fishergirl and dance the tarantella that I learnt at Capri.

MRS. L. I see; you are going to keep up the character.

NORA. Yes, Torvald wants me to. Look, here is the dress; Torvald had it made for me there, but now it is all so torn, and I haven't any idea——

MRS. L. We will easily put that right. It is only some of the trimming come unsewn here and there. Needle and thread? Now then, that's all we want.

NORA. It *is* nice of you.

MRS. L. (*sewing*). So you are going to be dressed up tomorrow, Nora. I will tell you what—I shall come in for a moment and see you in your fine feathers. But I have completely forgotten to thank you for a delightful evening yesterday.

NORA (*gets up and crosses the stage*). Well, I don't think yesterday was as pleasant as usual. You ought to have come down to town a little earlier, Christine. Certainly Torvald does understand how to make a house dainty and attractive.

MRS. L. And so do you, it seems to me; you are not your father's daughter for nothing. But tell me, is Doctor Rank always as depressed as he was yesterday?

NORA. No; yesterday it was very noticeable. I must tell you that he suffers from a very dangerous disease. He has consumption of the spine, poor creature. His father was a horrible man who committed all sorts of excesses, and that is why his son was sickly from childhood, do you understand?

MRS. L. (*dropping her sewing*). But, my dearest Nora, how do you know anything about such things?

NORA (*walking about*). Pooh! When you have three children you get visits now and then from—from married women who know something of medical matters, and they talk about one thing and another.

MRS. L. (*goes on sewing. A short silence*). Does Doctor Rank come here every day?

NORA. Every day regularly. He is Torvald's most intimate friend and a friend of mine too. He is just like one of the family.

MRS. L. But tell me this—is he perfectly sincere? I mean, isn't he the kind of man that is very anxious to make himself agreeable?

NORA. Not in the least. What makes you think that?

MRS. L. When you introduced him to me yesterday he declared he had often heard my name mentioned in this house, but afterward I noticed that your husband hadn't the slightest idea who I was. So how could Doctor Rank——

NORA. That is quite right, Christine. Torvald is so absurdly fond of me that he wants me absolutely to himself, as he says. At first he used to seem almost jealous if I mentioned any of the dear folks at home, so naturally I gave up doing so. But I often talk about such things with Doctor Rank because he likes hearing about them.

MRS. L. Listen to me, Nora. You are still very like a child in many things, and I am older than you in many ways and have a little more experience. Let me tell you this—you ought to make an end of it with Doctor Rank.

NORA. What ought I to make an end of?

MRS. L. Of two things, I think. Yesterday you talked some nonsense about a rich admirer who was to leave you money——

NORA. An admirer who doesn't exist, unfortunately! But what then?

MRS. L. Is Doctor Rank a man of means?

NORA. Yes, he is.

MRS. L. And has no one to provide for?

NORA. No, no one; but——

MRS. L. And comes here every day?

NORA. Yes, I told you so.

MRS. L. But how can this well-bred man be so tactless?

NORA. I don't understand you at all.

MRS. L. Don't prevaricate, Nora. Do you suppose I don't guess who lent you the two hundred and fifty pounds?

NORA. Are you out of your senses? How can you think of such a thing! A friend of ours, who comes here every day! Do you realize what a horribly painful position that would be?

MRS. L. Then it really isn't he?

NORA. No, certainly not. It would never have entered into my head for a moment. Besides, he had no money to lend then; he came into his money afterward.

MRS. L. Well, I think that was lucky for you, my dear Nora.

NORA. No, it would never have come into my head to ask Doctor Rank. Although I am quite sure that if I had asked him——

MRS. L. But of course you won't.

NORA. Of course not. I have no reason to think it could possibly be necessary. But I am quite sure that if I told Doctor Rank——

MRS. L. Behind your husband's back?

NORA. I must make an end of it with the other one, and that will be behind his back too. I *must* make an end of it with him.

MRS. L. Yes, that is what I told you yesterday, but——

NORA (*walking up and down*). A man can put a thing like that straight much easier than a woman.

MRS. L. One's husband, yes.

NORA. Nonsense! (*Standing still.*) When you pay off a debt you get your bond back, don't you?

MRS. L. Yes, as a matter of course.

NORA. And can tear it into a hundred thousand pieces and burn it up—the nasty dirty paper!

MRS. L. (*looks hard at her, lays down her sewing and gets up slowly*). Nora, you are concealing something from me.

NORA. Do I look as if I were?

MRS. L. Something has happened to you since yesterday morning. Nora, what is it?

NORA (*going nearer to her*). Christine! (*Listens.*) Hush! There's Torvald come home. Do you mind going in to the children for the present? Torvald can't bear to see dressmaking going on. Let Anne help you.

MRS. L. (*gathering some of the things together*). Certainly—but I am not going away from here till we have had it out with one another. (*She goes into the room on the left as* HELMER *comes in from the hall.*)

NORA (*going up to* HELMER). I have wanted you so much, Torvald dear.

HEL. Was that the dressmaker?

NORA. No, it was Christine; she is helping me to put my dress in order. You will see I shall look quite smart.

HEL. Wasn't that a happy thought of mine, now?

NORA. Splendid! But don't you think it is nice of me, too, to do as you wish?

HEL. Nice?—because you do as your husband wishes? Well, well, you little rogue, I am sure you did not mean it in that way. But I am not going to disturb you; you will want to be trying on your dress, I expect.

NORA. I suppose you are going to work.

HEL. Yes. (*Shows her a bundle of papers.*) Look at that. I have just been in to the bank. (*Turns to go into his room.*)

NORA. Torvald.

HEL. Yes.

NORA. If your little squirrel were to ask you for something very, very prettily——

HEL. What then?

NORA. Would you do it?

HEL. I should like to hear what it is first.

NORA. Your squirrel would run about and do all her tricks if you would be nice and do what she wants.

HEL. Speak plainly.

NORA. Your skylark would chirp, chirp about in every room, with her song rising and falling——

HEL. Well, my skylark does that anyhow.

NORA. I would play the fairy and dance for you in the moonlight, Torvald.

HEL. Nora—you surely don't mean that request you made of me this morning?

NORA (*going near him*). Yes, Torvald, I beg you so earnestly——

HEL. Have you really the courage to open up that question again?

NORA. Yes, dear, you *must* do as I ask; you *must* let Krogstad keep his post in the bank.

HEL. My dear Nora, it is his post that I have arranged Mrs. Linde shall have.

NORA. Yes, you have been awfully kind about that, but you could just as well dismiss some other clerk instead of Krogstad.

HEL. This is simply incredible obstinacy! Because you chose to give him a thoughtless promise that you would speak for him I am expected to——

NORA. That isn't the reason, Torvald. It is for your own sake. This fellow writes in the most scurrilous newspapers; you have told me so yourself. He can do you an unspeakable amount of harm. I am frightened to death of him.

HEL. Ah, I understand; it is recollections of the past that scare you.

NORA. What do you mean?

HEL. Naturally you are thinking of your father.

NORA. Yes—yes, of course. Just recall to your mind what these malicious creatures wrote in the papers about Papa and how horribly they slandered him. I believe they would have procured his dismissal if the Department had not sent you over to inquire into it and if you had not been so kindly disposed and helpful to him.

HEL. My little Nora, there is an important difference between your father and me. Your father's reputation as a public official was not above suspicion. Mine is, and I hope it will continue to be so as long as I hold my office.

NORA. You never can tell what mischief these men may contrive. We ought to be so well off, so snug and happy here in our peaceful home, and have no cares—you and I and the children, Torvald! That is why I beg you so earnestly——

HEL. And it is just by interceding for him that you make it impossible for me to keep him. It is already known at the bank that I mean to dismiss Krogstad. Is it to get about now that the new manager has changed his mind at his wife's bidding?

NORA. And what if it did?

HEL. Of course!—if only this obstinate little person can get her way! Do you suppose I am going to make myself ridiculous before my whole staff, to let people think I am a man to be swayed by all sorts of outside influence? I should very soon feel the consequences of it, I can tell you! And besides, there is one thing that makes it quite impossible for me to have Krogstad in the bank as long as I am manager.

NORA. Whatever is that?

HEL. His moral failings I might perhaps have overlooked if necessary——

NORA. Yes, you could—couldn't you?

HEL. And I hear he is a good worker too. But I knew him when we were boys. It was one of those rash friendships that so often prove an incubus in afterlife. I may as well tell you plainly, we were once on very intimate terms with one another. But this tactless fellow lays no restraint on himself when other people are present. On the contrary, he thinks it gives him the right to adopt a familiar tone with me, and every minute it is "I say, Helmer, old fellow!" and that sort of thing. I assure you it is extremely painful for me. He would make my position in the bank intolerable.

NORA. Torvald, I don't believe you mean that.

HEL. Don't you? Why not?

NORA. Because it is such a narrow-minded way of looking at things.

HEL. What are you saying? Narrow-minded? Do you think I am narrow-minded?

NORA. No, just the opposite, dear—and it is exactly for that reason——

HEL. It's the same thing. You say my point of view is narrow-minded, so I must be so too. Narrow-minded! Very well—I must put an end to this. (*Goes to the hall door and calls.*) Helen!

NORA. What are you going to do?

HEL. (*looking among his papers*). Settle it. (*Enter* MAID.) Look here; take this letter and go downstairs with it at once. Find a messenger and tell him to deliver it and be quick. The address is on it, and here is the money.

MAID. Very well, sir. (*Exit with the letter.*)

HEL. (*putting his papers together*). Now then, little Miss Obstinate.

NORA (*breathlessly*). Torvald—what was that letter?

HEL. Krogstad's dismissal.

NORA. Call her back, Torvald! There is still time. Oh, Torvald, call her back!

Do it for my sake—for your own sake—for the children's sake! Do you hear me, Torvald? Call her back! You don't know what that letter can bring upon us.

HEL. It's too late.

NORA. Yes, it's too late.

HEL. My dear Nora, I can forgive the anxiety you are in, although really it is an insult to me. It is, indeed. Isn't it an insult to think that I should be afraid of a starving quill driver's vengeance? But I forgive you nevertheless, because it is such eloquent witness to your great love for me. (*Takes her in his arms.*) And that is as it should be, my own darling Nora. Come what will, you may be sure I shall have both courage and strength if they be needed. You will see I am man enough to take everything upon myself.

NORA (*in a horror-stricken voice*). What do you mean by that?

HEL. Everything, I say.

NORA (*recovering herself*). You will never have to do that.

HEL. That's right. Well, we will share it, Nora, as man and wife should. That is how it shall be. (*Caressing her.*) Are you content now? There! there!—not these frightened dove's eyes! The whole thing is only the wildest fancy! Now you must go and play through the tarantella and practice with your tambourine. I shall go into the inner office and shut the door, and I shall hear nothing; you can make as much noise as you please. (*Turns back at the door.*) And when Rank comes tell him where he will find me. (*Nods to her, takes his papers and goes into his room and shuts the door after him.*)

NORA (*bewildered with anxiety, stands as if rooted to the spot and whispers*). He was capable of doing it. He will do it. He will do it in spite of everything. No, not that! Never, never! Anything rather than that! Oh, for some help, some way out of it! (*The doorbell rings.*) Doctor Rank! Anything rather than that—anything, whatever it is! (*She puts her hands over her face, pulls herself together, goes to the door and opens it. RANK is standing without, hanging up his coat. During the following dialogue it begins to grow dark.*)

NORA. Good day, Doctor Rank. I knew your ring. But you mustn't go in to Torvald now; I think he is busy with something.

RANK. And you?

NORA (*brings him in and shuts the door after him*). Oh, you know very well I always have time for you.

RANK. Thank you. I shall make use of as much of it as I can.

NORA. What do you mean by that? As much of it as you can?

RANK. Well, does that alarm you?

NORA. It was such a strange way of putting it. Is anything likely to happen?

RANK. Nothing but what I have long been prepared for. But I certainly didn't expect it to happen so soon.

NORA (*gripping him by the arm*). What have you found out? Doctor Rank, you must tell me.

RANK (*sitting down by the stove*). It is all up with me. And it can't be helped.

NORA (*with a sigh of relief*). Is it about yourself?

RANK. Who else? It is no use lying to one's self. I am the most wretched of all my patients, Mrs. Helmer. Lately I have been taking stock of my internal economy. Bankrupt! Probably within a month I shall lie rotting in the churchyard.

NORA. What an ugly thing to say!

RANK. The thing itself is cursedly ugly, and the worst of it is that I shall have to face so much more that is ugly before that. I shall only make one more examination of myself; when I have done that I shall know pretty certainly when it will be that the horrors of dissolution will begin. There is something I want to tell you. Helmer's refined nature gives him an unconquerable disgust at everything that is ugly; I won't have him in my sickroom.

NORA. Oh, but, Doctor Rank——

RANK. I won't have him there. Not on any account. I bar my door to him. As soon as I am quite certain that the worst has come I shall send you my card with a black cross on it, and then you will know that the loathsome end has begun.

NORA. You are quite absurd today. And I wanted you so much to be in a really good humor.

RANK. With death stalking beside me? To have to pay this penalty for another man's sin! Is there any justice in that? And in every single family, in one way or another, some such inexorable retribution is being exacted.

NORA (*putting her hands over her ears*). Rubbish! Do talk of something cheerful.

RANK. Oh, it's a mere laughing matter; the whole thing. My poor innocent spine has to suffer for my father's youthful amusements.

NORA (*sitting at the table on the left*). I suppose you mean that he was too partial to asparagus and pâté de foie gras, don't you?

RANK. Yes, and to truffles.

NORA. Truffles, yes. And oysters too, I suppose?

RANK. Oysters, of course; that goes without saying.

NORA. And heaps of port and champagne. It is sad that all these nice things should take their revenge on our bones.

RANK. Especially that they should revenge themselves on the unlucky bones of those who have not had the satisfaction of enjoying them.

NORA. Yes, that's the saddest part of it all.

RANK (*with a searching look at her*). Hm!

NORA (*after a short pause*). Why did you smile?

RANK. No, it was you that laughed.

NORA. No, it was you that smiled, Doctor Rank!

RANK (*rising*). You are a greater rascal than I thought.

NORA. I am in a silly mood today.

RANK. So it seems.

NORA (*putting her hands on his shoulders*). Dear, dear Doctor Rank, death mustn't take you away from Torvald and me.

RANK. It is a loss you would easily recover from. Those who are gone are soon forgotten.

NORA (*looking at him anxiously*). Do you believe that?

RANK. People form new ties, and then——

NORA. Who will form new ties?

RANK. Both you and Helmer, when I am gone. You yourself are already on the highroad to it, I think. What did that Mrs. Linde want here last night?

NORA. Oho! You don't mean to say that you are jealous of poor Christine?

RANK. Yes, I am. She will be my successor in this house. When I am done for, this woman will——

NORA. Hush! Don't speak so loud. She is in that room.

RANK. Today again. There, you see.

NORA. She has only come to sew my dress for me. Bless my soul, how unreasonable you are! (*Sits down on the sofa.*) Be nice now, Doctor Rank, and tomorrow you will see how beautifully I shall dance, and you can imagine I am doing it all for you—and for Torvald too, of course. (*Takes various things out of the box.*) Doctor Rank, come and sit down here, and I will show you something.

RANK (*sitting down*). What is it?

NORA. Just look at those!

RANK. Silk stockings.

NORA. Flesh colored. Aren't they lovely? It is so dark here now, but tomorrow—— No, no, no! You must only look at the feet. Oh well, you may have leave to look at the legs too.

RANK. Hm!

NORA. Why are you looking so critical? Don't you think they will fit me?

RANK. I have no means of forming an opinion about that.

NORA (*looks at him for a moment*). For shame! (*Hits him lightly on the ear with the stockings.*) That's to punish you. (*Folds them up again.*)

RANK. And what other nice things am I to be allowed to see?

NORA. Not a single thing more, for being so naughty. (*She looks among the things, humming to herself.*)

RANK (*after a short silence*). When I am sitting here talking to you as intimately as this I cannot imagine for a moment what would have become of me if I had never come into this house.

NORA (*smiling*). I believe you do feel thoroughly at home with us.

RANK (*in a lower voice, looking straight in front of him*). And to be obliged to leave it all——

NORA. Nonsense, you are not going to leave it.

RANK (*as before*). And not be able to leave behind one the slightest token of one's gratitude, scarcely even a fleeting regret—nothing but an empty place which the firstcomer can fill as well as any other.

NORA. And if I asked you now for a—— No!

RANK. For what?

NORA. For a big proof of your friendship——

RANK. Yes, yes!

NORA. I mean a tremendously big favor——

RANK. Would you really make me so happy for once?

NORA. Ah, but you don't know what it is yet.

RANK. No—— but tell me.

NORA. I really can't, Doctor Rank. It is something out of all reason; it means advice and help and a favor——

RANK. The bigger a thing it is, the better. I can't conceive what it is you mean. Do tell me. Haven't I your confidence?

NORA. More than anyone else. I know you are my truest and best friend, and so I will tell you what it is. Well, Doctor Rank, it is something you must help me to prevent. You know how devotedly, how inexpressibly deeply Torvald loves me; he would never for a moment hesitate to give his life for me.

RANK (*leaning toward her*). Nora—do you think he is the only one——

NORA (*with a slight start*). The only one—— ?

RANK. The only one who would gladly give his life for your sake.

NORA (*sadly*). Is that it?

RANK. I was determined you should know it before I went away, and there will never be a better opportunity than this. Now you know it, Nora. And now you know, too, that you can trust me as you would trust no one else.

NORA (*rises deliberately and quietly*). Let me pass.

RANK (*makes room for her to pass him but sits still*). Nora!

NORA (*at the hall door*). Helen, bring in the lamp. (*Goes over to the stove.*) Dear Doctor Rank, that was really horrid of you.

RANK. To have loved you as much as anyone else does? Was that horrid?

NORA. No, but to go and tell me so. There was really no need——

RANK. What do you mean? Did you know? (MAID *enters with lamp, puts it down on the table and goes out.*) Nora—Mrs. Helmer—tell me, had you any idea of this?

NORA. Oh, how do I know whether I had or whether I hadn't? I really can't tell you. To think you could be so clumsy, Doctor Rank! We were getting on so nicely.

RANK. Well, at all events you know that you can command me body and soul. So won't you speak out?

NORA (*looking at him*). After what happened?

RANK. I beg you to let me know what it is.

NORA. I can't tell you anything now.

RANK. Yes, yes. You mustn't punish me in that way. Let me have permission to do for you whatever a man may do.

NORA. You can do nothing for me now. Besides, I really don't need any help at all. You will find that the whole thing is merely fancy on my part. It really is so—of course it is! (*Sits down in the rocking chair and looks at him with a smile.*) You are a nice sort of man, Doctor Rank! Don't you feel ashamed of yourself now the lamp has come?

RANK. Not a bit. But perhaps I had better go—forever?

NORA. No indeed, you shall not. Of course you must come here just as before. You know very well Torvald can't do without you.

RANK. Yes, but you?

NORA. Oh, I am always tremendously pleased when you come.

RANK. It is just that that put me on the wrong track. You are a riddle to me. I have often thought that you would almost as soon be in my company as in Helmer's.

NORA. Yes—you see, there are some people one loves best and others whom one would almost always rather have as companions.

RANK. Yes, there is something in that.

NORA. When I was at home of course I loved Papa best. But I always thought it tremendous fun if I could steal down into the maids' room, because they never moralized at all and talked to each other about such entertaining things.

RANK. I see—it is *their* place I have taken.

NORA (*jumping up and going to him*). Oh, dear, nice Doctor Rank, I never meant that at all. But surely you can understand that being with Torvald is a little like being with Papa——

(*Enter* MAID *from the hall.*)

MAID. If you please, ma'am. (*Whispers and hands her a card.*)

NORA (*glancing at the card*). Oh! (*Puts it in her pocket.*)

RANK. Is there anything wrong?

NORA. No, no, not in the least. It is only something—it is my new dress——

RANK. What? Your dress is lying there.

NORA. Oh yes, that one; but this is another. I ordered it. Torvald mustn't know about it.

RANK. Oho! Then that was the great secret.

NORA. Of course. Just go in to him; he is sitting in the inner room. Keep him as long as——

RANK. Make your mind easy; I won't let him escape. (*Goes into* HELMER'S *room.*)

NORA (*to the* MAID). And he is standing waiting in the kitchen?

MAID. Yes; he came up the back stairs.

NORA. But didn't you tell him no one was in?

MAID. Yes, but it was no good.

NORA. He won't go away?

MAID. No; he says he won't until he has seen you, ma'am.

NORA. Well, let him come in—but quietly. Helen, you mustn't say anything about it to anyone. It is a surprise for my husband.

MAID. Yes, ma'am, I quite understand. (*Exit.*)

NORA. This dreadful thing is going to happen! It will happen in spite of me! No, no, no, it can't happen—it shan't happen! (*She bolts the door of* HELMER'S *room. The* MAID *opens the hall door for* KROGSTAD *and shuts it after him. He is wearing a fur coat, high boots and a fur cap.*)

NORA (*advancing toward him*). Speak low—my husband is at home.

KROG. No matter about that.

NORA. What do you want of me?

KROG. An explanation of something.

NORA. Make haste then. What is it?

KROG. You know, I suppose, that I have got my dismissal.

NORA. I couldn't prevent it, Mr. Krogstad. I fought as hard as I could on your side, but it was no good.

KROG. Does your husband love you so little then? He knows what I can expose you to, and yet he ventures——

NORA. How can you suppose that he has any knowledge of the sort?

KROG. I didn't suppose so at all. It would not be the least like our dear Torvald Helmer to show so much courage——

NORA. Mr. Krogstad, a little respect for my husband, please.

KROG. Certainly—all the respect he deserves. But since you have kept the matter so carefully to yourself, I make bold to suppose that you have a little clearer idea than you had yesterday of what it actually is that you have done?

NORA. More than you could ever teach me.

KROG. Yes, such a bad lawyer as I am.

NORA. What is it you want of me?

KROG. Only to see how you were, Mrs. Helmer. I have been thinking about you all day long. A mere cashier, a quill driver, a—well, a man like me—even he has a little of what is called feeling, you know.

NORA. Show it then; think of my little children.

KROG. Have you and your husband thought of mine? But never mind about that. I only wanted to tell you that you need not take this matter too seriously. In the first place there will be no accusation made on my part.

NORA. No, of course not; I was sure of that.

KROG. The whole thing can be arranged amicably; there is no reason why anyone should know anything about it. It will remain a secret between us three.

NORA. My husband must never get to know anything about it.

KROG. How will you be able to prevent it? Am I to understand that you can pay the balance that is owing?

NORA. No, not just at present.

KROG. Or perhaps that you have some expedient for raising the money soon?

NORA. No expedient that I mean to make use of.

KROG. Well, in any case it would have been of no use to you now. If you stood there with ever so much money in your hand, I would never part with your bond.

NORA. Tell me what purpose you mean to put it to.

KROG. I shall only preserve it—keep it in my possession. No one who is not concerned in the matter shall have the slightest hint of it. So that if the thought of it has driven you to any desperate resolution——

NORA. It has.

KROG. If you had it in your mind to run away from your home——

NORA. I had.

KROG. Or even something worse——

NORA. How could you know that?

KROG. Give up the idea.

NORA. How did you know I had thought of *that?*

KROG. Most of us think of that at first. I did too—but I hadn't the courage.

NORA (*faintly*). No more than I.

KROG. (*in a tone of relief*). No, that's it, isn't it—you hadn't the courage either?

NORA. No, I haven't—I haven't.

KROG. Besides, it would have been a great piece of folly. Once the first storm at home is over—— I have a letter for your husband in my pocket.

NORA. Telling him everything?

KROG. In as lenient a manner as I possibly could.

NORA (*quickly*). He mustn't get the letter. Tear it up. I will find some means of getting money.

KROG. Excuse me, Mrs. Helmer, but I think I told you just now——

NORA. I am not speaking of what I owe you. Tell me what sum you are asking my husband for, and I will get the money.

KROG. I am not asking your husband for a penny.

NORA. What do you want then?

KROG. I will tell you. I want to rehabilitate myself, Mrs. Helmer; I want to get on, and in that your husband must help me. For the last year and a half I have not had a hand in anything dishonorable, and all that time I have been struggling in most restricted circumstances. I was content to work my way up step by step. Now I am turned out, and I am not going to be satisfied with merely being taken into favor again. I want to get on, I tell you. I want to get into the bank again, in a higher position. Your husband must make a place for me——

NORA. That he will never do!

KROG. He will; I know him; he dare not protest. And as soon as I am in there again with him then you will see! Within a year I shall be the manager's right hand. It will be Nils Krogstad and not Torvald Helmer who manages the bank.

NORA. That's a thing you will never see!

KROG. Do you mean that you will——

NORA. I have courage enough for it now.

KROG. Oh, you can't frighten me. A fine, spoilt lady like you——

NORA. You will see, you will see.

KROG. Under the ice, perhaps? Down into the cold, coal-black water? And then, in the spring, to float up to the surface, all horrible and unrecognizable, with your hair fallen out——

NORA. You can't frighten me.

KROG. Nor you me. People don't do such things, Mrs. Helmer. Besides, what use would it be? I should have him completely in my power all the same.

NORA. Afterward? When I am no longer——

KROG. Have you forgotten that it is I who have the keeping of your reputation? (NORA *stands speechlessly looking at him.*) Well, now, I have warned you. Do not do anything foolish. When Helmer has had my letter I shall expect a message from him. And be sure you remember that it is your husband himself who has forced me into such ways as this again. I will never forgive him for that. Good-by, Mrs. Helmer. (*Exit through the hall.*)

NORA (*goes to the hall door, opens it slightly and listens*). He is going. He is not putting the letter in the box. Oh no, no! that's impossible! (*Opens the door by degrees.*) What is that? He is standing outside. He is not going downstairs. Is he hesitating? Can he—— (*A letter drops in the box; then* KROGSTAD'S *footsteps are heard, till they die away as he goes downstairs.* NORA *utters a stifled cry and runs across the room to the table by the sofa. A short pause.*)

NORA. In the letter box. (*Steals across to the hall door.*) There it lies—Torvald, Torvald, there is no hope for us now!

(MRS. LINDE *comes in from the room on the left, carrying the dress.*)

MRS. L. There, I can't see anything more to mend now. Would you like to try it on?

NORA (*in a hoarse whisper*). Christine, come here.

MRS. L. (*throwing the dress down on the sofa*). What is the matter with you? You look so agitated!

NORA. Come here. Do you see that letter? There, look—you can see it through the glass in the letter box.

MRS. L. Yes, I see it.

NORA. That letter is from Krogstad.

MRS. L. Nora—it was Krogstad who lent you the money!

NORA. Yes, and now Torvald will know all about it.

MRS. L. Believe me, Nora, that's the best thing for both of you.

NORA. You don't know all. I forged a name.

MRS. L. Good heavens!

NORA. I only want to say this to you, Christine—you must be my witness.

MRS. L. Your witness? What do you mean? What am I to——

NORA. If I should go out of my mind—and it might easily happen——

MRS. L. Nora!

NORA. Or if anything else should happen to me—anything, for instance, that might prevent my being here——

MRS. L. Nora! Nora! you are quite out of your mind.

NORA. And if it should happen that there were someone who wanted to take all the responsibility, all the blame, you understand——

MRS. L. Yes, yes—but how can you suppose——

NORA. Then you must be my witness, that it is not true, Christine. I am not out of my mind at all; I am in my right senses now, and I tell you no one else has known anything about it; I, and I alone, did the whole thing. Remember that.

MRS. L. I will, indeed. But I don't understand all this.

NORA. How should you understand it? A wonderful thing is going to happen.

MRS. L. A wonderful thing?

NORA. Yes, a wonderful thing! But it is so terrible. Christine, it *mustn't* happen, not for all the world.

MRS. L. I will go at once and see Krogstad.

NORA. Don't go to him; he will do you some harm.

MRS. L. There was a time when he would gladly do anything for my sake.

NORA. He?

MRS. L. Where does he live?

NORA. How should I know? Yes—(*feeling in her pocket*)—here is his card. But the letter, the letter!

HEL. (*calls from his room, knocking at the door*). Nora!

NORA (*cries out anxiously*). Oh, what's that? What do you want?

HEL. Don't be so frightened. We are not coming in; you have locked the door. Are you trying on your dress?

NORA. Yes, that's it. I look so nice, Torvald.

MRS. L. (*who has read the card*). I see he lives at the corner here.

NORA. Yes, but it's no use. It is hopeless. The letter is lying there in the box.

MRS. L. And your husband keeps the key?

NORA. Yes, always.

MRS. L. Krogstad must ask for his letter back unread, he must find some pretense——

NORA. But it is just at this time that Torvald generally——

MRS. L. You must delay him. Go in to him in the meantime. I will come back as soon as I can. (*She goes out hurriedly through the hall door.*)

NORA (*goes to* HELMER'S *door, opens it and peeps in*). Torvald!

HEL. (*from the inner room*). Well? May I venture at last to come into my own room again? Come along, Rank, now you will see—— (*Halting in the doorway.*) But what is this?

NORA. What is what, dear?

HEL. Rank led me to expect a splendid transformation.

RANK (*in the doorway*). I understood so, but evidently I was mistaken.

NORA. Yes, nobody is to have the chance of admiring me in my dress until tomorrow.

HEL. But, my dear Nora, you look so worn out. Have you been practicing too much?

NORA. No, I have not practiced at all.

HEL. But you will need to——

NORA. Yes, indeed I shall, Torvald. But I can't get on a bit without you to help me; I have absolutely forgotten the whole thing.

HEL. Oh, we will soon work it up again.

NORA. Yes, help me, Torvald. Promise that you will! I am so nervous about it—all the people—— You must give yourself up to me entirely this evening. Not the tiniest bit of business—you mustn't even take a pen in your hand. Will you promise, Torvald dear?

HEL. I promise. This evening I will be wholly and absolutely at your service, you helpless little mortal. Ah, by the way, first of all I will just—— (*Goes toward the hall door.*)

NORA. What are you going to do there?

HEL. Only see if any letters have come.

NORA. No, no! Don't do that, Torvald!

HEL. Why not?

NORA. Torvald, please don't. There is nothing there.

HEL. Well, let me look. (*Turns to go to the letter box.* NORA, *at the piano, plays the first bars of the tarantella.* HELMER *stops in the doorway.*) Aha!

NORA. I can't dance tomorrow if I don't practice with you.

HEL. (*going up to her*). Are you really so afraid of it, dear?

NORA. Yes, so dreadfully afraid of it. Let me practice at once; there is time now, before we go to dinner. Sit down and play for me, Torvald dear; criticize me and correct me as you play.

HEL. With great pleasure, if you wish me to. (*Sits down at the piano.*)

NORA (*takes out of the box a tambourine and a long variegated shawl. She hastily drapes the shawl round her. Then she springs to the front of the stage and calls out*). Now play for me! I am going to dance!

(HELMER *plays and* NORA *dances.* RANK *stands by the piano behind* HELMER *and looks on.*)

HEL. (*as he plays*). Slower, slower!

NORA. I can't do it any other way.

HEL. Not so violently, Nora!

NORA. This is the way.

HEL. (*stops playing*). No, no—that is not a bit right.

NORA. (*laughing and swinging the tambourine*). Didn't I tell you so?

RANK. Let me play for her.

HEL. (*getting up*). Yes, do. I can correct her better then.

(RANK *sits down at the piano and plays.* NORA *dances more and more wildly.* HELMER *has taken up a position by the stove and during her dance gives her frequent instructions. She does not seem to hear him; her hair comes down and falls over her shoulders; she pays no attention to it but goes on dancing. Enter* MRS. LINDE.)

MRS. L. (*standing as if spellbound in the doorway*). Oh!

NORA (*as she dances*). Such fun, Christine!

HEL. My dear darling Nora, you are dancing as if your life depended on it.

NORA. So it does.

HEL. Stop, Rank this is sheer madness. Stop, I tell you! (RANK *stops playing, and* NORA *suddenly stands still.* HELMER *goes up to her.*) I could never have believed it. You have forgotten everything I taught you.

NORA. (*throwing away the tambourine*). There, you see.

HEL. You will want a lot of coaching.

NORA. Yes, you see how much I need it. You must coach me up to the last minute. Promise me that, Torvald!

HEL. You can depend on me.

NORA. You must not think of anything but me, either today or tomorrow; you mustn't open a single letter—not even open the letter box——

HEL. Ah, you are still afraid of that fellow——

NORA. Yes, indeed I am.

HEL. Nora, I can tell from your looks that there is a letter from him lying there.

NORA. I don't know; I think there is; but you must not read anything of that kind now. Nothing horrid must come between us till this is all over.

RANK (*whispers to* HELMER). You mustn't contradict her.

HEL. (*taking her in his arms*). The child shall have her way. But tomorrow night, after you have danced——

NORA. Then you will be free. (*The* MAID *appears in the doorway to the right.*)

MAID. Dinner is served, ma'am.

NORA. We will have champagne, Helen.

MAID. Very good, ma'am. (*Exit.*)

HEL. Hullo!—are we going to have a banquet?

NORA. Yes, a champagne banquet till the small hours. (*Calls out.*) And a few macaroons. Helen—lots, just for once!

HEL. Come, come, don't be so wild and nervous. Be my own little skylark, as you used.

NORA. Yes, dear, I will. But go in now, and you too, Doctor Rank, Christine, you must help me to do up my hair.

RANK. (*whispers to* HELMER *as they go out*). I suppose there is nothing—she is not expecting anything?

HEL. Far from it, my dear fellow; it is simply nothing more than this childish nervousness I was telling you of. (*They go into the right-hand room.*)

NORA. Well!

MRS. L. Gone out of town.

NORA. I could tell from your face.

MRS. L. He is coming home tomorrow evening. I wrote a note for him.

NORA. You should have let it alone; you must prevent nothing. After all, it is splendid to be waiting for a wonderful thing to happen.

MRS. L. What is it that you are waiting for?

NORA. Oh, you wouldn't understand. Go in to them, I will come in a moment. (MRS. LINDE *goes into the dining room.* NORA *stands still for a little while, as if to compose herself. Then she looks at her watch.*) Five o'clock. Seven hours till midnight; and then four-and-twenty hours till the next midnight. Then the tarantella will be over. Twenty-four and seven? Thirty-one hours to live.

HEL. (*from the doorway on the right*). Where's my little skylark?

NORA (*going to him with her arms outstretched*). Here she is!

ACT III

THE SAME SCENE—*The table has been placed in the middle of the stage with chairs round it. A lamp is burning on the table. The door into the hall stands open. Dance music is heard in the room above.* MRS. LINDE *is sitting at the table idly turning over the leaves of a book; she tries to read but does not seem able to collect her thoughts. Every now and then she listens intently for a sound at the outer door.*

MRS. L. (*looking at her watch*). Not yet—and the time is nearly up. If only he does not—— (*Listens again.*) Ah, there he is. (*Goes into the hall and opens the outer door carefully. Light footsteps are heard on the stairs. She whispers.*) Come in. There is no one here.

KROG. (*in the doorway*). I found a note from you at home. What does this mean?

MRS. L. It is absolutely necessary that I should have a talk with you.

KROG. Really? And it is absolutely necessary that it should be here?

MRS. L. It is impossible where I live; there is no private entrance to my rooms. Come in; we are quite alone. The maid is asleep, and the Helmers are at the dance upstairs.

KROG. (*coming into the room*). Are the Helmers really at a dance tonight?

MRS. L. Yes, why not?

KROG. Certainly—why not?

MRS. L. Now, Nils, let us have a talk.

KROG. Can we two have anything to talk about?

MRS. L. We have a great deal to talk about.

KROG. I shouldn't have thought so.

MRS. L. No, you have never properly understood me.

KROG. Was there anything else to understand except what was obvious to all the world—a heartless woman jilts a man when a more lucrative chance turns up?

MRS. L. Do you believe I am as absolutely heartless as all that? And do you believe it with a light heart?

KROG. Didn't you?

MRS. L. Nils, did you really think that?

KROG. If it were as you say, why did you write to me as you did at the time?

MRS. L. I could do nothing else. As I had to break with you, it was my duty also to put an end to all that you felt for me.

KROG. (*wringing his hands*). So that was it. And all this—only for the sake of money!

MRS. L. You mustn't forget that I had a helpless mother and two little brothers. We couldn't wait for you, Nils; your prospects seemed hopeless then.

KROG. That may be so, but you had no right to throw me over for anyone else's sake.

MRS. L. Indeed, I don't know. Many a time did I ask myself if I had the right to do it.

KROG. (*more gently*). When I lost you it was as if all the solid ground went from under my feet. Look at me now—I am a shipwrecked man clinging to a bit of wreckage.

MRS. L. But help may be near.

KROG. It *was* near, but then you came and stood in my way.

MRS. L. Unintentionally, Nils. It was only today that I learned it was your place I was going to take in the bank.

KROG. I believe you, if you say so. But now that you know it, are you not going to give it up to me?

MRS. L. No, because that would not benefit you in the least.

KROG. Oh, benefit, benefit—I would have done it whether or no.

MRS. L. I have learned to act prudently. Life and hard, bitter necessity have taught me that.

KROG. And life has taught me not to believe in fine speeches.

MRS. L. Then life has taught you something very reasonable. But deeds you must believe in.

KROG. What do you mean by that?

MRS. L. You said you were like a shipwrecked man clinging to some wreckage.

KROG. I had good reason to say so.

MRS. L. Well, I am like a shipwrecked woman clinging to some wreckage—no one to mourn for, no one to care for.

KROG. It was your own choice.

MRS. L. There was no other choice—then.

KROG. Well, what now?

MRS. L. Nils, how would it be if we two shipwrecked people could join forces?

KROG. What are you saying?

MRS. L. Two on the same piece of wreckage would stand a better chance than each on their own.

KROG. Christine!

MRS. L. What do you suppose brought me to town?

KROG. Do you mean that you gave me a thought?

MRS. L. I could not endure life without work. All my life, as long as I can remember, I have worked, and it has been my greatest and only pleasure. But now I am quite alone in the world—my life is so dreadfully empty and I feel so forsaken. There is not the least pleasure in working for one's self. Nils, give me someone and something to work for.

KROG. I don't trust that. It is nothing but a woman's overstrained sense of generosity that prompts you to make such an offer of yourself.

MRS. L. Have you ever noticed anything of the sort in me?

KROG. Could you really do it? Tell me—do you know all about my past life?

MRS. L. Yes.

KROG. And do you know what they think of me here?

MRS. L. You seemed to me to imply that with me you might have been quite another man.

KROG. I am certain of it.

MRS. L. Is it too late now?

KROG. Christine, are you saying this deliberately? Yes, I am sure you are. I see it in your face. Have you really the courage, then——

MRS. L. I want to be a mother to someone, and your children need a mother. We two need each other. Nils, I have faith in your real character—I can dare anything with you.

KROG. (*grasps her hands*). Thanks, thanks, Christine! Now I shall find a way to clear myself in the eyes of the world. Ah, but I forgot——

MRS. L. (*listening*). Hush! The tarantella! Go, go!

KROG. Why? What is it?

MRS. L. Do you hear them up there? When that is over we may expect them back.

KROG. Yes, yes—I will go. But it is all no use. Of course you are not aware what steps I have taken in the matter of the Helmers.

MRS. L. Yes, I know all about that.

KROG. And in spite of that have you the courage to——

MRS. L. I understand very well to what lengths a man like you might be driven by despair.

KROG. If I could only undo what I have done!

MRS. L. You cannot. Your letter is lying in the letter box now.

KROG. Are you sure of that?

MRS. L. Quite sure, but——

KROG. (*with a searching look at her*). Is that what it all means?—that you want to save your friend at any cost? Tell me frankly. Is that it?

MRS. L. Nils, a woman who has once sold herself for another's sake doesn't do it a second time.

KROG. I will ask for my letter back.

MRS. L. No, no.

KROG. Yes, of course I will. I will wait here till Helmer comes; I will tell him he must give me my letter back—that it only concerns my dismissal—that he is not to read it——

MRS. L. No, Nils, you must not recall your letter.

KROG. But, tell me, wasn't it for that very purpose that you asked me to meet you here?

MRS. L. In my first moment of fright it was. But twenty-four hours have elapsed since then, and in that time I have witnessed incredible things in this house. Helmer must know all about it. This unhappy secret must be disclosed; they must have a complete understanding between them, which is impossible with all this concealment and falsehood going on.

KROG. Very well, if you will take the responsibility. But there is one thing I can do in any case, and I shall do it at once.

MRS. L. (*listening*). You must be quick and go! The dance is over; we are not safe a moment longer.

KROG. I will wait for you below.

MRS. L. Yes, do. You must see me back to my door.

KROG. I have never had such an amazing piece of good fortune in my life! (*Goes out through the outer door. The door between the room and the hall remains open.*)

MRS. L. (*tidying up the room and laying her hat and cloak ready*). What a difference! What a difference! Someone to work for and live for—a home to bring comfort into. That I will do, indeed. I wish they would be quick and come. (*Listens.*) Ah, there they are now. I must put on my things. (*Takes up her hat and cloak.* HELMER's *and* NORA's *voices are heard outside; a key is turned, and* HELMER *brings* NORA *almost by force into the hall. She is in an Italian costume with a large black shawl round her; he is in evening dress and a black domino which is flying open.*)

NORA (*hanging back in the doorway and struggling with him*). No, no, no!— don't take me in. I want to go upstairs again; I don't want to leave so early.

HEL. But, my dearest Nora——

NORA. Please, Torvald dear—please, *please*—only an hour more.

HEL. Not a single minute, my sweet Nora. You know that was our agreement. Come along into the room; you are catching cold standing there. (*He brings her gently into the room in spite of her resistance.*)

MRS. L. Good evening.

NORA. Christine!

HEL. You here so late, Mrs. Linde?

MRS. L. Yes, you must excuse me; I was so anxious to see Nora in her dress.

NORA. Have you been sitting here waiting for me?

MRS. L. Yes; unfortunately I came too late—you had already gone upstairs— and I thought I couldn't go away again without having seen you.

HEL. (*taking off* NORA'S *shawl*). Yes, take a good look at her. I think she is worth looking at. Isn't she charming, Mrs. Linde?

MRS. L. Yes, indeed she is.

HEL. Doesn't she look remarkably pretty? Everyone thought so at the dance. But she is terribly self-willed, this sweet little person. What are we to do with her? You will hardly believe that I had almost to bring her away by force.

NORA. Torvald, you will repent not having let me stay, even if it were only for half an hour.

HEL. Listen to her, Mrs. Linde! She had danced her tarantella, and it had been a tremendous success, as it deserved—although possibly the performance was a trifle too realistic—a little more so, I mean, than was strictly compatible with the limitations of art. But never mind about that! The chief thing is, she had made a success—she had made a tremendous success. Do you think I was going to let her remain there after that and spoil the effect? No indeed! I took my charming little Capri maiden—my capricious little Capri maiden, I should say—on my arm, took one quick turn round the room, a curtsey on either side, and, as they say in novels, the beautiful apparition disappeared. An exit ought always to be effective, Mrs. Linde; but that is what I cannot make Nora understand. Pooh! this room is hot. (*Throws his domino on a chair and opens the door of his room.*) Hullo! it's all dark in here. Oh, of course—excuse me. (*He goes in and lights some candles.*)

NORA (*in a hurried and breathless whisper*). Well?

MRS. L. (*in a low voice*). I have had a talk with him.

NORA. Yes, and——

MRS. L. Nora, you must tell your husband all about it.

NORA (*in an expressionless voice*). I knew it.

MRS. L. You have nothing to be afraid of as far as Krogstad is concerned, but you must tell him.

NORA. I won't tell him.

MRS. L. Then the letter will.

NORA. Thank you, Christine. Now I know what I must do. Hush!

HEL. (*coming in again*). Well, Mrs. Linde, have you admired her?

MRS. L. Yes, and now I will say good night.

HEL. What, already? Is this yours, this knitting?

MRS. L. (*taking it*). Yes, thank you. I had very nearly forgotten it.

HEL. So you knit?

MRS. L. Of course.

HEL. Do you know, you ought to embroider.

MRS. L. Really? Why?

HEL. Yes, it's far more becoming. Let me show you. You hold the embroidery thus in your left hand and use the needle with the right—like this—with a long easy sweep. Do you see?

MRS. L. Yes, perhaps——

HEL. Yes, but in the case of knitting—that can never be anything but ungraceful; look here—the arms close together, the knitting needles going up and down—it has a sort of Chinese effect. . . . That was really excellent champagne they gave us.

MRS. L. Well—good night, Nora, and don't be self-willed any more.

HEL. That's right, Mrs. Linde.

MRS. L. Good night, Mr. Helmer.

HEL. (*accompanying her to the door*). Good night, good night. I hope you will get home all right. I should be very happy to—— But you haven't any great distance to go. Good night, good night. (*She goes out; he shuts the door after her and comes in again.*) Ah!—at last we have got rid of her. She is a frightful bore, that woman.

NORA. Aren't you very tired, Torvald?

HEL. No, not in the least.

NORA. Nor sleepy?

HEL. Not a bit. On the contrary I feel extraordinarily lively. And you?—you really look both tired and sleepy.

NORA. Yes, I am very tired. I want to go to sleep at once.

HEL. There, you see it was quite right of me not to let you stay there any longer.

NORA. Everything you do is quite right, Torvald.

HEL. (*kissing her on the forehead*). Now my little skylark is speaking reasonably. Did you notice what good spirits Rank was in this evening?

NORA. Really? Was he? I didn't speak to him at all.

HEL. And I very little, but I have not for a long time seen him in such good form. (*Looks for a while at her and then goes nearer to her.*) It is delightful to be at home by ourselves again, to be all alone with you—you fascinating, charming little darling!

NORA. Don't look at me like that, Torvald.

HEL. Why shouldn't I look at my dearest treasure?—at all the beauty that is mine, all my very own?

NORA (*going to the other side of the table*). You mustn't say things like that to me tonight.

HEL. (*following her*). You have still got the tarantella in your blood, I see. And it makes you more captivating than ever. Listen—the guests are beginning to go now. (*In a lower voice.*) Nora—soon the whole house will be quiet.

NORA. Yes, I hope so.

HEL. Yes, my own darling Nora. Do you know, when I am out at a party with you like this, why I speak so little to you, keep away from you and only send a stolen glance in your direction now and then?—do you know why I do that? It is because I make believe to myself that we are secretly in love and you are my secretly promised bride and that no one suspects there is anything between us.

NORA. Yes, yes—I know very well your thoughts are with me all the time.

HEL. And when we are leaving and I am putting the shawl over your beautiful young shoulders—on your lovely neck—then I imagine that you are my young bride and that we have just come from our wedding and I am bringing you, for the first time, into our home—to be alone with you for the first time—quite alone with my shy little darling! All this evening I have longed for nothing but you. When I watched the seductive figures of the tarantella my blood was on fire; I could endure it no longer, and that was why I brought you down so early——

NORA. Go away, Torvald! You must let me go. I won't——

HEL. What's that? You're joking, my little Nora! You won't—you won't? Am I not your husband? (*A knock is heard at the outer door.*)

NORA (*starting*). Did you hear——

HEL. (*going into the hall*). Who is it?

RANK (*outside*). It is I. May I come in for a moment?

HEL. (*in a fretful whisper*). Oh, what does he want now? (*Aloud.*) Wait a minute. (*Unlocks the door.*) Come, that's kind of you not to pass by our door.

RANK. I thought I heard your voice, and I felt as if I should like to look in. (*With a swift glance round.*) Ah yes!—these dear familiar rooms. You are very happy and cosy in here, you two.

HEL. It seems to me that you looked after yourself pretty well upstairs too.

RANK. Excellently. Why shouldn't I? Why shouldn't one enjoy everything in this world?—at any rate as much as one can and as long as one can. The wine was capital——

HEL. Especially the champagne.

RANK. So you noticed that too? It is almost incredible how much I managed to put away!

NORA. Torvald drank a great deal of champagne tonight too.

RANK. Did he?

NORA. Yes, and he is always in such good spirits afterward.

RANK. Well, why should one not enjoy a merry evening after a well-spent day?

HEL. Well-spent? I am afraid I can't take credit for that.

RANK (*clapping him on the back*). But I can, you know!

HEL. Exactly.

NORA. Doctor Rank, you must have been occupied with some scientific investigation today.

HEL. Just listen!—little Nora talking about scientific investigations!

NORA. And may I congratulate you on the result?

RANK. Indeed you may.

NORA. Was it favorable, then?

RANK. The best possible, for both doctor and patient—certainty.

NORA (*quickly and searchingly*). Certainty?

RANK. Absolute certainty. So wasn't I entitled to make a merry evening of it after that?

NORA. Yes, you certainly were, Doctor Rank.

HEL. I think so too, so long as you don't have to pay for it in the morning.

RANK. Oh well, one can't have anything in this life without paying for it.

NORA. Doctor Rank—are you fond of fancy-dress balls?

RANK. Yes, if there is a fine lot of pretty costumes.

NORA. Tell me—what shall we two wear at the next?

HEL. Little featherbrain!—are you thinking of the next already?

RANK. We two? Yes, I can tell you. You shall go as a good fairy——

HEL. Yes, but what do you suggest as an appropriate costume for that?

RANK. Let your wife go dressed just as she is in everyday life.

HEL. That was really very prettily turned. But can't you tell us what you will be?

RANK. Yes, my dear friend, I have quite made up my mind about that.

HEL. Well?

RANK. At the next fancy-dress ball I shall be invisible.

HEL. That's a good joke!

RANK. There is a big black hat—have you ever heard of hats that make you invisible? If you put one on, no one can see you.

HEL. (*suppressing a smile*). Yes, you are quite right.

RANK. But I am clean forgetting what I came for. Helmer, give me a cigar—one of the dark Havanas.

HEL. With the greatest pleasure. (*Offers him his case.*)

RANK (*takes a cigar and cuts off the end*). Thanks.

NORA (*striking a match*). Let me give you a light.

RANK. Thank you. (*She holds the match for him to light his cigar.*) And now good-by!

HEL. Good-by, good-by, dear old man!

NORA. Sleep well, Doctor Rank.

RANK. Thank you for that wish.

NORA. Wish me the same.

RANK. You? Well, if you want me to sleep well! And thanks for the light. (*He nods to them both and goes out.*)

HEL. (*in a subdued voice*). He has drunk more than he ought.

NORA (*absently*). Maybe. (HELMER *takes a bunch of keys out of his pocket and goes into the hall.*) Torvald! What are you going to do there?

HEL. Empty the letter box; it is quite full; there will be no room to put the newspaper in tomorrow morning.

NORA. Are you going to work tonight?

HEL. You know quite well I'm not. What is this? Someone has been at the lock.

NORA. At the lock?

HEL. Yes, someone has. What can it mean? I should never have thought the maid—— Here is a broken hairpin. Nora, it is one of yours.

NORA (*quickly*). Then it must have been the children.

HEL. Then you must get them out of those ways. There, at last I have got it open. (*Takes out the contents of the letter box and calls to the kitchen.*) Helen! Helen, put out the light over the front door. (*Goes back into the room and shuts the door into the hall. He holds out his hand full of letters.*) Look at that—look what a heap of them there are. (*Turning them over.*) What on earth is that?

NORA (*at the window*). The letter—— No! Torvald, no!

HEL. Two cards—of Rank's.

NORA. Of Doctor Rank's?

HEL. (*looking at them*). Doctor Rank. They were on the top. He must have put them in when he went out.

NORA. Is there anything written on them?

HEL. There is a black cross over the name. Look there—what an uncomfortable idea! It looks as if he were announcing his own death.

NORA. It is just what he is doing.

HEL. What? Do you know anything about it? Has he said anything to you?

NORA. Yes. He told me that when the cards came it would be his leave-taking from us. He means to shut himself up and die.

HEL. My poor old friend. Certainly I knew we should not have him very long with us. But so soon! And so he hides himself away like a wounded animal.

NORA. If it has to happen, it is best it should be without a word—don't you think so, Torvald?

HEL. (*walking up and down*). He had so grown into our lives. I can't think of him as having gone out of them. He, with his sufferings and his loneliness, was like a cloudy background to our sunlit happiness. Well, perhaps it is best so. For him, anyway. (*Standing still.*) And perhaps for us too, Nora. We two are thrown quite upon each other now. (*Puts his arms round her.*) My darling wife, I don't feel as if I could hold you tight enough. Do you know, Nora, I have often wished that you might be threatened by some great danger, so that I might risk my life's blood and everything for your sake.

NORA (*disengages herself and says firmly and decidedly*). Now you must read your letters, Torvald.

HEL. No, no; not tonight. I want to be with you, my darling wife.

NORA. With the thought of your friend's death——

HEL. You are right; it has affected us both. Something ugly has come between us—the thought of the horrors of death. We must try and rid our minds of that. Until then—we will each go to our own room.

NORA (*hanging on his neck*). Good night, Torvald—good night!

HEL. (*kissing her on the forehead*). Good night, my little singing bird. Sleep sound, Nora. Now I will read my letters through. (*He takes his letters and goes into his room, shutting the door after him.*)

NORA (*gropes distractedly about, seizes* HELMER'S *domino, throws it about her while she says in quick, hoarse, spasmodic whispers*). Never to see him again. Never! Never! (*Puts her shawl over her head.*) Never to see my children again either—never again. Never! Never! Ah! the icy black water—the unfathomable depths—if only it were over! He has got it now—now he is reading it. Good-by, Torvald and my children! (*She is about to rush out through the hall when* HELMER *opens his door hurriedly and stands with an open letter in his hand.*)

HEL. Nora!

NORA. Ah!

HEL. What is this? Do you know what is in this letter?

NORA. Yes, I know. Let me go! Let me get out!

HEL. (*holding her back*). Where are you going?

NORA (*trying to get free*). You shan't save me, Torvald!

HEL. (*reeling*). True? Is this true, that I read here? Horrible! No, no—it is impossible that it is true.

NORA. It is true. I have loved you above everything else in the world.

HEL. Oh, don't let us have any silly excuses.

NORA (*taking a step toward him*). Torvald!

HEL. Miserable creature—what have you done?

NORA. Let me go. You shall not suffer for my sake. You shall not take it upon yourself.

HEL. No tragedy airs, please. (*Locks the hall door.*) Here you shall stay and give me an explanation. Do you understand what you have done? Answer me! Do you understand what you have done?

NORA (*looks steadily at him and says with a growing look of coldness in her face*). Yes, now I am beginning to understand thoroughly.

HEL. (*walking about the room*). What a horrible awakening! All these eight years—she who was my joy and pride—a hypocrite, a liar—worse, worse—a criminal! The unutterable ugliness of it all! For shame! For shame! (NORA *is silent and looks steadily at him. He stops in front of her.*) I ought to have suspected that something of the sort would happen. I ought to have foreseen it. All your father's want of principle—be silent!—all your father's want of principle has come out in you. No religion, no morality, no sense of duty—— How I am punished for having winked at what he did! I did it for your sake, and this is how you repay me.

NORA. Yes, that's just it.

HEL. Now you have destroyed all my happiness. You have ruined all my future. It is horrible to think of! I am in the power of an unscrupulous man; he can do what he likes with me, ask anything he likes of me, give me any orders he pleases—I dare not refuse. And I must sink to such miserable depths because of a thoughtless woman!

NORA. When I am out of the way you will be free.

HEL. No fine speeches, please. Your father always had plenty of those ready too. What good would it be to me if you were out of the way, as you say? Not the slightest. He can make the affair known everywhere; and if he does, I may be falsely suspected of having been a party to your criminal action. Very likely people will think I was behind it all—that it was I who prompted you! And I have to thank you for all this—you whom I have cherished during the whole of our married life. Do you understand now what it is you have done for me?

NORA (*coldly and quietly*). Yes.

HEL. It is so incredible that I can't take it in. But we must come to some understanding. Take off that shawl. Take it off, I tell you. I must try and appease him in some way or another. The matter must be hushed up at any cost. And as for you and me, it must appear as if everything between us were just as before—but naturally only in the eyes of the world. You will still remain in my house, that is a matter of course. But I shall not allow you to bring up the children; I dare not trust them to you. To think that I should be obliged to say so to one whom I have loved so dearly and whom I still—— No, that is all over. From this moment happiness is not the question; all that concerns us is to save the remains, the fragments, the appearance——

(*A ring is heard at the front-door bell.*)

HEL. (*with a start*). What is that? So late! Can the worst—can he—— Hide yourself, Nora. Say you are ill.

(NORA *stands motionless.* HELMER *goes and unlocks the hall door.*)

MAID (*half dressed, comes to the door*). A letter for the mistress.
HEL. Give it to me. (*Takes the letter and shuts the door.*) Yes, it is from him. You shall not have it; I will read it myself.
NORA. Yes, read it.
HEL. (*standing by the lamp*). I scarcely have the courage to do it. It may mean ruin for the both of us. No, I must know. (*Tears open the letter, runs his eye over a few lines, looks at a paper enclosed and gives a shout of joy.*) Nora! (*She looks at him questioningly.*) Nora! No, I must read it once again. Yes, it is true! I am saved! Nora, I am saved!
NORA. And I?
HEL. You too, of course; we are both saved, both you and I. Look, he sends you your bond back. He says he regrets and repents—that a happy change in his life—— Never mind what he says! We are saved, Nora! No one can do anything to you. Oh, Nora, Nora—— No, first I must destroy these hateful things. Let me see. (*Takes a look at the bond.*) No, no, I won't look at it. The whole thing shall be nothing but a bad dream to me. (*Tears up the bond and both letters, throws them all into the stove and watches them burn.*) There—now it doesn't exist any longer. He says that since Christmas Eve you—— These must have been three dreadful days for you, Nora.
NORA. I have fought a hard fight these three days.
HEL. And suffered agonies and seen no way out, but—— No, we won't call any of the horrors to mind. We will only shout with joy and keep saying, "It's all over! It's all over!" Listen to me, Nora. You don't seem to realize

that it is all over. What is this?—such a cold, set face! My poor little Nora, I quite understand; you don't feel as if you could believe that I have forgiven you. But it is true, Nora, I swear it; I have forgiven you everything. I know that what you did you did out of love for me.

NORA. That is true.

HEL. You have loved me as a wife ought to love her husband. Only you had not sufficient knowledge to judge of the means you used. But do you suppose you are any the less dear to me because you don't understand how to act on your own responsibility? No, no; only lean on me; I will advise and direct you. I should not be a man if this womanly helplessness did not just give you a double attractiveness in my eyes. You must not think any more about the hard things I said in my first moment of consternation, when I thought everything was going to overwhelm me. I have forgiven you, Nora; I swear to you I have forgiven you.

NORA. Thank you for your forgiveness. (*She goes out through the door to the right.*)

HEL. No, don't go. (*Looks in.*) What are you doing in there?

NORA (*from within*). Taking off my fancy dress.

HEL. (*standing at the open door*). Yes, do. Try and calm yourself and make your mind easy again, my frightened little singing bird. Be at rest and feel secure; I have broad wings to shelter you under. (*Walks up and down by the door.*) How warm and cosy our home is, Nora. Here is shelter for you; here I will protect you like a hunted dove that I have saved from a hawk's claws; I will bring peace to your poor beating heart. It will come, little by little, Nora, believe me. Tomorrow morning you will look upon it all quite differently; soon everything will be just as it was before. Very soon you won't need me to assure you that I have forgiven you; you will yourself feel the certainty that I have done so. Can you suppose I should ever think of such a thing as repudiating you or even reproaching you? You have no idea what a true man's heart is like, Nora. There is something so indescribably sweet and satisfying, to a man, in the knowledge that he has forgiven his wife—forgiven her freely and with all his heart. It seems as if that had made her, as it were, doubly his own; he has given her a new life, so to speak, and she has in a way become both wife and child to him. So you shall be for me after this, my little scared, helpless darling. Have no anxiety about anything, Nora; only be frank and open with me, and I will serve as will and conscience both to you—— What is this? Not gone to bed? Have you changed your things?

NORA (*in everyday dress*). Yes, Torvald, I have changed my things now.

HEL. But what for?—so late as this.

NORA. I shall not sleep tonight.

HEL. But, my dear Nora——

NORA (*looking at her watch*). It is not so very late. Sit down here, Torvald. You and I have much to say to one another. (*She sits down at one side of the table.*)

HEL. Nora—what is this?—this cold, set face?

NORA. Sit down. It will take some time; I have a lot to talk over with you.

HEL. (*sits down at the opposite side of the table*). You alarm me, Nora!—and I don't understand you.

NORA. No, that is just it. You don't understand me, and I have never understood you either—before tonight. No, you mustn't interrupt me. You must simply listen to what I say. Torvald, this is a settling of accounts.

HEL. What do you mean by that?

NORA (*after a short silence*). Isn't there one thing that strikes you as strange in our sitting here like this?

HEL. What is that?

NORA. We have been married now eight years. Does it not occur to you that this is the first time we two, you and I, husband and wife, have had a serious conversation?

HEL. What do you mean, serious?

NORA. In all these eight years—longer than that—from the very beginning of our acquaintance we have never exchanged a word on any serious subject.

HEL. Was it likely that I would be continually and forever telling you about worries that you could not help me to bear?

NORA. I am not speaking about business matters. I say that we have never sat down in earnest together to try and get at the bottom of anything.

HEL. But, dearest Nora, would it have been any good to you?

NORA. That is just it; you have never understood me. I have been greatly wronged, Torvald—first by Papa and then by you.

HEL. What! By us two—by us two who have loved you better than anyone else in the world?

NORA (*shaking her head*). You have never loved me. You have only thought it pleasant to be in love with me.

HEL. Nora, what do I hear you saying?

NORA. It is perfectly true, Torvald. When I was at home with Papa he told me his opinion about everything, and so I had the same opinions; and if I differed from him I concealed the fact, because he would not have liked it. He called me his doll child, and he played with me just as I used to play with my dolls. And when I came to live with you——

HEL. What sort of an expression is that to use about our marriage?

NORA (*undisturbed*). I mean that I was simply transferred from Papa's hands to yours. You arranged everything according to your own taste, and so I got the same tastes as you—or else I pretended to. I am really not quite sure which—I think sometimes the one and sometimes the other. When I look back on it it seems to me as if I have been living here like a poor woman—just from hand to mouth. I have existed merely to perform tricks for you, Torvald. But you would have it so. You and Papa have committed a great sin against me. It is your fault that I have made nothing of my life.

HEL. How unreasonable and how ungrateful you are, Nora! Have you not been happy here?

NORA. No, I have never been happy. I thought I was, but it has never really been so.

HEL. Not—not happy!

NORA. No, only merry. And you have always been so kind to me. But our home has been nothing but a playroom. I have been your doll wife, just as at home I was Papa's doll child; and here the children have been my dolls. I thought it great fun when you played with me, just as they thought it great fun when I played with them. That is what our marriage has been, Torvald.

HEL. There is some truth in what you say—exaggerated and strained as your view of it is. But for the future it shall be different. Playtime shall be over and lesson time shall begin.

NORA. Whose lessons? Mine or the children's?

HEL. Both yours and the children's, my darling Nora.

NORA. Alas, Torvald, you are not the man to educate me into being a proper wife for you.

HEL. And you can say that!

NORA. And I—how am I fitted to bring up the children?

HEL. Nora!

NORA. Didn't you say so yourself a little while ago—that you dare not trust me to bring them up?

HEL. In a moment of anger! Why do you pay any heed to that?

NORA. Indeed, you were perfectly right. I am not fit for the task. There is another task I must undertake first. I must try and educate myself—you are not the man to help me in that. I must do that for myself. And that is why I am going to leave you now.

HEL. (*springing up*). What do you say?

NORA. I must stand quite alone if I am to understand myself and everything about me. It is for that reason that I cannot remain with you any longer.

HEL. Nora, Nora!

NORA. I am going away from here now, at once. I am sure Christine will take me in for the night.

HEL. You are out of your mind! I won't allow it! I forbid you!

NORA. It is no use forbidding me anything any longer. I will take with me what belongs to myself. I will take nothing from you, either now or later.

HEL. What sort of madness is this?

NORA. Tomorrow I shall go home—I mean to my old home. It will be easiest for me to find something to do there.

HEL. You blind, foolish woman!

NORA. I must try and get some sense, Torvald.

HEL. To desert your home your husband and your children! And you don't consider what people will say!

NORA. I cannot consider that at all. I only know that it is necessary for me.

HEL. It's shocking. This is how you would neglect your most sacred duties.

NORA. What do you consider my most sacred duties?

HEL. Do I need to tell you that? Are they not your duties to your husband and your children?

NORA. I have other duties just as sacred.

HEL. That you have not. What duties could those be?

NORA. Duties to myself.

HEL. Before all else you are a wife and a mother.

NORA. I don't believe that any longer. I believe that before all else I am a reasonable human being just as you are—or, at all events, that I must try and become one. I know quite well, Torvald, that most people would think you right and that views of that kind are to be found in books; but I can no longer content myself with what most people say or with what is found in books. I must think over things for myself and get to understand them.

HEL. Can you understand your place in your own home? Have you not a reliable guide in such matters as that?—have you no religion?

NORA. I am afraid, Torvald, I do not exactly know what religion is.

HEL. What are you saying?

NORA. I know nothing but what the clergyman said when I went to be confirmed. He told us that religion was this and that and the other. When I am away from all this and am alone I will look into that matter too. I will see if what the clergyman said is true, or at all events if it is true for me.

HEL. This is unheard of in a girl of your age! But if religion cannot lead you aright, let me try and awaken your conscience. I suppose you have some moral sense? Or—answer me—am I to think you have none?

NORA. I assure you, Torvald, that is not an easy question to answer. I really don't know. The thing perplexes me altogether. I only know that you and I look at it in quite a different light. I am learning, too, that the law is quite another thing from what I supposed; but I find it impossible to convince myself that the law is right. According to it a woman has no right to spare her old dying father or to save her husband's life. I can't believe that.

HEL. You talk like a child. You don't understand the conditions of the world in which you live.

NORA. No, I don't. But now I am going to try. I am going to see if I can make out who is right, the world or I.

HEL. You are ill, Nora; you are delirious; I almost think you are out of your mind.

NORA. I have never felt my mind so clear and certain as tonight.

HEL. And is it with a clear and certain mind that you forsake your husband and your children?

NORA. Yes, it is.

HEL. Then there is only one possible explanation.

NORA. What is that?

HEL. You do not love me any more.

NORA. No, that is just it.

HEL. Nora!—and you can say that?

NORA. It gives me great pain, Torvald, for you have always been so kind to me, but I cannot help it. I do not love you any more.

HEL. (*regaining his composure*). Is that a clear and certain conviction too?

NORA. Yes, absolutely clear and certain. That is the reason why I will not stay here any longer.

HEL. And can you tell me what I have done to forfeit your love?

NORA. Yes, indeed I can. It was to-night, when the wonderful thing did not happen; then I saw you were not the man I had thought you.

HEL. Explain yourself better—I don't understand you.

NORA. I have waited so patiently for eight years; for, goodness knows, I knew very well that wonderful things don't happen every day. Then this horrible misfortune came upon me, and then I felt quite certain that the wonderful thing was going to happen at last. When Krogstad's letter was lying out there never for a moment did I imagine that you would consent to accept this man's conditions. I was so absolutely certain that you would say to him: Publish the thing to the whole world. And when that was done——

HEL. Yes, what then?—when I had exposed my wife to shame and disgrace?

NORA. When that was done I was so absolutely certain you would come forward and take everything upon yourself and say: I am the guilty one.

HEL. Nora!

NORA. You mean that I would never have accepted such a sacrifice on your part? No, of course not. But what would my assurances have been worth against yours? That was the wonderful thing which I hoped for and feared, and it was to prevent that that I wanted to kill myself.

HEL. I would gladly work night and day for you, Nora—bear sorrow and want for your sake. But no man would sacrifice his honor for the one he loves.

NORA. It is a thing hundreds of thousands of women have done.

HEL. Oh, you think and talk like a heedless child.

NORA. Maybe. But you neither think nor talk like the man I could bind myself to. As soon as your fear was over—and it was not fear for what threatened me but for what might happen to you—when the whole thing was past, as far as you were concerned it was exactly as if nothing at all had happened. Exactly as before, I was your little skylark, your doll, which you would in the future treat with doubly gentle care because it was so brittle and fragile. (*Getting up.*) Torvald—it was then it dawned upon me that for eight years I had been living here with a strange man and had borne him three children. Oh, I can't bear to think of it! I could tear myself into little bits!

HEL. (*sadly*). I see, I see. An abyss has opened between us—there is no denying it. But, Nora, would it not be possible to fill it up?

NORA. As I am now, I am no wife for you.

HEL. I have it in me to become a different man.

NORA. Perhaps—if your doll is taken away from you.

HEL. But to part!—to part from you! No, no, Nora; I can't understand that idea.

NORA (*going out to the right*). That makes it all the more certain that it must be done. (*She comes back with her cloak and hat and a small bag which she puts on a chair by the table.*)

HEL. Nora. Nora, not now! Wait till tomorrow.

NORA (*putting on her cloak*). I cannot spend the night in a strange man's room.

HEL. But can't we live here like brother and sister?

NORA (*putting on her hat*). You know very well that would not last long. (*Puts the shawl round her.*) Good-by, Torvald. I won't see the little ones. I know they are in better hands than mine. As I am now, I can be of no use to them.

HEL. But someday, Nora—someday?

NORA. How can I tell? I have no idea what is going to become of me.

HEL. But you are my wife, whatever becomes of you.

NORA. Listen, Torvald. I have heard that when a wife deserts her husband's house, as I am doing now, he is legally freed from all obligations toward her. In any case I set you free from all your obligations. You are not to feel yourself bound in the slightest way, any more than I shall. There must be perfect freedom on both sides. See, here is your ring back. Give me mine.

HEL. That too?

NORA. That too.

HEL. Here it is.

NORA. That's right. Now it is all over. I have put the keys here. The maids know all about everything in the house—better than I do. Tomorrow, after I have left her, Christine will come here and pack up my own things that I brought with me from home. I will have them sent after me.

HEL. All over! All over! Nora, shall you never think of me again?

NORA. I know I shall often think of you and the children and this house.

HEL. May I write to you, Nora?

NORA. No—never. You must not do that.

HEL. But at least let me send you——

NORA. Nothing—nothing.

HEL. Let me help you if you are in want.

NORA. No. I can receive nothing from a stranger.

HEL. Nora—can I never be anything more than a stranger to you?

NORA (*taking her bag*). Ah, Torvald, the most wonderful thing of all would have to happen.

HEL. Tell me what that would be!

NORA. Both you and I would have to be so changed that—— Oh, Torvald, I don't believe any longer in wonderful things happening.

HEL. But I will believe in it. Tell me. So changed that——

NORA. That our life together would be a real wedlock. Good-by. (*She goes out through the hall.*)

HEL. (*sinks down on a chair at the door and buries his face in his hands*). Nora! Nora! (*Looks round and rises.*) Empty! She is gone. (*A hope flashes across his mind.*) The most wonderful thing of all—— ?

(*The sound of a door shutting is heard from below.*)

[1879]

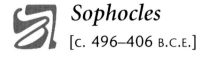

Sophocles
[c. 496–406 B.C.E.]

In ancient Greece, plays were performed annually at a religious festival for *Dionysus*, the god of wine. These performances were competitive, and the Athenian playwright SOPHOCLES remarkably earned approximately twenty first prizes in these drama contests. During his long lifetime, this master tragedian wrote an estimated one hundred plays, yet only seven remain: Oedipus the King, Electra, Antigone, Trachinian Women, Ajax, Philoctetes, *and* Oedipus at Colonus.

Ironically, the influential tragedy for which Sophocles is perhaps most famous—Oedipus Rex (Oedipus the King)—won only second prize. The three "Theban Plays"—Oedipus Rex, Oedipus at Colonus, *and* Antigone—*depict the fate of Oedipus, king of Thebes, and his children. Sophocles drew Oedipus, a man who unwittingly killed his father and married his mother, from familiar Greek myth. Through his dramatic depictions of Oedipus's life, Sophocles addressed the question of destiny and fate. These tragedies ask if man is master of his own fate, or if he is merely a puppet directed by the will of higher power. During the twentieth century, the Oedipus myth was famously invoked by the psychologist Sigmund Freud in his theory of the Oedipus Complex. Here, Freud hypothesized that a crucial stage in childhood development was characterized by the male child's desire for sexual involvement with the mother and the attendant rivalry with the father.

Sophocles is credited with a number of important theatrical innovations. He introduced props and scenic backdrops, which established for the audience the location of the the story. He reduced the size of the chorus and instituted the practice of providing a third actor on the stage. Traditionally, two actors performed all of the roles in classical drama; with the addition of this third actor, plots became more complex. Sophocles also began to present the whole of dramatic action in one play, rather than offering it in a trilogy, as his predecessor and teacher Aeschylus had done. This new plot structure, which often centered on inevitability and doubt, increased psychological depth for dramatic characters. Sophocles also provided readers and audiences with rich and complex characterizations of tragic women, such as Electra and Antigone.

Throughout his life, Sophocles was involved in public issues as a statesman, general, and priest. He lived through the height of Athenian power during the fifth century B.C.E. *and actively contributed to the rise of Athens following the Persian Wars. He died at age ninety, having witnessed the decline of Athens during the thirty-year Peloponnesian War waged among the Greek states.*

Oedipus Rex

SOPHOCLES

TRANSLATED BY DUDLEY FITTS AND ROBERT FITZGERALD

CHARACTERS

OEDIPUS,	King of Thebes, supposed son of Polybos and Merope, King and Queen of Corinth
IOKASTE[1],	wife of Oedipus and widow of the late King Laios
KREON,	brother of Iokaste, a prince of Thebes
TEIRESIAS,	a blind seer who serves Apollo
PRIEST MESSENGER,	from Corinth
SHEPHERD,	former servant of Laios
SECOND MESSENGER,	from the palace
CHORUS OF THEBAN ELDERS CHORAGOS,	leader of the Chorus
ANTIGONE and ISMENE,	young daughters of Oedipus and Iokaste. They appear in the Exodos but do not speak.
SUPPLIANTS, GUARDS, SERVANTS	

THE SCENE

Before the palace of Oedipus, King of Thebes. A central door and two lateral doors open onto a platform which runs the length of the facade. On the platform, right and left, are altars; and three steps lead down into the orchestra, or chorus-ground. At the beginning of the action these steps are crowded by suppliants who have brought branches and chaplets of olive leaves and who sit in various attitudes of despair. Oedipus enters.

---

[1]Iokaste has been translated as Jocasta in other versions of the play.

Translated by Dudley Fitts and Robert Fitzgerald. Copyright © 1949 by Harcourt, Inc. and renewed 1977 by Cornelia Fitts and Robert Fitzgerald. Reprinted by permission of Harcourt, Inc.

PROLOGUE[2]

OEDIPUS. My children, generations of the living
    In the line of Kadmos,[3] nursed at his ancient hearth:
    Why have you strewn yourselves before these altars
    In supplication, with your boughs and garlands?
    The breath of incense rises from the city   *5*
    With a sound of prayer and lamentation.
                                      Children,
    I would not have you speak through messengers,
    And therefore I have come myself to hear you—
    I, Oedipus, who bear the famous name.
    (*To a Priest.*) You, there, since you are eldest in the company,   *10*
    Speak for them all, tell me what preys upon you,
    Whether you come in dread, or crave some blessing:
    Tell me, and never doubt that I will help you
    In every way I can; I should be heartless
    Were I not moved to find you suppliant here.   *15*
PRIEST. Great Oedipus, O powerful king of Thebes!
    You see how all the ages of our people
    Cling to your altar steps: here are boys
    Who can barely stand alone, and here are priests
    By weight of age, as I am a priest of God,   *20*
    And young men chosen from those yet unmarried;
    As for the others, all that multitude,
    They wait with olive chaplets in the squares,
    At the two shrines of Pallas,[4] and where Apollo[5]
    Speaks in the glowing embers.
                              Your own eyes   *25*
    Must tell you: Thebes is tossed on a murdering sea
    And can not lift her head from the death surge.
    A rust consumes the buds and fruits of the earth;
    The herds are sick; children die unborn,
    And labor is vain. The god of plague and pyre   *30*
    Raids like detestable lightning through the city,

---

[2]Part of play that explains background and current action.

[3]Founder of Thebes.

[4]Pallas Athene, goddess of wisdom

[5]God of the sun.

And all the house of Kadmos is laid waste,
All emptied, and all darkened: Death alone
Battens upon the misery of Thebes.
You are not one of the immortal gods, we know;   35
Yet we have come to you to make our prayer
As to the man surest in mortal ways
And wisest in the ways of God. You saved us
From the Sphinx,⁶ that flinty singer, and the tribute
We paid to her so long; yet you were never   40
Better informed than we, nor could we teach you:
A god's touch, it seems, enabled you to help us.

Therefore, O mighty power, we turn to you:
Find us our safety, find us a remedy,
Whether by counsel of the gods or of men.   45
A king of wisdom tested in the past
Can act in a time of troubles, and act well.
Noblest of men, restore
Life to your city! Think how all men call you
Liberator for your boldness long ago;   50
Ah, when your years of kingship are remembered,
Let them not say *We rose, but later fell—*
Keep the State from going down in the storm!
Once, years ago, with happy augury,
You brought us fortune; be the same again!   55
No man questions your power to rule the land:
But rule over men, not over a dead city!
Ships are only hulls, high walls are nothing,
When no life moves in the empty passageways.
OEDIPUS. Poor children! You may be sure I know   60
All that you longed for in your coming here.
I know that you are deathly sick; and yet,
Sick as you are, not one is as sick as I.
Each of you suffers in himself alone
His anguish, not another's; but my spirit   65
Groans for the city, for myself, for you.

---

⁶Mythological winged creature with lion's body and human head that tormented Thebes by demanding the answer to this riddle: What has one voice and yet becomes four-footed and two-footed and
three-footed? When the riddle was answered incorrectly, she ate the respondent. Oedipus gives the
correct answer: A man crawls on all fours in infancy, walks on two feet when grown, and leans on a
staff in old age. After Oedipus answers correctly, the Sphinx kills herself.

I was not sleeping, you are not waking me.
No, I have been in tears for a long while
And in my restless thought walked many ways.
In all my search I found one remedy,   *70*
And I have adopted it: I have sent Kreon,
Son of Menoikeus, brother of the queen,
To Delphi,[7] Apollo's place of revelation,
To learn there, if he can,
What act or pledge of mine may save the city.   *75*
I have counted the days, and now, this very day,
I am troubled, for he has overstayed his time.
What is he doing? He has been gone too long.
Yet whenever he comes back, I should do ill
Not to take any action the god orders.   *80*

PRIEST. It is a timely promise. At this instant
    They tell me Kreon is here.

OEDIPUS. O Lord Apollo!
    May his news be fair as his face is radiant!

PRIEST. Good news, I gather! he is crowned with bay,
    The chaplet is thick with berries.

OEDIPUS. We shall soon know;   *85*
    He is near enough to hear us now. (*Enter Kreon.*) O prince:
    Brother: son of Menoikeus:
    What answer do you bring us from the god?

KREON. A strong one. I can tell you, great afflictions
    Will turn out well, if they are taken well.   *90*

OEDIPUS. What was the oracle? These vague words
    Leave me still hanging between hope and fear.

KREON. Is it your pleasure to hear me with all these
    Gathered around us? I am prepared to speak,
    But should we not go in?

OEDIPUS. Speak to them all,   *95*
    It is for them I suffer, more than for myself.

KREON. Then I will tell you what I heard at Delphi.
    In plain words
    The god commands us to expel from the land of Thebes
    An old defilement we are sheltering.   *100*
    It is a deathly thing, beyond cure;
    We must not let it feed upon us longer.

---

[7]Greek temple and oracle of Apollo.

OEDIPUS. What defilement? How shall we rid ourselves of it?
KREON. By exile or death, blood for blood. It was
    Murder that brought the plague-wind on the city.   *105*
OEDIPUS. Murder of whom? Surely the god has named him?
KREON. My Lord: Laios once ruled this land,
    Before you came to govern us.
OEDIPUS. I know;
    I learned of him from others; I never saw him.
KREON. He was murdered; and Apollo commands us now   *110*
    To take revenge upon whoever killed him.
OEDIPUS. Upon whom? Where are they? Where shall we find a clue
    To solve that crime, after so many years?
KREON. Here in this land, he said. Search reveals
    Things that escape an inattentive man.   *115*
OEDIPUS. Tell me: Was Laios murdered in his house,
    Or in the fields, or in some foreign country?
KREON. He said he planned to make a pilgrimage.
    He did not come home again.
OEDIPUS. And was there no one,
    No witness, no companion, to tell what happened?   *120*
KREON. They were all killed but one, and he got away
    So frightened that he could remember one thing only.
OEDIPUS. What was that one thing? One may be the key
    To everything, if we resolve to use it.
KREON. He said that a band of highwaymen attacked them,   *125*
    Outnumbered them, and overwhelmed the king.
OEDIPUS. Strange, that a highwayman should be so daring—
    Unless some faction here bribed him to do it.
KREON. We thought of that. But after Laios' death
    New troubles arose and we had no avenger.   *130*
OEDIPUS. What troubles could prevent your hunting down the killers?
KREON. The riddling Sphinx's song
    Made us deaf to all mysteries but her own.
OEDIPUS. Then once more I must bring what is dark to light.
    It is most fitting that Apollo shows,   *135*
    As you do, this compunction for the dead.
    You shall see how I stand by you, as I should,
    Avenging this country and the god as well,
    And not as though it were for some distant friend,
    But for my own sake, to be rid of evil.   *140*
    Whoever killed King Laios might—who knows?—

Lay violent hands even on me—and soon.
I act for the murdered king in my own interest.
Come, then, my children: leave the altar steps,
Lift up your olive boughs!

One of you go   145

And summon the people of Kadmos to gather here.
I will do all that I can; you may tell them that.

(Exit a Page.)

So, with the help of God,
We shall be saved—or else indeed we are lost.

PRIEST. Let us rise, children. It was for this we came,   *150*
And now the king has promised it.
Phoibos[8] has sent us an oracle; may he descend
Himself to save us and drive out the plague.

(Exeunt[9] Oedipus and Kreon into the palace by the central door. The Priest and the Suppliants disperse right and left. After a short pause the Chorus enters the orchestra.)

PARADOS[10]

Strophe[11] 1

CHORUS. What is God singing in his profound
Delphi of gold and shadow?
What oracle for Thebes, the Sunwhipped city?
Fear unjoints me, the roots of my heart tremble.
Now I remember, O Healer, your power, and wonder: 5
Will you send doom like a sudden cloud, or weave it
Like nightfall of the past?
Speak to me, tell me, O
Child of golden Hope, immortal Voice.

---

[8]Apollo

[9]They go out. (Latin)

[10]Song or ode the Chorus chants when they enter the stage.

[11]Song the Chorus sings as they dance from stage right to stage left.

Antistrophe[12] 1

Let me pray to Athene, the immortal daughter of Zeus,   *10*
And to Artemis[13] her sister
Who keeps her famous throne in the market ring,
And to Apollo, archer from distant heaven—
O gods, descend! Like three streams leap against
The fires of our grief, the fires of darkness;   *15*
Be swift to bring us rest!
As in the old time from the brilliant house
Of air you stepped to save us, come again!

Strophe 2

Now our afflictions have no end,
Now all our stricken host lies down   *20*
And no man fights off death with his mind;
The noble plowland bears no grain,
And groaning mothers can not bear—
See, how our lives like birds take wing,
Like sparks that fly when a fire soars,   *25*
To the shore of the god of evening.

Antistrophe 2

The plague burns on, it is pitiless,
Though pallid children laden with death
Lie unwept in the stony ways,
And old gray women by every path   *30*
Flock to the strand about the altars
There to strike their breasts and cry
Worship of Phoibos in wailing prayers:
Be kind, God's golden child!

Strophe 3

There are no swords in this attack by fire,   *35*
No shields, but we are ringed with cries.
Send the besieger plunging from our homes

---

[12]Song the Chorus sings as they dance back from stage left to stage right.

[13]Goddess of wild animals and the hunt.

Into the vast sea-room of the Atlantic
Or into the waves that foam eastward of Thrace—
For the day ravages what the night spares—   *40*
Destroy our enemy, lord of the thunder!
Let him be riven by lightning from heaven!

Antistrophe 3

Phoibos Apollo, stretch the sun's bowstring,
That golden cord, until it sing for us,
Flashing arrows in heaven!
Artemis, Huntress,   *45*
Race with flaring lights upon our mountains!
O scarlet god,[14] O golden-banded brow,
O Theban Bacchos in a storm of Maenads,[15]

(*Enter Oedipus, center.*)

Whirl upon Death, that all the Undying hate!
Come with blinding torches, come in joy!   *50*

SCENE 1

OEDIPUS. Is this your prayer? It may be answered. Come,
Listen to me, act as the crisis demands,
And you shall have relief from all these evils.

Until now I was a stranger to this tale,
As I had been a stranger to the crime.   *5*
Could I track down the murderer without a clue?
But now, friends,
As one who became a citizen after the murder,
I make this proclamation to all Thebans:
If any man knows by whose hand Laios, son of Labdakos,   *10*
Met his death, I direct that man to tell me everything,
No matter what he fears for having so long withheld it.
Let it stand as promised that no further trouble
Will come to him, but he may leave the land in safety.
Moreover: If anyone knows the murderer to be foreign,   *15*
Let him not keep silent: he shall have his reward from me.

---

[14]Bacchus, god of wine, creative ecstasy, and dramatic poetry

[15]Women who worship Bacchus.

However, if he does conceal it; if any man
Fearing for his friend or for himself disobeys this edict,
Hear what I propose to do:
I solemnly forbid the people of this country,   20
Where power and throne are mine, ever to receive that man
Or speak to him, no matter who he is, or let him
Join in sacrifice, lustration, or in prayer.
I decree that he be driven from every house,
Being, as he is, corruption itself to us: the Delphic   25
Voice of Apollo has pronounced this revelation.
Thus I associate myself with the oracle
And take the side of the murdered king.

As for the criminal, I pray to God—
Whether it be a lurking thief, or one of a number—   30
I pray that that man's life be consumed in evil and wretchedness.
And as for me, this curse applies no less
If it should turn out that the culprit is my guest here,
Sharing my hearth.
                 You have heard the penalty.
I lay it on you now to attend to this   35
For my sake, for Apollo's, for the sick
Sterile city that heaven has abandoned.
Suppose the oracle had given you no command:
Should this defilement go uncleansed for ever?
You should have found the murderer: your king,   40
A noble king, had been destroyed!
                        Now I,
Having the power that he held before me,
Having his bed, begetting children there
Upon his wife, as he would have, had he lived—
Their son would have been my children's brother,   45
If Laios had had luck in fatherhood!
(And now his bad fortune has struck him down)—
I say I take the son's part, just as though
I were his son, to press the fight for him
And see it won! I'll find the hand that brought   50
Death to Labdakos' and Polydoros' child,
Heir of Kadmos' and Agenor's line.[16]

---

[16]Labdakos, Polydoros, Kadmos, Agenor, father, grandfather, great-grandfather, and great-great-grandfather of Laios.

And as for those who fail me,
May the gods deny them the fruit of the earth,
Fruit of the womb, and may they rot utterly!   *55*
Let them be wretched as we are wretched, and worse!

For you, for loyal Thebans, and for all
Who find my actions right, I pray the favor
Of justice, and of all the immortal gods.
CHORAGOS. Since I am under oath, my lord, I swear   *60*
    I did not do the murder, I can not name
    The murderer. Phoibos ordained the search;
    Why did he not say who the culprit was?
OEDIPUS. An honest question. But no man in the world
    Can make the gods do more than the gods will.   *65*
CHORAGOS. There is an alternative, I think—
OEDIPUS.   Tell me.
    Any or all, you must not fail to tell me.
CHORAGOS. A lord clairvoyant to the lord Apollo,
    As we all know, is the skilled Teiresias.
    One might learn much about this from him, Oedipus.   *70*
OEDIPUS. I am not wasting time:
    Kreon spoke of this, and I have sent for him—
    Twice, in fact; it is strange that he is not here.
CHORAGOS. The other matter—that old report—seems useless.
OEDIPUS. What was that? I am interested in all reports.   *75*
CHORAGOS. The king was said to have been killed by highwaymen.
OEDIPUS. I know. But we have no witnesses to that.
CHORAGOS. If the killer can feel a particle of dread,
    Your curse will bring him out of hiding!
OEDIPUS.   No.
    The man who dared that act will fear no curse.   *80*

(*Enter the blind seer Teiresias, led by a Page.*)

CHORAGOS. But there is one man who may detect the criminal.
    This is Teiresias, this is the holy prophet
    In whom, alone of all men, truth was born.
OEDIPUS. Teiresias: seer: student of mysteries,
    Of all that's taught and all that no man tells,   *85*
    Secrets of Heaven and secrets of the earth:
    Blind though you are, you know the city lies
    Sick with plague; and from this plague, my lord,
    We find that you alone can guard or save us.

Possibly you did not hear the messengers?   *90*
Apollo, when we sent to him,
Sent us back word that this great pestilence
Would lift, but only if we established clearly
The identity of those who murdered Laios.
They must be killed or exiled.

                                                  Can you use   *95*
Birdflight[17] or any art of divination
To purify yourself, and Thebes, and me
From this contagion? We are in your hands.
There is no fairer duty
Than that of helping others in distress.   *100*
TEIRESIAS. How dreadful knowledge of the truth can be
    When there's no help in truth! I knew this well,
    But did not act on it; else I should not have come.
OEDIPUS. What is troubling you? Why are your eyes so cold?
TEIRESIAS. Let me go home. Bear your own fate, and I'll   *105*
    Bear mine. It is better so: trust what I say.
OEDIPUS. What you say is ungracious and unhelpful
    To your native country. Do not refuse to speak.
TEIRESIAS. When it comes to speech, your own is neither temperate
    Nor opportune. I wish to be more prudent.   *110*
OEDIPUS. In God's name, we all beg you—
TEIRESIAS.   You are all ignorant.
    No; I will never tell you what I know.
    Now it is my misery; then, it would be yours.
OEDIPUS. What! You do know something, and will not tell us?
    You would betray us all and wreck the State?   *115*
TEIRESIAS. I do not intend to torture myself, or you.
    Why persist in asking? You will not persuade me.
OEDIPUS. What a wicked old man you are! You'd try a stone's
    Patience! Out with it! Have you no feeling at all?
TEIRESIAS. You call me unfeeling. If you could only see   *120*
    The nature of your own feelings . . .
OEDIPUS.   Why,
    Who would not feel as I do? Who could endure
    Your arrogance toward the city?
TEIRESIAS.   What does it matter?
    Whether I speak or not, it is bound to come.

---

[17]Prophets predicted the future by observing the flight of birds.

OEDIPUS. Then, if "it" is bound to come, you are bound to tell me.   *125*

TEIRESIAS. No, I will not go on. Rage as you please.

OEDIPUS. Rage? Why not!

                        And I'll tell you what I think:

    You planned it, you had it done, you all but

    Killed him with your own hands: if you had eyes,

    I'd say the crime was yours, and yours alone.   *130*

TEIRESIAS. So? I charge you, then,

    Abide by the proclamation you have made:

    From this day forth

    Never speak again to these men or to me;

    You yourself are the pollution of this country.   *135*

OEDIPUS. You dare say that! Can you possibly think you have

    Some way of going free, after such insolence?

TEIRESIAS. I have gone free. It is the truth sustains me.

OEDIPUS. Who taught you shamelessness? It was not your craft.

TEIRESIAS. You did. You made me speak. I did not want to.   *140*

OEDIPUS. Speak what? Let me hear it again more clearly.

TEIRESIAS. Was it not clear before? Are you tempting me?

OEDIPUS. I did not understand it. Say it again.

TEIRESIAS. I say that you are the murderer whom you seek.

OEDIPUS. Now twice you have spat out infamy.

    You'll pay for it!   *145*

TEIRESIAS. Would you care for more? Do you wish to be really angry?

OEDIPUS. Say what you will. Whatever you say is worthless.

TEIRESIAS. I say you live in hideous shame with those

    Most dear to you. You can not see the evil.

OEDIPUS. Can you go on babbling like this for ever?   *150*

TEIRESIAS. I can, if there is power in truth.

OEDIPUS.   There is:

    But not for you, not for you,

    You sightless, witless, senseless, mad old man!

TEIRESIAS. You are the madman. There is no one here

    Who will not curse you soon, as you curse me.   *155*

OEDIPUS. You child of total night! I would not touch you;

    Neither would any man who sees the sun.

TEIRESIAS. True: it is not from you my fate will come.

    That lies within Apollo's competence,

    As it is his concern.

OEDIPUS.   Tell me, who made   *160*

    These fine discoveries? Kreon? or someone else?

TEIRESIAS. Kreon is no threat. You weave your own doom.
OEDIPUS. Wealth, power, craft of statemanship!
    Kingly position, everywhere admired!
    What savage envy is stored up against these,   *165*
    If Kreon, whom I trusted, Kreon my friend,
    For this great office which the city once
    Put in my hands unsought—if for this power
    Kreon desires in secret to destroy me!

    He has bought this decrepit fortune-teller, this   *170*
    Collector of dirty pennies, this prophet fraud—
    Why, he is no more clairvoyant than I am!

                                Tell us:
    Has your mystic mummery ever approached the truth?
    When that hellcat the Sphinx was performing here,
    What help were you to these people?   *175*
    Her magic was not for the first man who came along:
    It demanded a real exorcist. Your birds—
    What good were they? or the gods, for the matter of that?
    But I came by,
    Oedipus, the simple man, who knows nothing—   *180*
    I thought it out for myself, no birds helped me!
    And this is the man you think you can destroy,
    That you may be close to Kreon when he's king!
    Well, you and your friend Kreon, it seems to me,
    Will suffer most. If you were not an old man,   *185*
    You would have paid already for your plot.
CHORAGOS. We can not see that his words or yours
    Have been spoken except in anger, Oedipus,
    And of anger we have no need. How to accomplish
    The god's will best: that is what most concerns us.   *190*
TEIRESIAS. You are a king. But where argument's concerned
    I am your man, as much a king as you.
    I am not your servant, but Apollo's.
    I have no need of Kreon or Kreon's name.

    Listen to me. You mock my blindness, do you?   *195*
    But I say that you, with both your eyes, are blind:
    You can not see the wretchedness of your life,
    Nor in whose house you live, no, nor with whom.
    Who are your father and mother? Can you tell me?

You do not even know the blind wrongs   *200*
That you have done them, on earth and in the world below.
But the double lash of your parents' curse will whip you
Out of this land some day, with only night
Upon your precious eyes.
Your cries then—where will they not be heard?   *205*
What fastness of Kithairon[18] will not echo them?
And that bridal-descant of yours—you'll know it then,
The song they sang when you came here to Thebes
And found your misguided berthing.
All this, and more, that you can not guess at now,   *210*
Will bring you to yourself among your children.

Be angry, then. Curse Kreon. Curse my words.
I tell you, no man that walks upon the earth
Shall be rooted out more horribly than you.   *215*
OEDIPUS. Am I to bear this from him?—Damnation
    Take you! Out of this place! Out of my sight!
TEIRESIAS. I would not have come at all if you had not asked me.
OEDIPUS. Could I have told that you'd talk nonsense, that
    You'd come here to make a fool of yourself, and of me?
TEIRESIAS. A fool? Your parents thought me sane enough.   *220*
OEDIPUS. My parents again!—Wait: who were my parents?
TEIRESIAS. This day will give you a father, and break your heart.
OEDIPUS. Your infantile riddles! Your damned abracadabra!
TEIRESIAS. You were a great man once at solving riddles.
OEDIPUS. Mock me with that if you like; you will find it true.   *225*
TEIRESIAS. It was true enough. It brought about your ruin.
OEDIPUS. But if it saved this town?
TEIRESIAS (*to the Page*).   Boy, give me your hand.
OEDIPUS.   Yes, boy; lead him away.
    —While you are here
    We can do nothing. Go; leave us in peace.
TEIRESIAS. I will go when I have said what I have to say.   *230*
    How can you hurt me? And I tell you again:
    The man you have been looking for all this time,
    The damned man, the murderer of Laios,
    That man is in Thebes. To your mind he is foreign-born,   *235*
    But it will soon be shown that he is a Theban,

---

[18]As a baby, Oedipus was abandoned at this mountain.

A revelation that will fail to please.

A blind man,

Who has his eyes now; a penniless man, who is rich now;
And he will go tapping the strange earth with his staff.
To the children with whom he lives now he will be   *240*
Brother and father—the very same; to her
Who bore him, son and husband—the very same
Who came to his father's bed, wet with his father's blood.
Enough. Go think that over.
If later you find error in what I have said,   *245*
You may say that I have no skill in prophecy.

(*Exit Teiresias, led by his Page. Oedipus goes into the palace.*)

ODE[19] 1

Strophe 1

CHORUS. The Delphic stone of prophecies
    Remembers ancient regicide
    And a still bloody hand.
    That killer's hour of flight has come.
    He must be stronger than riderless   *5*
    Coursers of untiring wind,
    For the son of Zeus[20] armed with his father's thunder
    Leaps in lightning after him;
    And the Furies[21] hold his track, the sad Furies.

Antistrophe 1

    Holy Parnassos'[22] peak of snow   *10*
    Flashes and blinds that secret man,
    That all shall hunt him down:
    Though he may roam the forest shade
    Like a bull gone wild from pasture
    To rage through glooms of stone.   *15*

---

[19]Song sung by Chorus.

[20]Ruler of the Olympian gods.

[21]Goddesses of vengeance.

[22]Mountain sacred to Apollo.

Doom comes down on him; flight will not avail him;
For the world's heart calls him desolate,
And the immortal voices follow, for ever follow.

Strophe 2

But now a wilder thing is heard
From the old man skilled at hearing Fate in the wing-beat
    of a bird.   *20*
Bewildered as a blown bird, my soul hovers and can not find
Foothold in this debate, or any reason or rest of mind.
But no man ever brought—none can bring
Proof of strife between Thebes' royal house,
Labdakos' line, and the son of Polybos;[23]   *25*
And never until now has any man brought word
Of Laios' dark death staining Oedipus the King.

Antistrophe 2

Divine Zeus and Apollo hold
Perfect intelligence alone of all tales ever told;
And well though this diviner works, he works in his own night; *30*
No man can judge that rough unknown or trust in second sight,
For wisdom changes hands among the wise.
Shall I believe my great lord criminal
At a raging word that a blind old man let fall?
I saw him, when the carrion woman[24] faced him of old,   *35*
Prove his heroic mind. These evil words are lies.

SCENE 2

KREON. Men of Thebes:
    I am told that heavy accusations
    Have been brought against me by King Oedipus.

    I am not the kind of man to bear this tamely.

    If in these present difficulties   *5*
    He holds me accountable for any harm to him

---

[23]King who adopted Oedipus.

[24]Sphinx

Through anything I have said or done—why, then,
I do not value life in this dishonor.
It is not as though this rumor touched upon
Some private indiscretion. The matter is grave.   *10*
The fact is that I am being called disloyal
To the State, to my fellow citizens, to my friends.
CHORAGOS. He may have spoken in anger, not from his mind.
KREON. But did you not hear him say I was the one
Who seduced the old prophet into lying?   *15*
CHORAGOS. The thing was said; I do not know how seriously.
KREON. But you were watching him! Were his eyes steady?
Did he look like a man in his right mind?
CHORAGOS.   I do not know.
I can not judge the behavior of great men.
But here is the king himself.

(*Enter Oedipus.*)

OEDIPUS.   So you dared come back.   *20*
Why? How brazen of you to come to my house,
You murderer!
                              Do you think I do not know
That you plotted to kill me, plotted to steal my throne?
Tell me, in God's name: am I coward, a fool,
That you should dream you could accomplish this?   *25*
A fool who could not see your slippery game?
A coward, not to fight back when I saw it?
You are the fool, Kreon, are you not? hoping
Without support or friends to get a throne?
Thrones may be won or bought: you could do neither.   *30*
KREON. Now listen to me. You have talked; let me talk, too.
You can not judge unless you know the facts.
OEDIPUS. You speak well: there is one fact; but I find it hard
To learn from the deadliest enemy I have.
    KREON. That above all I must dispute with you.   *35*
OEDIPUS. That above all I will not hear you deny.
KREON. If you think there is anything good in being stubborn.
Against all reason, then I say you are wrong.
OEDIPUS. If you think a man can sin against his own kind
And not be punished for it, I say you are mad.   *40*
KREON. I agree. But tell me: what have I done to you?
OEDIPUS. You advised me to send for that wizard, did you not?
KREON. I did. I should do it again.

OEDIPUS.   Very well. Now tell me:
   How long has it been since Laios—
KREON.   What of Laios?
OEDIPUS. Since he vanished in that onset by the road?   45
KREON. It was long ago, a long time.
OEDIPUS.   And this prophet,
   Was he practicing here then?
KREON.   He was; and with honor, as now.
OEDIPUS. Did he speak of me at that time?
KREON.   He never did,
   At least, not when I was present.
OEDIPUS.   But . . . the enquiry?
   I suppose you held one?
KREON.   We did, but we learned nothing.   50
OEDIPUS. Why did the prophet not speak against me then?
KREON. I do not know; and I am the kind of man
   Who holds his tongue when he has no facts to go on.
OEDIPUS. There's one fact that you know, and you could tell it.
KREON. What fact is that? If I know it, you shall have it.   55
OEDIPUS. If he were not involved with you, he could not say
   That it was I who murdered Laios.
KREON. If he says that, you are the one that knows it!—
   But now it is my turn to question you.
OEDIPUS. Put your questions. I am no murderer.   60
KREON. First, then: You married my sister?
OEDIPUS.   I married your sister.
KREON. And you rule the kingdom equally with her?
OEDIPUS. Everything that she wants she has from me.
KREON. And I am the third, equal to both of you?
OEDIPUS. That is why I call you a bad friend.   65
KREON. No. Reason it out, as I have done.
   Think of this first: would any sane man prefer
   Power, with all a king's anxieties,
   To that same power and the grace of sleep?
   Certainly not I.   70
   I have never longed for the king's power—only his rights.
   Would any wise man differ from me in this?
   As matters stand, I have my way in everything
   With your consent, and no responsibilities.
   If I were king, I should be a slave to policy.   75
   How could I desire a scepter more
   Than what is now mine—untroubled influence?

No, I have not gone mad; I need no honors,
Except those with the perquisites I have now.
I am welcome everywhere; every man salutes me,   *80*
And those who want your favor seek my ear,
Since I know how to manage what they ask.
Should I exchange this ease for that anxiety?
Besides, no sober mind is treasonable.
I hate anarchy   *85*
And never would deal with any man who likes it.
Test what I have said. Go to the priestess
At Delphi, ask if I quoted her correctly.
And as for this other thing: if I am found
Guilty of treason with Teiresias,   *90*
Then sentence me to death. You have my word
It is a sentence I should cast my vote for—
But not without evidence!
You do wrong
When you take good men for bad, bad men for good.
A true friend thrown aside—why, life itself   *95*
Is not more precious!
In time you will know this well:
For time, and time alone, will show the just man,
Though scoundrels are discovered in a day.
CHORAGOS. This is well said, and a prudent man would ponder it.
    Judgments too quickly formed are dangerous.   *100*
OEDIPUS. But is he not quick in his duplicity?
    And shall I not be quick to parry him?
    Would you have me stand still, hold my peace, and let
    This man win everything, through my inaction?
KREON. And you want—what is it, then? To banish me?   *105*
OEDIPUS. No, not exile. It is your death I want,
    So that all the world may see what treason means.
KREON. You will persist, then? You will not believe me?
OEDIPUS. How can I believe you?
KREON.   Then you are a fool.
OEDIPUS. To save myself?
KREON.   In justice, think of me. *110*
OEDIPUS. You are evil incarnate.
KREON.   But suppose that you are wrong?
OEDIPUS. Still I must rule.
KREON.   But not if you rule badly.
OEDIPUS. O city, city!

KREON. It is my city, too!

CHORAGOS. Now, my lords, be still. I see the queen,
  Iokaste, coming from her palace chambers; 115
  And it is time she came, for the sake of you both.
  This dreadful quarrel can be resolved through her.

(*Enter Iokaste.*)

IOKASTE. Poor foolish men, what wicked din is this?
  With Thebes sick to death, is it not shameful
  That you should take some private quarrel up? 120
  (*To Oedipus.*) Come into the house.
                —And you, Kreon, go now:
  Let us have no more of this tumult over nothing.

KREON. Nothing? No, sister: what your husband plans for me
  Is one of two great evils: exile or death.

OEDIPUS. He is right.
                Why, woman I have caught him squarely 125
  Plotting against my life.

KREON.   No! Let me die
  Accurst if ever I have wished you harm!

IOKASTE. Ah, believe it, Oedipus!
  In the name of the gods, respect this oath of his
  For my sake, for the sake of these people here! 130

Strophe 1

CHORAGOS. Open your mind to her, my lord. Be ruled by her, I beg you!

OEDIPUS. What would you have me do?

CHORAGOS. Respect Kreon's word. He has never spoken like a fool,
  And now he has sworn an oath.

OEDIPUS.   You know what you ask?

CHORAGOS.   I do.

OEDIPUS.   Speak on, then.

CHORAGOS. A friend so sworn should not be baited so, 135
  In blind malice, and without final proof.

OEDIPUS. You are aware, I hope, that what you say
  Means death for me, or exile at the least.

Strophe 2

CHORAGOS. No, I swear by Helios, first in heaven!
  May I die friendless and accurst, 140

The worst of deaths, if ever I meant that!
It is the withering fields
That hurt my sick heart:
Must we bear all these ills,
And now your bad blood as well?   145
OEDIPUS. Then let him go. And let me die, if I must,
Or be driven by him in shame from the land of Thebes.
It is your unhappiness, and not his talk,
That touches me.

          As for him—

Wherever he goes, hatred will follow him.   150
KREON. Ugly in yielding, as you were ugly in rage!
Natures like yours chiefly torment themselves.
OEDIPUS. Can you not go? Can you not leave me?
KREON.   I can.
You do not know me; but the city knows me,
And in its eyes I am just, if not in yours.   155

(*Exit Kreon.*)

Antistrophe 1

CHORAGOS. Lady Iokaste, did you not ask the King to go to his
 chambers?
IOKASTE. First tell me what has happened.
CHORAGOS. There was suspicion without evidence; yet it rankled
 As even false charges will.
IOKASTE. On both sides?
CHORAGOS.   On both.
IOKASTE.   But what was said? 160
CHORAGOS. Oh let it rest, let it be done with!
 Have we not suffered enough?
OEDIPUS. You see to what your decency has brought you:
 You have made difficulties where my heart saw none.

Antistrophe 2

CHORAGOS. Oedipus, it is not once only I have told you—   165
 You must know I should count myself unwise
 To the point of madness, should I now forsake you—
 You, under whose hand,
 In the storm of another time,
 Our dear land sailed out free.   170
 But now stand fast at the helm!

IOKASTE. In God's name, Oedipus, inform your wife as well:
    Why are you so set in this hard anger?
OEDIPUS. I will tell you, for none of these men deserves
    My confidence as you do. It is Kreon's work,   *175*
    His treachery, his plotting against me.
IOKASTE. Go on, if you can make this clear to me.
OEDIPUS. He charges me with the murder of Laios.
IOKASTE. Has he some knowledge? Or does he speak from hearsay?
OEDIPUS. He would not commit himself to such a charge,   *180*
    But he has brought in that damnable soothsayer
    To tell his story.
IOKASTE.   Set your mind at rest.
    If it is a question of soothsayers, I tell you
    That you will find no man whose craft gives knowledge
    Of the unknowable.
                          Here is my proof: *185*

    An oracle was reported to Laios once
    (I will not say from Phoibos himself, but from
    His appointed ministers, at any rate)
    That his doom would be death at the hands of his own son—
    His son, born of his flesh and of mine!   *190*

    Now, you remember the story: Laios was killed
    By marauding strangers where three highways meet;
    But his child had not been three days in this world
    Before the king had pierced the baby's ankles
    And left him to die on a lonely mountainside.   *195*

    Thus, Apollo never caused that child
    To kill his father, and it was not Laios' fate
    To die at the hands of his son, as he had feared.
    This is what prophets and prophecies are worth!
    Have no dread of them.
                        It is God himself *200*
    Who can show us what he wills, in his own way.
OEDIPUS. How strange a shadowy memory crossed my mind,
    Just now while you were speaking; it chilled my heart.
IOKASTE. What do you mean? What memory do you speak of?
OEDIPUS. If I understand you, Laios was killed   *205*
    At a place where three roads meet.

IOKASTE. So it was said;
We have no later story.
OEDIPUS. Where did it happen?
IOKASTE. Phokis, it is called: at a place where the Theban Way
Divides into the roads toward Delphi and Daulia.
OEDIPUS. When?
IOKASTE. We had the news not long before you came   210
And proved the right to your succession here.
OEDIPUS. Ah, what net has God been weaving for me?
IOKASTE. Oedipus! Why does this trouble you?
OEDIPUS. Do not ask me yet.
First, tell me how Laios looked, and tell me
How old he was.
IOKASTE. He was tall, his hair just touched   215
With white; his form was not unlike your own.
OEDIPUS. I think that I myself may be accurst
By my own ignorant edict.
IOKASTE. You speak strangely.
It makes me tremble to look at you, my king.
OEDIPUS. I am not sure that the blind man can not see.   220
But I should know better if you were to tell me—
IOKASTE. Anything—though I dread to hear you ask it.
OEDIPUS. Was the king lightly escorted, or did he ride
With a large company, as a ruler should?
IOKASTE. There were five men with him in all: one was a herald;   225
And a single chariot, which he was driving.
OEDIPUS. Alas, that makes it plain enough!
But who—
Who told you how it happened?
IOKASTE. A household servant,
The only one to escape.
OEDIPUS. And is he still
A servant of ours?
IOKASTE. No; for when he came back at last   230
And found you enthroned in the place of the dead king,
He came to me, touched my hand with his, and begged
That I would send him away to the frontier district
Where only the shepherds go—
As far away from the city as I could send him.   235
I granted his prayer; for although the man was a slave,
He had earned more than this favor at my hands.

OEDIPUS. Can he be called back quickly?
IOKASTE.   Easily.
    But why?
OEDIPUS. I have taken too much upon myself
    Without enquiry; therefore I wish to consult him.   240
IOKASTE. Then he shall come.
                       But am I not one also
    To whom you might confide these fears of yours?
OEDIPUS. That is your right; it will not be denied you,
    Now least of all; for I have reached a pitch
    Of wild foreboding. Is there anyone   245
    To whom I should sooner speak?

    Polybos of Corinth is my father.
    My mother is a Dorian: Merope.
    I grew up chief among the men of Corinth
    Until a strange thing happened—   250
    Not worth my passion, it may be, but strange.
    At a feast, a drunken man maundering in his cups
    Cries out that I am not my father's son!
    I contained myself that night, though I felt anger
    And a sinking heart. The next day I visited   255
    My father and mother, and questioned them. They stormed,
    Calling it all the slanderous rant of a fool;
    And this relieved me. Yet the suspicion
    Remained always aching in my mind;
    I knew there was talk; I could not rest;   260
    And finally, saying nothing to my parents,
    I went to the shrine at Delphi.
    The god dismissed my question without reply;
    He spoke of other things.
                      Some were clear,
    Full of wretchedness, dreadful, unbearable: 265
    As, that I should lie with my own mother, breed
    Children from whom all men would turn their eyes;
    And that I should be my father's murderer.

    I heard all this, and fled. And from that day
    Corinth to me was only in the stars   270

Descending in that quarter of the sky,
As I wandered farther and farther on my way
To a land where I should never see the evil
Sung by the oracle. And I came to this country
Where, so you say, King Laios was killed.   *275*

I will tell you all that happened there, my lady.
There were three highways
Coming together at a place I passed;
And there a herald came towards me, and a chariot
Drawn by horses, with a man such as you describe   *280*
Seated in it. The groom leading the horses
Forced me off the road at his lord's command;
But as this charioteer lurched over towards me
I struck him in my rage. The old man saw me
And brought his double goad down upon my head   *285*
As I came abreast.
                                   He was paid back, and more!
Swinging my club in this right hand I knocked him
Out of his car, and he rolled on the ground.
                                                        I killed him.

I killed them all.
Now if that stranger and Laios were—kin,   *290*
Where is a man more miserable than I?
More hated by the gods? Citizen and alien alike
Must never shelter me or speak to me—
I must be shunned by all.
                                              And I myself
Pronounced this malediction upon myself!   *295*

Think of it: I have touched you with these hands,
These hands that killed your husband. What defilement!

Am I all evil, then? It must be so,
Since I must flee from Thebes, yet never again
See my own countrymen, my own country,   *300*
For fear of joining my mother in marriage
And killing Polybos, my father.
                                              Ah,

If I was created so, born to this fate,
Who could deny the savagery of God?

O holy majesty of heavenly powers!   305
May I never see that day! Never!
Rather let me vanish from the race of men
Than know the abomination destined me!
CHORAGOS. We too, my lord, have felt dismay at this.
    But there is hope: you have yet to hear the shepherd.   310
OEDIPUS. Indeed, I fear no other hope is left me.
IOKASTE. What do you hope from him when he comes?
OEDIPUS.   This much:
    If his account of the murder tallies with yours,
    Then I am cleared.
IOKASTE.   What was it that I said
    Of such importance?
OEDIPUS.   Why, "marauders," you said,   315
    Killed the king, according to this man's story.
    If he maintains that still, if there were several,
    Clearly the guilt is not mine: I was alone.
    But if he says one man, singlehanded, did it,
    Then the evidence all points to me.   320
IOKASTE. You may be sure that he said there were several;
    And can he call back that story now? He can not.
    The whole city heard it as plainly as I.
    But suppose he alters some detail of it:
    He can not ever show that Laios' death   325
    Fulfilled the oracle: for Apollo said
    My child was doomed to kill him; and my child—
    Poor baby!—it was my child that died first.

    No. From now on, where oracles are concerned,
    I would not waste a second thought on any.   330
OEDIPUS. You may be right.
                            But come: let someone go
    For the shepherd at once. This matter must be settled.
IOKASTE. I will send for him.
    I would not wish to cross you in anything,
    And surely not in this.—Let us go in.   335

(*Exeunt into the palace.*)

ODE 2

Strophe 1

CHORUS. Let me be reverent in the ways of right,
    Lowly the paths I journey on;
    Let all my words and actions keep
    The laws of the pure universe
    From highest Heaven handed down.   *5*
    For Heaven is their bright nurse,
    Those generations of the realms of light;
    Ah, never of mortal kind were they begot,
    Nor are they slaves of memory, lost in sleep:
    Their Father is greater than Time, and ages not.   *10*

Antistrophe 1

    The tyrant is a child of Pride
    Who drinks from his great sickening cup
    Recklessness and vanity,
    Until from his high crest headlong
    He plummets to the dust of hope.   *15*
    That strong man is not strong.
    But let no fair ambition be denied;
    May God protect the wrestler for the State
    In government, in comely policy,
    Who will fear God, and on his ordinance wait.   *20*

Strophe 2

    Haughtiness and the high hand of disdain
    Tempt and outrage God's holy law;
    And any mortal who dares hold
    No immortal Power in awe
    Will be caught up in a net of pain: *25*
    The price for which his levity is sold.
    Let each man take due earnings, then,
    And keep his hands from holy things,
    And from blasphemy stand apart—
    Else the crackling blast of heaven   *30*
    Blows on his head, and on his desperate heart.
    Though fools will honor impious men,
    In their cities no tragic poet sings.

Antistrophe 2

Shall we lose faith in Delphi's obscurities,
We who have heard the world's core   *35*
Discredited, and the sacred wood
Of Zeus at Elis praised no more?
The deeds and the strange prophecies
Must make a pattern yet to be understood.
Zeus, if indeed you are lord of all,   *40*
Throned in light over night and day,
Mirror this in your endless mind:
Our masters call the oracle
Words on the wind, and the Delphic vision blind!
Their hearts no longer know Apollo,   *45*
And reverence for the gods has died away.

SCENE 3

Enter Iokaste.

IOKASTE. Princes of Thebes, it has occurred to me
    To visit the altars of the gods, bearing
    These branches as a suppliant, and this incense.
    Our king is not himself: his noble soul
    Is overwrought with fantasies of dread,   *5*
    Else he would consider
    The new prophecies in the light of the old.
    He will listen to any voice that speaks disaster,
    And my advice goes for nothing. (*She approaches the
        altar, right.*)
                                        To you, then, Apollo,
    Lycean lord, since you are nearest, I turn in prayer   *10*
    Receive these offerings, and grant us deliverance
    From defilement. Our hearts are heavy with fear
    When we see our leader distracted, as helpless sailors
    Are terrified by the confusion of their helmsman.

(*Enter Messenger.*)

MESSENGER. Friends, no doubt you can direct me: *15*
    Where shall I find the house of Oedipus,
    Or, better still, where is the king himself?
CHORAGOS. It is this very place, stranger; he is inside.
    This is his wife and mother of his children.

MESSENGER. I wish her happiness in a happy house,   20
    Blest in all the fulfillment of her marriage.
IOKASTE. I wish as much for you: your courtesy
    Deserves a like good fortune. But now, tell me:
    Why have you come? What have you to say to us?
MESSENGER. Good news, my lady, for your house and your husband.   25
IOKASTE. What news? Who sent you here?
MESSENGER.   I am from Corinth.
    The news I bring ought to mean joy for you,
    Though it may be you will find some grief in it.
IOKASTE. What is it? How can it touch us in both ways?
MESSENGER. The word is that the people of the Isthmus   30
    Intend to call Oedipus to be their king.
IOKASTE. But old King Polybos—is he not reigning still?
MESSENGER. No. Death holds him in his sepulchre.
IOKASTE. What are you saying? Polybos is dead?
MESSENGER. If I am not telling the truth, may I die myself.   35
IOKASTE (*to a Maidservant*). Go in, go quickly; tell this to your master.
    O riddlers of God's will, where are you now!
    This was the man whom Oedipus, long ago,
    Feared so, fled so, in dread of destroying him—
    But it was another fate by which he died.   40

(*Enter Oedipus, center.*)

OEDIPUS. Dearest Iokaste, why have you sent for me?
IOKASTE. Listen to what this man says, and then tell me
    What has become of the solemn prophecies.
OEDIPUS. Who is this man? What is his news for me?
IOKASTE. He has come from Corinth to announce your father's
    death!   45
OEDIPUS. Is it true, stranger? Tell me in your own words.
MESSENGER. I can not say it more clearly: the king is dead.
OEDIPUS. Was it by treason? Or by an attack of illness?
MESSENGER. A little thing brings old men to their rest.
OEDIPUS. It was sickness, then?
MESSENGER.   Yes, and his many years. 50
OEDIPUS. Ah!
    Why should a man respect the Pythian hearth,[25] or
    Give heed to the birds that jangle above his head?

---

[25]Delphi

They prophesied that I should kill Polybos,
Kill my own father; but he is dead and buried,   55
And I am here—I never touched him, never,
Unless he died of grief for my departure,
And thus, in a sense, through me. No. Polybos
Has packed the oracles off with him underground.
They are empty words.

IOKASTE.   Had I not told you so?   60
OEDIPUS. You had; it was my faint heart that betrayed me.
IOKASTE. From now on never think of those things again.
OEDIPUS. And yet—must I not fear my mother's bed?
IOKASTE. Why should anyone in this world be afraid
     Since Fate rules us and nothing can be foreseen?   65
     A man should live only for the present day.

     Have no more fear of sleeping with your mother:
     How many men, in dreams, have lain with their mothers!
     No reasonable man is troubled by such things.
OEDIPUS. That is true, only—   70
     If only my mother were not still alive!
     But she is alive. I can not help my dread.
IOKASTE. Yet this news of your father's death is wonderful.
OEDIPUS. Wonderful. But I fear the living woman.
MESSENGER. Tell me, who is this woman that you fear?   75
OEDIPUS. It is Merope, man; the wife of King Polybos.
MESSENGER. Merope? Why should you be afraid of her?
OEDIPUS. An oracle of the gods, a dreadful saying.
MESSENGER. Can you tell me about it or are you sworn to silence?
OEDIPUS. I can tell you, and I will.   80
     Apollo said through his prophet that I was the man
     Who should marry his own mother, shed his father's blood
     With his own hands. And so, for all these years
     I have kept clear of Corinth, and no harm has come—
     Though it would have been sweet to see my parents again.   85
MESSENGER. And is this the fear that drove you out of Corinth?
OEDIPUS. Would you have me kill my father?
MESSENGER.   As for that
     You must be reassured by the news I gave you.
OEDIPUS. If you could reassure me, I would reward you.
MESSENGER. I had that in mind, I will confess: I thought   90
     I could count on you when you returned to Corinth.

OEDIPUS. No. I will never go near my parents again.
MESSENGER. Ah, son, you still do not know what you are doing—
OEDIPUS. What do you mean? In the name of God tell me!
MESSENGER. —If these are your reasons for not going home. 95
OEDIPUS. I tell you, I fear the oracle may come true.
MESSENGER. And guilt may come upon you through your parents?
OEDIPUS. That is the dread that is always in my heart.
MESSENGER. Can you not see that all your fears are groundless?
OEDIPUS. Groundless? Am I not my parents' son? 100
MESSENGER. Polybos was not your father.
OEDIPUS. Not my father?
MESSENGER. No more your father than the man speaking to you.
OEDIPUS. But you are nothing to me!
MESSENGER. Neither was he.
OEDIPUS. Then why did he call me son?
MESSENGER. I will tell you:
    Long ago he had you from my hands, as a gift. 105
OEDIPUS. Then how could he love me so, if I was not his?
MESSENGER. He had no children, and his heart turned to you.
OEDIPUS. What of you? Did you buy me? Did you find me by chance?
MESSENGER. I came upon you in the woody vales of Kithairon.
OEDIPUS. And what were you doing there?
MESSENGER. Tending my flocks. 110
OEDIPUS. A wandering shepherd?
MESSENGER. But your savior, son, that day.
OEDIPUS. From what did you save me?
MESSENGER. Your ankles should tell you that.
OEDIPUS. Ah, stranger, why do you speak of that childhood pain?
MESSENGER. I pulled the skewer that pinned your feet together.
OEDIPUS. I have had the mark as long as I can remember. 115
MESSENGER. That was why you were given the name[26] you bear.
OEDIPUS. God! Was it my father or my mother who did it?
    Tell me!
MESSENGER. I do not know. The man who gave you to me
    Can tell you better than I.
OEDIPUS. It was not you that found me, but another? 120
MESSENGER. It was another shepherd gave you to me.
OEDIPUS. Who was he? Can you tell me who he was?
MESSENGER. I think he was said to be one of Laïos' people.

---

[26]Oedipus means "swollen foot."

OEDIPUS. You mean the Laios who was king here years ago?

MESSENGER. Yes; King Laios; and the man was one of his herdsmen. *125*

OEDIPUS. Is he still alive? Can I see him?

MESSENGER.   These men here
    Know best about such things.

OEDIPUS.   Does anyone here
    Know this shepherd that he is talking about?
    Have you seen him in the fields, or in the town?
    If you have, tell me. It is time things were made plain. *130*

CHORAGOS. I think the man he means is that same shepherd
    You have already asked to see. Iokaste perhaps
    Could tell you something.

OEDIPUS.   Do you know anything
    About him, Lady? Is he the man we have summoned?
    Is that the man this shepherd means?

IOKASTE.   Why think of him? *135*
    Forget this herdsman. Forget it all.
    This talk is a waste of time.

OEDIPUS.   How can you say that,
    When the clues to my true birth are in my hands?

IOKASTE. For God's love, let us have no more questioning!
    Is your life nothing to you? *140*
    My own is pain enough for me to bear.

OEDIPUS. You need not worry. Suppose my mother a slave,
    And born of slaves: no baseness can touch you.

IOKASTE. Listen to me, I beg you: do not do this thing!

OEDIPUS. I will not listen; the truth must be made known. *145*

IOKASTE. Everything that I say is for your own good!

OEDIPUS. My own good
    Snaps my patience, then; I want none of it.

IOKASTE. You are fatally wrong! May you never learn who you are!

OEDIPUS. Go, one of you, and bring the shepherd here.
    Let us leave this woman to brag of her royal name. *150*

IOKASTE. Ah, miserable!
    That is the only word I have for you now.
    That is the only word I can ever have.

(*Exit into the palace.*)

CHORAGOS. Why has she left us, Oedipus? Why has she gone
    In such a passion of sorrow? I fear this silence: *155*
    Something dreadful may come of it.

OEDIPUS.   Let it come!
    However base my birth, I must know about it.
    The Queen, like a woman, is perhaps ashamed
    To think of my low origin. But I
    Am a child of Luck, I can not be dishonored.   *160*
    Luck is my mother; the passing months, my brothers,
    Have seen me rich and poor.
                              If this is so,
    How could I wish that I were someone else?
    How could I not be glad to know my birth?

ODE 3

Strophe

CHORUS. If ever the coming time were known
    To my heart's pondering,
    Kithairon, now by Heaven I see the torches
    At the festival of the next full moon
    And see the dance, and hear the choir sing   *5*
    A grace to your gentle shade:
    Mountain where Oedipus was found,
    O mountain guard of a noble race!
    May the god[27] who heals us lend his aid,
    And let that glory come to pass   *10*
    For our king's cradling-ground.

Antistrophe

Of the nymphs that flower beyond the years,
    Who bore you, royal child,
    To Pan[28] of the hills or the timberline Apollo,
    Cold in delight where the upland clears,   *15*
    Or Hermes[29] for whom Kyllene's[30] heights are piled?
    Or flushed as evening cloud,

---

[27]Apollo

[28]God of nature, shepherds, and fertility; associated with lechery, and often represented as half-man, half-goat.

[29]Messenger of the gods.

[30]Mountain that was birthplace of Hermes.

Great Dionysos,[31] roamer of mountains,
He—was it he who found you there,
And caught you up in his own proud   20
Arms from the sweet god-ravisher
Who laughed by the Muses'[32] fountains?

SCENE 4

OEDIPUS. Sirs: though I do not know the man,
    I think I see him coming, this shepherd we want:
    He is old, like our friend here, and the men
    Bringing him seem to be servants of my house.
    But you can tell, if you have ever seen him.   5

(*Enter Shepherd escorted by Servants.*)

CHORAGOS. I know him, he was Laios' man. You can trust him.
OEDIPUS. Tell me first, you from Corinth: is this the shepherd
    We were discussing?
MESSENGER.   This is the very man.
OEDIPUS (*to Shepherd*). Come here. No, look at me.
    You must answer
    Everything I ask.—You belonged to Laios?   10
SHEPHERD. Yes: born his slave, brought up in his house.
OEDIPUS. Tell me: what kind of work did you do for him?
SHEPHERD. I was a shepherd of his, most of my life.
OEDIPUS. Where mainly did you go for pasturage?
SHEPHERD. Sometimes Kithairon, sometimes the hills near-by.   15
OEDIPUS. Do you remember ever seeing this man out there?
SHEPHERD. What would he be doing there? This man?
OEDIPUS. This man standing here. Have you ever seen him before?
SHEPHERD. At least, not to my recollection.
MESSENGER. And that is not strange, my lord. But I'll refresh   20
    His memory: he must remember when we two
    Spent three whole seasons together, March to September,
    On Kithairon or thereabouts. He had two flocks;
    I had one. Each autumn I'd drive mine home
    And he would go back with his to Laios' sheepfold.—   25
    Is this not true, just as I have described it?

---

[31]Another name for Bacchus.

[32]Group of sister goddesses, patrons of poetry, music, art, and sciences.

SHEPHERD. True, yes; but it was all so long ago.

MESSENGER. Well, then: do you remember, back in those days,
That you gave me a baby boy to bring up as my own?

SHEPHERD. What if I did? What are you trying to say? 30

MESSENGER. King Oedipus was once that little child.

SHEPHERD. Damn you, hold your tongue!

OEDIPUS. No more of that!
It is your tongue needs watching, not this man's.

SHEPHERD. My king, my master, what is it I have done wrong?

OEDIPUS. You have not answered his question about the boy. 35

SHEPHERD. He does not know . . . He is only making trouble . . .

OEDIPUS. Come, speak plainly, or it will go hard with you.

SHEPHERD. In God's name, do not torture an old man!

OEDIPUS. Come here, one of you; bind his arms behind him.

SHEPHERD. Unhappy king! What more do you wish to learn? 40

OEDIPUS. Did you give this man the child he speaks of?

SHEPHERD. I did.
And I would to God I had died that very day.

OEDIPUS. You will die now unless you speak the truth.

SHEPHERD. Yet if I speak the truth, I am worse than dead.

OEDIPUS (*to Attendant*). He intends to draw it out, apparently— 45

SHEPHERD. No! I have told you already that I gave him the boy.

OEDIPUS. Where did you get him? From your house?
From somewhere else?

SHEPHERD. Not from mine, no. A man gave him to me.

OEDIPUS. Is that man here? Whose house did he belong to?

SHEPHERD. For God's love, my king, do not ask me any more! 50

OEDIPUS. You are a dead man if I have to ask you again.

SHEPHERD. Then . . .Then the child was from the palace of Laios.

OEDIPUS. A slave child? or a child of his own line?

SHEPHERD. Ah, I am on the brink of dreadful speech!

OEDIPUS. And I of dreadful hearing. Yet I must hear. 55

SHEPHERD. If you must be told, then . . .
They said it was Laios' child;
But it is your wife who can tell you about that.

OEDIPUS. My wife—Did she give it to you?

SHEPHERD. My lord, she did.

OEDIPUS. Do you know why?

SHEPHERD. I was told to get rid of it.

OEDIPUS. Oh heartless mother!

SHEPHERD. But in dread of prophecies . . . 60

OEDIPUS. Tell me.

SHEPHERD.   It was said that the boy would kill his own father.

OEDIPUS. Then why did you give him over to this old man?

SHEPHERD. I pitied the baby, my king,
>   And I thought that this man would take him far away
>   To his own country.
>   He saved him—but for what a fate!   *65*
>   For if you are what this man says you are,
>   No man living is more wretched than Oedipus.

OEDIPUS. Ah God!
>   It was true!
>   All the prophecies!
>   —Now,
>   O Light, may I look on you for the last time!   *70*
>   I, Oedipus,
>   Oedipus, damned in his birth, in his marriage damned,
>   Damned in the blood he shed with his own hand!

(*He rushes into the palace.*)

ODE 4

Strophe 1

CHORUS. Alas for the seed of men.
>   What measure shall I give these generations
>   That breathe on the void and are void
>   And exist and do not exist?
>   Who bears more weight of joy   *5*
>   Than mass of sunlight shifting in images,
>   Or who shall make his thought stay on
>   That down time drifts away?
>   Your splendor is all fallen.
>   O naked brow of wrath and tears,   *10*
>   O change of Oedipus!
>   I who saw your days call no man blest—
>   Your great days like ghosts gone.

Antistrophe 1

>   That mind was a strong bow.
>   Deep, how deep you drew it then, hard archer,   *15*
>   At a dim fearful range,

And brought dear glory down!
You overcame the stranger[33]—
The virgin with her hooking lion claws—
And though death sang, stood like a tower   20
To make pale Thebes take heart.
Fortress against our sorrow!
True king, giver of laws,
Majestic Oedipus!
No prince in Thebes had ever such renown,   25
No prince won such grace of power.

Strophe 2

And now of all men ever known
Most pitiful is this man's story:
His fortunes are most changed; his state
Fallen to a low slave's   30
Ground under bitter fate.
O Oedipus, most royal one!
The great door[34] that expelled you to the light
Gave at night—ah, gave night to your glory:
As to the father, to the fathering son.   35
All understood too late.
How could that queen whom Laios won,
The garden that he harrowed at his height,
Be silent when that act was done?

Antistrophe 2

But all eyes fail before time's eye,   40
All actions come to justice there.
Though never willed, though far down the deep past,
Your bed, your dread sirings,
Are brought to book at last.
Child by Laios doomed to die,   45
Then doomed to lose that fortunate little death,
Would God you never took breath in this air
That with my wailing lips I take to cry:

---

[33]The Sphinx

[34]Iokasate's womb

For I weep the world's outcast.
I was blind, and now I can tell why:
Asleep, for you had given ease of breath
To Thebes, while the false years went by.   *50*

EXODOS[35]

Enter, from the palace, Second Messenger.

SECOND MESSENGER. Elders of Thebes, most honored in this land,
    What horrors are yours to see and hear, what weight
    Of sorrow to be endured, if, true to your birth,
    You venerate the line of Labdakos!
    I think neither Istros nor Phasis, those great rivers,   *5*
    Could purify this place of all the evil
    It shelters now, or soon must bring to light—
    Evil not done unconsciously, but willed.

    The greatest griefs are those we cause ourselves.
CHORAGOS. Surely, friend, we have grief enough already;   *10*
    What new sorrow do you mean?
SECOND MESSENGER.   The queen is dead.
CHORAGOS. O miserable queen! But at whose hand?
SECOND MESSENGER.   Her own.
    The full horror of what happened you can not know,
    For you did not see it; but I, who did, will tell you
    As clearly as I can how she met her death.   *15*

    When she had left us,
    In passionate silence, passing through the court,
    She ran to her apartment in the house,
    Her hair clutched by the fingers of both hands.
    She closed the doors behind her; then, by that bed
    Where long ago the fatal son was conceived—   *20*
    That son who should bring about his father's death—
    We heard her call upon Laios, dead so many years,
    And heard her wail for the double fruit of her marriage,
    A husband by her husband, children by her child.   *25*

---

[35]Final scene

Exactly how she died I do not know:
For Oedipus burst in moaning and would not let us
Keep vigil to the end: it was by him
As he stormed about the room that our eyes were caught.
From one to another of us he went, begging a sword,   30
Hunting the wife who was not his wife, the mother
Whose womb had carried his own children and himself.
I do not know: it was none of us aided him,
But surely one of the gods was in control!
For with a dreadful cry   35
He hurled his weight, as though wrenched out of himself,
At the twin doors: the bolts gave, and he rushed in.
And there we saw her hanging, her body swaying
From the cruel cord she had noosed about her neck.
A great sob broke from him, heartbreaking to hear,   40
As he loosed the rope and lowered her to the ground.

I would blot out from my mind what happened next!
For the king ripped from her gown the golden brooches
That were her ornament, and raised them, and plunged them
    down
Straight into his own eyeballs, crying, "No more,   45
No more shall you look on the misery about me,
The horrors of my own doing! Too long you have known
The faces of those whom I should never have seen,
Too long been blind to those for whom I was searching!
From this hour, go in darkness!" And as he spoke,   50
He struck at his eyes—not once, but many times;
And the blood spattered his beard,
Bursting from his ruined sockets like red hail.
So from the unhappiness of two this evil has sprung,
A curse on the man and woman alike. The old   55
Happiness of the house of Labdakos
Was happiness enough: where is it today?
It is all wailing and ruin, disgrace, death—all
The misery of mankind that has a name—
And it is wholly and for ever theirs.   60
CHORAGOS. Is he in agony still? Is there no rest for him?
SECOND MESSENGER. He is calling for someone to open the doors
    wide
    So that all the children of Kadmos may look upon
    His father's murderer, his mother's—no,

I can not say it!

And then he will leave Thebes,   65

Self-exiled, in order that the curse
Which he himself pronounced may depart from the house.
He is weak, and there is none to lead him,
So terrible is his suffering.

But you will see:

Look, the doors are opening; in a moment   *70*
You will see a thing that would crush a heart of stone.

(*The central door is opened; Oedipus, blinded, is led in.*)

CHORAGOS. Dreadful indeed for men to see.
    Never have my own eyes
    Looked on a sight so full of fear.

    Oedipus!   *75*
    What madness came upon you, what demon
    Leaped on your life with heavier
    Punishment than a mortal man can bear?
    No: I can not even
    Look at you, poor ruined one.   *80*
    And I would speak, question, ponder,
    If I were able. No.
    You make me shudder.
OEDIPUS. God. God.
    Is there a sorrow greater?   *85*
    Where shall I find harbor in this world?
    My voice is hurled far on a dark wind.
    What has God done to me?
CHORAGOS. Too terrible to think of, or to see.

Strophe 1

OEDIPUS. O cloud of night,   *90*
    Never to be turned away: night coming on,
    I can not tell how: night like a shroud!
    My fair winds brought me here.

O God. Again

    The pain of the spikes where I had sight,
    The flooding pain   *95*
    Of memory, never to be gouged out.

CHORAGOS. This is not strange.
> You suffer it all twice over, remorse in pain,
> Pain in remorse.

Antistrophe 1

OEDIPUS. Ah dear friend   *100*
> Are you faithful even yet, you alone?
> Are you still standing near me, will you stay here,
> Patient, to care for the blind?

>> The blind man!

> Yet even blind I know who it is attends me,
> By the voice's tone—   *105*
> Though my new darkness hide the comforter.
CHORAGOS. Oh fearful act!
> What god was it drove you to rake black
> Night across your eyes?

Strophe 2

OEDIPUS. Apollo. Apollo. Dear   *110*
> Children, the god was Apollo.
> He brought my sick, sick fate upon me.
> But the blinding hand was my own!
> How could I bear to see
> When all my sight was horror everywhere?   *115*
CHORAGOS. Everywhere; that is true.
OEDIPUS. And now what is left?
> Images? Love? A greeting even,
> Sweet to the senses? Is there anything?
> Ah, no, friends: lead me away.   *120*
> Lead me away from Thebes.

>> Lead the great wreck

> And hell of Oedipus, whom the gods hate.
CHORAGOS. Your misery, you are not blind to that.
> Would God you had never found it out!

Antistrophe 2

OEDIPUS. Death take the man who unbound   *125*
> My feet on that hillside
> And delivered me from death to life! What life?

If only I had died,
This weight of monstrous doom
Could not have dragged me and my darlings down.   130
CHORAGOS. I would have wished the same.
OEDIPUS. Oh never to have come here
    With my father's blood upon me! Never
    To have been the man they call his mother's husband!
    Oh accurst! Oh child of evil,   135
    To have entered that wretched bed—the selfsame one!
    More primal than sin itself, this fell to me.
CHORAGOS. I do not know what words to offer you.
    You were better dead than alive and blind.
OEDIPUS. Do not counsel me any more. This punishment   140
    That I have laid upon myself is just.
    If I had eyes,
    I do not know how I could bear the sight
    Of my father, when I came to the house of Death,
    Or my mother: for I have sinned against them both   145
    So vilely that I could not make my peace
    By strangling my own life.
                            Or do you think my children,
    Born as they were born, would be sweet to my eyes?
    Ah never, never! Nor this town with its high walls,
    Nor the holy images of the gods.
                                        For I, 150
    Thrice miserable!—Oedipus, noblest of all the line
    Of Kadmos, have condemned myself to enjoy
    These things no more, by my own malediction
    Expelling that man whom the gods declared
    To be a defilement in the house of Laios.   155
    After exposing the rankness of my own guilt,
    How could I look men frankly in the eyes?
    No, I swear it,
    If I could have stifled my hearing at its source,
    I would have done it and made all this body   160
    A tight cell of misery, blank to light and sound:
    So I should have been safe in my dark mind
    Beyond external evil.
                            Ah Kithairon!
    Why did you shelter me? When I was cast upon you,
    Why did I not die? Then I should never   165
    Have shown the world my execrable birth.

Ah Polybos! Corinth, city that I believed
The ancient seat of my ancestors: how fair
I seemed, your child! And all the while this evil
Was cancerous within me!

For I am sick   170

In my own being, sick in my origin.
O three roads, dark ravine, woodland and way
Where three roads met; you, drinking my father's blood,
My own blood, spilled by my own hand: can you remember
The unspeakable things I did there, and the things   175
I went on from there to do?

O marriage, marriage!

The act that engendered me, and again the act
Performed by the son in the same bed—

Ah, the net

Of incest, mingling fathers, brothers, sons,
With brides, wives, mothers: the last evil   180
That can be known by men: no tongue can say
How evil!

No. For the love of God, conceal me

Somewhere far from Thebes; or kill me; or hurl me
Into the sea, away from men's eyes for ever.

Come, lead me. You need nor fear to touch me.   185
Of all men, I alone can bear this guilt.

(*Enter Kreon.*)

CHORAGOS. Kreon is here now. As to what you ask,
    He may decide the course to take. He only
    Is left to protect the city in your place.
OEDIPUS. Alas, how can I speak to him? What right have I   *190*
    To beg his courtesy whom I have deeply wronged?
KREON. I have not come to mock you, Oedipus,
    Or to reproach you, either.
    (*To Attendants.*)—   You, standing there:
    If you have lost all respect for man's dignity,
    At least respect the flame of Lord Helios:[36]   *195*
    Do not allow this pollution to show itself
    Openly here, an affront to the earth

---

[36]Helios: sun god.

And Heaven's rain and the light of day. No, take him
Into the house as quickly as you can.
For it is proper   *200*
That only the close kindred see his grief.
OEDIPUS. I pray you in God's name, since your courtesy
Ignores my dark expectation, visiting
With mercy this man of all men most execrable:
Give me what I ask—for your good, not for mine.   *205*
KREON. And what is it that you turn to me begging for?
OEDIPUS. Drive me out of this country as quickly as may be
To a place where no human voice can ever greet me.
KREON. I should have done that before now—only,
God's will had not been wholly revealed to me.   *210*
OEDIPUS. But his command is plain: the parricide
Must be destroyed. I am that evil man.
KREON. That is the sense of it, yes; but as things are,
We had best discover clearly what is to be done.
OEDIPUS. You would learn more about a man like me?   *215*
KREON. You are ready now to listen to the god.
OEDIPUS. I will listen. But it is to you
That I must turn for help. I beg you, hear me.

The woman is there—
Give her whatever funeral you think proper: *220*
She is your sister.
                                        —But let me go, Kreon!
Let me purge my father's Thebes of the pollution
Of my living here, and go out to the wild hills,
To Kithairon, that has won such fame with me,
The tomb my mother and father appointed for me,   *225*
And let me die there, as they willed I should.
And yet I know
Death will not ever come to me through sickness
Or in any natural way: I have been preserved
For some unthinkable fate. But let that be.   *230*

As for my sons, you need not care for them.
They are men, they will find some way to live.
But my poor daughters, who have shared my table,
Who never before have been parted from their father—
Take care of them, Kreon; do this for me.   *235*

And will you let me touch them with my hands
A last time, and let us weep together?
Be kind, my lord,
Great prince, be kind!

                          Could I but touch them,
They would be mine again, as when I had my eyes.   240

(*Enter Antigone and Ismene, attended.*)

    Ah, God!
Is it my dearest children I hear weeping?
Has Kreon pitied me and sent my daughters?
KREON. Yes, Oedipus: I knew that they were dear to you
    In the old days, and know you must love them still.   245
OEDIPUS. May God bless you for this—and be a friendlier
    Guardian to you than he has been to me!

Children, where are you?
Come quickly to my hands: they are your brother's—
Hands that have brought your father's once clear eyes   250
To this way of seeing—

                            Ah dearest ones,
I had neither sight nor knowledge then, your father
By the woman who was the source of his own life!
And I weep for you—having no strength to see you—,
I weep for you when I think of the bitterness   255
That men will visit upon you all your lives.
What homes, what festivals can you attend
Without being forced to depart again in tears?
And when you come to marriageable age,
Where is the man, my daughters, who would dare   260
Risk the bane that lies on all my children?
Is there any evil wanting? Your father killed
His father; sowed the womb of her who bore him;
Engendered you at the fount of his own existence!
That is what they will say of you.

                         Then, whom 265
Can you ever marry? There are no bridegrooms for you,
And your lives must wither away in sterile dreaming.

O Kreon, son of Menoikeus!
You are the only father my daughters have,

Since we, their parents, are both of us gone for ever.   *270*
They are your own blood: you will not let them
Fall into beggary and loneliness;
You will keep them from the miseries that are mine!
Take pity on them; see, they are only children,
Friendless except for you. Promise me this,   *275*
Great prince, and give me your hand in token of it.

(*Kreon clasps his right hand.*)

Children:
I could say much, if you could understand me,
But as it is, I have only this prayer for you:
Live where you can, be as happy as you can—   *280*
Happier, please God, than God has made your father.
KREON. Enough. You have wept enough. Now go within.
OEDIPUS. I must, but it is hard.
KREON.   Time eases all things.
OEDIPUS. You know my mind, then?
KREON.   Say what you desire.
OEDIPUS. Send me from Thebes!
KREON.   God grant that I may! *285*
OEDIPUS. But since God hates me . . .
KREON.   No, he will grant your wish.
OEDIPUS. You promise?
KREON. I can not speak beyond my knowledge.
OEDIPUS. Then lead me in.
KREON. Come now, and leave your children.
OEDIPUS. No! Do not take them from me!
KREON.   Think no longer
That you are in command here, but rather think   *290*
How, when you were, you served your own destruction.

(*Exeunt into the house all but the Chorus; the Choragos chants directly to the audience.*)

CHORAGOS. Men of Thebes: look upon Oedipus.
This is the king who solved the famous riddle
And towered up, most powerful of men.
No mortal eyes but looked on him with envy,   *295*
Yet in the end ruin swept over him.

Let every man in mankind's frailty
Consider his last day; and let none
Presume on his good fortune until he find
Life, at his death, a memory without pain.   *300*

[C. 430 B.C.E.]

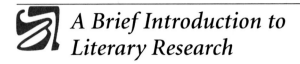 # A Brief Introduction to Literary Research

Why Do Literary Research?

Different kinds of writing assignments in literature classes ask the student to conduct different kinds of inquiry. Some, for instance, will ask you to focus closely on your own interpretation of a literary text, drawing evidence to support the claims made in the course of your paper solely from that text. Others will require that you perform extensive research into what are often called "secondary sources," texts that are not themselves the object of analysis, but instead provide a cultural, historical, theoretical, or critical lens through which a piece of literature might be understood. Included among such secondary sources are critical texts about the object of analysis, containing other scholars' interpretations and understandings of the text in question. This essay focuses on research into such critical writing about literature, as used to support your own writing and analysis.

Your research will have different purposes depending upon the assignment you have been given. You may be asked, for instance, to analyze the critical interpretations of a particular literary text as they have emerged over time; such a project will require you to uncover the debates among a number of scholars, how they agree and disagree with one another, and what the stakes of their various points of contention might be. Other assignments will ask you to write a research paper that is primarily focused on your own original argument about the literary text, but with attention to the responses of other scholars. In conducting this kind of research, you must guard against simply "trolling for quotes" and against an over-reliance on "authoritative" voices. The purpose of literary research is generally to enable you to enter into a field of critical discourse that is already in progress, to participate in an ongoing conversation about a literary text, and to stake out the significance of your way of approaching the text by acknowledging the approaches of other scholars and suggesting what questions have thus far been left unanswered.

Literary research, however, requires a particular set of skills, both in terms of finding appropriate sources and in reading, evaluating, and incorporating those into your own thinking. Your instructor will likely have some specific requirements for your research; what follows should be taken as general advice, a good set of strategies for beginning your work, and not as a replacement for any methods preferred by your instructor.

Step 1: Go to the Library

This step is not suggested facetiously: in fact, the first and most important piece of advice that you can receive is to get to know the research or reference librarians at your school's library. These librarians are specialists in information retrieval, and they will therefore have the best insights into the databases and bibliographies subscribed to by your library, as well as the other engines through which the material in your library may be found. They will also be of help in tracking down sources that may be difficult to obtain, whether through a consortial lending arrangement that your library participates in or through a broader interlibrary loan program. Your school's reference librarians may have areas of specialization within the curriculum, so you should consult your library's website to find out whether there are one or more librarians focused on research in literature. These librarians will be your best resource for finding the right material within the sea of possible information sources, so you should talk with them early and often.

Formulate Your Research Question

Though they are experts in information retrieval, your librarians will likely not be able to help you unless you have a sense of *what* information you are looking for. The first task you must undertake, then, is to figure out the basic parameters of your search. You must thus begin by formulating a basic research question. This question may, and in fact should, change as you progress in your research, as the arguments presented by other scholars will affect the way that you frame your own ideas; because of that, your initial research question will likely not be a fully elaborated thesis, but rather a general area of interest. This focus should not be too broad, however; beginning your research with an area of interest like "Hemingway" will result in more secondary sources than you can reasonably manage. Be as specific as you can: "representations of bullfighting in Hemingway" as a starting point will produce better results.

Consult a Wide Variety of Sources

The next task in front of you will be to find out what published texts will be of interest in your research. The most important sources for the kinds of research that you are undertaking will be scholarly books and journals. It's important to ensure that you consult a broad range of such sources: using only books as sources for your research may cause you to inadvertently exclude some of the most recent and significant analyses of the texts you are studying (because books generally take a lot longer to get into print than do journal articles), but using only journal articles may likewise cause you to inadvertently over-look some of the most important sustained arguments about your primary text. Your paper may wind up only citing one or the other form of publica-tion, but you should be certain that your research involves both forms.

Use the Right Database

These searches should be conducted primarily through scholarly databases, accessible either in your school's library or, often, through your library's web-site. Google is generally not a good site through which to conduct serious research, both because of the overwhelming number of results that the search engine can produce for any given search terms and because of the often unre-liable nature of the documents that such searches turn up. And while Wikipedia can often be a good source for general (or even very specific or arcane) infor-mation about a particular subject, it is not usually considered an acceptable source to cite in a college-level research paper, for the same reasons that citing any encyclopedia would be considered inappropriate: encyclopedias do not contain the results of original research, but rather condensations and sum-maries of the ideas and arguments made elsewhere. Google and Wikipedia might be useful as you begin to formulate your research question, but the actual research you do should be conducted using scholarly sources.

A brief note here on Google Scholar: While the material that this engine catalogs and searches is, indeed, scholarly in origin, the cataloging method that Google Scholar uses isn't considered terribly reliable, and the material that is cataloged is overwhelmingly weighted toward the sciences and social sciences. A search of Google Scholar cannot hurt, but it should by no means be the only database you consult. Furthermore, there are many online repositories containing electronic versions of scholarly journals, including Project Muse, JSTOR, and so forth, all of which provide the ability to search their holdings. These will be excellent sources for articles that you'll want to consult, but you shouldn't begin your search from these sites, as they index a limited number of journals.

Evaluate Sources Critically

Whatever their provenance, however—whether in print or online, whether books or articles—all of the sources that you uncover in the process of your research will require careful evaluation as to their reliability and credibility. You should consider, for instance, with each source you consult, whether the pub-lisher or publication is an appropriate one. A university press will generally be considered more authoritative as a source of scholarly books than a "vanity" press. Similarly, a scholarly journal will often be considered more reliable than a popular magazine. However, different kinds of arguments will require different kinds of source material, so you will need to use your own judgment. You should also evaluate the credibility of your sources' authors: are the writers authorities on the subject? Have they done thorough research? Finally, you must evaluate the arguments themselves: are the claims made by the source warranted and supported by the evidence? In the end, you should only use sources that your careful evaluation suggests are reliable.

Search the MLA Bibliography

The best way to begin finding authoritative sources, again, will be by searching scholarly databases. In literary studies, the primary database that you will want to search is the MLA Bibliography, published by the Modern Languages Association of America (though there are of course other databases to which your library might subscribe as well, and you shouldn't overlook your library's catalog; consult your librarian for information about them). The vast majority of journals in literature and language studies are indexed in the MLA Bibliography, as are many books in the field. There are many different search engines that provide access to the MLA Bibliography, each with slightly different characteristics, so you may want to consult with your librarian for specific instructions on searching the database. Generally, however, the database will provide the ability to search by Keyword, by Title, and by Author, among other parameters. Note, however, that "Title" and "Author" here refer to the sources indexed in the database, and not the primary text about which you are researching; to find sources *about* Hemingway, you should search for "Hemingway" as a keyword.

However, as I write, a keyword search for "Hemingway" in the MLA database produces 3969 results, which suggests that the search is too broad. Your database's search engine will provide some means of what is called Boolean searching, which allows you to use connectors like AND and OR to further refine your searches. AND as a Boolean term narrows a search, as both terms connected by the AND must be present for the record to be included; OR, by contrast, broadens a search, as a record will be included if it contains either term. A search, for instance, for "Hemingway AND bullfight" produces 11 results, which might seem reasonable. However, using "bullfight" as a term doesn't necessary give access to results that use terms like "bullfights" or "bullfighting." Your search engine should give you the ability to use wildcards in your search terms, which instruct the engine to return related words; "bullfight*" as a search term would thus return any term that begins with "bullfight," no matter what characters complete the word (thus including bullfights, bullfighting, bullfighter, and so forth). A search for "Hemingway AND bull-fight*" produces 41 results, which is a very good place to begin.

Evaluate Your Search Results

Your job is now to sort through these citations and see which ones appear to be most relevant to your research question. A number of the article citations that result from the "Hemingway AND bullfight*" search, for instance, focus on the novel *The Sun Also Rises*, though you may be writing about the short story "The Capital of the World." It is up to you to determine whether those articles' arguments about the novel are applicable to your own analysis of the short story. Sometimes the database records will include an abstract, or a short précis of the article's argument, which may help you make a decision. Other times there will be no abstract included, but you can get more information about the article by examining the record closely, as it will contain certain descriptors designed to facilitate searches. The record for Kathy G. Willingham's article, "The Sun Hasn't Set Yet: Brett Ashley and the Code Hero Debate," includes the descriptors "characterization," "Ashley, Lady Brett," and "hero-ine," which suggests that the article might be applicable to research into the relationship between the representation of bullfighting in Hemingway's writing and questions about gender.

If your initial search turns up either too many or too few results, or results that don't provide the kinds of sources that you're really looking for, you should think about how to refine your search terms. Examine the kinds of descriptors that the database's records include, and think about how you might use those terms to find better results. For instance, if you are thinking about Hemingway's representations of women, rather than searching for "Hemingway AND women," you might try a search for "Hemingway AND female characters." A reference librarian may be of particular help as you refine your search. Throughout the search process, you should keep good records for yourself of the searches you've conducted and the results they've produced.

Go to the Source

Once you've accumulated a number of citations that appear to be applicable to your research question, the next stage is to obtain the sources themselves. Some libraries' database configurations will provide information about whether the source is contained in the library's holdings; my institution's MLA database, for instance, includes a "Get This Item" link on each record, which leads the user to a page with more information about how to obtain the article or book. Some such sources will be very easily obtainable, as the journals may be archived online; others may require you to track down print copies of the journal or book in the library's stacks, and still others may not be in the library's holdings at all, requiring you to use an interlibrary loan program to obtain them. *You must not restrict your research to digitally available sources.* Because many journals have only been digitized since the early 1990s, and because very few books are available digitally, many of the most important sources for your research will require you to leave the computer behind, and venture into the library's stacks. There's a great benefit to doing so, however, which is a kind of serendipity that no digital search has yet been able to mirror: when you are flipping through the print back issues of a journal, or scanning the spines of books on a shelf, looking for the source that your search uncovered, you are very likely to run into something promising that for whatever reason didn't turn up in your search. These accidental encounters are a key element of the research process; don't miss out on them by sticking too closely to what's electronically available.

Reading and Notetaking

Once you've gotten your first round of sources, the next step is, unsurprisingly, to read them. You might skim them quickly at first, to see whether they in fact seem as applicable to your research question as their citations made them appear, and then read them more closely in order to uncover the finer points of their reasoning, which will be helpful to you in constructing your own argument. You should be certain to take thorough, accurate notes as you read, particularly keeping detailed records of the bibliographic information from each source, which you'll need when you construct your "works cited" list, as well as scrupulously ensuring that any direct quotations or paraphrases that you draw from these sources are properly attributed to their authors. Failure to do so constitutes plagiarism, whether the failure is intentional or inadvertent, and plagiarism may carry quite severe consequences, including failure or, in some cases, expulsion. Be very careful in your notetaking to indicate clearly to yourself which notes are drawn from the texts you're reading, whether quotations or paraphrases, and which constitute your own thinking. Don't rely on your memory for this purpose, as memory can deceive you.

Repeat

It is important also to note that your research process should be recursive; after reading a couple of sources on your initial research question, you might discover that your question has shifted directions slightly, requiring a return to the database to see if there are sources that more closely approximate your new idea. Moreover, you might find as you read an article that its author cites a further source that sounds like it might be useful to you; explore the bibliographies included with the secondary texts that you read to see whether there are previous sources that you should consult.

Remember throughout the process, however, what the purpose of the research you're conducting is; a report on the critical interpretations of a particular text will require very different uses of the material that you uncover than will a research paper that is intended to be focused on your own original argument. For the former, you'll want to keep track of the debates among the critics that you read; what seem to be the key points about which they agree, and over which they disagree, and why? For the latter, you should think not just about ways that the critical texts support the argument you want to make, but also about your points of entry into the critical conversation; how does your own interpretation of the text differ from those of the critics you are reading, and why? What questions do the critical interpretations to this point raise? What gaps do you find in the critical conversation? What would your perspective add to a reader's understanding of the text you're studying?

Literary research, like any other form of research, requires a set of skills that can only be developed through practice. Your instructor and your librarian may have further advice to help you as you work, but the best way to learn how to conduct this kind of research is simply to plunge in, poke around in the databases, explore the sources, and see what turns up. With a flexible sense of how your search terms work, with careful attention to the credibility of the sources you uncover, and with conscientious notetaking, you should be able to find your way quickly into the critical conversation about your topic.

MLA Documentation

DOCUMENTATION IS LIKE TRAFFIC SIGNS AND SIGNALS. Everyone in a culture agrees to use them in a certain way. Everyone in a community of readers and writers agrees that they will identify their sources according to agreed upon rules. Sometimes the rules are logical and have written cues, like stop signs, and sometimes the rules are more like dinner manners: We begin with the salad fork because everyone has agreed to do it that way. There are several forms of documentation for particular areas of study and specific journals. The MLA format is used for English and American literature and foreign language literature in the United States.

MLA Manuscript Format

The Modern Language Association (MLA)
- Cites sources in the text, not in footnotes or endnotes.
- Lists sources alphabetically by author's last name in a Works Cited section.
- Uses hanging indention (first line flush against the margin, second and subsequent lines indented) in the list of sources.
- Uses no punctuation when designating a page number.
- Separates items with periods.

Place name, date, and course information in the upper left-hand corner of the first page, and double space between lines, and before the centered title. Leave at least one inch margins, indent the first line of each paragraph five spaces, and double space. Quotations longer than four typed lines should be indented five more spaces. Place page numbers in upper right-hand corner, one half inch from the top of the paper. Use last name or short title before the number for identification. Leave one space after all punctuation: MLA allows either single or double space after periods or question and exclamation marks. Form a dash with two hyphens, using no spaces. The works-cited page begins with the centered words "Works Cited" and is alphabetized by author's last name unless there is no author; then works are alphabetized by book or essay title. For second and subsequent uses of the same author's name in the list, use three hyphens.

MLA in text citation

1. AUTHOR NAMED IN THE PAPER:
   If the author is named in the text, only page numbers are given.

   > Barri J. Gold discusses the influence of poetry on science (449).

2. AUTHOR NOT NAMED IN TEXT:
   When the author is not named in the text, the name appears in the notation.

   > The argument of the 1800s ran that evolution was an optimistic idea (Gold 451).

3. TWO OR THREE AUTHORS:
   When two or three authors appear as one, they are cited as follows.

   > Linkon, Peckham, and Lanier-Nabors claim that working-class interests are influencing literature (149).

4. FOUR OR MORE AUTHORS:
   All four authors may be named in the text; or first author named, followed by "et al." (Latin for "et alia," which means "and others") may be referenced in parentheses.

   > Mentors with much teaching experience will give more help than mentors who have taught little (Duin, Lammers, Mason, and Graves 143).

   > Or, the reference can be written as: (Duin et al.).

5. UNKNOWN AUTHOR:
   The title substitutes for the author's name in the text or in parentheses.

   > "The Twin Corbies" is a poem about two crows (119).

6. CORPORATE AUTHOR:
   A corporate author can be named in either the text or in the parentheses.

   > Illinois State University has 264 professors (1).

7. TWO OR MORE WORKS BY ONE AUTHOR:
   When two or more works by one author appear on the works-cited page, either name the work in the text, or include a short form of the title in the parentheses.

   > In "Unto My Books—So Good to Turn," Dickinson praises books as her friends (296).

   If author and shortened form both appear in parentheses, use the form as follows: (Dickinson, "Unto My Books" 296)

8. A SOURCE QUOTED IN ANOTHER SOURCE:
   To show that one author is quoting another, use the abbreviation "qtd." in.

Orr's "All Morning," illustrates a poetic introduction with "All morning the dream lingers" (qtd. in McCormick, Waller, and Flower 54).

9. NOVEL, PLAY, OR POEM:

Give the title if not mentioned in text when the work is first referred to, then follow with specific information.

NOVEL: part or chapter.

Ged said, "I fear what follows behind me" (A Wizard of Earthsea 117: ch. 6).

PLAY: act and scene and line numbers in Arabic numerals.

"He who tells too much truth is sure to be hanged," cries Joan (St. Joan 1.6).

POEM: refer to the part (if applicable) and line numbers.

"Surely some revelation is at hand," muses Yeats' "The Second Coming" (10).

10. WORK IN AN ANTHOLOGY:

Cite the author's name, not the editor's name.

In his essay "On Stories," Lewis observes that "No book is really worth reading at the age of ten that is not equally worth reading at the age of fifty." (100).

11. ENTIRE WORK:

Name the author in the text or note in parentheses.

Freire was introduced to North American scholars in Freire for the Classroom (Shor).

Works Cited

Books

1. ONE AUTHOR:

LeGuin, Ursula K. A Wizard of Earthsea. New York: Ace, 1968.

2. TWO OR THREE AUTHORS:

Jensen, George H., and John K. Ditiberio. Personality and the Teaching of Composition. Norwood: Ablex, 1999.

3. MORE THAN TWO AUTHORS OR EDITORS:

Lawson, Bruce, et al., eds. Encountering Student Texts. Urbana: NCTE, 1989.

4. EDITOR:

Hooper, Walter, ed. The Letters of C. S. Lewis. New York: Macmillan, 1979.

5. AUTHOR WITH EDITOR:

Tolkien, J.R.R. The Tolkien Reader. Christopher Tolkien, ed. New York: Ballantine, 1966.

6. UNKNOWN AUTHOR:

Pearl. Boston: Houghton Mifflin, 1975.

7. CORPORATE AUTHOR:

Illinois State University. Facts 1998–9. Normal, IL: ISUP, 1999.

8. TWO OR MORE WORKS BY THE SAME AUTHOR:

Lewis, C. S. The Lion, The Witch, and The Wardrobe. New York: Macmillan, 1950.

—-. The Magician's Nephew. New York: Macmillan, 1955.

9. TRANSLATION

Tolstoy, L. N. Anna Karenina. Trans. Rosemary Edmunds. New York: Viking, 1954.

10. WORK IN AN ANTHOLOGY

Walsh, Chad. "The Reeducation of the Fearful Pilgrim." The Longing for a Form. Ed. Peter J. Schakel. Kent, OH: Kent State UP, 1977. 64–72.

Periodicals

1. NEWSPAPER ARTICLE
(Signed)

Flick, Bill. "This Year in History," The Daily Pantagraph 31 December 1998: A 14.

(Unsigned)

"Teachers Take Nashville" The Council Chronicle September 1998: 7.

2. MAGAZINE ARTICLES
(signed)

Gould, Stephen Jay. "Capturing the Center." Natural History December 1998: 14, 1–18, 20–24.

(unsigned)

"College Can Give You Grief." Psychology Today Oct. 1998: 20.

3. PERIODICAL ARTICLES
(with continuous page numbering from issue to issue within a year)

Barri J. Gold. "The Consolation of Physics: Tennyson's Thermodynamic Solution." PMLA 117 (May 2002): 449–464.

(with each issue paged separately)

> Boyd, Ian. "In Search of the Essential Chesterton." <u>VII</u> 1:1 (March 1980): 28–45.

(1:1 meaning vol. 1, issue 1)

Other Sources

1. THE BIBLE

   > <u>The New International Bible.</u> Colorado Springs: International Bible Society, 1972.

   (Note. The King James Bible need not be named or underlined. You need only note chapter and verse in parentheses in the text (Matt. 12.1–3). Translations of the Bible other than King James should be identified and underlined.)

2. LETTER TO THE EDITOR

   > White, Curt. Letter. The Vidette. February 18, 1999: 6.

3. PERSONAL OR TELEPHONE INTERVIEW

   > Kay, Martha. Personal interview. Danville, Illinois, 10 March 1999.

4. RECORD, TAPE, OR CD

   > Kingston Trio. *Greatest Hits*. Curb Records. D2–77385, 1991.

Electronic Sources

These sources include a variety of types of communication: personal e-mails between persons or among private group members; list servs among several individuals with common work or interests; or news groups that serve associations or subscribers. The World Wide Web connects the individual to a wider community, including businesses and other commercial groups. For all these sources, a writer should include the author's name (if known), the e-mail address in brackets, the date of publication or communication, the URL in angle brackets, and the date of access in parentheses.

1. E-MAIL

   (include name of sender, e-mail address in angle brackets, title, date of transmission, type of correspondence, and date of access in parentheses.)

   > Scharton, Maurice. <scharton@mail.ilstu.edu> "Editing Information." 3 Mar 1999. Personal email. (11 March 1999).

2. LISTSERVS AND NEWS GROUPS

   (include information for e-mail but add the address of the group cite in angle brackets before the date of access.)

Larkin, Gregory. <Gregory.Larkin@NAU.EDU> "The Problem with Listserves." 24 April 1997. <river97-l@NAUVAX.UCC.NAU.EDU> (10 March 1999).

3. CD-ROM

   1998 Compton's Interactive Encyclypedia. CD-ROM. Cambridge: The Learning Company, 1998.

4. WORLD WIDE WEB
   National Resource:

   Mengisteab, Kidane. Globalization and autocentricity in Africa's Development in the 21st Century. Africa World Press, 1996. <http://www.ilstu/ressub/subject/business/maynewkk.html> (11 March 1999).
   Library Resource:

   Hatfield, Edward, and Susan Sprecher. Men's and Women's Preferences in Marital Partners in the United States, Russia, and Japan. Journal of Cross-Cultural Psychology. 26(6):728–750, Nov. 1995. <http://www.milner.ilstu.edu> (22 January 1999).
   Note that the second date is always the date this site was accessed while the first date is the time of publication.

Professional Site

NCTE Home Page. 6 January 2004. National Council of Teachers of English. 4 March 2004 <http://www.ncte.org>.

A Personal Site

Neuleib, Janice Witherspoon. Home page. Illinois State University. 26 February 2004 <http://www.ilstu.edu/~jneuleib>.

A Book

Crane, Stephen. The Red Badge of Courage. Gutenberg Project. University of California Berkeley Archives. 4 September 1996. Sunsite Berkeley. 4 March 2004 <http://sunsite.berkeley.edu/Literature/Crane/RedBadge/>.

A Poem

Dickinson, Emily. "A Narrow Fellow in the Grass," *Poetry Archive.* <http://www.emule.com/poetry>.

An Article in a Reference Database

"On 'Behave.'" Oxford English Dictionary Online. Second Edition. 1989. Oxford English Dictionary. 5 March 2004 <http://dictionary.oed.com/cgi/entry/00019662>.

An Article in a Journal

Applebee, Arthur N., and Judith A. Langer. "Discussion-based Approaches to Student Understanding: Classroom Instruction in the Middle School Classroom." <u>American Education Research Journal</u> 40:3 (2003). 2 March 2004. <<u>http://www.ncte.org/about/research/articles/115102.htm</u>>.

An Article in a Magazine

Perkins, Sid. "Avalanche." <u>Science News On Line 2</u> March 2002. 16 February 2004 <http://www.sciencenews.org/articles/20020302/bob14.asp>.

Glossary of Literary Terms

ACCENT. The emphasis placed on syllables in the rhythm of a line of poetry.

ACCENTUAL METER. Accentual meter measures the rhythms in poetic verse based on the number of speech stresses per line. Different accents create different meanings, e.g., "government *by* the people, *for* the people, as opposed to government by the *people*, for the *people* . . . ."

ACT. The major division in the action of a play. Smaller divisions within acts are called *scenes*.

AFTERWORD. A final passage or scene following the conclusion of a story or play, also called an *epilogue*. The afterword often presents the narrator's assessment of the overall meaning of the story.

ALIENATION EFFECT. An effect, such as a mask or a surreal setting, designed to prevent audiences from becoming emotionally involved in a play. This technique was used by the German dramatist Bertolt Brecht to move audiences to political action.

ALLEGORY. A narrative in which the characters, action, and dialogue work to represent an abstract concept. The fable of the ant and the grasshopper, for example, is an allegory advocating industriousness.

ALLITERATION. The repetition of a sound, usually the initial sound, in a sequence of words, such as "Full many a flower is born to blush unseen" (Thomas Gray, "Elegy Written in a Country Churchyard").

ALLUSION. A reference, often to a historical figure, myth, or artwork, that exists outside the literary work. Allusions to the *Bible* are common in Western literature.

AMBIGUITY. A deliberate use of language to suggest multiple meanings. For example, Young Goodman Brown's adventure in Nathaniel Hawthorne's story of the same name may have been a dream, or may have actually occurred.

AMPITHEATER. Originating in classical Greece, a theater designed with a stage surrounded by tiers of seats arranged in a semicircle.

ANALOGY. A comparison between two apparently unlike things that share some common features; a reference to the familiar in order to help readers understand the unfamiliar.

ANAPEST. A metrical foot comprised two short syllables and one long syllable, e.g., like a child, like a ghost.

ANECDOTE. A brief episode within a longer work, designed to make a point or illustrate an idea.

ANTAGONIST. The character who opposes the lead character, or protagonist. Occasionally, when the conflict is internal, the antagonist is actually another side of the protagonist's own personality.

ANTICLIMAX. A failure to achieve the anticipated high point in a narrative, usually resulting in disappointed expectations.

ANTIHERO. A main character who does not possess the normal positive qualities of a hero; antiheroes appear primarily in modern works.

ANTISTROPHE. With *strophe* and *epode*, a stanza in a Greek Ode. The antistrophe represents the reverse of the strophe.

ANTITHESIS. The balancing of one word or expression against a contrasting word or expression, as in "It was the best of times, it was the worst of times" (Charles Dickens, *A Tale of Two Cities*).

APOSTROPHE. An address either to a person who is dead or not present, to an inanimate object, or to an abstract concept, designed in part to provide insight into a character's thoughts.

APPROXIMATE RHYME. Also referred to as slant or near rhyme, these rhymes share sound qualities or sounds within words. An example of such a rhyme is the feminine or half rhyme. Approximate rhymes are often repeated strategically within a perfect rhyme scheme in order to achieve a particular affect, e.g., told, woe.

APRON STAGE. Popularized by Elizabethan theater, a stage that extends toward the audience, beyond the arch of the stage.

ARCHETYPE. A character, place, or event that represents a universal truth, often of mythic proportions. The archetype appeals to what psychologist Carl Jung referred to as the "collective unconscious," or the sublimated memories of an entire race.

ARENA STAGE. A stage that is surrounded on every side by the audience, with actors entering and exiting through the aisles.

ARGUMENT. An introductory statement to a longer work of prose or poetry that summarizes the main point of the work.

ASIDE. In drama, a monologue spoken by an actor directly to the audience, outside the hearing of other characters onstage. The aside was relatively common in Elizabethan drama, used to express a character's inner thoughts; in modern drama, it is sometimes used for humorous effect.

ASSONANCE. A pattern of identical or similar vowel sounds, usually in stressed syllables of words with different end sounds. For example, the "o" sound is repeated five times in this line from George Gordon, Lord Byron's "Childe Harold": "Roll on, thou deep and dark-blue ocean, roll!"

ATMOSPHERE. The general feeling evoked through setting or dialogue. In Charlotte Perkins Gilman's "The Yellow Wall-Paper," for example, the early description of the narrator's house creates as sense of foreboding and unease in the reader.

AUBADE. A lyric poem in which two lovers express their regret over the coming of the dawn.

AUDITORY IMAGE. A mental perception that recalls a particular sound, specifically a word or words that refer to something heard.

AUGUSTAN AGE. The period of English literature encompassing the first half of the eighteenth century, featuring such writers as Jonathan Swift and Alexander Pope, who emulated the work of figures in ancient Rome such as Virgil and Horace.

AUTHORIAL VOICE. An idealized projection of the author, or someone to whom the reader must give approval, that is the beliefs, attitude, and tone of the author, as opposed to the narrator or any other character in a work.

AVANT GARDE. Any form of writing that deliberately rejects tradition, instead employing thoroughly innovative style or subject matter.

BACCHIC. In classical Latin poetry, a foot consisting of a short syllable followed by two longs or a weak syllable followed by two strong syllables.

BALLAD. A song or poem that tells a story and often features a repeated refrain. Because the ballad was originally an oral rather than written form, a single ballad may appear in a number of different versions.

BEAST FABLE. A short tale illustrating a moral truth, featuring animals as the main characters. Aesop's tales, such as the tortoise and the hare or the fox and the grapes, are the most widely known beast fables.

BEAT. The pattern of stress in a poem.

BEGINNING RHYME. The rhyme located in the first syllables of a poem, e.g., Why should I have returned?

BILDUNGSROMAN. A novel, often autobiographical, that recounts the development of a character from childhood to maturity, for example, Ralph Ellison's *Invisible Man*.

BIOGRAPHY. A full account of a person's life written by another. Biography moves beyond mere facts to create a portrait of the subject. *Autobiography* refers to such an account of the writer's own life.

BLANK VERSE. Unrhymed verse written in iambic pentameter. Considered to be the poetic form closest to normal speech patterns, blank verse is featured in Shakespeare's plays and in narrative poems such as John Milton's *Paradise Lost*.

BLOCKING. The positioning of actors on a stage, including their movements and physical interaction. The director is responsible for blocking.

BOX SET. A stage designed to represent a room realistically, with three walls and an invisible fourth wall facing the audience.

BROADSIDE BALLADS. Popular in sixteenth-century England, cheaply printed ballads, speeches, and diatribes.

BURLESQUE. A comedy presented in the style of a lofty, serious work but featuring gross exaggeration and distortion.

CACOPHONY. A series of discordant or harsh sounds used to jar the senses of the audience, as in Thomas Hardy's antiwar poem "The Man He Killed": "You shoot a fellow down / You'd treat if met where any bar is."

CAESURA. Any pause in a line of poetry, often in the middle of a line, sometimes used to create rhythmic effect, e.g., "Had we but world enough, and time."

CANON. Originally referring to the authenticated books of the Bible, now used to indicate those works considered by scholars to represent the best writing in a literary tradition, the masterpieces. Since the 1960s, many scholars have questioned more traditional interpretations of the canon because of the absence of works by women and writers from other marginalized groups. Canon may also refer to a comprehensive list of works by a specific author (e.g., the canon of Shakespeare).

CARPE DIEM. Latin for "Seize the day," a common theme in lyric poetry emphasizing the need to pursue sensual pleasure because life is short. The theme was prevalent in English love poems written during the sixteenth and seventeenth centuries.

CASTING. The selection of actors to play specific roles in drama.

CATASTROPHE. The conclusion of a tragic drama, in which the protagonist often dies. Based on Gustav Freytag's analysis of typical five-act plays, catastrophe follows introduction, rising action, climax, and falling action.

CATHARSIS. According to Aristotle, the purging of emotions at the end of a tragedy. During the play, audiences experience pity and fear as they identify with the tragic hero; a successful tragedy ends by reaffirming traditional human values, allowing the audience to experience catharsis.

CHARACTER. A person presented in either fiction or drama, whose behavior contributes to the plot and whose personality lends meaning to the narrative.

CHARACTERIZATION. The methods by which a writer brings a character to life, usually through the character's own words and actions, the responses of other characters, and the narrator's commentary.

CHORUS. In classical Greek drama, a group of actors set apart from the main action of the play, who commented regularly on the implications of the action. The chorus often wore masks and performed ritualized dance movements as they chanted.

CHRONOLOGY. The arrangement of time in a work. Some works follow a *linear* chronology, relating a story from beginning to end, while some begin *in medias res*, or in the middle, and move back and forth in time.

CLASSICISM. A value system based on the culture of ancient Greece and Rome, focusing on such features as balance, simplicity, clarity, order, and reason.

CLICHÉ. A figurative expression that has become trite from overuse, such as "raging inferno" or "ship of state." In drama and fiction, a character or setting can be a cliché, such as the prostitute with a heart of gold or the dark and stormy night.

CLIMAX. The high point, or point of greatest tension, in the plot. Climax is sometimes referred to as the turning point.

CLOSED COUPLET. A couplet consisting of two rhymed lines of poetry expressing a complete thought, e.g.,

> A dog starved at his Master's Gate
> Predicts the ruin of the State

CLOSED FORM. Closed form refers to any poem that conforms to established conventions for rhyme, meter, or stanza form, such as a sonnet or haiku.

CLOSET DRAMA. A play written primarily to be read rather than performed onstage.

COLLOQUIAL DICTION. Language representative of ordinary people speaking informally, often using slang, such as the language in Bobbie Ann Mason's "Shiloh."

COMEDY. Drama featuring a happy ending, designed to amuse the audience.

COMEDY OF MANNERS. Popular in late seventeenth-century England, drama that satirizes the behavior of sophisticated, high-society characters.

COMEDY OF THE ABSURD. A type of twentieth-century drama rooted in existentialism, portraying humans as isolated creatures living a meaningless existence. Such plays dismiss conventional plot, setting, and characterization.

COMIC RELIEF. A humorous character or scene, usually introduced in a serious play, whose jokes and buffoonery are intended as a brief break from the tension created by the main narrative. A character introduced for comic relief will often comment directly upon the absurdity of the protagonist's dilemma. Examples of such characters include the drunken porter in Shakespeare's *Macbeth*.

COMING-OF-AGE STORY. A narrative which takes as its subject the central character's emergence from childhood into some form of maturity; this emergence is often produced by a traumatic experience of the adult world. Examples of the coming-of-age story include Sharon Olds' "Rites of Passage" and Julia Alvarez' "Trespass."

COMMEDIA DELL'ARTE. A form of improvised drama that developed in Italy during the fourteenth century, and that flourished in the sixteenth and seventeenth centuries. Commedia dell'arte (or "comedy of the profession," pointing to its creation by professional performers) used stock characters and scenarios, usually farcical in nature, but required actors to embellish and develop their roles in order to maintain the attention of the audience.

COMPLICATION. In the Aristotelian model of a narrative's action, a complication occurs after the onset of the narrative's problem, interfering with the protagonist's attempts to restore the status quo or a state of equilibrium. Complications generally function to push the plot along and to heighten the audience's tension.

CONCEIT. An extended metaphor, often using an unusual image to show the resemblances between otherwise unlike things. Common conceits in Elizabethan poetry include the frequent comparison of the beloved to a flower or a garden. The "metaphysical" poets extended the conceit in ways that were often startling and provocative, such as John Donne's comparison between a flea bite and a sexual encounter in "The Flea."

CONCRETE DICTION. Language that describes qualities that can be perceived with the five senses. Concrete diction is defined in opposition to abstract language, which cannot be so perceived; an adjective such as "good" is thus abstract, while "sweet" is concrete.

CONCRETE POETRY. Poetry that is shaped on the page, often to resemble the object it describes. For example, George Herbert's "Easter Wings" creates those wings both typographically and through its imagery.

CONFESSIONAL POEM. A poem which focuses on its narrator's state of mind, often describing that state of mind in less-than-flattering terms. The chaos or trauma of the narrator's internal life is often intended as a metaphor for the world at large. Confessional poets include Anne Sexton, Sylvia Plath, and Robert Lowell.

CONFLICT. A struggle between two forces that drives a narrative's plot. The two forces in conflict can be two characters, a character and his or her environment or society, or two large social groups. Conflict can also be wholly internal to a character, as in narratives in which a character struggles with his or her psychological issues or conflicting desires.

CONNOTATION. The implied or figurative meaning that a word or image carries, as distinct from its literal or explicit meaning. Connotation often includes contextual or culturally specific overtones. For instance, "home" literally means the place one lives, but it often carries the connotations of safety and security. See denotation.

CONSONANCE. A pleasant combination of sounds; also, the repetition of consonants or groups of consonants, particularly at the ends of words. See also alliteration, assonance.

CONVENTIONS. Structures, devices, or other features that are traditional or expected within particular literary genres. For instance, an English sonnet's rhyme scheme is a convention; similarly, the *femme fatale* is a convention of hardboiled detective novels.

COSMIC IRONY. Irony related to a deterministic or fatalistic view of the world, usually implying that fate or some other cosmic force is toying with human lives.

COUPLET. Two successive lines of poetry of the same metrical length, usually rhyming, that form a complete unit.

COZY. A light English mystery novel, filled with suspense but typically avoiding gruesome bloodshed or terror. The detective in a cozy is generally an amateur sleuth, and often a sweet elderly lady likely not to seem a threat to a criminal. Agatha Christie's Miss Marple novels are typical of the genre.

CRISIS. The peak of a narrative's tension; the critical turning point of a narrative's action that usually leads to or produces its climax.

CRITICISM. The interpretive or analytical work performed by a serious reader of a text, in which the reader evaluates the textual evidence in order to more fully comprehend a text's meaning. Criticism is so named not because it is of necessity "negative," but rather because the critic asks difficult questions in performing such analysis.

CYBERPUNK. A sub-genre of science fiction, growing out of the work of writers including William Gibson and Bruce Sterling, often focused on a dystopian, heavily computerized near-future world. Cyberpunk combines the nihilism of the punk movement with an interest in the ways new technologies shape the future of human societies.

DACTYL. A three-syllable metrical foot composed of one stressed and two unstressed syllables. Examples include "strawberry" and "horrible."

DECORUM. Literary and dramatic appropriateness, particularly in terms of the use of appropriate language and form. Decorum is a key principle of classical rhetoric.

DENOTATION. The literal or explicit meaning that a word or image carries, as distinct from its implied or figurative meaning. Denotation usually disregards the cultural or contextual overtones of a term. Dictionary definitions are generally denotative. See connotation.

DENOUEMENT. The outcome or resolution of a narrative's action. "Denouement" derives from a French term meaning "unknotting" or "unwinding," and thus refers to the period after a narrative's climax, during which the status quo or equilibrium is restored.

DETECTIVE STORY. A branch of mystery stories focusing on the investigation of a crime. The genre of the detective story was established in Sir Arthur Conan Doyle's tales of Sherlock Holmes, and was later revolutionized by the work of Dashiell Hammett and Raymond Chandler. The detective story frequently focuses as much on the psychology of the detective him- or herself as on the puzzle he or she is charged with solving.

DEUS EX MACHINA. Literally, "god from the machine," the device often used to resolve Greek drama, whereby a god would be lowered onto the stage in order to bring a divine end to the play's conflict. The term has come to be used to describe any improbable or unrealistic solution to a narrative's plot.

DIALECT. The language of a particular class, ethnic group, or region, as represented in literature. Dialect is a method of characterization that uses spelling, grammar, and word choice to represent the sounds of that character's speech, often with the intent of distinguishing the character from others in the narrative. A famous example of the use of dialect can be found in Mark Twain's *The Adventures of Huckleberry Finn*.

DIALOGUE. The lines spoken by a character in a work of fiction or drama, and particularly a conversation between two characters.

DICTION. The particular word choices made by an author. Diction may be formal or informal, concrete or abstract; diction is a major contributor to an author's style.

DIDACTIC POETRY. Poetry that is instructive in aim, seeking to teach its reader a lesson, or otherwise convince its reader of a particular argument.

DIMETER. A poetic line consisting of two metrical feet.

DISCOURSE. Traditionally, a formal verbal expression or exchange, taking place in either speech or writing. "Discourse" has been adopted as a key term in recent critical theory to describe the ways in which meaning, and particularly ideology, is disseminated within a culture through its uses of language.

DOCUMENTARY THEATER. A recent mode of theatrical production that brings together ethnographic research with performance, creating a play which is both factual and dramatic. The term usually implies that the dialogue has been taken verbatim from interviews. Documentary theater has roots in the Depression-era Federal Theater Project and the German "theater of fact" of the 1960s. Examples of documentary theater include Anna Deveare Smith's *Fires in the Mirror* and the Tectonic Theater Project's *The Laramie Project*.

DOGGEREL. Comic verse composed in a loose, irregular measure. "Doggerel" is today most often used in a derogatory fashion, to refer to crudely written or otherwise bad poetry.

DOUBLE ENTENDRE. A French term for "double meaning." A double entendre is a deliberately ambiguous phrase, usually conveying a secondary meaning of a humorously sexual nature.

DOUBLE PLOT. Two interwoven plots contained in one narrative. Often one plot is treated more centrally than the other, producing a main plot and a subplot. An example of such a double plot is contained in Shakespeare's *King Lear*, one with Lear at its center and the other revolving around Gloucester.

DRAMA. A genre of literary work, written in either prose or verse, in which characters enact a narrative through dialogue and pantomime. Most drama is written to be performed on the stage, though "closet" drama is intended to be read rather than performed.

DRAMATIC IRONY. A dramatic device in which the reader or spectator knows something about a situation that a character does not, with the result that the character either behaves inappropriately or expects an outcome that is opposed to that which the reader knows is forthcoming. Dramatic irony runs rampant in Sophocles's *Oedipus Rex*, as Oedipus repeatedly curses the murderer of Laius, not knowing that he is in fact that murderer.

DRAMATIC MONOLOGUE. A poem narrated by an individual speaker who addresses either the reader or an implied listener. The poetry of Robert Browning includes many dramatic monologues, including "My Last Duchess."

DRAMATIC POETRY. Drama written in verse. Also, poetry that presents a character speaking directly to the reader or audience without additional authorial devices.

DYNAMIC CHARACTER. Also known as a round character; a complex character depicted as having psychological depth, particularly one who develops and changes over the course of a narrative. See flat character.

DYSTOPIA. Literally, "bad place." As opposed to a utopia (a good place, an idealized imaginary world), a dystopia is a nightmarish fictional future world, in which characters lead dehumanized, fear-filled lives. Dystopian narratives often focus on totalitarian regimes, and are often satiric commentaries on our own society. Examples of dystopian narratives include George Orwell's *1984* and Margaret Atwood's *The Handmaid's Tale*.

ECHO VERSE. A kind of literary resonance, in which a sound, or word, or image in a text recalls a similar effect in another text. As a poetic form dating back to late classical Greek poetry, the final syllables of the lines repeat in reply or commentary.

ELEGY. In classical literature, "elegy" referred only to poems written in strict elegiac meter, with alternating lines of hexameter and pentameter. Since the Renaissance, however, "elegy" has been used to describe any poem that conducts a sustained and formal lamentation, usually over the death of a particular person. The poem, usually longer than a lyric but not so long as an epic, generally contains a speaker and is delivered in the first person, often uses classical allusions and motifs, and frequently traces the speaker's path from grief through acceptance to joy.

ELISION. The omission of a letter or syllable, often combining two words into one, for metrical effect.

END RHYME. Rhyme occurring in the final words or syllables of two or more lines of poetry, as opposed to internal rhyme, which occurs within a line.

END-STOPPED LINE. One of two major types of line breaks in poetry. End-stopped lines generally end in conjunction with the end of a phrase or a sentence. Contrast with enjambment.

ENGLISH SONNET. Also known as a Shakespearean sonnet. The English sonnet typically contains three quatrains and a couplet, with an abab/cdcd/efef/gg rhyme scheme.

ENJAMBMENT. One of two major types of line breaks in poetry. Enjambed lines break in mid-phrase, and thus do not contain a sustained pause at the end of a line. Contrast with end-stopped line.

ENVIRONMENTAL THEATER. A form of political theater, related to performance art, in which the performance moves out of the restricted space of the theater and into the public arenas of streets or parks, intentionally blurring the lines between performance and audience, and between reality and illusion.

ENVOY. Also spelled "envoi," a brief postscript to a poem or a piece of prose writing, which often dedicates the poem to its patron or sends it on its way into the world. "Envoy" is also a term for the short concluding stanza of a ballad or sestina.

EPIC THEATER. Commonly associated with Bertolt Brecht, a form of theater in which the style of acting, the inclusion of multimedia effects such as film and electronic sounds, and the presentation of rational argument are used to create a shock of realization in the audience. Epic theater operates through what Brecht called the "alienation effect," which works to distance the viewer from the play's characters, maintaining a constant awareness of the spectacle's unreality. By preventing the audience from identifying with the play's characters, Brecht hoped to engage them intellectually in thinking about the play's issues.

EPIGRAM. Originally, an inscription in verse on a building, monument, or coin. "Epigram" is now used to refer to short, often witty verse, usually with a surprising turn at the end.

EPIGRAPH. A quotation or verse taken from another poem, used to introduce a literary text.

EPIPHANY. The sudden revelation or dawning insight that a character frequently reaches at the climax of a short story, usually sparked by ordinary circumstances but of such power that it is understood to be life-changing.

The term was most notably used by James Joyce to describe the experiences of characters such as Gabriel, the young central figure in "The Dead."

EPISTLE. A poem that imitates the form of a personal letter. An example is Alexander Pope's "Epistle to Dr. Arbuthnot."

EPITAPH. Literally, an inscription on a gravestone. "Epitaph" is also used to describe a brief poem in memory of a dead person, as well as the final words spoken by a character before his or her death.

ESSAY. An interpretive or analytical piece of literary writing. Essays can be personal or critical in focus; the essay nearly always treats its subject from the limited point of view of the author.

EUPHEMISM. The substitution of a more pleasant or agreeable word or phrase for one that might be considered rude or offensive. For example, "passed away" is a euphemism for "dead."

EUPHONY. A grouping of words that produces a pleasant, soothing sound, as opposed to the harsh sounds of cacophony.

EXACT RHYME. Also known as "perfect rhyme," a rhyme in which the final vowel and consonant sounds are the same, as in "rhyme" and "crime." Homophones (such as "die" and "dye") are sometimes included in discussions of exact rhyme. Contrast with inexact or imperfect rhyme, eye rhyme, half rhyme, or slant rhyme.

EXODUS. The last piece of a Greek tragedy, including or following the final choral ode.

EXPLICATION. A detailed analysis of a piece of prose or poetry, one which attempts to account for the meaning and function of all of the elements of the text.

EXPOSITION. The early portion of a play or story's narrative structure in which the characters and situations are introduced. Exposition is also used to refer to any parts of a narrative that provide background information necessary to understanding the story.

EXPRESSIONISM. A style of art or literature, particularly associated with early twentieth-century Europe, in which the artist or writer focuses upon the expression of his or her internal feelings and emotions. Expressionist literature emphasizes the psychological and emotional aspects of the text.

EXTENDED METAPHOR. A sustained metaphor that is elaborated over the course of an entire stanza or poem.

EXTENDED SIMILE. A sustained comparison between two things, using "like" or "as" to draw the connection.

EYE RHYME. Words that give the appearance of rhyming when in print, but that are pronounced slightly differently, as in "bury" and "fury." Contrast with exact rhyme.

FABLE. A legendary tale usually including animals as characters, who display and represent human foibles, and often having a moral or instructional aspect to the telling. Fables are often humorous, and the animals often take on stylized traits—the tricky fox and the clever rabbit.

FAIRY TALE. A tale that constructs a world of the imagination often with ancient settings and/or characters of either royal or peasant background interacting. Many of the old fairy tales were transmitted orally before they were collected and written down. These stories usually contain magical elements, including supernatural creatures, and suggest a world where anything but the ordinary is likely to happen.

FALLING ACTION. In the plot of a narrative the action rises to a particular point (a climax) and then begins to fall to the inevitable conclusion. (Also referred to as the fourth part of plot structure.)

FALLING METER. Poetry includes regular beats that are divided into feet which include accented and unaccented syllables. Falling meter occurs in trochaic and dactylic meters when a foot ends with an unaccented syllable or two unaccented syllables. Trochaic: fearsome. Dactylic: tragedy.

FANTASY. A fantasy must have magic and magical characters, and these characters must find themselves in amazing and imaginative situations. The stories often unfold in worlds far away or long ago, and the characters often find themselves doing and experiencing things quite impossible in the ordinary world.

FARCE. A play that includes the boisterous and even crude types of action that happen when characters indulge in horseplay and sexual humor. Characters usually speak in colloquial terms and may even knock one another about and tumble down with and upon one another.

FEMININE RHYME. In poetic metrical feet, a foot that ends in an unaccented syllable is said to have feminine meter. Feminine rhyme occurs when two lines with feminine meter rhyme: Today comedy, tonight tragedy.

FICTION. A narrative shaped or made (from the Latin *ficio*, to shape or make) from the author's imagination. Parts of a fictional story, novel, or drama may refer to factual reality, but the story and characters arise from the musings of the creator.

FIGURATIVE. Referring to the use of figures of speech, that is, language that explains through metaphors or similes, comparing one thing to another in order to enhance or underscore the meaning.

FIGURES OF SPEECH. An image that relies on the comparative imagination of the reader or listener, e.g., cold as ice, mad as a hornet.

FIRST PERSON NARRATIVE. Literary works appear in a variety of voices. The speaker may be a master narrator who tells the story from outside of the characters' worlds, or the speaker may know about the characters' thoughts but still not be in the story him or herself. Finally, the first person narrative speaks from the point of view of one character in the narrative. That person has complete control of the line of the narrative. Readers are dependent on the point of view of that narrator and must either trust or suspect the speaker throughout the narrative.

FIXED FORM. Poetic form may be either open or fixed. Fixed forms are those in which the poet decides to follow a particular form both for the effect on the reader and for the challenge of expressing the meaning through a controlled rhythm and rhyme scheme.

FLASHBACK. An interruption in the line of the narrative which occurs when a character suddenly remembers a past event so vividly that it takes over the line of action for a time. Flashbacks are used in both novels and film to enhance the story line or to add information that is necessary to the plot of the work. Often in stories of war or conflict, the character will suddenly find him or herself out of time and into an episode of memory. This memory may explain something in the current action or something in the motivation of the character.

FLAT CHARACTER. A character who usually carries the action of a narrative without adding emotional insight or plot development. E. M. Forster coined the term to describe a character with few traits. The parlor maid in a play or the sheriff in a cowboy movie may be a flat character if she or he is there merely to facilitate the scene.

FLEXIBLE THEATER. Also called experimental theater and sometimes referred to as a black box. The theater is small, often with space for 100–200 persons in the audience, often providing flexible seating and space, allowing for theater in the round, a proscenium arch or fourth wall, thrust staging, or other innovative designs.

FLY-ON-THE-WALL NARRATOR. A narrator who does not enjoy knowledge of the thoughts or feelings of the characters but tells what is seen from a distance. The narrator does not intrude in the action but also does not give emotional insight into the characters except through observation of action. This form of narration demands that the reader follow the narrator in the inferences that are made from the observations, though perhaps the reader may also be encouraged to guess at more than the narrator is revealing.

FOIL. A character that sets off or contrasts with another character maybe serving as a foil or opposite.

FOLK BALLADS. Ballads that were sung by minstrels for hundreds of years before being written down. They are usually in a set ballad form with set rhyme and often with a repeated chorus that begins to draw and hold the listener in the story. Often, ballads exist in several forms since they changed as they were sung and passed on from minstrel to minstrel.

FOLK EPIC. An oral tradition that tells the story of a nation's heroes, the folk epic may have a variety of versions, as do the great Norse and Celtic legends, or the epic may have been recorded so long ago that one author claims the tale as in Homer's *Iliad* and *Odyssey*.

FOLKTALE. A tale that has been passed down by oral tradition, usually not having found a set form in the manner of a fairy tale.

FOOT. In poetry, the means of measuring meter. A foot has either two or three syllables with varying accents.

FORESHADOWING. In a narrative work, events are constructed so that early events will suggest later events in the development of the plot; thus a gun in the first act of a play suggests that someone will be shot in a later act. Without foreshadowing, the reader or audience might not be prepared for the outcome of the narrative.

FORM. Humans want to see order in the world, and authors and their readers or viewers are no exception. Thus a work of art will have some kind of form, whether that be a traditional plot or a more experimental shape. Poetry especially can be constructed in prescribed forms or can take more inventive shapes, but finally the form must be there as an essential part of the telling and understanding.

FORMULA LITERATURE. Literary works fall into genres that have more or less predictable forms. When the form controls the literary work to the extent that the outcome may be predictable or even obvious, the narrative work is considered to be formulaic, e.g., romance novels or westerns or action movies. The formula does not necessarily mean that the work is of less value, but when the formula so dominates the work that the creative element bends to the expected form or shape, then the work may not please the reader.

FOUND POEM. The poet may notice words in an ad or in a conversation, write them down, and then rearrange them into a pleasing and meaningful pattern, thus, a found poem.

FOURTH WALL. A proscenium "wall" located between the curtain and the orchestra used in modern experimental theater to create space outside the stage itself for movement and action.

FRAME NARRATIVE. In a story within a story, the outside story is the frame narrative or the story that enfolds the second narrative. Shakespeare's *Midsummer Night's Dream* tells the story of a group of characters, some of whom in turn are working on their own story, the acting out of the old tale of star-crossed lovers who meet at a wall. In this play the frame is the main narrative, and the internal narrative is entertaining and also linked

591

to the main plot. In other narratives, such as *Heart of Darkness*, the narrator tells his own story and then that of another trip to the same dark place, the second tale being the main narrative of the story.

FREE VERSE. Free verse has no prescribed form or meter, but free verse does have form, often a form found by the poet while composing. Meter and rhythm vary according to the needs and demands of the poem itself.

FREYTAG'S PYRAMID. In 1863 Gustav Freytag (Technique of the Drama) suggested that the five parts of classical drama suggest a pyramid, the rising action peaking at the climax and leading to the falling action; the five are exposition, complication (conflicting elements), climax, catastrophe, and resolution.

GENRE. The literary form that an author chooses to follow, assuming that the reader or viewer will enter into the agreed upon pattern. Thus if a work begins with a rhymed couplet and continues with more couplets, the reader quickly knows that the genre is poetry and reads accordingly. If a playgoer sees a very silly master of ceremonies appear before the curtain, the viewer will assume that the genre is dramatic comedy.

GOTHIC FICTION. The genre of fiction suggesting terror and suspense, often with the use of heavy medieval architecture (also referred to as Gothic). Horace Walpole is credited with the first Gothic novel, *The Castle of Otranto*, in 1764, but the Bronte's and Poe have given the form is true shape.

HAIKU. An unrhymed form derived from Japan, requiring seventeen syllables in a set five, seven, five form and using imagery from nature; the poem often resolves into an observation about nature and meaning in the last line.

HALF-RHYME. In poetic form, the middle of the line and the end of the line rhyme.

HAMARTIA. The Greek word for error, but in drama the word has come to mean something more drastic. For example, Hamlet is too hesitant to think clearly about the political situation in which he finds himself. His hesitance is his fatal error that will lead to his death. This error is not one that the character intends to make but is rather a part of the personality that cannot be evaded or avoided but that will inevitably lead to disaster for all involved.

HARD-BOILED FICTION. The hard-boiled detective of either gender works in a dangerous world where criminals are vicious, deaths are violent, and only a tough character can survive and solve the crime. This world of fiction has evolved in the twentieth century as detective fiction moved from the polite mysteries of the drawing room and the tea parlor to the mysteries of the streets where everyone carries a weapon, and the criminals are most certainly not gentlemen or gentlewomen.

HEAVY-STRESS RHYME. A poetic rhyme involving a spondee (two accented syllables together) or a free-verse form that uses internal emphatic rhyme.

HEPTAMETER. A line of poetry that has seven feet, including seven primary stresses.

HERMENEUTICS. Originally meaning the close study and interpretation of the *Bible*, but in modern criticism it means the principles and systems used to interpret meaning in any text.

HERO/HEROINE. In Greek epics, the leading warriors were called by the term from which hero is derived (heros). The term came to mean the lead character in a narrative or drama, the character who saves the day or who triumphs over adversity. Heroine was used as a feminine term, but current usage applies hero to both genders.

HEROIC COUPLET. A couplet written in iambic pentameter, that is five feet per line, each foot being an iamb, or two beat syllable with the stress on the second syllable. The heroic couplet is a closed couplet, a form that sums up an idea in two lines, but the heroic couplet must follow the metric form as well. Heroic couplets often appear at the end of scenes in Shakespeare's plays to sum up the action of the scene and to send the actor off stage with an exact and effective closing line.

HEURISTIC. From the Greek word for the modern word *eureka* (*heureka*, meaning "I found it"), any method or technique that helps a writer or speaker come up with ideas for a topic or for developing a topic.

HEXAMTER. Poetic lines with six rhythmic feet are said to be written in hexameter.

HIGH COMEDY/VERBAL COMEDY. Comedy that derives its humor from witty and satirical conversations on the parts of the players. The comic wit is often at the expense of human foibles, especially in the Restoration form known as the comedy of manners in which romantic alliances among upper-class partners are played out through witty exchanges between the characters.

HUBRIS. From Greek drama, the term used to describe a character who is laid low by his pride and arrogance, inasmuch as these qualities make anyone unable to see his or her own weaknesses.

HUMOR. Occurs in literature in at least two distinct ways, one being the farcical action where actors or characters buffet one another about and speak in crude and colloquial language. The other form of humor occurs when more observant and reflective characters satirize the foibles of human nature.

HYMN. A song of praise, best shown by the psalms in the Judeo-Christian scriptures or by other poetic songs written in praise.

HYPERBOLE. An overstatement used to stress a point.

IAMB. A poetic foot consisting of at least two syllables. An iamb is a foot with one accented and one unaccented set of syllables: beside or demand are words which demonstrate an iamb. This meter is common in English poetry, for it reflects the form of many English words.

IDENTICAL RHYME. Occurs when the same word is used for a rhyme in a poem.

IDEOLOGY. A a system of beliefs and values belonging to an individual or to a group.

IDIOM. A particular means of expression used in a particular language. In American English one stands "in line," but in British English one stands "on line."

IMAGE/IMAGERY. In poetic writing the stress may be expressly on the image that is being described or envisioned. Imagery is also used in fiction to create a particular mood or impression. It is important to keep in mind that these images appeal to the senses, giving an evocative picture of that which is being described.

IMAGISM. This movement in American twentieth century poetry stressed the image above all, leaving behind the poetic forms that emphasized meter and rhyme. The imagists such as Ezra Pound owed much to the Japanese haiku form that stresses one vivid picture.

IMPERFECT FOOT. In poetic meter, a foot is usually one stressed and one unstressed syllable, or one unstressed and one stressed, two unstressed and one stressed, one stressed and two unstressed, or two stressed syllables. Any variation from these five patterns is considered an imperfect foot.

IMPERFECT RHYME. Imperfect rhyme, including slant rhyme, presents a rhyme that is almost a rhyme but not quite so: love/leave.

IMPRESSIONISM. In fiction, impressionism stresses the impact of the external world on the internal world of a character. Flannery O'Connor's intellectual characters often muse over the possible meanings of the various incidents that happen in rural southern Georgia.

IN MEDIAS RES. Literally translated from Latin to mean "in the middle of the circle." It is used to refer to an epic tale that begins in the middle of the story and then reveals the previous incidents. *Star Wars* was a movie series that began in medias res.

INCREMENTAL REPETITION. This poetic term refers to phrases or lines that occur regularly at particular points in a poem as do the choruses in ballads or the repeated lines in some set poetic forms such as a villanelle which repeats lines from the first stanza in set form throughout the poem.

INEXACT RHYME. Like imperfect rhyme, inexact rhyme refers to a poetic variation on the expected rhyme: heart/hearth; laugh/wrath.

INITIATION STORY. A story that provides the first experience of a person, usually young, who faces a great life experience for the first time, especially death, sex, or religious doubt and faith. James Joyce's collection of stories, *Dubliners*, includes these three types of initiation stories.

INTERIOR MONOLOGUE. In fiction, the place where a character muses over a problem or issue internally. This musing is written out in the voice of the character but is not spoken to another character.

INTERNAL ALLITERATION. Within the lines of a poem, vowels or consonants will be repeated so that the internal alliteration will strike the reader's or listener's ear almost unaware: the slippery snake hissed softly.

INTERNAL RHYME. Within the line of a poem, words will rhyme, affecting the ear more than the rhythm, as does a rhyme at the end of a line: with laugh the gaff was gone.

INTERTEXTUALITY. Texts constantly refer back to other texts, even when one text does not quote another. Speech and writing are full of references to well known stories or to the Bible or Shakespeare. Writers like the poet T. S. Eliot use intertextuality purposefully to emphasize meaning; at the end of his poem "Little Gidding" he quotes Dame Julian of Norwitch, "And all shall be well and/All manner of things shall be well," but he does not reference the quote, assuming that his intended reader will know and understand the reference. Cited references demonstrate intertextuality as well, showing the relationship between the text being written and earlier writers on the subject.

IRONY. Occurs in a literary work when the text operates on at least two levels of meaning. Dramatic or tragic irony occurs when the audience has information that the characters do not, as in *Romeo and Juliet* when the audience knows that Juliet is not dead but Romeo thinks she is. Situational irony occurs when the story turns out to be the opposite of the expected as in *The Open Window* in which the woman telling the story to the visitor has created a false story that will shock the visitor when the truth is known. Cosmic irony occurs when the character can do nothing to change the fate that is prepared, and verbal irony occurs when the words spoken are the opposite of the meaning intended.

ITALIAN SONNET. The Italian or Petrarchen sonnet consists of an octet (eight lines) of iambic pentameter (five feet of unaccented and accented syllables) which presents the argument or dilemma and a sextet (six lines) that answer the argument or sorts out the dilemma. The lines are rhymed aaba/aaba and cdecde or cdcdcd.

KINETIC IMAGERY. Imagery in motion; thus a poem or story will show a vivid image in action.

LIMERICK. A short form of poetry including five anapestic lines (two unaccented and one accented syllables) rhymed aabba. Lines one, two, and five have three feet, and lines three and four have two feet.

LINE. In drama, refers to words spoken by a particular character. In poetry, a line is one specific line of poetry that can be either metric or set off in free verse for emphasis.

LITERARY BALLAD. A narrative poem written in calculated imitation of the form and style of traditional, anonymous ballads. Unlike traditional ballads, a literary ballad is not sung; it is written for sophisticated readers.

LITERARY EPIC. A careful, conscious emulation in writing by an individual author of earlier oral folk epic. Literary epics, such as Virgil's *Aeneid* or Milton's *Paradise Lost*, frequently compare the present to the glorious past

LITOTES. An indirect affirmation, usually understated, made by the denial of its opposite, such as "I was not a little hungry" to mean "I was very hungry."

LOCAL COLOR. The use in fiction of distinctive though typically superficial regional material intended to provide realistic background. Regional particularities can be expressed in specific types of setting, dialect, dress, custom or habit.

LOW COMEDY/PHYSICAL COMEDY. Characterized by boisterous activity or clownish behavior without intellectual appeal. Low comedy attempts to incite laughter by employment of jokes, gags, or slapstick humor.

LYRIC. A short, emotionally expressive poem by a single speaker. Commonly written in the first person, lyric poetry is frequently emotional, highlighting personal moods, thoughts, feelings, perceptions, and states of mind. Lyric typically evokes a songlike or musical quality. In ancient Greece, "lyric" was sung to the accompaniment of a lyre.

MADRIGAL. Short, secular song, typically dedicated to love or pastoral themes, arranged in counterpoint for several voices without accompaniment. The madrigal originated in Italy during the fourteenth century and triumphed in England during the Elizabethan period.

MAGIC REALISM. Contemporary narrative that combines mundane events and descriptive details with fantastic and magical elements in a realistic framework. Though usually associated with Latin American fiction, magic realism has blossomed into an international trend.

MALAPROPISM. The mistaken, comic use of a word in place of another with which it shares a close resemblance. The inaccurate, inappropriate word choice derives from confusion between the two words. The term derives from the character Mrs. Malaprop in *The Rivals* (1775) by Richard Brinsley Sheridan.

MASCULINE RHYME. Rhyme consisting of single stressed syllables or of stressed final syllables in polysyllabic words.

MEDITATION. A contemplative essay or sermon.

MELODRAMA. A popular form of theater that features stereotyped characters, such as villains, heroes, and young lovers, engaged in sensational events, intrigue, and action. Melodrama presents suspenseful plots centered on exaggerated conflicts between good and evil. The term is often employed pejoratively to connote a lack of psychological depth and an excess of emotional excitement.

METAFICTION. A type of fiction that renounces the illusion of verisimilitude to explore or comment on, in a self-conscious and self-referential manner, its own fictional nature. Repudiating realism, metafiction concentrates on the role of author and reader in the creation and reception of fiction.

METAPHOR. A figure of speech, not meant to be factually true, in which one thing is compared or substituted for something else. Although the two things are not identical, they are associated in language to emphasize a similarity between them.

METER. A regular, recurring rhythm, or pattern of stresses and pauses, in lines of verse.

METONYMY. A figure of speech which substitutes the name of one thing with that of another with which it is closely associated in common experience. The use of the "White House" or "Oval Office" to refer to the United States presidency is a familiar example.

MIME. A non-literary performance that involves acting with movement and gesture, but without any words.

MIMESIS. Imitation or mimicry intended to represent or reproduce reality.

MINIMALISM. A form of contemporary fiction written in an austere style with a severe restriction of content and setting, such as the work of Raymond Carver.

MISE EN SCÈNE. French term referring to the elements of a dramatic production including costume, scenery, lighting, etc. In cinema, the term refers more specifically to the arrangement of action in front of the camera.

MONOLOGUE. A long speech by one person. In drama, the monologue provides the spoken thoughts of a single character. In fiction, an interior monologue can similarly represent the thoughts, not the actual spoken words, of a character.

MONOMETER. A verse line with one metrical foot.

MONOSYLLABIC FOOT. A unit of meter with a single syllable.

MOOD. The atmosphere or tone of a literary work, conveyed through diction, characterization, and setting.

MORALITY PLAY. A form of religious drama popular in Europe during the fifteenth and sixteenth centuries consisting of moralized allegories. Featuring a variety of personifications, morality plays showcase the struggle for the Christian soul and communicate simple messages of salvation.

MOTIF. Any element that is repeated and developed throughout a narrative. Motif also refers to an element that recurs in many different literary works. Motifs encompass a wide variety of possible elements such as image, idea, situation, action, incident, or theme.

MOTIVATION. The explicit or implicit reason provided for the actions of a character. In drama or fiction, motivation defines what a character desires.

MULTICULTURALISM. In literary studies, the attention to work produced by or about cultural "minorities."

MYSTERY PLAY. A popular, religious medieval play on biblical themes.

MYTH. Traditional, anonymous story derived from oral tradition usually involving supernatural or heroic figures. Adopting a cosmic perspective, myths offer accounts of origins of human, social, and natural phenomena in boldly imaginative terms. It is believed that the fictional narratives of myth embody the popular ideas, values, and belief systems of cultures that create them.

MYTHOPOEIC. A term employed to describe writing that uses myth as a source or that bears a strong resemblance to myth especially in subject matter.

NARRATIVE. The ordered account of a true or fictitious event, or of connected events. Narrative selects and arranges the recounting of these events in a particular sequence.

NARRATIVE BALLAD. A common form of narrative poetry.

NARRATIVE POEM. A class of poem that tells a story.

NARRATIVE STRUCTURE. See "plot."

NARRATOR. The voice or character who relates the story of the narrative. The narrator is different than the author. The degree of participation, perspective, and personality of the narrator varies greatly though the narrator generally provides information and commentary on other characters and events.

NATURALISM. An extreme, deliberate form of realism in fiction or drama in which human characters are inevitable products or passive victims of the natural or social environment or of a particular genetic inheritance. Writers promoting naturalism strove for precise, objective recording of reality capable of demonstrating laws of causality, and aspired to scientific status for their researched, detailed accounts of behavior.

NEAR RHYME. See "slant rhyme."

NEOCLASSICAL COUPLET. Due to its popularity during the Neoclassical Period (a.k.a. the Augustan Age), the neoclassical couplet is another name for a heroic couplet (two successive rhyming lines of iambic pentameter).

NEOCLASSICAL PERIOD. See "Augustan Age."

NEW COMEDY. In ancient Greece, a form of comedy developed between 400–300 B. C. E. New comedy, frequently associated with Menander, is witty and offers unexpected plot twists.

NOVEL. Extended fictional prose narrative of book length. As a genre, the novel is enormously open and flexible, admitting innumerable exceptions. The novel is distinguished from the short story by its greater number of characters, variety of scenes, and span of time covered.

NOVELLA. Novel or narrative story of intermediate length, longer than a short story but less complex than a novel.

OBJECTIVE CORRELATIVE. The external expression of an interior mood or feeling by the deliberate use of a specific object, scene, or event to evoke a particular emotion.

OBJECTIVE POINT OF VIEW. The dramatic third person point of view, when the narrator reports on events and speech, but does not comment on the thoughts of other characters.

OCCASIONAL POEM. A poem expressly written for or inspired by a specific, typically significant, event.

OCTAMETER. A verse line with eight metrical feet.

OCTAVE. An eight line stanza. Octave indicates the first eight verse line section of sonnets.

OCTOSYLLABIC COUPLET. A type of couplet with eight syllables per line.

ODE. A formal, elaborate lyric poem of exalted style and serious, elevated tone.

OEDIPUS COMPLEX. Term used to describe child's attraction to the parent of the opposite sex; applied most frequently to the attraction of male children to a mother figure, often including overtones of jealousy directed at the father.

OFF RHYME. See "Inexact rhyme."

ONE-ACT PLAY. A shorter dramatic work, most one-act plays take place in a single location, focus on a limited number of characters, and depict a single, powerful incident. Like a short story or a poem, the characterization, setting, and themes must be presented efficiently and, consequently, one-acts sometimes seem less subtle than longer plays.

ONOMATOPOEIA. The attempt to label a thing by forming a word from sounds associated with it.

OPEN FORM. Free verse without any formal scheme including meter, rhyme, or stanza pattern.

ORCHESTRA. In classical Greek drama, the orchestra was the space separating the audience and the players on the stage. The chorus would perform in this space.

ORGANIC FORM. A concept that equates literature to living organisms in so far as both, it is believed, are created by a natural growth process. Value is placed on the entire literary work itself, whereby the "whole" exceeds the "sum" of its parts.

ORGANIC UNITY. Belief in the indissoluble synthesis of form and content in a literary work.

OXYMORON. A condensed paradox combining two contradictory terms, such as bittersweet.

PANTOMIME. Dramatic entertainment employing gesture, posture, and facial expression without speech to convey meaning, mimic action, and express feeling.

PARABLE. Brief, usually allegorical, tale intended to teach a moral or lesson. Typically the moral is only implied and consequently open to different interpretations.

PARADOS. In classical Greek drama, the section of the play that allowed the chorus to enter and comment on the events described in the prologue.

PARADOX. A statement or expression playing on words that initially seems self-contradictory, but which provokes reflection on ways or contexts in which it might seem valid. Also called an "oxymoron."

PARALLELISM. Arrangement of words, phrases or similarly constructed clauses or sentences in sequence or in a similar grammatical or structural way that suggests a recognizable correspondence between them.

PARAPHRASE. Restatement of the meaning or sense of a passage in different words often with the intention of clarification.

PARODY. Mocking or exaggerated imitation of distinctive features of a literary work, author, or style for comic, humorous effect.

PARTICIPATORY DRAMA. A form of drama in which audience members are encouraged to join in the action taking place around them, such as the popular *Tony and Tina's Wedding*.

PASTORAL. Derived from the Latin word for "shepherd," the pastoral is a literary mode that celebrates the virtues of rural, agrarian life and love. Also called "idylls."

PATHOS. This Greek word for passions has come to designate any element of a text that evokes sympathetic feelings in the reader or audience.

PENTAMETER. A line of poetic verse that consists of five metrical feet.

PERFECT RHYME. A rhyme in which the rhymed sounds precisely correspond, as in cat/hat, master/plaster, or dedicate/medicate.

PERIPETEIA. As defined by Aristotle in *Poetics* (350 B.C.E.), perepeteia or "peripety" denotes a sudden, often tragic, reversal in the fortunes of a protagonist.

PERSONA. Derived from the Latin word for the mask, the term "persona" refers to any speaker or narrator of a literary text.

PERSONIFICATION. Also known as "anthropomorphism," personification is the attribution of human characteristics to an inanimate object or phenomenon.

PETRARCHAN SONNET. Named after the Italian poet Francesco Petrarca, also known as Petrarch (1304–1374), the Petrarchan or Italian sonnet is a poem that consists of fourteen lines divided into two sections—the eight line octave and the six line sestet. The octave rhymes abbaabba and presents some kind of problem or conflict that is conventionally resolved in the sestet (rhymed cdecde). Also see "Italian sonnet."

PHONETIC. This term applies to transcriptions of words or letters that reflect the sound of spoken language.

PICARESQUE. Originating in fifteenth-century Europe, this literary genre concerns the escapades and misadventures of a wandering rascal ("picaro" is the Spanish word for rogue). Picaresque narratives are generally satiric, episodic, and involve minimal character development. Prominent examples include Le Sage's Gil Blas (1715), Henry Fieldings's Tom Jones (1749), and Voltaire's Candide (1759).

PICTURE POEM. As its name implies, a poem with its lines arranged in the form of a visual image.

PIDGIN. Derived from a Chinese pronunciation of the English word "business," a pidgin is a language heuristically developed by speakers of mutually unintelligible languages for purposes such as commerce and trade.

PLAY. A literary text intended for dramatic performance.

PLOT. The series of events unfolded throughout the course of a narrative. A conventional plot is organized in terms of conflict, climax, resolution, and denouement.

POETIC DICTION. The highly elevated and formalized language that rejects everyday speech in favor of literary devices such as archaism (outmoded words and expressions), epithets (personalized adjectival phrases, as in Alexander the Great), and circumlocution (roundabout or indirect description).

POINT OF VIEW. The perspective from which a story is told. Third-person omniscient and first-person narration are the most common points of view.

PREFACE. A short introduction that explains the purpose or intent of a given literary text.

PROLOGUE. Originally applied to the introductory speech of a Greek tragedy, this term has come to signify the preface of any literary text.

PROPAGANDA. Any literature written with the intention of recruiting its readers to a given social, political, or religious cause.

PROPS. A shortened form of the word "properties," the physical objects used to create the setting or "mise en scène" of a stage drama.

PROSE POEM. A poetic text written in prose form.

PROSODY. The collective formal techniques of poetry, including rhythm and meter, versification, and diction.

PROTAGONIST. The main character—whether hero or anti-hero—of any given literary text.

PSALMS. Worship songs, most particularly the collection of 150 sacred songs of praise collected in the Biblical Book of Psalms.

PULP FICTION. The collective name for sensational crime, adventure, and science-fiction stories printed on cheap "pulp" paper and published in popular magazines of the 1920s, 30s, and 40s.

PUN. A kind of word-play that depends upon identical or similar sounds among words with different meanings.

PYRRHIC. Within the context of poetic technique, a metrical unit with two consecutive unstressed syllables.

QUANTITATIVE METER. A type of meter based on the interplay between "long" and "short" syllables rather than stressed and unstressed syllables. Common to Greek and Latin poetry, quantitative meter concerns the duration of the spoken word.

QUATRAIN. A verse paragraph that consists of four lines.

RAP. This sub-genre of Rhythm and Blues music involves heavily vernacular lyrics spoken with the accompaniment of music. Also known as hip-hop, rap music was developed by African-American artists throughout the 1970s, 80s, and 90s.

REALISM. Originating in eighteenth-century Europe, this literary mode promotes faithful representation of human life and experience. Realist texts reject idealistic and fantastic subject matter in favor of detailed, accurate description and frank treatment of pessimistic themes.

RED HERRING. A distraction meant to divert the reader from a central point or issue. This tactic is particularly relevant for mystery fiction, in which the writer often frustrates the reader's attempt to arrive at a solution.

REFRAIN. Sometimes called the chorus, the refrain is a recurring line or set of lines in a poem or song.

REGIONALISM. Attention to the ways in which geographical location influences or emerges from a given literary text or set of texts. Also see "Local color."

RESOLUTION. The outcome or conclusion of a narrative conflict. A literary work that withholds clear resolution may be termed an "open-ended" narrative.

RESTORATION PERIOD. The interval between 1660–1700, following restoration of the British monarchy. In 1649, Oliver Cromwell successfully led a revolution against King Charles I; these strict Puritan rebels banned theatrical performance, which they considered worldly and decadent. When the monarchy was restored in 1699, King Charles II reopened England's theaters, giving rise to the bawdy "Restoration Comedy."

REVENGE TRAGEDY. Originating in England during the Elizabethan and Jacobean periods, revenge tragedy is a dramatic genre that concerns the protagonist's self-destructive attempts to avenge the death of a loved one. Notable examples include Thomas Kyd's *The Spanish Tragedy*, William Shakespeare's *Hamlet*, and John Webster's *The Duchess of Malfi*.

REVERSAL. A radical change in the situation of a literary character. See also "peripeteia."

RHETORIC. A term used to describe the collective techniques of persuasive writing.

RHYME. Concurrence of similar or identical sounds within different words.

RHYME ROYALE. Invented by Chaucer in the fourteenth century, the rhyme or "rime" royale is a type of poetic stanza which adheres to iambic pentameter and a fixed rhyme scheme of ababccdd.

RHYME SCHEME. The pattern of repeated words-sounds throughout the course of an entire poem or stanza.

RHYTHM. With respect to any literary text, rhythm refers to the sound-patterns created by organization of stressed and unstressed or long and short syllables.

RISING ACTION. With respect to conventional narrative structure, the term rising action describes the series of events that build tension and lead to a climax.

RISING METER. A metrical foot—such as an iamb or anapest—that concludes with a stressed syllable.

RISING RHYME. Also known as a "masculine rhyme," a rising rhyme concludes with a stressed syllable.

ROMANCE. Originally applied to medieval narratives of courtly love, the term has come to designate any adventure story that concerns fantastic situations and exotic settings.

ROMANTICISM. A nineteenth-century European artistic movement that stresses individualism, personal spiritual development, and human interactions with nature. Often favoring lyric poetry, Romantic writers favor intimate autobiographical themes and radical formal innovations.

RONDEL. Related to the rondeau, a rondel is a fourteen line poem that holds only two rhyming sounds. In this type of poem, the same two lines are repeated at the beginning, middle, and end of the poem.

ROUND CHARACTERS. Realistic literary characters distinguished by depth, psychological complexity, and even self-contradiction.

RUN-ON LINE. A line of verse that concludes without a natural pause or "caesura." This disjunction between syntax and versification often creates a feeling of anxiety or discomfort.

SATIRE. A literary text that uses comedy toward the end of derision.

SCANSION. The process of determining a poem's rhythmic pattern through recognition of stressed and unstressed syllables.

SCENE. Either the physical set of a play or one of the discrete narrative units that comprises an act in a play.

SELECTIVE OMNISCIENCE. Applies to a narrator that reveals only the perspective of a single character.

SELF-REFLEXIVITY. Most pronounced in metafiction, the quality of self-awareness in a literary text. A self-reflexive text underscores and celebrates its own status as a work of fiction.

SENTIMENTALITY. A style of writing that appeals to human sympathy and emotion rather than reason. This literary mode originated in eighteenth-century England; notable examples include Oliver Goldsmith's *The Vicar of Wakefield*, Susanna Rowson's *Charlotte Temple*, and Harriet Beecher Stowe's *Uncle Tom's Cabin*.

SESTET. The last six lines of an Italian sonnet. This conclusive stanza conventionally offers a resolution or response to the problem posed by the poem's first eight lines, which are known as the octave.

SESTINA. A thirty-six line poem that consists of three stanzas: six sestets and a final three-line "envoy." The sestina form also requires that the six words found at the end of the first sestet's lines variously recur at the end of the following sestet's lines and in the envoy.

SET. The physical elements that represent the setting of a dramatic production.

SETTING. The time and place in which a narrative takes place.

SHAKESPEAREAN SONNET. The Shakespearean or English sonnet consists of three quatrains and a conclusive couplet; its most common rhyme scheme is abab/cdcd/efef/gg. In contrast to the octave/sestet structure of the Italian, the Shakespearean form posits a thematic break between the twelfth and thirteenth lines of the poem. Also see "English Sonnet."

SHAPED VERSE. A poem printed in such a way that its visual shape reflects its content.

SHORT STORY. A work of prose-fiction that consists of 15,000–20,000 words.

SIGNIFYIN'(G). Within various African-American communities, "signifyin'(g)" represents the practice of appropriating, parodying, and otherwise transforming cultural elements of the dominant or mainstream group. African-American slaves, in particular, found signifyin'(g) a valuable form of resistance culture.

SIMILE. In poetry, a figure of speech whereby two unlike objects are compared to each other with the word *like* or *as*, e.g., "My mistress' eyes are nothing like the sun."

SITUATIONAL IRONY. A type of irony in which an action differs markedly from audience expectations, resulting in surprise and sometimes discomfort. Herman Melville uses situational irony in *Benito Cereno*, for example, as readers discover at the end of the novella that the reality of the situation is the complete opposite of their (and the protagonist's) perceptions.

SKENE. A wooden structure used by actors in fifth century B.C.E. Greek dramas, it typically represented a palace or temple. The skene was located in the back of the stage, allowing the actors to switch costumes when changing roles.

SLANT RHYME. Also referred to as near rhyme, in slant rhyme the sound of the words is nearly alike. This is because such rhymes share the same vowel sound but have different consonant sounds, e.g., scored and word.

SOLILOQUY. A speech given by a character in a play revealing the character's state of mind or motivation.

SONNET. Meaning little sound or song, one of the most popular poetic forms, particularly for poems dealing with love. It is comprised of fourteen lines written in iambic pentameter. Also see "Italian Sonnet" and "English Sonnet."

SPEAKER. In poetry, the speaker refers to the voice of the poem, the self or persona created by the author.

SPECTACLE. In drama, a scene often included for its spectacular effect.

SPENSERIAN STANZA. A form created by Edmund Spenser for *The Faerie Queen*, comprised of nine lines, the first eight written in iambic pentameter, and the ninth written in iambic hexameter.

SPONDEE. The spondee in poetry is composed of a metric foot of two accented syllables, often created for emphasis, e.g., "oh joy!"

STAGE BUSINESS. In drama, refers to any nonverbal action intended to capture the audience's attention and reveal the feelings of a character.

STAGE DIRECTIONS. In the text of a play, the directions that represent the playwright's view of the positions of the actors on the stage and their physical expressions.

STANZA. The basic unit of a poem typically comprised of two or more lines. A stanza operates much as the paragraph does in prose.

STATIC CHARACTER. A character who does not grow or change throughout a narrative.

STEREOTYPE. An unrealistic character based on assumptions about common traits of a certain group (e.g., women, homosexuals, Asians). Tom in Harriet Beecher Stowe's *Uncle Tom's Cabin*, for example, is a stereotype of the long-suffering, docile African slave.

STOCK CHARACTER. A kind of character, usually one-dimensional, appearing regularly in certain types of literature: the wicked stepmother in fairy tales, for example.

STREAM-OF-CONSCIOUSNESS TECHNIQUE. A technique in modern fiction designed to approximate the uncensored, disorganized flow of thought running through the mind of a character. Two of the most notable examples of the technique are James Joyce's *Ulysses* and William Faulkner's *The Sound and the Fury.*

STRESS. In poetry, the emphasis given a syllable often for metrical, or musical, purposes, e.g., pro*ject* and *pro*ject are different words depending on the stress and part of speech.

STROPHE. In poetry, strophe often refers to a stanza that does not have a regular metrical or rhythmic pattern.

STRUCTURE. Pertaining to any genre, the structure of a work refers to the arrangement of its elements.

STYLE. The term used to capture an author's way of expressing. Style is conveyed through the author's use of language, such as diction, syntax, metaphor and other figurative language.

SUBJECT. Refers to what a literary work is about, as distinct from its meaning.

SUBPLOT. A secondary plot within a larger story, normally related to and often reflective of the main plot.

SUMMARY. The summary of a work captures its main idea and the subtopics that develop the idea. Summaries come in various forms and lengths.

SURREALISM. The movement in literature and art founded by the poet Andre Breton in the early twentieth century. This movement attempted to capture the deepest recesses of the unconscious and dream-life through imagery that explored, as described by Arthur Rimbaud, "the reasoned disorder of the senses." For example: "Chicago/The trams make a noise like doughnut batter/dropped in oil."

SUSPENSE. The tension and anticipation that develops in the audience with regard to the plot, usually focusing on what will happen to the main character.

SYLLABIC VERSE. Poetry in which an established number of syllables in a line is repeated in subsequent lines, e.g., "Do not go gentle into that good night . . . Though wise men at their end know dark is right."

SYMBOL. A symbol in a work of art is an element that stands for something beyond its literal meaning in the text. It embodies an idea, such as the way in which the white whale in *Moby-Dick* is invested with meaning.

SYMBOLIST MOVEMENT. A literary movement that began in France during the late nineteenth century with writers such as Charles Baudelaire and Paul Verlaine, focusing on the mysteriousness of life, and relying on suggestion and symbol rather than explicitness and description.

SYNECDOCHE. A synecdoche is a figure of speech in which a part signifies the whole or the whole signifies the part, e.g., in the phrase "All hands on deck," hands stand for people.

SYNESTHESIA. From the Greek, a term meaning "perceiving together." The experience of two or more senses stimulated simultaneously when only one of them is being addressed; for example, "seeing" a color while hearing an actual sound (visualizing the color blue while hearing the Blues played on instruments).

SYNESTHESIS. In literature, refers to the description of one kind of sense in terms of another, such as "sweet as moonlight."

SYNOPSIS. A summary of the main points of an artistic work. In a short story, novel, or play, it relates the main plot line.

SYNTAX. Syntax refers to the way words are put together in sentences. The syntax of a sentence can make significant contributions to an author's style, e.g., "Ask not what your country can do for you . . . ."

TERCET. In poetry, a three line stanza, each line ending in the same rhyme. For example:

> Whenas in silks my Julia goes,
> Then, then, methinks, how sweetly flows
> That liquefaction of her clothes.

TERMINAL REFRAIN. A terminal refrain is that which appears at the end of each stanza of a poem, such as the "Nevermore" refrain in Poe's "The Raven."

TERZA RIMA. A three-line stanza in which one rhyme is used in the first and third lines and the rhyme in the second line is used in the first and third lines of the next stanza. It is also referred to as an overlapping or interlocking rhyme scheme, e.g.,

> I have been one acquainted with the night.
> I have walked out in rain—and back in rain.
> I have outwalked the furthest city light.
> I have looked down the saddest city lane,
> I have passed by the watchman on his beat
> And dropped my eyes, unwilling to explain.

TETRAMETER. In poetry, a meter consisting of four metrical feet, e.g., "Had we but world enough, and time,/This coyness, lady, were no crime . . . ."

THEME. In poetry, fiction, or drama, the theme is the dominating idea in a work. For example, one might say that the theme of *Romeo and Juliet* is the problem of star-crossed love.

THESIS. Associated mainly with the essay, the thesis represents the writer's main idea or attitude toward the subject of the writing.

THRUST STAGE. In theatre, a thrust stage is a stage where the audience is seated on three sides of the acting area.

TONE. Tone signifies the mood of a work of literature. The mood may be ironic, sad, joyful, or pensive.

TRAGEDY. A drama in which the main characters suffer a catastrophic end for the purpose of arousing pity on the part of the audience. Often a tragedy involves the downfall of a person of great significance.

TRAGIC FLAW. In tragedies, the tragic flaw represents the defect in the hero that is the cause of his downfall.

TRAGIC IRONY. A tragic irony is that which conspires against the hero in spite of his best efforts to avoid his fate.

TRAGICOMEDY. A play that uses the elements of a tragedy, but ends happily, such as in Shakespeare's *The Merchant of Venice.*

TRILOGY. A trilogy is a long literary work in three parts, each part standing on its own. William Faulkner's *The Hamlet, The Town,* and *The Mansion* are referred to as The Snopes Trilogy.

TRIMETER. In poetry, a meter consisting of three metrical feet. For example:
> The idle life I lead
> Is like a pleasant sleep,
> Wherein I rest and heed
> The dreams that by me sweep.

TRIOLET. A French poetic form of eight lines and using only two rhymes. The first two lines are repeated as the last two lines. Here is a playful example of this lyric form:
> Easy is the triolet,
> If you really learn to make it!
> Once a neat refrain you get,
> Easy is the triolet.
> As you see!—I pay my debt
> With another rhyme. Deuce take it,
> Easy is the triolet,
> If you really learn to make it!

TRIPLE RHYME. A triple rhyme occurs when the rhyming stressed syllable is followed by two unstressed syllables, e.g., "meticulous" and "ridiculous."

TROCHEE. A foot comprised of a stressed syllable followed by an unstressed syllable. Here is an example of an unrhymed trochaic:
> There they are, my fifty men and women
> Naming me the fifty poems finished!
> Take them, Love, the book and me together:
> Where the heart lies, let the brain lie also.

UNDERSTATEMENT. A figure of speech making something appear less important or true than it really is. Understatement is used to intensify meaning of a statement, as well as for the purposes of irony, sarcasm, or humor. It is the opposite of hyperbole., e.g, "Nor are thy lips ungraceful, Sire of men, / Nor tongue ineloquent."

UNITIES. The unities refer to the qualities of good plots, which possess unity of action, time, and place. Unity of action adheres to a sense of cause and effect inevitability. Unity of time adheres to the natural cycle of twenty-four hours. Unity of place adheres to consistency of location.

UNIVERSAL SYMBOL. The notion that a literary work may have some organizing principle, by virtue of its symbolism, to which all parts are related.

UNRELIABLE NARRATOR. A narrator whose judgment cannot be trusted by the reader, either because of the narrator's naivete, prejudices, emotional state, or mental age. In Eudora Welty's "Why I Live at the P.O.," for example, Sister's emotional instability, coupled with her hatred of her family, makes her an unreliable narrator.

UTOPIA. From the Greek word meaning "no place," a type of fiction that describes an ideal—or utopian—world.

VERBAL IRONY. A figure of speech in which the implied meaning of something differs from the literal meaning, such as in a sarcastic remark.

VERISIMILITUDE. Pertains to the qualities that make a work of fiction true to life. A work achieves verisimilitude when events, characters, situations, and places are plausible to the reader.

VERS LIBRE. A Latin term meaning free verse, or poetry without any consistent, fixed form or pattern.

VERSE PARAGRAPH. A verse paragraph appears in a poem lacking stanzaic form, that is, the lines are not grouped together within a regular, recurring pattern.

VILLANELLE. A nineteen-line poetic form in six stanzas. It uses only two rhymes and repeats two of its lines according to a set pattern.

VOICE. Refers to the attitude of the author as conveyed through the style or tone of the speaker in a work of literature.

WELL-MADE PLAY. A term that applies to the logical inevitability within so-called problem plays, farces, or comedies of manners.